BRIAN DICKSON

A Judge's Journey

BRIAN DICKSON

A Judge's Journey

ROBERT J. SHARPE AND KENT ROACH

Published for The Osgoode Society for Canadian Legal History by
University of Toronto Press
Toronto Buffalo London

Printed in Canada

ISBN 0-8020-8952-6

Printed on acid-free paper

National Library of Canada Cataloguing in Publication

Sharpe, Robert J.
Brian Dickson : a judge's journey / Robert J. Sharpe and Kent Roach

Includes bibliographical references and index.
ISBN 0-8020-8952-6

1. Dickson, R.G. Brian.   2. Judicial opinions – Canada.
3. Canada. Supreme Court – History.   I. Roach, Kent, 1961–
II. Osgoode Society for Canadian Legal History

KE8248.D5S53 2003   347.71'03534   C2003-903942-0

University of Toronto Press acknowledges the financial assistance to its publishing
program of the Canada Council for the Arts and the Ontario Arts Council.

University of Toronto Press acknowledges the financial support for its publishing
activities of the Government of Canada through the Book Publishing Industry
Development Program (BPIDP).

Contents

Foreword

In this book, two highly qualified authors, Robert Sharpe, a justice of the Court of Appeal for Ontario, and Kent Roach, a law professor at the University of Toronto, provide us with a penetrating analysis of the brilliant yet surprising career of Brian Dickson, by common agreement one of Canada's greatest judges.

Brian Dickson, a successful Winnipeg corporation lawyer, astounded his colleagues in 1963 by accepting an appointment as a Manitoba trial judge. Over the next twenty-seven years, including seventeen at the Supreme Court of Canada, Dickson participated in and ultimately led a revolution in Canadian law. The Dickson years on the Supreme Court were a time of unprecedented constitutional controversy and legal change. On his arrival, the Court was preoccupied with routine disputes; by his retirement as chief justice in 1990, the Court had become a major national institution and its decisions were the subject of intense public interest and concern. As the present biography of Chief Justice Dickson demonstrates, this striking transformation in the Canadian judicial system was matched by his own personal transformation. Justice Sharpe and Professor Roach have written an engaging and accessible biography of one of Canada's outstanding legal figures.

Brian Dickson: A Judge's Journey is the third biography published by The Society of a judge of the Supreme Court of Canada. Like its predecessors, *Duff: A Life in the Law* by David Williams and *Judging Bertha Wilson* by Ellen Anderson, this volume adds enormously to our understanding of the Court's jurisprudence and of its ever evolving place in Canada's institutional structure. The Society's members are indebted to Justice Sharpe and Professor Roach for the skill with which they have carried out their task.

The purpose of The Osgoode Society for Canadian Legal History is to encourage research and writing in the history of Canadian law. The Society, which was incorporated in 1979 and is registered as a charity, was founded at the initiative of the Honourable R. Roy McMurtry, a former attorney general for Ontario, now chief justice of Ontario, and officials of the Law Society of Upper Canada. Its efforts to stimulate the study of legal history in Canada include a research-support program, a graduate student research-assistance program, and work in the fields of oral history and legal archives. The Society publishes volumes of interest to the Society's members that contribute to legal-historical scholarship in Canada, including studies of the courts, the judiciary, and the legal profession, biographies, collections of documents, studies in criminology and penology, accounts of significant trials, and work in the social and economic history of the law.

Current directors of The Osgoode Society for Canadian Legal History are Robert Armstrong, Jane Banfield, Kenneth Binks, Patrick Brode, Brian Bucknall, Archie Campbell, Kirby Chown, David Chernos, J. Douglas Ewart, Martin Friedland, Elizabeth Goldberg, John Honsberger, Horace Krever, Vern Krishna, Virginia MacLean, Roy McMurtry, Brendan O'Brien, Peter Oliver, Paul Reinhardt, Joel Richler, James Spence, Norm Sterling, Richard Tinsley.

The annual report and information about membership may be obtained by writing: The Osgoode Society for Canadian Legal History, Osgoode Hall, 130 Queen Street West, Toronto, Ontario. M5H 2N6. Telephone: 416-947-3321. E-mail: mmacfarl@lsuc.on.ca. Website: Osgoodesociety.ca.

R. ROY McMURTRY
President

PETER N. OLIVER
Editor-in-Chief

Preface

This study of the life and judicial career of Brian Dickson had a modest beginning. The Osgoode Society solicited an extended interview of Dickson for its oral history project. Dickson agreed to cooperate and Robert Sharpe, then dean of the Faculty of Law, University of Toronto, and formerly Dickson's executive legal officer at the Supreme Court of Canada, conducted the interviews from 1991 to 1993. Dickson also deposited a large collection of over two hundred boxes of his personal papers in the National Archives of Canada in 1995. It soon became apparent that Dickson's papers, together with the interviews, formed a rich and unusual resource. With the encouragement of Peter Oliver, editor-in-chief of the Osgoode Society, and with the cooperation of Brian Dickson, Robert Sharpe began work on a book-length study of Dickson's judicial career. Dickson had stipulated that both the oral history and his papers should be closed to public view for twenty-five years; however, he granted unrestricted access to Sharpe and to anyone working with him on the book. Progress with the book was hampered by Sharpe's appointment to the bench in 1995, but Kent Roach's involvement as co-author from 1999, combined with the authors' coincident periods of judicial study leave and sabbatical leave in 2002–3, made completion of the book possible. We thank our colleagues at the Faculty of Law, University of Toronto, and the Court of Appeal for Ontario for making these periods of leave possible and for their warm support, encouragement, and helpful advice.

The scope of this book has been strongly influenced by our sources. The Dickson Papers provide a detailed record of the decision-making process of the judges of the Supreme Court of Canada from Dickson's appointment in

1973 to his retirement in 1990, while also telling us a great deal about his judicial colleagues and the Supreme Court during a period of unprecedented importance in its history. For the preparation of this book, the Dickson Papers have been invaluable; we are aware of no other Canadian judicial biography based on a judge's working files. On the personal side, however, Dickson valued his privacy as well as that of his family. The papers he deposited in the National Archives relate almost exclusively to his judicial work and there are few personal letters. When interviewed, he tended to maintain a similar focus. As a result, while we have done our best to offer a full account of Dickson's life and career, our focus is necessarily on the latter.

Included in the Dickson Papers are his personal working files from almost every case on which he sat throughout his seventeen years as a member of the Supreme Court of Canada. They contain Dickson's annotated copies of the crucial documents filed by parties – lower court judgments, the written arguments filed by the litigants, and the crucial documents, cases, and statutes. Dickson's case files also include material that many judges discard or destroy and that is not usually accessible to the public. Some of the material in this category was generated by Dickson's law clerks, with whom he always worked closely. For virtually every case, he asked his law clerk to prepare a pre-hearing 'bench memo' in which the clerk would summarize the facts, issues, and arguments and provide the judge with the clerk's own legal analysis and recommendation for how the appeal should be decided. If Dickson undertook to write reasons, the law clerk would usually be asked to prepare a more extensive research or, as Dickson called it a 'judgment memo,' analysing the facts, lower court judgments, and relevant authorities in considerable detail. The clerk prepared these memos after detailed discussion with Dickson about the case and about the way he intended to decide it. The memo provided Dickson with a starting point for his writing and sometimes amounted to a draft judgment. In many cases, substantial portions of the law clerk's memos have been destroyed or reduced to ribbons by Dickson's scissors-and-paste method of writing, but as much as possible of what is left has made its way into the case files deposited in the National Archives.

If another judge were writing, Dickson would often ask his clerk to review the colleague's draft judgment and prepare a memorandum commenting on the reasons and recommending that Dickson concur, suggest changes, or write his own concurring or dissenting reasons. Dickson appears to have retained most of these memos in his case files along with the draft judgments his colleagues prepared.

Perhaps the most interesting items found in Dickson's case files are the conference memoranda he prepared shortly after the oral argument of each appeal. During his time on the Court, it was the practice for the judges to retire to the conference room after hearing oral argument to discuss the case.

Starting with the most junior judge, each member of the Court who sat on the case was invited to explain how and why he or she proposed to decide the appeal. A tentative decision was made and one judge would volunteer or be asked by the chief justice to prepare reasons. It was understood that the judges were not bound by the views they expressed at conference, and quite often they changed their minds after further reading and reflection. Dickson took handwritten point-form notes during the conference discussion. At the end of the day, when he returned to his chambers, he called in his secretary and the law clerks and dictated a memorandum summarizing the conference discussion. Virtually all of Dickson's case files include copies of these conference memoranda indicating the tentative views of his colleagues after they had heard oral argument but before there had been any attempt to prepare written reasons for judgment.

Post-conference discussions between the judges appear, for the most part, to have been oral and informal. However, certain judges, including Dickson, often recorded their thoughts in written form, especially when they wished to record a significant substantive point for other members of the Court to consider. Some of Dickson's case files contain memoranda to and from other members of the Court commenting on draft judgments.

Dickson's case files often contain copies of draft judgments written by Dickson and by other members of the Court that differ from the final judgment. Dickson typically went through several drafts before circulating a draft to his colleagues. In some cases, there were still further drafts in which he made changes at the suggestion of another member of the Court. Similarly, in cases where another judge wrote the decision, the case file often contains drafts that were amended or even completely rewritten in response to suggestions or discussions.

We have thoroughly reviewed Dickson's case files and used them extensively as an important source for this book. Since many of these files reveal the thoughts and disclose the out-of-court deliberations of other judges, the important issue of the confidentiality that attaches to judicial deliberations must be addressed. Confidentiality provides judges with a zone of privacy within which they can engage in free and open discussion. If every comment or tentative thought were exposed to public view and scrutiny, discussions among judges could be inhibited and judicial decision making might be adversely affected. A judge might well hesitate to explore ideas or test views with his or her colleagues if no discussion could be kept private. A judge could be embarrassed by the disclosure of a tentative view once held but later rejected. Confidentiality of out-of-court judicial deliberations may also foster public confidence in the justice system. Litigants are entitled to a final judgment. Undue exposure of the twists and turns of collegial decision making could impair the integrity and finality of the judicial process.

Yet, despite its importance, the precise scope and extent of this rule of confidentiality has not been precisely described or defined in law. The very different question of the extent to which judges may be compelled to explain their decisions has been considered. The Canadian Judicial Council has a statutory mandate to inquire into allegations of judicial misconduct, and it may require judges to explain their actions. However, the investigative powers of other bodies have been interpreted narrowly and judges are immune from being compelled to explain their decisions to the executive or legislative branches of government.

The Dickson Papers present no question of compulsion and no clash between the judiciary, on the one hand, and the legislative and executive, on the other, and the issue of judicial immunity does not arise. The issue we have had to consider is whether statements freely made in the deliberative process must forever remain secret or whether there is a time when they may be openly explored by legal or historical scholars with a view to compiling a full and accurate record of Canada's legal heritage. We concluded that, with certain self-imposed qualifications, it was appropriate to use Dickson's case files as the principal source for this book. It is difficult to draw the precise line at which confidentiality yields to disclosure, but we will describe here where and why we have drawn the line.

Confidentiality is rarely, if ever, absolute. The interests of confidentiality must be balanced with the public interest in the free and open discussion of important issues of public concern. Confidentiality yields at the point where the interests protected by secrecy are outweighed by the public's right to know. As time passes, matters that required the protection of confidentiality have passed into history. The interest of confidentiality wanes and the public's right to know prevails.

Although the matter is not entirely without controversy in the United States, the American judicial practice is to allow biographers to make use of materials disclosing judicial deliberations. American Supreme Court justices routinely deposit their papers in public archives, often without restriction, fully expecting scholars to probe them for insights into the judicial process.

We accept that, for current cases and for sitting judges, the public interest is best served by protecting out-of-court judicial deliberations from the glare of public scrutiny. However, a rule of perpetual confidentiality is not required to protect the integrity of the judicial process. Indeed, public confidence in the judicial process might well be harmed if the law imposed a shroud of absolute secrecy. At a certain point, the interest of secrecy diminishes and another element of the public interest prevails. The Supreme Court of Canada is an important national institution. It now plays a pivotal role in the governance of this country. The public has an important interest in knowing how the Court has evolved to this position. In certain circumstances, the confidentiality surrounding judicial deliberations yields to the public interest in knowing the history of one of Canada's most important public institutions and the journey of one of our most notable judges.

We are fortified by the fact that this view seems to have been shared by Dickson himself. While Dickson did not explicitly record his views on the point, any other conclusion is impossible to reconcile with his actions. Dickson consciously chose to preserve his case files and to deposit them in the National Archives with a view to encouraging scholarly work. And he gave us unrestricted access to his papers for the purposes of writing this biography. Since he knew what his files contained, he must have concluded that in certain circumstances and after a certain period of time, the public interest permitted the disclosure of the Court's deliberations.

We have also operated under several significant constraints that, in our view, eliminate any risk of harm to the important interests protected by the confidentiality of out-of-court judicial discussions. Dickson himself imposed the first constraint. A meticulous and cautious judge, he was meticulous and cautious about what he deposited in the National Archives. Dickson carefully vetted every file and removed any material that he thought should not be disclosed, even under the restrictive terms he imposed upon the deposit. The fact that Dickson culled his case files weakens our ability to present a complete historical account since we have worked with an incomplete record. However, Dickson's careful vetting of the files strengthens our argument for using them in this study. He removed material that he thought should never be disclosed.

We ourselves have added certain qualifications. The first and most important is a product of the time it has taken to bring this project to completion. We avoided rushing to publication when the cases decided by Dickson and his colleagues were matters of current interest. Dickson retired from the Court in 1990 and this book appears more than a decade later, in 2003. The judicial exchanges disclosed here took place between thirteen and thirty years ago. Simply put, the events we describe have passed from the realm of current events to the realm of history. The need to protect them from public scrutiny has waned and the interest of compiling an accurate historical record prevails.

A second and related qualification concerns the interests of the individual judges who participated in the deliberations we describe. Arguably, a sitting judge deserves the protective umbrella of confidentiality. We have decided that we should not disclose anything revealed by Dickson's Papers of the deliberations of a still sitting judge. Here again, the passage of time from Dickson's retirement has largely solved the problem. During his seventeen years as a member of the Supreme Court of Canada, Dickson sat with twenty-three colleagues. Of these, nine survive and only one, Chief Justice Beverley

McLachlin, is still a sitting judge. We have avoided disclosing any of Chief Justice McLachlin's out-of-court deliberations that are revealed by Dickson's case files although we have included her own account of events, as well as those of Dickson's other surviving colleagues, who have generously consented to interviews for the purposes of this biography. Subject to these constraints, we believe that it was appropriate for us to make full use of the out-of-court judicial deliberations revealed by Dickson's case files. As will be seen from the pages that follow, these discussions do not discredit the Court or any judge, nor could there be any serious thought that their disclosure will inhibit judicial deliberations in the future. To the contrary, they reveal a group of dedicated and hard-working judges attempting to decide cases according to the law and to the best of their ability.

The Dickson Papers open an unusual window onto the career of one of Canada's most important judges and onto the judicial process at the Supreme Court of Canada in the period from 1973 to 1990. We believe that by looking through that window, as Brian Dickson said we could, we are fostering a better understanding of decision making at our highest court and thereby enhancing public confidence in the judicial process.

Many friends and colleagues read an earlier draft and provided us with helpful comments and suggestions for improvement. We thank the following for their important contribution to this book: Martin Friedland, Philip Girard, Linda Helson, James MacPherson, Patrick Macklem, Patricia McMahon, Peter Oliver, Howard Roach, Carol Rogerson, Geraldine Sharpe, William Stormont, Stephen Toope, and Stephen Waddams. We also thank an anonymous referee who provided us with many insightful and helpful comments and suggestions.

We are indebted to Peter Lawson and Patricia McMahon, both professional historians as well as lawyers, who provided detailed research essays giving us invaluable background information on Dickson's life before his appointment to the bench. A long list of students from the Faculty of Law, University of Toronto, worked on this project as research assistants. We thank the following for their important contribution: Oren Bick, Stephanie Chong, Mark Crow, Michael Dunn, Elizabeth Evans, Marie Irvine, Tycho Manson, Jeffrey Piercy, Adam Taylor, and Marko Vesely. We also thank Melanie McNaught and Megan Stephens, law clerks at the Court of Appeal for Ontario, for their research and editorial help; and Curtis Fahey for his fine copy editing of the manuscript. Finally, we owe special thanks to Barbara Dickson, Peter Oliver, and Marilyn MacFarlane for their patience and encouragement.

Our work was supported by a research grant from the Social Sciences and Humanities Research Council for which we are most grateful.

PART ONE

Introduction

1

A Judge's Journey

Brian Dickson's judicial career spanned a period of twenty-seven years, from his appointment as a trial judge in Manitoba in 1963 to his retirement as chief justice of Canada in 1990. He spent seventeen years on the Supreme Court of Canada, six as the nation's chief justice, and retired as Canada's dominant judicial figure. The Dickson era was a period of dramatic social and legal change. During this period, the Supreme Court of Canada emerged from relative obscurity to become a powerful national institution that dealt with some of the most controversial issues of the day. Brian Dickson was at the centre of this transformation of Canadian law and political life.

The child of Irish immigrants, Dickson grew up in small-town Saskatchewan. His father was a bank manager and his mother a university-educated woman who taught her two sons the importance of reading and education. The Dicksons lived in relative prosperity during the dark days of depression and drought in the 1930s. Although the security of his father's position allowed him to escape poverty and despair, the image of 'nothing but tumbleweed and sand blowing and abandoned houses and fences down' made a lasting impression on the teenaged Dickson.[1]

By the time he was ready for university, the family had moved to Winnipeg. After a rocky start in arts, where he demonstrated more interest in his fraternity than his grades, Dickson switched to law. In 1938, after four years of law school in the mornings and law office work in the afternoons, Dickson graduated at the top of his class. But economic times were still tough and Canada's future chief justice could not find work as a lawyer. He took a job with a Winnipeg insurance company as a clerk and sometimes sold policies door to door.

Dickson enlisted in the Royal Canadian Artillery shortly after the outbreak of war in 1939. He spent the early war years in England and returned to Canada in 1943 for officer training and to marry Barbara Sellers, the daughter of a wealthy and prominent Winnipeg businessman, whom he had started dating before going overseas. A quick crash course in officer training at the Royal Military College (RMC) in Kingston provided him with what he later described as his best education. Dickson volunteered for overseas service and, in the spring of 1944, joined the Allied assault in Normandy. He arrived in France shortly after D-Day and narrowly escaped death when he was severely wounded near Falaise. Military doctors amputed his leg in a field hospital. After a lengthy convalescence in England, a still weakened Dickson returned to Winnipeg the day before the birth of his first son.

At the age of twenty-nine, Brian Dickson finally started his legal career with Aikens MacAulay, a leading Winnipeg firm. He was bright and exceptionally hard working, and he enjoyed the blue-chip connections provided by his father-in-law, Henry Sellers. In addition to law, Dickson served on the boards of many large corporations and was actively involved in community service. In 1950, as president of the Red Cross, he took a leading role in coordinating with military precision the relief of victims of the Winnipeg Flood. By the mid-1950s, he had established his reputation as a leading commercial lawyer and a pillar of the Winnipeg community. He held senior positions in legal, religious, and community organizations. The Dicksons raised a family of four children and enjoyed a prosperous life that included a farm outside Winnipeg, where he could engage in his passion for horseback riding, a summer home in Minaki, and winter holidays in Mexico.

In 1963, at the age of forty-seven, Brian Dickson abruptly changed direction. Seemingly out of the blue, and to the bewilderment of his law partners, he accepted an appointment to the Manitoba Court of Queen's Bench. If Dickson had simply wanted a change from the practice of law, he had other attractive options. A senior and lucrative position in commerce was there for the asking and, only a year earlier, the federal Liberals had tried to entice him into politics. But Dickson, who had rarely seen the inside of a courtroom, chose the bench. He was now a trial judge, dealing with murders, rapes, divorces, personal-injury actions, disputed inheritances, and a myriad of other human conflicts that bore little resemblance to the problems he had confronted in corporate boardrooms. Dickson loved his new job. As he travelled from town to town on circuit, he was moved by the plight of his fellow citizens who came before him. He also gained an enormous respect for the common sense of Manitoba juries. His methods were not always orthodox. Before he sentenced anyone, he insisted on knowing more about the consequences for the accused. He frequently visited jails and penitentiaries in Manitoba to find out what would become of the offender.

Dickson was appointed to the Manitoba Court of Appeal in 1967. There, he missed the human drama of courtroom trials but welcomed the intellectual challenge of appellate work. He developed a clear and direct writing style. Although there were occasional flashes of the innovative judge he would later become, his carefully researched judgments generally followed established legal doctrine.

In 1973 Prime Minister Pierre Trudeau appointed Dickson to the Supreme Court of Canada. Dickson and his family moved to Ottawa to join an institution that was poorly understood by the Canadian public and frequently described as disappointing in the legal community. For the most part, the Court spent its time dealing with technical legal questions and resolving run-of-the-mill disputes. Most judges thought that their job was to apply precedents and the clear letter of the law, leaving questions of law reform and social justice to the elected legislatures. Judgments were written for a strictly legal audience; there was little scope for the consideration of the relevant historical, social, and political context. Broader issues of theory and policy were not confronted openly in judicial decision-making and the judges rarely strayed from traditional legal sources.

Yet, by the time Dickson retired as chief justice of Canada in 1990, the Court had become a major national institution, very much in the public eye and at the centre of political life in Canada. Scarcely a week seemed to pass without a front-page story on the Court, and Supreme Court judgments became familiar fodder for editorial-page writers. Under the 1982 Canadian Charter of Rights and Freedoms,[2] the Court confronted extraordinarily difficult issues of human rights and social policy. Debates about fundamental rights and freedoms replaced routine personal injury and property disputes on its docket. In the process, the Court's audience expanded beyond lawyers and legal academics to the Canadian public at large. Its decisions had implications for all Canadians and were the subject of intense public debate. No longer was the Court criticized for being too cautious, narrow, and legalistic. By the time of Dickson's retirement, some observers were asking whether the Court had become too willing to play an active role in Canadian political life.

Brian Dickson was the leading figure in this transformation of the Supreme Court and Canadian law. After his early years on the Court, when he often deferred law reform to the legislatures and applied precedents that he would later reshape, Dickson began to adapt the law to keep it in tune with a changing society. Even before the Charter, Dickson stressed the need to treat prisoners, aboriginal people, the injured, the accused, and women fairly. At first, Dickson often wrote in dissent, but many of these dissents were accepted by a majority of a changing Court in the 1980s. By the time he retired, he was revered in the legal community as a judge of exceptional ability. He wrote in a refreshingly lucid style, and he crafted strong and enduring precedents in Canadian law notable for their compassion.

We start our account of Dickson's journey with a study of two of his most important cases. Both involve Dr Henry Morgentaler's defiance of Canada's abortion law. In 1975, to the dismay of pro-choice advocates, Dickson and the Supreme Court reversed a jury acquittal and sent Morgentaler to prison. In 1988 Dickson and the Supreme Court struck down the same abortion law as infringing fundamental rights. The arguments against the abortion law were virtually identical in both cases. However, in the interval between them, Canada, its Supreme Court, and Brian Dickson had changed.

The First Morgentaler Case

Morgentaler was charged under the 1969 amendments to the Criminal Code that allowed abortions only if they were performed in a hospital and approved by a committee of doctors prepared to certify that the continuation of the pregnancy would endanger the woman's life or health.[3] Morgentaler defied the new law that made it an offence to perform abortions under any other circumstances. He sent letters to various politicians stating that he had performed over 5,000 illegal abortions and he published an article in a medical journal about his use of the quicker and less expensive technique of suction abortion. He even performed an abortion on television on Mother's Day, 1973. It was only a matter of time before he would be charged. At his trial, he argued that he was justified by the defence of necessity in performing an abortion on Verona Parkinson, a twenty-six-year-student from Sierra Leone. The trial judge allowed the novel defence of necessity to go to the jury and they acquitted Morgentaler, who the very next day continued his defiance of the abortion law in his Montreal clinic.[4]

The Quebec Court of Appeal reversed the acquittal on the grounds that there was no evidence of an emergency that could justify the necessity defence. Rather than follow the usual course and order a new trial, the Court of Appeal convicted Morgentaler on the basis that he had no possible legal defence. It denied Morgentaler bail pending his appeal to the Supreme Court and ordered the trial judge to impose a sentence. Morgentaler remained defiant, stating that 'I cannot believe that an immoral law will be upheld for long and I still believe very strongly that what I did was not only morally right, but legal as well.' These arguments did not impress the trial judge, who sentenced Morgentaler to eighteen months in prison for 'his massive and public flouting of the law.'[5] Morgentaler's fate was now in the hands of the Supreme Court.

For four days in October 1974, national attention was focused on the Supreme Court of Canada as lawyers gathered in the austere granite building in Ottawa to argue Morgentaler's final appeal. The case was front-page news, one of the few in the history of the 'quiet Court in an unquiet country'[6] to receive such attention. In an unusual move at the time, the Court allowed not only the accused's lawyer and the prosecutor to argue the case but also lawyers representing a women's group, a civil-liberties group, and three pro-life groups. Morgentaler's lawyers were joined by the crusading Toronto lawyer Clayton Ruby, representing Women in Crisis, and by Edward Greenspan, already well on the way to establishing himself as one of the country's leading defence lawyers, who represented the Canadian Civil Liberties Association (CCLA). They asked the Court to strike down the abortion law under the Canadian Bill of Rights[7] as a denial of women's privacy and equality rights. In doing so, they looked south of the border for inspiration, since a year earlier the United States Supreme Court had declared a woman's right to an abortion in her first trimester of pregnancy in *Roe v. Wade*.[8] They also relied on a 1970 Supreme Court of Canada decision under the Canadian Bill of Rights that struck down a discriminatory law that made it an offence for an Indian to be drunk off a reserve.[9] That was the first time the Supreme Court had ever used the statutory Bill of Rights to strike down a piece of federal legislation. It gave Morgentaler hope that Canada's highest judges might follow the example set by their American colleagues. Even if the abortion law was valid, Morgentaler maintained that the jury's acquittal should stand. He argued that his actions were justified to avoid a greater evil and to protect the woman's health. The student, who could not afford a hospital abortion, might do 'something foolish' if she was not allowed to end her pregnancy in Morgentaler's clinic.

The pro-choice advocates looked to Dickson as a likely ally. On the Manitoba Court of Appeal, he had written a decision under the Bill of Rights striking down a federal law that discriminated against Indians.[10] He had also demonstrated a healthy respect for the difficult decisions made by trial judges and juries, who, unlike judges on appeal courts, saw and heard all the evidence. With the exception of the reform-minded chief justice, Bora Laskin, the fifty-eight-year-old Dickson seemed as likely as any member of the Court to side with Morgentaler.

Although he had been appointed to the highest Court in only March 1973, Dickson was no longer the Court's most junior member. By now, Prime Minister Trudeau had appointed Louis-Philippe de Grandpré, the former president of the Canadian Bar Association and leader of the Quebec bar, directly from his practice to the Supreme Court. De Grandpré was definitely in the hot seat for the Morgentaler appeal. Following the Court's tradition, as the junior judge he would be the first to speak when the judges retired to their conference room to discuss the case after having heard argument from the lawyers. What no one expected, however, was the opening move from Morgentaler's lawyers. They asked that de Grandpré be barred from hearing the case on account of anti-abortion comments he had made the year before his appointment to the Court. This was a risky strategy; the last time a lawyer had asked a judge of the Supreme Court to be removed, he was found in contempt of court and fined $2,000 or sixty days in jail.[11] De Grandpré withdrew to his chambers while the remaining eight judges retired to consider whether he could sit. They did not take long to decide. Bora Laskin read the decision: 'This Court is not concerned in this appeal with the public debate on abortion. Its sole concern is with the exercise of its jurisdiction to hear this appeal on questions of law.'[12] This was not a good sign for Morgentaler.

The next order of business was the argument that the Court should strike down the 1969 abortion law under the Canadian Bill of Rights on the theory that the right not to be deprived of 'life, liberty or security of the person ... except by due process of law' included the right to an abortion. The prochoice side also argued that women were denied fair hearings because they could not appear before the hospital committees that decided their fate and because different committees applied different standards. These arguments went nowhere. Louis-Philippe Pigeon, a former lecturer in constitutional law at Laval University, told Morgentaler's counsel that some of his arguments were 'an insult to us.' Even the more liberal Bora Laskin told Greenspan that he was asking for 'an extraordinary application of the *Bill of Rights*.' Ruby's argument that the unavailability of committees to authorize abortion in some communities resulted in 'compulsory pregnancy' drew a pointed comment from the Court's most senior judge, the stern Ronald Martland: 'No one is forced to get pregnant.'[13]

The Court adjourned after two days of argument from the Morgentaler side. The next morning, Chief Justice Laskin told the Quebec prosecutor and the intervening pro-life groups that they did not have to answer the arguments concerning the validity of the abortion law under the Canadian Bill of Rights. This was devastating news for Morgentaler. The Court was unanimously rejecting the Bill of Rights argument as so hopeless that it did not warrant a response. Morgentaler recalled that 'the contrast between my expectations and the reality of the Supreme Court – with all the old judges who barely listened, and the others who peppered the lawyers with impolite and downright hostile questions – was depressing.'[14] Even though his liberty was on the line, Morgentaler did not bother to stay to hear the rest of his case.

Bora Laskin took on the task of writing the judgment dismissing Morgentaler's Bill of Rights argument. Laskin was known as the Court's leading civil libertarian, inclined to interpret the statutory Bill of Rights more generously than his colleagues. But even Laskin was not prepared to follow *Roe v. Wade.* Canadian judges had to pay 'due regard to the obvious differences that exist between the statutory *Canadian Bill of Rights* and the guarantees of the Constitution of the United States' and they had no business 'dividing the normal gestation period into zones of interests, one or more to be protected against state interference and another or others not.' He was also unimpressed by the argument that the abortion law was so unevenly applied that it failed to provide women with 'due process of law.' The courts should not supervise the 'administrative efficiency of legislation' and 'any unevenness in the administration' of the abortion law was 'for Parliament to correct and not for the courts to monitor.'[15] Dickson signed on to this judgment without hesitation. He was even more concerned than Laskin that the Court not intrude into Parliament's role in making and reforming the law.

'If I were trying the case with a jury'

The issue of whether the jury acquittal should stand was more difficult. Vince Orchard, Dickson's law clerk and a recent outstanding law school graduate, wrote a pre-hearing 'bench memorandum' arguing that Morgentaler's appeal should be dismissed and his conviction affirmed because there was no evidence that Morgentaler had tried to find out whether Verona Parkinson, who was six to eight weeks pregnant, could have complied with the abortion law.[16] Initially, Dickson was not convinced. His experience as a trial judge in Manitoba taught him not to overturn jury verdicts lightly or to deny juries the right to consider defences or evidence. Dickson was usually a polite listener in court, rarely posing many questions, and did not 'ride counsel'[17] as some of his colleagues did. Nevertheless, in this case, he grilled the Quebec prosecutor with the suggestion that maybe there was enough evidence to justify allowing the jury to decide whether Morgentaler had a defence of necessity: 'There was evidence that the girl had made telephone calls to doctors and hospitals in Montreal without success. There was also evidence in the trial that the girl, living in Montreal with only $200 a month for her college expenses, was in anguish over her condition.' Dickson suggested that 'it was up to juries to make judgments on such facts, not appeal courts'.[18] Despite his wealth and corporate law background, Dickson had sympathy for the impoverished and desperate Verona Parkinson. Life on the prairies during the Depression and his near-death wartime injury made Dickson acutely aware of poverty and human despair. The plight of a pregnant, young, single woman was far from anything he experienced, but he would have understood why she decided to seek out a quick, safe, and inexpensive way to end her pregnancy.

Dickson followed his usual practice of dictating a detailed memorandum of the judges' post-hearing conference. In this memo, he recorded that there was a general consensus to allow Morgentaler's appeal from the Court of Appeal's extraordinary decision to enter a conviction. He noted that, 'on a proper reading of the evidence of Dr. Morgentaler,' there was 'some evidence' to allow the jury to consider the defence of necessity. 'It seems to me that if I were a judge trying the case with a jury, I would have charged the jury on necessity as a possible defence. If this be correct, it was not in my view open to the Court of Appeal to substitute the verdict of "Guilty" for the jury verdict of "Not Guilty."' This accorded with Dickson's usual view that juries should be trusted with all relevant evidence and all relevant defences. Dickson noted that Morgentaler had testified that he was aware of Parkinson's 'state of penury and that it would be impossible for her with her financial resources to obtain an abortion at one of the Montreal general hospitals.' As he had pointed out to the Quebec prosecutor at the hearing, it was for the jury, not an appellate judge, to determine Morgentaler's creditability on this point. Dickson's conference notes indicate that his initial view was supported by seven of the Court's nine judges, with only Martland and de Grandpré clearly of the view that Morgentaler should be convicted. Even the normally conservative Pigeon indicated that the jury's verdict 'must stand, however perverse.' It looked like the Supreme Court would overturn Morgentaler's conviction.[19]

No Escape from the Discipline of the Statute

Some time between his conference memo of October 1974 and the release of the Court's judgment in March 1975, Dickson changed his mind. He ended up writing a judgment for the majority of the Court to uphold the Court of Appeal's decision to convict Morgentaler. As Dickson took a closer look at both the law and the facts of the case, he became more convinced that Morgentaler's conviction had to stand. In his early years on the Court, Dickson was reluctant to make radical changes to the law and from the start, he had been uneasy about the necessity defence. In his notes he described it as 'a very rare bird' that 'has never been recognized in English jurisprudence although some of the professorial writers have given it recognition.' Dickson respected the writings of legal academics and, as he prepared his judgment, he read all the available academic writings on necessity and abortion. Although some academics supported the defence of necessity, others did not and even the supporters did not believe that a pregnant woman's suicide threat was enough to excuse an illegal abortion.[20]

Dickson was also troubled by the lack of judicial precedents or explicit statutory authority for the novel necessity defence. The idea that any individual could disobey the law in order to satisfy some higher objective did not sit well with his conservative instincts. Parliament had provided a legal means to obtain an abortion and Morgentaler had 'deliberately flouted' the law. In one of his many drafts of the judgment, Dickson wrote: 'I refuse to recognize any principle of law which would entitle a person to violate the law because in his view the law conflicted with some higher social value ... Any rational judicial system worthy of the name must operate with a body of determined or determinable rules. So when Parliament, the legislative arm, has clearly spoken and declared the law, it is the duty of the Courts, as I conceive it, to give effect to the will of the legislature and not to frustrate that will by the facile recognition of ad hoc subjectivism in response to antagonistic ideas of societal needs.'[21] As he often did in his early years on the Court, Dickson deleted this strongly worded passage from his final judgment, but it reflected well his belief that courts should follow clear precedent and defer to clear expression of legislative will.

Dickson debated the issue with Bora Laskin, who felt very strongly that the trial judge had properly allowed the jury to consider the necessity defence. Dickson's files contain a memo written by Laskin's law clerk urging that the jury's acquittal be restored on the basis that the jury 'collectively *knew* that Verona Parkinson could not get an abortion in Montreal – it was practically impossible. And I would suggest that such a cognition is precisely why the institution of criminal trial by jury has been preserved.' The Laskin clerk had pulled out all the stops. He stressed the 'fundamental and practical significance' of the acquittal by jurors who 'know their community, its standards, its sentiments, and its subtle and intricate workings.' He went on to argue that Morgentaler's evidence suggested that Parkinson, whom he described as a 'poor, foreign, black student without means or friends,' was suffering 'severe emotional, physical and psychological trauma. Surely there was evidence for the reasonable jury to conclude that Morgentaler in fact performed the surgery, fearing the woman would either commit suicide or submit to a back-alley butcher.'[22]

Neither Bora Laskin nor his clerk's forceful arguments persuaded Dickson. Dickson's annotations to the clerk's memo reflected a deep concern for upholding the sanctity of the law. The evil avoided by breaking the law had to be greater than the evil of breaking it. There had to be objective evidence beyond Morgentaler's subjective views of the impossibility of compliance and the urgent need to preserve life. Dickson decided that Morgentaler had no defence and that the jury should not have been allowed to acquit him. There was no need for another trial. Morgentaler should be convicted and start serving his sentence of eighteen months' imprisonment without further ado.

In his judgment, Dickson concluded that Morgentaler was attempting 'to escape the discipline of the statute' by resorting to 'an ill-defined and elusive concept' of necessity that had 'little support in the cases.' He echoed the fears of some English judges that 'necessity would open a door which no man could shut,' 'provide an excuse for all sorts of wrongdoing,' and 'very easily become simply a mask for anarchy.'[23] If the necessity defence existed at all,[24] it could 'go no further than to justify non-compliance in urgent circumstances of clear and imminent peril where compliance is demonstrably impossible. No system of positive law can recognize any principle which would entitle a person to violate the law because on his view the law conflicted with some higher social value.'[25]

Dickson tried to distance himself from 'the loud and continuous public debate on abortion.' As he wrote and rewrote the judgment, he took pains to eliminate passages that might be construed as entering into the political or moral debate about abortion. In an early draft of his judgment, he changed a reference to the 1969 amendments having 'ameliorated' the law on abortion to the more neutral phrase 'modified.' He also changed a reference to Morgentaler 'bluntly' admitting to performing the abortion to the more neutral word 'openly.' He cut a passage that suggested 'in an abortion two lives are involved, the mother's and the unborn child's.' Whatever his own view about abortion (and they are not known), Dickson was determined to avoid the controversial abortion debate.

For Dickson, Parliament had conclusively decided the question and 'the desire of a woman to be relieved of her pregnancy is not, of itself, justification for performing an abortion.' He read the 1969 abortion law as 'a comprehensive code on the subject of abortions' and refused to apply the Criminal Code provision that authorized necessary surgical operations. Dickson did not mince his words about the need to defer to Parliament's scheme: 'We must give the sections a reasonable construction and try to make sense and not nonsense of the words. We should pay Parliament the respect of not assuming readily that it has enacted legislative inconsistencies or absurdities.' In 1975, in the age of parliamentary supremacy, Dickson firmly believed that the Court's role was limited: 'Whether one agrees with the Canadian legislation or not is quite beside the point. Parliament has spoken in clear and unambiguous language ... Justice must be done within the framework of, and according to, the rules set out in the *Criminal Code*.'[26]

Despite his often expressed faith in the wisdom of juries, Dickson decided that the Court of Appeal was entitled to substitute a verdict of guilty without ordering a new trial. Pigeon, an expert in statutory interpretation, had found that even though it was 'a major departure from the traditional principles of English criminal law,' the Criminal Code of Canada authorized an appeal court to enter a conviction over a jury's acquittal. This extraordinary power should 'be used with great circumspection,' but it was appropriate in Morgentaler's case because 'there cannot be any doubt concerning the commission of the offence by the accused.'[27]

Laskin dissented with the concurrence of the two other judges from Ontario,

Wishart Spence and Wilfred Judson. As Dickson had originally thought, Laskin believed that Morgentaler's testimony that he 'feared that the pregnant woman might do something foolish' was enough to leave the necessity defence with the jury. Laskin saw this as a way to protect the mental or physical health of women in circumstances where there was no access to 'the elaborate procedures'[28] of the abortion law.

The disagreement between Dickson and Laskin reflected their more fundamental disagreement over the role of judges as lawmakers. Laskin took a creative approach to judicial lawmaking, certainly more creative than Dickson was prepared to follow at the time. He believed that courts had a duty to balance conflicting interests, a matter Dickson preferred to leave to Parliament. A few months later, Laskin and Dickson had another famous disagreement in *Harrison v. Carswell*[29] over whether the courts were free to reinterpret laws to meet changing social and economic conditions. Dickson deferred to what he believed the legislature had intended to be a comprehensive scheme and refused to allow striking workers to trespass in a public shopping centre in order to picket one of its stores. Laskin, again in dissent, was prepared to respond to the deficiencies that he saw in the operation of the legislation in light of modern realities.

A Convicted Criminal

Hours after the Court released its judgment sending Morgentaler back to prison, Justice Minister Otto Lang, known for his anti-abortion views, made it clear that he would not grant Morgentaler the royal prerogative of mercy.[30] Just before entering prison, Morgentaler observed that he was prepared to go to jail because he had 'probably saved a few hundred women from death, and maybe a few thousand from injury, humiliation and stress.' He stated that, if he lived south of the border, he would have been considered a 'great specialist' not a 'convicted criminal.'[31]

The majority decision to convict Morgentaler was controversial. Pro-choice supporters were obviously opposed to the conviction of their hero, but others, including former prime minister and defence lawyer John Diefenbaker, disagreed with the decision to reverse the jury's verdict. Parliament responded to the controversy by amending the Criminal Code to require appeal courts to order a new trial in every case in which they overturned a jury acquittal. Dickson was sensitive to the criticism that the Court had received for usurping the jury's role by convicting Morgentaler. In a case eight years later in which the Court overturned an acquittal, he wrote in his conference memo that 'having regard to the criticism which the Court attracted in *Morgentaler* in approving the Quebec Court of Appeal's action in entering a conviction, I am not much in favour of entering a guilty verdict.'[32] In an interview after his retirement from the Court, Dickson admitted that he thought 'in retrospect' that it 'may not have been the wisest thing' for the Court to have convicted Morgentaler in the face of the jury's acquittal and that the better course would have been to order a new trial.[33]

Morgentaler did not fare well in jail. The conditions reminded him of the Holocaust concentration camp he had survived, he lost weight, and he frequently argued with his guards. He was denied parole, got divorced, and had his medical licence temporarily suspended. He had heart problems and was eventually transferred to a convalescent home, but this only had the effect of signalling to him his 'impending death.'[34] While in jail, Morgentaler was tried on another charge of violating the abortion law, but was again acquitted by a jury. This time the Quebec Court of Appeal did not overturn the acquittal and the Supreme Court refused to hear the crown's appeal. A new minister of justice then ordered that Morgentaler be retried on the original charges so that he could have the benefit of Parliament's new law that required appeal courts to order retrials when reversing jury acquittals. In 1976 Morgentaler was acquitted by yet another jury and ended up serving only ten of his eighteen months' sentence of imprisonment.[35] Dickson followed these proceedings closely and believed that in all cases the trial judge 'told the jury that there was no defence of necessity and in effect almost told them to convict, but every time the jury, as they were perhaps entitled to do, felt that this was not a case in which a conviction should be entered.'[36] Late in 1976 René Lévesque's newly elected Parti Québécois government announced that it would not enforce the federal abortion law, leaving Morgentaler free to operate his Montreal clinic. The Supreme Court and Dickson would not see Morgentaler again until 1986, four years after the enactment of the Charter of Rights and Freedoms as Canada's constitutional bill of rights.

The Second Morgentaler Case

Henry Morgentaler's second trip to the Supreme Court of Canada case arose out of 1983 charges stemming from the operation of an abortion clinic in downtown Toronto. Morgentaler and several other doctors were charged with conspiracy to violate the Criminal Code by performing abortions outside a hospital and without the approval of a hospital committee. The conspiracy charges meant that the case would not turn on the plight of a particular woman. The abortion law remained as it stood in 1974, but this time Morgentaler's lawyers argued that it violated the newly enacted Charter of Rights. They focused their arguments on section 7, which guarantees 'the right to life, liberty and security of the person and the right not to be deprived thereof except in accordance with the principles of fundamental justice.' Despite the striking similarity with the arguments that had failed so misera-bly in 1974, pro-choice advocates hoped for victory now that the courts had a constitutional mandate to protect fundamental rights and freedoms. They introduced evidence about the uneven application of the law by committees throughout the country and the fact that in some communities there were no committees and no legal abortions. Relying in no small part on the Court's unanimous 1975 judgment dismissing these same arguments, government lawyers defending the law did not bother to call evidence. They argued that abortion was still a matter for Parliament not the courts.

Few Lawyers Care for the Doctor's Chances

The trial judge rejected the argument that the abortion-committee procedures violated basic requirements of procedural fairness that Dickson and his col-leagues had articulated in a number of administrative-law cases. He also rejected Morgentaler's Charter argument in much the same way that Laskin had dismissed his Canadian Bill of Rights arguments a decade earlier. The enactment of the Charter did not mean that Canadian courts must follow *Roe v. Wade*. The fact that abortion at any stage of a woman's pregnancy had been illegal in Canada 'for well over 100 years'[37] meant that there was no right to abortion under the Charter. However, the trial judge allowed the defence of necessity to go to the jury. Morgentaler's lawyer, Morris Manning, took this one step further by telling the jury that they had a right to say that the law 'shouldn't be applied'. The trial judge admonished the jury that it was 'improper for a law-yer to suggest to a jury that they should break the law.'[38] Nevertheless, after six hours of deliberation, the Toronto jury acquitted Morgentaler.

A unanimous panel of five senior and respected judges of the Ontario Court of Appeal had little trouble dismissing Morgentaler's Charter argu-ments. Because abortion had historically been illegal, a right to abortion was not 'so deeply rooted in our traditions and way of life as to be fundamental.'[39] They rejected the argument that the abortion law discriminated against women, relying on a highly controversial 1979 Supreme Court decision which held that the denial of unemployment insurance during pregnancy did not amount to sex discrimination because 'any inequality between the sexes in this area is not created by legislation but by nature.'[40] Citing a recent Dickson judgment that limited the defence of necessity to emergency situations where it was impossible to comply with the law,[41] the Court of Appeal held that there was no evidence of necessity. They stressed, as Dickson had, that the necessity defence could never justify a premeditated decision to break the law.

It seemed that Morgentaler's second case was on the same trajectory as his first. On the eve of the Supreme Court hearing, the *Globe and Mail* observed that 'although the Supreme Court of Canada under Chief Justice Brian Dickson has gained a reputation as the most liberal court in the land, few lawyers familiar with the Morgentaler case care for the doctor's chances ... the Ontario Court of Appeal [decision] was unanimous, framed in extremely strong language and written by five of the court's most eminent members.'[42]

A Changed Court

The rights guaranteed by the 1982 Charter of Rights and Freedoms were similar to those found in the Bill of Rights but the Charter was part of the constitution, and Parliament was no longer supreme. Dickson and his colleagues had written several Charter decisions striking down federal and provincial laws. The cautious days of the Bill of Rights were over. In fact, even before the enactment of the Charter, Dickson and the Supreme Court had become more creative. In 1975 Parliament had altered the role of the Court by allowing it to decide what cases it would hear. The Court was no longer preoccupied with routine cases and considered only matters of public importance. It had boldly reformed important areas of criminal, public, and private law and Dickson had written many of these judgments. The composition of the Court had also changed. Only Dickson and Beetz remained from the Court that heard *Morgentaler I* and the Court now included its first woman, Bertha Wilson, as well as other energetic reform-minded judges.

Canadian attitudes towards the role of women had also changed. During the week of the Court's hearing in October 1986, the federal government announced a policy to allow women to assume combat support positions in the military while not ruling out actual combat positions.[43] This can be contrasted with debates in October 1974, the month the Court heard *Morgentaler I*, when the stories of the day included discussions in the 'women's section' of the *Globe and Mail* about whether children should receive sex education and a controversy over the fact that officials had awarded the crown in the Miss Seaway Valley beauty contest to the wrong eighteen-year-old 'girl.'[44]

There was even more public attention focused on the Court than in the first Morgentaler case. In late 1985, Norma Scarborough of the Canadian Abortion Rights Action League wrote Dickson to tell him that 'a letter writing campaign is underway amongst those who oppose all access to abortion in Canada.' Dickson had his executive legal officer, James MacPherson, reply: 'The Chief Justice has asked me to thank you for the letter and to tell you that the only factor that influences the Court in making its decisions is its understanding and interpretation of the law.'[45] Dickson received many letters from those opposed to abortion. The Victory Life Fellowship in Calgary sent Dickson, 'at our personal expense,' a book by United States President Ronald Reagan entitled *Abortion and the Conscience of the Nation*. In part because of Reagan's judicial appointments, the right to early abortions recognized in the 1973 *Roe v. Wade* decision was very much up for grabs south of the border. Dickson again had MacPherson reply: 'The Chief Justice has asked me to thank you for both the letter and the book.'[46] The replies reflected Dickson's polite and courtly manner, as well as his belief that a judge must keep an open mind until all the evidence was in.

'All or nothing'

On 7 October 1986 Henry Morgentaler took a seat in the front row of the small courtroom, which was packed to capacity with his supporters and his opponents. The room must have brought back unpleasant memories for him, for it was there, twelve years earlier, that the Supreme Court had quickly dismissed his arguments that the abortion law should be struck down under the Bill of Rights. Morgentaler thought that, of the seven judges who sat on the case, there were 'three for us, three against us, and Brian Dickson down the middle'. For whatever reason, he saw Dickson, the man who had previously written a judgment sending him to jail, as 'the enigma in the whole thing.'[47]

Morgentaler's lawyer, Morris Manning, addressed the Court first. Manning had started his career as a prosecutor, but, influenced by his wife, who was a doctor, he was totally committed to the pro-choice cause. He took a scholarly approach to the law and had written several books including a five-hundred-page treatise on the Charter. Manning argued that a woman's right to an abortion was a protected liberty. If the Court did not step in, Manning argued, society could ban 'abortion altogether, and contraceptives, for that matter. Or conversely, it could compel abortion as a means of population control.'[48] As Morgentaler's lawyer had more than a decade earlier, Manning relied heavily on American cases, particularly *Roe v. Wade*. He cited seventy-one American precedents and twenty American law review articles.[49] In marked contrast to the 1974 hearing, the Court asked Manning few questions about his argument that the law should be struck down. But he received a much rougher ride on the jury nullification issue. Dickson, always concerned with the rule of law, pointedly asked Manning to show him a case 'that says a jury has the right not to apply the law.' Manning had little to offer, prompting an unusually scathing comment from Dickson: 'So your best authority is a dissenting opinion of an American court?'[50]

The government lawyers argued that the Court should defer to Parliament's compromise between protecting the foetus and allowing women some access to abortion. The judges, sensitive to criticisms that the court had been too deferential under the Bill of Rights, were not content with such arguments for judicial deference. They peppered the government lawyers with questions about the lack of committees in some communities. Making a point that would very much remain in the Court's mind, Willard 'Bud' Estey, the down-to-earth former chief justice of Ontario, asked whether 'some kind of local option has slid into the *Criminal Code*?' In a voice that retained a discernable accent from her native Scotland, Bertha Wilson said that she had 'difficulty understanding' why the government thought it was adequate to rely on the fact that there were plenty of committees in Toronto, when there were so few committees in other parts of the country.[51] The federal government's lawyer reminded the Court that most Canadians supported some restrictions on abortions and argued that the Court was faced with the 'all or nothing' proposition of accepting the abortion law with its flaws or striking it down.[52]

After the oral hearing, the Court took the weekend off before holding its conference to discuss the case. The first judge to speak at the conference was the most junior member, Gérard La Forest. La Forest, a former legal academic and civil servant, often took a restrained approach under the Charter to matters of social policy. Dickson's conference notes suggest that La Forest indicated that section 7 of the Charter was designed to avoid the American 'substantive due process' doctrine that allows the courts to review the substantive justice of the law. La Forest stressed 'the right of Parliament to legislate on the matter.' He recognized that there were problems with the uneven application of the law, but he suggested that rather than strike the law down, the Court could handle the issue by allowing the defence of necessity to apply in a province such as Prince Edward Island that had no committees to authorize legal abortions.

Bertha Wilson, who had been appointed to the Court by Prime Minister Trudeau a few weeks before the Charter came into force, was the next to speak. Dickson's conference notes suggest that she was already well on her way to her famous sole judgment striking down the abortion law as an unjustified infringement of a woman's liberty and freedom of conscience. According to Dickson's notes, Wilson argued: 'The liberty interest assures individual autonomy respecting the person and privacy.' Wilson acknowledged a competing interest in protecting the foetus, but Parliament would have to justify any restriction on a woman's freedom under section 1 of the Charter, which allowed only 'reasonable limits' on *Charter* rights that were 'prescribed by law' and 'demonstrably justified in a free and democratic society.' The Court had decided in other cases that section 1 established a 'stringent standard of justification.' Wilson thought that Parliament might be able to justify restricting abortion 'in the later stages of pregnancy or those performed in the back room by some quack,' but the 1969 legislation was such 'a mess' that it could not be justified: 'Even if [the abortion law] was intended to protect health and life, if the woman lives in P.E.I., she does not get that protection ... It is up to Parliament to go back to the drawing board ... Perhaps we should go the U.S. route. There may be an area of privacy which the State cannot enter.' She added that Parliament might be assisted if the Court showed it 'where it went wrong'[53] La Forest and Wilson, the first two judges to speak, had defined the poles of the debate between judicial deference to Parliament's policy choices and judicial intervention to protect the autonomy and liberty of women. As he would in so many Charter cases, Dickson would provide a halfway house between these two poles.

Estey and Antonio Lamer, the former chair of the Law Reform Commission, both indicated that the abortion law should be struck down, but on narrower grounds than those contemplated by Wilson. The problem for them was not so much the substance of the law but the way it was applied: 'There are areas in the country where a woman cannot get a certificate and therefore cannot get an abortion.'[54] William McIntyre, a respected British Columbia judge named to the Court in 1979, who often took a much more restrained approach to the Charter than his colleagues, stated that he would follow the Ontario Court of Appeal's ruling on the basis that 'freedom of choice' was not enshrined in section 7 of the Charter. According to Dickson's notes, Jean Beetz, a careful and brilliant judge who often agonized over difficult judgments, indicated that he agreed with La Forest and McIntyre. Beetz's initial views were consistent with the decision that both he and Dickson made in the first *Morgentaler* case to dismiss a challenge to the same abortion law under the Bill of Rights.

'Brian Dickson down the middle'

Morgentaler's instincts about the Court were correct. After the hearing, it was split three to three, with Wilson, Lamer and Estey wanting to strike the abortion law down and La Forest, McIntyre, and Beetz wanting to uphold it. Dickson, who as chief justice spoke last at the post-hearing conference, would break the preliminary tie.

It must have been a dramatic moment. Would Dickson follow Beetz and reject Morgentaler's arguments, as he had done twelve years earlier? Or would he change course under the Charter and strike down the abortion law? Dickson's notes indicate that he said the law 'should be struck down.'[55] His colleagues pressed their chief justice: 'How can you say that because the procedure is faulty everyone gets abortion on demand?' The procedure of the abortion law 'was imperfect but Parliament went about it the only way it could have.' Dickson was firm and recorded in his notes: 'I indicated that if the procedure ... violated both security of the person and fundamental justice,' the abortion law must be struck down. Lamer suggested that it might be possible to fix the law by striking down only parts of the committee procedure, but Dickson indicated that he 'did not wish to get into chopping and changing' the abortion law. The law's procedural defects were so fundamental that, in Dickson's view, it had to be struck down. Indeed, the federal government's lawyer had told the Court that the law 'must remain as it is found in the *Criminal Code* or fall completely ... It is all or nothing.'[56] Dickson's vote meant that it was nothing.

The views expressed at conference were only tentative and much work remained to be done in researching further points of law and writing judgments. Typically, a judge in the majority would be assigned to draft a judgment to be considered by the other judges. They would then decide whether to agree or write their own judgments. They might also make suggestions for improvement or conditions for agreement. The Court did not release its judgment in *Morgentaler II* until January 1988, almost fifteen months after oral argument; in contrast, the Court had taken less than six months to deliver its judgment in *Morgentaler I*. The delay in 1988 reflected the fact that the Court was struggling under the burden of many early Charter cases and was preparing a number of lengthy judgments.

There was speculation in the press that Dickson would write because, as he neared retirement 'he would doubtless like to leave a milestone *Morgentaler* decision as part of his legacy.'[57] The speculation was correct, for Dickson did indeed prepare first reasons. As chief justice, Dickson hoped that the Court could speak with a clear and unified a voice. When he circulated his draft judgment at the end of June 1987, he stated in his covering memo to his colleagues: 'As you are well aware, this appeal is of great public importance and I believe that it would be very helpful if the Court could present as united a front as possible. To that end, I have attempted to write very narrowly, hoping to provide a core for agreement.'[58] Dickson had little or no power to secure unanimity, since each judge was entitled and bound by their oath of office to decide cases according 'to the best of my skill and knowledge.'[59] For the independent-minded members of the Court, this often meant writing their own judgments.

In view of his decision in *Morgentaler I*, it is not surprising that Dickson began his judgment with a discussion of what had changed in the past decade. He recalled that, in *Morgentaler I*, he had stressed that the Court had 'not been called upon to decide, or even to enter, the loud and continuous public debate on abortion.' Although the Court could still not 'resolve all of the competing claims advanced in vigorous and healthy public debate' or develop 'complex and controversial programmes of public policy', Dickson pointed to a fundamental change in the Court's role and in Canadian law. The Court was 'now charged with the crucial obligation of ensuring that the legislative initiatives pursued by our Parliament and legislatures conform to the democratic values expressed in the *Canadian Charter of Rights and Freedoms*.'[60] The values of the Charter, not the values of Parliament, now governed.

But Dickson tried to avoid making sweeping pronouncements. He knew that he would never persuade his more cautious colleagues to accept an obviously 'pro-choice' judgment based on a woman's freedom of conscience or her liberty interests, and he also knew that a pronouncement of that nature would engulf the Court in controversy. In his view, it was not necessary 'to tread the fine line between substantive review and the adjudication of public policy' or to decide, as the American courts had in *Roe v. Wade*, whether the Charter protected a right to privacy or complete freedom of choice in the first trimester of pregnancy.[61] The case should be decided on narrower grounds. As he had indicated at conference, Dickson concluded that the fact that a woman could be imprisoned for having an abortion without committee approval was enough to bring the Charter's right to security of the person into play. The procedural flaws of the law were sufficient to decide that it did not comport with the principles of fundamental justice.

Dickson avoided deciding whether the abortion law violated a woman's liberty or freedom of conscience, as Wilson maintained, but he made some moves in the direction of her more expansive approach. He argued that the abortion law interfered 'with a woman's bodily integrity in both a physical and emotional sense. Forcing a woman, by threat of criminal sanction, to carry a foetus to term unless she meets certain criteria unrelated to her own priorities and aspirations, is a profound interference with a woman's body and thus a violation of security of the person.' He stressed that delays in access to abortions caused by the cumbersome committee procedure forced significant numbers of women to undergo a second-trimester saline- induced abortion which required them to give birth to a dead foetus. He quoted at length evidence from a doctor that such abortions were 'cruel.'[62]

Dickson now accepted many of the same arguments that had failed to move him or any member of the Court in the *Morgentaler I*. Many hospitals in Canada did not have committees to approve abortions and those with committees applied different standards governing when an abortion was necessary to protect a woman's life or health. 'For some committees, psychological health is a justification for therapeutic abortion; for others it is not. Some committees routinely refuse abortions to married women unless they are in physical danger.' The vagueness of the abortion law meant that 'it is not typically possible for women to know in advance what standard of health will be applied by any given committee.'[63]

Finally, Dickson found that the government had not justified the abortion law as a reasonable limit on the rights of women. Dickson characterized Parliament's objective as balancing the competing interests of the woman and the foetus. Here as well, Dickson tried to avoid saying any more than he had to about the controversial abortion debate. He wrote that it was not necessary to decide whether the foetus had rights or even how far Parliament could go in protecting the unborn. The abortion law could not be justified because it failed to implement the very balance that Parliament itself had established. The 'cumbersome' and 'often arbitrary and unfair' administrative structure denied women access to abortions even when the continuation of their pregnancies would satisfy Parliament's own standard of endangering the life or health of the woman.

While this was enough to decide the case, Dickson insisted on setting out his strong views on the jury-nullification argument. He thought that it was improper for Morgentaler's lawyer to invite the jury not to apply the law and he wanted to say so. Jury nullification offended Dickson's strong belief in the need to ensure respect for the law. The rule of law bound everyone, including the jury. For Dickson, one of the 'frightening implications' of the jury nullification argument was that 'a jury fueled by the passions of racism could be told that they need not apply the law against murder to a white man who had killed a black man.'[64]

Only Lamer agreed with Dickson's judgment. Beetz decided to abandon the cautious approach he had taken on *Morgentaler I*, but he thought that Dickson's draft went too far. Beetz wrote a more cautious judgment, emphasizing the immediate threat to a woman's health posed by delay and the requirement for committee approval. Estey, who had at an early juncture started writing his own judgment, ended up agreeing with Beetz.

Wilson agreed that the law should be struck down, but she knew that Dickson's cautious approach would not end the abortion debate. She emphasized that a women's liberty and freedom of conscience were at stake and suggested that Parliament could justify restrictions on a woman's freedom of choice only 'somewhere in the second trimester.' In a memorable passage, Wilson wrote that it was 'probably impossible for a man to respond, even imaginatively' to the dilemma of an unwanted pregnancy and that the right to reproduce or not was 'an integral part of modern women's struggle to assert *her* dignity and worth as a human being.'[65]

As soon as McIntyre saw Dickson's draft, he made his views known. In a memo to Dickson he observed: 'I feel that possibly you have overlooked the constitutional question which is not whether abortion is a good thing or a bad thing, but whether or not it is in the constitutional power of the Federal Government or Parliament to enact the section of the *Code*.'[66] McIntyre's dissent was only somewhat less forceful. In his view, the Charter did not create the right to an abortion. He criticized Dickson's broad interpretation of security of the person, dryly noting that even the Income Tax Act interfered with people's priorities and aspirations. McIntyre agreed with Dickson that, since *Morgentaler I*, the courts had been given the additional duty of 'ensuring that the legislative initiatives pursued by our Parliament and legislatures conform to the democratic values expressed in the Canadian *Charter of Rights and Freedoms*.' However, he warned that 'the courts must confine themselves to such democratic values as are clearly found and expressed in the Charter and refrain from imposing or creating other values not so based.'[67] La Forest, who advocated a more restrained approach to Charter issues that implicated competing social values, joined McIntyre's dissent.

Abortion Law Scrapped

The Court's five-to-two decision striking down the abortion law predictably drew banner headlines: 'Abortion law scrapped; women get free choice.' Morgentaler, who announced that he would immediately open more clinics, told reporters that the decision was 'beyond my wildest dreams ... The decision today is the culmination of everything I felt the *Charter of Rights and Freedoms* stands for.'[68] He was particularly pleased with Wilson's bold judgment. In a 1993 letter inviting her to his seventieth birthday party, Morgentaler commented that 'while the other judges in the majority ruling decided the matter on narrow procedural grounds you, and only you, were upholding articulately human dignity, female self-esteem, freedom of religion and fundamental freedoms ...'[69]

Not everyone was pleased with the Court's decision. Roman Catholic Cardinal Gerald Emmett Carter, an adviser to the pope who had a year earlier ordered a Toronto church not to allow a girl to be an altar server at mass, declared the decision 'a disaster ... It is uncivilized. Abortions will become commonplace.'[70] For months and months, Dickson and Wilson received a large volume of vitriolic correspondence attacking their judgments. Joe Borowski, a former Manitoba provincial cabinet minister and well-known anti-abortion crusader whose case claiming rights for the foetus was pending in the Court, declared the decision 'scandalous and shocking ... The Supreme Court has canonized anarchy and law-breaking.'[71] Rocks were thrown at the window of Morgentaler's Montreal clinic and a hole, presumably to insert explosives, was cut in the roof of his Toronto clinic which was later bombed.[72]

Laura McArthur, president of the Right to Life Association, lodged a complaint with the Canadian Judicial Council, a body of judges (then chaired by Dickson as chief justice) which hears complaints of judicial misconduct.

McArthur pointed out that the Court had relied on a 1987 report which found that most of Ontario's hospitals did not have abortion committees, even though the report was not in evidence when the case was argued in 1986. Dickson had anticipated this objection. When he circulated his draft judgment to the Court, he indicated that he had placed 'some reliance on the very useful information provided by the Powell Report (1987), a public report on access to therapeutic abortions in Ontario ... Because the Report was released only this year, it did not form part of the record. I am inclined to use the Report because it is so helpful. My instinct is to write counsel asking for their comments on the Report.'[73] Dickson did not, however, follow his instinct, probably because of the Court's growing practice under the Charter to rely on published social-context material, even when not formally entered as evidence. The complaint was promptly dismissed – Dickson did not participate in the decision – on the basis that it raised 'no issue of judicial misconduct' and because it was 'not unheard of' for the Court 'to cite articles, books or other publications which might not have been referred to by the parties to the litigation.'[74] This ruling reflected the reality that the Court was now much more concerned with issues of social policy than it had been only a decade earlier.

The Distance Travelled

The two Morgentaler cases provide an overview of the significant journey taken by Brian Dickson and the Supreme Court from the early 1970s to the late 1980s. In *Morgentaler I*, Dickson and his colleagues deferred to Parliament's balance of the competing interests in the volatile abortion debate. No one on the Court, not even the liberal-minded Bora Laskin, was prepared to strike down Parliament's abortion law under the statutory Canadian Bill of Rights. Dickson could not countenance the defence of necessity in the absence of clear precedents. He went against his first instincts to defer to the jury and he sent Morgentaler to prison.

By 1988, both the Court and Dickson had changed. The Canadian Charter of Rights and Freedoms gave the Court a new mandate to strike down laws that were fundamentally unjust, while Dickson himself had grown as a judge and become more confident in the Court's ability to make law. He and most of his colleagues were determined to make something of the Charter and to avoid the criticisms that they had let the Canadian Bill of Rights die in the 1970s. Dickson never wavered from his original views expressed at conference that the abortion law must be struck down because it violated the Charter. As he well knew, *Morgentaler II* dealt with a controversial and divisive issue that directly affected the lives of ordinary Canadians and provoked the most passionate and divided of opinions. Perhaps more clearly than any other early Charter decision, it announced the emergence of the Supreme Court of Canada as the nation's moral compass.

But if Dickson had travelled a long way since *Morgentaler I*, he also had done his best to remain on the same road. Though the Court had moved to centre stage on one of the most controversial issues confronting Canada, Dickson continued to insist that his task as a judge remained legal. The broader philosophic, political, scientific, and theological matters concerning abortion could still, in his view, be left to Parliament. He continued to react sharply to arguments that jurors or anyone else were justified in disobeying the law because of their own views about higher values. Dickson also continued to seek the middle ground even though the Charter had shifted the terrain. He avoided the extremes of attempting to impose a detailed judicial solution to the abortion controversy or abdicating the new responsibilities of judicial review because the Charter did not specifically mention the word abortion. He urged his colleagues to decide the case on a relatively narrow basis that would not cut off public debate on the controversial abortion issue. His judgment left Parliament room to devise new abortion legislation, although it ultimately failed to do so.

PART TWO

Life before the Bench, 1916–1963

2

Prairie Upbringing

Robert George Brian Dickson was born on 25 May 1916 at Yorkton, Saskatchewan. His mother and father were Irish Protestant immigrants. Dickson's father, Thomas, the youngest of six children, was born in 1886 on a modest family farm in County Down in what is now Northern Ireland. He got a job with the Bank of Ireland after completing grammar school, but his economic prospects in Ireland were not bright. In 1913 Thomas decided to seek his fortune in Canada and take up a position with the Bank of British North America in Darlingford, Manitoba.

Dickson's mother, Sarah Elizabeth Gibson, was born in 1884 in the town of Mohill, County Leitrum, in the present-day Republic of Ireland. Known to friends and family as Lillian, she was the youngest of four children. Lillian's mother and father both died when she was very young; a childless cousin, married to a prosperous businessman, raised her. Lillian was one of the few women of the day to study at Trinity College, Dublin. She graduated with a degree in classics in 1912.

Lillian and Thomas met after her graduation while she was teaching at a private girls' school. The next year, Thomas left for Canada. With her superior education and the financial backing of her adoptive parents, Lillian had a future in Ireland, but in 1915 she followed Thomas to Canada. Thomas met her in Montreal where they were married on 13 August 1915.

Irish Immigrants

The Dicksons arrived in Canada on the crest of a wave of immigration. The Liberals, elected in 1896, had embarked on an ambitious program to populate the Canadian west with newcomers who would help realize Prime Minister Laurier's dream that the twentieth century would belong to Canada.[1] Thomas Dickson joined over 400,000 other new Canadians in 1913, recruited from the United States, the British Isles and Europe, with the promise of fertile farmland and the hope of a better life. The impact on Canada was enormous. Over two and a half million immigrants arrived between 1896 and the outbreak of the First World War, swelling Canada's population by more than a third. Wheat fields replaced grasslands as Canada's western frontier expanded.

By the early years of the twentieth century, immigration from central and eastern Europe started to alter dramatically the west's early mix of English, French, and aboriginal inhabitants. Many came from the Ukraine, Scandinavia, Russia, Poland, Italy, Germany, and Austria to add to Canada's cultural and linguistic diversity. However, it would take many years for non-English speakers to rise in the Anglo-Protestant-dominated social hierarchy. Irish immigrants, most of whom had arrived much earlier, did not rank particularly high in the social structure, but they were better placed than those from central and eastern Europe. Thomas and Lillian Dickson more or less escaped these rigid classifications. The Dicksons had Protestant roots, and, in a society that had yet to embrace the values of multiculturalism and cultural diversity, they avoided overt Irish self-identification. They quickly became, first and foremost, Canadians and settled with relative ease into the Anglo-Protestant elite that essentially controlled the political, economic, and cultural life of the Canadian west. As a boy, Brian Dickson's friends and acquaintances were overwhelmingly white and Protestant.[2]

Brian and his younger brother Thomas, who was born on 22 October 1918, were raised with a strong sense of pride in their parents' adopted country. Their parents' pro-Canadian point of view was reinforced at school where the pre-First World War focus on the British Empire gave way to a growing sense of Canada as an independent nation and of pride in Canada's accomplishments.[3]

Small-Town Saskatchewan

Thomas Dickson spent his entire working life with the bank that eventually became part of the Bank of Montreal. Bank managers were routinely moved from one branch to another every three or four years. Shortly before Brian's birth, Thomas was moved from Darlingford, Manitoba, to Wynyard, Saskatchewan, a tiny community on the Canadian Pacific Railway line between Edmonton and Saskatoon. When the Dicksons arrived, Wynyard was still a new community populated by Icelandic, Scottish, Ukrainian, Polish, and English immigrants. In 1916, the year Brian Dickson was born, the population of Wynyard was only 682. The town had no modern hospital and no electric power and, until 1925, the streets were illuminated at night by a few gas-lights.[4] Because of the rudimentary facilities available in Wynyard, Lillian was taken to nearby Yorkton to give birth to Brian.

In 1922 the Dicksons moved to Unity (population 747, according to the 1926 census), a small Saskatchewan town in the northern part of the province west of Saskatoon. Four years later, in 1926, the family moved to Weyburn, population 4,119, in the southern end of the province near the American border. Next came a stint in Regina from 1929 to 1932 and a promotion for Thomas to bank inspector. The family moved to Winnipeg in 1932 when Brian was part way through his final year of high school.

In small-town Saskatchewan, the bank was typically a solid redbrick building on a prominent corner. In Wynyard, the young Dickson family lived in an apartment provided for the manager on the second floor of the bank building. In Unity, other members of the bank staff occupied the apartment above the bank and the Dicksons had to rent a house, but in Weyburn the family again lived above the bank. These apartments were simple but respectable, and the local bank manager was regarded as an important member of the community.

Brian Dickson was raised in a modestly prosperous, closely knit, and conservative family. Thomas Dickson started as a junior manager, falling into what was known as the 'two and under' class. This meant that he earned less that $2,000, probably about $1,200, enough to maintain a family at a simple but decent standard. Lillian did not resume her career as a teacher in Canada, instead devoting herself to her family. As Thomas progressed in his banking career, the family prospered. Thomas bought a motorcar in 1924, and Lillian could soon afford live-in help to look after cleaning and household duties. Neither Thomas nor the boys were expected to help about the home. Lillian also enjoyed the luxury of trips home to Ireland to visit her relatives.

Thomas and Lillian Dickson led a quiet life focused on work, family, and the church. Lillian enjoyed cooking, and the family had regular meals together. Never far from home during the working day, Thomas regularly lunched with Lillian and the boys. Lillian, raised in the Church of Ireland, was very devout, and both Brian and his brother were baptized as Anglicans. Thomas had less interest in religion, but he attended church regularly with Lillian and the boys. Raised as a Unitarian, he did not share Lillian's preference for the Anglican Church. They chose the Presbyterian Church as an acceptable middle ground for the family in both Weyburn and Regina. In the later 1920s, the Presbyterians were the rump that had resisted the merger between the majority of their co-religionists, the Methodists, and the Congregationalists which had created the United Church of Canada. The predominant mood of the Presbyterians remaining after the schism was conservative and this, too, suited Thomas. The Presbyterian Church remained essentially silent on the causes of and solutions to the Depression and its only official response was to promote relief work by individual congregations.[5]

Lillian was strict about Sunday observance. Brian and his brother Tom dressed in their Sunday finest to attend church and Sunday school. Games or cards were forbidden on the Sabbath; the afternoon was spent in quiet activities such as reading. Religious observance was also an important part of daily life. The family always said grace at meals, and the children were taught to say their prayers at night. Lillian and Thomas took an active role in the life of the church. Lillian sang in the choir and Thomas was often asked to attend to the congregation's books and financial affairs.

Lillian's religious outlook had a lasting impact upon her sons. Brian became an Anglican and years later as a prominent Winnipeg lawyer, served as the chancellor to the bishop of Rupert's Land, the bishop's senior lay adviser. Like his father, Brian's younger brother Tom became a banker. However, he took early retirement, moved to Mexico, and spent two years studying Spanish and religion. He lived out the last ten years of his life as an Episcopalian parish priest in Guadalajara, and also put his banking experience to use as the bishop's right-hand man and financial adviser.

In addition to Sunday school, Brian and his brother took part in many other social activities – cubs, scouts, picnics, and sporting events. Brian particularly enjoyed the mock trials organized by the scout troop when he was about 12 years old. He took his turn at all the roles – defence counsel, prosecutor, and judge. It was his first exposure to the law, and when he was first appointed to the bench in 1963, he mentioned these Boy Scout mock trials as planting the seed for his future career in the law.[6]

Thomas and Lillian were conservative in their personal and social habits. As manager of a local bank, Thomas had cordial social relationships with business associates and the local doctors and lawyers. The Dicksons enjoyed playing bridge with friends. Lillian's education was superior to that of her husband, who had not gone beyond grammar school. Few of her friends or acquaintances shared her intellectual interests. She read widely and continued to derive pleasure from reading the classical works she had first encountered at Trinity College. Small-town Saskatchewan offered little to satisfy Lillian's intellectual interests, but if this concerned her, she did not show it. She was a positive woman who adored her family and put all her effort into nurturing her children, looking after her husband, and attending to her duties at the church.

Brian Dickson was close to his younger brother Tom. Only two years apart in age, the boys spent a great deal of time together, playing sports and enjoying outdoor activities. In the winter, every prairie town offered lots of hockey on outdoor rinks. The boys also enjoyed Saturday afternoon silent 'cowboy' movies accompanied by piano. Brian was a keen stamp collector and, by the time the family had moved to Regina, he was displaying his collection at the Boys Fair. In the summer, the boys swam, played baseball, and often went to a Boy Scout camp at a nearby lake for a few weeks. In addition, the family regularly went to a cottage or resort for Thomas's annual three-week vacation.

Years later, as a prosperous lawyer in Winnipeg, Brian Dickson acquired a substantial working farm where he kept cattle and horses. After he moved to Ottawa, he bought a farm in Ottawa where he rode his prized Morgan horses and kept a herd of fallow deer. Dickson's interest in animals and the outdoors was kindled as a boy in Saskatchewan. While living in Unity, Brian and Tom acquired a young coyote they kept as a pet in a wire cage for a couple of years. They enjoyed showing off their prize, pulling it in a cart at the annual Dominion Day Parade. Dickson's passion for horseback riding was also nurtured while he was a boy in Saskatchewan. The family did not own a horse, but friends and neighbours did. There was no formal instruction; it was 'just a matter of going out and getting on a horse and hoping that you could stay there.'[7]

Dickson remembered another adventure with animals with a profound sense of injustice. When Brian was about ten years old, the boys decided to keep white rats. They got an old upright piano box and filled it with hay and straw to provide a nesting place for the animals. The animals were quick breeders and the pack grew. Brian and Tom enjoyed having the rats crawl up their arms and around their necks. Unfortunately, the affection the boys had for these pets was not shared by some of the neighbours, who called in the local police constable. One day, Brian came home from school for lunch to find that all of his rats had been killed. The constable gave no warning before carrying out the deed. Years later, after his retirement from the bench, the incident was still vivid in his mind: 'I have never forgiven him. I thought it was a very cruel thing to have done.'[8] This long-remembered early brush with a perceived abuse of authority plainly left its mark on Canada's future chief justice.

Summer or part-time employment was uncommon, especially during the Depression when jobs were virtually non-existent. However, even as a boy, Brian Dickson was ambitious and he made two unsuccessful efforts to find work and earn some pocket money. When he was about eleven years old, he helped a milkman during the summer. To his dismay, the milkman failed to pay him what he had been promised. This was another early experience that made an impression on Brian, who later as a judge would hold people to their promises and use the law to ensure that people were not unjustly enriched by the hard work of others. At age fourteen, Brian applied for a job as an usher at the local cinema, a position that would provide both cash and free admission to the films. Again, he was disappointed. The proprietor came one night after he had gone to bed to inform Lillian that he thought Brian was too young for the work. Lillian was left to convey the news to her son.

The Depression

These early financial disappointments left their mark, but they were nothing compared to the economic devastation that was visited upon Saskatchewan farmers during the Depression. The wheat boom brought prosperity to the Canadian west by the mid-1920s, so much so that the Canadian prairies became the world's breadbasket. Western Canadian farmers, aided by low freight rates and relatively low tariffs on farm equipment, were producing as much as 50 per cent of world wheat exports.[9] However, the prairie economy was precariously focused on wheat, making it particularly vulnerable to the ravages of the Great Depression. The collapse of world wheat prices combined with natural disaster to bring economic devastation. The ruinous drought of 1929 was followed by windstorms in 1931 that turned the once rich topsoil into clouds of dust. A Saskatchewan provincial cabinet minister described the situation in a letter to Prime Minister R.B. Bennett pleading for help: 'the air ... is permeated with absolute dust, requiring lights on the cars even in the day time. The farmers ... are already in desperate circumstances. I find that only about one half of them have seeded and a considerable portion of that seed has blown out. The soil has drifted completely over fences and to a depth of two feet on one road that I travelled last year.'[10] A grasshopper plague in 1932 took what little else the land had to offer. Saskatchewan's per capita income of $478 had been the fourth-highest in Canada in 1928, but by 1933 it had fallen to a meagre $135. The government was essentially bankrupt and the once-proud prairie farmers had to depend upon trainloads of food and used clothing sent as charity from the east.[11] The Saskatchewan that had offered the Dicksons such hope when they arrived in 1913 had become Canada's poorest province.

Thanks to the security of Thomas Dickson's position with the bank, the family escaped the destitution that surrounded them. However, it was not an easy time to be a bank manager. Once prosperous farmers could not keep up the loan payments that Thomas Dickson was expected to collect and they were driven from their farms. Thomas had to face many heartbreaking situations. On occasion, he took young Brian along with him to make his discouraging calls. These visits to wasted prairie farms had a lasting impact on Dickson. He never forgot the humiliation and despair of the hard-working farmers who had lost everything through no fault of their own.

Although his father's position with the bank shielded Dickson from the worst of the Depression, he grew up in a climate of grave economic uncertainty and he was keenly aware that his future prospects could be limited. Young people had great difficulty finding work, and Saskatchewan teachers were distressed by the dim prospects their graduates faced. The board of Moose Jaw Collegiate adopted a resolution in 1934 urging the politicians to initiate a work program since, for the previous four years, only 10 per cent of its graduates had found employment. This was a demoralizing situation for which the young 'are in no wise responsible' and, said the board, 'unless something is done so that these young men and young women be given an opportunity to become self-supporting members of society, it will only result in a direct loss to us as a nation, and a loss to them of their self-respect ...'[12]

While Brian Dickson's outlook was plainly affected by the Depression, he also enjoyed some luxuries unimaginable to the average boy growing up in Saskatchewan. Most notable was his early and, for the times, unusual exposure to travel. Twice, Lillian took both her sons to Ireland, first in 1924 for a three-month visit and again for a longer visit in 1929. In Belfast they stayed with Thomas's brother Sam, a successful businessman known to Brian and Tom as the 'rich uncle.' They visited Lillian's unmarried sisters Sophie and Minnie in Mohill, and another sister Adelaide who lived with her family in Inniskilin. The second visit was for nine months, and Brian and Tom went to school in their mother's hometown, Mohill. Dickson met his cousins and one of Adelaide's daughters, Dorothy, was pretty and caught his eye, prompting 'a puppy love affair' for the thirteen-year-old Brian. Again, his recollections of animals were significant. In his retirement, Dickson recalled killing a pig, birthing a foal, and keeping a donkey that could be persuaded to move only by placing a thistle under its tail as memorable events from his times in Ireland. These early overseas adventures opened Dickson's eyes to the world beyond Saskatchewan and kindled a love for travel.

Early Education

Lillian Dickson's intellectual interests and love of learning and music made a strong impression on Brian, and indeed her example was a forceful influence throughout his life. In small-town Saskatchewan, the impact of Lillian's classical education sometimes surprised Dickson's friends. As a boy in Weyburn, Dickson went for a meal to the home of his friend Perry Millar. Mrs Millar asked Brian if he would like a second helping, to which Dickson replied: 'Oh no, Mrs. Millar, thank you. I have had *quantum sufficit*.' This early display of Dickson's erudition was long remembered in the Millar family.[13]

Lillian Dickson encouraged her children to read. Brian responded, although he was not as voracious a reader as his mother. Lillian ordered children's books by mail or procured them from the library when the Dicksons lived in a town that had one. Brian enjoyed the popular books for boys written by G.A. Henty and Horatio Alger. Henty was a British soldier in the Crimea and later a war correspondent. He wrote over thirty popular historical romances for boys. Horatio Alger was a nineteenth century American writer with a Harvard

Divinity degree who was forced to leave the pulpit in 1866 following allegations of sexual improprieties with boys. Within a year he had achieved success with the publication of *Ragged Dick*, the story of a poor shoeshine boy who rises to wealth. The theme proved to be popular and enduring and he proceeded to write over one hundred books for children that essentially relied on the rags-to-riches formula. Dickson read many of them. 'They all followed pretty much the same format. A young fellow from very modest beginnings would work hard and end up a great success. They were quite stimulating and inspirational for a lot of us to think that this was possible. They probably had a fair influence on our later lives.'[14]

The young Dickson took an active interest in drama. He acted and directed, sometimes in the same play. One memorable role was that of a young soldier in J.M. Barrie's sentimental *The Well Remembered Voice*.[15] The play portrays a First World War soldier, killed in action, who revisits his grieving parents and sweetheart in a seance. Praising his father for carrying on despite his loss, the soldier asks why his mother cannot stop wallowing in grief. He also asks his father why they did not spend more time together when he was alive and regrets his fear of asking his girl to marry him. The message that one should seize the moment to make the most of life was certainly not lost on Brian.

Dickson's elementary and secondary education was in the public schools of Unity, Weyburn, and Regina. Thomas and Lillian both took an active interest in their sons' schooling. Homework was regularly reviewed with mother, while father could be counted on for help in the preparation of a speech. Brian usually enjoyed school, but his enthusiasm for study depended to a large degree on the competence of his teacher. He shared his mother's passion for music and took piano lessons from a young age; he played in local festivals and in Weyburn his efforts were rewarded with a medal. Encouraged by a friend to join the Weyburn high school orchestra, Brian applied and was told by the orchestra leader that a flutist was needed. Brian saved his money and bought a flute and the leader taught him to play. He continued with the Regina junior symphony but then abandoned his orchestral career when the conductor told him that his flute was in the wrong key and that he should buy another. Piano playing remained a life-long source of pleasure and relaxation for Dickson.

Lillian followed the events of the day closely and she encouraged her sons to take part in family discussions at the dinner table. As a bank manager, Thomas thought it best to steer clear of politics, but he did watch current affairs with the cautious and conservative eye of a small-town banker. Although they were both Irish Protestants, Lillian and Thomas strongly disagreed about Irish independence. Lillian came from the south and had strong sympathy for the republican cause, a point of view that was strengthened with each visit home. Thomas was a staunch Ulsterman who held an equally strong view that at least part of Ireland should forever remain British. Discussion of Irish politics always generated a heated debate in the Dickson household. This early experience of being exposed to starkly different views on a controversial subject probably helped to develop Brian's ability to see both sides of disputes and honed his instinct to seek the middle ground.

Regina: An Introduction to Law and Politics

The Dicksons moved to Regina in 1929. They were more fortunate than most rural families who were moving to Regina at the time.[16] The city had become a destination for dispossessed farmers unable to find work, but, already suffering from high unemployment, it had no work to offer. In the summer of 1930, a General Motors plant that employed eight hundred men closed. The burgeoning number of unemployed led to increased government spending on make-work relief projects; almost $2 million was spent by the city, provincial, and federal governments in the years 1929–32. Even these projects were discontinued in 1932, leaving twenty percent of the city's population seeking relief. A family of four on 'the dole' got a meagre $16 a month, barely enough to survive. There was no work and virtually no welfare for hundreds of unemployed single men. In the early 1930s, May Day in Regina saw marching unemployed workers carrying red banners with radical slogans that incensed conservative onlookers. In 1933 Regina hosted the national convention for the socialist Co-operative Commonwealth Federation, precursor of the New Democratic Party (NDP), and the city gave its name to the famous Regina Manifesto that announced the new party's program.

At the Regina Collegiate Institute, Dickson was in the same class as Sandy MacPherson and William Lederman. MacPherson and Dickson 'paid attention in class and studied adequately, but did not pound the books.'[17] Lederman was the most serious student of the three. As Dickson remembered, 'there was never any doubt who was going to stand first in the class. That was Bill Lederman. The contest was over second place. With Sandy and me, it was pretty close to a dead heat.'[18] The trio went to school together, played hockey, and attended the same Presbyterian Sunday school. Dickson often went to the MacPhersons' summer place in the Qu'Appelle valley. MacPherson remembered Brian Dickson as a rather serious teenager who had inherited from his parents an 'even-tempered, patient, inquisitive and modest' nature.[19]

Murdoch MacPherson,[20] Sandy's father, whom Dickson later described as 'a great Canadian,'[21] was Saskatchewan's attorney general. He gave the trio an important early exposure to law and politics. 'Murdo' MacPherson was a Nova Scotian and a Dalhousie law graduate who came to Saskatchewan after being wounded during the First World War. Quickly becoming involved in Conservative politics, he lost in the federal election of 1921 but won provincially in both 1925 and 1929 and served as attorney general from 1929 to 1934 and as provincial treasurer from 1931 to 1934.

After school, the three boys often walked to the provincial legislature, where they headed directly for the attorney general's office. They could roam the government members' corridor and, if there was anything interesting in the House, listen to the debate from the gallery. Often they stayed in Murdo MacPherson's office and did their homework, sometimes dipping into the law books pretending to be lawyers. Murdo MacPherson was the first lawyer Dickson and Lederman got to know. He loved to entertain the boys with his stories of law and politics. 'He would lean back in his chair, light his pipe, and think out loud about the practice of law and the life of a politician.'[22]

Murdo MacPherson's subsequent legal career did not match those of the boys he entertained in his office. He was defeated in 1934 and promised an appointment to the Saskatchewan Court of Appeal by Prime Minister Bennett, but he was thwarted at the last minute by a political rival. MacPherson then returned to his law practice and made a serious run at the federal Conservative leadership in 1942, losing to John Bracken at the Winnipeg convention. William Lederman went on to study law at the University of Saskatchewan and then, like Dickson, served in the Royal Canadian Artillery in the United Kingdom and northwest Europe from 1941 to 1945. The two school friends often met during the war years. After the war, Lederman won a Rhodes Scholarship to study law at Oxford and he returned to Canada to a distinguished academic career, first at his alma mater in Saskatchewan and later at Dalhousie and Queen's, where he served as dean of law. He became one of Canada's greatest constitutional law scholars, and, after he became a judge, Dickson would frequently refer to and quote Lederman's writings in his decision.[23] Sandy MacPherson followed his father into practice and was later appointed a judge of the Saskatchewan Court of Queen's Bench.

Winnipeg: University and Law School

In 1932, part way through Brian's final year of high school, the Dicksons moved from Regina to Winnipeg. It was a larger city than Regina, but it too had been hit hard by the Depression. Often called 'the gateway to Western Canada,' Winnipeg's prosperity in the period following the First World War had rested on the grain trade. The collapse of world wheat market and the prolonged prairie drought had a devastating impact. By 1932, Winnipeg's unemployment rate was the second-highest in Canada and Vancouver had overtaken Winnipeg as Canada's third-largest city. Difficult economic circumstances produced significant social unrest. Unemployed men took to riding the rails and pleas were heard for the deportation of eastern European immigrants to protect jobs for the native born. Dickson was keenly aware of the economic difficulties, although, as in Saskatchewan, his father's success as a banker isolated the family from their effects. The Dicksons settled into a comfortable home in one of the city's most prosperous areas.

Dickson completed Grade 12 by writing the Saskatchewan examinations. In the fall, at the age of sixteen, he entered first year at the University of Manitoba. It was a momentous time for the university. The economy was stalled by the Depression and many young people, who might otherwise have found jobs, decided to continue their studies. The University was expanding despite the perilous financial situation it faced. However, just as the university was in the process of establishing its new site at Fort Garry, the debt-ridden province reduced its grant, forcing it to increase student fees, cut academic salaries, and reduce staff.[24]

In his first year, Dickson took courses in English, history, calculus, analytical geometry, political science, Latin, and logic. He joined a fraternity – Zeta Psi – that provided him with a group of friends to whom he stayed close for years to come. His fraternity brothers included the children of Winnipeg's social elite. Particularly notable were George and Edward Sellers, sons of a prominent entrepreneur and brothers of Dickson's future wife, Barbara. Ross Cooper, a medical student who lived at the fraternity, literally saved Dickson's life on the Normandy battlefield in 1944. Another fraternity brother was Clarence Shepard, who preceded him by a year in law school and stood as best man at his wedding in 1943.[25] Dickson enjoyed fraternity life and succumbed to the temptation of partying to the point of jeopardizing his studies. On the whole, his academic performance was mixed. He did very well in logic and reasonably well in Latin and political science, but he barely managed to scrape through calculus and analytic geometry, two subjects he expected to fail. After a second mediocre year as an arts student, Dickson worked for a few months as a junior teller in a branch of the Bank of Montreal. He knew that he did not want to spend his life working his way up in the bank as his father had done and so he turned to the law.

Dickson seems to have taken little or no interest in student activities or political action at university. In later life, he was strongly opposed to any form of discrimination, yet as a student he seems not to have been concerned by the fact that his fraternity followed the contemporary norm and excluded Jews. The only undergraduate course that made a lasting impression was a second-year history course on the French Revolution taught by the chair of the history department, Professor Noel Fieldhouse, an Oxford graduate with an imposing presence who had come to Manitoba in 1928. Fieldhouse was a legend to Dickson's generation of Manitoba undergraduates. Marshall McLuhan described him as the 'most inspiring' teacher he ever had. Others thought that he had dangerously ambiguous views about the rise of fascism.[26] Dickson remembered Fieldhouse as 'a superb teacher. He just made it come alive. You felt you knew each one of the characters, as if you were watching the guillotine operating and saw the Bastille overthrown. You could hardly wait to hear his next lecture and you can't say that about many lecturers.'[27]

Dickson's preoccupation with fraternity life and apparent lack of interest in the pressing social and political issues of the day was typical of his times. Canadian university students tended to be conservative and conformist during the early 1930s; the Depression inspired caution rather than radicalism. However, by 1935, the rise of fascism and the ominous signs of war in Europe started to provoke concern among some students. Pacifists conducted peace vigils reflecting anti-war sentiments. President Sidney Smith wrote in the 1938 'Brown and Gold' university yearbook that the university 'cannot reside and thrive upon a high mountain-top removed from the people on the slopes and in the valleys' and observed that 'democracy is dangerous because it is founded in conflict – the conflict of ideas.' In the same yearbook, Law Dean Thomas Laidlaw observed: 'In this changing world, both liberty of the subject and democratic institutions are being openly challenged as they have not been challenged in modern times. Economic conditions exist in all lands which none can justify and all should seek to remedy.'[29]

Dickson entered law school in 1934. He was only eighteen years old and he lived at home with his mother and father. His choice of career seems to have been something of an accident, although the seed had been planted by his enjoyment of family dinner-table debate, the Boy Scout mock trials, and listening to the tales of his friend's father, Murdoch MacPherson.

Just as Brian Dickson made the decision to become a lawyer, the Manitoba legal establishment was shaken by two controversies that cast the legal profession in a very bad light. In 1932 it was discovered that J.A. Machray, a highly respected lawyer and a prominent member of the Winnipeg establishment, had embezzled the university's endowment fund to cover some of his own bad investments. Machray had chaired the university's Board of Governors and was also the chancellor of the Anglican Diocese of Rupert's Land, two posts that Brian Dickson would later fill with considerably more distinction. Machray's fraud also involved church funds and has been described as 'the most shocking instance of misappropriation of client's funds in the history of the province.'[30] He pleaded guilty to fraud and died in prison after serving one year of his seven-year sentence. Shortly after being rocked by the precipitous fall of J.A. Machray, Manitoba's legal community was again hit with a controversy, this time involving Lewis St George Stubbs, a county court judge. Stubbs was a committed socialist who quite openly acted on his political views when deciding cases. In one notorious case he published a pamphlet criticizing the Court of Appeal for reversing him in an estate matter. Stubbs was forced to resign in 1933.[31] On the other hand, some prominent Manitoba lawyers made a more positive mark during the same period. Isaac Pitblado was elected president of the Canadian Bar Association (CBA) in 1934, and A.B. Hudson, the province's former attorney general, became the second Manitoban to be named to the Supreme Court of Canada in 1936. Brian Dickson would be the third, thirty-seven years later.

In the mid-1930s, the profession controlled legal education in Manitoba. Manitoba had followed the example of Ontario's Osgoode Hall with a program of professional instruction combined with hands-on experience in a law office. The program of the Manitoba Law School, jointly offered by the Law Society and the university, was established just before the First World War. It consisted of classes in the morning at the law courts and articling in a law office in the afternoons. Saturday mornings and summers were also spent at the office.

In 1934, Dickson was articled to the firm of Scarth, Guild and Honeyman. The pay was nominal – $11 a month until his fourth year, when his salary was increased to $15, still considerably less than fraternity brother Clarence Shepard, who received $25 a month from the City of Winnipeg legal department. Tuition was $100 in his first year of law school but the fees were increased to $125 in his second year, an amount that ate up the lion's share of Dickson's modest earnings. The firm had six lawyers, three partners and three associates. Even senior associates were poorly paid. One associate, George Dees, was a veteran of the First World War who supported his wife and children on $150 a month. The other two, Fred Christie and Wilbur Boyd, got $125 and $100 respectively. The partners were St Clair Scarth, a commercial lawyer, Charles Guild, a litigator, and Bert Honeyman, a successful local politician who served for years as a Winnipeg alderman. Guild had a reputation as a first-rate advocate and taught civil procedure and advocacy at the law school. Dickson was the only articling student.

Winnipeg was still in the grips of the Depression and much of Dickson's work as an articling student involved collections, mortgage foreclosures, and tax sales, matters with which he was all too familiar from his visits with his father to destitute farmers. Dickson also handled some family-law files and was expected to deliver letters and documents. Lectures commenced at 9:00 A.M. and concluded at 11:00 or 11:30. Most students stopped by the Land Titles office to do searches after class, had lunch, and then worked at the office until about 5:00 P.M. During the summer, students worked full-time at the office. The experience varied considerably depending on the interests, abilities, and inclinations of the principal. The work was routine and geared to the needs of the firm, with little or no thought of the educational experience it offered.

Dickson's class of '38 had about a dozen students, all of them men. The Law School's total enrolment was just over thirty. There were only three women, one of them Eva Mary Adamson, the daughter of Chief Justice J.E. Adamson. Most classes were taught by practitioners. There were only four professors with full-time appointments. Thomas Laidlaw was the dean. Though not a legal scholar, he was an able and well-liked administrator who guided the Law School from the difficult years of the Depression to the end of the war. Another full-time law teacher was Peter Tallin, 'a man with an awesome range of interests and accomplishments: Rhodes Scholar, champion athlete, prize winning typist, distinguished lawyer, voracious reader, teacher of mathematics and public speaking as well as of law, and dedicated soldier in both world wars.' He was proud of his physical fitness and, according to one law school legend, used to lie on the floor and invite students to stand on his midsection to prove his strength. Stories about Tallin were 'as numerous as his former students' but it was 'not always easy to distinguish fact from myth.'[32] Charles Rhodes Smith, another Rhodes Scholar and First World War veteran, was appointed a full-time professor in 1925. By Dickson's time as a student, Smith was mixing law teaching with practice. After the Second World War, he had a career in politics as Manitoba's minister of labour and attorney general, and in 1952 he was appointed chair of the Restrictive Trade Practices Commission in Ottawa. Smith was appointed to the bench at the same time as Dickson in 1963 and eventually became the province's chief justice.

During the early 1920s, in what has been described as its 'golden age,' the Manitoba Law School had taken a decidedly academic turn with the adoption of the Canadian Bar Association's model curriculum, the abolition of articles in two of the three years, the establishment of a library, and the hiring of two full-time professors. Unfortunately, by Dickson's time as a student, this bold experiment in academic legal education had been abandoned. The law school course had reverted to a four-year professional- and practice-oriented program of part-time study combined with articling. The predominant teaching style was the lecture method. The Law School had abandoned its early experiment with the Harvard-inspired case method of grilling students in a Socratic dialogue on the facts and reasoning of decided cases, a teaching style that would predominate in Canadian law schools after the war. Dickson studied from textbooks rather than casebooks and the curriculum included a standard range of legal subjects geared exclusively to what was perceived as being required for the practice of law. The focus was strictly on 'black letter' law. The Law Society had made a conscious decision to emphasize bread-and-butter professional training. Students were expected to learn legal rules and doctrine with little or no emphasis on policy, theory, or the social or economic context in which the law operated.[33] They had little or no choice of subjects. As Dickson explained to a graduating class in 1990, in his time 'the curriculum was limited to traditional legal subjects, and while we were well trained in black letter law, there was little of a theoretical or speculative nature for the more intellectually curious.'[34] It was not until the early 1960s that, partly at Dickson's urging, a completely university based law faculty was established in Manitoba.

The 1934 Law School calendar stated that students must attend 80 per cent of their lectures, which extended from 17 September to 21 December and from 3 January to 5 April. It also contained a warning that office duties would not excuse students from attendance at lectures. Many of the courses relied on English legal texts. For example, criminal law was taught from a standard English text, Kenny's *Outlines of Criminal Law*, and a copy of the Canadian Criminal Code. Students were reminded that 'in all cases where English textbooks are referred to, the points of divergence between the English law, and the corresponding Canadian law must be carefully observed.'

At law school, Dickson quickly reversed his mediocre arts record. In his first year he stood second in his class. His lowest marks were 66 per cent in criminal law and 72 per cent in contracts and 74 per cent in both civil procedure and accounting. His highest marks were 92 per cent in torts, 88 per cent in personal property, 87 per cent in the history of English law and English constitutional law, and 86 per cent in real property. In his second year, Dickson again stood second in his class, excelling in courses on equity, wills, agency and partnership, and real property. By his third year, he was first in his class, earning high marks in equity, corporations, and Canadian constitutional law. His worst mark – 65 per cent – was in a rather dismal sounding course called practical statutes, which required students to read the Bank Act, the Interest Act, and the Pawnbroker's Act. His second-worst subject, ironic given his subsequent contributions to the field, was in family law or, as it was called, 'domestic relations,' where he earned a 75 per cent. Dickson received the $40 Carswell Prize at the end of the year. Standing first in his fourth year, he graduated with the gold medal overall. He received marks of 90 per cent in jurisprudence and commercial finance and transaction, and his lowest marks were in the litigation-related subjects of criminal procedure (76 per cent) and civil practice and procedure (78 per cent). The Dickson family photo album contains clippings indicating that Dickson received $60 for the Isbister Scholarship in 1935 and 1936, $80 for 1937, and the Law Society prize of $50 when he graduated at the top of his class in his final year.

While Dickson excelled in jurisprudence, the course he took appears to have been based on the accepted wisdom of the nineteenth-century English common law. The assigned texts were Salmond on *Jurisprudence*[35] and Pollock's *First Book of Jurisprudence.*[36] These two texts were intended to introduce the new law student to the broad concepts underpinning the law. Unfortunately for Canadian law students like Dickson and his classmates, they focused almost exclusively on the British common law. For instance, at least half of Salmond was devoted to British property law. Pollock also concentrated on private law. While Salmond canvassed a wider variety of legal concepts, including natural law, his central focus was also 'civil' or state-made law. In addition, both texts used a considerable amount of Latin and referred extensively to Roman law.

The intellectual outlook typified by Salmond and Pollock has been described as 'the rule of law' approach. 'Its essential elements were the equality and autonomy of individuals, a division between the public and private realms, and the paramountcy of common law and courts.'[37] Legal reasoning was conceived in purely formal terms. The common law was seen as an internally coherent body of principles that could be derived from decided cases and applied deductively to resolve disputes. It assumed that common law principles could be derived and applied objectively and without reference to the political or social context. Roscoe Pound, a great American legal scholar of the early twentieth century, labelled this approach 'mechanical jurisprudence' since it assumed that decisions could be reached by 'rigorous logical deduction from predetermined conceptions' without regard to the social context.[38]

Some Canadian scholars, influenced by the American realist and sociological schools of jurisprudence, challenged the classic English common law approach to the study of law.[39] While Dickson was receiving his traditional and professionally oriented legal education, Bora Laskin, his future judicial colleague and his predecessor as chief justice of Canada, studied in W.P.M. Kennedy's innovative undergraduate law program at the University of Toronto and then went on to take a graduate degree at Harvard. Laskin was exposed to scholars who challenged the tenets of legal formalism and the strict separation of law and politics and argued that judicial decision making was not simply a matter of applying 'neutral' and abstract principles. They argued that the common law should not, and could not, be divorced from its social context; they tried to lay bare the values that actually drove legal decision making; and they distinguished 'the law in books' from 'the law in action' and were concerned not with what 'the courts have said that they were doing' but with what 'they have actually done in practice.'[40] This new wave of scholars also rejected the paramountcy of courts and urged greater attention to, and respect for, legislative and administrative decision making.[41] At Dickson's professionally oriented law school, these ideas were simply not in vogue.

The Sellers Connection

During law school, Dickson continued to spend time at the fraternity. He enjoyed swimming, hunting, golf, and tennis for recreation. Two fraternity brothers, George and Edward Sellers, became particularly close friends. George was a year older than Dickson and also studied law. Edward, the same age as Dickson, studied medicine. Their father, Henry E. Sellers, was a wealthy and successful businessman. The Sellers family lived in a very large house not far from the Dicksons' more modest dwelling. Harry and his wife, Irene, enjoyed travelling to the south in the winter. While they were away, Edward invited Dickson to spend a couple of months at the Sellers house. Dickson had his own room, a quiet place to study, and the luxury of a house with servants.[42] Another attraction was George and Edward's sister, Barbara, then only a fourteen-year-old school girl but eventually to become the love of Dickson's life.

Both George and Edward had attended Ridley College in Ontario and then returned to Winnipeg for university. Edward Sellers was a brilliant student and graduated from medical school with the gold medal the year after Dickson took the medal in law. George Sellers was a less serious student and did not complete his law degree. In 1936 he married Margaret Anne Aikens, the daughter of Harold Aikens, a prominent Winnipeg lawyer, friend of Henry Sellers, and future partner of Dickson. Dickson was fascinated by George's dashing and entrepreneurial spirit and he greatly admired Edward Sellers's intellectual achievements. Like Dickson, the Sellers brothers served overseas in the Second World War. George followed his father as a successful business-man and became one of Dickson's most important clients. Edward had a distinguished medical career at the University of Toronto, where he served as chair of pharmacology.

'Simply No Employment'

Dickson had his sights set on a career as a litigator but, despite his fine academic record, he could not find employment as a lawyer upon graduation. At about the same time, another future chief justice was having the same difficulty, although for different reasons. After graduating from Harvard, Bora Laskin was not hired as a law teacher at either Osgoode Hall or the Manitoba Law School because he was a Jew; he ended up writing summaries for the *Canadian Abridgment* for fifty cents a note.[43] Dickson made one or two overtures to Winnipeg law firms, but there simply were no jobs, not even for the Law School's gold medalist. As Dickson told a large assembly of young lawyers just called to the bar almost fifty years later: 'I thought the legal community would beat a path to my door. It didn't. There was simply no employment for a young graduate.'[44]

Dickson found a non-legal job with the Great West Life Assurance Company. He started in the agency department with David Kilgour, who later became president of the company. The work consisted of reporting on the work and sales of agents and company branches and included some door-to-door selling. After a year, he moved to the investment department, where his legal training was more relevant since much of the work involved vetting the documentation for mortgage investments. Dickson worked closely with Great West's legal advisers at Aikens MacAulay, the prestigious firm he would join after the war. His work included the enforcement of mortgages and he often had the unpleasant task of deciding to foreclose and seize the property of an unfortunate owner unable to keep up payments. Perhaps more interesting was his early exposure to the world of finance, gained from dealing with the investment of insurance premiums in mortgage and bond portfolios. In the end, however, employment at Great West provided Dickson with only modest satisfaction. He knew that he was not cut out to be an insurance salesman and the work on mortgages was uninspiring.

Since he could not find a job as a lawyer, Dickson decided not to pay the rather hefty Law Society fee for admission to the bar. It was not until 1940, after he had joined the army and was on his way overseas, that he was called to the bar as a fully fledged lawyer. As he explained in the letter he wrote in May 1940 to the secretary of the Law Society applying for membership: 'Since the 15th of June 1938 I have been employed by the Great West Life Assurance Company. Engaged in the Mortgage Investments Department of this firm, my duties are those of a mortgage clerk.'

Dickson's romance with Barbara Sellers started shortly after he graduated from law school. Dickson was able to use his success in his first-year logic course to advantage. Barbara was taking the course and her brother Edward recalled Dickson's high mark in the subject. Dickson agreed to tutor Barbara. She was, in Dickson's words, 'very beautiful and very wonderful.'[45] When she broke her leg skiing, he took her flowers and fruit and their romance blossomed.

Dickson became something of a fixture around the Sellers household. He spent much of his leisure time there. In the summer, he was invited to the Sellers summer home at Minaki, where he met George Tritschler and Bob Curran, young lawyers with Aikens MacAulay. Tritschler and Curran were seen as 'dashing social figures' and Dickson enjoyed their company. 'Picnics were the big thing. Everybody got dressed up. We went down Saturday night to a dance at the Yacht Club or at Minaki Lodge. Tritschler and Curran were always there. Tritschler was older than I was but I got to know them and we became good friends. They were just dashing around and so was I.'[46] The 'dashing around' was perhaps more of a wish than a fact. Barbara Dickson recalls her future husband as a serious young man who seemed almost envious of his carefree friends. In any event, the 'dashing around' was brought to an abrupt halt in 1939 with the outbreak of war in Europe.

3

Off to War

Canada declared war on 10 September 1939, following Germany's invasion of Poland on 1 September and Britain's declaration of war on 7 September. Brian Dickson had already enlisted as a member of the non-permanent active militia with the 38th Field Battery, 5th Field Brigade, Royal Canadian Artillery. By late 1939, Dickson's involvement with the regiment was taking up more and more of Dickson's time, and by early 1940 it had become an almost full-time endeavour. Dickson entered the Canadian Officers Training Corps and spent the summer of 1940 at Camp Shilo, near Brandon, Manitoba, training with field guns. Further training at the Fort Osborne barracks in Winnipeg followed.

Despite the enthusiasm of local militia units, Canada was ill-prepared for war. The military had been a natural target for government cutbacks during the Great Depression, with the result that in 1939 Canada's armed forces were seriously understaffed and poorly equipped. Dickson's militia unit trained with guns left over from the First World War. On the political front, Canada's ever-cautious prime minister, Mackenzie King, thought that an activist foreign policy, particularly one tied to Canada's membership in the British Empire, risked reopening the wounds of the bitter and divisive conscription debate of 1917. But King was an Anglophile at heart and he knew that English Canada would insist upon going to war at England's side.

Canada started to send its First Division to England in late 1939, but in these early days of the war the government had a limited war policy with no plans for full-scale mobilization or a large expeditionary force. From the autumn of 1939 until the spring of 1940, the Germans and the British waged what came to be known as the 'phoney war,' with little military activity on the battlefield. That ended when Germany invaded Denmark and Norway in April and, a month later, on 10 May 1940, the Germans unleashed their 'Blitzkrieg' attack first on Belgium and then the Netherlands and France. Germany now posed an immediate and direct threat to Britain. In late May the British Expeditionary Force, sent to help in the defence of France, was pushed back and threatened with annihilation. The miraculous evacuation of 338,000 British and Allied troops at Dunkirk was a defining moment for the Canadian public. A disastrous defeat had been narrowly avoided, but France was teetering and a German invasion of Britain seemed likely to follow. On 14 June 1940 the Germans walked into Paris, left undefended by the demoralized French army. These harrowing events had a strong impact upon the Canadian public and the Canadian government significantly expanded its war effort. As the historian C.P. Stacey recorded: 'The heavens, it seemed, were falling; and in the emergency the manhood of Canada came forward generously, eager to share the honour and the peril of the moment ...'[1]

Enlistment

Brian Dickson was part of a flood of volunteers for active military service in the summer of 1940. On 31 August he went with Clarence Shepard to Winnipeg's Minto Armories to enlist. George and Edward Sellers, his two closest friends, enlisted as well – George in the air force and Edward in the navy. Soon after, Dickson's brother Tom also enlisted in the army. Brian Dickson's militia regiment was mobilized as the 15th Light Anti-Aircraft Battery, Royal Canadian Artillery, and he was commissioned as a second lieutenant.

Dickson remained in Winnipeg with his regiment throughout the autumn of 1940. The situation in Europe was more and more ominous. Having easily taken France, Hitler launched his aerial bombardment of Britain, seemingly the first step of a planned invasion. From early July to mid-September, German bombers tried to bring the British to their knees and the Battle of Britain ensued. While the British were enduring the Blitz, Canadian efforts were focused on mobilization, recruitment, and training. The first phase of training, conducted in Canada, involved individual training, while the second phase, conducted overseas, focused on collective preparation as part of a fighting unit. At home, recruits learned basic military skills and the handling of weapons and equipment.[2] Dickson and the 15th Light Ack-Ack Battery trained in downtown Winnipeg. Though he had trouble with his mathematics course at the University of Manitoba, he and the other men in his unit took courses in electricity, mathematics, trigonometry, and geometry, mixed with sports and parade-ground training.[3]

Dickson's age, twenty-four, was a year older that the average age in the unit. As he prepared to go overseas, his romance with Barbara Sellers was becoming serious and the two talked about getting married. Henry and Irene Sellers were fond of Dickson, but they thought that Barbara was too young to marry and, in any case, Dickson would soon be off to war, perhaps never to return. Brian and Barbara's plans were put on hold.

England

After four days' embarkation leave in late January 1941, Dickson left Winnipeg by train for Halifax on 3 February. 'The scene at the station on leaving home was unforgettable. There were thousands of people on the platform and milling about the station saying good-bye to their loved ones and friends.'[4] The train stopped a few times for marches and exercises and arrived in Halifax on the 6th, in the midst of a heavy snowstorm. Dickson and his fellow artillerymen marched directly from the station to the docks, where they immediately boarded the *Warwick Castle*, formerly a Mediterranean luxury liner. The ship remained at anchor for two weeks awaiting the formation of the convoy that would take it across the North Atlantic. The boredom of waiting was broken when a freighter, laden with over-proof rum, pulled alongside and proceeded to sell its cargo to the troops. Some of the men got drunk and began throwing empty bottles. Dickson, who had been named the ship's adjutant, had to convey the necessary orders to end the party.

Between November 1939 and May 1945, more than 368,000 Canadian military personnel crossed the Atlantic. Although only one ship was lost, German U-boats were a constant threat. Troop convoys left Halifax under the escort of Canadian destroyers, while British battleships provided ocean escort across the open Atlantic and British destroyers accompanied the convoy in the dangerous waters around the British Isles.[5] The passage of the *Warwick Castle* in early February 1940 was rough. Dickson described the crossing forty five-years later: 'The weather was foul. The convoy speed was that of the slowest vessel. We were protected by destroyers of the Navy. In the heavy winter weather in mid Atlantic, these destroyers seemed literally to dive into the gigantic waves. One would think they would never reappear.'[6] At one point, a grand piano went through a wall in the main salon of the ship. Some of the men were violently ill and scarcely slept; Dickson himself resisted sea-sickness by following the advice of the ship's doctor, who recommended healthy doses of gin and bitters. As the voyage neared its end, Dickson was moved by the sight of the green Irish coast and the memory of his childhood visits. 'I could hardly wait until the end of the war to get back to Ireland.'[7]

Dickson and his unit disembarked at Gournock in the Clyde in Scotland on

1 March 1941 and proceeded to Colchester in Essex on England's southeast coast. Canadian troops arriving in Britain 'had attained only the most elementary standard of training' and 'there was much to do.'[8] The 15th Light Ack-Ack Battery received its intensive training from English instructors, the focus being the defence of Britain against a feared German invasion. Light anti-aircraft guns were in short supply, which complicated the training routine. Meal hours were staggered to maximize use of the available equipment.

Dickson was soon involved in active defensive duty. Every afternoon, a gun battery would go to the coast at Clacton-on-Sea, set up its guns, and watch for German bombers. The men took sleeping bags, hoping for a bit of rest, but often were up all night. The unit's first success involved an early encounter with the strict code of military discipline. 'Our battery had the good fortune, or bad fortune, to knock down the first enemy aircraft that came along that coast. The aircraft had been wounded. One of our gunners, called the number 4, had the firing peddle. He didn't wait for the command by the sergeant who was in command of the gun. He just pressed the firing pedal and the thing went firing away. Suddenly there was a great flash and the aircraft, a Junkers 52, went into the sea. The number 4 thought he was going to get a medal for this. Instead, he got court-martialled by the colonel for not waiting for the command to fire from the sergeant.'[9]

After a few months at Colchester, the regiment was stationed at various towns in Surrey, Sussex, and Kent. In addition to the usual air-defence role, the regiment was involved in extensive training exercises to practise its skills in anticipation of an invasion. Dickson served as the acting adjutant for the 3rd Light Anti-Aircraft Regiment for several weeks in December 1941. In March 1942 he was transferred to the staff of the First Anti-Aircraft Brigade Headquarters in Colchester. This meant a welcome move from spartan barracks to the comfortable house that had been requisitioned for brigade headquarters. He continued to spend part of his time with his unit, assigned to the air defence of Great Britain. Once, he encountered an early version of a German 'buzz bomb' – a self-propelled bomb sent flying towards its target from afar. 'I had the troops out on a route march. We heard a sort of wonking sound and looked up ... It had a heavy roar and seemed to be a little bit uncertain. Suddenly the motor cut out and the thing went into the ground about five hundred feet away. It dug a pit about ten feet deep and threw metal all over the place. We broke off and everyone went running to find out what this thing was all about.' The men collected pieces of scattered metal, and not long after 'about 20 people from London with Homburg hats' arrived. British defence experts had been anticipating this new German weapon and wanted to study the debris. 'So we lined up everybody and went along and collected all the things which were taken back to London for examination.'[10]

At the end of August 1942, Dickson moved to the headquarters of the Royal Canadian Artillery and, in October, he moved to the headquarters of the 1st Canadian Corps Artillery at East Grimstead as a 'Staff Learner.' There he worked on the plans for the invasion of Sicily. He returned to the Royal Canadian Artillery in December as a staff officer with the rank of acting captain and, in the spring of 1943, he was confirmed in the appointment of captain.

Many Canadian soldiers grew restless in England with the never-ending routine of training and waiting for something to happen. They had volunteered to fight and they were anxious to finish the war and go home. But Dickson did not complain. 'It was an exciting, exhilarating experience to put oneself on the line of defence for Canada.'[11] The threat of invasion and the uncertainties of the war brought people together in a fundamental common endeavour. Dickson also enjoyed life in England. Every couple of weekends, he was able to go to London, where the finer things of life were then affordable, even on a captain's pay. 'You could stay at the Dorchester or the Berkeley, the Grosvenor House, or the Savoy for, as I recall, nineteen shillings a night, which was pretty much of a bargain. We would go in for two or three nights. We would sightsee during the day, and then go to a nightclub at night.'[12] On several leaves, Dickson travelled to Dublin to visit his Irish cousins. Ireland was neutral in the war but welcoming. Food was more readily available than in England and Dickson enjoyed bacon and eggs instead of spam and brussels sprouts, as well as frequent visits to the Abbey Theatre.

Return Home, Marriage, and RMC

From the early days of the war, the demand for officers in the Canadian forces could not be met by the pool of pre-existing commissioned officers and military college graduates. To overcome the shortage, the Department of Defence adopted a policy of merit-based commissions, appointing men from the ranks in a process as free as humanly possible of political influence.

Dickson had impressed his superiors when appointed as a staff learner and then staff officer. The task of a staff officer was 'to give form to the commander's plan by ensuring that the appropriate troops arrive in the correct order, with the necessary equipment, at the right place and at the right time.'[13] Staff officers were the nerve-centre of the military. They were expected to gather and sift information, both strategic and tactical, and to provide operational assistance in the execution of the plan. The 'ideal' characteristics of a successful staff officer were loyalty to the command, 'military knowledge and practical experience, discretion, an ability to cooperate, a logical and flexible brain, imagination, foresight, an open mind, intellectual honesty, self-confidence, enthusiasm, stamina, singleness of purpose, and imperturbability.'[14]

Dickson had these qualities and his superiors identified him as someone with promise. During the early years of the war, aspiring Canadian staff officers were trained in Britain at Camberly or Sandhurst, but, from the middle of 1941, staff-officer training was conducted in Canada at the Royal Military College in Kingston. In the spring of 1943, Dickson was asked whether he would like to return to Canada to take the staff-officer course. Dickson was an ambitious man, and formal staff-officer training would definitely enhance his prospects in the military. He had also been away from home for more that two years and he very much wanted to get back so that he could marry Barbara Sellers, with whom he had maintained an active correspondence. He eagerly accepted the offer and returned to Canada on 6 June 1943.

On their fiftieth wedding anniversary, Dickson described the joy of returning home to Barbara in 1943: 'I will never forget the ecstasy returning to Winnipeg, to be greeted by a girl who had waited 2½ years. She was so very beautiful and I loved her dearly, more than the spoken word can tell. We became engaged in the Assiniboine Park Zoo, by the bear pit.'[15] On 18 June 1943 Brian Dickson and Barbara Sellers were married at Holy Trinity Anglican Church, Winnipeg. Dickson's best man was his fraternity brother and lifelong friend, Clarence Shepard, then an artillery captain as well. The ushers included George Sellers, then an air force wing commander, and future judicial colleague R.D. Guy.

The young couple left for a quick honeymoon at the Seigneury Club, Montebello, Quebec. Then, from 26 June to 16 October, Dickson attended the Seventh Canadian War Staff Course 1943 at the Royal Military College in Kingston, Ontario. He and his new bride lived in the hot attic of a house on Earl St that was built for one family but housed several during the war. The ceilings were low and when Dickson's tall law school friend and best man, Clarence Shepard, one of the ninety-six officers in the course, came to visit, he had to bend his head when he stood. On his fiftieth wedding anniversary, Dickson remembered a friend of Barbara's visiting them in Kingston. When she saw where the Dicksons lived, she said: 'Poor Barbara!'[16]

The Royal Military College had trained officers for the Canadian military since 1876. In 1939 there were 200 cadets enrolled in the college's four-year program. By the end of 1940, they all had left the college with commissions and the officer-training course was shortened to two years.[17] Even with this shortened program, however, the college could not hope to meet the needs of the military. In 1942 the regular program was suspended and the RMC facilities were devoted entirely to the staff-officer program that Dickson attended.

The course was a formative experience and, throughout the rest of his life, Dickson drew on the method and approach to problem solving that he learned at RMC. Candidates were nominated by their commanding officers and then selected by a committee from the list of nominees. The selection criteria included age, physical fitness, experience, and character. However, the Canadian military was desperate for staff officers and the formal criteria were not always met. By 1943, the minimum age had been lowered from twenty-five to twenty-two.[18] Staff-officer trainees put in long hours during their sixteen-week stay at RMC. Families were allowed but not encouraged;[19] the newly married Dicksons were an exception. Each morning, Dickson rode a bicycle across town from Earl St to RMC. From Monday to Friday, classes began at 9 A.M. and finished at 6 P.M. On Saturday, there were classes from 8 A.M. to 12:30 P.M. The bare minimum for study time outside class hours was three hours a day. Dickson found the course to be rigorous and demanding. To complete his assignments for the next day, Dickson was often up until 2.00 or 3.00 A.M. From these early days of their marriage, Brian and Barbara Dickson were a team, and Barbara was an important part of her husband's success. At RMC, she became fully engaged with Brian's work, sitting up with him while he pored over the books and papers, discussing the problems, and typing assignments.

The first phase of the course, five weeks in duration, concentrated on basic knowledge of all aspects of the staff officer's duties. This information included basic staff duties, organization, and equipment, as well as the preparation of written analysis and orders. Instruction took the form of lectures and discussions, with particular attention to the movement and stages of war. Students submitted written assignments and draft orders. The program included physical training during the early weeks, two hours a day were devoted to sports and students were also expected to learn to ride a motorcycle.[20] The final ten weeks of the course focused on tactical exercises and problems.

Dickson described the course in the following terms: 'It was really quite an education ... I guess mental discipline would be the central training. How to prepare command orders, how to direct an army formation ... how to plan an attack, how to plan a defence ... It was a very intensive form of discipline, and a lot of hard work for everybody. Everybody worked around the clock, almost seven days a week. Because it was wartime, everyone wanted to do well.'[21] Dickson found the course to be his most intensive educational experience. This opinion was shared by Clarence Shepard, who lost fifteen pounds during the course, largely on account of a lack of sleep, and claimed that he never worked harder.[22] The course stressed 'a method of thinking and a method of approaching a problem. What your objective is, what your alternatives are, and how to plan and implement each of those alternatives.'[23] This was a more modern, functional, and purposive approach than Dickson had been exposed to at the Manitoba Law School, where the emphasis was on the application of formal rules.

Upon completion of the RMC course, Dickson was appointed brigade major, with an acting rank of major, and posted to the headquarters of the Royal Canadian Artillery, 6th Canadian Division, in British Columbia, where he remained from the beginning of November 1943 through the end of March 1944. The course ended in mid-October and Dickson had two weeks' leave to get to Victoria. On the way, he and Barbara stopped in Edmonton to see his mother and father. There he learned that, because of a Japanese submarine threat, divisional headquarters was moving from Victoria to Prince George, British Columbia. The promise of 'a rose-covered cottage' and 'two bicycles'[24] in Victoria fell through.

In early November 1943 the Dicksons arrived in Prince George, then a frontier town with unpaved streets, wooden sidewalks, and 'a large number of drunken people at any hour of the day or night reeling down the street.'[25] Barbara managed to find a simple house to rent, which Dickson described as being a cut above the converted chicken coops some of their friends inhabited. One of Dickson's regular assignments was to meet visitors at the train that passed through at 3 A.M. The posting was far from ideal. By October 1943, the Pacific Command had been reduced and the remaining division, known derisively as 'the Fighting 6th,' was comprised largely of men who did not volunteer for overseas service. It is not entirely clear why Dickson was sent to Prince George, but the most likely reason was a questionable medical diagnosis. The military doctor had found a 'little bit of a skip' in his heart.[26]

Anxious to return to England, Dickson managed to persuade the medical authorities that there was no problem with his heart. As the Allied forces were preparing for the Normandy invasion, he left Barbara in Winnipeg and embarked for England on 30 April 1944 at the rank of captain. He was taken on strength in the No. 2 Canadian Artillery Reserve Unit on 11 May. On D-Day, 6 June 1944, still in England, Dickson was appointed general staff officer III (liaison), Headquarters, 1st Canadian Army. Barbara Dickson, anxiously awaiting his return to Winnipeg, was expecting a child, to be born in mid-December.

Normandy

Approximately 130,000 Allied troops landed in Normandy on 6 June and within a week the number had more than doubled to over 300,000. Harbours were hastily assembled so that the massive amounts of equipment and supplies needed for the assault could be landed. The German forces had been stretched and strained by heavy losses on the eastern front. Hitler did not expect the Allies to invade Normandy and many German units on the French coast were staffed by soldiers ordinarily considered too young or too old for war. However, the Germans who were there fought hard to resist the Allied advance. The D-Day assault met fierce resistance from well-fortified enemy positions overlooking the Normandy beaches and Allied losses were heavy. The D-Day objective of Caen, some nine miles from the coast, was reached only after thirty-three more days of bitter and costly fighting.

Dickson remained in England until late July. On 1 August he was appointed general staff officer III to Headquarters, 2nd Army Group, Royal Canadian Artillery. He passed through Caen, devastated by shelling and bombing. It was a terrible scene, the city was reduced to smouldering rubble and the air heavy with the stench of death.

The Allies had a firm grip on the Normandy coast and continued to push the German forces hard. The Americans, led by General George Patton, penetrated down the western side of Normandy to Avranches on the Atlantic coast and were in position to drive south and east to encircle the Germans, while the British and Canadians had taken Caen and were pushing south towards Falaise. The German generals saw a perilous situation developing and wanted to withdraw to a more defensible position at the Seine. However, at the best of times, Hitler tended to ignore the advise of his military experts, and to make matters worse, in late July a group of dissenting generals made him even more wary by attempting to assassinate him. Refusing to draw back, Hitler ordered his forces to gather to deliver what he hoped would be a fatal counter-attack against the Americans. British intelligence intercepted the German plan and the Allies saw an opportunity to trap the German forces in a pocket between the Americans on the left and the British and Canadians on their right. Vital to that plan was the advance on Falaise. If that objective could be achieved, the gap between the American and British forces would be closed, as would the German supply and escape routes.

In early August, General Montgomery, the commanding officer of the Allied armies in Normandy, instructed the 2nd Canadian Corps to take Falaise. Lieutenant-General Guy Simonds, Canadian corps commander, launched Operation Totalize to open the way to Falaise. Despite early success on 7 August, the Canadian forces met fierce resistance from enemy forces that included an S.S. division led by General Kurt Meyer[27] and within four days the operation was called off. The Germans had stopped the Canadians about eight miles from Falaise.

'Tractable,' a second operation, involved two armoured brigades and four infantry brigades as well as a British and a Polish armoured division, all under the command of Simonds's 2nd Canadian Corps. The plan was to proceed down the Falaise road with the support of Royal Air Force and Royal Canadian Air Force bombing. The assault began on 14 August, 'a beautiful summer day.'[28] The pounding of artillery and bombs, together with the rapid movement of two hundred and fifty tanks through open wheat fields, produced a massive cloud of dust and smoke that Simonds hoped would provide cover. Although it did obscure the Canadian advance from the enemy, it also caused problems for some of the armoured vehicle drivers who became disoriented when heading straight into the sun. The enemy anti-tank defences responded with heavy shellfire, and Dickson was severely wounded just as the assault was getting under way.

Dickson rarely talked about his war injury and when he did, the discussion was brief. His son Brian says that, 'even when something specific would come up, an anniversary of a date or something ... when you asked him, "What do you remember about that," he would say "Not very much. It sure is a nice day out isn't it?"'[29] However, in an interview conducted in 1992, Dickson gave the following account: 'I had been asked to go and try to salvage vehicles which were under heavy attack. I had some transport guys with me. It was about midday. We were trying to get these vehicles out of a particular area that was under very heavy assault. Something happened and the next thing we knew, half a dozen of them were dead. I was wounded.'[30] He did not explain the 'something' that happened. In fact, Dickson's near fatal wound and the loss of his right leg was the result of a tragic accident, as it is now called, 'friendly fire.' For the second time in a week, Allied aircraft had dropped their bombs short of the enemy lines on their own troops, with devastating effect. On 8 August it had been American bombers. This time it was RAF and RCAF bombers.[31]

Simonds's plan called for bombers to hit the enemy lines just as the assault was launched. The use of bombers for close support was inherently risky, and the whole operation required careful planning and coordination. Even a slight error could land bombs intended for the enemy on Allied troops. The bomber crews, who faced incredible risks, could easily bomb short when hit with enemy flak while flying straight into the target. Another problem was that the bomber crews were not accustomed to daylight raids and Operation Tractable was to be launched mid-day. These risks were explained to the Canadian army when it made its request for bomber support for 'Tractable.' Simonds decided that the risk of attacking without bomber support was greater.

The bombing operation was massive. Over 800 airplanes were involved: 417 Lancasters, 352 Halifaxes, and 42 Mosquitoes. They dropped 3,723 tons of bombs. Only two aircraft were lost; one of them, itself a victim of friendly fire, was shot down by Canadian anti-aircraft guns. Fewer than 10 per cent of the airplanes bombed short, and 44 of the 77 that did were RCAF. The losses were heavy: 156 killed and 241 wounded.[32]

Dickson refused to make anything of the fact that he had been hit by friendly fire. He simply did not want to blame anyone. He knew of the risks that bomber crews faced and he also knew that their casualty figures were staggering. In his mind, all involved in the fighting were doing their best in unfamiliar and difficult circumstances and accidents were inevitable.

While Dickson would not discuss the matter or blame anyone for his injury, there seems to be little doubt that the accident could have been avoided. Plans called for the bombers to time their runs precisely from the moment they reached the French coastline, but some of the pilots neglected to do so and relied entirely on visual recognition of targets. Troops on the ground had been told to use yellow flares to identify themselves as friendly forces; unfortunately, the bomber crews were told that no signals would be used. When the troops on the ground saw the bombers coming close, they set off the yellow flares. Some of the bomber crews thought that the yellow smoke indicated the position of the enemy.[33] Rather than ward off friendly fire, the flares attracted it. The incident could have been avoided if the Canadian army had given the air force proper information about the use of flares to mark its position and if the pilots had followed instructions to time their runs. Dickson was precise, punctilious, and well trained in the importance of careful military planning and it is remarkable that he did not resent the fact that he nearly lost his life to carelessness. He was probably aware that several people were disciplined and suffered demotions in rank, reprimands, and 'starring' from participation in similar raids unless they underwent retraining.[34] One pilot's fate illustrates precisely what Dickson wanted to avoid. The pilot's commanding officer described a bombing run a few months later when the pilot encountered heavy anti-aircraft fire and was severely wounded: 'Having been chastised by me for bombing short at Falaise, [the pilot] was determined to prove that this time he had bombed where he was supposed to have. He hung on long enough to enable the bomb-aimer to drop the bombs, and then for another couple of minutes to take the picture of where the bombs hit.'[35] The pilot was wounded and he collapsed. The remaining crew members managed to bring the crippled four-engine Lancaster home although they had never before landed an aircraft.

The *Official History* notes that the incident that nearly cost Dickson his life 'had momentarily a severely depressing effect on the morale of the units and formations that suffered. Men naturally overlooked the fact that the vast majority of the bombs had gone down precisely where they were intended to.'[36] Whatever he might have thought at the time, years after the war, Dickson's attitude was very different from that recorded in the *Official History*.

Bill Lederman was nearby and, although unaware that Dickson had been hit, saw the disaster unfold.[37] Clarence Shepard also witnessed the incident and described it in a letter home written shortly after:

The first vivid memory is of our being bombed by the RAF heavies by mistake at the opening of the second phase of the battle towards Falaise. It was a beautiful warm summer afternoon, and our spirits were high because we knew that 900 RAF heavies were on their way to soften up the German lines. They flew over low in perfect formation and I remember watching the bomb doors swing open and the bombs drop away in a graceful pattern. But I was horror-struck to see some of the bombs landing in the fields next to our headquarters. I knew that our troops were there. It was one of these bombs that cost Brian Dickson his leg. Soon the telephone in our operations' vehicle was jammed with frantic calls from our brigades to call off the bombing. As the staff officer responsible for divisional air support, all I could do was to get on the phone to my opposite number at Corps headquarters, but the bombers came for another 20 minutes before they stopped.[38]

Dickson suffered a compound fracture of his right femur. This was a common but serious wartime injury and required surgery as quickly as possible. Getting the patient to a surgical centre was the primary objective. Treatment, however, had to begin on the battlefield, where the wound was packed with dressings to control bleeding; the limb was then immobilized in a splint before the patient could be transported on a stretcher to the nearest medical unit. The patient was kept on the same stretcher until physicians were sure that shifting him would not worsen his condition. Most often, this meant that the patient was on the same stretcher until after surgery. Compound femur fractures were classified as high-priority injuries and given preference for treatment at advanced surgical centres.[39]

Dickson knew at the time that he had suffered a life-threatening injury and he thought he might die and never return to Canada. He also knew that Barbara was pregnant and expecting the birth of their first child in December. He credited a fraternity brother, in charge of the medical triage of wounded soldiers, with saving his life:

I got my leg shot off. We all carried some morphine in a pack in our battle dress that I never expected to use. I put that into my arm, and then went off into a sort of doped sleep. Fortunately, the recovery of wounded people was superb. I guess within a matter of minutes I was on ambulance jeep, being carried to a military hospital, where they laid us out as though we were logs of wood. I came enough alive to see somebody walking past who looked very familiar. In fact he had lived in the fraternity house. He was a surgeon, Dr. Ross Cooper. I said 'Hi, Coops.' He looked down and said, 'My God, now get this guy on to the operating table.' And they did. Dr. Cooper came back a little while later. By this time I was reasonably conscious. He said I had lost one leg and was badly wounded in the other, but that everything was going to be all right.[40]

In the confusion created by so many unexpected casualties, Dickson was fortunate to receive immediate attention. Available medical services were severely strained. Over the course of the day, the two available casualty-clearing stations received almost 550 casualties. Two Canadian field-dressing stations admitted approximately 570 wounded. Two other casualty-clearing stations had to be opened where almost 700 casualties were treated over the course of the day.[41]

According to a letter and a medical record he received long after the war,[42] Dickson was taken to a station at Carpiquet, just outside Caen. His medical care was administered in a canvas tent in a grain field, with an air raid in progress. Dickson received a blood transfusion and anaesthetic of ethyl chloride induction followed by ether vapour. Sometime around midnight, his right leg was amputated above the knee.

The bombing error of 14 August was only one incident in a day of difficult fighting. The Canadian Broadcasting Corporation's war correspondent was on the scene and described the battle for the home audience: 'There's still no swift rush southward. We're not yet in Falaise. The German Army is not disintegrating. Not yet. In fact, they're still putting up a bitter fight for every village. They know, as we know, that if we break through there, it's the beginning of the end of the German Army in the West. And slowly, we are breaking through. And we all know that history is alive right here among us.'[43] By the end of the day on 14 August, the Canadian forces were within striking distance of Falaise. Some 15,000 men had advanced five miles. Operation 'Tractable' was judged a success, although it was less than complete since the gap had not been completely closed. Some of the enemy units the Allies had hoped to trap had slipped through to fight another day. There was still much more fighting to be done, but, for Brian Dickson, the war was over.

Dickson was taken to a hospital at Bayeux and then to the military hospital at Aldershot in England. A frequent visitor at Aldershot was Colonel George Tritschler, the lawyer Dickson knew from his pre-war visits to the Sellers' summer home at Minaki. Tritschler was serving with the judge advocate general in London. The visits meant a great deal to Dickson and the two became close friends. Tritschler was a partner in Aikens MacAulay, the firm Dickson would join after the war, and years later became chief justice of the Manitoba Court of Queen's Bench and enticed Dickson to the judiciary.

Return to Canada

Shortly after 14 August, Barbara received an ominous telegram informing her that her husband had been wounded. Wartime security and limited means of communication denied her more information. She received another telegram when Dickson made it to the hospital in England, but even then the message was cryptic and gave little comfort. It was apparent to her that Brian had suffered a devastating injury. George Tritschler's letter provided her with more details, but he described Dickson's condition as 'frail,' hardly reassuring news. Even the details of Dickson's return to Canada were shrouded in military secrecy. Barbara was informed that he would be embarking on a hospital ship, but she was not given any details of when it would arrive. She later learned that the ship had arrived in Halifax, but again, no details were given about the train that would bring him to Winnipeg. While George Sellers managed to discover what day Dickson's train would arrive in Winnipeg, the authorities could not say precisely what time. On 11 December, George took Barbara, now nine months pregnant, to the station where they spent all day with a large crowd of women and children awaiting the return of their wounded husbands and fathers. Dickson, looking thin and frail, finally emerged from the train in a wheelchair. Barbara and George took Brian to the Sellers home and, shortly after getting him to bed, Barbara realized that she was about to give birth. She left her father in charge of Dickson and got the gardener to drive her to the hospital. The Dicksons' son Brian was born early the next day. It was a remarkable homecoming, but Dickson still needed time to recover from his ordeal. He had lost thirty pounds and his wounds needed further attention. He spent a few months at Deer Lodge Hospital where he underwent another operation on his leg to allow it to take a prosthesis.

Dickson's brother Tom also suffered a seriously debilitating leg injury. Tom was posted to the west coast late in the war, and the brothers met when Brian went to British Columbia following the staff-officer course. Both were anxious to go overseas. Brian encouraged Tom to apply for what was called the 'Canada Loan,' a program that provided Canadian army officers for shorthanded British infantry units that had lost officers in action. Tom was accepted and saw action with a British regiment in Holland. Like Brian, he suffered a severe leg wound from which he suffered pain for the rest of his life. Brian believed that his brother Tom would have been better off had his leg been amputated and always felt a pang of guilt for having facilitated Tom's assignment overseas.[44]

A Wounded Soldier

Dickson was profoundly affected by his war experience. It influenced and shaped his outlook and his thinking for the rest of his life. He readily adopted a rigorous military approach to organization, planning, and coordination, and he approached his professional work as a lawyer and a judge with military-like organization. Every task or project was meticulously planned and plotted from beginning to end in a logical fashion. He carefully assigned specific tasks to his juniors or law clerks and rigorously monitored their progress.

Antonio Lamer, who served with Dickson for ten years on the Supreme Court, described Dickson's demands on those who worked with him as follows: 'Sunday, I've got to see you and that's all, I mean to say, we are going to war ... I don't think it was selfishness, I think it was a sense of duty ... He battled like the army, so if you attack on Sunday, you attack, you are there.'[45] Dickson was even more demanding of himself, adhering relentlessly to his rigorous, self-imposed schedule. Problems and issues were identified and scrutinized from every possible angle until a rational and principled solution emerged. His judicial colleagues were struck by Dickson's military approach. Beverley McLachlin describes him as 'very organized,' 'very correct,' and 'very military,' and adds that he had a strong sense of decorum. 'Decorum, I always felt, it was terribly important for him. You had to behave properly and somehow, without ever saying it, he instilled in the judges who worked with him a sense that you were expected to maintain a certain standard of correctness.'[46] Claire L'Heureux-Dubé remembered that her first conversation with Dickson immediately after her appointment to the Supreme Court 'sounded like the regiment master or the chief of staff saying, "You are in my army and come" and there was no saying "no" ...'[47] But they all agree with Gérard La Forest that Dickson 'was a *nice* general.'[48]

Dickson's military experience also made a lasting impression on his compassionate side. Fate had dealt him 'an unfortunate, unexpected blow early in his life,' an experience that made him sensitive to the misfortunes of others.[49] Fighting alongside people from a wide diversity of backgrounds in a life-and-death struggle for fundamental values influenced his vision of Canada as an inclusive society.[50] In addition his near-death experience and the injury he suffered gave depth to his understanding of human suffering. He knew what it was to risk one's life for a cause, and he showed remarkable courage, grit, and determination in making the most of his life despite the limitations imposed by his own injury. The commitment to the great cause of the war years imbued him with a dedication to public service, a hatred of tyranny and cruelty, and a profound love for Canada and its ideals of fairness, acceptance, and opportunity for all.

Dickson suffered pain from his war injury for the rest of his life. After the war, he progressed from a wheelchair to two crutches, then two canes, one cane, and finally none. He walked with an obvious limp, but he walked on his own, almost always without a cane until he was well into his seventies. His prosthesis was a complicated affair involving an artificial leg and a harness around his shoulder. There can be no question that his war injury had a profound effect upon his life and his outlook. However, Brian Dickson was a proud and determined man who simply refused to allow his life to be limited or defined by his disability. As he said in an interview in 1985: 'It wasn't a question of "will I or won't I," the decision wasn't mine. It was done and that was it. From then on it was as if I was born with blue eyes or brown eyes. You accept it with no cavil.'[51] He did not like any notice to be taken of his disability and he pushed himself to the limit, and sometimes beyond, to get about on his own and do things unaided. 'Fiercely independent and proud,' he wanted no special favours because of his war injury.[52]

At times, Dickson suffered severe pain from his injury that could not be relieved by medication. Yet he had the ability to endure pain and never complained, even to his close family. As his son Brian recalls: 'When his leg was acting up, he would have those terrible grimaces. You could see a jolt of pain going through him and he would say "I'm all right. Don't bother. Don't worry about me."'[53]

Recalling the War

On 19 March 1945 Brian Dickson was discharged from the army. At the age of twenty-eight, almost seven years after graduating from law school, he was about to begin his career in the law. For the next forty years, Dickson had little involvement with military matters. His only link with the military was membership in the Royal Canadian Legion. Though he did not attend Legion meetings, he supported the organization nonetheless because he worried that the government might abandon veterans. He explained in a letter written in 1984, when he accepted an appointment as honorary colonel of the 30th Field Regiment (RCA) in Ottawa, that from the time he was invalided home in 1944 'my interest in the law did not permit me to continue with militia activities.'[54]

In the early 1970s, Dickson and Barbara enjoyed a vacation in France. They drove through Normandy and Dickson realized that he was only a few miles from the scene of his injury. He kept driving. He had no desire to revisit the shattering experience he had barely survived. Although he remained reluctant to discuss his own wartime experience, he sometimes did reveal his profound feelings about the tragedy of war. In March 1989, on a visit to the Austrian Constitutional Court in Vienna, Dickson was introduced to Dr Karl Müller, an Austrian judge who had also lost a leg during the war.[55] The two men limped towards each other and shook hands. They said nothing about the war nor did they mention the incidents than nearly cost them their lives. There was an unspoken but deeply felt bond between these two men of the law who, on opposite sides of the combat, had been maimed almost fifty years earlier. It was a moving moment for them and for those who witnessed it.

On a similar visit to what was still the Soviet Union in September 1989, Dickson, Barbara, Bertha Wilson, and her husband, John, visited the memorial in Leningrad where nearly 470,000 victims of the twenty-eight month siege during the Second World War are buried. The city, which has now reverted to its pre-revolutionary name of St Petersburg, lost over one-third of its inhabitants from the fighting and from starvation, yet its remarkable resistance was a turning point in the war and played an important part in the Nazi defeat. The memorial marks the horror of the war, the courage of the Russian people, and the enormous suffering they endured. The Canadian visitors and the Russian hosts shared a moment of silence broken only when Dickson strode a few steps towards the monument, seemingly without a limp, stood to attention, and, with tears in his eyes, snapped a military salute. His deeply moving gesture, like his career, was a remarkable combination of military precision and human compassion.[56]

4

Law and Business:
Family and Community

From 1945 until his appointment to the bench in 1963, Brian Dickson worked very hard to become a prominent member of the Winnipeg legal, business, and social establishment. He rose quickly through the ranks of Aikens MacAulay, one of Winnipeg's leading law firms, to become a firm partner and leader, his clients including many of the city's most important corporations. He was also deeply involved in the affairs of his profession, becoming president of the Manitoba Law Society and holding senior office in the Canadian Bar Association. Dickson, however, was more than a lawyer. He had a keen business sense and obtained appointments to many corporate boards, including a prestigious appointment to the board of one of Canada's chartered banks. At the same time, his commitment to public service was remarkable. He played a leading role in the relief effort during the Winnipeg Flood in 1950, and his name frequently appeared as a board member of community organizations.

Aikens MacAulay

In January 1945 Harold Aikens, a close friend of Dickson's father-in-law, Henry Sellers, invited Dickson to join the prestigious firm of Aikens MacAulay. The offer was eagerly accepted. The firm had been founded in 1879 by James Aikens, Harold Aikens's father.[1] James Aikens was a successful lawyer with a strong commitment to public service. He conceived the role of the lawyer to be that of an intellectual and moral leader with duties to society that transcend the narrow interests of his clients. Aikens played a significant part in developing the Manitoba Law School. Urging the profession to adopt an academic program rather than one that focused on professional training,[2] he explained his vision for the legal profession at the opening of the Manitoba Law School in 1914, when he told the students to see a legal career as a life of public service. Each one should 'not only to aspire to be the thorough lawyer, but to be the best Canadian.' Aikens told the fledgling lawyers 'that they should aim to be leaders in thought, promoters of the intellectual and moral development of our young nation, so that it may become a strong, and forceful leader in the Empire.'[3] Many years after Aikens's death in 1929, the firm he founded continued to espouse his conception of the ideal lawyer and to emphasize public service.

Aikens was also politically active. He was elected to Parliament as an anti-reciprocity Borden Conservative in 1911. In 1915 the provincial Tories were tainted by a scandal involving corruption in the construction of the provincial legislature, and they hoped that with Aikens as leader they could present a clean slate. Sir James resigned his seat to assume the leadership of the provincial Conservative party but the venture was a disaster. Only five Tories – not including Aikens – were returned in the provincial election that same year. Sir James did not, however, disappear from public life. He was appointed lieutenant governor of the province in 1916, a post he held for ten years.

Aikens was the driving force behind the creation of the Canadian Bar Association, the national voluntary association of lawyers founded in 1914, and served as the CBA's president until 1927. More than fifty years later, after his appointment as chief justice of Canada, Dickson recalled Aikens's ideals for the profession at a CBA meeting, noting 'his devotion to excellence in legal work, his deep commitment to improvement in legal education, his insistence on lawyers' responsibility to the community ... his estimation that ... a lawyer's crowning virtue is his personal integrity ... [and] a life-long preoccupation ... with national unity.'[4]

Dickson's wartime friend, George Tritschler, joined the firm in 1926, three years before the death of Sir James Aikens, and established a reputation as a fine litigator. Tritschler, a future Manitoba chief justice, juniored for E.K. Williams, another eminent counsel who preceded Tritschler as chief justice.

When Dickson joined the firm, it consisted of about ten lawyers. Harold Aikens, known to all by his military rank 'Colonel,' was an ambitious, talented, and energetic man who joined his father's firm in 1910 after graduating from the University of Chicago. He served his country during the First World War and, like Dickson, suffered the loss of a leg. Though a successful lawyer, he lacked his father's personal charm and displayed irascibility and what many regarded as an excessively stiff and formal manner. Despite their very different personal styles, Dickson was able to work closely with Aikens in the early years of his practice. They shared a family connection – Dickson's brother-in-law George Sellers was married to Aiken's daughter – and their similar military experiences and injuries no doubt also helped to forge a close bond between them. Aikens kept a close eye on Dickson's legal work and quickly saw that the firm had landed a rising star.

John MacAulay was the driving force in the firm when Dickson joined it. According to Dickson, MacAulay 'was brilliant, dominating, domineering, but very charming. He did everything and he did it brilliantly.' MacAulay was born on a farm near Morden, Manitoba, in 1892. He studied law as an extramural student while teaching school. His studies were interrupted by the First World War, he served with the Medical Corps and, after articling with the firm's founder, Sir James Aikens, was called to the bar in 1919. He began his legal career as a litigator but gradually shifted the focus of his practice to corporate work. He travelled widely and loved to tell stories. 'He always laughed at them. You would hear them twenty times, and he would laugh just as much at them the twentieth time as he did the first.'[5]

Dickson's story of how MacAulay attracted Safeway Stores, one of the firm's best clients, illustrates MacAulay's magnetic charm. In 1928 MacAulay was in California on business and he went out for a game of golf. He was regaling his golfing partners with one of his stories in the locker room. The fellow beside him 'was much taken by MacAulay's personality and asked what he did. He answered he was a lawyer and the fellow said, "Well, I am head of Safeway in the States and we need a legal firm to represent the whole company in Canada. How would your firm like to take that on?"'[6] MacAulay eagerly accepted the offer and, from that point on, turned his attention away from litigation to corporate law and business. By the mid-1950s, MacAulay was a prominent figure in both business and legal circles. He earned a reputation as a successful tax lawyer, served on the boards of a number of major corporations, and was vice-president of the Bank of Montreal.

Dickson quickly gained the respect and admiration of his colleagues. The firm's history says that he 'displayed unfailing courtesy, good humour, and concern for the well-being of others.'[7] Dickson's first year or so of practice was spent in the real estate department, and one of the firm's most important clients was his first employer, Great West Life. Most of the work involved mortgages, an aspect of Great West's affairs Dickson already knew first hand. The firm's mortgage practice had fallen into disarray, and Donald Thompson, one of the firm's leading corporate lawyers, credited Dickson with turning it around within a year.[8]

In addition to the mortgage work, Dickson assisted in drafting insurance policies. He was already well on his way to developing a distinct writing style based on careful choice of words, multiple drafts of documents, meticulous attention to detail, and the use of short, clear sentences. Dickson was personable but also a 'hard task master' who was 'tough minded' and 'did not suffer fools gladly.' Articling students and secretaries were warned on 'fear of their lives' not to assist Dickson should he fall, as he frequently did in the early days as he struggled to adjust to his artificial leg.[9]

The Winnipeg Flood

In 1950, just as Dickson was settling into the practice of law and raising a young family, he became involved in a military-like relief operation almost by accident. The combination of heavy winter snowfall and an unusually late spring caused serious flooding in southern Manitoba. Many rural communities were inundated and acres of farmland were under water, and Winnipeg, too, faced disaster as both the Assiniboine and Red rivers rose inexorably. Dickson worked day and night for six weeks to organize and coordinate the Red Cross relief effort to feed, clothe, and house thousands of Winnipegers who were driven from their homes by the flooding. His efforts identified him as a public-spirited citizen with remarkable organizational abilities.

This chapter in Dickson's life began when one of Henry Sellers's business associates asked him if he would like to become president of the Manitoba Red Cross. Work for the Red Cross was something of an Aikens MacAulay tradition – John MacAulay was very active in the organization – and so Dickson could hardly decline the offer despite his lack of prior involvement. Dickson asked MacAulay what he would be expected to do. 'About a meeting a month' was the answer. 'You just preside, and that's it. It lasts about an hour, maybe two. You will find it interesting.'[10]

Dickson accepted, and a few months later, in early May, he travelled to Toronto for a Red Cross meeting. While there, he received an urgent call from the premier's office in Winnipeg asking him to return for discussions on what could be done to help the flood victims. Dickson rushed back to a meeting in middle of the night in the cabinet room at the Manitoba Legislature. In attendance were Premier Douglas Campbell; the former premier, Stuart Garson, by then federal minister of justice; Brigadier Ronald Morton, head of the local military district; the city engineer, W.D. Hurst; and Chief of Police Charles MacIver. Farmlands and several small communities had already suffered extensive damage, and it appeared that the dikes at Fort Garry, a residential area of Winnipeg, were not going to hold. The premier declared a state of emergency. Brigadier Morton, a D-Day veteran, assumed control and asked Ottawa for permission to use military personnel and equipment to fight the flood. 'As we left the Legislative building just at dawn,' Dickson later remembered, 'I was walking with Brigadier Morton and suddenly the sirens went off, like wartime, which meant that the flooding of Fort Garry had started.'[11]

Dickson installed a bed at the Red Cross office and worked around the clock. He did not see Barbara or his son Brian for three weeks and was not at his law office for six weeks. Again, the call of duty took Dickson from his wife's side at an important time. While he worked on the flood-relief effort, which involved an extraordinary volunteer force that would grow to 4,400 workers, Barbara was home in bed expecting the birth of their second child, Deborah. Dickson described the work of the Red Cross in a press interview:

> The Red Cross is working day and night doing everything humanly possible to meet this tragic situation. Housing accommodation and food have already been provided for approximately 300 evacuees from flooded areas. Coffee and sandwiches paid for by Red Cross funds are served to flood workers by Boy Scouts, St. John's Ambulance and other organizations. Every available boat has been rented by the Red Cross on free loan. More than 1,000 pairs of hip waders have been loaned by Red Cross on request from municipalities. Besides these, literally thousands of requests for aid are each day channelled to proper sources such as the army, government or municipality. Manitoba Red Cross will continue to tap its energies to the utmost to meet this terrible emergency.[12]

By 7 May thousands of Winnipegers had been evacuated from their homes and patients at local hospitals had to be moved as dikes broke. The army brought in sandbags, boats, pumps, and other supplies by road, rail, and air, although the flooding seriously disrupted surface transport. On 8 May the body of a volunteer who had been swept away while working on a dike was discovered. That same day, it was announced in Ottawa that Premier Campbell's plea for federal financial aid would be favourably received. Farmers in southern Manitoba feared that they would have no crops and struggled to save livestock. Relief aid poured in from other parts of Canada. A special plea was made for potato sacks to serve as sandbags.

Dickson quickly put together a team of young businessmen to assume responsibility for various facets of the Red Cross Society's relief work. The Red Cross office on Osborne Street soon proved inadequate and on 9 May its operations were moved to Winnipeg's Civic Auditorium which also served as an evacuee reception centre. On 10 May, Brigadier Morton advised the evacuation of all women and children to homes or summer cottages outside Winnipeg to relieve overtaxed facilities, and workers struggled to maintain electric power and the city's gas supply. Although the call for evacuation was a request and not an order, an estimated 60,000 citizens left within a few days. An enormous burden fell on the Red Cross to coordinate the humanitarian aspects of the evacuation and arrange for food, clothing, housing, and transportation. The Manitoba Flood Relief fund was established with an executive committee that included Dickson's law partner John MacAulay, his father-in-law, Henry Sellers, and a number of other prominent Winnipegers. The flood crested after eighteen days in late May, but the evacuation continued since food and supplies had to be conserved for those engaged in relief work.

The governor general, Viscount Alexander, travelled to Winnipeg to review the relief operations. Upon his arrival, he was met by George Sellers, who held a rank in the reserve as group captain and who served as Alexander's aide-de-camp for the visit. The governor general donned a pair of hip waders and proceeded to inspect the city. He had been a military officer and he did not hesitate to offer his advice about the evacuation plans. Prime Minister Louis St Laurent followed the governor general to Winnipeg to assure Manitoba that federal financial aid to repair the vast damage would be available. St Laurent visited Red Cross flood headquarters, where he met Dickson.

At the peak of the flood, an estimated 600 square miles of farmland and 2,000 farms were covered in water to a depth of one to fifteen feet. One hundred thousand people were evacuated and 80,000 were left homeless. The relief effort put an enormous strain on the modest financial resources of the Red Cross. Dickson discussed the matter with John MacAulay and a prominent Toronto lawyer active in the Red Cross, Leopold Macaulay (no relation to John). They decided that the province would have to help and they made an appointment to see Premier Campbell. The premier, not known for his largesse with public funds, was told bluntly that $1 million was required immediately if the Red Cross effort was to continue. He seemed taken aback, but, after discussing the matter with his colleagues, he delivered the cheque to Dickson the next day. However, the Red Cross fundraising effort was very successful and, when it was all over, Dickson 'had the pleasant task of going back to Mr. Campbell and handing him a cheque for one million dollars payable to the Province of Manitoba from the Canadian Red Cross Society.'[13]

Winnipegers demonstrated remarkable calm and resolve in the face of the disaster, and Dickson and the others who threw themselves into the effort took justifiable pride in the depth of public spirit shown by their fellow citizens. The flood posed a war-like threat to the community, and, as he had ten years earlier when the threat was actual war, Dickson willingly rose to the challenge. As well as demonstrating his public spirit, Dickson proved himself an able and efficient administrator. After only five years in practice and at the relatively young age of thirty-four, he made his mark in difficult and demanding circumstances in full view of the political and business elite of Manitoba.

Within a year, Premier Douglas Campbell asked Dickson to come to his office early one morning. The province had been governed by a Liberal-Progressive coalition since the 1930s when it was first formed under Progressive leader John Bracken. Bracken left the premier's office in 1942 for federal politics, succeeding Arthur Meighen as leader of the newly named 'Progressive Conservatives.' Liberal Stuart Garson succeeded Bracken as premier of Manitoba, but he also left for federal politics in 1948, at which point Liberal Douglas Campbell succeeded him. Described as 'articulate, reasonable, and a shrewd judge of people,' Campbell positioned himself as the leader of a non-partisan coalition that he claimed 'eliminated politics from the business of government and ... made up for what it lacks in colour by gaining in efficiency.'[14] He saw Brian Dickson as a man who would enhance this image and he offered Dickson the office of attorney general.[15] The appointment would be immediate and Dickson would run in the forthcoming election. Dickson was mildly tempted by the offer, but Barbara had no interest in political life, and within a day or so he declined.

Two years later, in October 1953, Premier Campbell had more luck. This time he asked Dickson to chair the Civil Service Commission. The commission's mandate was essentially to ensure that the public service was free from patronage. It had general supervisory authority over appointments and promotions in the public service, made recommendations with respect to salaries and terms of employment, and heard appeals from dismissals. The previous chairman had resigned to run for office and was sitting as an opposition Conservative member of the legislature. Dickson accepted the premier's offer to serve as the commission's chair, but he refused to accept any salary to protect the independence of the office. The commission included a full-time member and senior members of the Manitoba public service. It met regularly, one afternoon every week or ten days, and made regular visits to the major provincial institutions, including mental hospitals and penal institutions, Headingly Jail, and the Home for Juvenile Delinquents, places that Dickson would later visit as a trial judge attempting to determine appropriate sentences for convicted offenders.

Law and Business

Dickson's early years in practice coincided with the post-war economic boom. After the desperate poverty of the 1930s and the peril and uncertainty of the war years, Canadians enjoyed a period of prosperity and calm. Fears that the economy would slump as it had after the First World War were quickly dispelled. Canada's industrial capacity had grown exponentially during the war, fed by government contracts, grants, and tax incentives, and that capacity could now be adapted to the requirements of peacetime. There was enormous pent-up consumer demand for housing, cars, and household appliances, while Canada's rich natural resource base became even more bountiful with the discovery of oil at Leduc, Alberta, in 1947.

Dickson found himself ideally placed to make the most of these highly favourable economic conditions. Bright, hard-working, and ambitious, he worked for a blue-chip law firm and his connection with the Sellers family opened up the world of business and ensured him a steady supply of challenging and lucrative work. Dickson certainly did not let opportunity pass him by.

He enjoyed working at Aikens MacAulay, but, as is so often the case with a law firm comprised of energetic and ambitious individuals, there were many stresses and strains. From 1945 to 1954, the firm had only two partners, Harold Aikens and John MacAulay. This was hardly a situation likely to produce harmony. George Tritschler and Don Thompson were senior and accomplished lawyers, but MacAulay was a tough negotiator and was reluctant to agree to anything that did not weigh heavily in favour of the existing partners. This was a misguided strategy. As the firm's history states, 'excruciating gradualism by the senior partners, result[ed] in growing restlessness on the part of the younger, expansion-minded members of the firm.'[16] In 1952, at the age of fifty-one, Tritschler was appointed a judge, lured to the Queen's Bench by his former mentor and Aikens MacAulay alumnus from the pre-war years, Chief Justice E.K. Williams. Tritschler was one of the top counsel in the province and, from the firm's perspective, this was a significant loss. The next year, Don Thompson left to join Clarence Shepard and form a rival firm that gave his name the prominence it deserved. In 1954 Aikens MacAulay lost another experienced solicitor, Herb Pickard, who joined Canadian Pacific. When Harold Aikens died in 1954, John MacAulay was the only partner.

While these losses were difficult for the firm, they did not hurt Dickson's career. Known for his 'intelligence, drive, and forthrightness,'[17] he quickly proved himself capable of assuming more responsibility. In 1953, after only eight years of practice, he was appointed Queen's Counsel. When Don Thompson left that same year, Dickson assumed senior responsibility for the corporate side of the firm's work for Great West Life and several other major clients, including the Bank of Montreal, the Winnipeg *Free Press*, and Safeway. By the mid-1950s, he had started to build an impressive list of directorships. MacAulay, it would seem, did not want to lose Dickson the way he had lost Tritschler and Thompson, and in 1954 he made Dickson his partner. The firm continued to attract talented young lawyers and the MacAulay tradition was strengthened when John's son, Blair MacAulay, joined the firm in 1960 to work as Dickson's junior.

By the early 1960s, John MacAulay was more and more interested in his outside pursuits and less and less involved in the day-to-day practice of law. He became deeply committed to the work of the International Red Cross. He started as the organization's Manitoba president, a position he would later entice Dickson to accept, in 1950 he became chairman of the Canadian Council, and in 1957 he was selected as chair of the International Humanitarian Law Commission at the Red Cross conference in New Delhi. Eventually, he rose to the office of president of the Board of Governors of the League of Red Cross Societies and by the early 1960s was spending much of his time in Geneva. In 1963 he accepted the Nobel Peace Prize on behalf of the Red Cross.

In MacAulay's absence, Dickson assumed much of the responsibility for the management of the firm. His corporate work covered the range of local, national, and international business and introduced him to many different facets of business and the country. The firm's history attributes Dickson's early success to his practicality and his 'readiness to accept the inevitable and concentrate his efforts on the achievable.'[18] His involvement in corporate Canada covered most major sectors of the Canadian economy. The Sellers family grain-trade business involved him in agriculture and transportation, and Dickson was also heavily involved in the natural-resources sector, largely through working with his entrepreneurial brother-in-law, George Sellers, the financial-services industry and, as legal counsel to the Winnipeg *Free Press*, the media.

Dickson's introduction to corporate Canada was provided by his close family connection with the Sellers family. His father-in-law, Henry Sellers, known to his friends as 'Harry,' was a successful businessman who had built a fortune on the grain trade. At the turn of the century, when he was sixteen, Harry Sellers, the eldest of nine children, came to Winnipeg from Fort William with nothing. Winnipeg was the natural centre of the grain trade, a business that was severely battered during the Depression with the collapse of wheat prices and the ravages of drought. He started at the bottom but by 1929, when the market crashed, was in a position to buy elevators and rescue Federal Grain Ltd. In the following years, he turned it into one of the world's largest private grain companies, with terminals at the Lakehead and on the west coast supplied by hundreds of grain elevators across the prairies.[19] During the 1950s, Federal Grain earned annual profits of between $3 million and $4 million and in the early 1960s it was described as, 'in all probability, the largest privately owned company of its kind in the world.'[20] Harry Sellers became one of Dickson's mentors and was a major force behind Dickson's business success.

The law firm's sterling reputation and solid performance with major financial institutions also provided Dickson with many opportunities. Aikens MacAulay did legal work for a number of financial institutions, including the Bank of Montreal, the Imperial Bank, and Canada Trust, and Dickson worked for each of them. The firm's relationship with these financial institutions was important for Dickson. He was involved in many aspects of the financial- services industry, including securities, and dealt with the Ontario Securities Commission and the United States Securities and Exchange Commission. The firm offered its clients more than strictly legal advice. Senior partners were often active in their corporate clients' business operations: Harold Aikens was on the board of directors of the Imperial Bank and his good friend Harry Sellers was vice-president, and MacAulay was a vice-president of the Bank of Montreal. Dickson proved himself every bit as capable as his senior partners, both as a lawyer and as a businessman. He had 'a terrific business mind'[21] and, at the young age of thirty-eight, was appointed to the Board of Directors of the Imperial Bank.

George Sellers was another important business connection for Dickson. He was not only Dickson's brother-in-law and close friend but also one of Dickson's best clients. Dickson described him as 'an entrepreneur par excellence, who liked to create companies, get them up and running, bring in management and then let them run themselves.'[22] George Sellers was very much involved in the post-Second World War natural-resource boom that was so important in the Canadian west. He created Jet Oils Ltd soon after the Leduc discovery. Dickson did the company's legal work, including a merger with Bailey, Selburn Oil, and Gas Ltd, and he put together the initial public offering that required prospectus clearance in both the United States and Canada. The offering was highly successful and Dickson was appointed to the board of the merged company. George Sellers also sat on the board of Federal Grain and became the company president after his father retired, although running a large company on a day-to-day basis did not play to his entrepreneurial strengths.

Dickson was also heavily involved in the affairs of Trans-Prairie Pipelines of Canada,[23] another local Winnipeg-based company. Dickson was Trans-Prairie Pipelines' legal counsel and vice-president. The company transported crude oil from the Daly and Virden-Roselea fields, located in northwest Manitoba, at a rate of approximately 5,000 barrels of oil per day.[24] In 1956 the company changed its name to Northwest Transmission Company Ltd,[25] and two years later the it expanded into Saskatchewan and moved its head office from Winnipeg to Edmonton.[26] Dickson's story of raising the necessary capital the day before the deadline for filing the application to build the Saskatchewan pipeline provides a glimpse of how, as an established and trusted member of the Winnipeg legal and business establishment, he was able to conduct business. Trans-Prairie made a last-minute decision to proceed and at 6 P.M. Dickson needed a letter of credit from a bank.

> I phoned the manager of a Royal Bank branch in Winnipeg whom I knew very well ... I said we need a letter from you saying you are going to underwrite this application to the extent of x-million bucks ... He said you go to the front door of

the branch and I will be there in an hour ... Within the hour we met ... he sat at his secretary's desk and he said write out what you want to say ... I wrote it out in handwriting and he sat down at the typewriter and typed it out and signed it and handed it to us ... [in] about 15 or 20 minutes committing the bank to quite a large amount of money ... Nothing had gone to the main office in Manitoba much less to the head office of the Royal Bank in Montreal. He didn't ask for any personal guarantees. He knew the people he was dealing with and so he said okay, here is your letter. So we went to Saskatchewan and at the end of the hearing we got the pipeline we wanted.[27]

In the natural-resources sector, Dickson was also a director of Martin Paper Products, which was related to the Powell River Pulp and Paper Company. When Powell River acquired Martin Paper, Aikens MacAulay was involved in the transaction, with Dickson responsible for overseeing the purchase. After the transaction had been completed, Dickson was appointed to the board of Martin. Later, the company was purchased by MacMillan-Bloedel.

Dickson became deeply involved, too, in a Winnipeg tannery with his fraternity brother Conrad Riley. Riley, who came from a prominent Winnipeg family, purchased Dominion Tanners in 1948. Dickson was both an investor and legal adviser, and, in due course, he became a member of the board. The business succeeded and expanded to Edmonton in 1957 and later to Toronto. In this venture as well, the family connections of the Winnipeg establishment were important. Also on the board was entrepreneur George Black, who was married to Conrad Riley's sister. Riley was married to Sir James Aikens's granddaughter.

Dickson and George Sellers were also active participants in the aeronautics industry. George was an avid pilot and flew his own Twin Beech, often accompanied by Dickson, sometimes in risky circumstances. One harrowing trip took them to Calgary in the depth of winter:

We put down at Swift Current or some place and they said nobody should be flying. George said, 'Let's go,' so we got into the air. It was just pea soup, you couldn't see a foot ahead of the plane, and suddenly he said, 'The radio's gone.' We were heading west, the next thing we were going to do was run into the Rocky Mountains. I was sitting behind him just doing some reading. I looked up and he looked back at me and the perspiration was coming on. It was about forty below outside and the plane wasn't much warmer. He is usually as cool as a cucumber, and he'd done an awful lot of flying. As we got where he thought we might be approaching Calgary, he said, 'here's a map, I'll go down and we will see if we can find an elevator and see if we can find out where we are.' So we went down. It is pretty scary stuff when you are down about fifty feet in a twin airplane. I suddenly saw a very peculiar crossroad, a sort of three-pronged one with a railway track on it, so I said I know exactly where we are. I showed him on the map, 'Just turn left now and follow the track and you are going to end up in Calgary.' By that time I was sweating too. That was the sort of experience you always had with George.[28]

George Sellers, the bold risk taker, and Dickson, the meticulous planner, made an excellent team.

One of Dickson's best-known clients was the Winnipeg *Free Press*, originally named the Manitoba *Free Press*, a legend among Canadian newspapers. The *Free Press* was founded by Sir Clifford Sifton, Laurier's minister of the interior and superintendent-general of Indian affairs from 1896 to 1905. Sifton's plan for the settlement of western Canada started the immigration wave that had brought Dickson's parents to Saskatchewan. The *Free Press* was made famous by its founding editor, John Wesley Dafoe, a powerful and independent voice in Canadian political debate from 1901 to 1944. By Dickson's time, Clifford Sifton's son Victor ran the *Free Press*, and by 1954 another prominent Liberal, Tom Kent, an Oxford-educated economist who came to Canada in the early 1950s after a stint with the Manchester *Guardian*, was its editor. John MacAulay was the *Free Press*'s principal lawyer, but, as he gradually withdrew from active practice, Dickson became more and more involved. The Dickson network had grown 'to include some of the more important media personalities in Manitoba.'[29]

Dickson took special pleasure in his appointment to the board of the Imperial Bank of Canada, a post that gave him national corporate exposure. As vice-president of the bank, Henry Sellers recommended his son-in-law for the board after the death of former board member Harold Aikens in May 1954. The board, comprised of a small group of prominent business leaders, met every two or three weeks, usually in Toronto. Dickson loved Imperial's clubby atmosphere: 'We would have our meeting in the morning and then go to lunch at the Toronto Club, sit around and talk about the Maritimes or Vancouver or Winnipeg or what have you, and we all became good friends.' Travel arrangements for the bank's meetings were first- class and the directors were whisked about in limousines and provided with superb dinners. The twenty-four directors became close friends; Dickson often stayed with James Walker, a prominent Toronto lawyer with McCarthy and McCarthy whom he had first met during the war at RMC. The Imperial Bank's annual meeting was regularly held in late November in Toronto, often coinciding with Grey Cup weekend. Managers, accountants, and other senior staff and their spouses made their way to Toronto by train.

In 1959 Dickson addressed the Imperial Bank's meeting on behalf of the board. His topic was the Canadian Bill of Rights, which was about to be introduced into Canadian law. This was an unusual subject for a commercial lawyer to discuss at the annual meeting of a bank. According to the Imperial Bank's newsletter, he 'spoke with the fluency and erudition of a lawyer' and 'dealt with this controversial subject without taking sides, but with the fairness we have come to expect from an impartial and judicial mind.'[30] Dickson's choice of topic suggests that, by 1959, the range of his legal interests transcended the limits of his corporate-law practice. But from his early years in practice, Dickson had had progressive views. He was responsible for Aikens MacAulay hiring its first female lawyer, Betty Morrison, perhaps foreshadowing the sympathetic attitude Dickson displayed years later as a judge when dealing with legal issues affecting women.[31]

Things changed after the Imperial Bank merged with the Bank of Commerce to form the Canadian Imperial Bank of Commerce in 1961. Neil McKinnon, president of the Bank of Commerce, suggested the merger to Stuart Mackersy, president of the Imperial Bank, who agreed. The Bank of Commerce was much larger and Dickson felt that its executives, especially McKinnon, easily dominated those of the Imperial Bank. The deal was negotiated on a cross-country train ride. Directors were collected in each city and, by the time the train arrived in Vancouver, the deal was sealed. Directors of both banks became directors of the new bank, but the group was very large and the intimacy and friendship of the Imperial Bank days was lost.

While Dickson's practice rarely took him to court, he appeared as counsel before several boards, tribunals, and commissions. This was as close as he got to litigation and it provided him with a valuable lesson in the work of administrative tribunals.[32] In the early 1960s he was counsel for the grain trade before the Royal Commission on Transportation, appointed to inquire into problems relating to the railways. Murdoch MacPherson, the former attorney general of Saskatchewan who had introduced Dickson to law and politics twenty-five years earlier in Regina, chaired the commission. Dickson appeared as well before the Highway Traffic and Motor Transport Board, the Air Transport Board, the Winnipeg City Council, and various legislative committees. He also represented the Manitoba Dental Association, which was engaged in an ongoing battle with denturists regarding the right to make and sell false teeth.

Blair MacAulay, his junior, says that Dickson was an 'unbelievably hard worker' and 'task master' with a superb intellect. Completely focused on his work and on providing his clients very immediate results, he worked longer and harder than the other lawyers in the firm. Indeed, he approached his work 'with wartime dedication.'[33] A late-afternoon meeting with a client typically ended with a promise from Dickson that the documents would be ready at 9 A.M. the next morning. 'There were just no excuses.' Social or family commitments could not stand in the way of getting the work done. Dickson worked evenings and weekends and expected others to do so as well. 'He was just relentless.' Dickson also had an uncanny ability to spot errors, a trait his juniors and law clerks marvelled at. Again to quote Blair MacAulay: 'If I had drafted a twenty-five page document and there was a spelling error on the fifteenth page, he had an unbelievable ability to spot [it] ... he could ... find [it] ... in the space of thirty seconds.' But Dickson drove himself every bit as hard as he drove others and law clerks and juniors alike described working for Dickson as 'a phenomenal learning experience.'[34] He did his best to avoid any sign of stress or strain, but, until he became a judge, he was a heavy smoker, especially when pushed at work.

Family and Community

In addition to his many business activities and his busy law practice, Brian Dickson was a committed husband and father, who somehow also managed to lead a remarkably active life as a leading light in the Winnipeg community. Dickson's work during the 1950 flood was just the first in a long list of significant voluntary contributions; in fact, he seems to have been every bit as driven and compulsive in his community work as he was in his law practice.

Barbara Dickson was very involved in her husband's career. They had a strong marriage and were partners in every sense of the word. While Barbara allowed Dickson to take centre stage, she was a powerful influence in his success. A woman of intellect, wealth, and social grace and standing, she was a rock for Dickson and he constantly relied upon her. She provided him with shrewd common-sense advice which became especially important after his appointment to the bench in 1963, and, though she was not involved in the details of his law practice, she certainly helped him steer a steady course in his multifaceted legal, business, and community activities. Barbara was also a gracious hostess for social events and a devoted mother for their four children.

In 1945, the Dicksons bought a house on Waterloo Street in Winnipeg: 'This was a very nice house on a nice street in what they call Crescentwood. A fellow called John Flanders who ran a real estate company owned it. He had it listed for $10,000 which I thought was a huge amount of money for a house. It was about twice what any house pre-war would have cost. I was haggling a bit with him and Mr Sellers was in the act and helping us out. He was a friend of Flanders. And Flanders said, "Well, as a friendly gesture, I will knock off $250." So we bought it for $9,750.00.'[35]

The Dicksons' daughter Deborah was born in 1950 and, even before the arrival of twins, Barry and Peter, in 1954, the family needed more room. In 1951 the Waterloo Street house was sold for $16,000 and, for $35,000, the Dicksons bought a more substantial four-bedroom home on Wellington Crescent, one of the best streets in Winnipeg. They improved the house with an addition and purchased the adjoining lot.

The Dicksons loved the outdoors and, from Brian's early years in practice, owned a county retreat. The first was a cottage on about seventeen acres on the Assiniboine River at Kirkfield, a few miles outside Winnipeg; where they had a huge garden with vegetables and prize-winning gladiolas. Harry Sellers, a keen gardener, often joined the Dicksons on the weekends. Dickson enjoyed working with his hands and spent time puttering with garden equipment and water pumps, installing docks, and building garden walls.

While Dickson enjoyed physical exercise, the loss of his leg imposed obvious limitations. Before the war he had enjoyed riding but it was not until a family trip to Arizona in 1958 that he resumed the activity. Until then, he had assumed that he could no longer ride but at the Arizona ranch he was encouraged to give it a try. After three days, he had graduated to the 'fast ride.' Shortly thereafter, he and Barbara decided to buy a farm of several hundred acres about thirty-five miles outside Winnipeg. This allowed him to resume what would be, from that point on, a life-long interest in horseback riding. 'We had six horses and then we got a hundred or more cattle. We had a feeder operation. We had Hereford cattle. It was real farming, a real farming operation.'[36]

On the weekends, Dickson led the entire family on early-morning rides even in the depth of winter, in the bitter Manitoba wind and cold, leading the charge with a 'big furry hat and a big sheep skin coat.'[37] These weekend rides often included a visit to the nearby Hutterite colony of some one hundred and fifty traditional inhabitants. The Hutterites fascinated Dickson. He asked them about their children and their farming. He and Barbara were often invited to Hutterite weddings despite the fact that outsiders were rarely included. Community leaders came to see him to discuss problems with families who wanted to leave, a legal issue he would confront a few years later as a trial judge.

Dickson relaxed at the farm, but there, as at work, he compiled lists of things to be done. Tasks were assigned and progress towards completion carefully monitored. Most weekends were spent at the farm, which Dickson kept until his appointment to the Supreme Court of Canada in 1973. He then sold it to hockey star Bobby Hull, recently acquired by the Winnipeg Jets of the new World Hockey Association. While riding was a sport for the wealthy, Dickson's fitness program also exposed him to those of more modest means – in Winnipeg he swam at lunchtime at the YMCA. Dickson was a strong swimmer and he developed powerful chest and arm muscles as partial compensation for the loss of his leg.

Minaki

The Dicksons eventually took over the Sellers summer home on an island at Minaki in Lake of the Woods. The ninety-acre island had a substantial house and had been in the Sellers family from the 1920s. Henry Sellers sold it to Dickson at 'a give-away price.' The family enjoyed summers at Minaki. George and Edward Sellers had nearby summer homes and the Dickson children often played with their cousins. The Dickson property included boathouses with sleeping quarters that were usually occupied by the children of friends from Winnipeg. Barbara and the children went for two months each summer. Dickson travelled from Winnipeg to be with them on weekends, rarely staying more than a few days at a time. When he was there, Dickson loved to fish, swim, and go boating. In the early years, access was by train but later on it was possible to travel by car.

The Minaki summer home was near the Whitedog Reserve and, from his early days on the island, Henry Sellers had regular contact with the local native community. He hired men from the reserve to cut wood and do odd jobs at his property, and he enjoyed talking to them about hunting and fishing. Like Sellers, Dickson was fascinated by aboriginal people and their very different way of life. Both men also shared the belief that aboriginals had not been treated fairly, and they both bristled at racist and derogatory remarks about 'lazy' or 'drunken Indians.'[38] Dickson carried on the Sellers' tradition and hired Joseph Wawence, who lived at Whitedog, to work at the cottage. In earlier times, Henry Sellers had employed Wawence's father in a similar capacity. The Dicksons were impressed by Wawence and asked him if he would be prepared to work at their farm near Winnipeg. Wawence agreed and moved to the farm, where he worked and lived with his family for a year. After he had moved back to Whitedog, Wawence called Dickson to tell him that his daughter Gloria was very ill and had been taken away. Dickson intervened and found that the child had been taken to a hospital in Winnipeg. Incensed by the high-handed and inconsiderate treatment of the aboriginal family, he arranged for Wawence and his wife to travel to Winnipeg by train, and went to the station to meet them. The Dicksons visited the ten-year old girl in hospital the day before she died and they helped the Wawence family with the funeral arrangements. After the tragic death of his daughter, Joseph Wawence's life fell apart. He had a drinking problem and ended up in the penitentiary after committing a serious crime.[39] Dickson was deeply affected by his dealings with Wawence. He realized that the Wawence tragedy was not an isolated one, and his social conscience was troubled. He and Barbara

decided to establish scholarships for aboriginal children at a Winnipeg private school, but this gesture did not succeed since the children could not settle
in such a different environment and returned home to their families after a
few months.[40]

Lessons in Language

In the early 1960s, Dickson accepted the invitation of one of his clients, the
president of Aero Naves, to spend ten days at his house in Acapulco. The
Dicksons were captivated by Mexico but their social conscience was plagued
by the low wages paid to the four household servants. Dickson was also
embarrassed by his inability to communicate with the servants in their own
tongue; he had to manage the details of meals and other arrangements with
his Berlitz phrase book. Eager to return to Mexico, he decided that he should
learn Spanish and he hired a University of Manitoba student from the Philippines to teach him. The Dicksons returned to Mexico often and on one trip
took the student from the Philippines along. They eventually bought a house
near Acapulco where they socialized with the family of a close friend their son
Brian had made when he went to work in a Mexico City law firm to learn
Spanish. When Winnipeg hosted the Pan American games, Dickson, by then a
judge, offered his services as a translator and envoy with Spanish-speaking
teams.

Dickson also did his best as a busy practising lawyer to learn French. He
had taken French in high school but found that it 'was taught as [a] subject
akin to mathematics, but somewhat less interesting' and that 'one struggled
with the grammar and with the vocabulary, but at the end of it all one could
not, in French, order a meal in a restaurant or ask for directions in a street.'[41]
As with Spanish, an embarrassing incident prompted him to study the language. While in Quebec City, Dickson got into a taxi. The driver spoke no
English and, unable to communicate, Dickson had to leave the cab and go in
search of a bilingual driver.[42] Dickson, the proud Canadian, felt humiliated by
his inability to communicate and decided that it was time to learn some
French. Barbara had studied French in university and shared his interest. They
engaged a French teacher who spoke little English to come regularly to their
home for dinner, conversation, and French grammar lessons. She even spent
time with the family at Minaki. This effort at bilingualism was much to the dismay of the Dickson children, who were expected to participate in the exercise.

Discipline and Hard Work

Dickson's life was hectic, 'a constant struggle to figure out what the right life
was, and how much time we should spend at each.'[43] The fact that he was

exceptionally well organized, however, allowed him to make time for his wife and four children despite an intense work schedule. As his son Brian says: 'I always think of him as being very disciplined, a very hard worker. But he seemed to do it reasonably effortlessly. He didn't say, "I can't do anything right now because I am up to my eye balls in something – would you go away and come back tomorrow." He always seemed to have things worked out. "We'll do that right now" or "we'll do that at 10 o'clock" ... You never got the impression that he was putting the family in second place to his work.'[44]

The Dicksons spent a great deal of time with Harry Sellers and also with Lillian and Thomas Dickson, who had retired to Winnipeg to be near their grandchildren. Barbara had helped her father with his own entertaining since her mother's death in the early 1940s and, despite her own busy life and four children, she continued to play that role in his later years. She also developed a very close relationship with Dickson's mother and was touched by the fact that Lillian referred to her as the daughter she had never had.

Dickson had high standards for himself and for his children and he did not hesitate to let them know when he was disappointed. He had a no-nonsense approach and liked things to be done properly. He encouraged the children to finish what was on their plates with a favourite phrase that summed up his approach to life: 'Eat it and like it.' When his suggestions for family activities were received with comments such as 'that's really boring,' Dickson's response was: 'We are going to have fun. No damn fooling.' He was generous with advice and with money and was a supportive father. As his son Brian explains: 'When you had a problem, or an idea, or needed support, he was always there and ready to provide it whether it was some advice or whether you needed a bit of money to do something.'[45]

Just as his own mother and father had encouraged family debates on the burning issues of the day, Dickson engaged in some lively discussions with his children. He disagreed with Brian about the war in Vietnam. Dickson thought that, if your country asked, it was your duty to serve. He was unsympathetic to American war-resisters who sought refuge in Canada and he urged Brian, who was studying at Princeton, not to get involved in anti-war activities. Yet, despite his strong views on the subject, Dickson was careful never to let these debates interfere with his relationship with his son. Brian says: 'One of the good things about him was, even when you had a fairly heated argument, he would always cool it off at the end. He would say; "Well you know, you've got your opinions, I've got mine and I am an older guy, you are a younger guy. We don't have to agree on everything and isn't it a great day outside."'[46]

Dickson had an interest in collecting art that had been sparked by his father-in-law, Harry Sellers, and by his partner, John MacAulay. Sellers regularly visited art galleries when he travelled and he often bought the works of young artists. Many of his acquisitions were passed on to the Dicksons, including a work of art by the acclaimed artist Michael Snow, who produced an important sculpture for the Ontario pavillion at Expo 67. A.Y. Jackson, a leading member of the Group of Seven and a friend of Sellers, presented him with a painting of a Federal Grain elevator. MacAulay was much more serious about art and managed to assemble a very fine personal collection of impressionist and Group of Seven paintings. The Dicksons, too, acquired many Canadian paintings, including several Jacksons and a Cornelius Krieghoff, and their collection also included works by Manet and Renoir.[47]

Dickson followed his mother's example as a committed church member. Although not particularly religious in his outlook, he had 'a serious spiritual' side.[48] The Dickson family regularly attended the downtown parish where the Sellers family had been active for many years and where Barbara taught in the Sunday school. From 1960 to 1971, Dickson served as chancellor of the Diocese of Rupert's Land, senior lay adviser to the bishop. In this capacity, he provided the bishop with financial and legal advice and also assisted on matters of discipline and with any other sensitive issues where outside counsel was needed.

Dickson also took an active interest in the affairs of the University of Manitoba and played an important role in modernizing legal education. From 1948 to 1954, he was a special lecturer at the Law School, teaching corporation law, bankruptcy, and civil procedure. More significant was his work as a member of the Law School's Board of Trustees, which he joined in the mid-1950s.[49] Legal education was in a state of flux during the 1950s. In Manitoba, as in most provinces, the profession maintained almost complete control over legal education. Things had hardly changed from Dickson's days as a student – a combination of apprenticeship, through articling, and courses mostly taught by practitioners on a part-time basis. Fully academic, university-based law schools were emerging across Canada to replace the professional model, but not without significant resistance from the profession.[50] The Manitoba profession favoured maintaining the status quo. When a Law Society committee recommended in 1962 that students spend their entire first year at the Law School, recently retired chief justice E.K. Williams was doubtful: 'The sooner a man gets thrown into the practical life of the practice of law the better for him.'[51]

Dickson did not share these traditional professional attitudes. He had serious reservations about the state of legal education and favoured the university-based model. His experience as an articling student had been less than satisfactory. While some students got good articles, the training was uneven and there was little or no control over their work or supervision. From an academic perspective, Dickson believed that the professional model left a great

deal to be desired. Busy practitioners had a wealth of knowledge and experience to convey, but, as part-time lecturers, they had their limitations and could
not match the intellectual depth of a full-time academic. Years later, as a judge,
Dickson urged law schools 'to provide an education in a broad sense, not just
professional training.'[52] Dale Gibson, a 1950s graduate and historian of the
Manitoba profession, describes Dickson as 'probably the most influential force
on the Board' on this issue.[53] Dickson avoided taking an overtly public stand,
but, behind the scenes, he pushed quietly and steadily for improvements in
Manitoba's system of legal education. Gradually, more full-time faculty members were hired. Some trustees favoured hiring retired judges as professors,
but Dickson successfully resisted that initiative, believing that would perpet-
uate old ways of thinking and that, if it were implemented, the chance to introduce students to the most current trends in legal thought would be lost. He
also persuaded his fellow trustees to pay the academics higher salaries and
provide more resources to improve the Law School's program.

It was not until the early 1960s, during Dickson's tenure as president of the
Law Society, that a fully academic program was established. Dickson led Manitoba's 'quiet revolution in legal education,'[54] which culminated in a full-time
university based program. Ironically, the final push came from the Law Society
of Upper Canada, the governing body of the Ontario profession that had so
strongly resisted change to its own system a few years earlier.[55] Ontario refused
to accept Manitoba graduates unless Manitoba established a full-time LLB program.[56] This proved to be the catalyst to reform. The Law Society finally relinquished its role and decided in April 1964 to establish a full-time academic
program. The Faculty of Law was created at the University of Manitoba, and
the Law School eventually moved from the law courts to a new building at the
university. In Dale Gibson's words, the final result 'was another unmarked
monument to the career of a remarkable behind-the-scenes lawyer.'[57]

Dickson's involvement in the affairs of the University of Manitoba continued after his appointment to the bench. In the late 1960s, the Faculty of Arts
and Science was in a state of disarray: 'The scientists felt that the people in the
arts faculty did nothing but talk ... and the people in arts thought that the scientists were insufferable.'[58] Hugh Saunderson, the president, and Peter Curry,
the chancellor, came to Dickson's chambers at the courthouse to ask him to
head an inquiry to address the question of whether there should be one faculty or two. After hearing everyone out, it became apparent that virtually
everyone wanted a divorce and Dickson's recommendation to that effect was
accepted and implemented. In 1970, after his appointment to the bench, Dickson was asked to sit on the university's Board of Governors. He accepted and,
in 1971, became chairman of the board, a position he filled until his appointment to the Supreme Court of Canada in 1973.

The list of Dickson's community activities goes on and on. He served on the board and the executive committee of the Winnipeg General Hospital, and later on the board of the Health Sciences Centre. He was on the board of the Winnipeg Foundation, a community-based charity for the underprivileged that attracted significant contributions from the Winnipeg elite. Dickson was also a member of the board of the Winnipeg Blue Bombers football team and acted as the team's lawyer. He remained a Blue Bomber fan throughout his life, rejoicing at their victories but often having to pay lost bets to friends when they suffered defeat.

A related activity that took a great deal of time was Winnipeg Enterprises. City officials wanted to replace the city's rundown amphitheatre and football stadium. They had to get public approval, but more than once, referenda to provide financing were defeated. Dickson and three friends formed a non-profit company called Winnipeg Enterprises and borrowed almost $5 million for the construction of a stadium and arena. The loans, guaranteed by the city, were repaid in time and the Winnipeg got two important sports facilities at no cost to the municipal, provincial, or federal governments.[59] Dickson's active community work was encouraged by Barbara, who herself was active with the Junior League and at the Winnipeg General Hospital.

On top of all of this, Dickson was deeply involved in the affairs of his profession. He was first elected a bencher of the Law Society of Manitoba in 1956, and he served as chair of the discipline committee. This could be an onerous duty since it involved sitting in judgment on professional colleagues whose careers were on the line. However, the legal profession in Manitoba was close-knit and collegial. In Dickson's circle, 'a lawyer's word was as good as his bond.' Rightly or wrongly, discipline was administered in a manner consistent with the close and club-like nature of the Manitoba bar. Dickson certainly did not lack compassion for his professional colleagues who stepped out of line. 'Usually it was just a matter of telling people that they had to sharpen up ... I think we were all inclined to be a little sympathetic.'[60]

Dickson was a bencher for many years and became president of the Law Society in June 1962, a little more than a year before his appointment to the Manitoba Court of Queen's Bench. He was on holiday in Spain when he was elected president and his fellow benchers passed a resolution 'to send a cable to Mr. Dickson, wherever he may be, informing him of his election and congratulating him.'[61] During Dickson's year as president of the Law Society, the benchers faced the usual fare of business from the trivial to the serious. The executive committee debated whether 'it was desirable to continue the practice of serving refreshments prior to Benchers meetings.' They decided that it was, but that the meetings should start at 12:30 in the afternoon. Business became more serious when an emergency meeting had to be held to deal with the discovery that a Swan River solicitor had a $33,000 shortfall in his trust accounts.[62]

The Aikens MacAulay tradition made high office in the Canadian Bar Association almost inevitable. Sir James Aikens, who founded the association in 1914, was only the first member of the firm to serve as its president. His son Henry filled the office, as did E.K. Williams, John MacAulay, and Lorne Campbell, all partners in the firm. It was a standing joke at the firm that, to collect their pay cheques, firm members had to show their CBA membership cards. Dickson was appointed to the executive committee in 1958 and he thereafter served in a variety of capacities, including treasurer. He was in line to be named president in 1963 when he was appointed to the bench.

A Change in Direction

By the early 1960s, Brian Dickson's career could have gone in any one of several directions. According to Blair MacAulay, 'there was no question that if my father stepped aside, that the firm would be headed by Brian.'[63] Dickson's corporate experience and shrewd business acumen could also have led easily to a leadership position with a major corporation. Running Federal Grain would have been an obvious possibility and no doubt there were others as well.[64]

Still another possibility was a career in politics. As already noted, Dickson turned down an attractive offer to enter public life in 1951. Subsequently, the Federal Liberals actively recruited him to run in the 1963 election. After their devastating defeat in 1958 to the Progressive Conservatives, led by John Diefenbaker, Liberal Party organizers sought to attract high-profile candidates across the country. The Liberal campaign strategy was to build a strong 'Liberal Team' of star candidates to bolster the chances of their leader, Lester Pearson, who struggled as a campaigner. Among the many prominent candidates were future cabinet ministers Mitchell Sharp, Walter Gordon, Donald Macdonald, Maurice Lamontagne, Charles 'Bud' Drury, Maurice Sauvé, John Turner, former NDP stalwart Hazen Argue and political scientist Pauline Jewett. Perhaps the best- recognized name among these new Liberal recruits was Red Kelly, a star hockey player with the Toronto Maple Leafs. Dickson knew Lester Pearson, whose wife, Marion, came from Winnipeg. He often saw the Pearsons at social functions, and his partner, John MacAulay, had excellent connections in the Liberal Party. Despite his passion for public service, however, Dickson said no to the Liberal recruiters. He was not interested in elected office or in a life of part-time living in Ottawa and lengthy periods away from Winnipeg and his family.

When he was offered a judicial appointment in 1963, Dickson's law partners and associates were astounded that he was about to abandon his highly successful business-law career to become a judge. Although George Tritschler had left the firm for the bench, unlike Dickson, he had been a litigator and it was not apparent that he would one day lead the firm. John MacAulay was deeply concerned about losing a key member of the firm and his son Blair, Dickson's junior, says that when he heard of Dickson's decision 'it was the most frightening day in my life ... It absolutely stunned me ... It was a shock'.[65] Another lawyer at Aikens MacAulay at the time described Dickson's departure for the bench as very surprising and a 'devastating blow to the firm.'[66] The firm was losing a lawyer who, as the president of the Law Society of Manitoba and the next president of the Canadian Bar Association, was at the top of the legal profession. Dickson was also at the apex of corporate Canada, with his multiple directorships and business and social connections from coast to coast and a track record of tireless service to the Winnipeg community. Even Barbara Dickson was surprised by her husband's decision. She thought that, after his very busy life in practice, he might find the bench too quiet and she wondered if he would find enough in the job to maintain his interest.[67]

But, after spending eighteen years in the business world, Dickson had decided that it was time to focus on the law. He had a strong commitment to public service. He also had achieved financial security for himself and his family and could afford the significant cut in salary that would follow accepting a judicial appointment and resigning from Aikens MacAulay and his corporate directorships. In the years to come, he would prove that his wide experience as a soldier, trusted business adviser, tough-minded corporate lawyer, and community-minded volunteer were ideal qualifications for the bench. He had truly lived up to the ideals of his firm's founder, James Aikens. Dickson thought that 'dedication to public service is the mark of the professional' and he described a legal career as 'a life of public service' with multifaceted responsibilities 'to the state, to the court, to the client, to his fellow lawyers and to himself.'[68] Rejecting the view that lawyers were 'value-neutral technicians,' he argued that 'technically competent lawyers who fail to recognize the moral quality of their work misunderstand the nature of their calling and ignore their larger responsibilities to society.'[69] He consistently promoted the 'vision of a lawyer as a wise counsellor, skilled advocate, contributor to the improvement of the legal system, an unselfish and courageous leader of public opinion and a professional willing to answer the call for public service.'[70] Shortly after his appointment to the bench, Dickson urged young lawyers being called to the bar to dedicate their 'lives to the service of the public, in the cause of truth and justice ... a life of unselfish service to others.'[71] He was troubled by 'disturbing signs' of declining public confidence in the profession and by the perception that 'lawyers are more interested in making money than in living up to the best standards of their calling.'[72]

In 1963 Dickson had the makings of a 'lawyer-statesman – possessed of great practical wisdom and exceptional persuasive powers, devoted to the public good but keenly aware of the limitations of human beings and their political arrangements.'[73] One feature of a 'lawyer-statesman' is the ability to see different sides of an issue. And as Chief Justice Beverley McLachlin says Dickson was 'always open.' She believes that this breadth of vision 'was such an important part of his personality, whether we call it imagination, whether we call it flexibility ... that was the way he approached problems: lets' look at all sides of it. I learned an enormous amount from him about judging, about putting yourself in other people's shoes, about considering the problem from all sides.'[74]

Dickson went to the bench with a strong sense of citizenship and public duty and a remarkable grasp of how best to blend principle with pragmatism. As he demonstrated in his practice, he had an acute legal mind. But he was never a legal technocrat. In his law practice as in his judicial work, Dickson displayed mature legal judgment, not raw legal expertise. As one of his former law partners put it, Dickson was 'more sound than brilliant'.[75] From the early days of his practice, he acted 'without professional veneer,'[76] keeping his clients out of trouble by steering them towards practically achievable solutions that balanced expediency with principle. As a judge, he was faithful to the law and demonstrated remarkable intellectual rigor in his legal analysis, but he never lost the corporate lawyer's perception of the law as a means to an end. Though he revered the law, he always saw it in terms of the human problem that was posed. Dickson the corporate lawyer used the law to help his clients achieve their goals. Dickson the judge did his best to use the law to improve the lot of his fellow citizens. He had the lawyer-statesman's prudential wisdom to assess problems from a broad perspective, and judiciously to reconcile competing rules and values in a principled fashion.

Twenty-seven years later, as he was about to retire as chief justice of Canada, Dickson articulated the vision of the lawyer as statesman when he told a graduating class of lawyers that leading a well-rounded life would make them better lawyers:

Involve yourself in your community and dedicate yourselves to its betterment. Taken an interest in physical and outdoor activities and maintain your fitness. Expand your horizons through travel. Develop an interest in another country, its language, culture, perhaps even its legal system. These extra-curricular non-professional activities will not only enrich your lives, they will make you a better lawyer. There is more to the law than cases and statutes, contracts and deeds of trust. The law involves people and their relations with each other. To understand and advise your clients properly, you need to understand and experience the world at large.[77]

PART THREE

A Judge in Manitoba, 1963–1973

5

Queen's Bench

Samuel Freedman, a highly respected member of the Manitoba Court of Appeal, was the first person to ask Dickson to consider the possibility of a judicial appointment. Freedman had been a judge since 1952, when he was appointed as a trial judge at the age of forty-four. He was a brilliant and witty speaker, widely regarded as one of Canada's finest judges, and a strong candidate for an appointment to the Supreme Court of Canada. It would not have occurred to Freedman that Dickson, the man he was recruiting for the bench, was the one the prime minister would select ten years later when it came time to appoint a westerner to the nation's highest court. Freedman had been discussing the need to attract good lawyers to the bench with George Tritschler, then chief justice of the Court of Queen's Bench. Freedman and Tritschler realized that, because of the corporate nature of Dickson's practice, he might be overlooked for the judiciary. They decided to see what could be done to promote his candidacy.[1]

Despite his remarkable success as a lawyer, Dickson was not an obvious candidate for the bench because of his limited experience as an advocate. The task of a good commercial lawyer is to avoid litigation and Dickson's work had rarely taken him to court. However, his reputation for efficiency, hard work, and acute legal analysis made him an attractive candidate. He was forty-seven, an ideal age for appointment to the bench, had gained enough experience in the world to be wise, and still had the energy of a younger man. As well, he combined legal acumen with a distinguished war record and a demonstrable commitment to public service.

Freedman and Tritschler decided that Freedman should raise the matter with Dickson. One evening, Dickson and Freedman were both attending a dinner and Freedman mentioned that the Court of Queen's Bench was having problems. As the province's superior trial court with jurisdiction over all matters, ranging from civil disputes to serious criminal cases, the Queen's Bench was at the very heart of the administration of justice in Manitoba. However, the court was falling behind in its work and badly needed an infusion of talent and energy. Two of its seven members were ill and a third, William Ferguson, was unable to cope with the workload. Ferguson was appointed to the bench after a successful career as a crown prosecutor, but he found the burden of deciding cases too heavy. Plagued by indecision and an increasing backlog of reserved judgments, he wanted to leave the Queen's Bench and become a county court judge in his hometown, Minnedosa. The minister's office would not agree to a transfer and Ferguson decided to resign.

Freedman asked Dickson if he had ever thought about becoming a judge. Dickson's reply was, 'Well no, I never gave it a thought.' Freedman responded, 'Well maybe you should.'[2] Freedman took Dickson's non-committal answer to indicate that his mind was open to the prospect. Tritschler wrote a letter to the federal minister of justice, Lionel Chevrier, urging him to consider Dickson for judicial appointment despite Dickson's lack of trial experience: 'If persons of this calibre were frequently appointed to the Bench, mistakes might still occur but, very soon the Canadian Judiciary would begin to reflect the aura of a new strength that would deserve the admiration of the bar and public.'[3]

On 31 October 1963 Doug Everett, a neighbour and well-known Liberal (he was later appointed to the Senate), asked Dickson to stop by for a drink on his way home. Two more future senators, Gil Molgat, Liberal leader of the opposition in the Legislative Assembly, and another well-known party member, Margaret Konantz, were there when Dickson arrived. After a few minutes of small talk, the question was posed: 'If you were offered a judgeship, would you accept?' Dickson was clearly interested, but careful. 'Before I give you an answer to that, I would like to know whether it is a firm offer, and if I do accept am I assured of an appointment?'[4] He had no intention of putting his name on a list of possible candidates, raising the matter with his family, law partners, and key clients, only to find that the position was not his. The trio undertook to contact the minister of justice to determine how firm the offer was.

Later the same evening, at a banquet at the Marlborough Hotel in Winnipeg, Dickson received word that the minister had been contacted and that if he wanted the job, it was his. The cabinet would be meeting the next day and Dickson was given until 10 o'clock the next morning to decide.

I spoke to my wife and I spoke to my partners and they were all very accommodating. I had had about eighteen years of very active corporate practice, but with quite a few appearances before boards and tribunals and a lot of travel. It seemed to me that this would offer a change of pace and an opportunity to do public service ... When you are doing corporate work, in a sense you are not really a lawyer, because you are more a businessman, figuring out the bottom line, and particularly when you are running companies, on the boards of companies, it is very much business oriented. The idea of getting back really to learning about law and working in a law library appealed to me a great deal when I thought about it.[5]

One of Dickson's law school professors, Charles Rhodes Smith, was appointed to the Queen's Bench the same day as Dickson.

Less than a month later, on 29 November 1963, Dickson was sworn in as a judge of the Manitoba Court of Queen's Bench. He told those who gathered to mark the occasion: 'I begin my new work, conscious of my shortcomings, but dedicated to the cause of justice ... attempting at all times to do what is fair between man and man and between man and the state.' 'Justice,' he said, is a 'product not of the intellect but of the spirit, not transient but eternal.'[6] During his twenty-seven years on the bench, Dickson tried to live by this approach and keep basic questions about the fairness and decency of the law foremost on his mind.

While there 'were some who sniggered' because of Dickson's lack of trial experience, his appointment was widely applauded. Chief Justice Tritschler described it as 'the position seeking the man' and was confident that his new colleague would 'add lustre to this bench.' The president of the Manitoba Bar Association, T. Mackay Long, drew a laugh at the swearing-in ceremony when he indicated that he had not heard 'a single remark that was in any way critical or derogatory of the appointment – and I must say, that's extremely unusual.'[7] The Winnipeg *Free Press* congratulated the government for 'placing legal and personal qualifications ahead of political considerations' and for setting 'an excellent standard for itself in future appointments to the bench.'[8] The Winnipeg *Tribune* applauded the appointment in a glowing editorial describing Dickson in terms of the lawyer-statesman ideal. 'Mr. Justice Dickson is a man of wide interests and experience ... a gold medallist in law school ... a distinguished war record ... an outstanding member of the bar and a lecturer in corporation law at the Manitoba Law School ... and has made notable contributions to business and industry in this province.' The newspaper saw Dickson as far more than a sound lawyer: 'Mr. Justice Dickson's experience in diverse fields of activity in addition to his knowledge of the law will serve him in good stead on the bench. But in some ways even more important are the qualities of mind and will with which he has been endowed. The new justice has insight, kindliness and an appreciation of human foibles and aspirations, as well as the gift of decision. Mr. Justice Dickson should make a notable contribution to the bench of this province.'[9]

A Working Judge

As a trial judge, Dickson was expected to do anything and everything, anywhere in the province. George Tritschler described the constituency of the Court of Queen's Bench as 'extending from the United States border to the North West Territories and the shores of Hudson Bay, with a multiformity of population spread unevenly over the whole area ...' There was 'a plentiful variety of civil and criminal cases' and the work was definitely hands-on. In the days before computers, fax machines, executive assistants, and professional court administrators, 'we did our own administration, revised the rules, arranged court sittings and then assigned rotas for ourselves on circuit.'[10]

Dickson was in line to become president of the Canadian Bar Association. Judges had served as president in the past and Dickson thought that he could manage both jobs, but Tritschler wanted his energetic and efficient new colleague to help clear out a backlog of cases. He strongly discouraged Dickson from accepting the position so soon after accepting judicial office and Dickson withdrew his name.

In the early 1960s, new judges received no training yet they were expected to deal with everything. Dickson turned to his colleagues for advice. Justice Israel Nitikman, who had practised criminal law before being appointed to the bench, occupied the next office at the courthouse in Winnipeg. Dickson described Nitikman as 'a very sound, wonderful judge and a wonderful man ... a Godsend as far as I was concerned.' He also relied on Tritschler, his old friend and mentor. Tritschler was obviously delighted to have a man of Dickson's intellect and energy as a judicial colleague. His admiration for Dickson was reciprocated. 'Chief Justice Tritschler was one of the brightest and best legal scholars I ever ran into. He was virtually self-taught because they did not have a law school at the time.' Tritschler was an imposing figure, with a quick mind and a military bearing and manner. A lifelong bachelor and a committed Catholic, he wrote short but well-crafted judgments and was rarely reversed on appeal. Dickson recalled him as 'very down to earth, very dedicated, very devout ... a man of the highest integrity and highest intelligence.'[11]

While Dickson benefited from the advice of Nitikman and Tritschler, collegiality between Queen's Bench judges was not particularly strong. Trial judges work alone; a point can be discussed with another judge, but most of the work is done independently. In addition to the nature of the work, the physical arrangements at the courthouse in Winnipeg contributed to the isolation. There were no common dining facilities and the judges were often away on circuit in other parts of the province.

After his appointment, Dickson faced a period of adjustment from the busy working and social life of corporate counsel and director. In the early 1960s, perhaps even more than today, judges led a relatively sheltered social life. 'The first and most telling impression upon the new appointee is the trauma of isolation.'[12] The Dicksons' involvement in the social and commercial life of Winnipeg was significantly curtailed. As Dickson explained: 'The door closes on that portion of your life and a lot of people who are your friends, you find you are not really able to associate with them on a social basis for fear of issues coming before the court which might affect their particular financial concerns.'[13] On the other hand, in the early 1960s, judges were freer to pursue certain community activities than they are today. Believing that it was important for judges to maintain contact with the community, Dickson continued to serve on the Board of Governors of the University of Manitoba, and for two years was its chairman, a position he relinquished only when he moved to Ottawa to take up his appointment to the Supreme Court of Canada. He also served, while a judge, on the board of the Winnipeg General Hospital and the Board of the Winnipeg Art Gallery, and continued his role as chancellor of the Anglican Diocese of Rupert's Land.

Years later, however, Dickson would conclude with considerable regret activities of this nature were no longer appropriate for sitting judges. In 1986 a Saskatchewan judge wrote to Dickson, by then chief justice of Canada, to ask if he should accept an appointment as chancellor to his local bishop, the very post Dickson had filled when he was a trial judge. Dickson recorded his advice in a memorandum: 'I have given the matter more thought and have advised [the judge] this morning against accepting the Chancellorship for the reasons that the Anglican Church, indeed more church groups, seem to be becoming more activist in sensitive areas such as the South African problem, abortion and labour disputes.'[14] Even so Dickson still thought that the isolation of judges from their communities was unfortunate. He explained the dangers of isolation in a lecture on the role of judges. 'It affects the ability of the judge to perceive social change and to know the needs of the law. There is the danger of losing touch with the reality of the market place and with non-legal views and experiences.'[15]

One method Dickson used to keep in touch with reality was to discuss his judicial work with Barbara. This was a radical change from his days in practice when Dickson felt that respecting client confidentiality severely limited his ability to discuss his work at home. In constrast, his judicial work was public and, throughout his entire judicial career, he relied significantly upon Barbara's intelligence and common sense. She, in turn, took a strong interest in what he was doing and became very familiar with the detail of his cases and the moral dilemmas they posed. Later, when Dickson sat as an appellate judge, Barbara sometimes read the written arguments filed by the parties and discussed them with her husband.[16]

At home, Barbara continued to provide a steady and stable environment for the family. When Dickson was appointed to the Queen's Bench, his children were still young. Brian, the eldest, was eighteen years old and off to Princeton to study political science and languages. Deborah was just entering her teens, and the twins, Barry and Peter, were only nine years old.

Dickson never regretted his decision to accept the appointment to the bench. He found the work interesting and fulfilling and he enjoyed the independence. He had been his own boss as a senior member of his firm, but life on the bench freed him from the demands of clients and the concerns of running a large law practice. A further attractive feature of the job for a man of Dickson's capacity for getting things done was that, once the work assigned for the week was completed, 'the rest of the time is your own and you can spend it reading or going hunting or fishing or whatever.'[17] Summer sittings were exceptional, perhaps a few days on motions, with the rest of July and August free. Without the continued pressures of clients to please, he stopped smoking and had more time for his family, the farm and the pleasures of the outdoors.

The Most Difficult Task

As a Queen's Bench judge, Dickson tried many criminal cases. The Queen's Bench dealt with the most serious crimes – murder, manslaughter, rape, and robbery – and most trials were before a jury. Shortly after his appointment, Dickson confessed that he would have to do some studying in the area of criminal law. His initiation to the criminal courts did not take long. Within a week of his swearing-in, Dickson took on the task of running the Criminal Assizes in Winnipeg. There were two rape cases on the list. Both accused entered pleas of guilty. These cases had an indelible impact on Dickson. One accused was a handsome young man who stood at the top of his high school class. He forced sex upon a young mother, threatening to smash her baby's head if she refused.[18] The other case was equally disturbing – a serial rapist who attacked women in a parking garage near the legislative buildings in Winnipeg.[19] Dickson was faced with the daunting task of sentencing these two offenders. He later described sentencing as 'the most difficult task a trial judge performs.'[20]

Dickson had known that sentencing was going to be an important aspect of his work as a Queen's Bench judge, and he decided that before he sentenced anyone, he had to find out more about the available correctional facilities. Few, if any, judges have undertaken this sort of investigation, reasonable though it may seem. What Dickson found was not reassuring. 'I went first of all to Stoney Mountain Penitentiary and spent a day out there with the warden' and some of the prison staff. Dickson asked what they thought should be done with sex offenders and was told that prison was not the best place for them. In the view of the prison officials, these individuals suffered from mental illness and, with eight hundred inmates and one part-time psychiatrist, the chances of getting help were poor. The prison officials 'didn't want any part of these guys. Most of the time they had to keep them in confinement to protect them from other inmates who might well want to kill them.' Dickson proceeded to visit the Selkirk Mental Hospital and spent a day there with the superintendent and his staff, who gave him an equally discouraging message about sex offenders: 'We don't want these guys because we have no custodial care. We appreciate that they are not really proper for penal institution and they fall between the two.' The only place that combined security with treatment was Penetanguishene in Ontario, and it was always full. 'There is really no institution in Manitoba where they can be sent.'[21]

In the end, Dickson sentenced both men to seven years' imprisonment. He took another unusual step in making an effort to follow their lives afterwards. The serial rapist, 'expected to be a recidivist, turned out to be a very good guy.' The student, 'for whom they had great hopes after his release, repeated the same type of crime and found himself back in the pen.'[22]

Another difficult sentencing case arose on Dickson's first trip to The Pas as circuit judge in June 1964. The case involved charges against a young native boy, Alan Canada, who lived on the Oxford Lake Reserve. One night, he struck his brother on the head with a piece of firewood during an argument. The brother was knocked unconscious and died after being flown out to hospital. It was found that he had an unusually thin, or 'egg shell,' skull. Alan Canada was charged with his brother's murder and the case came before Dickson. By the time the trial began, the charge had been reduced to manslaughter and Canada had agreed to plead guilty. He spoke no English and a young native girl acted as interpreter. They both broke into laughter as she interpreted the formal language of the charge. Dickson asked what was so funny and was told that it was simply not possible to translate 'the Eastern Judicial District of the Province of Manitoba' into Ojibway. The usual sentence for a crime of this nature by a native accused was, at the time, three years. However, the more Dickson heard about Alan Canada, the shorter it seemed the sentence should be. The boy was a model member of the community and a local clergyman had posted bail and taken Alan into his home, where he acted as babysitter. Alan had also shone at a Minaki conference for young aboriginals. 'As his sterling qualities were recited, the term for which I had planned to sentence him decreased rapidly. In the end, he was sent for a few months to an outdoor work camp.'[23]

Dickson thought that the traditional approach to sentencing was circumscribed and unimaginative. The judge charged with this awesome task 'knows little about the offender, however complete the pre-sentencing report. The range of punishments which he may impose is narrow.' Greater heed, Dickson believed, should be paid to the experience of other jurisdictions where alternatives to incarceration were in more frequent use. 'Our present method of divorcing imposition of punishment from criminology and penology, combined with the complete lack of follow-up on the part of the sentencing authority, is unlikely to make for an optimum result.' A few years later, after his appointment to the Court of Appeal, Dickson attended a sentencing seminar in a prison where 'half of those taking part were inmates who had been on the receiving end of the sentencing process.' Dickson expected to hear a litany of complaints, but there was little bitterness or recrimination. 'With one or two exceptions related to sentences for the possession of marijuana, all felt that they had been fairly treated.' Everyone agreed, however, on one point – 'that no young offender should ever be committed to a jail or penitentiary if there was any other possible means of dealing with him.'[24]

Dickson continued his prison visits for years to come, even as a judge of the Court of Appeal, when he and Chief Justice Samuel Freedman would visit both provincial jails and the federal penitentiary at Stoney Mountain at regular intervals, usually showing up unannounced.[25] Dickson and Barbara also volunteered, together with other lawyers and judges, to visit the prison for concerts and sales of arts and crafts made by the inmates. On one visit, the prisoners performed a musical skit based on the popular film 'Three Coins in a Fountain.' The prison version was 'Three Cons on a Mountain.' The Dicksons laughed along with the inmates, and Barbara graciously purchased the wares the prisoners had to offer. Dickson's prison visits and the trouble he took to find out what actually happened to the people he sentenced reflected his determination to see the inmates as fellow human beings, deserving of dignity and respect despite their transgressions.

Dickson's Time Bomb

In 1979 Dickson told a law school audience: 'For the new trial judge, a criminal jury case can be a somewhat harrowing experience. It is like a time bomb. One never knows when it will explode.'[26] The trial of Henry Acoby in March 1965 at Portage la Prairie for the murder of Rafael Gagnon proved to be Dickson's time bomb.[27] He described it as 'the most strange and unusual' case he tried. 'It was a seamy case, replete with much drinking and sex.'[28] Four young native people, two males and two females, bought a dilapidated car in Portage la Prairie and returned to the reserve late at night. They were drinking heavily and decided to go deer hunting. One of the women passed out and the others, Acoby and Gagnon and Agnes Mennow, went out with a rifle and a flashlight to 'night-light.' Ten days later, a farmer found Gagnon's body in a field. He had been shot in the back of the head. Mennow told the police that Acoby shot Gagnon because Gagnon had tried to rape her. Acoby was charged with murder and Mennow repeated the same story at the coroner's inquest and at the preliminary inquiry.

At the trial, it was clear that Mennow's testimony would be crucial to the prosecution. 'It was all very coherent until she came to the actual killing and then she clammed up.' Dickson threatened her with contempt and her response was, 'I am not going to talk.' She was put in jail overnight and the trial adjourned to the next day. That night she attempted suicide. The next day, the courtroom was full of some rather threatening looking people and she maintained her refusal to give evidence about the shooting. By the third day, Dickson was advised that she wanted to speak to the defence counsel, Harvey Pollock. Dickson called counsel into his chambers and advised them of Mennow's request. Crown counsel agreed to allow Pollock to see her. Pollock returned after his interview with Mennow 'just as white as a sheet, and he said, "I have an ethical problem."'[29] Dickson arranged for Pollock to go down to Winnipeg to discuss the matter with Chief Justice Tritschler.

The trial resumed the next day. Crown counsel said that he had no more questions. Pollock asked Mennow in cross-examination: 'Who did the shooting?' The answer was unforgettable: 'She let out a scream that you could have heard a block away and she said; "You know who did it, I did it." The press people were out the door in a shot, and everybody was in a state of shock, including the crown prosecutor and including me.'[30] Pollock asked for a directed verdict of acquittal, but Dickson insisted that the matter go to the jury. The crown called further evidence in an attempt to salvage its case, but to little avail. Dickson gave a charge understandably favourable to the accused. The jury quickly decided upon a verdict of not guilty.

There remained the question of what should happen to the witness in light of her apparent admission of guilt. 'That presented a bit of a problem because her evidence was given very much under duress. It wasn't a voluntary statement in any sense because we had her in jail and we threatened her with everything but hanging, drawing and quartering if she didn't talk.' In the end, it was decided to release her without charge. 'To this day I don't know whether she was telling the truth when she said that she had done it, or whether she was just so frightened by what would happen to her if this fellow was found guilty.'[31]

Dickson was strongly affected by these trips to remote parts of Manitoba to preside over trials involving aboriginals. He was very struck not only by the difficult lives aboriginal Canadians lived but also by 'their traditions, their deep sense of humanity and the warmth in which he was received.' Despite his radically different life experience, Dickson always felt comfortable with and 'very supported by aboriginal peoples.'[32]

Dickson tried three murder cases as a Queen's Bench judge at a time when capital punishment was still in effect. 'We had the black cap ready, and the sentence of hanging drafted and dated and the jail where the fellow would be hanged if found guilty of capital [murder].'[33] The government's policy was to commute the death penalty, but even so, Dickson, who was strongly opposed to capital punishment,[34] never had to pass the sentence. 'Most of the killings, I am unhappy to say it, in Manitoba at the time concerned native people and most of the crimes were committed when they were under the influence of alcohol.' Dickson 'charged the jury that if the fellow was so intoxicated he didn't have the capacity to form the intent to kill, then the verdict should be manslaughter.' Invariably, the verdicts were either manslaughter or second-degree murder.[35]

'An abundance of common sense'

Dickson enjoyed working with juries and became a great believer in the jury system. As a trial judge, 'it was always a great relief to be able to charge the jury and leave them to decide the facts.'[36] He found that jury members took their task seriously. On several occasions, people who had served on a jury in his court later told him how significant the experience had been. Although he almost invariably agreed with the jury, Dickson did not think it appropriate to indicate his views either before or after the verdict had been rendered. The law permits a trial judge to offer his or her views on the credibility of the witnesses, but Dickson found this difficult to reconcile with the primary rule that the members of the jury were the sole finders of the facts and that the expression of the judge's views on the facts threatened the appearance of impartiality. He thought that either congratulations or chastisement from the trial judge 'at best are unnecessary and at worst are demeaning to the jurors and to the judicial system.'[37]

During Dickson's time as a trial judge, criminal jury trials were simpler matters than they are today. Jury selection proceeded quickly; each side had a certain number of peremptory challenges, but even these were used sparingly and Dickson never had to deal with a challenge for cause, where potential jurors are questioned about bias or prejudice. Trials typically took a few days. A week-long trial was unusual, even for serious murder cases.

There was surprisingly little material available to assist trial judges in the preparation of jury charges. Dickson exchanged notes and ideas with two experienced trial judges in other provinces, Bruce Smith, the chief justice of Alberta, and George Alexander Gale, the chief justice of the High Court in Ontario. 'We all worked on common charges, the standard sort of criminal charge in major types of cases. We exchanged these among ourselves and tried to keep them up to date and pick up any new wrinkles that might come from the Court of Appeal or the Supreme Court of Canada.'

Dickson was not a believer in lengthy jury charges that reviewed the evidence in detail. He followed George Tritschler's rule of thumb that, no matter how serious the offence, 'any jury charge that went beyond forty-five minutes was too long.' Most people, Dickson felt, simply could not absorb more information at a single sitting. 'These charges that go on for two or three days, I just can't understand.' On the other hand, the trial judge must also consider that, in the event of an appeal, the charge will be dissected before the Court of Appeal. The task is to write something simple enough to be comprehensible to twelve ordinary citizens unschooled in the law, yet sufficiently sophisticated to survive microscopic examination by defence counsel on appeal. Dickson favoured the simpler approach followed by many English judges, who 'place the matter before juries simply and effectively, using the pungent colloquial terms with which one addresses the average person.' He thought that, while juries were 'endowed with an abundance of common sense,' they were 'not students of logic or accustomed to subtle reasoning' and that it was 'difficult for the average jury to absorb in an hour the teachings which would challenge a superior law school class.'[38]

Typically, Dickson would draft his jury instructions in longhand in the evening, sometimes working until 2:00 or 3:00 in the morning. Every word was written down. He followed Tritschler's advice 'never to say a word in the jury charge' that had not been committed to writing. This avoided the problem encountered by some judges who found themselves reversed on appeal because of an ill-advised remark that had not been fully considered. 'I don't think I was ever reversed in a criminal case. The nice thing about being a trial judge, once you deliver your charge, then you sit back and relax and say, "Well, from now on it is up to the jury, and if I made a mistake then there will be the Court of Appeal to correct me."'[39]

The experience of explaining technical points of law to juries had a lasting effect on Dickson. It shaped his attitude as an appellate judge when a jury charge was under attack. 'You realize the pressures the trial judge is under and you don't nit-pick and you don't quibble about small, unimportant aspects.' As an appellate judge, Dickson became known for his clear and readily understandable writing style and insisted that judicial writing should be accessible to the ordinary Canadian. This he attributed to his experience as a trial judge explaining technical points of law to a jury: 'I think you learn perhaps a better understanding of how to write in a way which will be understood by the man in the street, the person who hasn't got legal training.'[40]

The Harsh Realities

The bulk of Dickson's work as a Queen's Bench judge consisted of civil cases ranging from divorce and matrimonial law to property, contract, and commercial disputes. The variety was enormous: 'automobile accidents of all shapes and sizes, insurance claims, damaged machinery, corporate battles, interpretation of wills, partnership disputes, cattle rustling, forgery, bankruptcy, interpretation of municipal by-laws and argument over ownership of mineral rights. This was some of the grist which feeds the mill of a trial judge.'[41]

While his criminal cases may have been more dramatic, many of the civil cases Dickson tried were heart-rending in their portrayal of the harsh realities of life in western Canada. This was not the world that Dickson had encountered in his corporate law practice. In one case two brothers contested ownership of the family farm, and a handwriting expert had to be called as an expert witness to help Dickson decide whether documents had been forged.[42] Another case involving a dispute in a Ukrainian family over the sale of a farm, saw emotions running so high that on the first day Dickson carefully noted: 'recess because plaintiff wept.'[43] A case heard in Winnipeg in September 1965 dealt with the claim of one German immigrant against another.[44] The defendant had married the plaintiff's daughter, but he was unwilling to accept her disabled son; the child's grandfather sued for the $40 a week the defendant had promised to pay for the child's keep. Another tragic case involved a fatal-accident claim brought by an aboriginal woman and her children on account of the death of their husband and father.[45] At the time of his death, Peter Lathlin lived with his wife and eight children, the oldest being eleven years old, in a log cabin which he had built on the reserve. Described by The Pas Indian agent as a 'good provider' who was 'never on the relief rolls,' Lathlin was run over on the road on a cold December night by a driver who fled the scene. The agent testified that the deceased 'drank but didn't let it interfere with his job or family life.' The post-mortem examination revealed that Lathlin was highly intoxicated at the time he met his death. In his carefully written decision, Dickson rejected the defence submission that the claim should be dismissed outright on the ground that Lathlin was the author of his own misfortune, but he did find the deceased contributorily negligent and reduced the award by 50 per cent. In another fatal-accident case, the widow's claim was diminished when she had to admit that her husband was a womanizer: 'When he wasn't with me he said he lived at hotels and other women's homes.'[46]

Divorce cases were decided in Winnipeg on Tuesday mornings. Dickson took his turn presiding over Divorce Court at least once a month, when between ten and fifteen petitions for divorce would be heard, and he also heard divorces on circuit. When Dickson was appointed, the only legal ground for divorce was adultery, and the evidence was often fabricated: 'In a lot of them, you had the suspicion that it was pretty much a set-up. They would usually find the husband in some motel with some girl that he shouldn't have been with.'[47] In 1968 the grounds for divorce were broadened 'and the former business of detectives and all that sort of business passed out of the picture, fortunately.'[48] In most cases, all that was left of the marriage by the time the case was heard was a bare legal formality, but Dickson recognized that 'each represents a personal tragedy to those immediately concerned.'[49] Custody issues were difficult and bitter; maintenance and support were particularly important to women in an age when most stayed at home to look after the children. Dickson took his turn in divorce court but he had no stomach for the bitterness and acrimony of family disputes and later said that he 'detested' the work.[50]

Personal-injury cases arising from motor-vehicle accidents and other causes formed a significant component of the Queen's Bench judge's work on the civil side. In June 1967 Dickson dealt with a tragic case arising from an activity with which he was very familiar.[51] A young girl, about fourteen, was killed at a riding stable her second time out. In a detailed written judgment demonstrating his extensive knowledge of horses and riding, Dickson found that two of the guides supplied by the riding stable were 'clearly incompetent.'[52] He dismissed the argument that the stable could excuse its negligence on the basis of a sign reading 'Riders Ride at Their Own Risk' since the sign had not been brought to the young girl's attention.

Assessing damages for personal injuries, like sentencing in criminal cases, is a subjective and difficult task. Dickson thought that the traditional approach of awarding damages was narrow and that innovative techniques ought to be considered. The central problem is that damages are assessed once and for all at the time of trial and the law offers no possibility for revisiting the situation. The prognosis and future prospects of the injured party have to be assessed on the basis of the information available and the resulting award often represents little more than an educated guess that could provide a windfall or prove to be inadequate. Dickson favoured a scheme of periodic payments to avoid the guesswork.[53]

On Circuit

An important aspect of the life and work of a Queen's Bench judge was going on circuit. Dickson regularly travelled by car to the county towns of rural and northern Manitoba – Dauphin, Brandon, Portage la Prairie, Minnedosa, The Pas – to try whatever cases needed to be heard. The typical assignment was for a week, but the time could be shorter if the cases settled or pleas of guilty were entered, or longer if there was a complex case to be heard. In most towns, there was a room with a desk and bed for the judge on the second floor of the courthouse. These quarters were adequate but spartan and the visiting judge led a monastic life. 'Sometimes it was just above the lock-up which was down below and you would be wakened by the sound of the prisoners going for breakfast. The fellow who made their breakfast would bring you up a cold plate of bacon and eggs and a cup of coffee and pieces of dry toast.'[54]

Dickson was wary of social contact with members of the local bar. 'The ones who were wanting to welcome you frequently turned out to be the very people who were going to be before you a few days later.' Lunch and dinner would be taken at a restaurant or hotel. 'Sometimes you would see the lawyers who had been before you that day. You might say 'hello' but that would be about it.'[55]

Brandon, Dauphin, and Portage la Prairie were Dickson's most frequent destinations as a circuit judge. Two weeks after he was sworn in as a judge, Dickson went to Dauphin for a week to hear civil cases. This was followed by a short stay in Minnedosa in February, then back to Dauphin in March when a civil case had to be adjourned because the court reporter was marooned in Neepawa on account of a blizzard. To make up the time, Dickson ordered that the case be heard two days later in the evening, but the weather thwarted that plan as well when the defendant was snowbound. That week in Dauphin, Dickson tried his first criminal jury case, a relatively complex case of fraud and forgery which lasted a week. In April he spent a day in Portage la Prairie, followed by a week in The Pas in June. In the fall, it was a day in Brandon when all cases settled and Dickson was left only uncontested divorces to resolve, and then two days in Dauphin to hear a civil dispute between two brothers fighting over cattle and farm tools. The first year was completed with two trips to Portage la Prairie in November and December. There, Dickson tried a civil case against a veterinarian who had caused a horse to fall and break its leg while being gelded. Dickson found in favour of the owner of the horse and awarded $1,650 damages.[56]

'Without fuss and with distinction'

On the bench, Dickson took detailed notes of the evidence, while a shorthand reporter kept a verbatim account of the proceedings. A full transcript was prepared only in the event of appeal but Dickson routinely marked 'get' in his notes opposite the crucial portions of the evidence, and would have the reporter read back the verbatim account when it came time to write a judgment or prepare a jury charge. He carefully identified the rare occasions when he asked a question himself with the notation – 'Question by the Court.' Evidence was noted precisely as given by the witness and in rural Manitoba this frequently involved grammatically incorrect and uncouth language. Dickson's notes rarely contained any of his own observations or impressions but occasionally he would indicate what a witness was wearing to distinguish in his mind that witness from the others. In a case involving a man who had been badly burned, Dickson noted the extent of the plaintiff's disfigurement.[57] In the case involving the young girl killed while riding, he indicated that one of the guides responsible for supervision was 'very immature, a young child' while the other was 'very dumb, unreliable.'[58] Dickson studied his notes carefully when preparing reasons for judgment or a jury charge and meticulously underlined the crucial passages in red. In most cases, the arguments of counsel were recorded in skeletal fashion, although careful note was taken of all case citations. Often, at the conclusion of a civil case, Dickson would reserve judgment and ask counsel to submit written argument so that he could carefully consider the legal issues.

Dickson's work as a Queen's Bench judge was solid, though few of his trial decisions could be described as being particularly notable or groundbreaking. Earning a reputation as a 'no nonsense' judge, conducting trials, in the words of his mentor Tritschler, 'without fuss and with distinction,'[59] he produced a steady stream of concise, readable judgments that reflected the diversity of subject areas coming before the trial court. Trial judges assess witnesses, find facts, and apply established legal principles to the cases they decide. They are expected to be prompt and predictable. Dickson fulfilled those expectations. Shaping and changing the law is primarily the task of the appellate courts, which command a broader perspective of the judicial system.

However, these early judgments of Dickson do exhibit the clarity of style and attention to detail evident in his later work on the Supreme Court of Canada. The analysis is clear and precise, and legal propositions are carefully supported by ample citations of the leading authorities. Dickson did not hide the fact that on occasion his own research on a point went beyond the cases cited by counsel.[60]

Dickson's writing gradually took on a confident and distinctive manner. He admired the refreshingly unconventional, plain-language writing style of the great English judge Lord Denning, who often started his judgments with a simple and well-crafted sentence that set the stage for what was to follow. Instead of the conventional: 'This is an action by the plaintiff for damages for personal injuries occasioned as a result of a motor vehicle accident,' one finds Dickson writing: 'Shortly after 1:00 A.M. on Sunday, September 27, 1964, defendant fell asleep while driving his car.'[61] These opening sentences fix in the reader's mind first and foremost the human dimensions of the case.

While Dickson's work as a trial judge does not reveal any particular judicial philosophy or jurisprudential approach, there are occasional hints in his trial judgments of thinking that would become more apparent in later years on the Supreme Court of Canada. Dickson's insistence upon the utmost clarity in his writing and analysis is matched by his impatience with technical positions or arguments. This was exhibited in both criminal[62] and civil cases. In an action brought by an insurance company, Dickson carefully disposed of all the arguments advanced in support of the claim and concluded: 'The concept of this action seems to lie in technical ingenuity, but it is so wanting in other attributes that one wonders at it having been brought.'[63] Another theme Dickson would later develop on the Supreme Court of Canada was deference to the specialized expertise of administrative boards and tribunals. As a trial judge, Dickson insisted that 'where injustice is done by a non-statutory arbitration board, there must be some means whereby an aggrieved party can reach the courts and obtain redress. The power of the court to intervene in a proper case is founded on its jurisdiction to protect property and civil rights.'[64] However, where the parties had submitted their dispute to arbitration and the arbitrator's interpretation of the collective agreement was 'one which the language ... will reasonably bear,'[65] judicial deference was called for and he refused to interfere with the arbitrator's decision. The Manitoba Court of Appeal disagreed[66] but the case was appealed to the Supreme Court of Canada[67] where Dickson's judgment was restored.

Dickson loved his work as a trial judge and always described it as the best job in the world. He enjoyed the independence, the intellectual challenge, and the opportunity to work with juries and lawyers, particularly on criminal cases. In a series of lectures at the University of Toronto in 1979, six years after his appointment to the Supreme Court of Canada, Dickson described the role of trial judge as follows:

> A trial judge determines credibility, finds facts, draws vital inferences and is at liberty, within the confines of legal principle, to determine the litigation. A trial judge enjoys a freedom, and an independence, which is not open to an appellate judge. As he moves from trial court to chambers, to divorce court, to circuit, he goes alone. Subject to appeal the decisions are his and his alone. He may consult with his colleagues on a point of difficulty but the final responsibility is his. He is at the pulse of the litigation. Though his role is to adjudicate, he is in the trenches of the warfare, along with counsel, the witnesses, the jury. His involvement is more immediate, more intense, at times more dramatic and in certain ways more challenging than that of his counterpart on the appellate bench. He is

in control of proceedings which are essentially adversarial. Day after day he observes witnesses, listens to their responses during examination-in-chief and later in cross-examination. He learns by experience how to distinguish between those telling the truth and the few who attempt to deceive. The trial judge has the comfort of knowing that if he errs, his error will be corrected in the courts above. He must also endure an occasional reversal. The rejection by a court of appeal of one's *chef-d'oeuvre* can be a chastening experience, particularly on the first occasion. Thereafter, the pain subsides as one comes to realize that it is all part of the judicial process.[68]

The Essentials of Communal Living

Dickson's longest and most significant civil trial was *Hofer et al. v. Hofer et al.*,[69] a three-week case heard in March and April 1966. The case involved a clash between property rights and the religious integrity of a colony of Hutterites. The plaintiffs in the suit complained that they were being wrongly expelled from the colony and sought a division and distribution of their share of the colony's assets, valued at over $1 million. The defendants alleged that the plaintiffs threatened the religious integrity of the colony and that they had no right to a share of the colony's communal property.

Dickson knew a great deal about Hutterite practices from his visits to the colony near his farm. Hutterite colonies are founded upon specific religious principles and all property is owned communally. This practice allowed Hutterites to accumulate large and prosperous tracts of farming land, making them somewhat unpopular on the prairies.[70] In the *Hofer* case, the two plaintiffs had developed an interest in the 'Radio Church of God' and subscribed to a magazine called 'The Plain Truth.' Both the radio program and the magazine promoted beliefs seriously at odds with those of the Hutterite Brethren. Of particular concern were the magazine's claim that the Sabbath should be celebrated on Saturday rather than Sunday and its assertion that pork was 'unclean' and should not be eaten. The Hutterites were Sunday observers who raised pigs and for whom the production of pork products was a major enterprise.

Ministers of the colony insisted that the four Hofer brothers not read *The Plain Truth* and lengthy discussions ensued as to whether views advocated by this magazine were supported by the Bible. It was decided that the plaintiffs should be punished by the penalty of *unfrieden*, which meant that they could not associate with any other member of the colony, including their own wives. They refused to accept the punishment and were expelled.

During the trial, extensive evidence was heard about the teachings and beliefs of both the Hutterian Brethren and the Radio Church of God. Major and fundamental doctrinal differences existed, touching upon the Sabbath, dietary laws, observance of Christian festivals, and community of property. The plaintiffs took the position that, although the Hutterian Brethren Church claimed to follow the primitive Church of the Apostles, it did not practise what it preached. In effect, the court was asked to declare that, for the preceding four hundred years, Hutterite practices were at variance with Hutterite preaching, and that the early leaders and those who followed them were theologically in error.

The case raised some difficult issues. Could a court become embroiled in this debate over religious dogma? The difficulties are obvious, yet if the court refused to entertain the plaintiff's contentions, was it not possible that they would be deprived of valuable property rights without cause? There was a clear clash between the claims of individual property rights and the communitarian claims of the Hutterite religion. Dickson took several months to write a careful decision. He held that the rights of the religious community had to prevail despite the harsh consequences for the plaintiffs, who would be expelled without any compensation for their years of hard work. He refused to declare that one religion or doctrine was right and the other wrong. Rightly or wrongly, the Hutterian Brethren Church held certain beliefs which were fundamentally at odds with those promulgated by the Radio Church of God and it was impossible for the adherents of the former to co-exist with those of the latter. Although the plaintiffs had been treated harshly, Dickson respected the decision of the religious community to uphold its beliefs in the face of dissent. He found that, for the Hutterite community, 'the totality of religion permeates all life and uniform doctrinal belief is essential to survival.' In this setting, the doctrines chosen by the plaintiffs had 'disruptive force' and by adopting such views, Dickson concluded, the plaintiffs had 'excluded themselves from the spiritual community of which they had previously been a part' and the 'full unanimity of faith, life and work essential to communal living' had ceased.[71]

The implications for the plaintiff Hofer brothers were severe. At stake was all the wealth they had worked to create, not just property attaching to the church itself. Dickson held, however, that because of the belief in community of property, the plaintiffs never acquired a personal interest in the property and that there was no basis to accord them one as they departed, despite their stated intention of forming a separate colony based on similar community-property concepts. Those remaining had the right to expel the plaintiffs without giving them a share of the community's property. Dickson, in effect, upheld the rights of the larger religious community over the property and unjust-enrichment claims of the dissenting Hofer brothers.

Dickson's decision was appealed to the Manitoba Court of Appeal and then to the Supreme Court of Canada. Both courts upheld his ruling.[72] As he learned a few years later when he joined the Supreme Court of Canada, the care he had taken to prepare his reasons was rewarded in another important way. The judges of the Court were impressed by his work on this difficult case and marked him as one of the judges from western Canada suitable to replace Emmett Hall, who was approaching retirement.[73]

The *Hofer* judgment provides an insight into the complex weave of individualistic and communitarian values in Dickson's judicial philosophy. Reconciling claims of individual rights with the interests of the community would become one of his preoccupations when, as chief justice of Canada, he led the judiciary into the age of the Charter of Rights and Freedoms. *Hofer* shows that, well before his landmark Charter judgments, Dickson had a profound respect for religious diversity and for distinctive communal arrangements. He was quite prepared to deny individual rights that were incompatible with the continued survival of a distinctive community. From his early years as a judge, Dickson was not a single-minded defender of individual rights and was receptive to legal arguments that had a communitarian basis.

6

Court of Appeal

In June 1967, after almost four years as a trial judge, Dickson was appointed to the Manitoba Court of Appeal. The appointment 'just seemed to be a sort of natural progression' and Dickson did not hesitate to accept when Canada's flamboyant new minister of justice, Pierre Elliott Trudeau, called. 'It was a further opportunity to learn a little more law in a different environment and it was a very congenial court at the time.' The 'spartan digs in some of those minor Manitoba towns' were starting to get 'a little tiresome.' It was also a pleasant change to have a more permanent situation in Winnipeg and to avoid the perils of winter driving to the remote corners of the province.[1]

'A breath of fresh air'

The experience of sitting as an appellate judge was not entirely new to Dickson. In Manitoba, as in several other provinces, superior court trial judges are also appointed as ad hoc judges of the Court of Appeal. This designation allows them to sit in the Court of Appeal, where illness or absence of one member may create a pressing need for temporary help. Before his appointment to the Court of Appeal, Dickson already had the experience of sitting on over half a dozen appeals as an ad hoc judge.[2]

Dickson first sat as an ad hoc appellate judge in December 1965 and, on that occasion he amply demonstrated his talents for appellate work. His decision, *R. v. Bannerman*,[3] involved the difficult issue of the reliability of the evidence of children in sexual-assault prosecutions. Dickson wrote a judgment of considerable significance in a delicate and sensitive area of the law. The judgment reflects many of the underlying values and principles that would become more apparent years later when Dickson was a Supreme Court judge deciding Charter cases.

The appellant had been convicted of serious sexual offences against two native children, a boy aged thirteen and his sister aged twelve. The key issue on appeal was the reliability of the evidence offered by the victims. Bannerman's lawyers argued that the boy did not have adequate religious knowledge of the consequences of lying under oath and that the trial judge should not have allowed the boy to give sworn testimony. The boy had been questioned at the trial about his religious beliefs. When asked what would happen to him if he did not tell the truth, the boy said that he did not know. Bannerman relied on earlier decisions that appeared to say that, before a child could give sworn evidence, the child had to show an awareness that superhuman punishment, such as going to hell, would be the consequence of telling of a lie.

Dickson disagreed. Sceptical of technical rules that kept evidence from the jury, he dissected the case law, said to require knowledge of the 'consequences' of an oath, and concluded that this emphasis was unwarranted. Dickson thought that the 'fire and brimstone' code of the earlier cases was based on shaky and outmoded theological grounds. He observed that one's beliefs as to the consequences of an oath necessarily depended upon the nature of one's religious convictions, a point of some significance given that these were native children. It could not be assumed that every witness was a Christian, or that every Christian held precisely the same religious beliefs. Dickson offered examples of diverse customs or practices from other religious cultures designed to elicit the truth. Drawing upon his own knowledge of religion – he was still the chancellor of his Anglican diocese – he held that, even from a purely Christian perspective, the question put to the child posed a theological problem of some complexity. The Christian doctrine of forgiveness of sins meant that only God could know what would happen to the child if he lied. As Dickson put it, 'the most learned moral theologian compelled to answer that particular question must have given the same answer as [the boy]. By his answer this child was not admitting his ignorance in an area where he ought to have been better informed.'[4]

Dickson concluded that the old cases ought no longer to be followed and that 'all that is required when one speaks of an understanding of the "consequences" of an oath is that the child appreciates it is assuming a moral obligation ... The object of the law in requiring an oath is to get at the truth relative to the matters in dispute by getting a hold on the conscience of the witness.' The boy had shown an understanding of the moral obligation to tell the truth and this, Dickson held, was enough to support the trial judge's decision to allow the boy to give sworn evidence. Dickson insisted that the judgment of the trial judge was to be respected and he proceeded gently to lecture his temporary colleagues on the Court of Appeal on the importance of giving trial judges adequate latitude. 'This judge had the very great advantage of observing and talking to the child ... Each case will depend on its own facts, and the impression that the child makes upon the judge will be of great importance.'[5]

The Supreme Court of Canada upheld Dickson's judgment without further reasons.[6] His decision remains the leading Canadian authority on the point today and, building on its thinking, Parliament overhauled the Evidence Act to facilitate receiving the evidence of children.[7] The *Bannerman* decision reflects Dickson's moderately progressive notion of judicial lawmaking in the late 1960s.

The thinking that motivated the *Bannerman* decision linked three future chief justices of Canada. Dickson's judgment more or less coincided with Bora Laskin's dissent in the Ontario Court of Appeal on the same point. Laskin said that, as a legal test, the fear of devine retribution was 'highly talismanic' and added: 'The common law deserves better than that at the hands of the judiciary in the 20th century.'[8] *Bannerman* later caught the eye of another future chief justice of Canada, Beverley McLachlin, when she was a law professor teaching evidence at the University of British Columbia. McLachlin recalls the decision as her first encounter with Dickson: ... 'I was very impressed with that decision ... It was a breath of fresh air, it was liberal and wasn't tied to the old British traditions ... Something struck me as different and remarkable in its reasoning, its willingness to take a fresh look at a difficult area.'[9]

As he left the trial court for the Court of Appeal in 1967, Dickson described his philosophy in the following terms:

> Judges are sometimes accused of creating law. In a sense they do. Law takes shape only at the moment when it is fitted to the facts of an actual case. It is thus moulded in the process of adjudication. The body which adjudicates has final say as to what is and what is not law. As new conditions arise judges apply and adapt to them old precepts and principles. New law thus arises and law instead of being fixed and static becomes a living, changeable entity shaped to satisfy the needs of society. Progressive growth and adaptation therefore become, and must become, the principal characteristic of our legal system to the end that social control, growth and development are achieved.[10]

In *R. v. Bannerman*, Dickson had refused to be tied down by rigid adherence to 'fixed and static' rules based upon outmoded attitudes about children and religious belief. He applied and adapted the fundamental underlying legal principles to craft a modern approach that better reflected current social reality. Dickson's *Bannerman* judgment exhibits several features that would characterize his later jurisprudence: insistence upon clear and understandable rules that make sense in modern Canadian society, attention to religious and other forms of diversity that render traditional legal rules suspect, distrust of technical rules that exclude evidence, and deference to first-level decision makers.

Family Matters

Within a few months of his appointment to the Court of Appeal, Dickson's son Brian entered law school at the University of Toronto. A strong student with a flair for languages, an interest his father encouraged, Brian had just spent a year in France after graduating from Princeton. Following a stint in Mexico working at a law firm, he was fluent in both French and Spanish. Upon graduation from law school in 1970, he embarked on a successful career with the Department of External Affairs, taking him to postings in Romania, India, Guatemala, and Washington. Brian's spouse, Kate, pursued a career in the field of international development.

Deborah, seventeen years old when Dickson moved to the Court of Appeal, wanted to become a nurse. To reach that goal, she needed to take chemistry but had a weak teacher and was floundering. Though Dickson knew next to nothing about chemistry, he decided to help her. He went to the books and father and daughter overcame the subject together. In Barbara Dickson's words: 'They both hated it, but they made their way through the course and Deborah succeeded on her examination' and eventually became a nurse.[11] Shortly after graduating, Deborah met Chris Shields, a neurosurgery resident from northern Ontario. They married in 1971 and were living in Winnipeg. In 1973, their first daughter, Lisa, the Dicksons' first grandchild, was born. Still at home with the Dicksons were the twins Barry and Peter, thirteen years old in 1967, then at high school. The Dickson home was a popular gathering spot for their wide circle of friends.

The Dickson family faced the loss of all three grandparents in rapid succession. Lillian Dickson died the same year Dickson was appointed to the Court of Appeal. They had always been close and Dickson was very conscious of her strong influence on him and his children. It was only after his father's death four years later, in 1971, that Dickson learned that Lillian was two years older than Thomas. Henry Sellers, active in community and philanthropic pursuits to the end, passed away in 1970. Even in his later years, Sellers was constantly raising money for his church and for the hospital and quietly contributing to various causes. He established the Sellers Foundation in the 1930s and he added a substantial sum on his death when he left the foundation in the hands of Barbara Dickson and her brothers, George and Edward Sellers.

In the years to follow, Barbara assumed her full share of responsibility for the affairs of the Sellers Foundation which made a substantial grant to the Health Science Centre in Winnipeg for research into diabetes and another to the Sick Children's Hospital in Toronto for research on cystic fibrosis.

Appellate Judge

In Dickson's time, the Manitoba Court of Appeal was not a busy court, and he found appellate work easier to manage than the work of a trial judge. There was no travel, fewer cases to decide, and more time for thinking and reflection. Collegiality was an important factor since the court sat in panels, usually of three but occasionally five for major cases. During his tenure on the court, the judges worked well together. 'We all fitted in very well and there was a good esprit. Winnipeg is not a very big city and particularly the legal profession was not too numerous, so we knew each other very well.'[12]

Dickson's appointment coincided with the elevation of Charles Rhodes Smith, his former professor and Queen's Bench colleague, who was named chief justice of Manitoba. Dickson described Rhodes Smith as 'a very gentle man, great for collegiality and people liked him very much.'[13] Samuel Freedman was Dickson's most distinguished colleague on the Court of Appeal. An outstanding jurist who wrote clear and scholarly judgments, Freedman was a Russian-born Jew who had come to Canada at the age of three. His father was a junk dealer in Winnipeg's north end. Freedman was appointed to the Queen's Bench in 1952 at the age of forty-four and to the Court of Appeal in 1960. In 1971 he was named chief justice of Manitoba.[14] Dickson had high regard for Freedman's 'technical legal acumen, as well as for his deep and perceptive insights into the larger function of the law' and for the 'rich background of culture and learning' reflected in his judgments.[15] Alfred Monnin, another future chief justice of the province, had been on the Court of Appeal for five years when Dickson was appointed in 1967. Monnin was a Franco-Manitoban who had been appointed to the Queen's Bench in 1957 when he was only thirty-seven years old. Another of the court's judges was a friend of his from law school days who had been an usher at his wedding, R.D. Guy. Known as 'Doc,' Guy had been active in the Conservative Party and was appointed directly from the bar to the Court of Appeal by the Diefenbaker government in 1961.

Most cases were decided on the spot and disposed of by short oral reasons immediately after the completion of argument. For the more difficult cases, the practice was to have an informal meeting after the appeal had been argued to discuss the case and determine who should write the judgment. In Dickson's time, there were no law clerks to assist in the tasks of research and writing. Dickson was meticulous in his determination to track down all the relevant authorities and he often found it necessary to look at legal sources beyond those cited by counsel. As he explained to an audience of law students in 1979, he relied on counsel to identify the key facts, but 'with respect to the law ... an appellate judge will place far less reliance on counsel.' After reviewing the cases and statutes cited by counsel, he felt free to 'do further independent research if ... the importance of the matter requires it, or if a point is inadequately researched by counsel.'[16] Dickson recalled the lawyers to give them a chance to argue any new issues revealed by his research, but not where the research only supported a conclusion on a point that had been argued.

The role of a provincial appellate court in Canada is complex and delicate. These courts are intermediate between the trial courts, which mete out justice first-hand, and the Supreme Court of Canada, which has the final say. A provincial court of appeal serves to see that justice is done in each case, but, in so doing, it must also chart the course the law is to follow in other cases. Dickson said that the 'principal function' of intermediate appellate courts 'is to correct errors of law in the decisions of lower courts.' But, he added, this review function 'involves development of a uniform and consistent body of law which, while drawing on the legal rules that embody the collective experience and judicial wisdom of our culture, assures that the law continues to meet the changing needs of society.' According to Dickson, an 'intermediate appellate court must seek justice in the individual case, but it must do so mindful always of its duty to develop a rational and systematic body of law'. He described this combined function as 'treacherous ground.'[17] It is sometimes said that judges of intermediate appellate courts are prisoners of the trial courts, which find the facts, and the Supreme Court, which decides the law. Yet provincial appellate courts also have the right and duty to correct egregious factual errors and, in areas of law unique to the province, they are the court of last resort.

Dickson's appellate judgments reflect the same meticulous care with the facts that he had exhibited in his trial judgments. He frequently began with a pithy paragraph composed of simple but powerful sentences that explained the essence of the case and its human dimension. An appeal from a sentence of preventive detention commences: 'This case concerns a sentence of preventive detention imposed upon the appellant, McAmmond, by Keith, C.C.J. McAmmond is 31 years of age. He suffers from a mental disorder. He is a sexual deviate. He molests young children. He does this furtively. There is no evidence that he has ever resorted to violence.'[18] A case involving the liability of deer hunters for the accidental shooting of a farmer is introduced as follows: 'We are here concerned with the law affecting deer hunters who each fall, in increasing number, invade the bush lands and woodlands of the province in search of game, and their accountability for accidental injuries inflicted by them.'[19]

Dickson's appellate judgments were also characterized by a clear and direct style. He took great pains to express himself as clearly as possible and routinely went through several drafts before he was satisfied with the result. He deliberately avoided legalese and jargon. For the most part, his opinions are short and concise, certainly shorter than has now become common. He thought that giving proper reasons was a discipline integral to the judicial function and he deplored the occasional failure of provincial appellate courts to give reasons: 'It is unfair to the litigants, to the bench and bar of the province and to the court of final appeal.'[20]

Dickson's judgments had a scholarly flavour, although they were certainly less ambitious than his later work on the Supreme Court of Canada. He routinely reviewed the case law in a careful and thorough manner. His citation of American, Australian, and New Zealand authorities was considerably more frequent than the prevailing practice. Similarly, while his reliance on scholarly writing did not approach the practice he established years later on the Supreme Court, it was more ample than the prevailing judicial norm. In part, this was a reflection of the fact that at the time legal scholars were neither numerous nor prolific. Dickson constantly urged the academic community to write more. A writing stylist would find little to criticize in Dickson's judgments except, perhaps, a tendency to quote authorities at length rather than provide a synopsis or synthesis in his own words. Again, in comparison to the later work on the Supreme Court, there is relatively little explicit discussion of policy issues but, of course, far fewer of the cases coming before the Manitoba Court of Appeal in the late 1960s and early 1970s raised issues that lent themselves to that sort of discussion.

Even in decisions of sufficient jurisprudential significance to find their way into the law reports, the Manitoba Court of Appeal was, during Dickson's time, usually unanimous. Dickson rarely wrote a dissenting opinion. In all but two[21] reported cases, he carried the majority, and in one of those two, his dissent was only partial.[22] When the court was divided, the judge with whom Dickson was in most frequent disagreement was Guy. In a number of these cases, Guy dissented from a tightly reasoned Dickson opinion based upon a close reading of the case law. Guy was inclined to a more instinctive 'apply the equities' approach.

Next to Guy, the judge with whom Dickson most frequently disagreed was Freedman. This is surprising since both men had liberal- leaning views and both brought a decidedly scholarly approach to their work. On the other hand, their backgrounds could hardly have been more different. Freedman was a respected jurist, but, as a Jew in the early 1970s, he was still something of an outsider to the Winnipeg establishment while Dickson was a solid member. Freedman was very involved in the activities of the Jewish community, whereas Dickson belonged to the staid Manitoba Club, the site of high-powered business lunches and elite dinners. The club still excluded Jews. Dickson tried to break the unspoken but clearly understood ban by proposing for membership Ernest Sirluck, the newly appointed Jewish president of the University of Manitoba. However, Sirluck refused to serve as the token Jew and, for the time being, the anti-Semitic exclusion remained.[23]

While on the Manitoba Court of Appeal, Dickson was perhaps more likely than Freedman to follow the letter of the law, even if that led him to a harsh result. As we shall see in the next chapter, in his early years on the Supreme Court of Canada, Dickson's cautious approach to judicial law reform led him to have even sharper disagreements with Bora Laskin. Freedman and Laskin shared many traits. They both brought a learned and scholarly approach to their judicial work, and they also shared a willingness to reshape the law where they thought that change was necessary for the law to meet changing social and economic conditions. In contrast, Dickson's early inclination was to insist that law reform be left to the legislature. In the famous case of *Harrison v. Carswell*, he insisted that the letter of the law allowed a Winnipeg shopping centre owner to exclude workers picketing their employer in the course of a lawful strike.[24] Dickson overruled Freedman's judgment upholding the rights of the picketing workers.[25] At the Supreme Court, Laskin dissented and, like Freedman, insisted that the law of trespass and the statute making trespass an offence could not be rigidly applied to defeat the rights of workers.

In Dickson's only fully dissenting opinion, he insisted upon a strict interpretation of a statute, even though it produced an awkward result, and disagreed with Freedman's strong majority judgment interpreting the statute according to what he thought it should mean. This case arose from winding up the Bank of Western Canada.[26] The trial judge dealing with this complex corporate tangle had ordered that one aspect of the matter – entitlement to over three million dollars' worth of shares held by an Ontario trust company – be dealt with in Ontario by an Ontario judge. This highly unusual procedure was authorized by a section in the federal statute stating that the courts and the judges of the various provinces 'are auxiliary to one another.'[27] An appeal was taken from an order of the Ontario judge and the question was whether the appeal was to be heard by the Ontario Court of Appeal or by the Manitoba Court of Appeal. Five judges were assembled to hear the matter. The statute said that the appeal was to be heard by the court of final resort in the province where the 'proceeding originated.' Was the 'proceeding' the original winding-up petition or the question of the shares in Ontario?

Samuel Freedman persuaded Smith and Guy that the appeal had to be heard in Ontario. Basing his analysis upon the practicalities of the situation, Freedman wanted no part of sitting in judgment on the rulings of judges from other provinces, some of whom operated under a very different legal regime. How, he asked, could the Manitoba court deal with the matter if it involved a transfer to Quebec, proceedings in French, and a ruling on a point of civil law? Freedman supported this conclusion by observing that the section had been redrafted without any apparent intention to alter the law and that under the previous version the appeal would have been heard in Ontario.

Dickson disagreed and pointedly observed: 'What we are here concerned with is not what the legislation should provide but what in fact it does provide.' He was dismissive of the historical argument: if 'the plain meaning' of the statute now differs from what appeared in the past, 'I can only conclude that parliament, in its wisdom, made a change.' However inconvenient the result, Dickson could not escape the fact that, as he read it, the statute contemplated appeals being heard in one province from orders made in another.[28]

Dickson and Freedman were both mentioned as candidates for the Supreme Court of Canada and both men were ambitious. They shared a genuine mutual respect, but there can be little doubt that there existed a certain rivalry between them. Still, the extent of the differences between Dickson and Freedman should not be exaggerated. Freedman dissented in only three reported cases on which he sat with Dickson[29] and wrote separate concurring opinions in two others.[30]

Commercial Realty

A fundamental issue to be resolved in commercial cases is the competing claims of freedom of contract and legal doctrines designed to ensure fairness and protect weaker parties. One might expect that Dickson's experience as a corporate lawyer would incline him to favour the sanctity of contract but his judgments reflect a more subtle approach. In one appeal, Dickson applied a protective doctrine to overcome a harsh contractual term in an equipment lease.[31] The borrower had defaulted and the equipment had been repossessed and sold. The finance company was not satisfied just to recover the equipment and any outstanding payments and sued to enforce the strict terms of the lease, which appeared to give it the right to recover all remaining payments as if the borrower still had the equipment. After a detailed review of the case law – which must have involved his own research since the debtor did not appear to argue the case – Dickson found against the finance company. He concluded that the clause relied upon by the finance company amounted to an unenforceable 'penalty clause', a contractual provision that coerced a defaulting party to perform rather than providing a genuine pre-estimate of the innocent party's loss.

On the other hand, Dickson was a pragmatic judge who tried to decide cases according to the reasonable expectations of the parties. His experience as a corporate lawyer inclined him to apply the letter of contracts in cases involving sophisticated parties of equal bargaining power. While he was still a trial judge, Dickson sat ad hoc in a case involving a contractual dispute between the owner of a shopping centre and a commercial tenant.[32] The tenant disputed the right of the owner to lease space to a new tenant who would directly compete with the existing tenant, but could point to nothing in the lease that limited the owner's rights. For reasons not apparent from the judgment, the case was seen to be of sufficient importance to warrant a five-judge panel. The court divided on whether the existing tenant had the right to prevent the owner from leasing space to a competitor. Dickson wrote the majority judgment, holding in favour of the owner. He had negotiated and carefully drafted hundreds of commercial agreements, and he rested his judgment on the commercial realities of the situation. The lease was the result of 'protracted and intense negotiations over a period of months by men of experience.' If the tenant wanted to protect itself, it 'should have done so by clear words.' Drawing on his experience as a corporate solicitor, Dickson explained: 'Such a covenant, in precise and detailed terms, is, I venture to suggest, not unusual in leases of this nature.'[33]

In estates cases, Dickson exhibited a similar tendency, insisting on following the letter of the words used in the will even if the result seemed unfair.[34] His refusal to depart from the stated intention of a testator led him to reverse his mentor, George Tritschler, who had upheld a challenge to the will of a ninety-year-old man dividing his modest estate equally among his four children.[35] One son had remained on the farm, the only significant asset in the estate, and claimed that his father had promised it to him. Tritschler was moved by the claim and ruled that the son was entitled to the farm. In the Court of Appeal, Guy agreed with Tritschler's approach to the equities of the case. Dickson, however, insisted that the intent of the father when drafting his will had to be upheld. He reasoned that the court 'was never intended to rewrite the will of a testator' and that it should not 'except in plain and definite cases, restrain a man's right to dispose of his estate as he pleases.'[36] Dickson's detailed judgment, amply supported by references to English, Australian, and Canadian cases and reversing Tritschler, attracted the support of the third judge, Freedman, and reflected his characteristic blend of legal and pragmatic arguments. He was skceptical of both the equity and the economics of the claim. The son had been compensated for his work on the farm and, since it was a marginal operation, Dickson thought that selling it and investing the proceeds would produce a better return. Moreover, one of the brothers was in a state of greater financial need. In Dickson's view, Tritschler had gone too far in rewriting the will.

Care and Caution

Dickson did not hesitate to impose liability in relation to carelessness in the everyday activities of rural Manitoba. Deer hunters who discharged their guns without sufficient heed to the possible presence of a farmer near his barn were held to account.[37] So was the father who allowed his fourteen-year-old son to operate a snowmobile when the boy was not competent to do so.[38]

Only one tort case involved a difficult legal issue, and in this instance Dickson was cautious and, according to Bora Laskin's judgment in the Supreme Court of Canada, correct.[39] The case arose from a long-standing dispute that twice went all the way to the Supreme Court of Canada. It involved a proposed high-rise apartment block on Wellington Crescent, the street where Dickson lived. A Winnipeg developer had persuaded the city to enact a zoning change to permit the construction, but homeowners association successfully challenged the zoning change in the courts.[40] Stopped in his tracks, the developer sued the city to recover money spent in preparatory work on the project. The trial judge dismissed the claim and the developer appealed. The appeal raised difficult legal issues and was heard by a five-judge panel. The court was badly divided; three judgments were delivered. Dickson and Guy wrote separate opinions dismissing the appeal, while Freedman dissented and would have allowed the developer's claim.

One might expect that a clash on a legal issue of this importance would bring out the best in Dickson and Freedman but both wrote restrained and cautious judgments. Dickson found that a person affected by a zoning by-law, passed in good faith but later found to be defective, had no claim. The developer had no contract, express or implied, with the city and Dickson refused to accept that a municipality could be sued for negligence. Passing a by-law was either a legislative or quasi-judicial function that had never attracted civil liability. An important decision of the House of Lords[41] made liability for negligent misstatement possible; however, Dickson held that, by enacting the by-law, a municipality was not making a representation or giving advice that could form the basis for a claim. Even if there was a basis for liability, Dickson ruled that the claim was barred by a statute that required actions against public officers to be brought within six months. He cited one of his own trial judgments that had had been upheld by the Court of Appeal holding that the statute applied to municipalities.[42] Freedman, in contrast, thought that the city could be held to account for negligence. He believed that Dickson's earlier judgment on the limitation point was wrong and urged his colleagues to overrule their own previous decision upholding it. Freedman took a liberal view of the power of the court to overrule one of its own decisions: '... the practice of rigid adherence to a court's earlier decisions is not quite so deeply rooted in Manitoba, or indeed in Canada' as in England.[43]

Sentencing and the Plight of Prisoners

Appeals against sentences in criminal cases represented a significant component of the work of the Court of Appeal. Dickson continued to exhibit his concern about sentencing and the plight of prisoners by visiting the prisons to assess for himself the consequences of imprisonment. He often went with Samuel Freedman.

For Dickson, the most tragic sentence appeals involved native people who came before the court without counsel. He worried that the court did not have the means to deal properly with their appeals. Many 'were inarticulate and almost incoherent.' There was no legal-aid scheme in place to ensure that they got adequate representation. The best the court could do was to arrange 'to have a native woman come and represent some of these people and tell their side of the story and just why they thought they were being badly treated if they were sentenced to so many years for such and such a crime.'[44]

On one appeal, Dickson's often-expressed concern for the plight of young offenders sentenced to adult facilities led him to increase a sentence. Three prisoners had subjected a young prisoner to a violent sexual assault. The victim 'appeared to be a mild and submissive person' and was in custody awaiting psychiatric care. The magistrate who tried the case took a casual approach and felt that the infrequency of such assaults and the lax attitude of prison authorities justified a rather lenient sentence. Dickson strongly disagreed and was plainly troubled by attitudes that implicitly condoned victimization and sexual exploitation of young prisoners. 'A person in prison custody is entitled to the protection of law no less that a person outside and he should not be subjected to maltreatment such as occurred here.' He ruled that the magistrate was wrong to consider insufficient surveillance by the guards as a mitigating factor. This case demonstrates Dickson's firm belief that prisoners did not lose their rights or claims to be treated with decency just because they were imprisoned.[45]

None of the criminal cases Dickson heard as an appellate judge could match the drama or interest of his criminal trials while on the Queen's Bench. They were, for the most part, routine cases that did not challenge his intellect or flair for writing. Dickson was unsympathetic to arguments that evidence should be excluded.[46] As in his days as a trial judge, he was routinely dismissive of technical arguments[47] and insistent upon a straightforward, common-sense approach that would ensure that the judge and jury dealt with the substance of the matter, unburdened by formal constraints. Usually this meant rejecting arguments advanced on behalf of the accused.[48]

'A growing tendency to challenge tradition'

In the late 1960s, traditional public moral values were challenged and Dickson, who still had two teenaged sons living at home, was very aware of the temper of his times. Speaking to lawyers being called to the bar, he noted the 'growing tendency ... to challenge tradition and traditions, to challenge constituted authority whether it be religious, governmental, judicial or parental, and to challenge those representative of authority.' Despite his conservative corporate-law background, Dickson welcomed re-examining basic concepts 'to separate wheat from chaff, to separate those features of a system which are archaic and outmoded, having outlived their usefulness, from those features which are of continuing validity and worth and utility.'[49]

The most significant criminal cases Dickson heard as an appellate judge dealt with the relationship between law and morality. Is society justified in punishing sexual conduct between consenting adults because the majority considers it to be immoral or disgusting? The Canadian Criminal Code, drafted in the Victorian era, still punished certain sexual acts on purely moral grounds. However, the notion that the law had a legitimate role in enforcing standards of sexual behaviour, well accepted at the time the Criminal Code was drafted, was under attack. In 1967 Justice Minister Pierre Elliott Trudeau proclaimed: 'There's no place for the state in the bedrooms of the nation.'[50] Trudeau echoed a theme struck in an unusually public academic debate. A prominent English legal philosopher, H.L.A. Hart of Oxford University, had joined issue with Lord Devlin, a prominent English judge.[51] Hart challenged Devlin's defence of the criminalization of homosexual conduct and provided a philosophic and jurisprudential foundation for the argument that the state had no business criminalizing behaviour solely on the ground that it was morally unacceptable to the majority.

Dickson confronted the issue in a case decided in January 1968, a month after Trudeau made his famous proclamation but before Parliament amended the Criminal Code to decriminalize private acts between consenting adults.[52] Late one night, just after 2 A.M., the police went to a dwelling in Winnipeg hoping to find evidence of an infraction of the provincial liquor laws. Upon entering the vestibule of the house, they peered through a window in the door and could see a man and a woman in the kitchen engaged in the act of fellatio. The male participant, identified in the law reports only as 'P,' was charged with the offence of committing an act of gross indecency. The Criminal Code provision contained no definition of 'gross indecency,' but regarded the offence as a serious one with a penalty of up to five years' imprisonment. At trial, the evidence clearly established that the accused and his female partner were adult common law spouses, that they had both fully consented to the act, and that it had been performed within the privacy of their home. 'P' was acquitted in the magistrate's court and the crown appealed.

The case came before Dickson, Smith, and Monnin. The court divided sharply on the question of whether the conduct was punishable under the Criminal Code. Monnin was convinced that it was. Citing the writings of Lord Devlin, he concluded that 'public decency has been outraged and the conduct complained of deserves punishment by the state.' Dickson disagreed and wrote a short but compelling judgment based upon the principle that it was not for the courts to sit in judgment on what passes in private between consenting adults. In Dickson's decidedly liberal view, 'parliament never intended, in enacting [the gross indecency section], to impose upon the courts the authority or the responsibility of being arbiters of the private heterosexual sex behaviour of consenting adults.'[53] While he couched his reasons as an interpretation of the existing legislation, Dickson was accomplishing the very reform that Trudeau had proposed. Smith agreed with his former student Dickson and 'P' was acquitted of gross indecency. Dickson's judgment was applauded in the *Criminal Law Quarterly* for reflecting 'a commonsense view of the proper purposes of the criminal law' and for the pains he had taken to consider the broader social and philosophical implications of the issue.[54]

'To be unemployed is not a crime'

Another case in which Dickson demonstrated a liberal judicial philosophy was a 1969 decision[55] involving a clash between the law and the 'hippie sub-culture.' A young man named Heffer had hitch-hiked to Winnipeg from Vancouver in early July 1969. He had four dollars in his pocket and proceeded to the unemployment insurance office in search of casual employment. He then went to an organization called CRYPT (Committee Representing Youth Problems Today) and was told where he could find a free bed for the night. Early the next morning, while sitting on the steps of the Centennial Centre with several other youths, some of whom he had met the night before, he was arrested and charged with vagrancy. He was released from custody and then tried before a police magistrate a few days later. The magistrate convicted. Heffer was represented by Roland Penner, the province's future attorney general, then a well-known Winnipeg criminal lawyer who often took on the causes of the dispossessed and disadvantaged. Heffer agreed to have his case taken to the Manitoba Court of Appeal as a 'test case' to determine the limits of the vagrancy law frequently used by the Winnipeg police to rid the city of 'undesirable elements.'

The Criminal Code section under which Heffer was charged was notoriously vague. It allowed the police to arrest anyone who had no 'apparent means of support' and who was 'found wandering abroad or trespassing' and could not 'justify his presence in the place where he is found.'[56] Dickson wrote a judgment that was applauded in the press as striking 'a blow for the rights of the individual.'[57] The police, said Dickson, had no basis to lay the charge. 'There is nothing untoward about resting on the steps of a public building.'[58] The accused, politely referred to by Dickson as 'Mr. Heffer,' had sought employment and had done nothing to suggest even remotely that he had or was about to engage in criminal activity. The police had asked no questions but simply ordered Heffer to get into the police car.

The vague language of the Criminal Code gave the police a powerful and conveniently ill-defined weapon. This did not sit well with Dickson who, despite his background as an establishment lawyer, empathized with the youthful urge to roam and drew upon his experience travelling in Europe, where, he observed, 'it has long since been the custom of many young people of little means to roam from place to place, aided in some countries by the provision of youth hostels where bed and breakfast can be had at little cost.'[59] As he recalled years later: 'I thought this was barbarous, this idea of arresting the young man without any crime except for the fact that he only had four dollars in his pocket.'[60] Dickson also related the decision to his boyhood experience on the prairies. As he told an audience of law students: 'During the years of the depression ... the charge of vagrancy was used to rid the community of those who seemed to be footloose and unemployed and, therefore, undesirable.' This offended him: 'Poverty is not a crime. To be unemployed is not a crime.'[61]

R. v. Fuller[62] dealt with another technique employed by the police and the magistrates courts to rid Winnipeg of 'undesirable' youth. A young man, arrested on a charge of possession of marijuana, was taken before a magistrate where he immediately pleaded guilty. An unusually heavy sentence of nine months' imprisonment was imposed, but the magistrate directed that the warrant directing committal to prison be withheld for seven days and added: 'I assume Mr. Fuller that you are planning to leave the city.' This was known as issuing a 'floater' and had become common practice in western Canada. Not surprisingly, Fuller left town, but once again, Roland Penner took an appeal to challenge the legality of the scheme. Dickson had little hesitation in finding that the practice was illegal. It offended both individual rights and community values. From the perspective of the rights of the individual, Dickson found that the practice 'finds no legal justification in the statute; it is likely to induce an accused, in the hope of escaping imprisonment, to plead guilty to a charge to which he might otherwise plead not guilty.' From the communitarian perspective, issuing 'floaters' amounted to one community passing off its problems to another. This offended Dickson, who viewed Canada's communities as 'interdependent' and thought that 'relations between them should be marked by mutual respect and understanding.' Allowing one community 'to rid itself of undesirables by foisting them off on other communities violates this basic concept of consideration for the rights of others and should not be tolerated.'[63]

'On the wrong side of any line which could possibly be drawn'

Dickson's decisions in the cases dealing with gross indecency, vagrancy, and 'floaters' were rightly hailed as reflecting a liberal and progressive view of the law. However, as a provincial appellate judge, Dickson was by no means uniformly liberal in his approach. As would become increasingly apparent from his work on the Supreme Court of Canada, Dickson was prepared to limit individual rights where he thought it necessary to protect fundamental communitarian values. This tendency was revealed in his 1970 decision in *R. v. Great West News Ltd,*[64] a case involving obscenity. The issue was whether, as required by the criminal code, the crown had established that the exploitation of sex in a number of magazines, including *Nude Living,* which featured pictures of female genitalia, was 'undue.' Dickson referred to the material as 'dirt for dirt's sake' and concluded that 'if a dominant characteristic of the publication is the undue exploitation of sex, it is obscene and it does not, it seems to me, become any less obscene by putting on the cover a sticker bearing the word "adult" and enclosing it in a plastic cover,'[65] a view he would depart from years later on the Supreme Court of Canada.[66] Dickson rejected the defence argument that evidence was required to establish the community standard. That, he found, was a question for the judge to decide on the basis of the 'contemporary standards of the Canadian community.' Dickson adopted a passage from Lord Devlin's famous book defending the use of law to enforce morality, the same authority he had rejected in the gross-indecency case. He accepted the principle that 'all organized societies have sought in one manner or another to suppress obscenity' and that 'the right of the state to legislate to protect its moral fibre and well-being has long been recognized.'[67] The community standard was to be determined, according to Lord Devlin, not 'by the opinion of the majority' or by 'the counting of heads' but by the standard 'of the reasonable man ... not to be confused with the rational man.' The law simply applied 'principles which every right-minded person would accept as valid' – what another English writer called "practical morality," which is based not on theological or philosophical foundations but "in the mass of continuous experience half-consciously or unconsciously accumulated and embodied in the morality of common sense."'[68]

This thinking is difficult to reconcile with his gross-indecency judgment, but Dickson never approached judging as an exercise in logic or legal theory. He recognized that the regulation of human affairs by law was an extraordinarily complex and varied exercise where one could not hope to find a simple formula to decide all cases. Some legal principles are rooted in liberal individualism while others derive from communitarian values. Dickson thought that it would be wrong for a judge to have a pre-determined agenda or always to prefer one theory to another. His personal views tended to favour individual rights, but he also believed that individual rights are meaningless without a community and, as we shall see, he would frequently prefer community values even in cases involving the Charter of Rights.

A few months later, Dickson rejected an even more direct challenge to obscenity law.[69] The charges involved 29 magazines featuring nude pictures and 227 paperbacks featuring stories about sex. Freedman, who had prefaced his earlier judgment with the catchy statement, 'I am not greatly enamoured of censorship, judicial or otherwise,'[70] concluded that the magazines and the books were obscene, but only after quoting in some considerable detail the lurid details. He was lenient on sentence and would have reduced the corporate defendant's $10,000 fine to $2,000, whereas Dickson did not find the fine excessive. Monnin, who had dissented from Dickson's liberal gross-indecency decision, agreed with his more hefty obscenity fine in this case. As in the earlier case, the more conservative Dickson avoided discussing the details of the publications, relying on Freedman's graphic and somewhat bemused description. Dickson stuck to the law and surveyed the law of Canada, the United States, and England. He conceded that it 'is sometimes difficult to draw a line between that which is obscene and that which is not. It is not unlike having to draw a line between night and day. There is dusk.' However, he also concluded that these books plainly fell 'on the wrong side of any line which could possibly be drawn.'[71]

The accused also argued that the obscenity law violated freedom of expression under the Canadian Bill of Rights. Once again, Dickson had no difficulty in accepting a law intended to fortify community values of decency. 'Quite unmoved by this argument,' he wrote that freedom of speech 'is not unfettered' and that, while the Canadian Bill of Rights was intended to protect 'basic freedoms of vital importance to all Canadians ... it does not serve as a shield behind which obscene matter may be disseminated without concern for criminal consequences.'[72]

Divorce was another area where Dickson did not always follow his liberal moral instincts. As we have seen, before the reforms of the late 1960s, the only ground for divorce in Canada was adultery. Many unhappy couples wishing to end a marriage resorted to creating the evidence they needed. What was the appropriate judicial response – bend the rules or insist that the law be strictly applied? In an appeal brought in 1969 by the Queen's Proctor, a crown officer with power to intervene in the public interest in divorce proceedings, Dickson resisted a strong dissenting opinion written by Samuel Freedman and instead sided with the more conservative Alfred Monnin in refusing a divorce. The case had a tortured history and had gained notoriety in the profession as something of a test case. The woman with whom the husband was said to have committed adultery was incorrectly named in the divorce petition, and she been not been served as required by the rules of court. The petitioner wife appealed, relying on another rule that dispensed with service where the identity of the co-adulterer was unknown or could not be found. Freedman wanted to grant the divorce. Adultery had been proved and he could see little point in prolonging the misery. As he put it: 'I do not know what further can reasonably be expected of the petitioner.' However, Dickson dismissed the appeal. He held that divorce proceedings transcend the interests of the litigants and implicate the public interest. The petitioner had made insufficient effort to find the co-adulterer and, with what could only be described as an unusually strict approach, Dickson insisted upon compliance with the letter of the rules.[73]

'A negation of the principle of equality'

As a member of the Manitoba Court of Appeal, Dickson rarely confronted the broad issues of human rights that would preoccupy him years later as chief justice of Canada. However, he did write a significant judgment in *Canard v. Attorney General of Canada*,[74] dealing with a discriminatory provision of the Indian Act that denied an aboriginal woman the right to administer her deceased husband's estate. Dickson declared the section of the act inoperative under the Canadian Bill of Rights. Flora Canard, a status Indian, lived on Fort Alexander Indian Reserve No. 3. After her husband was killed in a motor-vehicle accident, she consulted a lawyer who took the usual steps to allow her to deal with her husband's estate and to sue the party responsible for the accident. But she discovered that an Indian Affairs official had already been appointed administrator of the estate and a wrongful-death action had already been commenced. The Indian Act vested all authority with respect to the affairs of deceased Indians in the minister and authorized him to appoint executors and administrators. Flora Canard decided to challenge this startlingly paternalistic provision as discriminatory and in conflict with the promise of equality in the Canadian Bill of Rights.

Early decisions had given limited effect to the Bill of Rights and had balked at striking down legislation that offended its guarantees. However, the Supreme Court's 1970 decision in the *Drybones* case[75] had taken the legal community by surprise. There, the Court had found that the Bill of Rights promise of equality was paramount and precluded Parliament from making it an offence for members of a specified racial group, Indians, to do something (being drunk off a reserve) which all other Canadians could do with impunity. Fortified by *Drybones*, Dickson found that the statutory provisions depriving Flora Canard of the right to administer her husband's estate were contrary to the guarantee of equality and therefore inoperative. By denying her the right to administer her husband's estate, the law was 'a negation of the principle of equality and places Mrs. Canard in a state of inferiority vis-à-vis other Canadians. The discrimination to which she is subjected stems from the fact that she is an Indian. It is discrimination by reason of race.'[76]

The federal government tried to save the law by arguing that the beneficial provisions of the Indian Act would also have to go if the court found the racial criteria unacceptable. This argument raised a central problem in equality theory, namely, how to treat benefits conferred upon disadvantaged groups. From one perspective, affirmative measures singling out a group disadvantaged by reason of race in order to improve its lot enhance the value of equality. However, those denied the same benefits because they are not members of the racial group singled out for special treatment often contend that their right to equality is being denied. Does 'the right to equality before the law ... without discrimination by reason of race' mean that all racial classifications are precluded? Is it possible or acceptable for courts to pick and choose between appropriate and inappropriate racial classifications? While it would be misleading to suggest that Dickson had a fully worked out theory of equality when he decided *Canard*, he was convinced that aboriginal people could challenge the disadvantages of discrimination without forgoing their preferential legal rights. He read the Bill of Rights as 'intended to erase all marks of servitude based on race, national origin, colour, religion or sex' and thought that 'it is not consonant with reason or justice' to insist that Indians had to forfeit those rights to gain the benefits of the Indian Act. 'The freedoms expressed in the *Bill of Rights* cannot be bartered away.' Dickson was equally scathing of the traditional paternalistic approach that saw aboriginal people as children in need of protection. 'If the *Bill of Rights* means anything, it means that no racial group shall be deemed inferior to any other racial group in the enjoyment of basic human rights and fundamental freedoms.'[77]

In the early 1970s, Dickson's *Canard* judgment went too far for the Supreme Court. Shortly after Dickson's appointment in 1973, the Supreme Court did an about-face on the *Drybones* decision and severely curtailed the application of the Canadian Bill of Rights.[78] The federal government appealed Dickson's *Canard* judgment and, over the strong dissent of Chief Justice Bora Laskin, a majority at the Supreme Court reversed it.[79]

In his later judgments on the Supreme Court, Dickson emphasized the special place and distinctive rights of Canada's aboriginal peoples. However, in the late 1960s and early 1970s, he tended to follow the prevailing view that native Canadians should be treated the same as anyone else. Indeed, this was the approach advocated in a controversial 1969 White Paper released by the federal government that would have eliminated special status for Indians under Canadian law.[80] Most of the time, as in *Canard*, the idea that aboriginal peoples should be treated the same as non-aboriginal peoples helped the aboriginal litigant. In a 1968 decision dealing with the custody of a child born to a native mother and a European father, Dickson refused to be swayed by the father's arguments that an Indian reserve was not an appropriate place for the child. He was certainly aware of the difficult living conditions. The father 'gave a rather lurid description of the overcrowded and unsanitary condition of the house ... However, from his description the house would appear to be typical, neither better nor worse than the house one frequently finds on an Indian reservation.'[81] Dickson insisting that the case had to be decided on strictly legal principles, ruled that the trial judge had erred in awarding custody to the father on the basis of the 'best interests of the child' test. The parents were unmarried and the native mother was entitled to rely on the common law rule establishing that the mother was entitled to custody of an illegitimate child and that the father had no rights. She could be deprived of her rights only in exceptional cases, and certainly not because of a relative lack of material and financial advantages. Dickson's approach in this case may also have been influenced by his firm belief that 'poverty is not a crime.'

The 'Chicken and Egg' War

Dickson decided a number of cases involving the reconciliation of provincial regulatory authority to enact marketing schemes for farm products with the federal power to regulate trade and commerce. By the early 1970s, it was well established that the federal power extended to international and interprovincial trade but that the provinces had the right to regulate intraprovincial trade and business. However, in an integrated national economy, the line between interprovincial and intraprovincial trade was fuzzy.

Manitoba's farmers were caught in the crossfire of the 'chicken and egg' war between Ontario and Quebec. Ontario farmers produced a surplus of eggs while Quebec farmers produced a surplus of chickens. Both provinces created marketing schemes, with Ontario fixing minimum prices for chickens and Quebec fixing minimum prices for eggs. Both provinces created their schemes to protect their own producers from extraprovincial competition, and both schemes had an adverse effect on Manitoba's efficient farmers who consistently produced surplus products for the interprovincial market. Manitoba urged the federal government to act, but the political process appeared to be deadlocked and so it decided to challenge the marketing schemes in the courts. To bring the issue before its own Court of Appeal, the Manitoba government adopted a highly unusual strategy. It presented a phantom regulatory scheme – a carbon copy of the Quebec marketing law – controlling the sale of extraprovincial eggs in Manitoba. The government then referred the constitutionality of the scheme to the Manitoba Court of Appeal. Manitoba had no intention of proceeding with this scheme, but the strategy allowed it to test the constitutionality of the Quebec law in the courts of Manitoba.[82]

Dickson undoubtedly knew that the reference had been trumped up, but he made no mention of that fact in his judgment holding the scheme to be unconstitutional. He decided the case as if Manitoba was serious about its marketing scheme, carefully traced the jurisprudence, and discerned a trend towards 'broadening of the federal trade and commerce power'[83] that placed a corresponding limit on the capacity of a province to limit free trade. The proposed marketing scheme embraced the marketing of all eggs in the province, whatever their provenance. A province could regulate marketing farming products within its own borders, but this scheme went too far. In Dickson's view, it fell outside provincial jurisdiction, infringed the federal trade and commerce power, and constituted an unacceptable interference with interprovincial trade. He ruled that Manitoba's proposed regulation had to be struck down, hardly a loss for the province since the government's strategy was to attack the Quebec scheme. Manitoba appealed its so-called loss to the Supreme Court of Canada, which upheld Dickson's ruling.[84] The 'chicken and egg' case was an important one. By striking down the protective scheme, the courts bolstered free trade within Canada and limited the capacity of provinces to erect barriers to protect local producers and interfere with the free flow of goods across provincial borders.[85]

But Dickson also respected provincial powers and, in another case, he upheld a provincial law regulating the sale of farm products.[86] Under the law, Manitoba-grown potatoes could be marketed only through the Manitoba Vegetable Marketing Commission. The reach of this legislation, enacted in concert with federal measures, was explicitly limited to products produced and sold in Manitoba, making it, Dickson ruled, fully within provincial legislative authority. Dickson did not allow views about the politics of marketing boards, which required farmers to market their products through a government agency, to influence his own thoughts about whether they were within or beyond provincial jurisdiction.

Dickson's final contribution as a Manitoba judge to the conundrums of the trade and commerce power came in a judgment released shortly before his appointment to the Supreme Court of Canada. Again, the case concerned the marketing of natural products, this time hogs. Three Manitoba meatpacking companies wanted to import hogs from Saskatchewan. Manitoba legislation prohibited packers from slaughtering hogs not purchased from a provincial marketing board. The companies attacked the scheme, alleging that it constituted an illegitimate interference with interprovincial trade. Dickson upheld the Manitoba law on the basis that it was not 'designed to restrict or limit the free flow of trade between the provinces as such, but rather to develop and maintain the orderly marketing of the regulated product' within Manitoba.[87] This time, however, the Supreme Court disagreed with Dickson and, in a decision described by some as 'extreme,'[88] struck down the scheme as an unconstitutional interference with interprovincial trade.[89]

Dickson wrote these constitutional judgments in a relatively restrained manner. For the most part, his analysis consisted of lengthy quotations from the leading cases, with no bold strokes and no sweeping statements. The approach is cautious and somewhat formal, certainly less bold than his later writing on the trade and commerce power as a member of the Supreme Court of Canada.[90] However, the results are generally consistent with Dickson's later significant contributions to the complex jurisprudence of federalism. First, his approach is deferential. He tended to uphold regulatory schemes. The hog-marketing case in particular indicated Dickson's willingness to accommodate provincial regulation for provincial purposes, even if it affected interprovincial trade. However, a second (and to some extent inconsistent) tendency is his willingness to bolster the federal trade and commerce power. The *Manitoba Egg Reference* suggests that, faced with the stark choice between deference to legislative judgment and a generous ambit for federal power, he tended to choose the later. These early decisions also reflect a third important feature of Dickson's subsequent federalism jurisprudence, namely, his determined search for a balanced approach that accommodated to the greatest extent possible both provincial and federal powers.

Law as 'an integral part of the social process'

After four years as a trial judge and six years on the Court of Appeal, Dickson had proved himself to be one of Canada's finest judges. Writing his judgments in a refreshingly clear and lucid style, he had made an important mark in the area of law and morality by excluding the application of the criminal law to private sexual conduct between consenting adults. His refusal to countenance unlimited police or judicial power with respect to wandering youth, his equality-rights judgment in *Canard*, and his federalism judgments dealing with the trade and commerce power revealed an essentially progressive view that saw the law in terms of the broader social, political, and economic context. In a 1970 address to students at the University of Winnipeg, Dickson spoke of the need to recognize the legal system 'as an integral part of the social process' and argued that 'as increasing recognition is given to the social problems of the nation – poverty law, the rights of the dispossessed, the poor, the mentally ill, illegitimate children – it is increasingly apparent that we must seek to develop a legal system that provides both "equality before the law," and justice to the particularities of individual cases.'[91]

On the other hand, Dickson was a careful and cautious judge. His approach to judging was lawyerly and pragmatic, not theoretical or philosophical. He could not be accused of having any particular agenda. To the extent that he had taken essentially liberal positions in the morality and equality cases, he was probably displaying his essentially open-minded attitude and his willingness to listen to new ideas, rather than revealing any predetermined or fixed philosophy. He did not hesitate to apply obscenity law as necessary to protect the community's moral fibre or to follow the existing law in requiring proof of adultery for a divorce. In federalism cases, he took a balanced approach that displayed no obvious inclination to favour either federal or provincial power.

PART FOUR

The Supreme Court, 1973–1984

7

Starting Slowly

Brian Dickson served on the Supreme Court of Canada from 1973 to 1990. During that time, both he and the Court changed a great deal. Dickson joined a Court that decided many cases but did so in a manner that added little to the development of the law. It was strongly criticized for having 'an outmoded and unduly narrow conception of the role of law'[1] and for failing 'to examine in depth the legal principles' or 'the philosophy of law' that animated its decisions,[2] which were unfavourably compared in terms of their intellectual quality with those of the United States Supreme Court, the British House of Lords, and the Australian High Court. Each of those final courts had the power to hear only cases important to the development of the law. In contrast, the Canadian court was required by law to hear any appeal if more than $10,000 was in dispute, even if the appeal raised no point of legal or public importance.[3] The Court that Dickson joined was also criticized for its restrictive interpretation of the statutory Canadian Bill of Rights.[4] In the early 1970s, it would have been difficult to imagine that Dickson would preside over a Court in the 1980s that would occupy a central policy-making role in the country and would revive a constitutional bill of rights to the point of being criticized by some for usurping the role of the elected legislature.

The Dickson Court that shaped the Charter and aboriginal rights in the 1980s contained only Dickson and Jean Beetz from the earlier era. It was an institution with changing members while Dickson was a man with relatively settled views about the world and the role of judges. Nevertheless, Dickson did change during his judge's journey. As seen in chapter 1, the judge who convicted Henry Morgentaler for violating the abortion law in 1974 became the judge who in 1988 would strike the abortion law down under the 1982 Canadian Charter of Rights and Freedoms. The enactment of the Charter was the most important development in this transformation, but Dickson changed as well. In order to understand Dickson's journey as a judge and its elements of both continuity and change, it is important to understand his early years on the Supreme Court.

From 1973 to 1975, Dickson was comfortably in the mainstream of a Court that was criticized for resolving disputes by applying precedents and deferring law reform to the legislatures. During this time, Dickson frequently disagreed with Bora Laskin, at the time the judge most willing to take a policy-oriented and creative approach to law making. Their most famous dispute was *Harrison v. Carswell*. Dickson, for the majority, concluded that the Court should apply the clear language of Manitoba's trespass law and a prior precedent to prohibit striking workers from picketing a private shopping mall. In dissent, Laskin argued that the Court had a duty to update the ancient doctrine of trespass to take into account modern realities and the legitimate interests of striking workers. *Harrison v. Carswell* was the most famous disagreement between Laskin and Dickson, but there were others. Many others.

The Call to Ottawa

Dickson replaced Emmett Hall of Saskatchewan, whose retirement was seen as a significant loss to the Court. Hall is best known for his important role as a chair of the royal commission on health care, but he also was an activist and civil-libertarian judge. He was the only judge to dissent from the Court's decision to affirm Stephen Truscott's murder conviction, and found, again in dissent, that the Nisga'a had un-extinguished aboriginal title to their lands in British Columbia and that an act that deprived women but not men of Indian status when they married a non-Indian violated the equality guarantees of the Canadian Bill of Rights.[5] In a 1986 speech, Dickson praised Hall for exhibiting 'genuine compassion for individual human beings, especially the most disadvantaged members of our society,'[6] but it was far from clear in 1973 that Dickson would follow in Hall's footsteps.

Although Hall and Dickson had both been successful lawyers who were deeply involved with their communities on the prairies, Dickson had a more conservative reputation.[7] He had represented and sat on the boards of large corporations whereas Hall had represented those charged in the Depression-era Regina riots and doctors charged with violating the abortion law. Hall also had a high profile while Dickson was 'an almost complete stranger to the general public' who many believed 'will certainly not attract the attention his predecessor did.'[8] Justice Minister Otto Lang, or perhaps his Justice Department speechwriter, seemed to have expected and even hoped that Dickson would be less creative than Hall. During Dickson's swearing-in ceremony, Lang explained that he was 'not one who believes that the Court should second guess the legislators by doing their job. It is in our tradition, and I would not like to see it changed, to leave the pressures on the law makers to do their job.'[9] For Lang and the Department of Justice, the lawmakers in 1973 were the elected legislators, not the judges of the Supreme Court.

Dickson's appointment, announced on 26 March 1973, came within a month of Hall's retirement. Hall had replaced a judge from British Columbia. Since the last judge from British Columbia had retired in 1962 and the last judge from Manitoba had retired in 1946, it was Manitoba's turn. Thomas Berger, who had been on the British Columbia Supreme Court since 1971, may have been considered. Berger had been a NDP representative in British Columbia in the 1960s and had represented the Nisga'a in the landmark *Calder* aboriginal land claim. In 1973, however, he was only forty years old, and the following year the federal government would appoint him to head a royal commission to examine whether a pipeline should be built in the Mackenzie valley.[10] A more obvious alternative was Samuel Freedman, who had been on the bench since 1953 and had been chief justice of Manitoba since 1971. But Freedman was just a month shy of his sixty-fifth birthday and still new in his position as Chief Justice of Manitoba; besides, although he denied them, there were rumours that he had health problems. Religion may also have been a factor. Trudeau's only Supreme Court appointment before Dickson had been Laskin, and regrettably, even as late as the early 1970s, the appointment of a second Jewish justice might have been controversial.

Dickson would have attracted the attention of Prime Minister Trudeau for a number of reasons. Some of Dickson's decisions applying the Canadian Bill of Rights and interpreting the Criminal Code showed that he shared Trudeau's concern for civil liberties. Dickson was also a strong proponent of bilingualism and had made an effort to learn French. In Canada's centennial year, 1967, Dickson told lawyers being called to the bar in Manitoba that in order to be competent lawyers, they must understand French. He argued that bilingualism was a source of 'strength not a weakness' in the country and praised the bilingual origins of Manitoba.[11] This attitude, rare in the west at the time, reflected both Dickson's sense of Canada and his ambition to become a member of the Supreme Court of Canada. It likely attracted the attention of decision makers in Ottawa.

The Move to Ottawa

Dickson eagerly accepted the appointment to the Supreme Court. He was ambitious and ready for new challenges. There had been a certain amount of good-natured rivalry with Freedman while they were both on the Manitoba

Court of Appeal and there was not enough work on the Court of Appeal to occupy Dickson's time fully. Accepting the appointment, however, meant moving from a comfortable situation in Winnipeg. Had the offer come a few years earlier, Dickson would have refused it. He and his wife were devoting considerable time and attention to Dickson's aged mother and father and to his father-in-law, Harry Sellers. By 1973, Dickson's parents and father-in-law had passed away, and he was free to go. His son Brian had graduated from Princeton and from law at the University of Toronto and was well on his way to a successful career with the Department of External Affairs. Daughter Deborah had completed her training as a nurse, married Chris Shields, and moved to the United States, first to Vermont and then to Louisville, Kentucky, where Shields pursued his career as a neurosurgeon. The most difficult aspect of the move to Ottawa was forcing the twins, Peter and Barry, who were just completing secondary school, to leave their wide circle of friends in Winnipeg. The boys desperately wanted to stay, but they had no choice but to pack up and move.

Barbara took charge of the move with her usual calm efficiency, and helped her husband find and furnish temporary living quarters in an Ottawa apartment. Dickson was soon fully occupied and absorbed with his work at the Court and Barbara returned to Winnipeg to dispose of the house and the farm. The Dicksons wanted a country property, but they had to cope with a provision in the original 1875 Supreme Court Act that required the judges to live within five miles of the city. They decided to buy a city apartment to satisfy the law and went in search of a suitable country property. Soon they discovered a nineteenth-century stone farmhouse with many acres of land along the banks of the Ottawa River at Dunrobin, about twenty miles outside the city. The property, called 'Marchmont,' was ideal, combining an elegant historic home with the space the Dicksons needed for their horses. They made an offer, but the owners changed their minds about selling and took the property off the market. The Dicksons bought a much smaller house and farm on the Quebec side near Aylmer and the Gatineau Park, but they were not happy there. The house was small and there were only a few acres of land for the horses. Within a few months, the owners of Marchmont decided to sell after all, and the Dicksons were on the move again. The dislocation and moving from house to house was undoubtedly a strain on the family, especially with Peter and Barry longing for Winnipeg.

Ottawa did have some advantages to offer. The city, spruced up for the centennial year, had plenty of green space and a newly opened National Arts Centre. The Dicksons soon adjusted to the Ottawa social scene, entertaining Supreme Court colleagues and gradually becoming welcome additions to embassy dinners and social gatherings of the Ottawa elite. In some ways, the move to Ottawa simplified their life. Marchmont offered the pleasures of country life within striking distance of the city and the Dicksons no longer had to divide their time between city and country as they had in Winnipeg.

For the next seventeen years, Dickson essentially devoted all of his time and energy to his judicial work. Twelve-hour days were the rule rather than the exception and he usually worked over the weekend as well. Some of his colleagues thought that Dickson was a 'workaholic' even by their own strict standards.[12] The law clerks made frequent trips to the farm, both during the week and on weekends. On sitting days, Dickson was driven to the Court and arrived shortly after 9 A.M. He dealt with correspondence, discussed the day's case with his law clerks, and then often visited one or two of his colleagues for informal discussion of the day's case or work in progress on a judgment. In the early days, the judges usually had lunch at the Rideau Club, then situated directly across from the Parliament Buildings on Wellington Street, where they had a reserved table. After the Rideau Club was destroyed by fire in 1979, Dickson ate lunch at his desk until Chief Justice Laskin established the judges' dining room on the third floor of the Supreme Court building. When Court finished at 4 P.M., Dickson spent another hour and a half in his chambers, meeting the clerks to discuss the day's case, dealing with correspondence and other routine matters, and often spending a few moments with colleagues. Evenings and weekends were devoted to reading for the cases to be heard and writing judgments. If the Court was not sitting, Dickson preferred to stay at the farm, where he would read for upcoming cases or work on the judgments he was writing.

Dickson rarely went to movies or plays nor did he have time for any significant reading outside the law apart from the odd mystery novel or biography while on vacation. He did, however, read legal periodicals and academic legal writing and he was an avid newspaper reader. He followed current political events closely, with a sharp eye for anything that might affect the work of the Court. His non-legal interests included playing the piano, and he also followed football, especially if his beloved Winnipeg Blue Bombers were playing. Dickson continued his hobby, dating to his boyhood, of stamp collecting and he and Barbara maintained and added to their significant art collection.[13] Dickson's most significant non-legal activity was time with his family. He and Barbara remained close to their four children. Barry and Peter survived the dreaded move to Ottawa and both became commercial pilots. Later, they both went into business, Barry in Oakville as a farm- and garden-equipment dealer and Peter in Vancouver as a real estate investor and developer. The Dickson family would eventually include five grandchildren. Deborah's daughters, Lisa and Karen, were followed by Brian's boys Graham and Eric and then by Barry's son Brian. Dickson was a proud grandfather and he and Barbara were very involved in the lives of their five grandchildren. Whenever possible, they attended concerts, sporting events, graduations, birthdays, and other celebrations, even if it meant travel to Louisville, to one of Brian's postings, or to Oakville. They made a point of calling their grandchildren every Sunday.

Dickson's main recreation was his daily morning ride. He typically began his day by rising early and going to his stables. His farm manager, Blake Ross, 'would have two horses saddled every morning, winter and summer ... groomed and ready to go.' Accompanied by Ross, Dickson would ride his favourite Morgan horse, 'Rosedale,' for forty-five minutes to an hour every morning. He was perhaps attracted to the Morgans because, not unlike himself, they were tough and stocky but also a bit flashy. Antonio Lamer recalled that, when he told Dickson it was crazy to ride in the early morning when 'it was darn cold and freezing,' Dickson 'would just laugh and say the horses loved it. And so did he.'[14] Marchmont's many acres along the banks of the Ottawa River gave the Dicksons the land they needed to keep as many as six horses as well as a herd of fallow spotted deer and several African barbary sheep. Dickson purchased some of the animals from an old army friend, Colonel Daley, who had established the African Lion Safari near Hamilton, Ontario. As he told an interviewer in 1992: 'We usually have a couple of dogs, we have more cats ... I think the cat population is about twelve right now. So if you are interested in a cat we can provide one for you. And we have pigeons and we have had rabbits. Blake Ross's girls like rabbits so we have rabbits.'[15]

The Dicksons led a gracious life at Marchmont. Acres of well-tended lawns and gardens surrounded the stone house, the route to which passed through a stone gate with a brass plaque stamped 'Marchmont. R.G.B. Dickson,' and then along an impressive sweeping drive. The property included barns for the animals and a house for the full-time farm manager and his family. The Dicksons also employed two full-time domestics to do housework and cooking. Dickson, the judge who had an unusual empathy for the poor and downtrodden, lived a life that few Canadians could imagine, let alone afford.

The Court That Dickson Joined

In a 1974 speech, Dickson described that, on a visit to the Supreme Court, 'one would see five or seven or nine men, sometimes referred to as 'old,' but I might take issue with that. They sit at a raised bench. They are dressed in the usual black legal gowns except at the opening of term when red robes trimmed in ermine ... are worn. At the back of the courtroom, there is seating for about 25 people. Few members of the public come to observe ... As there are no witnesses and seldom any histrionics, visitors do not normally remain for long.' He went on to observe that the Court 'hears cases involving every

area of law – civil, criminal, maritime, income tax, copyright, patents, expropriation. There is no particular area that predominates.' There was 'no time
limit on oral argument' and 'counsel usually take time to expand on what they
feel are the important points of evidence and of law relevant to the case.'[16]

Dickson had no difficulty adjusting to his new surroundings. The other
judges were pleased by his appointment and they welcomed him as an important new member of the team. Unlike Laskin, who rarely joined the rest of the
Court for lunch at the Rideau Club,[17] Dickson felt utterly at home in such surroundings. He admired and liked Laskin from the start, and the Dicksons and
Laskins saw each other socially.[18] After his death, Dickson remembered Laskin
as a 'great judge' who 'made a lasting impression on the jurisprudence of our
country and a major contribution to Canadian social thought and action.'
Dickson noted that Laskin was 'ever sensitive to injustice and ready at all
times to reject the notion that whatever is, is right. He had a moral grandeur
without the slightest taint of self-righteousness, a moral distinction that could
quite literally be felt.'[19] Dickson also got on very well with another leading
judge on the Court, Ronald Martland from Alberta. In fact, Dickson had more
in common with Martland than Laskin. They were both westerners who had
represented large corporations in practice and both had served as chancellors
in the Anglican Church.

Dickson may have felt a bit intimidated by his new colleagues. Laskin had
done graduate work at Harvard and had a distinguished career as a law professor. Martland was a former Rhodes Scholar who had won the prestigious
prize of Vinerian Law Scholar at Oxford.[20] Dickson's half-time education at
the Manitoba Law School, even supplemented by his crash officer-training
course at the Royal Military College, did not compare.

The Court in 1973 was an aging and conservative institution. It had long
abandoned its bold approach to the protection of civil liberties in the 1950s
and now embraced a follow-the-rules approach. With the exception of Bora
Laskin, who was only four years older than Dickson, most of judges were in
their seventies or close to it. While Laskin had been on the Court for only
three years, he was already viewed by legal scholars to be the Court's leading
light, especially after the departure of Hall. But Laskin was not yet chief justice nor was he expected ever to occupy that post. Gérald Fauteux, a former
prosecutor and commissioner for the 1946 Gouzenko spy inquiry, was chief
justice. When he retired near the end of 1973, both the Court and Court-
watchers fully expected that Martland, as the Court's most senior member
and its jurisprudentially conservative 'centre of gravity,' would succeed
him.[21] Martland had been appointed by Prime Minister Diefenbaker in 1958
straight from his distinguished law practice. He believed that legislatures as
opposed to judges should make the law and, as the 'archtypical judge of the

sixties,'[22] adhered to a strictly 'black letter' approach to the law (after his retirement, he would criticize the Charter as an invasion of parliamentary supremacy). He had written for the majority of the Court in denying Irene Murdoch an interest in a ranch that she had helped to develop, and had received much public criticism because of his comments that Mrs Murdoch had done 'the usual work of a farm wife.' Laskin's dissent in that case, which had stressed that legislative family-law reform might be preferable but that 'the better way is not the only way,' had been widely praised.[23]

Pierre Trudeau surprised many by appointing Laskin as chief justice at the end of 1973. One Toronto lawyer went so far as to argue in the *Globe and Mail* that Laskin's promotion to chief justice over more senior colleagues 'was wrong' and that Trudeau had taken the decision because 'he prefers a court which will legislate to a court which leaves legislation to Parliament.' The same lawyer noted that, as a 'very great gentleman,' Martland 'has been true to the traditions of his office and remained silent.'[24] This was true but Laskin's appointment came as a shock to Martland. Just before Laskin's appointment was announced, Martland told Dickson that he had received a call from the Prime Minister's Office indicating that he would be the next chief justice.[25] He would 'remain sensitive to the perceived slight for his final nine years on the Court.'[26] Even Laskin was surprised. When Dickson went to congratulate him, 'he was in a state of shock.'[27] The press continued to speculate about tensions on the Court, with one story suggesting that Laskin's comments shortly before he took over as chief justice that 'it's too easy for judges to say that if the law needs to be changed that it is the responsibility of Parliament' had 'probably alienated him totally and forever from the diehard traditionalists.'[28] Feeling awkward about the Martland situation, Laskin, the new chief justice, asked Brian and Barbara Dickson to take the lead in arranging Fauteux's retirement dinner at the Chateau Laurier, a sign that the still newly arrived handsome, energetic, and gracious couple from Winnipeg were well accepted by both the new chief justice and the traditionalists at the Court.

The Court that Dickson joined had many long-serving members besides Martland. Wilfred Judson, a former Latin teacher and trial judge from Ontario, had been on the Court since 1958. Dickson would remember Judson as a man 'of few words and very acerbic' who wrote 'very succinct judgments.'[29] Roland Ritchie, who had served as counsel for a royal commission on Newfoundland's entry into Confederation and came from a prominent Nova Scotia family, had been on the Court since 1959. He was best known as the author of the Court's first decision striking down a law under the statutory Canadian Bill of Rights. This case, however, was something of an aberration, since Ritchie would go on to write often-criticized judgments that upheld laws that discriminated against Indian women and pregnant women.[30] Ritchie, like

Martland, was a cautious and conservative black-letter lawyer for whom strict adherence to precedent was all important.[31] Dickson would later recall Ritchie as a 'wonderful man' and a hard working and productive member of the Court. Like Dickson, Ritchie had been wounded in Normandy during the Second World War. He required a metal plate in his head and this would later cause him health problems that forced him to retire in 1984, during Dickson's first year as chief justice. Ritchie's family would remember that, after Ritchie's retirement, Dickson 'cheered him greatly' by not forgetting him and including him 'in court occasions.'[32]

Louis-Philippe Pigeon, a former legal adviser to Quebec Premier Jean Lesage, the author of a book on legislative drafting, and a former constitutional law professor at Laval University, was one of the three judges that were required by law to be members of the Quebec bar. Speaking at a conference after Pigeon's death, Dickson recalled Pigeon's 'encyclopedic knowledge of Quebec Civil Law, an outstanding ability in interpreting statutes and a deep understanding of Canadian constitutional law.'[33] Two new judges from Quebec, Jean Beetz, a former Rhodes Scholar, law dean of the University of Montreal, and legal adviser to Prime Minister Trudeau, and Louis-Philippe de Grandpré, a former head of the Montreal and Quebec bars and the Canadian Bar Association, were appointed by Trudeau on New Years Day, 1974. These appointments added new blood to the Court and relieved Dickson from his position as the Court's most junior judge, who was required to speak first at conferences after oral hearings. Dickson's office was next to de Grandpré's and the two judges became friendly, with the Dicksons often inviting the de Grandprés to their farm. However, de Grandpré was never entirely comfortable as a judge and he served on the Court for only three years. His views were very conservative, even for the Court of the early 1970s, and he was frequently at odds with the more liberal and centralist views of Laskin. One study of the Court suggests that de Grandpré's resignation was a protest against what he regarded as Laskin's 'blind centralism.'[34] De Grandpré was replaced by Yves Pratte, another prominent Quebec litigator appointed straight from the bar. However, Pratte did not last as long as de Grandpré and left the Court after less than two years. Dickson was extremely concerned about the possible separation of Quebec, especially after the election of a separatist government in 1976, and the unwillingness of these Quebec judges to stay on the Court worried him greatly.

Jean Beetz, however, was a constant and important force during most of Dickson's time on the Court. Dickson especially respected Beetz's strong and scholarly views about federalism, and he often found himself torn between Laskin's inclinations towards a strong role for the federal government and Beetz's inclinations towards strong provincial governments that would accommodate Quebec. Beetz, rather than Dickson, might have been appointed chief justice after Laskin had it not been for his aversion to administration and his 1982 heart attack. Dickson and Beetz served together on the Court for fourteen years. Dickson would fondly remember that, over these years, he had developed 'a warm friendship and a close personal relationship' with Beetz, a 'gentle, modest, brilliant man.' After Beetz, ill with cancer, retired from the Court in 1988, Dickson visited him in Montreal. He recalled that 'Jean was as witty, charming and erudite as ever ... he faced his final battle with the same courage, dignity and integrity with which he had lived his life.'[35]

Wishart Spence had been on the Court since 1963 and during that time had chaired a royal commission to examine allegations of a security breach in the affair between Gerda Munsinger and a cabinet minister. Like Laskin, Spence had done graduate work in law at Harvard and took a liberal and creative approach to the law. He joined Laskin in dissent in upholding Dickson's decision on the Manitoba Court of Appeal invalidating, under the Canadian Bill of Rights, a law depriving Indians of the ability to administer their spouse's estate.[36] Dickson would eventually join Laskin and Spence in dissent so much that they were jokingly known in legal circles as LSD. However, the LSD trio rarely came together in Dickson's first few years in the Court.

From Dickson's early years on the Court until his retirement, the judges had a post-hearing conference in each case to discuss the result and to decide who would write the decision. In the early years, Martland, Pigeon, and Laskin were most forceful in these discussions. Martland was 'usually quite succinct, concise and definite.' Laskin 'was always quite forceful' and Pigeon 'was always quite definite.' During his brief time on the Court, de Grandpré tended to have a clear point of view 'which he always expressed quite firmly.' Beetz would sometimes be slow reaching decisions. Ritchie 'was never too aggressive' and Judson, who was known for being taciturn, 'rarely said anything at conference.'[37]

Deciding Cases of 'little, if any ... importance'

From 1973 to 1975, Dickson spent a considerable amount of time deciding disputes that raised no important legal issues but could be appealed to the Supreme Court as of right simply because the matter in dispute was greater than $10,000. As a rookie justice and a former corporate lawyer with a wealth of commercial experience, he was assigned a fair share of these cases. Although the legal issues were not particularly daunting, it often took much time and many pages to outline the often complex facts of the case and the rulings of the court below. Dickson decided these cases with typical care and deliberation, but they were hardly the type of intellectual challenge that he thought should occupy the attention of the nation's highest Court.

Many as-of-right cases involved run-of-the-mill traffic accidents in which Dickson recalled that 'the only identifiable issue was which car entered the intersection first, and the only persons interested in the outcome would be two insurance companies.'[38] Another case concerned whether the architects or the contractor were responsible for a leaky roof that caused over $10,000 damages to a doctor's home. Soon after his appointment, Dickson concluded that private-law appeals as of right should be abolished. After only eight months at the Court, he told an interviewer that 'some cases come before the court in which there is little, if any, legal question of importance' while 'other cases which perhaps have no monetary significance may present major legal questions and legal principles, and these are sometimes delayed while the other cases are cleared.' In Dickson's view, it was 'absolutely essential to have some very major control over the number of cases which come before the court.'[39] The nine-judge Court sat in panels of five and frequently delivered oral judgments from the bench in order to process over 160 appeals in some years. When Dickson came to the Court, there were over 100 cases ready for hearing and another 100 awaiting the lawyers' final submission of the necessary documents.[40] Dickson agreed with a 1973 report of the Canadian Bar Association that recommended that the Supreme Court be able to decide whether a case had 'some element of public importance beyond the purely individual concerns of the parties to the case' to justify hearing the appeal. Dickson's high school classmate, Queen's University law professor William Lederman, had served as research officer for this influential report.[41] Not everyone was a fan of the proposal. Retired Supreme Court judge Roy Kellock wrote an editorial warning that the Court should not solely be concerned with cases that raised large issues and scoffing at the idea that the Court would ever have its docket dominated by cases involving the constitution and the Bill of Rights. An unnamed 'prominent Toronto lawyer' expressed his concerns about a more policy-oriented Court less tactfully: 'Why don't they just apply the bloody law and not worry about changing it.'[42]

The 1975 amendment to the Supreme Court Act that gave the Court the ability to decide whether to hear a case because it raised issues of 'public importance' was presented by Minister of Justice Otto Lang as a response to the Court's crushing workload. He also noted that, 'in this day and age', the amount of money in dispute should not be the deciding factor.[43] But the abolition of appeals as of right, combined with Laskin's elevation to chief justice, sent a clear signal to the Court. The chair of the 1973 CBA report, Toronto lawyer and future judge Bert MacKinnon, made it no secret that he thought that the Court's judgments paled beside those of high courts in the United States, the United Kingdom, and Australia.[44] Having to hear appeals as of right certainly affected the style of the Court's judgments. Law professor Paul Weiler predicted in a 1974 book that giving the Court control of its own docket would cause the court 'to adopt a very different' and more policy-oriented 'stance in disposing of those cases.'[45] Weiler's book was extremely critical of the Court and caused a bit of a scandal in legal circles,[46] but Weiler was certainly not alone in criticizing the Court for its narrow and excessively legalistic approach.

The abolition of appeals as of right had an important effect on the Court. In a 1975 *Canadian Bar Review* article, Laskin proclaimed that now the Supreme Court's 'main function is to oversee the development of the law ... to give guidance in articulate reasons ... on issues of national concern.' This, he added, 'is surely the paramount obligation of an ultimate appellate court with national authority.'[47] In a number of speeches, Dickson cited the abolition of appeals of right as a 'development of the highest importance' that was causing the Court to take a more policy-oriented approach in its judgments.[48] In one 1980 speech in St John's, Newfoundland, Dickson remembered that until the Court gained control of its own docket: it 'reviewed appeals on a case by case basis, meting out justice between the parties, restricting judgment, in many instances, to the very facts of the case.'[49] This was the very fact-specific style of reasoning that had led Weiler to be so critical of the Court. By introducing leave to appeal, Parliament invited the Court to consider both the public importance and the underlying principles of the cases it heard. Dickson saw this as a clear mandate to shape and develop the law.

Dickson followed the debates around the amendment to the Supreme Court Act that abolished civil appeals as of right for another, more personal reason. When appointed to the Court in 1973, he had respected the requirement in the Supreme Court Act that all judges had to live within five miles from Ottawa, but he was irked by it. The law had been in place since the Supreme Court was created in 1875, when, as Dickson observed, it was 'based on travel by sleigh or buggy' and 'meant something. Today the automobile makes the five miles meaningless.'[50] In part at Dickson's urging, the 1975 amendments allowed members of the Court to live up to twenty-five miles outside the newly created National Capital Region. Some would have gone further and abolished the residence requirement as trivial, obsolete, and difficult to administer. The residence requirement had been a bone of contention since the Court's creation and had contributed to the decision of several people to refuse an appointment to the Court and even to resign their appointment once accepted.[51] Dickson, who was happy to be appointed to the Court and had a strict sense of duty, would not have taken such a drastic stance, but the change in the residence requirement, sometimes known as the 'Dickson amendment,' was important to him since Marchmont was just inside the new statutory limit.

Certainty and Predictability in the Law

Dickson brought a wealth of corporate experience to the many contracts and business disputes heard by the Court. One of his earliest decisions demonstrated his commitment to fundamental principles, as well as some of his differences with Laskin. Dickson upheld a by-law of a golf club that required the shareholders to approve the transfer of shares to another person. In doing so, he appealed to the fundamental principles of contract law by arguing that the original shareholders had agreed to this as part of the articles of incorporation.[52] Laskin, with Spence's agreement, dissented. He was concerned that a publicly incorporated company was being allowed to 'turn itself into a private club.'[53] This disagreement reflected the different perspectives of the two men. Laskin, a Jew, had suffered discrimination from private clubs and other bodies. Dickson, a former corporate lawyer, had belonged to private establishment clubs and trusted the contractual nature of businesses. Laskin was prepared to regulate arbitrary exercises of private power whereas Dickson was concerned that the Court would exceed its legal authority if it went behind the text of the articles of incorporation.

Another early contracts case highlighted Laskin and Dickson's different attitudes towards the obligation to follow the Court's prior precedents. A buyer agreed to purchase land on the condition that zoning approval be obtained. Before the deal closed, it became clear that there would be no zoning approval. The buyer decided that he wanted to buy the land in any event, but the vendor no longer wanted to complete the sale because he had received a better offer for the land. The buyer sued and 'cited a number of American and English authorities which support the broad proposition that a party to a contract can waive a condition that is for his benefit.'[54] The vendor relied on a much-criticized 1959 precedent of the Supreme Court which held that failure to achieve a 'true condition precedent' that depended on a 'future uncertain event' would void the contract even if the party that would benefit from the condition was prepared to waive the requirement.[55] At conference, Dickson noted that 'there is much to be said for the idea that the purchaser should be able to waive'[56] a clause intended for his benefit, but in the end he applied the Court's 1959 precedent that such a condition could not be waived, even though that precedent had been criticized as overly formalistic. He stressed the importance of 'certainty and predictability in the law' and worried about disturbing a precedent that lawyers might have relied upon in drafting the agreement.[57]

Laskin, dissenting with Spence, would have allowed the purchaser to waive the requirement for zoning approval. He disagreed with 'my brother Dickson' that allowing the purchaser to waive the condition of zoning approval amounted to rewriting the contract. In Laskin's functional view, the vendor would not be harmed by the waiver of a provision intended to benefit the purchaser.[58] His judgment was described as 'in the finest tradition of policy-oriented reasoning,'[59] while Dickson's was criticized as 'hollow,' 'unconvincing,' and running the risk of allowing a vendor 'an escape not bargained for.'[60] Dickson's formalistic approach in this early case was consistent with his respect for precedent and his desire to avoid introducing uncertainties in the law. Katherine Swinton, Dickson's law clerk during the 1975–6 term, recalls that 'he was still, for such an amazing judge, somewhat unsure of himself.' She notes that he became more and more sure of himself and the Court's role over the years, 'but he was still feeling his way when I was there.'[61]

Harrison v. Carswell

Dickson's most famous judgment in his early years on the Court and his most famous disagreement with Laskin was *Harrison v. Carswell*.[62] Sophie Carswell worked at the Dominion grocery store in the Polo Park Mall in Winnipeg. Her union was in a legal strike with Dominion's. The manager of the shopping centre informed Carswell that she could not picket the store on the mall's property. Carswell continued to picket. On four separate days she was charged with trespass, convicted, and fined $40 under Manitoba's Petty Trespass Act. Her convictions were reversed by a majority of the Manitoba Court of Appeal.[63] Dickson described the Court of Appeal decision, written by his former colleague Samuel Freedman, as one that 'balanced the public interest in picketing with the public interest in private right of property ownership, and followed two California cases decided in favour of the right to picket.'[64] Represented by Dickson's old firm, the shopping centre appealed to the Supreme Court. The case involved a clear conflict between the rights of unions and others to picket in shopping centres and the competing rights of corporations who owned shopping centres to control access to them and respond to the wishes of their tenants. The case was made more important by the fact that large shopping centres like Polo Park were replacing the public spaces of the downtown core as the key shopping and meeting places in Canadian cities.

It was clear after oral argument that Dickson and Laskin would disagree and that Dickson would command a majority, with only Spence and Beetz supporting Laskin. Dickson's conference notes suggest that, for him, the case was a simple matter of following the court's prior precedents. In a brief 1971 oral judgment, the Court had upheld a trespass conviction of a person who, in an effort to boycott California grapes, had picketed a Safeway store in a shopping centre in Ontario.[65] For Dickson, it was 'difficult to make a meaningful distinction between a picketer who tells people not to go to Safeway because of a labour dispute in California and a picketer who tells people not to go to Dominion Stores because she and her fellow employees are on strike.' Dickson somewhat tersely added in his conference notes: 'Although the Chief Justice was a member of the Court in ... [the 1971 case], he does not wish to follow that decision.'[66]

Laskin, who had taught labour law and been a labour arbitrator, believed that there was a meaningful distinction between consumer and labour picketing. He did not hesitate to try to pull rank on Dickson, arguing that both he and Spence had sat on the 1971 grape boycott case and that, for them, the case decided only the 'narrow question' of whether a shopping centre could ever bring a trespass charge. In his judgment, Laskin argued that his views as a member of the 1971 panel 'should give pause to any suggestion that ... [the 1971 case] because it was so recently decided, has concluded the issue now before us.' He warned that 'this Court, above all others in this country, cannot be simply mechanistic about previous decisions.'[67] Laskin's views were not shared by all on the Court. Roland Ritchie wrote Dickson a memo because he thought that Dickson 'might be interested in the views of this member of the Court who sat' in the 1971 case but who disagreed with Laskin and Spence about its meaning. Ritchie believed that the case was 'controlling authority' and added that he 'did not share the view' that the practice of following precedent 'should be lightly abandoned as a governing principle in our system of law.'[68]

Laskin wrote his vigorous dissent with experience and authority. While doing graduate work at Harvard, he had published a 1937 article criticizing Canadian courts for following precedent and applying the common law to labour pickets.[69] In the same year, Dickson had been slogging through courses such as Practical Statutes at the Manitoba Law School while working at a law office. Laskin sounded like a law professor lecturing a student when he warned against a 'mechanical deference to *stare decisis*'[70] which would use 'a previous decision involving a "brown horse," by which to judge a pending appeal involving a "brown horse"'[71] and would 'take merely one side of a debatable issue and say that it concludes the debate without the need to hear the other side.'[72] Using a sociological and policy-oriented approach to law making, Laskin argued that the court must create 'an appropriate legal framework for new social facts'[73] such as the privately owned shopping centre that had an open invitation to the public. His reasoning demonstrated what Dickson would later describe as Laskin's 'academic' approach to the law but also his ability to 'be very cold and very biting.'[74] Dickson may have been a bit intimidated by Laskin. Bertha Wilson, a colleague of both Laskin and Dickson, would later recall that she thought that Dickson 'thought of Bora as in some ways superior, of having a better intellect than he himself had ... I always thought that Brian underestimated himself ... I didn't think his own assessment of himself was fair because ... the wonderful thing about him was his larger view of life ... '[75]

Dickson's conference memo suggests that he had originally hoped to decide the case solely on the basis of precedent and that it did 'not seem to me that there is any need for me to get into the policy aspect.' This was consistent with Dickson's other early judgments in which he followed precedents closely and without much question. Laskin, however, had thrown down a strong intellectual challenge for Dickson to justify his more restrained approach to judicial law making and Dickson soon felt compelled to respond. Writing and rewriting his judgment, he concluded that the main issues were the appropriate division of labour between courts and legislatures, the need for the courts to follow precedents, and the need for courts to avoid making arbitrary choices best left to the legislature. He had his law clerk research the academic literature on the role of the judge. With reference to Benjamin Cardozo's famous statements about judges making law only in a incremental fashion, and to other works of jurisprudence from Canada, Australia, and England, Dickson argued: 'The submission that this Court should weigh and determine the respective values to society of the right to property and the right to picket raises important and difficult political and socio-economic issues, the resolution of which must, by their very nature, be arbitrary and embody personal economic and social beliefs. It also raises fundamental questions as to the role of this Court under the Canadian constitution. The duty of the Court, as I envisage it, is to proceed in the discharge of its adjudicative function in a reasoned way from principled decision and established concepts.'[76] The Manitoba legislature had not chosen to make any exceptions for peaceful picketing in its trespass act even though other provinces had done so.[77] For Dickson, it was 'the Legislature, which is representative of the people and designed to manifest the political will,'[78] that was in the proper position to change the law. The courts were not in a position to balance property rights against the right to picket because the balance raised political and economic issues that should be decided by the legislature.

In a passage from an early draft that was deleted in the judgment, Dickson pointedly warned that 'proponents of legal activism' overlooked the fact that such 'activism can operate in two directions, and that in interpreting profoundly political issues, restraint must be applied if justice is to be attained.'[79] In other words, the freedom that Laskin was claiming for judges could be used for both good and bad. Dickson may well have believed that workers should be allowed to picket in shopping centres, but he believed that this was a matter for legislatures. Dickson was not anti-labour. He refused to write into his judgment a distinction that Ritchie had urged that would allow 'canvassers or collectors for a recognized charity' into a shopping centre, but not those who were expressing 'a view which was in direct conflict with the policy of the company which owned the premises.'[80] Dickson did not believe that it was possible for the Court to distinguish good trespassers from bad or the labour picketers in this case from the consumer picketers in the 1971 case. He was concerned about 'the uncertainties and very real difficulties which emerge when a court essays to legislate as to what is and what is not a permissible activity within a shopping centre.'[81] Judicial creativity was justified only when supported by clear and manageable principles. If there were no such principles, Dickson believed that the Court should defer to the legislature, which was better suited to engage in either 'arbitrary' or 'political' line drawing. In later years, Dickson would be fond of creating innovative halfway houses to bridge competing legal rules. However, in *Harrison v. Carswell*, he could see no manageable halfway house or compromise between the rights of the property owner and the rights of the picketers. In his view, the Petty Trespass Act meant that property rights should prevail.

At Laskin's urging,[82] Dickson added a passage to his majority judgment stating that the Court was capable of acting 'creatively – it has done so on countless occasions.' His subsequent decisions, certainty provide many examples both of judicial creativity and a willingness not to let precedents stand in the way of developing the law. They can perhaps be reconciled with his decision in *Harrison v. Carswell* by a passage that Dickson drafted for inclusion in that judgment but that, at the suggestion of Pigeon,[83] he deleted a few weeks before the judgment release. In the deleted passage Dickson adopted Lord Reid's statement that appellate tribunals should develop the common law and not be deterred by 'old cases,' but that they must do so on the basis of 'fundamental principles' as opposed to 'arbitrary conditions or limitations.' Judicial creativity was justified in cases dealing with '"lawyer's law"' as opposed to matters that 'are the subject of public controversy and on which layman are as well able to decide as are lawyers. On such matters it is not for courts to proceed on their view of public policy for that would be to encroach on the province of Parliament.'[84] A decade later, Dickson would agree to a similar distinction between matters that were protected under the Charter because they were 'in the inherent domain of the judiciary as guardian of the justice system' and matters within 'the realm of general public policy.'[85] There are questions about whether this distinction between law and politics is maintainable or has been maintained, but it was an important one in Dickson's mind.

The immediate commentary on the case favoured Laskin's dissent. Two student commentaries echoed Laskin's criticisms of Dickson for not adapting the concept of trespass to modern realities.[86] Court critic and labour law scholar Paul Weiler was perhaps more cautious. He observed that 'prima facie, the court is the appropriate institution for renovating' the outmoded common law doctrine of trespass, but also warned that courts should generally leave it to 'the legislature to adopt new legal policies which tilt the delicate balance of economic power' between unions and employers.[87] Speaking at a 1976 conference after another judge had praised Laskin's dissent, Dickson, who was sensitive to any criticisms of his judgments, somewhat defensively stated 'that I have not the slightest intention of discussing *Harrison v. Carswell* ... My views are found in Supreme Court Reports.' He went on, however, to argue that 'the judicial role is interstitial. What the courts are really effecting is an incremental elaboration of the law.' He stressed the importance of stability in the law and the expectation that judges will 'have due regard to the existing rules in the legal order and abide by the rules which existed at the time of the action.'[88] In another 1976 speech, he argued that 'the law must be adaptable to change but not become a weather cock.' As he had in his disagreements with Laskin over contract law, Dickson emphasized the importance of people being able 'to order their affairs in the knowledge that certain courses of action will have predictable legal consequences.'[89] Echoing the deleted passage from *Harrison v. Carswell*, Dickson warned that 'once you recognize a very large activist role for the judiciary, you must also accept that that activist role can be reflected in more than one direction' and that 'many judges are sufficiently modest to wonder whether their own values are the proper ones.' He added a significant and prophetic caveat by noting that the situation was different in the United States, where there was a constitutional bill of rights and the courts had an 'undoubted right and duty ... to be creative.'[90]

In subsequent years, there was a subtle shift in Dickson's extrajudicial commentary about the role of the judge. In a 1978 convocation address at the University of Saskatchewan, he spoke of the Court being 'at a threshold of a new era of judicial decision-making' in which there would be 'a growing recognition of social and economic conditions in the formulation of decisions of the Court' and 'more relaxed attitudes' towards following precedents. 'The change made in 1975 in the jurisdiction of our Court, with emphasis on issues of public importance, is part of the same trend.' He indicated that courts should revise 'old rules' that 'no longer make sense in contemporary society' or that 'no longer fulfill the purposes for which they were erected.' Taken by itself, this could have supported the Laskin dissent in *Harrison v. Carswell*. At the same time, however, Dickson still maintained that judicial change, unlike legislative change, 'must be supported by legal principles and materials' and aim to achieve 'adjudicative' as opposed to 'distributive justice.'[91] He reiterated his familiar theme that judges had no place in making arbitrary choices and should instead concentrate on effecting only those changes required by legal principle.

Aboriginal Rights and Private Property

As in *Harrison v. Carswell*, Dickson's early cases on aboriginal rights demonstrated the same concern for following legal authority and respecting private property. In his first hunting-rights case, Dickson affirmed the conviction of four treaty Indians from the Long Plain Reserve in Manitoba who were charged with hunting deer without due regard for the safety of others. There was little doubt that they had been hunting dangerously. They had fired high-power rifles shortly after midnight in a farmer's alfalfa field; the farmer was awakened by the sound of rifle shots and by a light flashing through his bedroom window. Although it was not strictly necessary to decide the case, Dickson went on to express 'grave doubt' that the Indians had lawful access to the farmer's field simply because the farmer had failed to post 'no hunting' signs on his property. He feared that such an approach would mean that 'the carrying of a fire-arm immunizes an act which would otherwise be trespass.' Dickson, who had owned a farm in Manitoba, also expressed concern that farmers would have to engage in the 'tiresome and costly business' of posting signs in order to protect their land from trespass.[92] His preference in this case, released on the same day as *Harrison v. Carswell*, was again for the right of the property owner.

In another Manitoba hunting case, Dickson affirmed the conviction of Lawrence Mousseau, a treaty Indian, who shot a deer from a public highway in Manitoba.[93] Dickson rejected the Manitoba Court of Appeal's conclusion that had interpreted his first hunting-right case to mean that Indians could hunt on public roads so long as they did not do so in a dangerous fashion. As in *Harrison v. Carswell*, Dickson was concerned that the courts would be drawn into the difficult job of drawing lines, in this case about what sort of hunting was dangerous and what was not. In his conference notes, he rejected the 'extreme position ... that if any member of the public had any right of access to land,' Indians could hunt on that land. He believed that such an argument would 'reach the absurd point that an Indian could hunt in a shopping centre or a golf course, or at a public beach or picnic ground, or in Assiniboine Park in Winnipeg, and nothing would prevent shooting the tame deer which abound in the park.'[94] Dickson, who kept deer at Marchmont, did not want anyone shooting them.

Even in early cases in which Dickson recognized an aboriginal right to hunt for food, he took a more restrictive approach than he would in later cases. In a 1977 case, he held that Alex Frank had an aboriginal right to hunt for food in Alberta even though he resided in Saskatchewan. Dickson noted that Treaty 7 between the queen and the Plains and Wood Cree extended over provincial borders. He did not, however, rely on the moral obligation to give treaties a generous interpretation favourable to the Indians that he would subsequently stress. Rather, he relied on 'statutory construction' of the Natural Resource Agreement.[95] He parsed the words of that agreement and not the treaty to find that it provided the right to hunt for food to 'Indians who, at any particular moment, happen to be found within the boundaries of the Province of Alberta, irrespective of normal residence.'[96] This approach risked subsuming the broader treaty right under the narrower statutory right. During his last year on the Court, a majority would use Dickson's decision to support such a conclusion. By that time, however, Dickson would join Bertha Wilson and argue in dissent that the broader treaty right should prevail.[97]

In another 1977 case, Dickson had little trouble concluding that the aboriginal right to hunt for food which was recognized in the prairies did not apply in British Columbia. No treaties had been signed in British Columbia and the Natural Resource Agreement did not apply. 'However receptive one may be ... on compassionate grounds,' Dickson could not accept the argument of the British Columbia Indians that they had not surrendered their rights and 'should not be placed in a more invidious position than those who entered into treaties.'[98] This absence of legal authority for Dickson meant that Indians in British Columbia, unlike Indians on the prairies, could be convicted of hunting for food without a licence on unoccupied crown lands. Dickson was also influenced by the clear language of the Indian Act, which stated that, in the absence of a treaty or federal law, provincial laws of general application applied to the Indians. One commentator criticized Dickson's judgment for reducing aboriginal rights to the level of mere 'compassion.'[99] Dickson, however, saw matters differently. For him, rights required clear legal authority and compassion alone was not sufficient to justify a judicial decision.

Dickson also avoided the larger issue of whether hunting rights in British Columbia could be found in either the Royal Proclamation of 1763 or the existence of aboriginal title over the land. He believed that there was insufficient evidence to decide such momentous issues. In an often-quoted passage, he concluded for the Court that 'Claims to aboriginal title are woven with history, legend, politics and moral obligations. If the claim of any Band in respect of any particular land is to be decided as a justiciable issue and not a political issue, it should be so considered on the facts pertinent to that Band and to that land, and not on any global basis.'[100] At one level, this conclusion relied on a distinction between law and politics. Law was objective and determined on the basis of precise evidence while politics concerned issues of history and legend and considerations of morality and compassion. In subsequent cases, however, Dickson would draw more freely on history, moral considerations, oral evidence, and aboriginal perspectives in defining the legal nature of aboriginal rights. He would also subsequently write about the importance of compassion to law. Dickson's approach to aboriginal rights and to judicial decision making became more generous and less positivistic over time.

Neglect of Fault Principles in Criminal Law

Upon his retirement Dickson was praised for 'his consistent and principled approach to criminal law'[101] and recognized as 'a great judge and a wonderful scholar of criminal law.'[102] He did not, however, start that way. Although Dickson would later be associated with the liberal, pro-accused, and law-reform-minded LSD (Laskin, Spence, Dickson), the dissenting wing of the Court, he frequently wrote for a majority and in disagreement with Laskin and Spence during his first years on the Court.

In these early years, Dickson considered himself bound by precedent even if that meant a result that he would have avoided as unfair later in his career. One such decision was *Hill v. The Queen.*[103] Barbara Hill was driving home one afternoon in a busy section of Toronto when the taxi cab in front of her stopped suddenly to avoid a pedestrian. Hill's car touched the rear of the taxi, causing minor damage to its bumper. Believing that no damage had occurred, Hill then drove home. She was subsequently charged under the provincial highway traffic act with failing to remain at a scene of an accident. The case raised a fundamental issue of criminal law: Can a person be guilty if he or she is unaware or mistaken about the facts which make the conduct illegal? In his conference memo after oral argument, Dickson characterized Edward Greenspan's argument on behalf of Hill as a 'subjective one' that left it 'to the accused to decide whether damage has been caused necessitating a stop.'[104] This was an appeal to the principles of subjective fault that Dickson would later champion, but it did not convince him during this his first year on the Court.

Dickson affirmed Hill's conviction on the basis that 'whatever Mrs. Hill believed or did not believe was irrelevant' because the offence was not a 'crime in the "true sense"' but rather a provincial traffic offence. He interpreted the offence as one of no-fault liability in which a conviction followed from the act of leaving the scene of the accident without regard to whether the accused was at fault. All that mattered was that 'there was an accident on a highway in which she was directly involved; she failed to remain at or return immediately to the scene and was, therefore, properly convicted ... ignorance in this case affords no greater defence than in the case of a driver who unwittingly exceeds the speed limit or inadvertently goes through a red light.' Dickson was not persuaded by a Spence and Laskin dissent that argued that the offence was 'designed to penalize an attempt to escape civil liability for damage caused, not to needlessly impede the proper movement of traffic.'[105]

Dickson followed often-criticized Supreme Court precedents which drew a dichotomy between true crimes that required subjective fault and all other offences that required no fault. Many lower court judges interpreted Dickson's judgment as precluding the development of a 'halfway house' approach that allowed an accused who acted reasonably and without fault to be acquitted of regulatory offences that were not true crimes.[106] In just five years time, Dickson himself would create such a halfway house in his landmark *Sault Ste Marie* decision.[107] In 1973, however, Dickson applied the Court's existing precedents, even if that meant the conviction of a person who may not have been at fault.

Even when Dickson agreed with Laskin, his early criminal cases were not always consistent with his later positions. In a 1975 dissent joined by Laskin, Dickson concluded that the crime of criminal negligence in the Criminal Code should be determined on the basis of an objective standard. In other words, what mattered was whether a reasonable person as opposed to the accused, would have recognized the prohibited risks. The majority of the Court took an approach more favourable to the accused and concluded that the prosecutor must prove that the accused subjectively recognized the prohibited risk.[108] In 1989 Dickson would change his mind and agree with a Bertha Wilson judgment that argued that a criminal-negligence conviction required proof that the accused was subjectively at fault.[109]

A Limited Judicial Role

Dickson disagreed with Laskin in a 1973 case concerning the proper procedure to be followed by trial judges in accepting guilty pleas. The case again reflected their different approach to precedents and judicial law making. The twenty-one-year-old accused had been reluctant to plead guilty to breaking and entering an associate's cottage, perhaps because he thought that he had permission to stay at the cottage.[110] Dickson believed there was no reason to second-guess the trial judge's discretionary decision to accept the guilty plea. He was reluctant to complicate the trial judge's task by imposing mandatory duties when accepting routine guilty pleas. He also relied on a 1969 precedent in which the Supreme Court had refused to reopen a guilty plea in a far more serious case in which a twenty-one-year-old man had pled guilty to non-capital murder in order to avoid a possible death sentence. Laskin again disparaged the idea that the Court 'must pay a mechanical deference' to its past precedents. Certainly, in this instance, the precedent was troubling, involving an aboriginal man who required a Cree interpreter and whose own lawyer confessed to not understanding his client's 'mind or intent.'[111] Dickson, who as a trial judge had experience with the poor representation that some aboriginal people received, should have been concerned about the precedent, but he loyally applied it. As Dale Gibson commented in a 1974 article about Dickson, if precedents 'do not permit an outcome that he would regard as equitable, he normally accepts that the matter is out of his hands.'[112]

Another early case involved a man named Marcoux who was forced by the police to participate in a line-up where he was identified by a crime victim as the man who stole his wallet.[113] Marcoux argued that requiring him to participate violated his right against self-incrimination. Dickson's conference memo suggested that he was attracted to the idea that 'an accused has a legal right to refrain from taking part in a lineup' and that the jury should not be allowed to 'draw an adverse inference from the exercise by the accused of his legal right.'[114] Nevertheless, as in *Morgentaler I*, Dickson did not go with his first and liberal instincts to side with the accused. He eventually wrote a judgment for a unanimous Supreme Court that concluded that the accused's right against self-incrimination had not been violated. Following established authority, he reasoned that the right against against self-incrimination protected the accused only from being forced to be a witness at his trial and did not influence what happened in the police station. Dickson and the Court would decide similar issues very differently under the 1982 Charter of Rights.[115]

Dickson's early decisions reveal a slow and cautious start at the Supreme Court. In many cases, he followed precedents and deferred the task of law reform to the legislature. He often followed what Paul Weiler identified in his influential 1974 critique of the Supreme Court as 'the formal style of legal reasoning ... The judges write their opinion as if there is already an established legal rule which binds them. The rule is applied because the law requires it, not because the judges believe it is a desirable rule.'[116] His famous disagreement with Laskin in *Harrison v. Carswell* over adherence to precedent and the limits of judicial law making was not an aberration. Dickson was less willing to depart from precedents than Laskin in many other cases. In the absence of established legal principles, he left law reform to the elected legislature because of concerns that the judiciary should not make what Dickson saw as arbitrary or political choices. He erred on the side of property rights rather than in favour of the rights of picketers and aboriginal hunters. He also erred on the side of allowing a conviction to occur in the absence of fault rather than require even a halfway house of negligent conduct. However, as we shall see in the next chapter, by the late 1970s, Dickson was quickly gaining ground and becoming significantly more creative in his approach to judicial lawmaking.

8

Gaining Ground

If Dickson started slowly and cautiously in his first few years on the Supreme Court, he soon made up for lost time. From 1976 to 1983, he developed as one of the Court's leading figures, a judge prepared to innovate and, if necessary, to dissent. Despite his frequent disagreement with Laskin during his early years on the Court, Dickson now moved closer to Laskin's views.

This middle stage in Dickson's career was one of striking change on the Court. A Court that had been criticized in the early 1970s for following precedents and not recognizing the broader implications of its rulings began to reform large areas of public and private law. Dickson was well aware of these changes. In a 1978 speech, he spoke of the Court being 'at a threshold of a new era of judicial decision-making' in which it would be more concerned with broad questions of policy and in which it would adapt and change the law.[1] The boldness of the Supreme Court in the period immediately before it began hearing cases under the 1982 Charter of Rights and Freedoms is often neglected, but it clearly emerges from an account of Dickson's career.

Dickson made his mark on public law at a slightly earlier stage than on private or criminal law, topics that will be examined in subsequent chapters. Many of Dickson's early public-law judgments were dissents that would be accepted by majorities of the Court in a few years time. As in other areas, Dickson was influenced by critical ideas expressed by legal academics about the traditional law. Academics in turn praised Dickson and helped create some of the momentum that saw his dissents win the adherence of his supreme court colleagues.

Dickson's public-law decisions connected with his personal interests and experiences. A significant number of cases dealt with the obligations of law societies and universities to treat their members fairly. Dickson, as a former head of the Law Society of Manitoba and a member of the University of Manitoba's Board of Governors, understood how these institutions worked. An even larger number of cases dealt with claims by prisoners that they had not been treated fairly. From the start, Dickson was receptive to these claims. Before his appointment to the Supreme Court, as we have seen, Dickson had visited many prisons, and he had a rather benevolent view of prisoners as disadvantaged: 'They were largely uneducated, some of them committed crimes under some degree of intoxication and they are part of the Canadian community which I think we can feel rather sorry for in most cases.'[2]

'Not a liberal in the classical sense'

Dickson's concerns about prisoners and others affected by the exercise of state power reflected a liberal's concerns about the rights of the individual. His concern about disadvantaged groups and his sense that the state should set an example, however, also reflected a more conservative world-view. Consistent with his early decisions on the Manitoba Court of Appeal in which he appealed at different times to both the liberal individualism of H.L.A. Hart and the conservative community values of Lord Devlin, Dickson was a liberal with a conservative or communitarian streak or what some have called a 'tory touch.'[3] A wealthy man and a former military officer, Dickson believed that it was important for the more advantaged to assist the less advantaged. He became increasingly willing over the years to accept the rights of disadvantaged groups – prisoners, religious and linguistic minorities, workers, aboriginal people – that some liberals were less willing to recognize.

Dickson's 'tory touch' also manifested itself in frequent deference to state regulation and expertise in various fields such as labour relations. The state owed its citizens fair treatment, but, as long as it acted with basic decency, its regulatory activities should be accepted by both citizens and courts. As Dickson's former law clerk Joel Bakan observes, Dickson 'was not a liberal in the classic sense ... he wasn't a person who saw the state as the enemy ... He believed in the state, he believed in order and he had a quite benevolent view of the state as a force for good in society.' In Bakan's view, Dickson was concerned about communities and vulnerable groups and had a 'sort of noblesse oblige' in which he believed 'that things have to be fair, things have to be just ... these communities have to be empowered but not to the point where they challenged the overarching community which is the state.'[4]

Dickson's administrative-law decisions combined a liberal concern with protecting individuals from unfair treatment by the stronger state with a more communitarian concern about recognizing the legitimate role of the state in promoting social values. There was no tension between individualistic and communitarian values for Dickson because he believed that the public interest would be advanced by treating individuals fairly while individuals in turn should honour the rule of law as represented by fair decisions about the public interest. This combination of fairness and deference would come to full fruition in his approach to the Charter of Rights.

Halfway Houses

Although he could insist on some principles without compromise,[5] Dickson also had an exceptional ability to formulate creative compromises – what he called 'halfway houses' – between extreme positions. The halfway house was a recurring and important theme in Dickson's jurisprudence and it reveals much about the man himself. One was Dickson's openness to all sides of a question. Dickson was willing to listen and learn and he continued to grow throughout his judicial career. He believed that a judge should try to understand all sides of an issue and consider all the evidence before reaching a decision. Whether in the courtroom with lawyers or in chambers with clerks or at the dining room table with his family, Dickson welcomed the expression of competing and even extreme views and he took an almost bemused pleasure in listening to competing positions argued with vigour and flair. At the same time, Dickson was a moderate who was not often comfortable with extreme or doctrinaire positions. His inclination was to move towards the middle and try to convince others that his halfway houses accommodated both sides of the debate and provided a firm foundation for going forward. Dickson's inclination to seek halfway houses that accommodated competing positions made him something of a judge's judge. He was perceived not as having a set agenda but rather as trying to make the best decisions only after listening to both sides and considering all the material that could help him improve the law. Even though Dickson had effectively sent him to jail in the 1970s, Henry Morgentaler went into his second hearing before the Supreme Court in 1986 describing Dickson as 'down the middle' and an 'enigma.'[6]

Dickson's preference for halfway houses may have been in part a reflection of his background in the corporate world. Long before he became a judge, Dickson had experience in listening to competing interests and making pragmatic and prudent compromises that would, he hoped, allow a common enterprise to flourish. The history of Dickson's former law firm takes special note of his 'practicality' and ability to 'concentrate his efforts on the achievable.'[7] Dickson's preference for accommodation also reflected his keen appreciation and love of Canada as a diverse and complex country. In subsequent chapters we will examine how he recognized the need for both provincial autonomy that would accommodate Quebec and a strong national government; the need to respect the rights of both individuals and groups; and the need to ensure that people were treated fairly but also the need to accept reasonable and fair choices made by democratically elected governments. Dickson's penchant for halfway houses and creative compromises made him the type of judge who was ideally suited to play an increasingly important role in the governance of Canada.

Challenging the Rigid Dichotomies of Administrative Law

When Dickson came to the Supreme Court, administrative law was based on two contested dichotomies. The first was that the powers that the state exercised over individuals were either 'administrative' or 'quasi-judicial.' An administrative decision included the revocation or withholding of a privilege but was often circularly defined as a decision that was not quasi-judicial. If a decision was categorized as administrative, the state had no duty to give the affected person a hearing or even an opportunity to reply. In contrast, a quasi-judicial decision would generally require a full hearing according to the rules of 'natural justice' that were observed in courts. It was all or nothing. The individual was either entitled to no procedural rights at all or to receive a court-like hearing. Everything depended on the classification of the state power as administrative or quasi-judicial, but this classification process was uncertain, arbitrary, and subject to much litigation.

The second dichotomy was between matters within an administrative agency's jurisdiction and matters outside its jurisdiction. The courts would generally allow the agency to make unreasonable findings in matters within its jurisdiction but would correct even the slightest error if they believed that the agency exceeded the ambit of its jurisdiction. The jurisdictional/non-jurisdictional dichotomy, like the administrative/quasi-judicial dichotomy, meant that the courts either took important decisions away from administrative agencies or refused to intervene even if they made perverse decisions. The distinction between matters inside and outside jurisdiction was hazy and the subject of much technical analysis and litigation.

Dickson successfully challenged both rigid dichotomies by developing new, flexible, and creative compromises or halfway houses that allowed the courts to play a supervisory role without insisting that every agency have a full court-like hearing and without second-guessing the agency on every decision it made. Dickson and Laskin developed the doctrine of fairness to bridge the gap between requiring court-like procedures and not requiring any procedural rights for administrative decisions. Dickson thought that the state should always be required to observe the basic tenets of fairness. He did not think of fairness as a technical legal term of art. It was an attribute of common humanity and basic respect for the dignity of each and every individual.

Dickson's influential view that courts should correct only 'patently unreasonable' decisions can also be seen as a creative compromise between the extremes of courts substituting their views for those of expert administrators and courts holding that even perverse administrative decisions were final and unreviewable by the courts. He was a proponent of judicial deference towards administrative decisions, but he did not believe in judicial abdication.

'The rule of law must run within penitentiary walls'

Since his appointment to head the Manitoba Civil Service Commission in the early 1950s and during his time on the Manitoba courts in the 1960s, Dickson took an unusual interest in custodial institutions and the treatment of prisoners, making annual trips with his colleague Samuel Freedman to Manitoba's imposing Stoney Mountain Pententiary and, with Barbara, attending 'social nights' to watch plays put on by the prisoners and to purchase their handicrafts.[8] Dickson's files on prisoner cases contain an unusual amount of press clippings about corrections. The 1970s were a time of intense controversy about prisoners' rights. A 1971 riot at Kingston Penitentiary had, in an echo of much more intense violence at Attica in upper New York State, resulted in the death of two inmates and the transfer of some four hundred more to Millhaven. The transfer had not gone well because, as Dickson observed in one of his cases, the prisoners 'were made to run a gauntlet of guards who struck them with clubs as they entered the institution.'[9] A small and dedicated group of Canadian prison lawyers relentlessly litigated cases in which they maintained that prisoners had been treated unfairly, and they also made their arguments for fairness to prisoners in the academic journals.[10]

Dickson's decisions concerning prisoners displayed a compassionate concern that they be treated fairly. Dickson believed that imprisonment 'isn't all a matter of simple punishment. They are still human beings, they still have wives or friends or family, or girlfriends. And the idea that you put them in penitentiary and forget about them for five years or ten years, twenty years, I think is just dead wrong. ... the idea of having been confined, they should be demeaned by this or that form of minor denigration, denied the right to vote, denied the right to this, denied the right to that, I think is wrong.'[11] A file in one of Dickson's many prison cases contains a pamphlet from the John Howard Society. Dickson heavily underlined a passage that argued that most prisoners came from a 'deprived background' such as a 'broken home, parental neglect or brutality, foster homes or institutions.'[12]

Dickson's concern about prisoners was evident from the start of his career at the Supreme Court. In 1974 he concluded that indeterminate detention for habitual offenders who did not present 'a real and present danger to life or limb' was not lawful.[13] The case involved forty-eight year-old Robert Hatchwell, who had twenty-eight criminal convictions, most relating to car thefts. For Dickson, the car thief with a 'fixation about cars' was more a 'nuisance' than a 'menace'. Hatchwell's crimes were 'not motivated by gain nor by any destructive urge; for in every case, according to the evidence, the property taken was recovered undamaged. The appellant drives the stolen vehicles until such time as he is apprehended. Of late he has shown a preference for large tractor-trailer units.'[14] Martland and Ritchie dissented and would have imposed indeterminate detention on the basis that Hatchwell was 'an incorrigible criminal, whose criminal activities will continue indefinitely if he is not detained.'[15]

In a decision dealing with the censorship of a prisoner's mail, Dickson rejected a trial judge's ruling that prisoners lost the benefits of solicitor-client privilege. In Dickson's view, the case should be approached 'on the broader basis that i) the right to communicate in confidence with one's legal adviser is a fundamental civil and legal right, founded upon the unique relationship of solicitor and client, and ii) a person confined to prison retains all of his civil rights, other than those expressly or impliedly taken from him by law.' He recognized that 'nothing is more likely to have a "chilling effect" upon the frank and free exchange and disclosure of confidences' than prison officials examining the mail.[16] Beverley McLachlin, then a law professor, praised Dickson's decision on the basis that 'prisoners, as much as, if not more than, other persons, need the opportunity for free and frank communication with their lawyers, whether with respect to pending trials and appeals or issues arising out of their treatment after sentencing.'[17] Dickson was not, however, prepared to say that prisoners had an absolute right not to have their mail opened.[18] He balanced the rights of the prisoners with the state's interest in prison discipline by indicating that prison officials should examine letters only to 'the minimum extent necessary to establish whether it is properly the subject of solicitor-client privilege.'[19] This case foreshadowed Dickson's approach to the Charter, in which he accepted state objectives but insisted that they be pursued in a proportionate manner that infringed rights as little as possible.

Another important prisoners' rights issue was whether the state had to provide hearings when they revoked parole. One important case involved Lenard Howarth, who was on parole after serving two years of a seven-year sentence for armed robbery. Howarth had a job and was taking sociology classes at Queens University when he was charged with indecent assault. He insisted that he was innocent and, after a month, the charges were dropped.

Four days after the charges were dropped, however, Howarth's parole was revoked without any hearing or explanation. As Dickson dryly commented in judgment: 'The Parole Board says it is under no duty to enlighten Mr. Howarth nor to give him an opportunity to be heard.'[20] In a decision written by Pigeon, the majority of the Court denied Howarth relief on the basis that the Parole Board's decision was an administrative one and hence not subject to judicial review. The majority decision was typical of the Court's reasoning in this era in that it applied past precedents and relied on the wording of the Federal Court Act without exploring the principles at stake. Howarth's arguments about 'the duty of fairness lying upon all administrative agencies' was dismissed by Pigeon as 'completely irrelevant in the present case.'[21]

Dickson tried to influence his colleagues by circulating a *Globe and Mail* editorial entitled 'Parole and the Rule of Law.' The editorial called for Canadian courts to follow the United States Supreme Court in granting procedural rights to parolees.[22] Dickson followed public affairs in the newspapers closely and was likely more aware of developments concerning prisoners' rights than many of his colleagues. Even with the help of the *Globe and Mail*, however, Dickson could not gain a majority and ended up writing one of his first dissents on the Court. Significantly, both Laskin and Spence signed on to Dickson's judgment. This was the first time that the three judges, who were soon to be known in the law schools and the legal profession as LSD, wrote together in dissent.

Dickson started his dissent from the proposition that the seriousness of the consequences for the individual affected was the most important factor in determining whether the Parole Board had a duty to act fairly. He distinguished restrictive precedents on the basis that they did not stand 'in the way of assuring a paroled inmate minimal procedural safeguards.' Although Howarth was a convicted armed robber, Dickson rejected 'out of hand any suggestion that because a paroled inmate is a convicted criminal he stands denuded of civil rights.' Parole was not 'a mere privilege or act of grace and favor, conferring no rights on the parolee and subject to withdrawal at will,' but rather 'a right' to 'release upon conditions.' Dickson placed himself in Howarth's shoes as a parolee who had been 'given his liberty and an opportunity to be re-united with his family and friends, to further his education, to seek and obtain employment and subject to the terms of his parole and the statute to enjoy the privileges of a free man and the prospect of ultimate restoration of full civil status. All of this is a precious right.'[23]

Dickson concluded that the Parole Board should have given Howarth 'some indication of what has been said against him and an opportunity to respond. Failure to do so can surely only engender bitter feelings of injustice.'[24] This followed some recent developments in England which suggested that duties of fairness were not limited to quasi-judicial functions, as well as criticisms by academics that the distinction between quasi-judicial and administrative functions was uncertain and depended on the result that the judge wanted to achieve. Dickson would not have required a full-blown trial, but he thought that Howarth should have been allowed to respond in some way to the decision to revoke his parole and return him to the penitentiary. His dissent was praised by academics. In an article that Dickson kept in his file, law professor Patrice Garant strongly criticized the majority judgment of Pigeon as 'une argumentation de technicien du droit, formé à l'école du droit privé, qui ramène la construction du droit administif à un jeu d'interprétation du droit statutaire.'[25] A comment in the *Canadian Bar Review* praised Dickson's judgment for giving 'credence and respectability to the common law notion of "duty to act fairly," thus providing another tool for ensuring accountability on the part of our administrative bodies.'[26] A year later, however, Dickson ended up in dissent with Laskin in a similar parole-revocation case. The strongly worded dissent won critical praise, but the commentators were not optimistic that the Court would move beyond the 'fruitless characterization exercise' of whether revocation of parole was an administrative or quasi-judicial decision.[27]

The commentators were wrong. By the end of the 1970s, the Court was indeed prepared to recognize a general duty of fairness. Yet this victory did not come without a struggle. One prisoner went to the Supreme Court twice in three years before the Court recognized that he should have some procedural rights. The case arose over a minor incident in which two inmates, Martineau and Butters, were charged with two prison disciplinary offences. Martineau pled guilty to the offence of being in a cell with another inmate, Butters, without authorization, but he contested the second charge which alleged that he had engaged in homosexual acts in the cell. Martineau was convicted of being in an indecent position before a board of three prison officials and sentenced to fifteen days in punitive isolation on a restricted diet. He argued that he was treated unfairly because he was not allowed to be present when Butters testified. An earlier study of disciplinary proceedings in the same British Columbia penitentiary had concluded that disciplinary proceedings were conducted without the basic features of fairness and that the inmates 'almost to a man, felt that Warden's Court was a kangaroo court ... they were automatically guilty notwithstanding anything they said.'[28]

On Martineau's first trip to the Supreme Court, the majority of the Court dismissed his claim. Pigeon held, that despite internal directives requiring a fair hearing, the disciplinary board's decision was an unreviewable administrative matter. It was an error to conclude 'that whenever the decision affects the right of the applicant, there is a duty to act judicially.'[29] Dickson's conference notes indicate that he believed that the board's decision was quasi-judicial because the directives governing disciplinary proceedings 'speak of a charge notice ... defence appearing personally, full answer and defence, weighing of evidence and award of punishment.'[30] Whether or not one accepted that the duty of fairness was restricted to quasi-judicial decisions, this was a case in which the Court should intervene. Some members of the Court were concerned that, if they accepted Martineau's argument, 'there will be a flood of appeals from the recipients of penitentiary discipline.' In their dissenting judgment, Laskin and Dickson dismissed such concerns as 'entirely irrelevant' and argued that the notion that a disciplinary authority could depart from its own procedural rules was 'too nihilistic a view of law ... to accept.'[31]

Having lost the battle to have the disciplinary decision categorized as 'quasi-judicial,' Martineau and his dedicated prisoners' rights lawyer, John Conroy, did not give up. They revived alternative proceedings and asked that that Court recognize a general duty of fairness that would give Martineau procedural rights even if the disciplinary matters were not 'quasi-judicial.' If past cases were any indication, it would be difficult to convince the courts to intervene. By the time Martineau returned to the Supreme Court a second time, however, Laskin and Dickson had persuaded the Court to change the law. Ironically for the prisoners' rights movement, this change was made in a case in which a police constable had been dismissed from his position.

'No right to be arbitrary ... there is a halfway house'

The police case involved a probationary constable named Nicholson. Regulations in Ontario provided an explicit right to a hearing only when actual constables as opposed to probationary ones were dismissed. In his conference notes, Dickson characterized the issue as 'whether the Regulation means what it says, or whether there is an inherent right to be heard.' Although he noted that many of his colleagues believed that, given the wording of the regulation, Nicholson was 'out of luck,' Dickson 'took the view that there was a halfway house between a full-hearing and a right to be arbitrary. I do not think the legislation intended the granting of an arbitrary right or of unfair treatment.' His rough, handwritten notes simply state; 'no right to be arbitrary ... there is a halfway house.'[32] Although Dickson noted that Laskin had been 'doubtful' at conference, Laskin went on to write a landmark decision to which Dickson and three other judges agreed. The narrow majority held that the probationary constable had a right to be treated fairly in the sense that he 'should have been told why his services were no longer required and given an opportunity, whether orally or in writing as the Board might determine, to respond.' Laskin picked up Dickson's language and described the new duty of fairness 'as a halfway house ... between the observance of natural justice ...

and arbitrary removal.'[33] Dickson's dissent in *Howarth*, proclaiming a general but flexible duty of fairness, had become the law only five years after it was penned.

When Martineau's case reached the Supreme Court the second time, more than the law concerning fairness had changed. A parliamentary committee chaired by Mark MacGuigan had issued a damning report after a series of prison riots. MacGuigan argued that 'there is a great deal of irony in the fact that imprisonment – the ultimate product of our system of criminal justice – itself epitomizes injustice' because of the absence of a fair system of justice behind the walls. The committee had concluded: 'It is essential that the Rule of Law prevail in Canadian penitentiaries.'[34] Yet some judges still took a hands-off approach. The Federal Court of Appeal had dismissed Martineau's second case on the traditional basis that, where a prisoner has a grievance with respect to decisions that were not classified as quasi-judicial, 'his remedy is political.'[35] The Supreme Court, however, was no longer willing to accept this restrictive line of reasoning.

Dickson was assigned the task of writing a majority judgment.[36] He rejected 'narrow or technical' approaches to when a person's rights were affected because the task of the courts was not only to protect formal rights but also 'to assure the proper functioning of the machinery of government.'[37] Fairness for Dickson was more than a duty owed to individuals; it was, as well, a vital component of proper governance in the public interest. The state's duty of fairness went beyond the individual interests at stake to encompass the principle that all state power should be exercised with human decency and within the limits of the rule of law. Dickson's understanding of fairness was an amalgam of a liberal's insistence that individuals be treated fairly and a communitarian's concern that the state not abuse its powers.

Dickson concluded that the disciplinary board had a duty to act fairly because its decision deprived the prisoner 'of his liberty by committing him to a "prison within a prison." In these circumstances, elementary justice requires some procedural protection. The rule of law must run within penitentiary walls.'[38] This last statement echoed the recommendations of the MacGuigan committee, but with the added force of a Supreme Court decision. As a commentator noted, Dickson's elegant phrase took on a life of its own and was cited by Canada as fulfilling its international obligations to respect the rights of prisoners.[39] The Court's decision established 'for the first time in Canada that prisoners are not totally without a claim to procedural protection for disciplinary steps taken against them during their confinement,' and, in doing so, it 'opened the modern era of prison law and exposed internal parole and prison processes to judicial scrutiny.'[40]

The rule of law under Dickson's expanded view of fairness did not necessarily mean a court-like hearing. He cautioned judges that 'the power of judicial review must be exercised with restraint. Interference will not be justified in the case of trivial or merely technical incidents.'[41] Dickson was concerned that prisoners be treated fairly before important decisions such as the denial of parole or the imposition of discipline were made, but he was also reluctant to require that they be given a full court-like hearing. Compromises were not without their risks. Some commentators expressed concerns that the new doctrine of fairness was 'diluted "natural justice"'[42] For Dickson, however, it was better to run this risk than to have no duty of fairness for most state decisions affecting individuals.

Another factor in Dickson's approach was his rejection of fine or arbitrary distinctions and his growing enthusiasm for a flexible and functional approach to legal questions. In Dickson's view, it was 'wrong ... to regard natural justice and fairness as distinct and separate standards.' The ultimate issue 'in all cases dealing with natural justice and with fairness' was whether 'the tribunal on the facts of the particular case acted fairly towards the person claiming to be aggrieved.'[43] This holistic approach reflected Dickson's distaste for complex, uncertain, and artificial categories in the law. Rather than investing energies on fine and technical points of classification, Dickson believed that judges should rely on their common sense and their basic sense of fairness and decency.

Dickson worked hard on his *Martineau II* judgment, going through six drafts, two of which he wrote out by hand. His expansive and flexible approach turned out, however, to be too sweeping to command a majority at the time. Pigeon ended up writing a short judgment for the majority. Yet even he had to concede that administrative decisions were now subject to a duty of fairness.

A final case involving prisons demonstrates that, while Dickson's views of the obligations of governments to act fairly were broad, they were not limitless. Significantly, the case involved a claim that a prison guard as opposed to a prisoner had been treated unfairly. The guard, named Evans, had been denied a promotion after a parliamentary committee had criticized him for precipitating a riot at Millhaven Penitentiary in 1976 by telling the inmates over a loudspeaker, 'Come on girls, pick up your skirts and pull it. No stabbings in the yard tonight, the blood bank is running low.' Dickson provided the context, noting that Millhaven was a prison with a history of violence since its opening 'in an atmosphere of brutality borrowed from the violence of Kingston Riot' of 1971.[44] The majority of the Court was concerned that the civil service appeal board had not made an independent determination of whether the parliamentary committee's criticism of Evans was correct and held that the guard had not been treated fairly when he was denied a promotion.

Dickson disagreed. He pointedly observed that 'when there is whiff of injustice in the air arising from possible misapprehension of facts, the natural tendency of the courts is to case about for some means of ascertaining the true state of affairs and put matters right. But there are limits.' Dickson believed that the prison guard's reputation, whether deserved or not, was relevant to his merit for promotion. It was 'impractical' to give 'every candidate the opportunity of refuting evidence adverse to his or her candidacy.'[45] Dickson drew a contextual distinction between the disadvantaged position of prisoners who had parole revoked or were punished in solitary confinement and the comparatively advantaged position of a prison guard who was denied a promotion because a parliamentary committee concluded that he had provoked a prison riot. Everyone had a right to fair treatment, but context mattered. It was most important that the weakest be treated with decency and fairness.

'To hear both sides'

Dickson was even more familiar with universities than prisons, having served on the Board of Governors of the University of Manitoba until his departure to Ottawa to take his place on the Supreme Court. His respect and belief in the mission of Canadian universities was so profound that he courted public controversy in the mid-1980s when he spoke publicly against the decisions of governments to cut their funding.[46] Dickson's fondness for universities did not mean, however, that they did not have to treat their students and faculty fairly. For Dickson, fairness would only enhance the stature and respect due to universities.

As in the prison cases, Dickson first wrote in dissent in cases involving universities, with the majority of the Court eventually moving closer to his views. A 1979 case involved a social-work student, George Harelkin, who had been required to discontinue his studies at the University of Regina. Harelkin had not been able to appear before or submit material to the committee of professors who made the decision. The majority of the Court denied his appeal by relying on a 1969 precedent[47] and holding that, since he could take a further appeal to the university Senate, any unfairness in the committee's decision could be cured without resort to the courts. Dickson saw the case differently and, as in the prison cases, his dissent won praise from academic commentators.[48] He sympathized with the position of the student who 'was entitled to know why he was being expelled – be it unsatisfactory marks, as stated in the Dean's letter, or a tendency to be neurotic in his ideas, as stated by Professor Hanowski. And he was entitled to respond to and correct any statements prejudicial to his position.'[49] Dickson's conference notes indicated that he did not want 'to burden a University with a mountain of legalities,' but that the legislation provided two hearings and 'we would be acting improperly in denying him one of those hearings.'[50] The legislation required the committee of professors 'to hear' the case. To hear quite simply meant 'to hear both sides.'[51]

A year later, Dickson wrote for a majority of the Court in another case in which he concluded that a university had acted unfairly. A professor had been suspended without pay for three months by a university president for unauthorized use of computer facilities. The professor was allowed to present his case before the Board of Governors. The university president who had suspended him was by law part of the Board of Governors. He did not vote on the professor's appeal, but he did remain with the board as it deliberated on the matter over an evening meal and answered some questions about the case during that time. The suspended professor, of course, was not invited for dinner and did not have a chance to respond to the president's answers.

Dickson concluded that the whole process lacked the appearance of fairness. As a former chair of the University of Manitoba's Board of Governors, he was careful not to impugn 'the integrity or bona fides' of the governors, who 'normally serve without remuneration in the discharge of what is frequently an arduous and thankless form of public service.'[52] Nevertheless, he concluded that the board's dismissal of the professor's appeal must be overturned. Dickson again appealed to the basic meaning of a hearing. It required the governors not only to listen to both sides but also to allow each side an opportunity to correct or contradict the other's statements. In order to enjoy autonomy from the courts, the university must act fairly. Dickson dismissed Ritchie's argument in dissent that an opportunity to respond would have done the professor no good. For Dickson, the courts should not be concerned 'with proof of actual prejudice, but rather with the possibility or the likelihood of prejudice in the eyes of reasonable persons.' Justice must not only be done but seen to be done. Even if it would not change the outcome, a fair hearing had an intrinsic value while an unfair process would 'engender bitter feelings of injustice.'[53] Fairness for Dickson was a matter not only of treating individuals with respect but also of promoting the bonds of community.

Dickson's experience as a bencher of the Law Society of Manitoba who had served on its discipline committees made him familiar with the painful process of professional discipline. As with prisons and universities, Dickson's familiarity with the process did not lead him to be complacent about the need for fair treatment. In a 1974 case involving the discipline of a lawyer, members of a discipline committee who had found the person guilty of professional misconduct were present when their findings were reviewed by the entire governing body. Dickson found this troubling, stating, 'I do not like a judge to be sitting in appeal of his own decision.'[54] A majority of the Court, however, decided that the overlapping of functions was permissible because it had been clearly authorized by statute.[55] Dickson agreed with Laskin, who argued in dissent that the case 'cries out for judicial intervention in accordance with accepted principles of administrative law.'[56] When a similar case came back to the Court a year later, Dickson, with the concurrence of Laskin, Spence, and Ritchie, wrote that the idea of 'institutional bias or participation by association should not ... be rejected out of hand as a possible ground for apprehension of bias.' He also warned that 'to avoid criticism,' professional bodies should not rely on statutes which might authorize overlapping functions because they had a 'duty to be scrupulously fair to those of their members whose conduct is under investigation and whose reputation and livelihood may be at stake.'[57]

In most cases, statutes did not prevent Dickson from developing a common law bill of rights in the form of an implied duty that public bodies act fairly. In a 1978 case, Dickson argued that by requiring governmental bodies to act fairly, the courts were using the common law to fill 'the legislative omission ... in order to give such procedural protection as will achieve justice and equity without frustrating the parliamentary will as reflected in the legislation.'[58] A year later, he concluded even more strongly that 'natural justice and fairness are principles of judicial process deemed by the common law to be annexed to legislation, with a view to bringing statutory provisions into conformity with the common law requirements of justice.'[59] Dickson's administrative-law decisions did not demonstrate the concerns about overextending the judicial role that had led him to part company with Laskin in *Harrison v. Carswell*.

'Boards make mistakes – as do courts'

Dickson's insistence that the state owed those affected by its decisions a judicially enforceable duty of fairness was accompanied by an insistence that courts should take a relatively deferential approach to the review of governmental decisions on matters that did not concern fairness. This might be seen as a paradox in Dickson's thought, as well as in the Supreme Court's approach to administrative law. Yet such a reading underplays Dickson's insistence that, even when courts defer to the state, they must not abdicate their role in reviewing governmental action. At a more philosophical level, it also ignores how communitarian strands in his fairness cases laid some of the theoretical ground for the deference cases. Fairness was important not only for the individual but also for the community. At the same time, fairness should not be applied in such a way that would unreasonably impair the regulatory interests of the community. A similar misreading of Dickson might lead some to characterize his later Charter cases, when he more frequently deferred to the state and especially to state action designed to protect the disadvantaged, as inconsistent with other decisions that stressed liberal and individualistic values.

Dickson, however, did not see any conflict between liberal and communitarian strands of legal principle. For him, the state's claim to respect and deference from the courts depended on its willingness to observe the basic tenets of fairness and to offer reasonable justifications for its actions.

Dickson was prepared from the start to defer to the decisions of labour boards as long as they were reasonable and fair. In a 1973 case he upheld a labour board decision not to certify an association of nurses as a union on the basis that the association was dominated by the employer. He concluded that 'if the Board acts in good faith and its decision can be rationally supported on a construction which the relevant legislation may reasonably be considered to bear, then the Court will not intervene.'[60] A handwritten note in the case file reveals the essence of Dickson's approach. 'Boards make mistakes – as do courts ... Every mistake does not go to jurisdiction – merely reflection of an agency of humans. If honest and fair – have jurisdiction. Board with special expertise represents labour and management.' His notes also stressed that the judicial review was 'not an appeal.'[61] This early decision recognized that courts should defer to the legitimate range of decisions that could be made by administrative boards

Another case involved the application of the much-criticized 'jurisdictional fact doctrine.' This doctrine effectively allowed reviewing courts to substitute their views for the fact finding of administrative bodies if the facts were deemed necessary to give the administrative body jurisdiction over the matter. The case involved a probationary civil servant named Jacmain who had been dismissed. He had previously gotten into trouble with his employer over what Dickson characterized as 'troublesome and abrasive' conduct. The civil servant claimed that he was entitled to a full hearing because he had been let go for disciplinary reasons. An adjudicator found this to be the case, but the majority of the Supreme Court held that the adjudicator had erred in finding that the dismissal was for disciplinary reasons. It classified the factual finding about the reasons for the dismissal as a 'jurisdictional fact' and applied a 1971 precedent which held that courts should intervene whenever they thought administrative tribunals had made a mistake in determining a 'jurisdictional fact.'[62]

Although the parties had not cited one piece of academic literature in their factums, Dickson's clerks fully briefed him on the savage academic criticism surrounding the Supreme Court's 1971 case.[63] Dickson knew that his judgment would be a dissent, with the support of only Laskin and Spence, but he worked hard to create a way out of the dichotomy between courts second-guessing agencies in their determination of 'jurisdictional facts' or not reviewing even perverse findings by agencies. Dickson wanted to avoid the extremes of either allowing an administrative body 'an unlimited power to determine the extent of its jurisdiction' or subjecting 'the correctness of every detail to retrial in the Court' with 'the opinion of a judge substituted for that of the tribunal.' Although the latter extreme came perilously close to what the Court's precedents stood for, Dickson followed the academic critics by arguing that it sacrificed 'the special experience and knowledge' of administrative bodies, as well their advantage of 'hearing and seeing the witnesses.'[64] Dickson again chose a 'halfway house.' On the one hand, jurisdictional review by the courts should not be abandoned because it was 'a useful tool to ensure that tribunals deal with the type of issues which the Legislature intended.' On the other hand, courts should not exercise a 'trial de novo' on jurisdictional facts. Rather, they should give the administrative tribunal 'some latitude' so long as it 'reached its decision honestly and fairly and with due regard to the material before it.' In a draft of his judgment, Dickson indicated that he thought that the adjudicator was right to hold that the troublesome employee had been dismissed for disciplinary reasons. But he quickly added that his views about the correctness of the decision were 'not important' and he eventually deleted the whole passage from his judgment.[65] The important point for Dickson was that judges should intervene only if the agency had made a manifest or grievous error. His innovative approach was praised by academic commentators, but even they pointed out that it was not supported by any of the Court's precedents.[66] As in the fairness cases, however, Dickson's approach was on the ascendancy and he would soon win a majority for his dissenting views.

'Patent unreasonableness'

A year later, Dickson's most famous administrative-law decision was released. Although it built on many of the themes in his previous dissent, it commanded the agreement of a unanimous Court. The case involved a public-sector labour dispute in New Brunswick. The union, the Canadian Union of Public Employees (CUPE), obtained a ruling from the Public Service Labour Relations Board that the employer had violated the law by having management do work in liquor warehouses and stores during the strike. Although Dickson ultimately deferred to the labour board's decision, his conference notes suggest that 'there seems, as a point of common sense, to be little reason why management personnel could not be used in a strike.' Had he been a manager, Dickson's instincts would have been to pitch in during a strike to keep the business going. Nevertheless, Dickson also could see the labour board's side of the story. If management did the work of the strikers, there might be 'no limit as to the persons who could be used.'[67] In a note that he jotted down during oral argument, Dickson reminded himself that 'this Court does not sit as an appeal tribunal and one cannot ask oneself what interpretation one would have if seized of the question' decided by the board.[68]

In his judgment, Dickson recognized that 'the question of what is and is not jurisdictional is often very difficult to determine' and that courts should not 'brand as jurisdictional, and therefore subject to broader curial review, that which may be doubtfully so.'[69] The labour board was 'not required to be "correct."' Whether 'rightly or wrongly decided,' its decision deserved respect because of the board's specialized experience in public-sector labour relations, which called for 'a delicate balance between the need to maintain public services and the need to maintain collective bargaining.' The board was also protected by a statutory provision which declared that its decisions were final and not to be questioned or reviewed in any court. Courts had traditionally found their way around such privative clauses, when it suited them. Dickson believed that such clauses should slow the courts down but not necessarily stop them from intervening. In what was to become one of the most important phrases in Canadian administrative law, he warned that the courts should intervene only if 'the Board's interpretation was so patently unreasonable that its construction cannot be rationally supported by the relevant legislation and demands intervention by the courts upon review.'[70] Despite his own inclinations to allow management to fill in during a strike, Dickson upheld the board's decision. Years later, he explained that 'unless the decision is one which is very offensive because it goes absolutely against all the evidence or all the arguments and is patently unreasonable, the decision should stand. It may be one that we agree with, it may be one that we disagree with, but if it is reasonable ... I didn't think the judiciary should take it upon itself to say, "you decided this incorrectly."'[71] Dickson's approach was based on deference to the agency and not on a general scepticism about whether there were right answers to legal questions.

CUPE was quickly heralded as a watershed judgment. David Mullan, a leading administrative-law professor, observed that it was a 'refreshing change' and a 'significant advance' because it recognized the 'autonomy and prerogatives of expert statutory authorities.'[72] The decision was so quickly accepted that, within five years, Dickson was able to cite it for the proposition that there was a 'customary judicial deference to specialized administrative tribunals.'[73] At the same time, however, *CUPE* was a halfway house that preserved a role for judicial correction of patently unreasonable errors. This was judicial deference, not judicial abdication.

In the mid-1980s, the Supreme Court reasserted its ability to determine if administrators had exceeded their jurisdiction, especially when ordering a remedy. In a judgment written by Beetz, but agreed to by Dickson, the Court indicated that 'once a question is classified as one of jurisdiction,' courts could not 'refrain from ruling on the correctness of that decision.'[74] The decision was criticized by a number of commentators as a retreat from the qualified deference of *CUPE*. In a 1988 decision involving a labour arbitrator,

Dickson moved the Court back towards a more deferential posture. Even if the arbitrator erred in law by restoring employees fired for misconduct during a strike, the error was not patently unreasonable and the courts should allow the body with expertise in labour relations to settle the dispute.[75] A year later, Dickson again deferred to an order by a labour arbitrator that an employer provide only certain facts when prospective employers asked for references about a former employee who had been wrongfully dismissed. Beetz dissented on the basis that such a restriction on the employer's free speech was 'totalitarian.'[76] Dickson was more willing to tolerate state intervention. He stressed that the arbitrator's order 'was a legislatively sanctioned attempt to remedy the unequal balance of power that normally exists between an employer and employee.' Prohibiting the arbitrator from restricting the employer's freedom of expression 'would be tantamount to condoning the continuation of an abuse of an already unequal relationship.'[77] Even with Charter concerns about the employer's freedom of expression added to the balance, Dickson still drew a contextual distinction between the advantaged position of the employer and the disadvantaged position of the wrongfully dismissed employee. As in the prison cases, it mattered to Dickson whether the person claiming relief from the Court was an advantaged employer or prison guard or a disadvantaged employee or a prisoner.

'In favour of the Indians'

In aboriginal rights, as with administrative law, Dickson began to find his own distinctive voice in dissent. The 1979 *Jack* case asked whether any fishing rights were protected in the Terms of Union under which British Columbia entered Confederation. Article 13 provided that the federal government agreed to take 'the charge of Indians' and to pursue 'a policy as liberal as that hitherto pursued by the British Columbia government.' In a short judgment for all members of the Court except Dickson, Laskin summarily concluded: 'I see nothing in art.13 that could possibly operate as an inhibition on federal legislative power in relation to fisheries.'[78] Laskin saw the case through his concern for federal power and without any particular sympathy for the position of aboriginal people.

Dickson dismissed arguments that federal regulation of the fishery was immune from judicial review as 'untenable.' As in administrative law, he would not abdicate the Court's role. He also rejected Laskin's idea that the traditional approach to Indian fishing rights was a matter of mere 'expediency.' If an issue about aboriginal rights was ambiguous, 'it should be so interpreted as to assure the Indians, rather than to deny to them, any liberality which the policy of the British Columbia government may have evinced prior to Union.' This was Dickson's first articulation of the principle that ambiguities should be resolved in favour of a generous interpretation of aboriginal rights. Dickson also suggested that 'one could suggest that "a policy as liberal" would require clear priority to Indian food fishing and some priority to limited commercial fishing over the competing demands of commercial and sport fishing.'[79] Here, he expressed for the first time the principle that the aboriginal fishery had priority over the non-aboriginal fishery. By the end of his career, he would convince a full Court to accept the principles of both generosity and priority with respect to aboriginal rights.

Dickson was generous in defining aboriginal rights, but he never saw them as absolute. He indicated that 'any limitation upon Indian fishing that is established for a valid conservation purpose overrides the protection afforded the Indian fishery by article 13.' This reflected his constant belief that aboriginal rights could be limited and regulated for conservation reasons. In the end, Dickson supported the majority's decision to affirm Jack's conviction for fishing for food on the basis that the government was permitted to prohibit all salmon fishing because of conservation concerns about below-average salmon runs and record-low precipitation. Even on this issue, however, Dickson attempted to link conservation concerns to aboriginal perspectives by noting that it appeared from the historical evidence that 'the Indians themselves practiced some form of self-imposed discipline for conservation purposes' and that 'they do not claim the right to pursue the last living salmon until it is caught.'[80] This represented an important first attempt by Dickson to incorporate aboriginal practices and perspectives into his decisions.

A year later, Dickson decided a hunting-rights case from Manitoba in a bolder and more generous fashion than his earlier cases.[81] He struck down a Manitoba law that restricted Indian hunting 'over great tracts of Crown land' on the basis that 'its sole purpose is to limit or obliterate a right Indians would otherwise enjoy.' Moreover, the provincial law invaded federal jurisdiction over Indians by singling them out.[82] Dickson strongly criticized Manitoba's actions as 'a blatant attempt to un-entrench ... and to derogate from rights granted to the Indians.' This would not be the last time that Dickson was critical of the attempt of his home province to take away the constitutional rights of minorities.[83] Unlike in his earlier Manitoba hunting-rights cases, Dickson supported his conclusions by reference to the treaties. The Cree and Salteaux had surrendered 'a large part of what is now the Province of Manitoba in exchange for reserves (one square mile for family of five), small cash payments, powder, shot, ball and twine and gardening and carpenters' tools' and the 'right to pursue their avocations of hunting, trapping and fishing throughout the tract surrendered ... '[84] Dickson's knowledge about the treaties and his implied doubts about their generosity influenced his expansive interpretation of the hunting rights.

As in his *Jack* dissent, Dickson stressed that the right to hunt should be given 'a broad and liberal construction' with any doubts being decided 'in favour of the Indians, the beneficiaries of the rights.' Even though several judges had been sceptical at the conference, Dickson indicated that 'the Indians' right to hunt for food ... is paramount and overrides provincial game law regulating hunting and fishing.'[85] His willingness to give Indians any benefit of a doubt and priority over non-aboriginal hunting and fishing, both articulated a year earlier in his *Jack* dissent, resurfaced, but this time in a unanimous judgment.

Dickson's changing approach to aboriginal issues can be explained by a number of factors. One was his growing confidence as a judge. Another was the fact that he could draw on more resources to assist him in understanding aboriginal legal claims. When Dickson first joined the Court, there were few law schools teaching native rights, and many people, including Prime Minister Trudeau, thought that the course of justice was to give aboriginal people the same rights as other Canadians.[86] In the late 1970s and early 1980s, however, the attitudes of many Canadians towards aboriginal people changed. Dickson and his law clerks took advantage of increased thinking and writing about aboriginal issues in the law schools and in the law reviews. Dickson closely followed the debates over the inclusion of aboriginal rights in the 1982 constitutional amendments. Although he did not express it in the same public way as Thomas Berger, Dickson had sympathy for aboriginal demands and he felt that Laskin had overreacted in his criticism when Berger, then a judge on the British Columbia Supreme Court, spoke out in favour of including aboriginal rights in the constitutional package.[87]

In 1983, one year after aboriginal rights were restored into the constitutional package, Dickson persuaded the whole Court to agree to the generous approach to interpreting aboriginal rights that he first had articulated in his solo 1979 judgment in *Jack*. Dickson declared the important interpretative principle that 'treaties and statutes relating to Indians should be liberally construed and doubtful expressions resolved in favour of the Indians.'[88] The case arose not from a treaty but attempts by Revenue Canada to collect income tax on the wages of an Indian logger living on a reserve. For Dickson, the 'plain and ordinary meaning' of the Indian Act demanded an exemption from taxation on wages earned on reserve. If there had been any ambiguity, however, Dickson was prepared to adopt the interpretation that was most favourable to the Indians. In the last half of the 1980s, he would rely on this principle to take an even more generous approach to aboriginal rights.[89]

Basic Decency and Fairness

Dickson and the Court were gaining ground in the late 1970s and early 1980s. In both administrative and aboriginal law, Dickson first articulated many of his innovations in dissent, often with Laskin's agreement. This contrasts with

Dickson's reluctance to dissent and his frequent disagreements with Laskin during his first few years on the Court. Dickson gradually became more confident in his own abilities and more certain of the Court's responsibilities to develop the law. He was clearly influenced by Laskin, whom he greatly admired, but he was also prepared to disagree with him and take a more generous approach to aboriginal rights. Dickson's jurisprudential innovations were driven by his impatience with arbitrary classifications, his search for creative compromises or halfway houses, and his overriding concern for treating people, especially the more disadvantaged, with basic decency and fairness.

Brian Dickson, 1984, chief justice of Canada

Sarah Elizabeth 'Lillian' Gibson
in Ireland

Thomas Dickson, 1926

Lillian and Thomas Dickson with Brian,
1916

Brian and Thomas Dickson
circa 1921

Brian and Tom riding a pony with
cousins in Ireland

Brian and Thomas Dickson growing up
in Saskatchewan

Brian and Tom, circa 1932

Family picnic – Tom, Lillian, Thomas and Brian

Regina, 1932. William Lederman and Sandy MacPherson (top row) and
Brian Dickson (middle row)

Law school graduation, 1938

In training at Camp Shilo, Manitoba, 1940

Canadian Officer Training Corps, England, 1943. Brian Dickson seated far right

Wedding day, Winnipeg, 18 June 1943

Prime Minister Louis St Laurent with Brian Dickson, Winnipeg Flood, 1950

Winnipeg Flood Headquarters, 1950. (l to r): Clarence Shepard, Brian Dickson, Governor General Viscount Alexander, Stuart Stanbury, George Sellers

Deborah, Barbara, and Brian with Peter and Barry, 1954

Brian Dickson, at Aikens MacAulay

Mianki: Harry Sellers, Brian and Barbara Dickson, and Brian Dickson, Jr.

Queen's Bench judge, 1963

Supreme Court of Canada, 1973

Chief Justice Bora Laskin, 1975

Supreme Court building, Ottawa

Supreme Court of Canada, 1975. (l to r seated): Wilfred Judson, Bora Laskin, Prime Minister Pierre Elliott Trudeau, Ronald Martland, Roland Ritchie; (standing): Jean Beetz, Louis-Philippe Pigeon, Wishart Spence, Brian Dickson, Louis-Philippe de Grandpré

Supreme Court of Canada, 1977. (l to r): Willard Estey, Brian Dickson, Wishart Spence, Ronald Martland, Bora Laskin, Roland Ritchie, Louis-Philippe Pigeon, Jean Beetz, Yves Pratte

Main courtroom, Supreme Court of Canada

Judges' conference room

Visit by American Chief Justice Warren Burger, September 1985. (l to r): Ambassador Tom Niles, Chief Justice Warren Burger, Prime Minister Brian Mulroney, Chief Justice Brian Dickson

Brian Dickson, Jr, hooding his father at honorary degree ceremony, University of Toronto, 20 June 1986

Riding at Marchmont

Supreme Court of Canada, 1987. (Seated, l to r): William McIntyre, Jean Beetz, Brian Dickson, Willard Estey, Antonio Lamer; (standing): Gérard La Forest, Bertha Wilson, Gerald Le Dain, Claire L'Heureux-Dubé

Supreme Court of Canada, 1989. (Seated, l to r): Gérard La Forest, Antonio Lamer, Brian Dickson, Bertha Wilson, Claire L'Heureux-Dubé; (standing): Peter Cory, John Sopinka, Charles Gonthier, Beverley McLachlin

Seventy-fourth birthday with law clerks and their families, May 1990

Gowning for court, June 1990, with Court attendant Lou Lefebvre

Riding with grandchildren at Marchmont, 1990. (l to r): Karen and Lisa Shields,
Eric and Graham Dickson

At Marchmont with Derry, 1990

Pierre Trudeau and Brian Dickson, luncheon at the Law Faculty Common Room, before Trudeau's convocation address at the opening of the Bora Laskin Law Library, 21 March 1991

Pierre Trudeau giving convocation address entitled 'Patriation and the Supreme Court of Canada' at Convocation Hall, University of Toronto, 21 March 1991

Brian Mulroney, Barbara Dickson, Brian Dickson, Mila Mulroney

Fortieth wedding anniversary, 18 June 1983

Fifty-fifth wedding anniversary, Marchmont, 18 June 1998. (Standing, l to r): Peter Dickson; Deborah, Chris, Lisa, and Karen Shields; Graham, Brian, Kate, and Eric Dickson; Brian, Dana, and Barry Dickson; (seated): Brian and Barbara Dickson.

9

Compassion and Equity

In the late 1970s and early 1980s, Dickson played an important role in reforming the private law. Especially where the legislature had not stepped in, he was willing to innovate in a bold and sometimes quasi-legislative manner. As in other areas, he was attracted to general and simple principles. The concerns about substantive fairness that animated Dickson's public-law decisions were present in his private-law decisions as well. He wrote several landmark judgments requiring that women have their contributions recognized when their marriages ended. He was also prepared to provide remedies for the abuse of power, whether by governments, corporations, or individuals. He demonstrated, too, considerable compassion to the injured. While not imposing civil liability in the absence of fault, he was opposed to arbitrary restrictions on liability for injuries caused by negligence and he insisted on full compensation for all the financial losses of personal injury. At the same time, Dickson imposed caps on damages for non-financial injuries such as pain and suffering. As a person who had suffered a serious injury, he knew the importance of full financial compensation but also the limited ability of money to repair pain and suffering.

'I couldn't have done it without my dear wife'

Following the liberalization of divorce laws in 1968, the courts were confronted with many more cases stemming from the dissolution of marriages. One of the most difficult issues was the division of property after a marriage had ended. Men traditionally had the legal title to the family home or the family farm, and women could not obtain their share unless the court was prepared to find that the man held the title in trust for the woman. The law contemplated a trust only if there was some concrete evidence of the couple's intention that the woman had an interest in the property. Couples who married during a time of low divorce rates rarely specified what should happen to the house or the farm if the marriage ended.

Dickson wrote an important series of judgments recognizing that women had valid claims to an equitable division of property acquired during their spousal relationships, even though legal title to the property was in their partner's name. In these judgments he used an innovative legal vehicle – the constructive trust – to recognize the contribution of women to the accumulation of property during a marriage. His decisions were based on the equitable principle that no one should be unjustly enriched at the expense of another. Breaking with the restrictive approach used by both the Supreme Court and other courts in the Commonwealth, and, in sharp contrast to his decision in *Harrison v. Carswell*, Dickson followed and advanced Bora Laskin's desire to reform the law to take on modern realities rather than waiting for legislative reform. In doing so, he took positions that Laskin had articulated in dissent and turned them into majority judgments. These decisions showed Dickson as a law reformer, but they were also guided by his sense that the flexible principles of equity could be applied and administered by the courts in a predictable manner.

Dickson's reforms in family law were very much in touch with the times. By the end of the 1970s, most provinces had enacted legislation to ensure a more equitable distribution of matrimonial property between men and women. As Dickson noted in a 1981 speech to other judges on family law, 'the legislative response has been to vest very wide discretionary powers in the judiciary, not noticeably different from that envisaged in the application of the law of constructive trust.' In his view, 'a wide discretion is inescapable' because of 'the complexity and subtlety of the myriad of marriage relationships.'[1]

The Supreme Court heard the (in)famous case of *Murdoch v. Murdoch* in March 1973, the month that Dickson was appointed to the Court. As often happened during this time of civil appeals as of right, the nine-man Court sat with only five judges, and Dickson was not one of them. The Court denied Irene Murdoch's claim to a ranching operation, despite the twenty-five years of hard physical labour that she had contributed to its development before her marriage ended. Martland, for the majority, concluded that Murdoch had not made direct financial contributions and that there was no evidence that the ranch, which was held in her husband's name, was intended to be shared should the marriage break down.

In a lone dissent, Laskin argued that Mrs Murdoch was entitled to a share in the ranch on the basis of the equitable vehicle of a constructive trust. In

Laskin's view, 'a court with equitable jurisdiction is on solid ground in translating into money's worth a contribution of labour by one spouse to the acquisition of property taken in the name of the other, especially when such labour is not simply housekeeping, which might be said to be merely a reflection of the marriage bond. It is unnecessary in such a situation to invoke present-day thinking as to the co-equality of the spouses to support an apportionment in favour of the wife.' Laskin conceded that legislative reform in this area might be preferable but, in a memorable phrase, argued that 'the better way is not the only way.'[2]

The case gained an unusual amount of publicity, almost all of it critical. Martland's comments that Mrs Murdoch's work was only 'the usual work of a farm wife'[3] led to a story in the popular press entitled 'The law as male chauvinist pig.' In a report calling for urgent legislative reform, even the Law Reform Commission of Canada declared that 'the conscience of Canadians was shocked by the application of the present law ... in *Murdoch* ... such law is no longer tolerable in a society that professes its laws to be both humane and just.'[4] As one historian of the Court has noted: 'The reputation of the Supreme Court was damaged in the minds of many while that of Laskin soared ... Within three months Laskin was to be named chief justice, passing over the other judges, and in particular Martland, who was the senior judge.'[5] Dickson later remembered that 'Bora, for his dissenting judgment, was declared the folk hero of Canada, and very much lauded and applauded, whereas the others were somewhat criticized and denigrated.'[6]

Despite the many disagreements between the two men about other cases at the time, Dickson's sympathies were clearly with Laskin. He remembered that, when Laskin showed him a draft of the *Murdoch* dissent, it seemed 'to be very fair and reasonable and just.'[7] In a 1977 speech to law students, Dickson praised Laskin for using the equitable device of a constructive trust 'in a novel but far-sighted remedial way in order to achieve an equitable result in a matrimonial property dispute,'[8] even though Laskin was writing in dissent and Dickson would not normally comment on such a division in the Court. Having grown up on the prairies, Dickson appreciated the important contribution of women to farm life. He also recognized that his own wife had brought many assets, intellectual, social, and financial, to his marriage and that these assets had contributed to his success as a lawyer and judge. The case was almost certainly a topic of discussion in the Dickson household since Barbara Dickson took an active interest in the cases before the Court and the notoriety of *Murdoch* could not have escaped family discussions.

Five years after *Murdoch*, Dickson had the opportunity to write a judgment in a similar case involving the claims of another farm woman, Helen Rathwell. Like the Dicksons, the Rathwells had been married shortly before Lloyd

Rathwell went overseas to fight in the Second World War. Dickson's conference notes started with the statement: 'This is the case in which the husband and wife were married during wartime. He was in the Army and she was in the Airforce.' Upon Lloyd Rathwell's return from overseas, the newly married couple put their wartime savings (about $700 each) into a joint bank account. This money was used to purchase four quarter-sections of farming land in 1946 and 1947 under the Veterans's Land Act. As required by that act and as was the custom in western Canada at the time, the title to the Rathwells' land was held in the husband's name. In 1958 and 1959, the Rathwells purchased more land from the joint account. Dickson's conference notes, but curiously not his judgment, indicate that in the late 1960s, 'for reasons which do not appear on record, the marriage broke up. One night at about 3.00 A.M. the husband phoned the wife stating that he was going to sell the farms. He was drunk at the time. The wife immediately retained a lawyer who filed a caveat in which she claimed a ten per cent interest.'[9] This incident was significant to Dickson. From his years as a trial judge hearing divorce cases – the only part of a trial judge's work that he did not like – Dickson often said that there was no such thing as a friendly divorce.

The trial judge dismissed Mrs Rathwell's case. He chauvinistically dismissed the fact that the Rathwells had referred to the land as 'ours': 'I am able to take judicial notice that husbands (other than a foolhardy and valiant few) who desire a life of peaceful co-existence within the matrimonial bailiwick rather than either a hot or cold war, habitually use the diplomatic and ambiguous "ours" rather than the forthright and challenging "mine" when referring to anything of monetary value.'[10] Dickson observed in his conference notes that the trial judge had 'reflected a marked bias against such a claim.'[11] The trial judge had also been influenced by the fact that Mrs Rathwell had been awarded $250 a month in maintenance and indicated that 'she's not going to get it both ways ... Somebody has to defend the men from the present mode of the women's liberation movement.'[12] Again Dickson noted 'bias' beside this quotation.

Dickson approached the case with an appreciation of the important role that women played on farms. Lloyd Rathwell had acknowledged that his wife 'contributed to an extent.' Dickson pointedly added: 'It was to a considerable extent. Mrs. Rathwell did the chores when her husband was busy on the land; she looked after the garden and canned the produce; she milked cows and sold cream; she drove machinery, baled hay, provided meals and transportation for hired help and kept the books and records of the farming operation. She raised and educated four children.' Dickson looked beyond the farm to the broader social context to observe that, because of 'a more enlightened attitude toward the status of women, altered life-styles, dynamic socio-economic changes,' 'increasingly, the work of a woman in the management of the home and rearing of the children, as wife and mother, is recognized as an economic contribution to the family unit.' Spouses could contribute through either 'money' or 'caring for the home and family.'[13] This went beyond Laskin's dissent in *Murdoch*, which did not recognize housekeeping or the raising of children as a contribution that might require the courts to impose a constructive trust to ensure that the husband was not unjustly enriched at the wife's expense.[14]

In some ways, given the law at the time, *Rathwell v. Rathwell* was an easier case than *Murdoch v. Murdoch* to decide in the wife's favour. Drawing on her wartime earnings as a clerk in the air force, Mrs Rathwell made an equal contribution to the couple's joint bank account after the war and the additional land was purchased from that bank account. Martland would have given Mrs Rathwell some interest in the land on the traditional basis of an intentional or resulting trust. Dickson, however, believed that the intent-based approach was artificial. 'It is not in the nature of things for young married people to contemplate the break-up of their marriage and the division, in that event, of assets acquired by common effort during wedlock.' Mrs Rathwell should be awarded a half-interest on the basis of equitable principles against unjust enrichment that operated regardless of the couple's intent. 'As a matter of principle, the court will not allow any man unjustly to appropriate to himself the value earned by the labours of another. That principle is not defeated by the existence of a matrimonial relationship between the parties ... .'[15] General principles were more important than the status of the parties. Although he noted that critics labelled it 'palm-tree justice,' Dickson embraced the 'justice and equity' approach favoured by Lord Denning, the reform-minded and sometimes renegade English judge.[16] Nor did Dickson shy away from the fact that this equitable approach gave judges considerable discretion. In his view, judicial discretion guided by the 'certainty of legal principle' was 'capable of redressing injustice and relieving oppression.'[17] Dickson was attracted to abstract and general principles because they helped simplify the law and were flexible enough to allow judges to achieve justice on the facts of the case.

Dickson's law clerks urged him to overrule *Murdoch*,[18] but he tried to sidestep the unpopular precedent by arguing that the constructive trust approach had not been fully argued or explicitly rejected in *Murdoch*. Dickson was prepared to say that he 'would not, with utmost respect, follow *Murdoch* to the extent that it stands in the way of recognition of constructive trust as a powerful remedial instrument for redress of injustice.' Dickson's expansive and equitable approach won the support only of Laskin and Spence, forming the reform-minded LSD triumvirate. The more restrictive intent-based approach of the majority meant that many women, who, unlike Mrs Rathwell, had made no direct financial contributions to the family property, would not receive any interest in houses and farms when the marriage ended.

Dickson relied on the work of academics to support his constructive-trust approach. His extensive working notes on the case are heavily annotated with cut-outs from various academic sources from the United States, England, and Canada. He was particularly influenced by Canadian scholars such as Donovan Waters, who argued that the traditional intent-based approach was 'in many cases a mere vehicle for giving the wife a just and equitable share in the disputed asset' and 'in fact a constructive trust approach ...'[19] and predicted that judges would manipulate the concept of intent to reach just results. Increasingly influenced as well by Laskin's more policy-conscious approach to legal doctrine, Dickson thought it best to acknowledge directly that the courts would find an equitable solution regardless of the couple's intent. Not surprisingly, his decision received attention in the law journals, where it was praised as a 'boldly innovative' and 'original and thoughtful contribution.'[20] Mr Rathwell's counsel, however, wrote a case comment criticizing the Dickson approach as 'judicial activism.'[21]

Dickson also got some feedback from the public. A.B. McGillivary wrote Dickson to ask why he had not fully repudiated *Murdoch* and suggested that legislation was necessary 'to ensure a wife one half the property of both upon divorce ... It should not be left to lawyers or judges to decide the degree of contribution made by each – not unless they have lived with them for at least 20 years.' Dickson, assuming the letter-writer to be male, addressed his reply to 'Mr. McGillivary': 'I was pleased to learn of your interest in this recent decision of the Court. It is a long-established and salutary custom that it is not open to members of the Court to expand on the specific matters contained in a case. The judgment must speak for itself. I was interested, however, to read your proposals for legislative change.'[22]

The intent-based approach that Dickson rejected was based on 'the very clear common law principle that the individual's right of property is fundamental to the system, and it is not for the courts to assume the power to take property from one person and give it to another simply because that seems to the particular court a fair solution.'[23] Dickson's usual concern for property rights and his deference to legislative reform might have led him to leave family-law reform to the legislature, however, in the late 1970s, he was starting to take a less absolute view of property rights and a more expansive view of judicial lawmaking. While acknowledging that the use of constructive trusts 'reflects a diminishing preoccupation with the formalities of real property law and individual property rights,' he argued that an approach stressing justice and equity was 'more in keeping with the realities of contemporary life.'[24]

In 1980 Dickson had another chance to persuade his colleagues to accept the constructive trust. The case involved Rosa Becker's claim against her common law spouse, Lothar Pettkus. They had been together for almost twenty years. For the first six years, they had lived on Rosa Becker's earnings. Pettkus used his income to purchase a bee farm held in his name. Rosa Becker worked hard on the bee farm and the couple bought more properties. With his usual attention to detail and human interest, Dickson noted that 'Miss Becker pulled her fair share of the load: weighing only 87 pounds, she assisted in moving hives weighing 80 pounds. Any difference in quality or quantum of contribution was small.'[25] Since Becker and Pettkus never married, their case was not subject to family-law legislation and its resolution would depend on how the judges developed the common law.

Rosa Becker, like Helen Rathwell, was treated poorly by the trial judge in large part because she was a woman. The trial judge concluded that Becker's payment of virtually all household expenses during the early years of the relationship was 'in the nature of risk capital invested in the hope of seducing a younger Defendant into marriage.' Pettkus was five years younger than Rosa Becker. Dickson, who now knew that his own mother was two years older than his father, bristled at the trial judge's biased remark and observed in his judgment that the passage lacked 'in gallantry.'[26] The trial judge awarded Becker only 40 of over 400 beehives, without bees, and $1,500, representing the earnings from the hives during the last few years. This was worse than Becker had received from Pettkus, who had thrown $3,000 on the floor and told her to take their 1966 Volkswagon and forty beehives with the bees. This incident was significant to Dickson at a number of levels. He again took note of the often ugly circumstances surrounding the break-up of a marriage. He also believed that Pettkus's actions supported the idea that Becker had a reasonable expectation to the assets.

Rosa Becker, who had left her common law relationship claiming emotional and physical abuse from Pettkus, fared better on appeal. In a judgment written by Bertha Wilson that relied on Dickson's judgment in *Rathwell*, the Ontario Court of Appeal awarded Becker a half-share in the bee farm by means of a constructive trust. Wilson realized that her judgment was 'a calculated risk' because she relied on the equitable constructive-trust approach articulated by Laskin in *Murdoch* and Dickson in *Rathwell* and ignored the fact that this approach had yet to win support from the majority of the Supreme Court.[27] Wilson would join Dickson as a colleague in 1982 when Prime Minister Trudeau made her the first woman to sit on the Court. *Pettkus v. Becker* was not her only innovative decision while on the Ontario Court of Appeal, she also wrote a decision recognizing a new civil action for discrimination that Laskin (with Dickson's agreement) reversed on the basis that the statutory human rights code precluded a separate civil action.[28] However, in *Pettkus v. Becker*, Dickson admired Wilson's attempts to reform the common law. He would later recall that Wilson's judgment represented an important effort to reform the law 'to reflect changes in our community's values' such as 'radical shifts' in the 1960s and 1970s 'towards marriage and divorce.'[29]

Only five judges were originally scheduled to sit on *Pettkus v. Becker*. Three days before the hearing, Chief Justice Laskin sent a memo to the Court that stated: 'I feel that a full Court should sit because it involves issues that were raised in *Rathwell* and on which not all members of the Court were agreed.'[30] The full Court would now decide between the traditional intent-based approach advocated by Martland and Ritchie and the more expansive constructive-trust approach championed by Laskin and Dickson. Dickson's conference memo indicates that the divisions on the Court were clear: 'Judge Ritchie plans to write and so do I. He will take the route of the resulting [or intentional] trust and I the route of the constructive trust.' As he would in many cases, Dickson did not allow the fact that a majority of the Court had not yet accepted his views to move him off his position. There were dangers, however, in not accepting the majority's approach. At the conference, Dickson had the clear support only of Laskin, and, since Spence had retired at the end of 1978, it was possible that the LSD position would be reduced to an even more isolated Laskin and Dickson dissent.

The Court that heard *Pettkus v. Becker* in June 1980 was, however, a much different court from the one that had heard *Rathwell* only three years earlier. Willard 'Bud' Estey had been appointed by Prime Minister Trudeau in September of 1977. At the time he was chief justice of Ontario and had already headed two royal commissions and the Ontario High Court. Like Dickson, Estey was born in Saskatchewan and had served in the Second World War, but, unlike Dickson, he had been a litigator and had done graduate work at Harvard. Estey's father had also served on the Supreme Court from 1944 to 1955. When appointed to replace Judson, most believed that Estey would gravitate towards the LSD wing of the Court.[31] Dickson played a significant role in Estey's appointment. Laskin lobbied hard for the appointment of his old friend, Charles Dubin, of the Ontario Court of Appeal, but got nowhere with the government and there was an impasse. Dickson invited the Laskins and 'a senior cabinet minister' to Marchmont for a Sunday lunch. 'After lunch the minister and the chief justice went for a walk along the shore and came back about two hours later all smiles.' Estey's appointment was announced the next day.[32]

William McIntyre had been appointed at the start of 1979 by Trudeau to replace Spence. He, too, had grown up in Saskatchewan and served in the war. He had been a respected trial and appeal court judge in British Columbia, best known for his decision that the death penalty was inconsistent with the Canadian Bill of Rights, a decision that the Supreme Court including Laskin and Dickson disagreed with.[33] McIntyre's appointment broke the usual convention of three Ontario judges. This was done to placate the British Columbia bar which thought the province had been ignored, and on an understanding with Ontario Attorney General Roy McMurtry that when Martland retired he would be replaced by someone from Ontario. Although McIntyre took a fairly restrictive approach to the Charter – as Dickson later put it, 'he anchored the right wing of the Court after Martland's retirement'[34] – he took an expansive view of equality and was a likely ally for Dickson in *Pettkus v. Becker.*[35]

Julien Chouinard had been appointed by Prime Minister Joe Clark later in 1979 to replace Yves Pratte. Although appointed by a Conservative government, it was reported that Chouinard 'was not expected to change the political balance of the court.' Chouinard was a former Rhodes Scholar, law teacher and senior Quebec civil servant. He had been on the Quebec Court of Appeal for four years but for three of those years had chaired a royal commission on bilingual air-traffic control. The junior member on the Court that would hear *Pettkus v. Becker* was Antonio Lamer, who was only forty-three years of age. Appointed in March 1980 by Pierre Trudeau, newly restored to power, Lamer had previously been a criminal law professor, the head of the Law Reform Commission of Canada, and a trial and appeal court judge in Quebec. Dickson befriended Lamer from the start of his time at the Supreme Court. Lamer would sometimes rise in the early hours of the morning so that he could arrive at Marchmont for Dickson's early morning rides and the Lamers and the Dicksons went to the Grey Cup together in Montreal.[36] Lamer's appointment was particularly symbolic and important. The energetic young law reformer replaced the traditional and cautious Pigeon, a pattern that would be repeated two years later when Trudeau appointed Wilson to replace the retiring Martland.

Even though there had been little support for his constructive-trust approach at conference, Dickson worked hard on his reasons in *Pettkus v. Becker* and hoped that he could convince the new members of the Court. Citing the famous Lee Marvin palimony case, Dickson concluded that there was no reason why the constructive-trust approach should not be applied to a common law relationship. 'This was not an economic partnership nor a mere business relationship, nor a casual encounter. Mr Pettkus and Miss Becker lived as man and wife for almost twenty years. Their lives and their economic well-being were fully integrated.'[37] In Dickson's view, the status of the litigants was not relevant to the principle of preventing unjust enrichment. He added, however, that he was not legislating a regime of equal property for common law partners, something that the Ontario legislature had not done in its family-law reform legislation, but only ensuring that no partner was unjustly enriched simply because they were not married.

Dickson instructed his clerk that he wished to '"fine-tune" the concept of constructive trust,' especially 'in light of comment, favourable or unfavourable, which attended the *Rathwell* decision.' Sensing the prospect of securing a majority, Dickson indicated to his clerk that he wanted 'to emphasize that there is nothing novel in the concept'[38] and he deleted a reference in a draft judgment that suggested he was overruling *Murdoch*, even though he would later make the following acknowledgment in a letter to Donovan Waters: 'I share your view that the Canadian law of matrimonial property would have been much improved had a majority of the Court accepted the minority views expressed by Bora Laskin in *Murdoch*.'[39]

In his judgment, Dickson argued that the constructive trust was a flexible and ancient tool of equity that could 'accommodate the changing needs and mores of society, in order to achieve justice.'[40] It was organized around the simple yet powerful principle of preventing unjust enrichment. Pettkus had been enriched at Becker's expense on account of her contributions and work, and there was no juristic reason to justify the transfer. Becker had a reasonable expectation that she would have a share of the bee farm. Pettkus had done nothing to disabuse her of that expectation and had freely accepted the benefits of her work. Equity would not be achieved if he was unjustly enriched. Dickson circulated a draft judgment that gave Rosa Becker only 40 per cent of the business and property, and not the 50 per cent that Bertha Wilson had awarded in the Court of Appeal. After objections from Laskin, Estey, McIntyre, and Lamer, however, he changed his judgment to order a 50/50 split. Chouinard also joined the opinion. The tables were turned and Dickson now had a majority, with only three judges, Martland, Ritchie and Beetz, supporting the more traditional intentional-trust approach.

Martland, the author of the now thoroughly discredited *Murdoch v. Murdoch*, wrote a particularly vehement dissent. The imposition of a constructive trust 'has very wide implications and involves judicial legislation in that it extends substantially the existing law.' Dickson's extension of the law was, in Martland's view, 'undesirable. It would clothe judges with a very wide power to apply what has been described as "palm tree justice" without the benefit of any guidelines. By what test is a judge to determine what constitutes unjust enrichment? The only test would be his individual perception of what he considered to be unjust.'[41] These were strong words of criticism from a colleague whom Dickson liked and respected. The next year Dickson responded at a national conference on family law, 'palm tree justice,' Dickson argued, was 'a catchy phrase' and a 'deprecatory epithet' but not one that should be directed at the constructive trust. The new remedy was 'not based on any notion of paternalism or unlimited judicial discretion but rather on the simple equitable principle' that no one should be unjustly enriched. He quoted academics who argued that the new approach was not 'likely to cause chaos or lessen predictability.' Dickson also noted that the many legislatures that enacted new family-law legislation in the late 1970s had also granted 'very wide discretionary powers in the judiciary, not noticeably different from those envisaged in the application of the law of constructive trust. And one might ask – how could it be otherwise? Matrimonial disputes do not readily lend themselves to resolution in a detailed and rigid formulary.'[42]

Dickson defended his equitable approach to a constructive trust in such broad and flexible terms that it could be applied to a broad array of business and individual relations. He observed that 'it would be undesirable, and indeed impossible, to attempt to define all the circumstances in which an unjust enrichment might arise.' The constructive trust was 'a useful tool in the judiciary armory' because it could apply whenever there was an unjust enrichment. This would occur whenever there was 'an enrichment, a corresponding deprivation and absence of any juristic reason for the enrichment.' The term 'juristic reason' was novel and made the general principles of fairness that animated the judgment seem more precise.[43] Dickson's approach laid the foundations for the subsequent development of the law of restitution based on the broad principles of unjust enrichment.

Dickson's decision was inspired not only by the principles of equity but also by Quebec's Civil Code. His formulation of the principle against unjust enrichment was remarkably similar to what he later praised as 'the elegant structure' and 'logical, clear and to the point approach' taken by Jean Beetz in a 1977 judgment that recognized the principle of unjust enrichment under Quebec's Civil Code.[44] Strangely, however, Dickson did not cite the Civil Code case, even though he had signed on to Beetz's opinion. Just as strange was that Beetz joined Martland's vehement dissent criticizing Dickson's unjust-enrichment approach as 'palm tree justice.' Both men may have been reluctant to cross-pollinate the Civil Code and the common law. At the same time, the parallels between the cases are striking. Dickson may have been more open to civilian influences than his other anglophone colleagues. Because of his willingness to work in French, Dickson sat on more than his share of Civil Code cases and he admired the way the civilian system used scholarly analysis to articulate general principles of law. Dickson respected the Civil Code as an integral part of Quebec's distinct society and would have disagreed with Pierre Trudeau, who, in the course of his opposition to the constitutional recognition of Quebec as a distinct society, argued that most of Quebec's laws 'are the product of a juridical culture far more closely related to that of other provinces than to the laws of New France or the Napoleonic Code.'[45] In a 1990 speech opening the World Congress of the Academy of Comparative Law, Dickson described the Supreme Court of Canada 'as a Mecca for Comparative Law' in which the judges were in an unique position to compare 'the basic values, principles and rules of both legal traditions' while also respecting the separate nature 'of these two "great" traditions.'[46] Dickson's judgment in *Pettkus v. Becker* followed his desire for a distinctively Canadian jurisprudence. It did not slavishly imitate either English or American law on the subject[47] and drew on Canada's bijuridical heritage.

Dickson's decision was warmly received in the media and by commentators. Whether 'consistent with precedent or not,' *Pettkus v. Becker* 'accepted the changing face of community expectations' both with respect to the equality of the sexes and the role of common law relationships.[48] The *Globe and Mail* in an editorial entitled 'Fair Shares,' praised Dickson's decision for its fairness and its recognition that in a common law relationship 'there is the same dependence, the same bond, the same sense of sharing – and the same feeling when the two parties separate that each has an interest in the fruits of the marriage.'[49] A spokesperson for the Ontario Status of Women Council lauded the decision as a 'a major change in the interpretation of the role of the woman in a common-law relationship.'[50] Doris Anderson, president of the Canadian Advisory Council on the Status of Women, was a little less glowing, observing that Dickson's judgment showed 'a glimmer of sensitivity to the criticism heaped upon the Court by those concerned with women's rights.'[51] A family-law scholar wrote that the decision 'indicates that the changing composition of the highest court has produced a Bench which is increasingly liberal and prepared to enter into the process of formulating "judicial legislation" ... The radical change of approach from *Murdoch* to *Pettkus* has demonstrated that to achieve ... the goal of accommodating "the changing needs and mores of society" ... the Court is prepared to disregard its own precedents, even those of recent vintage.'[52]

Although she was awarded a half-interest in the bee farm, valued at $150,000, and became a hero in the battle for women's rights, the matter did not end happily for Rosa Becker. She told reporters that she could not go out to celebrate the judgment delivered just before Christmas in 1980 because she 'was broke.' She foresaw trouble collecting from Lothar Pettkus because 'when it comes to giving money, he's very stingy. We may have a little battle with him.'[53] She was right: she and her lawyer had great trouble collecting the Court's award. While hospitalized in Ottawa in 1984, Rosa Becker sent Dickson a plaintive letter by registered mail: 'Dear your honour! I beg you to see me and listen to me.' The letter indicated that Becker's mental health had suffered. 'I see things before they happen.' She indicated that she had taken ill during her marriage because she 'could foresee what would happen to me when we sold the farm. What Pettkus did to me was very sickening.' The letter was also addressed to Dickson's new colleague on the Court, Bertha Wilson. Dickson showed Wilson the letter and Wilson commented, that it was indeed a 'sad case.' Dickson's secretary wrote Becker a courteous but firm reply that explained: 'The Chief Justice has asked me to say that he has read your letter, but it will not be possible for him to see you. After a judgment in a case has been delivered, it is not possible for any of the Judges to discuss the case or take part in subsequent events.'[54] A few years later, Rosa Becker committed suicide.[55]

Dickson wrote a third judgment solidifying the place of the constructive trust in family law. The case involved another common law farming couple, the Sorochans, who had lived together for forty-two years and raised six children. Dickson's handling of the case underlined the compassion that animated his approach. The case was crammed onto the last day of the Court's busy term, just before its summer recess, when it was struggling with its new responsibility under the Charter and had almost seventy judgments under reserve. Dickson had been informed that Mrs Sorochan was fatally ill and he wanted her to have a judgment during her lifetime. 'For the next three weeks, at a time when he must have been tired ... he worked incessantly to write the judgment'.[56] The Court summoned the parties back on 31 July 1986. The late July judgment day and the release of a judgment that had not yet been translated into French were rare and the atmosphere in the Court was emotional.[57] The press noted that 'the court had reached a decision in near record time after the woman ... in documents filed with the court ... said she believed she did not have long to live.'[58]

Dickson's decisions in these three family-law cases changed the law. It may have made a difference that in each case the claim was made by a farm woman. Dickson's detailed description of the work done by Helen Rathwell, Rosa Becker, and Mary Sorochan indicates his appreciation of the hard work of farming and the important role of women on farms. His decisions also reveal a strong inclination to view all marriages as equal partnerships, a view that was quickly adopted by most legislatures, albeit in legislation that was not always as sensitive to the circumstances of each individual case as Dickson's constructive-trust approach. Rathwell and Sorochan had assumed a traditional but valuable role as stay at home wives and mothers. Becker's role was somewhat less traditional, but Dickson refused to allow her status as a common law partner to affect the application of the principle against unjust enrichment. The overriding issue for Dickson was not the status of the parties but the principle of avoiding unjust enrichment.

Dickson's descriptions of the situation of the three women also suggests that he had genuine compassion for their situation. In a 1986 commencement address at the University of Toronto just before Dickson heard the Sorochan case on an expedited basis, he argued that compassion must be part of the law. 'For the law to be just, it must reflect compassion. For a judge to reach decisions which comport with justice and fairness, he or she must be guided by an ever-present awareness and concern for the plight of others and the human condition.'[59] Dickson looked to the flexible and discretionary remedies of equity and its tradition of basing decisions on broad principles of good conscience and justice to find a place for compassion in the law.

Dickson's approach to family law also reflected his own experience of marriage as an equal partnership. His career as a corporate lawyer and director of banks and other large companies had undoubtedly been assisted by Barbara Dickson's connections as the daughter of Henry Sellers, a wealthy and successful businessman. More important, Dickson's own marriage was an equal partnership. In a touching speech when the Dicksons returned to Montebello, Quebec, the site of their honeymoon, to celebrate their fiftieth wedding anniversary with family and friends, Dickson remembered his marriage as 'the time my life began.' He composed a poem about their life together:

> Perhaps as she listens to speech 44.
> Not an inkling she gives that she's heard it before
> And oh the postmortems that go on each night
> 'What do you think' and 'was it all right?'
> And when it's all over remember the person
> Who really has earned that glass of champagne, the speeches and toast
> Then comes that speech which is truer than most
> I couldn't have done it without my dear wife ...'[60]

Dickson's talent for judgment writing plainly surpassed his capacity for poetry, but it was from the heart and it contained much truth. Before marrying, Dickson had been a talented but underemployed clerk at an insurance company. During his marriage, he rose to the pinnacle of the legal, corporate, and judicial establishment of Canada. He genuinely believed that he could not have done so without his wife, and his family-law decisions demonstrated that, as a judge, he was prepared to recognize the important contributions that women made to other marriages.

'Common humanity'

Dickson had a faith in first principles, such as the prevention of unjust enrichment and responsibility for reasonably foreseeable harms in negligence or tort law, and he was willing to reject artificial but traditional restrictions on liability tied to the status of either the plaintiff or the defendant. In one early case, Dickson rejected what he saw as 'procrustean and often vain attempts' to limit liability because the injured party could be classified as a trespasser. Dickson, the outdoorsman, identified with a snowmobiler who was out 'for an evening of healthful recreation through woods and across lakes in Northern Ontario' when he was knocked off his snowmobile and seriously injured by an unmarked pipe. 'It has not been found easy to reconcile the Victorian landowner's unbridled rights with the modern law of negligence,' but the latter, in Dickson's view, should prevail. He rejected restrictions on civil liability tied to the plaintiff's status because they were complex and uncertain and because they imposed artificial restrictions on the general principles of negligence. The landowner had a duty to treat even a trespasser with 'common humanity' by responding to foreseeable risks.[61] The reference to the obligations of 'common humanity' revealed a compassionate side to Dickson's understanding of tort law.[62]

Dickson rejected the law's traditional preference for railways in personal injury cases. As he stated in conference notes dealing with one such case, 'the time has come to recognize that a railway is in no better or worse position than any other Canadian with respect to negligence ...'[63] He expressed the same concern in somewhat more cautious tones in his judgment. Restrictions on the liability of railways may have once been in 'the interests of a young and undeveloped nation' but in 'a more developed and populous nation this attitude of laissez faire may have to yield to accommodate the legitimate concern of society for other vital interests such as the safety and welfare of children.'[64] Dickson upheld the railway's liability for a seven-year-old boy who had lost both his legs when he had fallen under the wheels of a slow-moving, mile-long freight train. The railway should be liable for foreseeable risks caused to children regularly crossing railway tracks that had no barriers and no attendants. Dickson's rough notes for judgment contained what for him was the heart of the case: 'The basis of liability is the foreseeability of harm to the child. Considerations of common humanity.'[65] Dickson rejected the railway's argument that the boy or his parents bore responsibilities for the tragedy. Noting that the boy's mother was at home tending to a sick brother and that his father, who worked night shifts, was asleep, Dickson argued that 'the railway company knew, far better than the parents, when a train would be passing. The railway company created the danger and was in the best position, with the least inconvenience, to protect the children exposed to the danger.'[66] The fact that Dickson himself had lost his leg may have allowed him to empathize with the boy and the difficulties he would face throughout his life.

Dickson also rejected the idea that professionals were in a more favoured position when it came to holding them liable for their negligence. A 1976 case involved a claim by an investor in Moose Jaw, Saskatchewan, who had relied on an accountant's financial statements. An unsupervised student prepared the statements and they contained serious errors. When the investor lost his money, he sued the accountant. The accountant argued that he could not be held responsible for the economic losses of a person he had never known. Dickson's old high school friend, Sandy MacPherson, had been the trial judge and found for the investor on the basis that the accountant ought to have known that investors would rely on the negligent audit. The Saskatchewan Court of Appeal overturned MacPherson's judgment on the basis of a well-known American authority that expressed what Dickson later called the 'bogey man' of professionals being exposed to indeterminate and unlimited liability.[67] Writing for the majority of the Court, Dickson restored MacPherson's judgment, and in doing so he drew on his extensive experience with the corporate world, investments and accountants. 'The day when the accountant served only the owner-manager of a company and was answerable to him alone has passed. The complexities of modern industry combined with the effects of specialization, the impact of taxation, urbanization, the separation of ownership from management, the rise of professional corporate managers, and a host of other factors, have led to marked changes in the role and responsibilities of the accountant, and in the reliance which the public must place upon his work.' The 'added prestige and value' of accountancy for Dickson also produced 'a concomitant and commensurately increased responsibility to the public.'[68] Consistent with general principles of tort law, accountants should be liable to all those they ought to know would rely on their audits.

'Money cannot obliterate anguish and suffering'

In January 1978 the Court decided a trilogy of cases dealing with the assessment of damages arising from negligent accidents which left the victims severely injured. The lead case involved a twenty-one-year-old man, James Andrews, who had been rendered a quadriplegic in a traffic accident. Andrews had been awarded over a $1 million at trial, one of the highest ever awards in Canada at the time. The Alberta Court of Appeal halved this figure because the trial judge had contemplated home care for the plaintiff rather than less expensive institutional care. The Court of Appeal had also reduced the plaintiff's non-pecuniary damages for 'pain and suffering' from $150,000 to $100,000. Dickson's conference memo suggests that several members of the Court were concerned with the 'astronomic' award of damages for home care, which would include 'full-time orderlies per day, plus housekeeper, plus, plus,

plus!'[69] The conference note, however, suggests nothing of the surprising trade-off that Dickson would fashion so that a unanimous Court would accept the generous award for home care.

Dickson criticized the Court of Appeal for suggesting that the plaintiff desired home care because it was 'the most expensive.' In his view, it was reasonable for Andrews to have home care as opposed to having to 'languish in an institution which on all evidence is inappropriate to him.' There should be full damages for the 'injuries of the innocent party'[70] without regard, in the era of mandatory insurance, to the effects of damage awards on defendants. Years later, in a speech to American doctors preoccupied with high damage awards, Dickson explained that even though the cost of home care was more than four times the cost of institutional care, 'the difference in the quality of life these individuals would have at home was demonstrably superior to that available in an institution. We held that they were not required to mitigate their damages by accepting a less expensive, but inferior type of care.'[71] Dickson had experienced the differences between institutional and home care while recovering from his devastating wartime injuries.

Although he was generous in assessing the plaintiffs' financial needs, Dickson upheld the Court of Appeal's reduction of the pain and suffering damages to $100,000 and held that this was a new cap for all such damages. This cap was truly innovative and Dickson's case files contain no hint that he was inspired by the arguments of the lawyers in the case or by any law-reform proposal. Years later, he candidly explained that the cap on non-pecuniary damages was 'a trade-off' designed to respond to concerns about the total award being over a $1 million because of the generous award for the cost of home care.[72] The cap may have been a pragmatic compromise, but Dickson justified it by arguing that any award for pain and suffering would be 'arbitrary' because there was no market or 'medium of exchange for happiness.'[73] Courts should take a functional approach that would award money to provide solace to the plaintiff but not attempt to replace the irreplaceable. The Canadian cap was far from trivial, but it also stopped the growth of pain and suffering awards that were adding to the cost of insurance in the United States.

Although he restored the trial judge's award for pecuniary damages, Dickson worried that any calculation of a lump-sum award could miss the mark because, after judgment, 'new needs of the plaintiff arise and present needs are extinguished.'[74] Dickson himself had a second operation some time after his leg was amputated and had gone through long periods of adjustment to his injury. The wealthy former corporate lawyer who had represented Great West Life and even drafted some of its insurance policies strongly hinted that he would prefer to see legislatures bring in state-funded no-fault schemes for personal injuries that would avoid the cost and delay of litigation and the 'disturbing ... disparity resulting from lack of provision for victims who cannot establish fault ...' This statement revealed Dickson's communitarian side and his compassion for all injured people. At the same time, he believed that this type of wholesale reform would require legislation. In the meantime, the courts must apply fault-based principles and 'award damages which compensate accident victims with justice and humanity for the losses they may suffer.'[75]

Dickson was willing to legislate a cap on non-pecuniary damages and stick to it. In a 1981 decision in which the plaintiff had suffered extensive brain damage that made him unable to communicate with others, Dickson reduced non-pecuniary damages to the $100,000 level. He summarized his approach to full financial damages and capped damages for pain and suffering in clear and eloquent terms: 'Anything having a money value which the plaintiff has lost should be made good by the defendant. The first and controlling principle is that the victim must be compensated for his loss.'[76] At the same time, 'a lost limb or a lost mind are not assets that can be valued in monetary terms. Money cannot repair brain damage or obliterate anguish and suffering.'[77] Dickson knew from his own personal experience that even significant wealth could not compensate for the pain and suffering that accompanied serious injury.

'Inexcusable confusion and unnecessary complexities'

One of Dickson's most important private-law judgments dealt with the relevance of a breach of a statute for liability in tort. The case is also interesting because it allowed Dickson to re-visit a topic that he had addressed forty-five years earlier as a fourth-year law student at the Manitoba Law School when he wrote his undergraduate thesis on the same subject. The case involved a lawsuit by the Canadian Wheat Board to collect significant damages from the Saskatchewan Wheat Pool for the delivery of grain infected by rusty beetle larvae. The grain had been visually inspected and shown no signs of disease, but a more elaborate test revealed that the grain was infected. By the time the results were known, the grain was already on a ship that then had to be diverted and fumigated. The Canadian Wheat Board sought damages not on the basis that the Saskatchewan Wheat Pool had been negligent in delivering the infested grain, but rather on the basis it had breached a provision of the Canadian Grain Act that prohibited the delivery of infested grain. The trial judge found the Wheat Pool liable on the basis of breach of statutory duty as opposed to negligence. Dickson, who by this time had taken a strong stand against no-fault liability in criminal law,[78] noted that the trial judge's statutory duty approach made liability 'absolute and not qualified ... evidence of reasonable care on the part of the defendant ... was not sufficient to absolve the Pool of civil liability.'[79]

Dickson prefaced his judgment by noting that 'the commentators have little but harsh words for the unhappy state of affairs'[80] produced by the conflicting cases on the relevance of breach of a statute to civil liability. Things were no better than in 1938, when he had concluded in his unpublished student paper that 'a review of the cases reveals much inexcusable confusion, and a number of unnecessary complexities.'[81] In his 1983 judgment, Dickson confessed that 'arriving at a solution, from the disarray of cases, is extraordinarily difficult.'[82] Nevertheless with characteristic attraction to flexible first principles, Dickson proceeded to achieve an elegant solution from the 'disarray of cases.'

In a twenty-three-page judgment that quoted extensively from over ten academic sources from England, the United States, and Canada, Dickson concluded that breach of a statute should be considered only as evidence of negligence as opposed to a separate cause of action. This conclusion avoided the injustice of imposing heavy liability on a defendant who may not have been at fault, and it accorded with the general trend away from separate torts to a general theory of civil responsibility based on negligence. It was always open to the legislature to amend the legislation if indeed it intended that any breach of a statute should result in liability.

Dickson's judgment was also remarkably similar to the approach he had recommended as a fourth-year law student. In his 1938 paper he had warned that basing liability on breach of statute ran the danger of 'imposing liability without fault' in cases 'in which the standard set by the Legislature may [be] too lenient or too severe for the purpose of tort law.'[83] The Manitoba Law School had succeeded in teaching Dickson the importance of clarity and attention to basic principles. Even as a fourth-year law student, he had been keenly aware that a rigid rule could result in injustice and take away the ability of a jury to determine whether the defendant had acted reasonably in all the circumstances. As both a student and a judge, he approached the welter of cases on statutory breach with a focus on what was appropriate for the purpose of tort law and with a faith in general and flexible principles of liability based on negligence.

With its clear, numbered conclusions, its survey of cases and commentary, its reluctance to impose liability without fault, and its articulation of lucid and general first principles, Dickson's judgment was a classic that was lauded by the profession and the academy alike. His colleague Antonio Lamer wrote a memo stating, 'Your opinion is probably one of the best you have written to my knowledge, if not the best coming out of this Court (I have not read them all!).' Lamer added that Dickson's approach was similar to that used under Quebec's Civil Code and noted that, although convergence between the common law and the civil law 'is not a necessary endeavor in all matters, it surely is not unwelcome when it happens.'[84] Canada's leading tort scholar, Allen Linden, who had recently been appointed to the bench, also wrote Dickson a congratulatory letter. He stated that reading the decision had left him 'breathless. Once again, you have taken a complex area of the law and analyzed it in its historical context, evaluated the competing policies and articulated a fresh, clear and sensible approach to the problem.' Linden noted that he would have to rewrite portions of his text on tort law and that he would send a copy of the judgment to his mentor, Professor John Fleming, the world's leading torts scholar. Linden also raised three questions about the case. Dickson took the questions seriously and had a law clerk assist him in researching his replies. He wrote back to Linden that he had refused to make breach of a statute prime facie evidence of negligence because the ultimate question 'is not did the defendant breach the statute but was the statutory breach negligent.' Dickson also explained to Linden that both this decision and an early one rejecting no-fault liability in criminal law were designed to provide 'a workable regime' and a 'sensible solution' so that 'when someone breaches a statute through no fault of his own, he will be safe' from both civil and criminal liability.[85] Dickson's opposition to no fault-liability and his concern about fairness transcended the boundaries of private and public law.

Dickson's judgment was praised in law journals both at home and abroad. A comment in the *Oxford Journal of Legal Studies* noted that the judgment was in accord with 'fault' as 'a pervading theme in the present structure of tort liability.' A commentator in the *Cambridge Law Journal* wrote: 'It would be too much to hope that Wheat Pool will have much impact here.' John Fleming also wrote approvingly of the case in his textbook.[86] In some ways, Dickson never went far from the textbook tradition of the rule-of-law followed at the Manitoba Law School. Dickson, like many text writers, placed his faith in general and flexible principles and was prepared to reform those parts of the common law that placed arbitrary restrictions on the application of those principles.

In a sense, scholars have the last word after the Supreme Court has delivered its judgments. Dickson frequently wrote his judgments and especially his dissents with an eye on what scholars were saying about a particular subject. Indeed, one of the reasons so many of Dickson's dissents eventually became the law was that they were often inspired by academic critique of the law and praised by academics for their principled approach to the law. In 1982 Dickson dissented in an important case in which the city of Nepean tried to recover money it paid to Ontario Hydro as a surcharge on electricity after it was determined that Hydro did not have the statutory power to levy such a surcharge. The majority of the Court applied an old but much-criticized rule that money paid because of a mistake of law as opposed to a mistake of fact could not be recovered. It argued that the old rule was supported by concerns about 'certainty in commerce and public transactions' and the disruption of 'undoing ... past concluded transactions.'[87]

Dickson dissented with the agreement of Laskin. He took a common-sense approach: 'To the layman, the issue would be a clear one. Nepean should succeed. Good conscience and plain honesty would require Hydro to repay. To the lawyer trying to follow confused and contradictory authority the matter is not that simple.' Characteristically, Dickson reached a position that he believed was supported by both common sense and principle. 'In my view, honesty and common justice require that Ontario Hydro repay Nepean the monies paid in the mistaken belief that Ontario Hydro had the authority to exact them.' Citing over fifteen academic authorities from Canada, England, and the United States, Dickson stressed that the distinction between mistakes of law and mistakes of fact was uncertain and complex because of 'numerous exceptions and qualifications.' Most important for Dickson, the distinction was not supported by principle. 'Once a doctrine of restitution or unjust enrichment is recognized, the distinction as to mistake of law and mistake of fact becomes simply meaningless.' Certainty was important in commercial matters, but in this case it would 'be better served by the non-recognition of a rule which sows confusion and which has so little to recommend it.' The fact that the distinction between a mistake of fact and a mistake of law was so difficult to explain and that the tests had become so convoluted indicated that the law was not grounded in principle. Principles for Dickson should be clear and easy to explain. The court should abandon complex and unnecessary classifications of mistakes as matters of fact or law and instead allow judges to determine whether 'on general principles of equity, it would be unjust to allow the recipient of the benefit to retain it.'[88] This was a broad equitable test similar to the constructive-trust approach that Dickson had defended in the family-law cases.

Dickson's dissent in this case won praise from academic commentators. University of Toronto contracts professor John Swan wrote Dickson: 'I consider your arguments unanswerable. I am only sorry that they were not shared by all members of the Court ... It is always very encouraging to read a judgment that treats academic views as relevant and important.'[89] Dickson sent a copy of Swan's letter to Laskin and warmly replied to Swan: 'I was naturally very pleased to receive your letter ... As you observed, I found the views of academics to be of great interest.' Dickson added: 'Although the judgment did not attract a majority, I would hope that we will get a case before too long in which the point can be considered again ...'[90] Seven years later, the point did come up again and the Court adopted Dickson's dissent.

Gérard La Forest, a former law professor himself, praised Dickson's dissent as 'a thorough, scholarly and damning analysis of the mistake of law doctrine ... What the judgment reveals is a rule built on inadequate foundations, lacking in clarity (the distinction between a mistake of fact and mistake of law can best be described as a fluttering, shadowy will-o'-the-wisp), and whose harshness has led to a luxuriant growth of exceptions.'[91] Dickson's reliance on scholarly critiques of the existing law helps explain the durability of many of his judgments, including his dissents.

We Cannot Correct Every Error

The discretionary process of granting leave to appeal and its effects on the number of private-law cases became a matter of some controversy. In a 1982 letter to a contracts professor, Dickson expressed his 'wish for a greater number of private law cases. The difficulty of course arises at the time of granting leave and in determining whether the case concerns only the interests of the immediate litigants or presents for consideration some broader issue which may be of national concern.'[92] As chief justice, Dickson took the message that there was no policy against hearing private law cases to the bar. He told the Canadian Bar Association in 1984 not to fear that the Court would hear nothing but criminal and constitutional cases. 'To my mind that would be completely inconsistent with our jurisdiction as a *general* court of appeal ...'[93] A year later, he told lawyers in Toronto that the rise in the number of Charter cases was to be expected, but that this should not 'be at the expense of private law cases.' He did not want the Court to 'become a specialized tribunal dedicated only to the resolution of constitutional litigation.'[94] But the number of private-law cases were on the decline. In 1983, the year before the Court started hearing Charter cases, they constituted almost a quarter of the Court's cases; in 1984 they were only 11 per cent of the cases and in 1985 only 16 per cent.[95]

When Bryan Williams, president of the Canadian Bar Association, gave a speech in September 1986 stating that 'because of the Supreme Court's current understandable preoccupation with *Charter* cases, criminal appeals and constitutional matters, many important commercial cases are not being granted leave at the Supreme Court level,'[96] Dickson reacted sharply. He asked Williams to prove his case: 'I would be grateful if you could give me the names of the "many important commercial cases" which were not granted leave by this Court. I would like to run through the papers.'[97] Williams was forced to retreat. He could not name a single case and conceded that his remarks were based on the perceptions of the bar.[98]

Part of the controversy reflected a lack of understanding about the Court's criteria for granting leave to appeal. Lawyers wanted the Court to hear cases to correct a perceived injustice to their clients. In one case, a Vancouver lawyer who represented a thirteen-year-old boy who suffered serious brain injuries in a motor-vehicle accident wrote Dickson that he 'felt awkward in writing to you but I do not know where else to turn. The client is without a remedy ... the case has been on my mind every day.'[99] Dickson himself wrote to the lawyer, assuring him that the case had 'been reviewed carefully by the three judges who sat on the leave panel and by myself. Although this is a sad case, we have decided that the decision of the panel not to grant leave was the correct one.'[100] The lawyer thanked Dickson for 'your kindness in reviewing this matter,' adding that Dickson's 'sympathetic letter is appreciated by myself and my client.' At the same time, he stated that the case had convinced him of the 'need for a different system of appeals.'[101] In another case, Dickson wrote that he appreciated a lawyer's 'concern with the plight of the plaintiff' but insisted that 'injustice to one or other party of litigation ... is not the primary criterion used to determine whether a case comes to the Court. This Court does not regard itself as a court of error, obliged to correct every error alleged to have been committed by a provincial court of appeal. I see the role of the Court as rather that of developing basic and broad legal principles which will guide the development of Canadian jurisprudence in the years ahead.'[102] Although he was not prepared to accept that the Court would seldom hear private-law cases, Dickson was comfortable with the idea that the Court's job was to develop general principles of law for the entire nation, as opposed to resolving disputes between parties.

First Principles and Compassion

Dickson did not hesitate to take bold steps in reforming the private law and he wrote a series of landmark private-law decisions in the mid- to late 1970s and early 1980s which continue to influence the law today. They were characterized by an embrace of general first principles such as liability for negligence and the prevention of unjust enrichment and a distaste for arbitrary restrictions on those principles tied to the status of the parties or the classification of the dispute. Many of the decisions demonstrated Dickson's overriding concern with equity and his compassion for those who deserved compensation and recognition. His loss of his leg probably influenced his approach to damages, both in demanding full compensation for financial losses and in recognizing the impossibility of compensating for pain and suffering, and his own experience in marriage made him sensitive to the important contributions that women made to family assets.

There was an important connection between the substance and form of Dickson's judgments that will be explored in the next chapter. Dickson's focus on basic principle led him, quite naturally, to a plain-language approach in which he carefully crafted his judgments to make them as clear and simple as possible. It also caused him to be unusually open to the assistance he could receive from both law clerks and legal academics in improving the quality and justice of the law.

10

Write and Rewrite

Dickson quickly earned a reputation as a writer of remarkably clear judgments. It cannot be said that his competition on the Supreme Court at the time was particularly stiff. There was a pronounced preference for legalistic judgments that were based upon an arid recitation of the relevant statutes and case law. Reference to scholarly writing was rare.[1] Most judges considered it to be neither necessary nor appropriate to discuss underlying policy considerations or to locate the legal issues in their broader social, economic, or political context. The Court often spoke in an obscure and technical legal voice, making little or no effort to render judgments that would be accessible to the ordinary Canadian.

Dickson worked hard or, as he would say, 'sweated blood,' to make his judgments as clear as possible. He started with laborious hand written drafts and often went through as many as ten versions before settling on the final product. In crafting his judgments, Dickson worked closely with his law clerks – the top recent graduates from law schools. He asked his clerks to search for cases from many jurisdictions and to probe the writings of the world's leading legal scholars. Dickson's case files are thick with photocopied, annotated academic writings, even though, especially in the early years, these writings were not always cited by the lawyers who argued the case. His working files suggest that often, especially when writing a significant judgment that broke new ground, Dickson was more influenced by the research of his clerks than by the arguments of counsel. Most of Dickson's law clerks went on to become full-time law professors in Canada's law schools. Dickson admired legal academics and was always interested in any assistance that their writings could provide. In turn, his judgments were often praised by academics and used as teaching tools. As seen in the previous two chapters, scholarly praise of Dickson's judgments helped produce some of the momentum that saw many of his dissents become majority judgments.

Dickson's approach to judgment writing was not only a matter of style and his willingness to write many drafts. It also reflected his views about the Court as an important national institution and about the substance of the law. For Dickson, it was 'imperative that our judgments be understandable to people who have not had legal training. We are not writing simply for legal academics or other judges. The cases we deal with ... affect every man, woman and child in the country.' Even the legal community needed accessible and clearly written judgments. Dickson thought of the busy trial judge 'reading these judgments of the Supreme Court of Canada late at night preparing for a jury charge ... It is very much easier for them to read something which is written in everyday language.'[2] The form and substance of judgments were, for Dickson, intimately connected. 'It is obvious that a person cannot write more clearly than he thinks' and the 'identifying badge of a superior judgment is a focus on principle and reason.'[3] Dickson often found overly technical, uncertain, and arbitrary legal concepts to be both unjust and difficult to explain.

'Sweating blood'

From the start, Dickson worked hard to make his judgments both interesting and even stylish. One early judgment dealt with a technical point of statutory interpretation. A large and recently amalgamated corporation argued that it should not be held responsible for outstanding price-fixing charges against one of the smaller companies it had absorbed. Dickson rejected this argument. The 'vestigial remnants' of the original company had not, in Dickson's sceptical words, been placed in a state of 'ethereal suspension ... Such metaphysical abstractions are not, in my view, a necessary concomitant of the legislation. The effect of the statute, on a proper construction, is to have the amalgamating companies continue without subtraction in the amalgamated company, with all their strengths and their weaknesses, their perfections and imperfections, and their sins, if sinners they be. Letters patents do not give absolution.'[4] Such stylistic flourishes, not to mention religious imagery, were rare in the Court's judgments. Some of Dickson's judgments had traces of the intelligent boy who had grown up with a book-loving, Trinity College-educated mother and who had made an impression on neighbours by telling them that he had eaten 'quantum suffict.' Dickson was fond of consulting a dictionary and a thesaurus, but this sometimes resulted in the use of unfamiliar words. Lamer's memo praising Dickson's decision in *Saskatchewan Wheat Pool* added a playful P.S.: 'Apart from having learnt a great deal of common law from reading your opinion, I have also learned the word "jejune." I have taken note of it and will try it on a few of my English speaking friends – I will evidently take the precaution of having with me a photocopy of page 1129 of the Shorter Oxford Dictionary, 3rd edition.'[5] Dickson's literary flourishes did, at times, raise judicial eyebrows. McIntyre agreed that 'you could always read Dickson and his meaning without difficulty,' but he added, 'I think he was overly verbose at times.'[6] La Forest commented that 'I got the feeling occasionally, [Dickson's] judgments were written to catch the media. I wasn't the only one who thought that.'[7]

In 1981 Dickson explained his approach to a judicial seminar on judgment writing. A judgment should reflect the 'intense thought' that should precede its writing. Judgment writing was a discipline that 'minimizes snap judgments and casual theorizing' and 'compels thinking at its hardest.' A well-crafted judgment should assure the litigants and the public that there had been 'intensive and thoughtful study of the record, the briefs and the law.' Dickson was blunt about the shortcomings of some of the judgments he read. Many 'show a strong tendency to be wordy, unclear and dull.' Often this was simply the product of sloppy thinking. 'Thoughts straggle across the printed page like a gaggle of geese, without form, without beginning or end, lacking in coherence, conciseness, convincingness.'[8]

Dickson offered helpful practical tips on good judgment writing. He admired the method of the great English judge Lord Denning, who was famous for his writing and especially for his pithy and evocative first paragraphs. Dickson told the judges: 'Open with a strong paragraph. The importance of the first paragraph cannot be over-emphasized. Tell the reader what the case is about so that he may know what to look for as he proceeds. Don't leave him hanging until page 5 or 6. Don't bury him under a mountain of detail.'[9] Sometimes Dickson's opening paragraphs would focus on the facts and sometimes on the law. In either case, they were strong and set the stage for what was to come. In *Rathwell v. Rathwell*, for example, Dickson indicated that the appeal provided an opportunity to decide 'a continuing struggle between the "justice and equity" school ... with Lord Denning the dominant exponent,' and the 'intent school' reflected in the Supreme Court's *Murdoch* decision. 'The charge raised against the former school is that of dispensing "palm-tree" justice; against the latter school, that of meaningless ritual in searching for a phantom intent.'[10] The opening paragraph in *Pettkus v. Becker* focused on the facts: 'Lothar Pettkus, through toil and thrift, developed over the years a successful beekeeping business ... It is not to his efforts alone, however, that success can be attributed. The respondent, Rosa Becker, through her labour and earnings contributed substantially to the good of the common enterprise. She lived with Mr

Pettkus from 1955 to 1974, save for a separation in 1972. They were never married. When the relationship sundered in late 1974, Miss Becker commenced the action, in which she sought a declaration of entitlement to a one-half interest in the lands and a share of the beekeeping business.'[11]

Dickson told the judges to write the first draft of judgment in longhand. 'This avoids discursiveness and affords a strong inducement to write brief judgments.' He was adept at the 'scissors and paste' technique so that he could include quotations from reported cases, academic writings, and parts of the research memos prepared by the clerks and the factums or written briefs prepared by the parties. He made full use of all available sources, but the final product was unmistakably his. In his later years on the Court, word-processing technology made handwritten first drafts less commonplace. Some have criticized both the law clerks and word-processing technology for adding to the length of Supreme Court judgments, including Dickson's. In retirement, when Dickson had less assistance from others, he still wrote first drafts of important speeches and letters in his own meticulous handwriting and returned to non-electronic forms of 'cut and paste.'

Dickson urged judges to prepare logical outlines for their judgment and to use headings 'to break the text of a long judgment into manageable parts.' Headings also encouraged judges to discuss and dispose of 'each topic ... in a compartment by itself,' with a clear statement of the legal principle that decided each issue. This was one of Dickson's most important contributions to the art of judgment writing. He established a 'Dickson style,' involving opening paragraph headings, which remains the norm today for most judges. This approach reflects Dickson's penchant for organization but also his desire to demonstrate to litigants and the public that the entire case had been carefully considered. It did, however, have the unfortunate effect of extending the length of his judgments and, on that count, the Dickson style has its critics. McIntyre, who did his best to keep his judgments short, believed that Dickson wrote at 'too great length.' Matters got significantly worse after Dickson's retirement, when the annual production of Supreme Court judgments went from two to three volumes. As McIntyre dryly observed: 'To keep up with the present Supreme Court decisions would be like reading *War and Peace* every two weeks.'[12]

Dickson was a believer in 'plain language' long before it became a popular term of art. He also cautioned against unduly formal judgments that 'overemphasize precedents and case law.' Judges should avoid 'opaque language, obscure conceptualization,' which tends 'to leave the reader in a state of obfuscation.' 'What is needed,' he explained, 'is clear, succinct, forceful writing.' He warned his audience that good writing is not easy and that it takes time. But to 'sweat blood for a month' writing a judgment is worth it, he suggested, 'if we can expunge the clumsy legalese, tedious, obscure prose, over-blown phrases, the vagueness and verbosity which are neither good law nor good literature.' He urged judges to 'use the active voice – passive voice indicates a vague, anonymous thing.' They should avoid Latin phrases, trite phrases, distracting footnotes, cliches, and 'far-fetched, abstract circumlocutions ... There really is no need in legal writing to be formal and stuffy.' He also warned that phrases such as '"no citation or authority is needed"' will cause the reader to 'suspect that a citation was really needed but could not be found.' 'It is obvious,' 'it is clear,' 'it is too clear for words,' and 'undoubtedly,' in Dickson's view, often concealed similar weakness.

The most important lesson that Dickson conveyed to other judges was 'finally, write and rewrite ... I have found that the first draft of a judgment is usually a confusing mass of refractory, repetitive and, at times, contradictory material. Pride of authorship cannot get in the way of a polished final product ... Edit and re-edit so that the end product is clear, concise and readable.' Dickson took pride in carefully crafting and recrafting his judgments and his 'workaholic'[13] schedule made it possible for him to write many drafts and still deliver his judgments in a timely manner. But Dickson's multiple drafts were much more than a matter of style. The form of the judgment was a manifestation of its substance. A judgment that was difficult to read and understand was likely to contain confusing and arbitrary concepts that should have no place in the law. Conversely, an elegant and clear judgment would likely contain concepts that would make the law better. As he explained in a 1977 speech: 'The high task of the Supreme Court of Canada is the building and re-building of legal rules. The more expert it is at the task, the more will it appear to control the practices of the lower courts, for nothing has more binding force than a perfectly constructed legal rule which, in truth, is irresistible. If the Court does its task badly, the result will be confusion in the lower courts and among lawyers.'[14]

'The clerks can be most helpful, indeed indispensable'

Dickson struggled to craft the best and clearest judgments possible. But he did not struggle alone. In the same 1977 speech, he stated that the 'calibre' of the Court's justices was 'not even half of the story' in determining whether the Court successfully fashioned legal rules. Much depended on 'the legal culture of the country ... This legal culture continually leaks into the Court's work through the briefs and argument of counsel, the legal periodicals, the awareness and assimilation of foreign jurisprudence, the use of law clerks and informal interchange with the schools and the bar.' Dickson added that 'the law clerks of the Supreme Court serve many useful purposes, not the least of which, to my mind, is to bring to the Court an awareness of current teachings and attitudes in Canadian law schools. In researching the law, in the preparation of bench memoranda, in discussion, the clerks can be most helpful, indeed indispensable.'[15]

Changes in the nature of the Court's work enhanced the role of law clerks and made it necessary to have more of them. The abolition of appeals as of right and the introduction of the leave-to-appeal procedure in 1975 meant that some five hundred leave applications had to be analysed, digested, and decided each year. The cases that survived the filtering of the leave-to-appeal procedure raised difficult issues of law. At the same time, as the Court assumed more of a lawmaking role, the demands on the judges grew. More often than in the past, extensive research was required and reflective reasons for judgment were expected. These expectations and added burdens on the Court's workload were magnified still further with the advent of the Charter of Rights and Freedoms in 1982. As a consequence, more law clerks were hired. When Dickson had joined the Court, each judge had one clerk, as they had since their introduction in 1968. In 1982 the number of clerks increased to two for each judge.[16] Three years later Dickson recorded that there was a general consensus at conference 'that most of the clerks work many hours of overtime every week, including Saturdays and Sundays,'[17] and in 1989 the number of clerks for each judge increased to three. Not surprisingly, as the role of the Court changed and the number of clerks increased, the files for each case expanded. Indeed, there is a rough correspondence between the number of clerks and the number of volumes needed to contain the Court's yearly output.[18]

Initially, it was up to each judge to hire his or her own clerk as the judge saw fit and the hiring process was relatively informal. Katherine Swinton recalls that Dickson's phone message offering her the clerk's job was mislaid and she did not return Dickson's call for a week. A few years later, Patrick Monahan was summoned in the middle of a class to call Dickson, collect, from the payphone at the law school.[19] But by the mid-1980s, the selection process had become more systematic and centralized in the Office of the Chief Justice. With a law clerk position now a significant career credential for both law practice and the academy, law deans pressed for an open and fair selection process for their graduates and the Court recognized the need to regularize its hiring practices.[20] Individual judges still made their own selection, but the process resembled applications for an academic graduate program.

The role of law clerks in the work of the Court is not without controversy. Law clerks are young, inexperienced, and anonymous. They are also typically very bright and full of ideas they are keen to promote. They are accountable to no one, except the judge they serve. Some members of the legal profession have said that the clerks have too much influence. Dickson rejected this claim. In 1988 he stated that the clerks 'do not exert – or for that matter – attempt to exert undue or unwarranted influence in the process. We judges know how to decide a case and why. The clerks do, however, greatly facilitate the work of each member of the Court.'[21] In retirement, Dickson recalled: 'I never had any occasion in the years I was on the Court from 1973 to 1990 in which I felt the law clerk was trying to sell a bill of goods which I wouldn't otherwise have bought. I think they recognize that once the judge said this is the way I am going, that was it and if they had a different view, that was just too bad.'[22]

At the same time, the research done by the law clerks had an important impact on the style of the Court's judgments. Brian Morgan, who clerked for Dickson in 1978–9, wrote a thoughtful article, vetted by Dickson, about the role of law clerks. Morgan linked the law clerks to the shift away from the Court's 'previous adherence to narrow particular adjudication' and its increased willingness 'to lay down more general propositions of law which could offer better guidance for the country ... The primary potential of the law clerk is to add depth of scholarship to the strength of the judgment on the bench. The clerk can also help to keep the judicial process responsive to developments in legal thought ... ' Morgan argued that the clerks' work was 'particularly important now that the court is concerned primarily with issues of national importance, and major judgments tend increasingly to constitute broad reviews of the law.' Although Morgan rejected the idea of clerks 'as a shadow bench of second justices, wielding improper power by improper delegation,' he also conceded that 'it would be disingenuous to pretend that the clerk's contribution commences after the judge had concluded the result in each case.' He suggested that 'law clerks help to bring about a greater flexibility, which is essential if judicial law is to be vital in a period of rapid social change.'[23] The enhanced role and increasing number of law clerks was part of the process of the Court becoming an important national policy maker.

During his seventeen years on the Court, Dickson routinely heard arguments from the top barristers in Canada. As already indicated, he was a polite listener in court and would not generally 'ride counsel'[24] in the way that some of his colleagues would. His notes, written immediately after oral argument and the initial conference of the judges, occasionally mentioned that a particular lawyer had made a good point, but this was relatively rare. In any event, the impact of oral argument frequently diminished in the months it took the Court to produce its written judgments. In 1988 Dickson explained that 'if we feel that research or preparation of the parties has been inadequate or incomplete, and, regrettably, this happens more often than it should, we can ask the clerk to do the necessary research so that an authority or point can be properly explored before argument.'[25] There are frequent examples in the case files of clerks supplying Dickson with material, often academic articles and texts, that was not present in the parties' written arguments. Dickson would at times cut and paste material from the parties' written briefs into his judgments, but he did this much more frequently with his clerks' memos. For him, the Court's increased policy-making role meant that it could not rely solely on the material presented by the parties.

Dickson's practice was to have his clerks prepare a 'bench memorandum' for each case he sat on. He wanted more from the clerk than a summary of what the parties had provided in their written arguments. Dickson instructed his clerks to 'state issues either as formulated by the appellant or as reformulated by you.'[26] The clerks were asked to go beyond the authorities provided by the parties and to check Canadian, United States, and European authorities as well as learned journals. In 1979 Brian Morgan commented that one effect of the clerks was increased use 'of other Commonwealth and American authorities, and a greater awareness of the contents of legal journals.'[27] Many of the law clerks had been student editors of the law journals and they frequently liked to cite such articles.[28]

The clerk's bench memorandum would provide the core research for the judgment on cases in which Dickson wrote. In Dickson's early years on the Court, when he had just one clerk, some bench memos would be only a few handwritten pages and rarely would be more than twenty. Research was conducted through the use of indices of case reporters and by card catalogues. By the end of his time on the Court, each clerk had a word processor and access to computer data banks to conduct research.[29] It was not unusual then for bench memoranda to run from twenty to fifty typed pages. In an important case, the clerk who had prepared the bench memo would often sit in on the oral argument. Dickson's standard procedure was to return to his office at the first opportunity after the judges-only conference at the conclusion of the oral hearing and dictate a 'conference memorandum.' This recorded the views expressed by the other judges at the court conference following the hearing of the appeal. It also recorded Dickson's views and the Court's tentative decision on the case. The conference memoranda were dictated aloud to Dickson's secretary. The clerks were invited into chambers and listened with rapt attention. There was an element of drama and excitement. The clerk had invested enormous time and energy in the case, and it was now time to learn how his or her analysis compared with that of the nation's top nine judges. While the country would have to wait for months to learn the result, Dickson's clerks were the first to know which way the case was likely to be decided. Not all judges shared so fully with their clerks the details of what happened at the judges' conference.

When he finished dictation, Dickson would ask the clerks what they thought. He was quite willing to listen to what they made of the Court's tentative decision. In cases where the result was still up in the air, there would often be discussion of which way the case should be decided. Dickson might invite research on a point that appeared to be significant in light of the oral argument or on account of the views expressed by another judge at conference. In cases where the result was clear or where Dickson's own views were firm, the discussion would focus on the immediate task of getting on with the preparation of written reasons. The clerk who had prepared the bench memorandum remained charged with the file. The law clerks were fully involved in the drafting and redrafting of Dickson's judgments. When Dickson struggled with a point, he liked to have the clerk present, and clerks were often summoned to Dickson's farm to discuss how best to resolve issues or frame the argument. Indeed, Dickson's clerks were frequent visitors to his farm both on weekdays when the court was not sitting and on weekends when Dickson was hard at work. Dickson expected much from his clerks – some of his colleagues thought that he was too hard on them[30] – but, in return, he gave them a complete view of the judging process and they did not complain.

When Dickson received draft reasons for judgment from a colleague, he asked the clerk to prepare an analysis of the draft that set out 'the propositions of law which the judgment expostulates' and included the clerk's own comments on the judgment.[31] Dickson expected the clerk's detailed and considered assessment of the issues and of the possible and preferred analysis. The clerks took direction from the way the case was argued, from the conference discussion, and, most of all, from the views Dickson had expressed. However, Dickson made it clear that, in the end, he wanted the best possible product. If the clerk had a plausible angle on the case that others had overlooked, Dickson wanted to know about it. Joel Bakan, who clerked for Dickson in 1984–5, explained: 'I never felt, when I was working with him that intellectually he considered himself to be in a hierarchical relationship with me. I felt that he was treating me as a partner ... He wanted good ideas, he wanted good judgments, he wanted the right result and the right reasoning but he did not have the ... sense of having to have ownership over ideas.'[32] Katherine Swinton, who clerked for Dickson in 1975–6, similarly observed: 'He brought you into everything, he wanted you to challenge, because it was a way for him to challenge his own ideas or to find someone to check that he was on the right path.' Brian Morgan wrote shortly after his clerkship that 'the most rewarding experience of clerking, I found, was to become immersed with the judge in the heart of a case, from early research and memoranda to final draft, working together to craft the best possible reasons to support the decisions [Dickson] made.'[33]

Dickson looked to his clerks for help and advice in all aspects of his judicial work. Shortly after he became chief justice, he invited all of the law clerks to make suggestions for improvements to the work of the Court. The clerks eagerly responded with a twelve page memo asking for improved working conditions for themselves and recommending several significant changes in the Court's procedures. The clerks advised that 'delay in the hearing and disposition of appeals is a matter of great concern. We note that even in criminal cases, appeals sometimes sit on this Court's docket for upwards of two years before they are heard.' Many of the things the clerks recommended – greater selectivity in granting leave to appeal, deciding leave applications without oral argument, and setting time limits for oral argument – were later adopted. The clerks also pressed the Court to liberalize its policy on intervenors: '... the public as a whole has a significant interest in [Charter] decisions and the court should be reluctant to prevent people from making their views known. Furthermore, public interest groups can make a valuable contribution to the court's understanding of the factual context in which its decisions will be taken and the potential impact of those decisions.'[34]

Most of the clerks worked in close proximity to each other in a large collective office. Often, clerks assigned the same task by different judges would share views and research for bench memoranda. Morgan explained that 'due to their proximity, the law clerks are continually discussing cases among themselves, often in heated debate. Weak arguments are weeded out and strong approaches refined before being presented to the judge.'[35] There would often be more discussion about a case among the clerks of various judges than among the judges themselves. As draft judgments were being prepared, the debate and exchange among clerks would continue. There can be no doubt that these exchanges among the clerks influenced the advice given to the judges. Frequently, a judge might learn more from the law clerk about the way a colleague was leaning than from the colleague directly. At the same time, however, the clerks did not negotiate deals that could be presented as a fait accompli to their judges; the judges themselves always made the ultimate decision. Dickson's own clerks would share work among themselves. Because the clerks worked only for a year, cases would often have to be passed from an outgoing clerk to an incoming one. Dickson remained open to the insights of new clerks who looked at a case with a fresh eye.

The intense work and frequent visits to the farm meant that Dickson, more so than many other judges, developed close relationships with his law clerks. Two of Dickson's clerks, recalling their discussions with Laskin's clerks, have suggested that Dickson was more open than Laskin to the clerks' criticisms and input.[36] Dickson described his relationship with his clerks as 'extremely cordial, affectionate is perhaps the best word ... from my point of view one of the finest experiences I have ever had.'[37] He engaged in a regular correspondence with his former law clerks, who kept him informed of engagements, marriages, children, and new jobs. Brian Morgan started the annual tradition of law clerks and Dickson getting together to celebrate his birthday when he suggested to his predecessors, Katherine Swinton and Joe Magnet, that they join Dickson for lunch. Dickson was delighted. When Rollie Thompson, the clerk who followed Morgan, started to organize the next year's celebration, Dickson decided to invite all the former law clerks to the farm for lunch. The pattern had been established and each year, up to Dickson's retirement in 1990, his former clerks would travel to Ottawa in late May for the weekend. The clerks invited Dickson and his wife Barbara to dinner at a restaurant on Saturday night and the Dicksons hosted a luncheon at the farm on Sunday. As the years went by, these gatherings resembled a family reunion. Spouses were introduced and babies were proudly displayed. The clerks wanted the tradition to continue after Dickson's retirement from the court in 1990, but he and Barbara politely declined. The Dicksons knew that the gatherings would not be the same after the chief justice's departure from the Court and without the constant infusion of new clerks. They preferred to end the celebrations on a high note rather than have them limp along into an indefinite future.

During his seventeen years on the Court, Dickson had twenty-seven clerks.[38] He favoured clerks with strong academic records and excellent research and writing skills, and he looked to them to bring to the Court 'the most recent, up to-date views that were being expressed within the various law faculties in this country.'[39] Many of the clerks would also be either returning from graduate studies, generally in the United Kingdom or the United States, or embarking on such studies after their year at the Court. In a 1987 address to the Canadian law deans, Dickson commented that the law clerks 'work so closely with us that they become, in a very real sense, friends and confidantes. In addition to their intellect and their research capacity, they bring us the breath of fresh air that blows through law faculties, and they keep us in touch with new ways of thinking about the law and justice.'[40] Clerkship with Dickson became a recognized credential for an academic career. Of the twenty-seven clerks he employed, no fewer than sixteen went on to full-time professorial positions. Katherine Swinton remembers Dickson encouraging her to go to graduate school after her clerkship rather than accept an offer for a government job. She adds: 'He really did respect legal academics and so I think he was quite proud he had one of his clerks go off to do that.'[41] Swinton was the first Dickson law clerk to become a full-time legal academic, but she was later joined by Joseph Magnet, Rollie Thompson, Jamie Cameron, Patrick Monahan, Dianne Pothier, Joel Bakan, Colleen Sheppard, Stephen Toope, Patrick Macklem, Martha Shaffer, Craig Scott, Stephen Smith, Carl Stychin, and Shauna Van Praagh. Other Dickson clerks went on to distinguished careers at the bar. One Dickson clerk is now a superior court judge and others are bound to follow.

Dickson's many former clerks who became academics read the Supreme Court's judgments with a critical eye. Dickson was sensitive to criticism, but he appreciated the often critical role of academics. In one speech, he observed that 'academic writing often carries a sting, felt sharply by the judge whose opinion is being subjected to scholarly scrutiny, but in the end, we can only gain from imaginative and constructive comment by our academic colleagues.'[42] In a letter to former clerk Jamie Cameron, who had written to tell Dickson that she had said something critical of a Charter judgment, Dickson noted: 'You are a law professor and have an absolute duty to seek truth in the legal world. If that means that you are critical of some of our decisions, then so be it ... I will always read what you write with interest, including the article which you have enclosed and, although I may not agree with everything you write, I expect that I will always profit from it.'[43] Dickson had a similar exchange with Patrick Monahan, who had written several critical pieces. Monahan wrote to Dickson to say that he felt awkward about attending the annual birthday party. When he got the letter, Dickson picked up the phone to reassure Monahan that he was welcome and followed this up with a letter saying: 'I would be happy to sit down to talk with you at any time about the Court and the problems which come before it.'[44]

Judges and Academics: 'Allies in a common cause'

Dickson thought it important for judges to read scholarly writing. He believed that there were important parallels between universities and courts, both of which had to be independent in order to engage in their task of seeking the truth and educating the public.[45] Dickson looked to scholarly writing throughout his years on the Supreme Court for assistance in deciding cases and he maintained an active correspondence with a number of law professors. Here he joined Bora Laskin in leading the Court away from the anti-intellectual approach that had prevailed until the 1970s. As late as 1950, the chief justice of Canada refused to allow counsel to cite the *Canadian Bar Review* in oral argument.[46] It was considered inappropriate to cite living authors, presumably out of the fear that they might change their minds. Dickson derided this restrictive attitude and welcomed the broader view of law that looked to scholarly writing for any light it might bring to bear on a difficult point of law.[47]

When he gave the Goodman Lectures at the University of Toronto in 1979, Dickson chided the academy for not writing more. He argued that 'the quantity of good academic writing, published in any year, is meagre in relation to the number of legal scholars to be found in the law schools of the nation.' This was important to Dickson, because he believed that 'the quality of the law achieved by the courts bears a direct relationship to the quality of analysis offered by the academic community.'[48] The law school's Dean, future Supreme Court Justice Frank Iacobucci, invited Dickson to his office to view a large stack of books and articles published by members of the faculty. Dickson, however, was also concerned that legal academics often waited for the Supreme Court to render judgment before commenting on the issues before the Court. Dickson subsequently wrote to Iacobucci, quoting a paper given by Paul Weiler that decried the failure of the Canadian academic community in the field of legal theory. Weiler urged his academic colleagues to ask themselves how helpful they had been in offering scholarly analysis of a problem before writing 'some after-the-fact negative reinforcement to the judges through a slashing law review critique.' Dickson told Iacobucci that Weiler expressed very well 'the close and direct inter-relationship between the academics and the judiciary' that he thought would be helpful.[49] Dickson's reliance on Weiler's ideas also underlined how the Court had come to terms with scholarly criticisms. Many had viewed Weiler's 1974 book, strongly critical of the Court, as somewhat beyond the pale. By the end of the 1970s, however, the Court had gradually moved towards the more policy-oriented approach that Weiler had advocated. No doubt Dickson took mischievous pleasure in returning the volley by citing Weiler's challenge to the academy.

In October 1980 Dickson attended an academic workshop at the University of Toronto and was taken aback by the forceful criticisms of recent Supreme Court of Canada decisions on constitutional law made by a young scholar from the University of Victoria, James MacPherson. MacPherson had argued that recent federalism cases 'are unfortunate and unwise and are likely to have serious negative ramifications for the Canadian economy and citizen.'[50] After the seminar, Dickson took MacPherson aside and complimented him on his paper. He confided that, had he read it before concurring in one of the cases, he might not have agreed with the majority's opinion. He urged MacPherson, whom he would later hire as his chief executive legal officer, to keep writing, but suggested that it would be more helpful if he could offer his comments on cases before they reached the Supreme Court so that the judges would have the benefit of his views when they were deciding the case. Dickson took a similar approach when Professor Donovan Waters, a distinguished trusts scholar whose writings Dickson had frequently relied upon, sent him an offprint of an article[51] criticizing one of Dickson's judgments. Dickson replied politely but pointedly: 'I very much enjoyed reading your article and only wish that I had the benefit of its observations when the ... case reached this Court.'[52] Dickson's comments displayed the same openness that his law clerks experienced. If there was a problem with the law, Dickson wanted to know about it and fix it.

Jacob Ziegel wrote to Dickson suggesting that there were difficulties getting academic comment into print before cases reached the Supreme Court of Canada.[53] Ziegel, an experienced and well-respected scholar, had a point. Some of the practical problems with Dickson's suggestion that academics write on issues before the Court were highlighted by an exchange in 1982 with Barry Reiter, who had just left the University of Toronto Faculty of Law to go into practice. Mindful of Dickson's invitation to provide academic analysis that might help the Court decide a difficult case, Reiter sent Dickson a copy of an unpublished academic article. It concerned a case that had been argued and that was under reserve. Reiter explained that he had tried to get the comment published earlier, but that he had missed the journal's deadline. Reiter also sent copies of the article to counsel. Dickson returned the article unread. He repeated his strong belief in a partnership between the judiciary and the academy but refused to consider Reiter's comment. After the Court's judgment was released, Reiter reminded Dickson of the admonition he had given the academic community for being more ready with after-the-fact criticism than pre-judgment assistance.[54] Dickson's reply was polite but firm: 'However highly motivated the action might be,' the submission of an unpublished article by a third party 'could be perceived as an attempt by someone not directly involved in the litigation to influence the Court. Rightly or wrongly, those are my views.'[55] Dickson's desire for assistance in resolving the difficult issues before the Court had limits.

Dickson may also have been overly optimistic about the practical guidance that academic comment could provide. Some academics hope to influence the development of the law, but it is often unrealistic to expect them to focus on how a particular case should be decided. Deciding cases is the role of the courts, while scholarly criticism and commentary tends to be at a more general and abstract level. In any event, Dickson was attracted to the work of academics such as Peter Hogg, Don Stuart, Stephen Waddams, Donovan Waters, and Glanville Williams who write in a textbook tradition that emphasizes broad organizing principles for a mass of cases. Like these academics, he was often prepared to jettison arbitrary distinctions in the cases before the Court if he thought that this would make the law more principled. Dickson also remained open to trends in legal scholarship. Some of Dickson's later Charter judgments were receptive to the arguments made by critical legal scholars that the Court had not been sensitive enough to the distributional implications of its Charter decisions and ran the risk of striking down laws that were necessary to assist the disadvantaged.[56] In his last year on the Court, Dickson cited the arguments of critical-race theorists in a judgment upholding hate-propaganda laws and signed on to a judgment by Bertha Wilson that embraced feminist critiques of the law of self-defence.[57]

Dickson took a particular interest in the relation between academics and judges and delivered several speeches on the subject. In particular, he bemoaned the traditional neglect of scholarship in the development of the English common law and praised the important role that scholars play as a source of law in European civil law countries.[58] In a 1981 speech at Dalhousie Law School entitled 'The Relationship of Judges and Law Schools – "Allies in a Common Cause,"' Dickson urged Canadian lawyers to draw academic writings to the Court's attention. 'The quality of judging,' he said, 'is an echo of the quality of teaching. I have no doubt that the strength of the judiciary at any one time is a function of the strength of those whose primary concern is the scholarship of the law ... the door of the law must now be open for the integration of academic law into the mainstream of Canadian law if we are ever to develop a distinctively Canadian jurisprudence ... Together the judges and the law schools face the challenge and the opportunity to improve the Canadian legal system and the quality of justice within that system.'[59] In 1984 Dickson indicated that 'the Court's increasing consciousness of the wider implications of its decision has affected its relationship with the academic community. What was once largely a monologue has now turned into a dialogue, with the court welcoming and often incorporating academic research and opinion.'[60] Dickson's reliance on academics was not without critics. William McIntyre believed that 'the country was ill-served by the court in the first 10 years of the Charter' in part because Dickson and others responded to 'the pressure of all the propaganda in the newspapers and the academic world, all the professors were writing articles and there was a certain amount of hysteria about it.'[61]

From his appointment to the Supreme Court in March 1973 to 1976, Dickson gave few speeches at law schools. However, from 1976 on, he was a frequent visitor, lecturer, and honorary-degree recipient at law schools across Canada. Dickson enjoyed these visits and prepared as meticulously for a lecture to first-year law students as he would for a formal speech on receiving a honorary degree. His close relationship with the law schools and legal academics was a two-way affair. In a 1984 interview, he suggested that when scholars had 'gone to the trouble of writing in a learned journal in a constructive way, I think we are very unwise not to take the benefit of it.' He added that 'when we refer to the writings of the scholar then I would think that that encourages the scholars to write because they realize that people are reading their writings and getting support from them.' As the interviewer, Professor Gordon Bale, noted, Dickson's attention to scholarly writings was one of the reasons he had 'such a fine reputation' in the law schools.[62] Dickson was often praised by academics, who found his clear and principled decisions to be a useful teaching tool. One law professor, who had also appeared before Dickson as counsel, wrote to Dickson in retirement and commented on how he taught Dickson judgments to his students in several courses because they were 'models of both analytic lucidity and human compassion.'[63] After Dickson's retirement, two academic symposia honoured Dickson's work and many of his decisions continue to be taught in the law schools today.[64]

11

Fault and Free Will

Upon his appointment to the Manitoba Court of Queens Bench, Dickson, perhaps remembering that he had received some of his lowest marks in criminal law, had confessed that he would have to do some studying in the field. As it turned out, however, Dickson left a formidable and lasting impression on criminal law as the leading exponent of the requirement that accused should not be convicted unless they were at fault for committing harm. The fault principle meant that accused who committed a prohibited act would not be guilty if their mind was not directed to the crime. To take a familiar example, a person who possesses an illegal drug is not guilty if he or she honestly believes that the substance is sugar. Dickson believed that the requirement of fault was 'common to all civilized penal systems. It derives from our belief in freedom of the will. We believe that a person is accountable for what he wills, for what he does deliberately, or recklessly. But we do not punish conduct as criminal unless we are convinced beyond a reasonable doubt that the wrongdoing was done consciously.'[1] Dickson was applauded for establishing a revolutionary new presumption against punishment without fault, but his insistence on subjective fault in sexual-violence cases and for intoxicated or mentally disturbed accused was much more controversial.

As in other areas of law, in his first few years on the Court, Dickson followed precedents quite strictly, even when they led him to convict in the absence of fault. By the late 1970s, however, he was prepared to reform the law in a bold manner if he thought that the fault principle justified the change. As he matured as a Supreme Court justice, Dickson still paid attention to precedent, but his search for authorities became more far-reaching and extended to the United States and especially Australia. He was more willing to distinguish precedents that did not clearly decide cases in a principled manner. He also dissented more frequently. Dickson's dissents in the criminal law, however, were less likely to become the law than his dissents in the public- and private-law cases examined in chapters 8 and 9. He was unwilling to make compromises or develop halfway houses even in the face of criticisms that his approach would not protect the public, especially women, from violence by offenders who were intoxicated or mentally ill or had a mistaken perception of the circumstances.

Dickson's approach to the criminal law was also characterized by his usual quest for clarity and simplicity. Dickson always remembered the difficulty he had explaining uncertain and complex concepts of criminal law to Manitoba juries. At his swearing-in ceremony at the Supreme Court, he recalled how a trial judge 'toils into the night preparing a jury charge for the following morning ... The judge at such moments yearns for greater clarity and simplicity in the legal picture which he must paint for the jury. The minds of jurymen do not always respond with lively animation to fine legal distinctions.'[2] Dickson's approach was also influenced by his strong beliefs that the jury was entitled to hear all the evidence in the case and that they could be trusted to follow the judge's instructions about how to use the evidence.

A New Halfway House: The Due Diligence Defence

Regulatory offences are enacted by all levels of government to promote the public welfare by punishing individuals and corporations who violate laws designed to safeguard the environment, health and safety, and other public goods. Canadian law traditionally took a dichotomous approach in which most regulatory offences were treated as no-fault offences; all the prosecutor had to prove was that the accused caused the forbidden harm. The only other alternative was to treat the regulatory offence like a serious crime and require the prosecutor to prove beyond a reasonable doubt that the accused actually knew that his or her conduct would result in the harm prohibited by the statute. This dichotomy between no-fault and subjective fault placed courts in a difficult position. Interpreting a regulatory offence as requiring subjective fault often made it nearly impossible to convict an accused, especially a corporation, despite harmful conduct. On the other hand, only requiring the proof of a prohibited act could result in a conviction in cases in which an accused had done all that could reasonably be expected to prevent the harm. Indeed, Dickson's 1973 decision to interpret leaving the scene of an accident as a no-fault offence ran the risk of convicting those who left the scene of an accident but who did not even know that they had been involved in an accident.[3]

Future Supreme Court justice Louise Arbour, then a law professor, criticized Dickson's 1973 decision 'for its failure to engage in an in-depth analysis' about whether the stigma, penalty, or purpose of the offence required proof of subjective fault, though she herself looked to legislatures, not the courts, to reform regulatory offences.[4]

Legislative reform did not emerge and in 1978 Dickson, speaking for a unanimous Court, fundamentally changed the prosecution of regulatory offences. The case involved a pollution charge against the City of Sault Sainte Marie. The city hired a company to dispose of the town's garbage. As Dickson noted, 'the garbage and wastes in due course formed a high mound sloping steeply toward, and within twenty feet of, the creek. Pollution resulted.'[5] The disposal company was convicted, but not the city because of the difficulty of proving beyond a reasonable doubt that its senior officials knew that the garbage was being dumped in the water. At the Supreme Court, the parties focused their arguments on whether the pollution offence required subjective fault. In conference, many of Dickson's colleagues expressed the view that the offence was no-fault; indeed, this was the appropriate disposition suggested by the Court's own precedents, including Dickson's 1973 case on leaving the scene of an accident. Most of the conference discussion involved technical points that had been emphasized by counsel. There were few signs that the case would become a landmark one.

Dickson summarized the relevant literature and competing arguments before starting the first of many drafts of his judgment. His handwritten notes outlined the case for and against no-fault liability. On one side of the page, Dickson noted that regulatory offences did not have the same stigma as true crimes and no-fault liability might deter harmful conduct. On the other side, he noted that any prosecution 'necessarily attracts some of the stigma and effects on reputation which pervades' the traditional uses of the criminal law and that the 'injustice of convicting those not at fault dilutes the criminal law and leads to cynical disrespect for the law.'[6] These arguments closely followed the views of the Law Reform Commission of Canada[7] and a number of academics that there should be a halfway house that did not require proof of subjective fault but that did require some fault in the form of negligence. Despite the Supreme Court's previous decisions, some Ontario courts had been experimenting with requiring negligence for regulatory offences, as had courts in Australia. Although he had shown no interest or awareness of this approach in his 1973 case, Dickson now concluded that there was nothing 'novel about this solution. It is the approach advocated by almost all the writers on the subject.'[8] Dickson's judgment was an innovative tour de force, but it built on the prior work of academics, law reform bodies, and judges.

In his judgment, Dickson started from what for him was the bedrock proposition that true crimes required proof of subjective fault and that 'mere negligence is excluded from the concept of the mental element required for conviction.' As he would insist in a subsequent and controversial rape case, a person who 'fails to know facts he should have known is innocent in the eyes of the law.' Dickson warned that nothing in the judgment was 'intended to dilute or erode that basic principle.'[9] All true crimes should be presumed to require subjective fault in the form of intent or some knowledge of the facts that made the conduct criminal. Dickson was also not prepared to reverse the traditional burden on the crown to prove fault beyond a reasonable doubt in true criminal cases. 'Mere difficulty of enforcement cannot justify the shifting of a burden of proof of the mental element to the accused, for if that were the case one could easily justify doing away with the presumption of ... [fault] and the presumption of innocence in criminal law proper.'[10]

In the case at hand, however, Dickson rejected the conclusion that the pollution offence required proof of subjective fault. The offence was a provincial attempt to protect public welfare so that 'natural streams which formerly afforded "pure and healthy" water for drinking or swimming purposes' do not 'become little more than cesspools when riparian factory owners and municipal corporations discharge into them filth of all descriptions.'[11] As a person who loved nature, who went to great efforts to live outside first Winnipeg and then Ottawa, and who started each day with a horse ride on his extensive acreage, Dickson was concerned about pollution and the conservation of the natural environment. He was reluctant to allow corporations that polluted to escape unpunished simply because the government could not prove beyond a reasonable doubt that a high official in the corporation knew about the pollution. Dickson was also aware that many people were maimed and injured when individuals and corporations did not follow health and safety standards. Perhaps reflecting on his own injury in the military, he argued that 'potential victims of those who carry on latently pernicious activities have a strong claim to consideration.'[12] For him, regulatory offences were not 'victimless offences.'

Although the pollution offence did not require proof of subjective fault, Dickson no longer believed that it was acceptable to punish a person or a corporation that was without fault because of the 'generally held revulsion against the punishment of the morally innocent.' Dickson drew on his own experience in the corporate world to reach this conclusion. He knew that any conviction could affect the reputation of a corporation and its managers. A person or corporation accused of a regulatory offence was exposed to 'the loss of time, legal costs, exposure to the processes of the criminal law at trial and, however one may downplay it, the opprobrium of conviction.'[13] Accordingly, he set out a broad new presumption that a person or corporation charged with a regulatory offence would not be convicted if they could establish a defence of due diligence or lack of negligence. He dealt with objections that he was violating the presumption of innocence by requiring the accused to prove the defence of due diligence on the pragmatic basis that, under the previous law, 'the alternative is absolute liability which denies an accused any defence whatsoever.' As a former corporate lawyer and corporate director, Dickson was in an excellent position to give a functional defence for requiring the accused to establish due diligence. 'In a normal case, the accused alone will have knowledge of what he has done to avoid the breach and it is not improper to expect him to come forward with the evidence of due diligence. This is particularly so when it is alleged, for example, that pollution is caused by the activities of a large and complex corporation.' Henceforth, it would be people in the senior corporate positions that Dickson occupied who would have to establish the due-diligence defence. These officials could not 'slough off responsibility by contracting out the work.'[14] Corporate power, for Dickson, implied corporate responsibility.

Willard 'Bud' Estey, the newly appointed Ontario judge who, like Dickson, was fully familiar with the corporate world at first took a different view of the matter. He wanted to keep no-fault offences 'alive and well' and was concerned about the 'community being marched off into chaos under the banner of the defence of absence of negligence.'[15] In the end, however, Estey withdrew a draft dissent and signed on to Dickson's after Dickson added a sentence indicating that the subject matter of the legislation and the penalty might allow some regulatory offences to still be classified as no-fault offences.[16]

Dickson finessed his own 1973 decision that the provincial offence of failing to remain at the scene of an accident was a no-fault offence. He interpreted this recent case as standing for the proposition that regulatory offences did not require proof of subjective fault, but not as standing 'in the way of a defence of reasonable care in a proper case.'[17] At least one commentator found this distinction unconvincing.[18] Dickson also responded to concerns that the Court was creating sweeping presumptions that affected all criminal and regulatory offences by arguing that the concepts of both absolute-liability and regulatory offences were 'the product of the judiciary and not of the Legislature.'[19] Dickson was willing to reform the law in a bold matter if he thought that it was a matter of 'lawyer's law.' At the same time, his decision had a stunning impact on what at the time was estimated to be about 40,000 regulatory offences producing a total of 1.4 million convictions each year.[20] Henceforth there would be presumption that the accused would have a defence of due diligence in all these cases.

Dickson's judgment was well received because it added certainty, consistency, and fairness to the prosecution of regulatory offences. The next year the

Court found that there was a due-diligence defence to the offence of duck hunting within a quarter-mile of a baited area. Dickson illustrated the uncertainty of the pre–*Sault Ste Marie* law by noting that 'the three courts which have dealt with the matter to date have characterized the offence in three different ways.' Under the new law, however, the Court could easily reject both the accused's argument that the offence required subjective fault and the prosecution's argument that the offence did not require fault. Drawing this time on his experience as a duck hunter, Dickson indicated that hunters, many of whom 'hope to get into position before first light,' could not reasonably be expected 'to search through swamp, bog, creeks, corn fields, over land and in water in search of illegal bait.' The 'difficulty of enforcement is hardly enough to dislodge the offence' from the presumption that the innocent should not be punished.[21]

Dickson's judgment in *Sault Ste Marie* formed the basis for the Supreme Court's landmark 1985 decision in *Reference re B.C. Motor Vehicles* that the imposition of imprisonment for a no-fault offence violated the Charter. Antonio Lamer, who had been vice-chair of the Law Reform Commission when it wrote its influential report, relied heavily on *Sault Ste Marie* for the proposition that no-fault offences offended the fundamental principles of penal liability by punishing the morally innocent. Imprisoning innocent people was not reasonable given the alternative of allowing a due-diligence defence, 'the success of which does nothing more than let those few who did nothing wrong remain free.'[22] A year after Dickson's retirement, the Supreme Court held that any violation of the presumption of innocence entailed in requiring the accused to prove a defence of due diligence was justified in order to fulfil the public-welfare objectives of regulatory offences.[23] Dickson's innovative halfway house remains the law today.

No Halfway House: Rape and Contested Notions of Fault

Although Dickson was attracted to a halfway house for regulatory offences, he insisted on fault for true crimes without compromise. He applied the basic principles of requiring an overt act and subjective fault even when they caused discomfort in a society that was becoming more aware of the prevalence of sexual violence against women.

In 1978 Dickson decided a case involving two members of a Winnipeg biker gang, the Spartans, who had been convicted by a jury of raping a sixteen-year-old girl. The girl testified that the co-accused, Dunlop and Sylvester, were two of eighteen gang members who raped her. Dunlop and Sylvester testified that all they had done was deliver four cases of beer to a dump on the outskirts of Winnipeg and observed from a distance a woman having intercourse with a gang member. After deliberating for a few hours, the jury asked the judge whether the accused were guilty as an accomplice to rape if they were aware of a rape taking place in their presence and did nothing to prevent it. Dickson concluded that the trial judge erred by not answering with a simple 'no.' In what is still the leading case on the issue, Dickson stressed that something more than mere presence at the scene of a crime was necessary for an individual to be found guilty as an accomplice to the crime. 'A person who, aware of a rape taking place in his presence, looks on and does nothing is not, as a matter of law, an accomplice. The classic case is the hardened urbanite who stands around in a subway station when an individual is murdered.' He acquitted the accused on the basis that there was no evidence that they 'rendered aid, assistance or encouragement' to the gang rape or did 'any positive act or omission to facilitate the unlawful purpose.'[24] The judgment demonstrated the liberal and individualistic principles that, for Dickson, were at the heart of the criminal law. The most conservative and prosecution-minded members of the Court – Martland, Ritchie, and Pigeon – dissented and would have convicted the men of rape because of their membership in the gang and their delivery of beer to the site of the rape.

None of Dickson's criminal law judgments is more famous or controversial than his 1980 decision involving a Vancouver businessman named Pappajohn who was convicted of raping a female real estate agent. In his conference memo, Dickson noted that the two 'had a bibulous luncheon and post-luncheon fiesta at a restaurant and then retired to his home following which the stories are quite different. She says that she was pushed into a bedroom and that, despite her screams, she was repeatedly raped over a period of hours, culminating in the accused tying her hands and putting a bow tie around her neck. She finally escaped and ran nude to the adjoining house occupied by a priest.'[25] Pappajohn argued that, even if the woman did not consent to intercourse, he honestly believed that she had. The English courts had recently recognized the defence of honest but unreasonable belief in consent, but the case had caused so much controversy that the government had appointed an inquiry to examine the issue.[26] At conference, it appeared as if the Canadian Court would not follow the controversial English position. Dickson noted that his colleagues thought that the English case was a 'philosophic discussion of judges with little to do, and the defence of honest belief should not be part of our law.' Estey sent Dickson a memo indicating that he thought that the accused should have a defence only if his mistaken belief was both honest and reasonable.[27]

Dickson, however, believed that the mistake defence 'avails an accused who acts innocently, pursuant to a flawed perception of the facts, and nonetheless commits' the prohibited act, in this case rape. What mattered was whether the accused's mistaken belief in consent was honestly held, not whether it was reasonable. To require that a mistake be reasonable meant that the accused 'must have acted up to the standard of an average man, whether the accused is himself such a man or not ...' This would convert rape into a crime of negligence, something that Dickson could not accept for a true crime. At the time there was little feminist scholarship on the issue and Dickson, whose case file was full of academic material, was influenced by the fact that there was a 'virtually unanimous rejection of the added requirement of "reasonableness" ... in the scholarly writings.'[28] The universal principle of subjective fault should prevail over any contextual concerns about the particular crime.

Dickson also rejected the requirement that a mistake must be reasonable because of a fear of complicating the jury's task. It would be 'unfair to the jury, and to the accused, to speak in terms of two beliefs, one entertained by the accused, the other by a reasonable man, and to ask the jury to ignore an actual belief in favour of an attributed belief.' The jury should be allowed to consider all the evidence and not forced to find a fictional intent other than the one that the accused actually had. Paradoxically, however, Dickson also argued that the jury was unlikely to accept the accused's claim of an honest mistake 'unless the mistake is, to the jury, reasonable.' Perhaps trying to ward off criticisms that his approach would allow many rapists to go free, Dickson stressed that juries had in his experience a 'high degree of common sense' and an 'uncanny ability to distinguish the genuine from the specious.' Dickson predicted that 'it will be a rare day when a jury is satisfied as to the existence of an unreasonable belief.'[29] Dickson's combination of principle and pragmatism convinced all of his initially sceptical colleagues to accept the controversial defence of an honest but not necessarily reasonable mistaken belief that the woman had consented.

The Court split on whether Pappajohn could use this new defence. McIntyre, for the majority, insisted that there must be more evidence for the accused's claim than his belief that the woman had consented. Dickson dissented because, in his view, there was enough evidence to allow Pappajohn to raise the new defence. The woman's clothes had been neatly folded and her jewellery removed. She did not have any bruises. Dickson warned that 'there can be many ambiguous situations in sexual relationships...where each party interprets the situation differently, and it may be quite impossible to determine with any confidence which interpretation is right.' He thought it unjust to convict 'if the woman in her own mind withholds consent, but her conduct and other circumstances lend credence to belief on part of the accused that she was consenting.'[30] Having recognized the principle of subjective fault, Dickson refused to compromise in its application.

Although the majority of the Court affirmed Pappajohn's conviction, Dickson's decision on the defence of honest mistake was the object of immediate and sustained criticism. A representative of the Vancouver Rape Crisis Centre argued that the new defence of honest but unreasonable belief in consent condoned 'the male notion that a "no" sometimes mean "yes"'. Doris Anderson, the head of the Canadian Advisory Council on the Status of Women, expressed concerns that the decision would encourage attempts 'to discredit the woman, to make her look confused and unsure ... anything to prove that she led that poor man into thinking that she really wanted sex with him.' Nine Vancouver women's groups wrote a letter to the editor urging Parliament to abolish the defence that 'a man's honest belief, even if false and unreasonable, that a woman consented to sex is a valid defence in a rape case.' Citing statistics that 'a woman is raped every 17 minutes and 1 in 4 women will be sexually assaulted sometimes in her life,' they asked, 'Why is Canadian law making it easier for a man to violently attack a woman without any repercussions?'[31] These groups viewed the issue contextually while Dickson saw it as a matter of universal and abstract principle. They had much less faith than Dickson that juries and judges would reject specious claims of a man's mistaken belief in a woman's consent. Jamie Cameron, the law clerk who assisted Dickson on the judgment, was practising law in Vancouver before going on to graduate school and an academic career. She sent Dickson some of the negative press that *Pappajohn* had received in Vancouver. Dickson expressed hope in his reply that his former clerk was defending the judgment because it was 'sound in law,' though he recognized that 'this may not be a very convincing argument to the feminist groups of British Columbia.'[32] Feminist opposition to *Pappajohn* was neither temporary nor limited to British Columbia. Much of the subsequent movement for reform of sexual offences in both the 1980s and 1990s was built around opposition to Dickson's reasoning in *Pappajohn*.

Dickson's position in *Pappajohn* was supported by most academic writing at the time it was written, but it soon became more controversial. In a comment entitled 'Safeguarding Fundamental Principles,'[33] Queen's criminal law professor Don Stuart praised Dickson for his 'impressive attempt to expound a principled approach to our law of mistake.' However, Toni Pickard, Stuart's colleague, wrote a comment entitled 'Harsh Words on *Pappajohn*.'[34] She criticized Dickson for applying abstract principles without regard to the particular context of sexual violence. She argued that a negligence standard would encourage men to ascertain whether the women truly consented in an ambiguous situation.

The controversy did not fade. As part of the 1983 reforms that replaced the offence of rape with the offence of sexual assault, Parliament added a new provision which required judges to instruct juries that 'when reviewing all the evidence relating to the determination of the honesty of the accused's belief, to consider the presence or absence of reasonable grounds for that belief.'[35] This preserved the *Pappajohn* defence but codified Dickson's suggestions that jurors should turn their minds to the reasonableness of the accused's claims.

A few years later, the controversy was reignited after a trial judge acquitted a man named Sansregret who had twice broken into his ex-partner's apartment, threatened her with a butcher's knife, hit her, prevented her from phoning the police, and then had sexual intercourse with her. The trial judge concluded that no rational person would have believed the woman had consented, but she found that Sansregret 'saw what he wanted to see, heard what he wanted to hear, believed what he wanted to believe.' The facts of this case were too much for Dickson. His conference notes suggest that he thought Sansregret should be convicted under *Pappajohn* because 'if a man terrorizes a woman for over an hour with actual and threatened physical violence, it should be obvious his actions have created a risk that her consent is not genuine. If he fails to inquire into her consent, his indifference cannot be justified. Such indifference is recklessness ... I find it hard to see how a mistaken belief can be deemed an honest belief where it results from an indifferent attitude towards the consequences of actions ... For belief to be honest it must be based on inquiry.'[36] Dickson signed on to a unanimous decision written by McIntyre convicting Sansregret because he was wilfully and deliberately blind to whether the woman consented. McIntyre noted that the preclusion of mistakes based on wilful blindness 'is not to be taken as a retreat from the position taken in *Pappajohn* that the honest belief need not be reasonable,'[37] but Don Stuart and other academics questioned the distinction and suggested that the Court had run roughshod over the trial judge's factual findings.[38]

After Dickson's retirement, Parliament restricted the *Pappajohn* defence by providing that, in sexual-assault cases, the accused could not have a defence of mistaken belief in consent if he did not take reasonable steps, in the circumstances known to him at the time, to ascertain that the complainant was consenting.[39] This new standard combined subjective- and objective-fault elements in a manner that Dickson opposed. It has, however, been upheld under the Charter.[40] The new law also confirmed another position that Dickson disagreed with, namely, that self-induced intoxication could not be the basis for the defence of mistaken belief in a sexual-assault case.

No Halfway House: Intoxication and Sexual Violence

In a series of dissents, Dickson insisted that the jury should hear about evidence of intoxication even when the accused was charged with rape or sexual assault. The traditional law denied the accused any defence of intoxication if the crime was classified as one of 'general intent.' The rationale was that intoxication would be relevant only if the accused was charged with a 'specific intent' offence such as murder that required the accused to direct his mind to ulterior consequences. In *Leary*, a 1977 case, the majority of the Court applied its own 1960 precedent holding that intoxication could not be a defence to rape. Pigeon focused on the protection of society from drunken and violent offenders. He quoted an English judge who argued that it was not acceptable to 'let logic prevail even though public order be threatened.'[41] He also followed the English courts by concluding that, even if the accused was too intoxicated to recognize that the woman did not consent, his actions in voluntarily becoming intoxicated demonstrated sufficient fault to convict him of rape.

Dickson wrote a strong dissent that was subsequently widely praised in the academic literature. He was concerned that the distinction between specific- and general-intent offences was not found in the Criminal Code or known to psychology. The courts could not always agree on whether a crime such as rape should be classified as one of general or specific intent. Further, the dichotomy between general and specific intent complicated the work of judges and juries because they were required to consider intoxication for some charges but not for others. In Dickson's view, there was now 'little reason for retaining in the criminal law – which should be characterized by clarity, simplicity and certainty' – the difficult and uncertain dichotomy of general- and specific-intent offences. It was, in Dickson's view, 'an impossible task' to ask the jury to determine the accused's state of mind without considering evidence of intoxication. If the accused had been drinking, then intoxication was relevant. Juries should not be asked to 'find a fictional non-existing mental state as an ingredient of guilt.'[42] For Dickson, the path of common sense pointed in the direction of considering all the evidence.

The most important issue for Dickson was his belief that excluding consideration of intoxication could result in a conviction without fault. He rejected the idea that 'everyone who gets drunk is thereby reckless' because 'recklessness cannot exist in the air; it must have reference to the consequences of a particular act.' The requirement of subjective fault was not a technical or legalistic issue for Dickson. It was tied to his beliefs about the presumption of innocence and the social obligation to punish only those who, by the exercise of their free will, broke the law. In one of his more philosophical discussions of fault, Dickson argued:

> The notion that a court should not find a person guilty of an offence against the criminal law unless he has a blameworthy state of mind is common to all civilized penal systems. It is founded upon respect for the person and for the freedom of human will. A person is accountable for what he wills. When, in the

exercise of the power of free choice, a member of society chooses to engage in harmful or otherwise undesirable conduct proscribed by the criminal law, he must accept the sanctions which the law has provided for the purpose of discouraging such conduct. Justice demands no less. But to be criminal, the wrong-doing must have been consciously committed.[43]

He believed that 'society and the law have moved away from the primitive response' of punishing people simply for committing the criminal act.[44] History, principle, logic and the need for a clear and consistent criminal law were, in Dickson's view, all on the side of abolishing restrictions on when the jury could consider evidence of intoxication.

He insisted on subjective fault as a matter of principle, but Dickson also made pragmatic appeals in defence of his position. He addressed the majority's concerns about public safety by arguing that he had grave doubts that the restrictive law 'deters or is capable of deterring the intoxicated offender.' In any event, the Court should leave concerns for public safety to Parliament. 'If sanctions against drinking to excess be thought necessary,' in Dickson's view 'they ought to be introduced by legislation – as in a crime of being drunk and dangerous.' Dickson stressed that the intoxication defence would be successful only if intoxication had prevented the accused from realizing that the woman was not consenting. The fact 'that, by reason of drink, [the accused's] judgment and control relaxed so that he more readily gave way to his instinctual drives, avails him nothing.'[45] Dickson had faith that the jury would acquit men accused of rape only if they were truly not at fault.

In 1988 the Court returned to the issue of whether intoxication could be a defence to a crime of sexual violence. A man named Bernard had been convicted of sexual assault causing bodily harm but now argued that not allowing the jury to consider evidence of his intoxication violated his Charter rights. At conference, Dickson indicated that he intended 'to write to re-iterate' his dissent in *Leary*, which, he noted, was now 'supported by the *Charter*.' It seemed that Dickson had a majority, with Lamer, Wilson, and La Forest, the liberal wing of the Court on criminal-law matters, all indicating that they agreed with his earlier dissent. Beetz, who had agreed with the majority in *Leary*, not surprisingly believed that the trial judge had been right to take away the drunkenness defence, as did McIntyre and the newly appointed Claire L'Heureux-Dubé, who frequently sided with the state on criminal-law matters.[46] Gérard La Forest recalled in an interview that Dickson was a bit taken aback by the prospect that he might have a majority on this issue and quipped, 'I am afraid I am going to be in the majority!'[47] In a 1991 interview, Dickson himself stated: 'I sometimes wondered what would have happened if my point of view had been the majority, because Parliament would have had to bring in some legislation, such as a charge of committing such and such a crime while intoxicated. That was not impossible.'[48] Although Dickson would not compromise his principles of subjective fault, his moderate instincts made him uneasy at the prospect that his views about fault and intoxication might become the law of the land.

In the end, however, Dickson did not have to worry about the need for parliamentary intervention, for his defence of a wide-open intoxication defence remained a dissenting position. McIntyre and Beetz dismissed the accused's appeal by upholding the traditional law that drunkenness could never be a defence to a crime of sexual assault.'[49] Wilson, joined by L'Heureux-Dubé, was troubled by the notion that the recklessness of getting drunk could be sufficient for a sexual-assault conviction. She wrote her own 'halfway house' judgment that left open the new possibility that extreme intoxication might be a defence to sexual assault. In her 'tentative view,' substituting the fault of becoming drunk for the fault of sexual assault would violate the Charter. On the facts of the case, however, Wilson had no trouble affirming Bernard's conviction because he still 'had sufficient wits about him after the violent assault to hide a bloodied towel and pillowcase from the police.'[50]

Dickson's dissent candidly and confidently declared 'that nothing I have heard or read since the judgment in *Leary* has caused me to abandon or modify in the slightest degree the views of the dissent which I there expressed.'[51] He did, however, feel compelled to address the institutional issue of when a court should overrule its prior decisions. The traditional restrictions on the intoxication defence should be abandoned because they were inconsistent with other precedents, the most important being the *Pappajohn* defence of honest but unreasonable mistake about consent. The traditional rule should also be abandoned because it was uncertain and unfair to the accused and had been subjected to sustained scholarly criticism. The most important reason for overruling the traditional rule, however, was the enactment of the Charter. By presuming that the accused had sufficient fault regardless of intoxication, Dickson concluded that the traditional rule violated the accused's rights not to be deprived of liberty except in accordance with the principles of fundamental justice and his right to be presumed innocent. These violations could not be justified as reasonable because there was no evidence that public safety would be threatened by abandonment of the restrictions on the intoxication defence.

Four years after Dickson's 1990 retirement, a majority of the Court accepted Wilson's proposed halfway house and recognized a defence of extreme intoxication to sexual assault. Lamer and La Forest signed on to the majority decision while stating that they still agreed with the Dickson position 'which goes much further.'[52] The more moderate Wilson position, however, was unpopular. Both women's groups and the public at large were outraged with the possibility that a person who committed sexual assault might go free because of extreme intoxication. They were not persuaded by the Court's restrictions on the defence, such as requiring the accused to prove the defence with expert evidence. With all-party approval, Parliament quickly enacted a new law. This legislation did not create a new offence of being drunk and dangerous or committing sexual assault while intoxicated that Dickson had contemplated might be enacted should his position become the law. Rather, the new law took a tougher approach that reaffirmed the traditional law that Dickson opposed and deemed that the fault of becoming extremely intoxicated was sufficient for a sexual-assault conviction.[53] Dickson never compromised his abstract and principled approach to the intoxication defence, but his approach never became the law of the land.

Free Will and Mental Disorder

During his seventeen years on the Court, Dickson wrote judgments in almost every case that involved mentally disturbed offenders. Although the cases involved horrendous acts of violence which could easily trigger concerns about public safety and were filled with complex testimony from psychiatrists, Dickson consistently saw them through the lens of the importance of establishing that the accused was at fault for committing crimes. In a lecture to law students, he expressed concerns that public hostility to the insanity defence after it was used by John Hinckley Jr, as a defence to his attempted assassination of President Ronald Reagan might lead to a return to the days 'when insanity was dealt with by imprisonment rather than treatment.'[54] Dickson's generous approach to the insanity defence was related to his conviction that those who did not commit crimes intentionally and as a result of their own free will should not be punished.

In 1976 he dissented in two cases involving accused who had raised the insanity defence to murder charges. The first case involved a man who stabbed to death his wife of one week. The accused argued that a mental disorder, combined with his drinking, had deprived him of criminal responsibility. The majority of the Court upheld a rigid separation of the insanity and intoxication defences, as well as the man's murder conviction. Dickson dissented, with Laskin and Spence, because the accused's 'mental condition as well as the effect of alcohol are relevant to the critical question, not placed before the jury in this case, of whether the accused *had* the necessary intent.'[55] This case was an early example of Dickson's insistence that the jury should be allowed to consider all the evidence in determining whether the accused had the subjective intent to commit the crime.

The second case involved a man named Schwartz who had killed two people. Dickson initially thought it was a bad case in which the Court should never have given leave. Nevertheless, it became an important precedent. Following English and Canadian authority, the trial judge had instructed the jury that Schwartz had no insanity defence if he was capable of knowing that his actions was legally wrong. The majority of the Supreme Court upheld this traditional position, reasoning that it would be too 'subjective' to make the defence available to a person who knew that his actions were illegal but who believed that they were morally justifiable.[56] Dickson, in a dissent joined by Laskin, Spence, and Beetz, argued for a broader approach that would not punish those who, because of a mental disorder, thought that their crimes were not morally wrong. He was concerned about a woman who killed her child 'in the insane belief the voice of God had called upon her to offer a sacrifice and atonement'; a man who shot the king in the hope that he would be hanged and could respond to God's command 'to save mankind by the sacrifice of himself'; and a man who killed because 'the man-in-the-moon told me to do it' even though he knew he would be hanged.[57] Most of these examples were taken from Glanville Williams's leading text on criminal law.[58] Dickson also found support for his approach in the French language version of the insanity defence and the work of legal historians. Indeed, his use of a wide range of sources and his reliance on academics was striking. In a 1971 article highly critical of the Court's criminal law judgments, Paul Weiler had noted that the Court never used 'Canadian periodical writings' and only rarely cited British and American academics and then never 'to show that alternatives are available in the common law, or as a source of arguments favouring one alternative as more desirable and compatible with principle than another.'[59] In this 1976 judgment, however, Dickson relied on articles and books to this very end. His dissent was a tour de force that, not surprisingly, won praise from academics.

In Dickson's last case before retiring, his dissent in *Schwartz* became the law. The case involved a brutal murder in Winnipeg by two boys, aged fifteen and sixteen, who were convicted of first-degree murder because they were aware that killing was illegal. At conference, Dickson indicated that he still believed that his original dissent was correct and that 'wrong includes morally wrong.'[60] In a decision authored by Lamer, who had been appointed chief justice after Dickson's retirement, the Court overruled *Schwartz*.[61] A minority, however, expressed concerned that Dickson's approach was too subjective and could risk public safety. The teenagers received a new trial and were found not guilty by reason of insanity.

Dickson interpreted the insanity defence in a generous manner in most cases. In a 1980 murder case involving a thirty-one-year-old man with a borderline intelligence and a long history of psychiatric treatment, Dickson refused to have the insanity defence precluded because of a psychiatrist's testimony that the accused did not have a 'disease of the mind.' For Dickson, the insanity defence raised issues of free will and criminal responsibility that could not be resolved by medical opinion. 'The real question before the jury was the extent to which the accused's appreciation of the nature and quality of his act was impaired' when he attempted to rape and then strangled to death a fellow psychiatric patient. The insanity defence would apply if the accused was, because of a mental disorder, unable to appreciate that the victim would die. This was, for Dickson, 'simply a restatement, specific to the defence of insanity, of the principle that ... intention as to the consequences of the act, is a requisite element in the commission of a crime.'[62] Dickson's approach to the insanity defence was driven by the idea that an accused who was not subjectively at fault should not be convicted.

There were limits to how far Dickson would take his generous reading of the insanity defence. In 1982 the Court heard a case in which a psychiatrist had testified that a cocaine importer named Abbey had some delusional ideas that he was 'protected from punishment by some mysterious external source.' The trial judge and the British Columbia Court of Appeal accepted that this delusion rendered Abbey incapable of appreciating the nature and quality of his actions. Dickson did not. He usually started his insanity judgments with a discussion of the relevant legal principles. This one he started with the facts. Abbey admitted that, before leaving Canada for Peru, he had received money from three individuals to buy cocaine. When apprehended, he had stated: 'You got me ... It's coke.'[63] Common sense suggested that this accused was not insane. The fact that Abbey may not have appreciated that he would be punished and may have acted on the basis of 'an irresistible impulse' did not mean that he should not be punished. As Gérard La Forest recalled, even though Dickson took a principled and high-minded approach to the criminal law, he would not ignore his own beliefs that some accused were 'guilty as hell.'[64]

Dickson was unwilling to force an accused to accept an insanity defence that could lead to indeterminate detention for treatment if he believed that the accused was not mentally ill. He dissented in a 1980 case in which a twenty-year-old male university student named Rabey had assaulted a female student after a romantic rejection. The woman had told Rabey that he was 'just a friend' and Rabey had hit her on the head with a rock while screaming, 'You bitch, You bitch.' The majority of the Court concluded that, if the accused indeed had acted involuntarily, his only defence was insanity. They stressed that the ordinary person would not act involuntarily in response to a romantic rejection as opposed to some extraordinary shock.[65] Dickson criticized the majority for requiring the emotional blow to be so severe that an average person would go into an automatic state. 'As in all other aspects of the criminal law, except negligence offences, the inquiry ... [should be] directed to the accused's actual state of mind ... The fact that other people would not have reacted as he did should not obscure the reality that the external psychological blow did cause a loss of consciousness.' It was not only the intellectual principle of subjective fault that motivated Dickson, but also a concern about the proper disposition for the young accused. Dickson stressed that the student was 'a well-behaved young man until this incident' who had 'never lost his temper or displayed signs of anger.' Moreover, 'the medical experts gave him a clean mental bill of health.'[66] The consequence of an insanity verdict would have been automatically to subject the twenty-year-old to indeterminate detention at the lieutenant governor's pleasure. Dickson had visited institutions where the criminally insane were detained and he was not impressed with the way people were treated there.

As in his dissents on intoxication, Dickson recognized that the majority in *Rabey* was influenced by policy concerns about social protection. He argued that society was not endangered by the acquittal of a person like Rabey, who did not need treatment. Although praised by many academics for their principled approach, Dickson's dissents on both automatism and intoxication were criticized for giving too little weight to social protection and have not become the law.[67]

No Deliberate Disobedience of the Law

Dickson's concern about subjective fault and free will drove all of his important judgments touching on the mental capacity of the accused and led him to take an approach that was generous to the accused. When Dickson believed that the accused had acted intentionally, however, he was more minded to favour the prosecution. Dickson was reluctant to recognize a defence of necessity in *Morgentaler I* because of his concern about condoning an accused's deliberate decision to commit a crime.[68] In a 1984 case he recognized the necessity defence but retained much of his earlier caution. He concluded that the defence should apply only in emergency cases in which the accused acted in an involuntary manner. Although his judgment quoted a range of philosophers from Aristotle to Kant, Dickson characteristically used concrete examples to make his point. The lost mountain climber who breaks into a cabin 'on the point of freezing to death' was not acting voluntarily and could not realistically be deterred by the threat of punishment. 'His "choice" to break the law is no true choice at all; it is remorsefully compelled by normal human instincts. This sort of involuntariness is often described as "moral or normative involuntariness."' Dickson even suggested that the necessity defence would not apply if the danger was 'one that society would not reasonably expect the average person to withstand,'[69] even though an average-person standard was in tension with his normally subjectivist approach to issues of fault and voluntariness.

Dickson's commitment to the rule of law led him to maintain that necessity could excuse only an emergency decision to break the law in response to an immediate peril. It could never justify a deliberate and calculated decision to break the law. Bertha Wilson believed that Dickson's approach was too restrictive. She sent him a memo arguing that, in some cases, necessity could operate as a justification if the accused broke the law in the pursuit of a higher duty. In her subsequent solo judgment, she hinted that this might have some relevance to the abortion controversy. 'If one subscribes to the viewpoint articulated by Laskin C.J.C. in *Morgentaler*' the higher duty could include a doctor's 'legal obligation to treat the mother.'[70] Dickson's response to Wilson was firm. He suggested that Wilson's approach would allow people to break the law 'in the light of their allegedly laudable motivation' whereas, in his view, necessity should '*not* ... either justify or excuse those who choose to disobey the criminal law because it conflicts with their perception of a higher duty.' Dickson told Wilson that he still thought that his 1974 *Morgentaler* judgment 'that the courts cannot recognize obedience to "higher values" as a defence to a criminal charge ... is a correct one. If there is a legal way to cope with the danger, the law ought not to be broken.'[71] With respect to deliberate decisions to break the law, Dickson was more conservative than Wilson and his views prevailed.[72]

Dickson's commitment to the rule of law extended to his personal activities. If he thought there was any question that he himself might break the law, he would ask his law clerks to research the subject. The law clerks, who were busy writing bench and judgment memos, took Dickson's requests seriously, but somewhat tongue in cheek. Stephen Toope was asked to inquire whether a liquor licence was required for one of Dickson's parties. He replied that, as long as Dickson was not selling liquor to his guests, he should be fine because 'I can find no requirement for any license or permit for private parties of any number of people. See Regulation 581, Revised Reg. Ont. 1980 as amended (updated to 1986). Toope playfully added: 'My research was confirmed with a telephone call to the Ontario Liquor Control Board Regional Office. An employee, who said that he was not allowed to give his name, stated that no permit is required for private functions where liquor is not sold. By the way, I did not identify myself either!'[73] A few months later, Dickson asked another clerk, Patrick Macklem, to look into the legalities should Dickson decide to do some hunting on one of his morning horse rides. Macklem replied that, according to the Ministry of Natural Resources, 'it is lawful to carry an unloaded rifle on a horse on a public highway, but only during daylight hours. It cannot be loaded, however.' Macklem added that it was an offence to shoot a gun across a highway or to drive a horse 'furiously' on a highway. He warned the chief justice that he might be guilty of four offences 'if you chase and shoot your quarry on a public road at night.'[74]

Respect for Trial Judges

Dickson's respect for trial judges may have reflected his military experience. In the military, Major Dickson developed an appreciation of the important role played by each rank and the need for those at the top to trust and look after those who worked below them.

Dickson always bore in mind the difficult task of trial judges in charging juries about the law. He shaped the criminal law and the law of evidence with an eye on the difficulties that overly complex and uncertain distinctions would cause for trial judges. He rejected the qualified defence of honest but unreasonable self-defence that in some countries could reduce murder to manslaughter in large part because he feared that such a new defence 'would require prolix and complicated jury charges and would encourage juries to reach compromise verdicts to the prejudice of either the accused or the Crown.'[75] An experienced trial judge, John Holland, wrote Dickson thanking him for not further complicating the law because trial judges already had 'the almost impossible task of instructing juries in language which they may understand and at the same time pass the microscopic examinations' of appeal courts. In his reply, Dickson indicated that he was 'in entire agreement' with the trial judge's 'comment that undue complications in jury charges will lead to the death of the jury system' and expressed his concern that the complexity of the criminal law 'has made the task of the trial judge almost impossible.'[76]

Dickson's desire to simplify the work of trial judges explains his most important reform of the complex law of evidence. The case involved a complex drug conspiracy trial involving a man named Vetrovec. A crucial issue was whether any of the witnesses were accomplices of Vetrovec and thus deemed under the law at the time to be untrustworthy witnesses whose evidence required independent corroboration. The trial judge took six days to instruct the jury, in part because he was required to explain the complex legal definition of who was an accomplice and what constituted corroboration and to review the evidence that could constitute corroboration. These complex rules had been criticized by many academics and the Law Reform Commission of Canada had recommended their abolition. Dickson's conference notes reflected his concern for the difficult position of trial judges. 'We should not ignore the fact that trials are becoming increasingly long, complicated and sophisticated. The present trial lasted 100 days and it is simply nonsense to go through 100 days of trial, ask the judge to pick out items from the evidence capable of corroboration and then when he errs in one or two items start the whole process again.'[77]

In his judgment, Dickson noted that cases defining the test for corroborative evidence were numerous, complex, and difficult to reconcile. He was also concerned that the rules could detract from the jury's role in determining the credibility of all witnesses. 'To construct a universal rule singling out accomplices ... is to fasten upon this branch of evidence a blind and empty formalism. Rather than attempting to pigeon-hole a witness into a category and then recite a ritualistic incantation, the trial judge might better direct his mind to the facts of the case, and thoroughly examine all the facts which might impair the worth of a particular witness.' He advocated a common-sense approach that left the broad issue of credibility to the trier of fact. Trial judges should have discretion to decide when juries should be warned about accepting any witness's testimony. It was, in Dickson's view, impossible to codify common sense.[78] He subsequently explained his bold decision to law students as a example of a Supreme Court refusing to be a slave to an old rule that had 'become so technical and complex' that it had 'lost sight of the justice it sought to achieve.'[79]

Respect for the Jury

Dickson's desire to keep the law simple for trial judges, his faith in the jury, and his lack of sympathy for those who intentionally resorted to violence can all be seen in a 1986 case that dealt with the controversial defence of provocation. A successful defence of provocation reduces an intentional murder to manslaughter if the accused acts in the heat of passion in response to a wrongful act or insult that would deprive an ordinary person of self-control. The case involved sixteen-year-old Gordon Hill, who was charged with the murder of Vernon Pegg. The crown's theory was that the two were lovers and that, after a falling-out, Hill murdered Pegg by hitting him over the head with a hatchet and stabbing him to death with two steak knifes. Hill claimed both self-defence and provocation and argued that Pegg, who was his thirty-two-year-old volunteer 'Big Brother,' had made 'unexpected and unwelcome homosexual advances' and threatened to kill him.[80] The trial judge instructed the jury that, to find provocation, they must first find that Pegg's actions would have deprived an ordinary person of self-control, and he refused Hill's request that the jury be told to consider how an ordinary sixteen-year-old would react. The jury convicted Hill of second-degree murder and he was sentenced to life imprisonment without eligibility for parole for ten years.

The Supreme Court upheld Hill's conviction, Dickson writing for the majority. He started from the proposition that the provocation defence 'employs the objective standard of the reasonable person' in order 'to encourage conduct that complies with certain societal standards of reasonableness and proportionality.' The defence should not be available to 'an ill-tempered or exceptionally excitable person.' Although Dickson believed that it was 'fair to conclude that age will be a relevant consideration when we are dealing with a young accused person,' the question of who was the ordinary person should be left to 'plain common sense of the average Canadian jury.' In this case, the accused before them was 'male and young. I cannot conceive of a Canadian jury conjuring up the concept of an "ordinary person" who would be either female or elderly, or banishing from their minds the possibility that an "ordinary person" might be both young and male.'[81] In his conference notes, Dickson had indicated that he did 'not want to make things any more difficult for trial judges.'[82]

Wilson dissented, arguing that the trial judge should have instructed the jury to compare Hill's actions with those of an ordinary sixteen-year-old male. For her, the accused's sex was relevant to place the insult in context and Hill's age was relevant to the self-control expected from him. Wilson, who had gone directly from her Toronto Bay Street law practice to the Ontario Court of Appeal, had less faith in the common sense of the jury than Dickson, the former trial judge from the prairies. Wilson's approach of endowing the ordinary or reasonable person with some of the same characteristics as the accused was, however, on the ascendancy. Four years later, Dickson was persuaded by Wilson's landmark judgment that a woman's past experience as a battered woman should be considering in determining whether she had acted in reasonable self-defence.[83] Six years after Dickson's retirement, a slim majority of the Supreme Court ruled that the ordinary person in the provocation defence 'must be of the same age, and sex and share with the accused such other factors as would give the act or insult a special significance ...'[84] Unlike Dickson's decision in *Hill*, this approach does not rely on the common sense of the jury to endow the ordinary person with the appropriate experiences and characteristics. As society became more self-consciously diverse, faith in the jury system was challenged. Still, many criticize the Court's new approach as collapsing the distinction between subjective and objective standards and making it too easy for the accused, often an angry man, to benefit from the provocation defence.

Much of Dickson's approach to the criminal law was influenced by his faith in juries. He trusted that juries would use their common sense to reject specious claims of intoxication or a mistaken belief that victims of sexual offences consented. He also believed that juries would follow a trial judge's instructions about the proper legal tests and use of evidence. His belief in the jury system was unshakeable even in difficult cases. One case involved a man named Corbett who argued that he was denied a fair trial because, when he testified at his murder trial for a 1982 killing during a drug deal, the jury was told that he had been convicted of another murder in 1971. Dickson affirmed Corbett's murder conviction and trusted that the jury followed the trial judge's instruction to consider the prior murder conviction only to the extent that it reflected on his credibility as a witness and not on his propensity to murder again. Dickson argued that 'it is preferable to trust the good sense of the jury and to give the jury all relevant information, so long as it is accompanied by a clear instruction in law.' He believed that the jury should not 'be forced to decide the issue in the dark.' To make too much out of the risk that juries might not follow the trial judge's instruction could, in Dickson's view, 'seriously undermine the entire jury system.'[85] Gérard La Forest dissented and argued that Corbett had been denied a fair trial. He was influenced by social-science evidence that suggested that the accused would be prejudiced if jurors learned about prior convictions. La Forest later recalled that Dickson's faith in the jury 'was real, he trusted that jury.' For his part, La Forest still maintains: 'I just don't think the jury is that trustworthy.'[86]

Dickson's faith in the jury was obviously influenced by his own experience as a trial judge. Between 1963 and 1967, when he was a trial judge, Dickson rarely disagreed with the verdicts reached by Manitoba juries. Even though he was wealthier, better educated, and more travelled than the average jury member, he genuinely respected their collective common sense and wisdom. His wartime service, his involvement in community organizations such as the Red Cross, which mobilized much of the Winnipeg community during the 1950 Red River flood, and the Anglican Church also made him aware that lawyers and judges had no monopoly on wisdom or fairness. At the same time, the Manitoba juries that Dickson instructed were drawn from a relatively homogenous community. For example, there were few, if any, aboriginal people on Dickson's juries because Indian reserves were not required to submit the names of their residents for jury service in Manitoba until 1971.[87]

An Uncompromised Insistence on Fault

Dickson was repelled at the injustice of convicting a person in the absence of fault. Although his 1978 decision in *Sault Ste Marie* introduced a new halfway house based on the new defence of due diligence, it was driven by Dickson's belief that even a corporation should not be convicted of a regulatory offence if it was not at fault. Dickson would not compromise his commitment to subjective fault for true crimes even if it meant he was criticized for threatening the safety of women from sexual violence and the safety of the public from intoxicated and mentally disturbed offenders. He insisted on subjective fault without compromise, but, for better or worse, many of his decisions on these issues never became the law of the land.

12

Balanced Federalism

Brian Dickson served on the Supreme Court of Canada during a period of acrimonious constitutional debate and profound constitutional change. The constitutional battles of the 1970s and 1980s were fought on several fronts. The federal government was determined to modernize Canada's constitution, complete with an amending formula and a Charter of Rights. But the federal plan collided with a determined push for increased provincial powers, fuelled by the rise of Quebec nationalism and the claims of the western provinces for increased control over energy, natural resources, and the environment. These battles, complicated by an economic downturn and fights over diminishing tax revenues, placed severe strains on Canada's federal structure. They provoked a seemingly endless round of constitutional discussions between Ottawa and the provinces and frequent trips to the Supreme Court of Canada.

Canada's Constitution Act, 1867 (known until 1982 as the British North America Act, 1867) divides legislative powers between the Parliament of Canada and the provincial legislatures. Given the generality of the constitution's language and the changing political, economic, and social circumstances since Confederation, the courts have had to decide, on an ongoing case-by-case basis, the precise scope and limits of federal and provincial legislative authority.[1] Not surprisingly, given their importance, these judicial decisions have been the subject of fierce political and academic debate. Until 1949, the Judicial Committee of the Privy Council in the United Kingdom served as Canada's court of last resort and, in that capacity, established the basic ground rules for Canada's federal structure. The Privy Council tended to apply a classic vision of federalism resting on bright-line categories protective of provincial autonomy and deliberately ignoring the political, social, and economic context. Many scholars, including Bora Laskin, argued that the Privy Council skewed federalism by applying abstract reasoning and by according too much weight to claims of provincial autonomy and too little weight to broad federal powers, especially trade and commerce and the residual power to make laws for the 'Peace, Order and good Government' of Canada (POGG).[2] However, other scholars, including Jean Beetz and Louis-Philippe Pigeon, defended the Privy Council's record as properly reflecting the Confederation bargain and protecting provincial autonomy from being overwhelmed by sweeping centralist claims.[3]

By the time of Dickson's appointment, the Supreme Court had served for almost twenty-five years as Canada's final court of appeal. There can be little doubt that the Court had been moving away from the provincialism of the Privy Council. Some observers even claimed that Court was biased against the provinces.

Dickson did his best to steer a middle course in the treacherous seas of federalism review, exhibiting no discernable tendency to favour either the federal government or the provinces. He tended to be reluctant to strike down laws on federalism grounds, although he was quite prepared to assert judicial authority to protect individual and minority rights. The reasons for this variation in Dickson's attitude to judicial review are complex. It derives in part from the complex weave in his judicial philosophy of communitarian and individualistic values. Dickson saw federalism as involving the competing claims of governments. He thought that governments should cooperate to advance the general social good and that courts should not create obstacles, even if that meant leaving room for both levels of government to act. In federalism cases, Dickson favoured a judicial 'hands off' approach, generally refusing to strike down either federal or provincial laws, with the inevitable and – to Dickson – welcome result of overlapping spheres of federal and provincial authority.

Equally if not more important was Dickson's vision of Canada. He had a passionate belief in a strong and united Canada, but his prairie roots made him acutely aware of Canada's diversity and of the advantages of local solutions to local problems. He saw Canada as resting 'on a subtle equilibrium of contrasting forces' that had to be kept in balance. Canada, he said in a 1983 address at Dalhousie Law School in Halifax, 'balances two languages, two legal traditions and a multitude of cultural heritages.' The Constitution protected what he described as the 'basic bargain of Confederation' by protecting an 'equilibrium' of 'economic and geographical centralizing forces ... set off against similar decentralizing forces ... through a sensitive division of legislative powers between a central Parliament and provincial legislatures.'[4]

Dickson had no doubts about the fundamental importance of judicial review for federalism. He thought that 'the very nature of our federal system requires an impartial umpire of disputes between the federal and provincial governments'[5] and he saw the Supreme Court as the 'guardian of the federal bargain.'[6] In a 1977 case[7] he confronted a Saskatchewan statute immunizing the province from claims for the return of money paid under an unconstitutional tax. At the post-hearing conference, Dickson spoke of the 'necessity of the Court to monitor constitutional questions and preclude either power from immunizing itself from its own breach of the Constitution.'[8] Dickson wrote the Court's judgment striking down the law. While insisting that the courts would not question the wisdom of legislation, Dickson also asserted: 'It is the high duty of this Court to insure that the Legislatures do not transgress the limits of their constitutional mandate and engage in the illegal exercise of power.'[9]

Dickson did not dwell upon the maintenance of conceptual, abstract, and theoretical jurisdictional categories. He was more interested in crafting practical solutions to the multidimensional social and economic issues faced by modern governments. As he showed in his administrative-law decisions, discussed in chapter 8, Dickson did not distrust the state nor did he use the law of judicial review to enforce laissez-faire ideas of a minimal state. His basic posture in federalism, as in administrative law, was deference.[10] In a 1978 decision deciding that a province could establish an inquiry into organized crime despite section 91(27), which gave the federal government jurisdiction over 'the criminal law,' Dickson wrote: 'We should not lightly decide that enabling legislation is beyond the constitutional competence of the enacting body.'[11] Dickson was strongly attracted to legal doctrines that allowed for the operation of both federal and provincial laws. In a 1989 decision upholding a federal law that created a civil right of action, a matter ordinarily within section 92(13), the provincial power over property and civil rights,[12] Dickson observed: 'A law which is federal in its true nature will be upheld even if it affects matters which appear to be a proper subject for provincial legislation.'[13] He adopted the analysis of his former high school classmate, the eminent constitutional scholar William Lederman, who wrote that where one aspect of a matter falls within federal competence and another aspect is provincial, both laws should stand if 'the contrast between the relative importance of the two features is not so sharp.' [14] If the federal and provincial characteristics of a matter were more or less equal in importance, Dickson could see no reason 'to kill one and let the other live.'[15] This meant that overlapping federal and provincial laws could both be constitutionally valid.

Dickson welcomed overlapping federal and provincial laws as a natural result in a federal state, and thought that it encouraged cooperation between the two levels of government. He frequently observed in his judgments that 'overlap of legislation is to be expected and accommodated in a federal state.'[16] On this point as well, the influential thinking of Lederman was cited with approval: '... our community life – social, economic, political, and cultural – is very complex and will not fit neatly into any scheme of categories or classes without considerable overlap and ambiguity occurring.'[17]

Acceptance of overlapping federal and provincial legislation was further enhanced by Dickson's narrow definition of paramountcy, the judge-made rule that provides that in the event of conflict between validly enacted federal and provincial legislation, federal legislation prevails and the provincial law is rendered inoperative to the extent of the conflict. In a 1982 decision, Dickson was confronted with virtually identical Ontario and federal securities legislation regulating insider trading. Dickson later explained that he knew from his days in practice that the Ontario Securities Commission was 'at the centre of the financial world' and that, because its decisions were more or less accepted by other provinces, 'there is no need for a national securities commission.'[18] While he hinted in his judgment that Parliament had the constitutional authority to establish a national securities commission, he was not prepared to strike down or limit the Ontario scheme. He held both the federal and provincial laws valid since each level of government had a valid purpose in mind. Describing duplication as 'the ultimate in harmony,' Dickson held that 'mere duplication without actual conflict or contradiction is not sufficient to invoke the doctrine of paramountcy and render otherwise valid provincial legislation inoperative.' Duplication of proceedings or double recovery of damages could be readily controlled by the courts without striking down the law. He elaborated the narrowest possible definition of paramountcy, limiting its application to situations 'where there is actual conflict in operation as where one enactment says "yes" and the other says "no"; 'the same citizens are being told to do inconsistent things; compliance with one is defiance of the other.'[19]

Dickson's approach was sometimes at odds with that of two other dominant judicial thinkers on federalism with whom he served, Bora Laskin and Jean Beetz. Both Laskin and Beetz had been distinguished constitutional-law scholars before they became judges, and they took very different approaches to federalism. Laskin had a 'highly centralist vision of federalism.' He tended to interpret federal powers generously, and to limit what he saw as provincial incursions into broad federal spheres of authority. Beetz, on the other hand, was a 'classic federalist.' He was protective of provincial powers and he favoured clear and definite limits on broad federal powers that impinged upon provincial jurisdiction. Beetz's vision of federalism reflected his Quebec civil law background. His highly conceptual approach ensured clear jurisdictional lines that would protect the provincial powers essential to the preservation and enhancement of Quebec's distinctive language, culture, and legal tradition.[20]

Dickson's pragmatic and functional approach to federalism sometimes took him with Laskin and other times with Beetz. Dickson shared with Laskin the view that a strong federal government was desirable, particularly to deal with economic issues and to restrict provincial attempts to restrict civil liberties. He shared with Beetz an understanding of the importance of protecting provincial authority,[21] although he differed on how best to achieve that goal. Dickson understood Quebec's preoccupation with provincial autonomy as a guarantee of cultural and linguistic survival, but he took a decidedly less conceptual approach than Beetz and was more open to balancing federal and provincial interests. Once again, Dickson's judicial instincts led him to search for middle ground, halfway house solutions that would avoid tilting the federal balance too far in one direction or the other.

Peace, Order, and Good Government

The first landmark federalism case Dickson faced as a member of the Supreme Court was the 1976 *Anti-Inflation Reference.*[22] The Court's divided decision revealed fundamental differences between Laskin and Beetz, and Dickson's concurrence with Laskin demonstrated their shared belief in the importance of a strong national government with the capacity to deal with the economic health of the country as a whole.

Inflation was a matter of serious concern in the mid-1970s, and in the 1974 election wage and price controls were a central issue. The Liberals won with the promise of no controls, defeating Progressive Conservatives who had promised to introduce them. However, when faced with an alarming increase in the rate of inflation, Trudeau and the Liberals changed their minds. In 1975 Parliament established a wide-ranging scheme of wage and price controls to deal with the problem of inflation. In Parliament, the Liberal government rejected the opposition's plea that, to protect the law from constitutional attack, the scheme should be expressly declared to be emergency legislation. The federal government managed to get the provinces to agree to support the program, but, knowing that the constitutionality of the scheme was bound to be challenged by business or labour interests, the federal cabinet directed a reference to the Supreme Court of Canada to have the issue put to rest as soon as possible.

The case turned on the scope of the residual federal power 'to make Laws for the Peace, Order and good Government of Canada.' Read in isolation, the words suggest a broad general federal power and that appears to have been the view of Sir John A. Macdonald and other key political figures at the time of Confederation.[23] However, unless there are some limits, the POGG clause could swallow up virtually every subject and distort Canada's federal scheme. Particularly vulnerable is the provincial power over 'Property and Civil Rights,' a fundamental aspect of the Confederation bargain that is vital to the maintenance of Quebec's distinctive Civil Code, which regulates property and civil rights in that province.

Before their appointments to the bench, both Laskin and Beetz had written scholarly articles exploring the reach and the limits of POGG. Laskin, believing that Canada needed a strong central government to deal with the economy, argued in favour of a generous interpretation of POGG[24] and was highly critical of the narrower interpretation adopted by the Judicial Committee of the Privy Council to protect provincial autonomy. Beetz approached the question from a much different perspective. He argued that the general language of POGG had to be limited to safeguard the basic integrity of the federal scheme and to ensure that Quebec had the powers necessary to protect its distinctive language and culture.[25] Louis-Philippe Pigeon expressed similar views before his appointment to the Supreme Court, defending the Privy Council and the 'fundamental principle of provincial autonomy' from the attacks of Laskin and other anglophone scholars.[26]

It was well settled in the case law that, at a minimum, Parliament could invoke the POGG power to deal with national emergencies. The federal government argued in court that inflation had reached the level of a national emergency that justified resort to the POGG power. The difficulty with this argument was that the government had said nothing in Parliament about an emergency when enacting the law. The federal case also rested on the second, less well-developed 'national concern' branch of POGG jurisprudence. The case law suggested that, where 'the real subject matter of the legislation ... goes beyond local or provincial concerns or interests and must from its inherent nature be the concern of the Dominion as a whole,' it fell within the federal POGG power.[27] The problem was that inflation was such a general and all-pervasive phenomenon that, if it were accepted as a legitimate head of federal power, huge areas of provincial jurisdiction would be affected and the federal balance could be tilted too far in favour of Ottawa.

At the post-hearing conference, there was general agreement that the anti-inflation scheme should be upheld, but Dickson's memo identified the conundrum the case posed:

> The Chief Justice will draft the first reasons following which there will be a further conference.
>
> The principal point of concern ... is to ensure that the federal power cannot, in the future, by a mere declaration that a matter is one of serious national concern

invade the provincial sphere of jurisdiction under Section 92 of the BNA Act. The reasons should emphasise the special nature of the situation giving rise to the legislation and, in particular, the general provincial agreement and the temporary nature of the legislation which was enacted to meet the state of affairs existing at the end of 1975.[28]

In less than six weeks, the Court handed down a judgment upholding the federal scheme. Dickson concurred with Laskin's opinion upholding the law under the emergency branch of POGG. Laskin was prepared to excuse Parliament's failure to use the word 'emergency,' and Dickson later described Laskin's use of a huge volume of extrinsic evidence on the prevailing economic circumstances as 'a major breakthrough,'[29] although the evidence disputed the existence of an emergency. Without providing a convincing explanation of why or how,[30] Laskin found that the evidence, together with certain features of the act itself, was enough to show that the law was a response to what Parliament could reasonably regard as a national emergency. For Laskin, a key point was that the anti-inflation law was temporary, indicating that it was a response to an unusually pressing but transient problem. Having upheld the law on the emergency point, Laskin found it unnecessary to decide whether the law could also be upheld under the national concern doctrine, but there were strong hints in his judgment that he thought that it could.

Beetz wrote a powerful dissenting opinion, widely regarded as a judicial masterpiece of classic federalism.[31] Beetz held that, if Parliament intended to rely on the national emergency doctrine, it had to actually say that there was an emergency. If Parliament was not prepared to declare an emergency, it was not for the Court to proclaim one. Laskin, who often said that the media should do a better job covering the work of the Court, was irritated by an Ottawa *Citizen* editorial on the case that supported Beetz's opinion. The *Citizen* proclaimed: 'It's all very well to proclaim a national crisis. For that you can always get Supreme Court backing.'[32] Although this was more or less the very point Beetz had made in his dissent, Laskin took umbrage at the comment. Later, in a speech to the Canadian Press, he upbraided the press and described the editorial as an 'oversimplification which distorted the decision' and scored a point 'at the high cost of impugning judicial integrity.'[33]

Since he was not prepared to uphold the federal law as valid emergency legislation, Beetz also had to deal with the 'national concern' argument. To uphold the law on the ground that it dealt with a matter of 'national concern' would, Beetz thought, seriously disturb Canada's federal structure. Inflation involved so much that fell within provincial jurisdiction that Beetz could not accept it as a valid head of federal power. It was, he wrote, 'totally lacking in specificity' and 'so pervasive that it knows no bounds.' Drawing on articles written by future Justice Gerald Le Dain[34] and by William Lederman,[35] Beetz concluded that to accept inflation as a valid head of federal power 'would render most provincial powers nugatory.'[36]

Laskin's opinion attracted a majority on the national emergency doctrine, but a majority also agreed with Beetz on the national concern point.[37] That result addressed the concern that Dickson had expressed in his conference memo. The Court had managed to uphold the federal anti-inflation law on the narrower ground, avoiding any significant expansion of federal power. Why did Dickson not stick to the idea he expressed in his conference memo and agree with Laskin on the emergency point and with Beetz on the national concern doctrine? This was a natural halfway house in which Dickson could comfortably lodge. Dickson's conference notes suggest that he leaned towards Beetz's staunch defence of the 'federal principle' and his law clerk, Katherine Swinton, presented a case for affirming the 'classical federalism model' with 'two coordinate levels of government each dominant in its own sphere.'[38] Dickson, however, was solidly in Laskin's camp in the *Anti-Inflation Reference*. Indeed, he later claimed that he 'took quite an active part in the discussion and the drafting' of the judgment.[39] Dickson was certainly influenced by the fact that the federal scheme was supported by the provinces. Another point is that, by not ruling on the national concern issue, Dickson was exercising judicial restraint. Since he agreed with Laskin that the law could be upheld as emergency legislation, there was no need to say anything else.

Provincial Demands: Natural Resources and Broadcasting

In a 1978 judgment dealing with provincial control over natural resources, Dickson staked out some independent ground. He disagreed with a controversial majority judgment, written by Martland, striking down the Saskatchewan NDP government's 'royalty surcharge' on oil. The tax was imposed after world oil prices shot up as a consequence of the 1973 oil crisis. Saskatchewan decided to appropriate for the provincial treasury the windfall gains that would otherwise flow to its domestic producers. Martland held that the tax amounted to an export tax and that it interfered with Parliament's section 91(2) power to regulate interprovincial trade and commerce.

Dickson's instinct was to support a robust federal trade and commerce power, and indeed, at conference after oral argument, he agreed to write the Court's judgment holding 'that the legislation violated the constitution by trenching upon the federal trade and commerce power.'[40] However, after working closely on the case, he changed his mind and decided to allow the provinces the freedom of action to 'safeguard their legitimate interests as in their wisdom they see fit.' Dickson concluded that there was no evidence that the tax had in fact interfered with interprovincial trade. Saskatchewan oil continued to flow to markets outside the province and purchasers paid the same price for the oil as they would have paid without the tax. The only impact of the tax was that the province, not the producers, reaped the gain resulting from the dramatic rise in world oil prices. Dickson thought that the majority decision interfered with the plenary power of the provinces over their own natural resources. That power, he wrote, should be subject only 'to limits imposed by the Canadian constitution,' and, applying the presumption of constitutionality, he insisted that to prove invalidity 'the evidence must be clear and unmistakable; more than conjecture or speculation is needed to underpin a finding of constitutional incompetence.'[41]

The decision was a bitter disappointment for Saskatchewan Premier Allan Blakeney and for the resource-rich western provinces who saw it as an illegitimate interference with the right of a province to reap the benefits of its own natural resources. This grievance was further aggravated by subsequent decisions of the Court[42] and by the federal National Energy Program of the early 1980s.[43] Although Dickson kept his views private at the time, he was very sympathetic to these provincial concerns and he shared the perception of many westerners that the Trudeau Liberals ignored their interests.[44] The concerted provincial lobby for an accommodation of provincial interests eventually led to a constitutional amendment as part of the 1982 package that gave provinces the right to levy taxes on natural resources even for the export market.[45] Once again, a Dickson dissent became the law of the land, although this time it took a constitutional amendment.

Two other cases decided in 1978 involved another aspect of the federal-provincial conflicts of the late 1970s, namely, Quebec's insistence on the powers it needed to ensure its distinctive cultural and linguistic character. Both cases involved the regulation of cable television in Quebec.[46] Dickson agreed with Laskin's majority judgments holding that the federal government had exclusive jurisdiction over cable television, while the three Quebec judges, Pigeon, Beetz, and de Grandpré, dissented. These cases were important to Quebec since the regulation of broadcasting touched the very sensitive nerve of provincial control over language and culture. Quebec had introduced its own scheme after unsuccessfully lobbying Ottawa, with the support of Ontario and British Columbia, for jurisdiction over cable television at federal-provincial conferences in 1973 and 1974. The issue became even more explosive with the 1976 election of the separatist Parti Québécois. Given Dickson's usual sensitivity to provincial claims, his tolerance of overlapping regulatory schemes, and his concern about the isolation of Quebec judges and the alienation of Quebec, his concurrence with Laskin seems surprising. At conference, Dickson expressed doubt: 'Seven members of the Court [including Pigeon] seem satisfied that ... [a Privy Council decision on the regulation of radio] settles the matter and that the federal government has jurisdiction. De Grandpré and Beetz JJ and I have some doubts. We wish to look at it further ...'[47] However, the Privy Council decision[48] strongly supported federal competence and Laskin wrote a powerful judgment stating that it made no sense to distinguish cable transmission from other forms of broadcasting. From the perspective of national unity, there is much to be said for federal control over broadcasting and this, too, may have influenced Dickson.

The natural-resources and cable-broadcasting decisions were bitterly resented by diverse provincial interests. In the resource-rich west, the Court was attacked as Ottawa's instrument for centralization, while, in Quebec, it was attacked for its alleged insensitivity to the need for strong provincial powers to nurture the flowering of the French language and culture. The Court was criticized for its alleged centralist bias by editorial writers, legal scholars and, most colourfully, Quebec's separatist premier, René Lévesque: 'Comme la Tour de Pise, la Cour penche toujours du même bord.'[49] Bora Laskin saw these criticisms as a serious challenge to the Court's integrity and authority. He took the unusual step of responding publicly with a spirited defence against what he described as 'extravagances and distortions.'[50]

Ammunition for a Constitutional Bill of Rights

In two more important 1978 decisions, Dickson again sided with Laskin's strong plea for federal power, but in both cases they were in dissent. Both involved the federal power in relation to criminal law. *Nova Scotia Board of Censors v. McNeil*[51] concerned the validity of a provincial statute establishing a censorship scheme for movies and other forms of public entertainment. *Attorney General for Canada and Dupond v. Montreal*[52] involved an attack on a Montreal by-law that prohibited public assemblies or gatherings on public property for a period of thirty days. This extraordinary measure was prompted by the unusual circumstances of terrorist activities by fringe separatist groups.

Laskin always interpreted the federal criminal law power generously, seeing it as one element in the federal arsenal for the protection of civil liberties. As an academic, he had written extensively on the subject, arguing that fundamental rights and freedoms were exclusively within federal authority and that the courts could and should strike down offending provincial laws.[53] Not surprisingly, therefore, he viewed the Nova Scotia censorship scheme as an attempt to protect the public from obscene, indecent, and offensive material and this, he thought, fell within the federal government's exclusive competence over criminal law. As for the Montreal by-law, Laskin described it a 'mini-criminal code' to deal with the maintenance of public order. However, in neither case could Laskin persuade a majority of his colleagues. Spence and Dickson agreed with Laskin in both cases, forming the LSD trio that, at the time, often took liberal positions on criminal and public-law issues, but the majority of the Court held that both laws were constitutionally valid. Martland wrote the majority opinion in *McNeil*, upholding the censorship law as valid under the provincial powers with respect to 'property and civil rights' and 'matters of a merely local or private nature.' Beetz wrote the majority opinion in *Dupond*, upholding the by-law as a legitimate preventive measure and a matter 'of a merely local or private nature' and giving short shrift to the serious issues of freedom of expression and freedom of association.

By concurring with Laskin, Dickson departed from his usual inclination to allow for overlapping federal and provincial jurisdiction. However, both cases involved significant civil-liberties values, and, at least in these instances, such values trumped Dickson's usual tolerance of cooperative federalism. His conference memos show that, while he was reluctant to place undue limits on provincial authority, he was also troubled by the impact the challenged laws had upon freedom of expression and freedom of assembly. In *McNeil*, Dickson's initial inclination was to strike down the censorship law but at the same time to 'acknowledge that there is a valid provincial right to regulate and prohibit if it can be tied to a valid provincial purpose.'[54] In *Dupond*, though he was sympathetic to the attempt to control violent street demonstrations and inclined to uphold the by-law, he was more worried about the fundamental freedoms at issue. 'It seems to me that the legislation encroaches upon a basic and fundamental right – that of assembly and the right to protest – the regulation of which falls within federal power.'[55]

The majority's refusal in *McNeil* and *Dupond* to limit provincial laws impinging on civil liberties was a serious setback for Laskin, who had long advocated an expansive definition of the federal criminal-law power as a way to ensure respect for civil liberties. In a number of significant cases in the 1950s, the Supreme Court had demonstrated a remarkable ability to protect fundamental freedoms, and a leading constitutional law scholar suggested that the Court of the 1950s would have decided *McNeil* and *Dupond* differently.[56] In the 1970s, despite the ardent support of Laskin, the civil-libertarian spirit had been lost.[57] Once again, however, the Court's inclination ran counter to the flow of history and it may have had a bearing on the impetus for constitutional change. According to a leading political scientist, the majority decisions in *McNeil* and *Dupond* were a setback that 'provided additional ammunition for advocates of a Constitutional Bill of Rights.'[58]

'A careful and delicate division of power'

The earliest federalism judgments Dickson wrote as a member of the Supreme Court dealt with reconciling the federal power in relation to criminal law with the provincial power with respect to the administration of justice. Dickson was convinced that the constitution gave the provinces a pre-eminent role in the day-to-day administration of justice. He thought that history favoured a strong provincial role and that justice would be better administered by local officials familiar with local conditions. But here Dickson collided head-on with Bora Laskin, who insisted on limiting the provincial role to protect plenary federal authority in the important area of criminal law.

As is so often the case, the constitution's text was less than clear. Section 91 (27) of the *Constitution Act, 1867* gives the Parliament of Canada responsibility for the 'Criminal Law, except the Constitution of Courts of Criminal Jurisdiction, but including the Procedure in Criminal Matters,' while, under section 92 (14), the provinces have responsibility for 'the Administration of Justice in the Province, including the Constitution, Maintenance, and Organization of Provincial Courts, both of Civil and of Criminal Jurisdiction, and including Procedure in Civil Matters in those Courts.' There is an obvious tension between federal authority over the 'criminal law' and 'procedure in criminal matters,' on the one hand, and provincial competence in relation to 'the administration of justice in the province,' on the other. Dickson saw these provisions as an attempt to 'effect a careful and delicate division of power between the two levels of government in the field of criminal justice'[59] and he thought that the Courts should do their best to achieve a proper balance of federal and provincial authority. Laskin viewed the federal power as pre-eminent and was determined to protect it from provincial incursion.

The first case, *Di Iorio v. Warden of the Montreal Jail,*[60] decided in 1978, dealt with the validity of a Quebec commission of inquiry into organized crime. At conference[61] the Court was sharply divided. Martland and Pigeon thought that the province had the power to establish the inquiry and to give those conducting it the right to compel witnesses to attend and answer questions and to commit for contempt anyone who refused to comply. Laskin disagreed. He had always advocated a generous interpretation of the federal criminal-law power as a way of protecting civil liberties from provincial infringement.[62] He thought that requiring a witness to attend to be questioned in respect of criminal activities made the proceedings criminal in nature and that the province was intruding upon the federal power. Dickson was undecided. He was concerned about the inquisitorial nature of the inquiry and asked whether the province could revoke the right to silence. Although he was on the fence, Dickson agreed to write the judgment.

Dickson's initial concern with the procedural rights of those under investigation faded and he wrote a strong judgment that charted the course for his consistent defence of a significant provincial responsibility in the area of criminal justice. His judgment reflects the themes that pervade his federalism jurisprudence. He tried not to read any provision of the constitution narrowly and he was inclined to uphold legislation if at all possible. If that approach was to be applied even-handedly to both federal and provincial authority, it had to be mediated by Dickson's acceptance and encouragement of overlapping spheres of federal and provincial competence. He saw an element of overlapping powers as implicit in Canada's constitutional arrangements: 'One should not expect to be able to draw a fine line between two heads of power nor should one attempt to do so.'[63] The provincial inquiry was plainly concerned with criminal law, but it was general in nature. It did not deal with specific charges and its function was to investigate and report, not convict or acquit. The province was not purporting to add to the list of crimes defined by Parliament or to change the criminal law. Dickson thought that the inquiry could be supported under the province's authority over the administration of justice. His affirmation of provincial competence attracted a majority,[64] but it drew a strong dissent from Laskin, who saw the provincial inquiry as a direct invasion of exclusive federal competence over criminal law. He thought that allowing the province to establish inquiries into organized crime would open the door to provincial inquiries into other federal areas, such as bankruptcy, where they had no legislative competence.

When the Court heard argument in *R. v. Hauser*,[65] two years later, it seemed that Dickson's generous interpretation of provincial power in *Di Iorio* would be extended to include the right to prosecute criminal offences. Hauser was charged with possession of cannabis for the purpose of trafficking. He challenged the right of the attorney general of Canada to conduct the prosecution, arguing that the constitution assigned that responsibility to the provincial attorney general. At conference, the Court was unanimous. As Dickson put it in his memo: 'The Court seems quite content that *Di Iorio* was properly decided and that we should probably reinforce it by an affirmative statement as to the provincial rights under "administration of justice."' Dickson was assigned the task of writing an opinion that would recognize 'concurrency of jurisdiction' in the area of criminal law, allowing for provincial enforcement of federally enacted laws.[66]

However, in the year between oral hearing and judgment, it became clear that Dickson's generous interpretation of the provincial power over the administration of justice would not prevail. [67]The majority upheld the right of the attorney general of Canada to prosecute narcotics offences on the unlikely ground that the Narcotics Control Act should be characterized not as criminal law but rather as legislation under the federal POGG power. Dickson had to recast his draft judgment as a lengthy and compelling dissent. The Narcotics Control Act, he wrote, was criminal law: 'It is extremely difficult, indeed impossible upon the authorities, to characterize the Act as being little more than a stringent regulatory scheme for the control of narcotic drugs.'[68] The conclusion that the act could be sustained under POGG resurrected a discredited case from the 1880s upholding federal temperance legislation under POGG[69] and it went against the grain of the majority Beetz had attracted in the *Anti-Inflation Reference* three years earlier to limit a broad POGG power. Dickson insisted that narcotics offences were criminal and emphasized that responsibility over criminal justice was shared. The province had 'the right to direct the judicial process' but only 'in accordance with prescribed federal procedures.'[70]

As he often did when deciding federalism cases, Dickson drew upon historical evidence.[71] He was convinced that the Fathers of Confederation thought that decisions about the prosecution of crimes could best be made at the local level. By attempting to take control of prosecutions, the federal authorities were in 'breach of the bargain struck at the time of Confederation.' He thought that the overlapping authority of the federal power to deal with the rules of substantive and procedural criminal law and the provincial authority to administer the criminal law at the local level reflected an awareness of the 'need ... to maintain the "subtle balance" between national and local interests envisaged in our Constitution, leaving the administration of criminal justice in provincial hands where it could be more flexibly administered in response to local conditions.' Dickson did not rest his case on history alone. He argued that, from a functional perspective, it made sense to locate prosecutorial authority at the provincial level. Prosecution policies should be sensitive to local needs and concerns and it was desirable to achieve cohesion of the investigatory, policing, and prosecutorial functions of the enforcement of the criminal law.[72]

The issue of reconciling the federal criminal-law power and provincial competence with respect to the administration of justice arose again when Royal Canadian Mounted Police (RCMP) officers challenged the jurisdiction of an Alberta tribunal to investigate a citizen's complaint.[73] The majority of the Court, led by Chief Justice Laskin, unhesitatingly said 'no' to provincial jurisdiction. Laskin insisted that federal jurisdiction had to be protected and that, since the province could not discipline an RCMP officer, it had no business conducting an investigation.

Alone in dissent, Dickson again appealed to history and to the importance of local law enforcement. As a westerner, Dickson was perhaps more used to the RCMP acting as the local police than his colleagues from Ontario and Quebec. He refused to see the RCMP's performance of this function as resulting in the elimination of local control. He argued that 'if constitutional history teaches us anything it teaches that the Fathers of Confederation wished the substantive criminal law to be enacted at the federal level ... but the administration of justice within the province ... to be at the local level.' Dickson saw the maintenance of law and order as 'inherently of local concern...best managed by local officials, sensitive to the needs and idiosyncrasies of the community.' Effective law enforcement could not be managed by 'officials in Ottawa' but 'required, at the controls, a hand responsive to local needs.'[74] Dickson insisted that the province should be able to investigate the activities of the police.

A. G. Canada v. Canadian National Transportation Ltd.[75] dealt the final blow to Dickson's 'pro-province' administration of justice theory. The federal authorities prosecuted Canadian National (CN) on a charge of conspiracy to lessen competition under the Combines Investigation Act. Hoping that the Court would adopt Dickson's theory, at least in relation to the criminal law itself, CN argued that the offence was truly criminal in nature and that only the provincial attorney general could conduct the prosecution. The *Hauser* decision, said CN's lawyers, turned on the classification of the Narcotics Control Act as a law for the peace, order, and good government of Canada rather than as criminal law. Prior decisions classified the Combines Investigation Act as criminal law, and from the time of Confederation, as a matter of practice, the provincial attorneys general had prosecuted ordinary criminal offences.

The majority of the court was unimpressed by CN's argument. Laskin concluded that, even if the prosecution was truly criminal in nature, the federal attorney general was entitled to prosecute. He unequivocally repudiated Dickson's theory and wrote that provincial authority over the administration of justice did not include the right to prosecute criminal offences. Parliament had the right to decide who should conduct criminal prosecutions and existing provincial prosecutorial power with respect to ordinary criminal offences existed only by leave of the federal authorities.

Dickson maintained that the constitution accorded prosecutorial authority with respect to criminal offences to the provinces. In a memo to file, he had recorded: 'We must decide the case with the aid of experience and not necessarily logic' and 'the control by provincial attorney's general of criminal offence charges has been a fact of life for over 100 years.'[76] Despite his failure to convince his colleagues, Dickson wrote in his judgment: 'I remain unshaken in the view I expressed in *Hauser* ...' As in other areas of the law, Dickson was willing to repeat his dissents. Without any serious hope of persuading the other members of the Court, he made a final appeal to the functional and historical underpinnings of his argument. In his judgment, he wrote: '[A] page of history may illuminate more than a book of logic.' Dickson could not accept that the Fathers of Confederation contemplated 'that ultimate constitutional authority for the conduct and prosecution of all criminal offences – the multitude of cases arising daily in the hundreds of communities in what was then Canada – would centre in Ottawa.'[77]

Although Dickson was unable to persuade his colleagues with his arguments favouring provincial prosecutorial authority, it is fair to say that most commentators have favoured his position.[78] Moreover, in response to the majority decisions, the federal crown has delegated prosecutorial authority over most offences to the provincial attorneys general. The overlapping cooperative scheme envisioned by Dickson largely has been achieved in practice if not in constitutional law – and is yet another example of a Dickson dissent becoming the law of Canada.

'The true balance'

Canadian National firmly closed the door on Dickson's plea for provincial control over the administration of justice, but it also served as the starting point for his significant achievement in elaborating a workable theory to allow for general federal economic regulatory authority under the trade and commerce power. It was settled that the federal government could regulate interprovincial and international trade, but the courts had failed to articulate a workable test for the second or general branch that allowed the federal government to regulate 'trade affecting the whole Dominion.'[79] At what point does the regulation of economic activity transcend these legitimate spheres of provincial jurisdiction, especially property and civil rights, and fall within federal power? Can a line defining federal power be drawn with sufficient precision to leave appropriate scope for provincial competence to deal with the business of regulating most day-to-day commercial activity?

Dickson was keenly interested in economic issues and, in developing his perspective on the constitutional parameters of regulatory authority, he drew on his experience as a sophisticated commercial and corporate lawyer, a member of the board of directors of a chartered bank, and a member of the Manitoba Court of Appeal, where he had decided no fewer than four cases[80] involving the trade and commerce power. His combined business and legal experience led him to believe that there were economic issues, national in scope and affecting the 'economy as a single integrated national unit,'[81] that transcend provincial interests and provincial competence. At the same time, he had a strong belief in the need to protect provincial jurisdiction over the regulation of businesses, trades, and local economic activity. He was acutely aware that the country could not be ruled entirely from Ottawa and that provincial powers had to be preserved to deal effectively with local economic and business activity. The challenge was to unlock the constitutional barrier to federal regulatory power created by the failure to articulate appropriate scope for 'general regulation of trade affecting the whole Dominion', but to do so in a way that would not imperil 'the local autonomy in economic regulation contemplated by the constitution.'[82] A middle ground had to be found between an all-pervasive interpretation of the federal power, which would overwhelm the regulatory powers of the provinces in relation to their own local economic activities and, as Dickson would say in a judgment years later, 'an interpretation that renders the general trade and commerce power to all intents vapid and meaningless.'[83]

The law was in a murky state when Dickson wrote *Canadian National*.[84] He realized that it would be difficult, if not impossible, to state a precise test for the federal power. The limits of the federal power, he wrote 'are not fixed, and ... questions of constitutional balance play a crucial role in determining its extent in any given case at any given time.'[85] He described the competing values of provincial autonomy in relation to the regulation of particular trades and businesses and the need for federal capacity to deal with the economy as a whole.

To achieve a balance between vital federal and provincial interests, Dickson built upon a 1977 Laskin decision[86] that had identified the elements for a valid exercise of the general branch of the federal trade and commerce power. Laskin wrote that there had to be a general regulatory scheme monitored by the continuing oversight of a regulatory agency that was concerned with trade as a whole rather than with a particular industry. To 'ensure that federal legislation does not upset the balance of power between federal and provincial governments,' Dickson added two further crucial elements directly focusing on the dimensions of the problem being addressed in relation to provincial capacity '(i) the legislation should be of a nature that the provinces jointly or severally would be constitutionally incapable of enacting; and (ii) the failure to include one or more provinces or localities in a legislative scheme would jeopardize the successful operation of the scheme in other parts of the country.'[87]

The reference to provincial incapacity, a device later employed to allow for a contained expansion of the federal POGG power,[88] achieved the balance Dickson was seeking, protecting provincial regulatory authority where the matter remained local but affording scope for federal initiatives aimed at the national economy as a whole where the matter transcended provincial regulatory capacity. Only Beetz and Lamer agreed with Dickson's trade and commerce analysis, however. The other members of the Court sided with Laskin, who found it unnecessary to deal with the complex trade and commerce issue.

Yet, once again, a Dickson minority opinion would become the law. Six years later, on the eve of his retirement from the Court, Dickson wrote another judgment that put the crowning touch on his effort to give the general branch of the trade and commerce power meaningful existence. In *General Motors of Canada Ltd. v. City National Leasing*,[89] the Court ruled on the constitutional validity of a section of the federal Combines Investigation Act that created a private civil right of action in damages for certain violations of the act. City

National, represented by John Sopinka shortly before his appointment to the Court, sued General Motors for damages, relying on the statutory right of civil action. Ordinarily, an action for damages is a civil right that can be created only by a provincial legislature. The constitutional validity of the federal Combines Investigation Act had been upheld in earlier decisions under the federal criminal-law power. General Motors moved to strike out the claim on the ground that by creating a civil claim, Parliament had trespassed on the exclusive power of the provinces in relation to property and civil rights.

At conference there was considerable uncertainty[90] but in the end Dickson wrote for a unanimous Court to uphold the constitutional validity of the civil action. Dickson found the Combines Investigation Act to be valid under the general branch of the federal trade and commerce power. While Parliament's creation of a civil cause of action for violation of the federal competition law encroached upon the provincial power over property and civil rights, the right of action was sufficiently related to the overall scheme of the act that the intrusion into the provincial field was justifiable.

Dickson's judgment pulled together the threads of the evolution of the general branch of the federal trade and commerce power. Writing of the need to strike 'the true balance between property and civil rights and the regulation of trade and commerce,' he reiterated his familiar themes of judicial restraint and overlap between federal and provincial laws: 'Overlap of legislation is to be expected and accommodated in a federal state' and 'judicial restraint in proposing strict tests which will result in striking down such legislation is appropriate.'[91]

The Combines Investigation Act satisfied the requirements that he and Laskin had laid down for the valid exercise of federal power. There was 'a well-orchestrated scheme of economic regulation' aimed at the elimination of activities that reduce competition in the marketplace. The regulatory scheme 'operates under the watchful gaze of a regulatory agency' that was national in scope and 'aimed at the economy as a single integrated unit rather than as a collection of separate local enterprises.' Anti-competitive activities did not respect provincial borders and legislation to combat such conduct was effectively beyond the capacity of the provinces. Although the creation of civil rights of action fell within provincial competence, this provision, Dickson wrote, had to be judged in light of the overall scheme of the Combines Investigation Act. Parliament had not created a freestanding civil right of action as damages could only be awarded if a specific violation of the Act were established. The civil right of action was functionally related to the Act's operation, purpose, and philosophy and could not be dismissed as an illegitimate appendage.[92]

It is difficult to measure the impact of the Dickson view of the general branch of the federal trade and commerce power. There can be no doubt that, from a jurisprudential perspective, Dickson's judgments in *Candian National* and *General Motors* represent the most ambitious judicial attempt to carve out an area of legislative authority for Parliament to enact legislation affecting the Canadian economy as a whole. On the other hand, the recent trend towards deregulation of the economy in response to global competitive forces has discouraged reliance upon the broadly based federal regulatory schemes that lie at the heart of Dickson's analysis.

Overlapping Powers and Watertight Compartments

Just as Dickson's vision of a middle way of cooperative federalism that tolerated and even encouraged overlapping jurisdiction between the two levels of government collided with the strongly centralist opinions of Bora Laskin, so too did it confront the classical federalism of Jean Beetz. Their differences came to a head in a case argued in 1986, involving a challenge by the Ontario public servant employees union, OPSEU, to a provincial law banning them from political activity at both the provincial and federal levels.[93] OPSEU argued that the provincial legislature had no business restricting the right of Ontario citizens to engage in federal political activities. By the time the case reached the Supreme Court of Canada, the Charter had been enacted and the public servants wanted to rely on it as well. Both Laskin and Dickson approved the constitutional questions required to notify all attorneys general of the issues raised by the case, including the Charter issues.[94] However, at the oral hearing, OPSEU's lawyers, Stephen Goudge and a former Dickson clerk, Ian McGilp, were surprised when Blenus Wright, counsel for Ontario, objected.[95] The Court retired to consider the point and there was what Dickson described as a 'heated discussion in the conference room.'[96] Goudge and McGilp repaired to the coffee shop to plot an alternate strategy. McGilp came up with the idea of advancing the same arguments on the rather shaky ground of the pre-Charter 'implied bill of rights' theory that certain fundamental rights, especially those pertaining to the democratic process, were implicit in Canada's constitutional order and beyond the reach of restriction by provincial legislation.

When the judges came back into court, it was apparent that there had been a sharp disagreement. A red-faced Dickson announced that a majority had decided that the Charter arguments would not be heard since they had not been considered by the Ontario courts. He noted pointedly that he, together with Chouinard and Le Dain, disagreed with the majority. When Goudge outlined his argument and indicated that he would be relying on the theory of an implied bill of rights, Dickson chuckled. Beetz, who wanted to exclude the *Charter* arguments, seemed annoyed by Dickson's enjoyment of this end-run around the Court's ruling.

The implied bill of rights argument provoked an interesting discussion at conference. Some of the judges were concerned about the overlap with the Charter. There would be two sources for freedom of expression, one of which could be limited by section 1 (providing that the guarantee of rights is subject 'to such reasonable limits prescribed by law as can be demonstrably justified in a free and democratic society') or overridden by the notwithstanding clause. One judge suggested that perhaps the Court should take the position that the Charter did away with the implied bill of rights, but Dickson noted that 'this was strongly rejected for two reasons. First, there was felt to be some value in retaining what had been said about freedom of speech in some of the early cases. If at some time some provincial government or federal government arbitrarily sought to deny all freedom of speech and use s. 33 to avoid the Charter, it might be very helpful to have possible recourse to a constitutional value implicit through the preamble to the Constitution. The second argument against ... [the] proposal lay in the fact that to give effect to it would diminish freedom of speech which had existed prior to the *Charter.*'[97]

On the federalism point, the public servants relied on the Court's 1965 *McKay* decision exempting election signs in a federal campaign from a municipal by-law that prohibited all signs on residential property.[98] Goudge urged the Court to extend this principle to the situation of the public servants. The province, he argued, simply had no business restricting political activity in the federal sphere and the Court should limit the law's application accordingly.

Dickson wrote first reasons. He was cool to the argument for an implied bill of rights because he thought this to be an area where the province had to be given some leeway. As he put it, 'no single value ... can bear the full burden of upholding a democratic system of government.'[99] Dickson was also entirely unsympathetic to the attempt to whittle away at the provincial law because it impinged upon the federal sphere. The case offered him the opportunity to crystallize and reiterate his thinking on overlapping powers. He rejected the contention that there were spheres of federal authority immune from the impact of otherwise valid provincial legislation. In this respect, he dismissed a 1966 decision supporting federal immunity,[100] as unpersuasive, and, relying on the work of Peter Hogg, a leading constitutional law scholar, he wrote: 'The history of Canadian constitutional law has been to allow for a fair amount of interplay and indeed overlap between federal and provincial powers.' Arguments in favour of interjurisdictional immunity or viewing federal and provincial powers as 'watertight compartments ... have not been the dominant tide of constitutional doctrines; rather they have been an undertow against the strong pull of pith and substance, the aspect doctrine, and in recent years, a very restrained approach to concurrency and paramountcy issues.'[101] As for

McKay, Dickson simply said that the case had been wrongly decided and that it should be overruled. He adopted Hogg's criticism that *McKay* was inconsistent with the basic principle that otherwise valid legislation 'is not objectionable just because it affects a matter outside jurisdiction.'[102]

Dickson's judgment went too far in the direction of overlapping jurisdiction for Beetz, the classical federalist who insisted upon sharp lines defining exclusive spheres of authority. In his terse, toughly worded memorandum responding to Dickson's draft reasons, Beetz stated that he agreed with the result Dickson reached, but that 'I respectfully disagree with most of your reasons ... You summarily overrule two important decisions of this Court[103] which happen to incur the displeasure of Professor Hogg and a few academics.' Beetz was particularly annoyed by Dickson's dismissal of the 1966 case upon which he intended to rely in an important series of judgments he was working on. 'You probably pre-empt the reasons and the result in the trilogy I am working on.' Beetz thought that the election-signs decision could be distinguished, and he left no doubt where he stood: 'I will discuss with you and other members of the coram what should be done in this case. One thing is sure however: I cannot agree with your reasons as they presently stand.'[104]

Dickson responded with a memo the very same day. He told Beetz that he did not intend to overrule the 1966 case, but rather to limit its application. On *McKay,* Dickson was firm. 'I am persuaded that the thrust of our recent decisions ... [including one of Beetz's own judgments] indicates that *McKay* would be decided differently today ... I concluded that it was more honest to overrule it rather than try to distinguish it.'[105]

Beetz was unmoved and he wrote a concurring judgment, upholding the legislation as a valid exercise of provincial authority over the operation of an important aspect of the executive branch of the structure of the provincial government. He gave the implied bill of rights a surprising endorsement, holding that '... neither parliament nor the provincial legislatures may enact legislation the effect of which will be to substantially interfere with the operation of the basic constitutional structure.'[106] However, he also held that the provincial law at issue did not have that effect. Political activities at the federal level had to be included to ensure the impartiality of the public service. Rather than overrule *McKay,* Beetz distinguished it on the ground that it involved a complete ban on signs whereas the restriction of political activity at issue amounted to no more than regulation.

This exchange reflected a significant difference between Beetz and Dickson on the nature of Canadian federalism. Dickson resisted sharp lines of division between federal and provincial jurisdiction and he was strongly attracted to the idea of overlapping spheres of authority and cooperation between the two levels of government. Beetz insisted upon clean lines of authority, resisting what he saw as incursions by one level of government into the affairs of the other. The Beetz judgment won the day. Dickson garnered the support of only Lamer, but even that was qualified since Lamer wrote a one-line concurring judgment agreeing with both Beetz and Dickson.

'Prodigious judicial statecraft'

Dickson's pragmatic and functional approach to federalism, seeking if possible to locate authority at the level he perceived to be most adept at dealing with the problem, avoided any doctrinaire inclination or predisposition to favour either federal or provincial authority. He believed that the two levels of government should cooperate in finding the most appropriate solution to social and economic problems. As his judgments on the federal trade and commerce power show, he favoured a strong central government to deal with the economy as a whole. Yet, as his decisions on the administration of justice reveal, he was also keenly aware of the advantages of local solutions to local problems.

From a purely conceptual perspective, his thinking on federalism seems to have been less rigorous than that of either Laskin or Beetz, the two most influential federalism jurists of his era. But Dickson did not think that constitutional adjudication could or should be reduced to abstract legal rules. He saw the search for the proper meaning of the constitution's provisions dividing power between the federal government and the provinces 'not as an abstract exercise in statutory interpretation, but as a practical problem with foreseeable political consequences.'[107] He insisted that issues should be decided on a 'careful case by case analysis,'[108] not 'in a vacuum' but in light of 'currents in social, economic, and political thought.'[109] He mediated the poles of Laskin's centralism and Beetz's classical federalism, agreeing with Laskin on some issues with economic and civil-liberties implications and agreeing with Beetz on other issues concerning local powers and the need to restrain federal powers that could overwhelm the provincial jurisdiction over property and civil rights.

Dickson's pragmatism, functionalism, and balancing of federal and provincial interests may seem to render constitutional adjudication susceptible to subjectivity and unpredictability. However, as his former clerk, Katherine Swinton observes in her study of federalism jurisprudence, there is also much to be said for Dickson's approach.[110] Dickson paid appropriate heed to the constitution's text and to precedent, but he looked as well to history and to the underlying policy concerns. He was highly attentive to social and political context and to the changing needs of the Canadian federation. Dickson believed that there was an element of 'prodigious judicial statecraft'[111] in constitutional adjudication that could not be reduced to legal doctrine. He paid close attention to the shifts in the country's political mood and, if subsequent history is any guide, when he disagreed with his judicial colleagues, his views reflected more often than not the trajectory of Canadian federalism. Several of his dissenting or minority opinions carried the day in the end, adopted in later decisions, by legislation, and even by constitutional amendment.

Dickson was profoundly concerned about national unity and the threat of Quebec separation.[112] He was also deeply troubled by western alienation. Strongly disagreeing with what he regarded as Pierre Trudeau's dismissive attitude towards western Canada, he was especially upset by the Liberal government's National Energy Policy.[113]

Dickson took into account this sense of Canada and Canadian values when deciding constitutional cases. He had an instinctive belief that Canada's regional differences and tensions could not be accommodated by a purely conceptual approach to the constitution. To a large extent, his passionate belief in a strong and united Canada, balanced with his keen appreciation of the country's diversity and need for provincial integrity, reflected Canada's unresolved issues of national identity. He simply refused to come down cleanly on one side or the other. As we shall see in the next chapter, Dickson and the Supreme Court of Canada would played a vital role in maintaining that balance when very different visions of Canada clashed in the constitutional crisis of 1981.

13

Patriation of the Constitution

On 2 October 1980, Prime Minister Pierre Elliott Trudeau announced that, despite overwhelming provincial opposition, the federal government would proceed with a request to the United Kingdom Parliament to amend Canada's constitution. The federal proposal would ask Westminster to patriate Canada's constitution with an amending formula and a Charter of Rights and Freedoms. Trudeau proposed unilateral federal action following more than a decade of constitutional debate, confrontation, and impasse. It set the stage for a protracted constitutional battle between the federal government and the provinces, a battle involving fundamental political and legal issues fought at first ministers' conferences, in the corridors of Westminster, and in the Supreme Court of Canada.

Trudeau's Constitutional Agenda

Determined to complete what he saw as Canada's unfinished constitution, Pierre Trudeau fought hard for constitutional change from the late 1960s until the early 1980s, first as justice minister and then as prime minister. Canada's original constitution, the British North America Act, 1867, was simply a statute enacted by the United Kingdom Parliament. It contained no amending formula and could be changed only by another act of the Parliament at Westminster. Despite numerous attempts since the 1920s, federal and provincial leaders had never been able to agree on an amending formula. Trudeau was intent on patriating Canada's constitution and thereby wiping out the country's last vestige of legal colonialism.

The second crucial element in Trudeau's constitutional agenda was an entrenched bill of rights that would identify and protect the essential attributes of Canadian citizenship. Trudeau wanted a bill of rights that would include the usual rights and freedoms of a modern liberal democracy but would also guarantee language and education rights to assure Canadians that they had a home anywhere in the country and to avoid the creation of what he regarded as linguistic ghettoes. Trudeau believed that a bill of rights would give Canadians an identity and a sense of national purpose that would allow the country to rise above its regional differences. He believed passionately that Canada was greater than the sum of its parts and he saw the project of constitutional renewal as a necessary step in Canada's evolution as a nation.

While the Trudeau vision struck a resounding chord with many Canadians, it was strongly resisted by most provincial leaders, particularly those from Quebec and western Canada. For Quebec, the issue was the preservation and protection of the province's distinctive cultural and linguistic identity and the fear that emphasis on bilingualism and individual rights would inevitably lead to assimilation. For the western provinces, the concerns were control of natural resources and feelings of alienation stemming from a perception that Ottawa was unduly preoccupied with the cultural claims of Quebec and the economic well-being of Ontario.

Quebec Separatism and Western Alienation

Regionalism took an alarming turn in 1976 with the election of the separatist Parti Québécois government, an event that only strengthened Trudeau's belief in the urgency of constitutional reform. At the same time, western alienation was fuelled by federal policies relating to natural resources, which effectively required resource-rich provinces to share their bounty with the rest of the country. Central Canada saw these policies as essential to national economic prosperity, but the west considered them to be an outright expropriation of valuable provincial resources.

The country was presented with two competing and, it seemed, irreconcilable visions of the nation. The federal Liberal vision was that of a pan-Canadian citizenship that would unite all Canadians around shared individual and community values. Provincial leaders, led by Quebec and Alberta and supported by the federal Conservatives, argued that Canada was a community of communities and that Confederation was a compact of sovereign provinces.

The round of constitutional wrangling leading to Trudeau's unilateral federal proposals was directly linked to Quebec's unsuccessful sovereignty-association referendum in late May 1980. Trudeau had been returned to office in February 1980 after the surprising collapse of Joe Clark's Progressive Conservative government. Together with Justice Minister Jean Chrétien, Trudeau fought the referendum campaign with the promise of a new constitutional deal for Quebec, carefully avoiding any details. Quebec voted against sovereignty-association in the May 1980 referendum, and in early June 1980 Trudeau invited the provincial premiers to 24 Sussex Drive where he presented them with his 'people's package' of patriation, an amending formula, and a Charter of Rights and Freedoms, along with a 'governments' package' of increased power-sharing with the provinces.

Dickson was a passionate Canadian and he was deeply concerned by the unity crisis. His intense feelings about holding the country together grew from his military experience: 'I fought with French Canadians, I fought with other Canadians, they were representing a country, we weren't representing any section of the country.'[1] He followed the unity debates closely. The singing of 'O Canada' at a dinner shortly after the Quebec referendum brought tears to his eyes. In a convocation address in October 1980, he described the situation as 'the most serious constitutional crisis in our history,' but he took solace from the defeat of the sovereignty-association referendum and from the fact that 'Canadians are discussing, more or less dispassionately, but freely and democratically, basic and fundamental changes in our constitution and our national fabric.'[2]

Federal Unilateralism and Constitutional Impasse

A summer of difficult federal-provincial meetings failed to produce agreement. Most premiers resisted an entrenched Charter of Rights as an unjustifiable shift of power from the legislatures to the courts and as a threat to their own authority. They pressed demands for increased powers as a precondition to any agreement on an amending formula. The process of federal-provincial consultation and debate collapsed when a conference of first ministers ended without agreement in September 1980.

Trudeau's announcement in early October that he would proceed unilaterally caused consternation in several provincial capitals. Provincial anxieties were heightened by a new element in the amending formula. The federal package now allowed for amendments by popular referendum, an option that could be invoked only by the federal government. The message could not have been clearer. Ottawa was now asserting the right to go over the heads of the premiers with a unilateral request to Westminster, and in the future it could do the same by appealing directly to the Canadian people. Only the Conservative governments of Bill Davis in Ontario and Richard Hatfield in New Brunswick supported the federal unilateral action. British Columbia, Alberta, Manitoba, Quebec, Newfoundland, and Prince Edward Island – 'the gang of six' – were strongly opposed. At this point, Nova Scotia and Saskatchewan neither supported nor opposed Ottawa.

The constitutionality of a unilateral federal request to amend the constitution was uncertain. Trudeau's earlier unilateral attempt at Senate reform had been stymied by a Supreme Court decision holding that Parliament could not 'make alterations which would affect the fundamental features, or essential characteristics, given to the Senate as a means of ensuring regional and provincial representation in the federal legislative process.'[3] However, that initiative involved ordinary federal legislation, not the right of Parliament to ask Westminster for a constitutional amendment. Between 1867 and 1980, the British North America Act, 1867 had been amended some twenty-two times, always by the Westminster Parliament. All amendments had been made at the request of the Canadian Parliament, and, since the matter each time involved a request to an external state, there was a general consensus that only the Canadian Parliament could make it. Ottawa's position was simply that, unless and until the constitution was patriated with an amending formula, the letter of the law allowed the federal Parliament to request an amendment and required Westminster to act on any such request.

The opposing provinces asserted that the federal proposal lacked both legal and political legitimacy. They contended that the federal package of amendments – especially the Charter of Rights – would affect provincial jurisdiction and that Ottawa's unilateral action violated the important federal principle that each level of government had to respect the constitutional division of authority. The provinces argued that the federal government had no right to legislate in areas of provincial jurisdiction and that it could not evade the constitutional division of powers by going to London without their consent. A long line of prime ministers (with the notable exception of Pierre Trudeau) had accepted the need for provincial agreement. In its own 1965 White Paper, the federal government had stated that there is a 'general principle ... that the Canadian Parliament will not request an amendment directly affecting federal-provincial relationships without prior consultation and agreement with the provinces.'[4] Even if the letter of the law allowed Trudeau to go it alone, the opposing provinces argued that a unilateral federal request ran counter to established 'constitutional convention' and so lacked political legitimacy. Constitutional conventions are unwritten rules that have become established through practice. While they are accepted as important structural elements of the constitution, they are enforced by the political process rather than in the courts.

Behind this formal legal debate there lurked profound questions about Canadian nationhood. Where did Canadian sovereignty reside? Was Canada a compact of ten provinces, each possessed of powers that could not be eroded without consent? Or was Canada more than the sum of its provincial parts? If so, who spoke for the Canadian nation as a whole? Trudeau had no doubts on these questions. He insisted that Canada was more that the sum of its provincial parts and refused to see his project of constitutional change held hostage by the provincial premiers. If they would not agree, he would go over their heads and appeal to the entire nation. Only the Parliament of Canada could speak for all Canadians, and, as the prime minister of Canada with the full confidence of the House of Commons, Trudeau asserted the right to proceed in the best interests of the country as a whole.

The opposing provinces considered how best to challenge Trudeau. They immediately launched a campaign of intensive lobbying of members of the Westminster Parliament, a campaign that received a major boost when the British House of Commons Foreign Affairs Committee, chaired by Sir Anthony Kershaw, concluded that Westminster would not be bound to act on a unilateral request from Ottawa for a constitutional amendment that significantly affected the federal structure. The Kershaw Committee stated that Westminster should expect such a request to be made with at least the level of provincial support that would be required under the proposed amending formula. While the Kershaw Committee's report was not binding, Ottawa was put on notice that it should not assume that a unilateral request would be automatically enacted in Britain, and the opposing provinces were encouraged to continue their lobbying campaign of wining and dining British backbenchers.

The Gang of Six Goes to Court

The 'gang of six' also decided to challenge Trudeau's unilateral action in the courts. Both legal and political strategy dictated a pre-emptive strike. If the lobbying in London failed and the federal package was enacted by the United Kingdom Parliament, there was little hope that the courts would find that it lacked constitutional authority. Provincial legislation allowed provincial cabinets to refer legal questions directly to a province's court of appeal from which there was a right of appeal to the Supreme Court of Canada. The gang of six decided that there should be three references, directed to the courts of appeal of Manitoba, Newfoundland, and Quebec, asking essentially the same questions. Would the federal package affect provincial powers? If it would, did the law allow the federal government to make the request without provincial consent? Alternatively, was there a constitutional convention requiring provincial consent?

Many provincial leaders were wary of the Charter and, in an attempt to win provincial support during the summer of 1980, the federal government watered down many of its key provisions. Then, with the provinces disagreeing among themselves on the constitutional package, the federal government decided to create a committee that would hold public hearings on the matter. Many groups argued for a stronger Charter. The Advisory Council on the Status of Women and the Canadian Civil Liberties Association were particularly influential in persuading the committee members, and ultimately the federal cabinet, to strengthen the equality guarantee, the protection of legal rights, and the remedial provisions of the Charter while at the same time imposing a stricter test for allowing reasonable limits on Charter rights.

The Manitoba Court of Appeal was the first to pronounce on the constitutionality of the federal unilateral proposal, releasing its decision in early February 1981.[5] The court was divided, but a three-to-two majority, led by Dickson's former colleague Chief Justice Samuel Freedman, upheld the federal position. Freedman wrote that securing provincial agreement to any amendment involving the distribution of legislative power was desirable but not necessary. He found that the need for provincial consent was a matter of ongoing debate rather than settled practice, and that while we might well have been moving in the direction of a convention requiring provincial consent, we had not yet arrived at that destination.

At the end of March, the Newfoundland Court of Appeal shocked the federal government by coming to a very different conclusion – that both law and constitutional convention required provincial consent.[6] The court rested its analysis on the proposition that Canada had become a fully independent and sovereign nation with the passage of the Statute of Westminster in 1931. The Parliament of Westminster retained the formal legal authority to amend the Canadian constitution, but, since it renounced any effective sovereignty, it was a bare legislative trustee and could act only at the request of those parts of the Canadian community whose powers were affected. Provincial powers were clearly affected and, ruled the court, the federal unilateral position was inconsistent with the very nature of Canadian federalism.

In mid-April, only days after the re-election of René Lévesque and the Parti Québécois, the Quebec Court of Appeal rendered its four-to-one majority judgment upholding the federal position.[7] The constitution's written text, said the majority, made it clear that amendments could be made only by the Parliament of Westminster, that Westminster could act only on the request of the federal Parliament, and that such a request could not be refused. The court was far from persuaded that there was any convention that would limit the federal Parliament's power to ask Westminster for an amendment.

Lawyers for the federal government had tried to finesse the issue of provincial consent by arguing that its package of amendments did not affect provincial powers. The federal lawyers argued that, since the Charter of Rights would apply equally to the federal and provincial governments, it did not alter the federal-provincial equilibrium. This argument was rejected by the Newfoundland and Quebec Courts of Appeal and was not answered by a majority of the judges in Manitoba.

'It's a federal country'

An appeal to the Supreme Court of Canada was inevitable, especially after the decision of the Newfoundland Court of Appeal. The Court dealt with the case very swiftly. Argument started only days after the release of the Quebec opinion and proceeded over five days in late April and early May 1981. As it so often did, the federal government retained the formidable John Robinette to lead. Other counsel included three future chief justices and two future premiers who would later play a leading role in the national unity debate – Roy McMurtry represented Ontario, while Michel Robert from Quebec and Clyde Wells from Newfoundland both acted for Canada. Quebec's future separatist premier Lucien Bouchard was one of the lawyers to argue Quebec's case.

The judges worked on the decision over the summer months. Patrick Monahan, Dickson's law clerk at the time, sat with Dickson in his office reviewing one of the factums supporting Ottawa's unilateral position. As always, Dickson insisted on reducing complex legal arguments to what he saw as the basic principles. He observed: 'You know the thing about Canada is it's a federal country.' For Dickson, 'Canada as a federal country' was paramount and whatever the Court decided had to make sense in terms of that basic starting point.[8]

According to Dickson, the *Patriation Reference* required 'very many more' meetings and conferences than any other case on which he had sat, 'not only conferences with all the members of the Court, but also with groupings within the Court in order to try and decide the best manner of resolving the issue.' Unfortunately, for undisclosed reasons, he did not include his case file in the National Archives deposit and, so we know nothing about the conferences or discussions among the judges that led to the final decision. By the end of September, after a very busy summer, the Court produced its lengthy and complex judgment. Dickson described it as 'the most important case the Court has ever decided.'[9]

The political wrangling and posturing continued. Shortly before the Supreme Court released its decision, the Parti Québécois government, fearing the worst, distributed a brochure entitled *Minute Ottawa!* It showed on its cover a fist crumpling the Quebec flag and inside proclaimed that the federal constitutional package would cripple Quebec's capacity to control its own destiny. There was talk of a snap referendum. Trudeau speculated that he might resign in the wake of an unfavourable Court ruling.[10] Provincial leaders talked of the need for a further round of constitutional negotiations.

The Court's judgment took an unusual form. There were four separate opinions. The nine judges went in various directions on various issues, with different groups forming the majority and minority on each issue. However, there was a clear majority on the two critical issues and Dickson joined the three Quebec judges, Beetz, Chouinard, and Lamer, to form the core group in the majority on both issues. A seven-to-two majority accepted the federal argument that there was no legal requirement for provincial consent. Dickson agreed with Laskin, Beetz, Estey, McIntyre, Chouinard, and Lamer that, from a strictly legal perspective, Parliament could, without provincial consent, ask the Parliament at Westminster to amend the Canadian constitution even though the amendments affected provincial powers. Martland and Ritchie dissented on this point. They ruled that Parliament's request offended a legal principle of federalism. However, on the question of constitutional convention, a six-to-three majority rejected the federal position. Dickson agreed with Martland, Ritchie, Beetz, Chouinard, and Lamer that a substantial degree of provincial consent – to be determined by the politicians and not the courts – was required. On that issue, Laskin, Estey and McIntyre dissented. In their view, it could not be said with sufficient certainty that such a convention existed.

The judgments were written without individual attribution. Dickson later explained in an interview that 'we just brought it out in the names of those who took a particular point of view without identifying any particular author because we all had quite a bit of input into each of the judgments to which we subscribed.'[11] However, the majority judgment on the legal issue and the dissenting judgment on the question of convention bear the unmistakable marks of Bora Laskin's style and tone. It is more difficult to divine the author of the majority judgment on constitutional convention. It has been suggested that Martland wrote the opinion,[12] but this is more or less contradicted by some of Dickson's later statements. In a tribute to Beetz, Dickson wrote: 'Jean Beetz's role in the process whereby the Supreme Court of Canada reached a conclusion was extremely important.'[13] Dickson also suggested that the difference between the two opinions on the convention point reflected Beetz's Oxford training in the British legal tradition, which accepted conventions as binding, and Laskin's Harvard training in the American tradition, which was hostile to the notion.[14] The judgment also resembles Dickson's style and, although there is nothing in his files to indicate what role he played, it would be surprising if he had not made some contribution as well.

On the legal issue, the majority opinion drew a sharp line between political and legal limitations and held that there was no legal impediment to federal unilateralism. The majority was unmoved by the argument that inherent in the federal division of powers was a legal constraint preventing the federal Parliament from infringing upon provincial authority by asking Westminster to amend the constitution without provincial consent. 'What is desirable as a political limitation does not translate into a legal limitation, without expression in imperative constitutional text or statute.' The majority could find nothing 'that casts any doubt in law as to the undiminished authority of the Parliament of the United Kingdom over the *British North America Act*' and insisted that 'the law knows nothing of any requirement of provincial consent, either to a resolution of the federal Houses or as a condition of the exercise of United Kingdom legislative power.'[15]

By joining the majority's tightly reasoned opinion on the legal question, which was based on a strict textual reading of the constitution, Dickson was disagreeing with the opinion of his old friend and eminent constitutional scholar, William Lederman, who argued that there was a legally enforceable convention requiring provincial consent for amendments to the Canadian constitution.[16] Lederman did not pull his punches. He criticized the majority's opinion as 'narrowly positivistic and historically static.'[17] Dickson carefully read what his old friend from high school days in Regina had to say. Any sting that Dickson may have felt from this tough criticism was soothed by Lederman's praise for what the other majority said about the constitutional convention. Dickson later wrote a glowing tribute to Lederman's scholarly contributions, quoting at length the extracts from his *Patriation Reference* paper praising the majority on the convention issue and essentially avoiding any mention of Lederman's highly critical treatment of the majority on the legal issue.[18]

Although Dickson was not willing to impose a legal impediment on the federal government that had no support in the text of the constitution, he stuck to his basic point that Canada 'is a federal country.' He joined a different majority, consisting of Martland and Ritchie, who believed that a unilateral request was illegal, and the three Quebec judges, Beetz, Chouinard and Lamer, to rule that there was a constitutional convention requiring a substantial measure of provincial consent. Conventions, explained this majority, are essential rules that form part of the Canadian constitution. For example, the obligation of the government to resign if the opposition obtains a majority in an election and the rule that the prime minister should have the support of the majority in the House of Commons are conventions rather than part of the written constitution. These rules are enforced by political sanction rather than by court order. However, the majority explained, they are firmly established constitutional rules and, indeed, 'may be more important than some laws.' The 'main purpose of constitutional conventions is to ensure that the legal framework of the constitution will be operated in accordance with the prevailing constitutional values or principles of the period.' Conventions are based not on judicial precedents but 'on precedents established by the institutions of government themselves.' They generally conflict with the legal rules enforced by the courts – the legal right of the sovereign queen to refuse royal assent is nullified by the convention that assent should not be refused on the ground of disagreement with the policy behind the bill. Yet, if assent were withheld, a court could not apply the law. Similarly, should the government of the day refuse to resign after defeat at the polls, a court could not remove it from power and would be legally required to enforce orders or regulations it made.[19]

Although a court could not enforce a convention, it could, said the majority, recognize one. The majority proceeded to review the evidence. Proponents of the convention could point to the fact that, apart from Pierre Trudeau, a long list of prime ministers and other federal ministers had consistently stated that they felt bound to obtain provincial consent before seeking a constitutional amendment. The majority also found that a pattern emerged from the amendments that had been made. Although most of the twenty-two amendments had been made without provincial consent, only five directly affected the powers of the provinces, and those amendments supported the existence of a convention requiring some measure of provincial consent. There had been provincial agreement on every amendment affecting provincial authority and no amendment altering provincial powers had been made where the province affected had withheld agreement. The majority concluded that there was a convention requiring provincial consent that coincided with 'the federal principle' and that this convention 'cannot be reconciled with a state of affairs where the modification of provincial legislative powers could be obtained by the unilateral action of the federal authorities.'[20]

Was there any room between the extremes of the federal unilateral position that no provincial consent was required and the provincial position that all provinces had to agree? If something less than unanimity would do, what level of provincial consent was required? The point was of particular concern to Dickson, who characteristically was searching for a compromise and who pressed the lawyers several times during oral argument for some 'middle position.' On this crucial point, Saskatchewan broke with the dissenting provinces and won the day with the majority. Saskatchewan's counsel Ken Lysyk, himself a constitutional scholar, argued that it was unnecessary to specify the degree of provincial consent required. He urged the court to find:

> First: there is a constitutional requirement for a measure of provincial agreement for constitutional amendments of the type described; and
> Second: the situation before the Court does not disclose a sufficient measure of provincial agreement.[21]

This offered Dickson and the other judges in the majority the middle ground they were looking for:

It would not be appropriate for the Court to devise in the abstract a specific formula which would indicate in positive terms what measure of provincial agreement is required for the convention to be complied with. Conventions by their
nature develop in the political field and it will be for the political actors, not this
Court, to determine the degree of provincial consent required.

It is sufficient for the Court to decide that at least a substantial measure of provincial consent is required and to decide further whether the situation before the
Court meets with this requirement. The situation is one where Ontario and New
Brunswick agree with the proposed amendments whereas the other eight provinces oppose it. By no conceivable standard could this situation be thought to
pass muster. It clearly does not disclose a sufficient measure of provincial agreement. Nothing more should be said about this.[22]

The majority stopped short of endorsing the compact theory of confederation,
but the opinion was in harmony with what Lederman described as 'the classic
model' according to which 'federalism is an equal partnership' between the
provinces and the federal government.[23]

Laskin, joined by Estey and McIntyre, doubted that the convention question
was justiciable and refused to consider the middle-ground position. They
insisted that, at most, the Court should answer only the precise questions that
had been posed by way of reference. The question asked whether the consent
of *all* the provinces was required and the Court should only answer that question. But even if the 'middle ground' was open for consideration, the dissenters
stated that the vague answer it yielded was so lacking in precision as to undermine the case for finding a convention in the first place: 'If there is difficulty in
defining the degree of provincial participation, which there surely is, it cannot
be said that any convention on the subject has been settled and recognized as
a constitutional condition for the making of an amendment.'[24] The dissenting
judges assessed the evidence of past practice very differently from the majority
and found that it revealed little more than ongoing debate and controversy:
'The degree of provincial participation in constitutional amendments has been
a subject of lasting controversy in Canadian political life for generations. It cannot be asserted, in our opinion, that any view on this subject has become so
clear and so broadly accepted as to constitute a constitutional convention.'[25]

The dissenting judges used unusually strong language to characterize the
majority conclusion: 'It is unrealistic in the extreme to say that the convention
has emerged.' As for the 'federal principle' said to support the convention,
the dissenting judges accepted that 'each of the two levels of government
must be protected from the assault of the other' but they also observed that
the British North America Act, 1867 did not create a 'perfect or ideal federal
state.' There were several items in the list of federal powers – disallowance,

the declaratory power, the power to make laws for the peace, order, and good government for the entire country, the criminal-law power, and the principle of federal paramountcy – that indicated a predominant federal power. Of particular relevance was the fact the federal government was the 'sole conduit for communication'[26] with Westminster.

Back to the Constitutional Bargaining Table

Chief Justice Laskin took the unusual step of allowing television cameras into the courtroom when he announced the Court's decision. This brave judicial experiment with modern media verged on the disastrous. Laskin's voice was barely audible to an expectant nation and this, combined with the complexity and subtlety of the Court's split decision, made it next to impossible to understand exactly what the Court had decided. But before long, the legal experts had examined the written text and the principal players reacted.

Federal Justice Minister Jean Chrétien immediately declared the decision a federal victory. Pierre Trudeau, who was in Korea on a trade mission the day the Supreme Court of Canada released its decision, was more cautious.[27] The Court's decision confirmed the federal government's legal authority to proceed. While the Court had also found that constitutional convention required provincial consent, the Court had, as Trudeau put it, 'ducked the question of how many provincial governments should agree.' This, said Trudeau, left things as they were before. The federal government would prefer to have provincial agreement, but if the provinces were not prepared to agree, the federal government would proceed: 'So grave are the constitutional questions facing the country, so long have successive governments been trying to come to grips with them, that we must be prepared to do what the Supreme Court has clearly and massively indicated we have the legal authority to do. This is not a matter of legal trickery; it is a matter of law.' Trudeau refused to put the constitution on the back burner. 'At what point,' he asked, 'is the use of these conventions to force the Canadian people into giving this or that federal power to this or that provincial government going to stop?' To deal with the problems of separatism and regional alienation, immediate action dealing with 'the inadequacies of our fundamental law' was imperative. But he had to concede that the Court's decision left the door slightly ajar: 'I see no alternative but to press on. But I assure you that we will do so prudently, conscious of the magnitude of our enterprise and sensitive to real and meaningful change in the attitude of provincial governments.'

The provincial premiers were every bit as determined as their federal counterparts to take solace in the Court's decision. British Columbia Premier William Bennett spoke on behalf of the eight dissenting provinces: 'The court makes it clear that the Trudeau government proposals are unconstitutional.'[28]

René Lévesque regarded the decision as a major boost to Quebec's opposition to the federal constitutional proposals: 'Even if the court cannot stop it in the strict narrow legal sense, this manoeuvre by Ottawa is totally unacceptable on a constitutional basis, not to say unconscionable.'[29] Manitoba Premier Sterling Lyon stated that Trudeau's proceeding in the face of the Court's decision 'would be immoral, [it] would be acting not only unconstitutionally, but with deception.'[30] Alberta Premier Peter Lougheed insisted that Trudeau 'abandon' his attempt at unilateral patriation.[31] Opposition Leader Joe Clark joined in vowing to fight hard against any federal unilateral action.

Would Canadians tolerate unilateral federal action in the face of the Court's solemn pronouncement that the constitution required substantial provincial agreement? Would Westminster act on a unilateral federal request? Could the provinces ignore the Court's explicit warning that it could not legally enforce the convention requiring substantial provincial agreement? As lawyers, politicians, and editorial writers pored over the decision, it became clear that the Court had sent the key players back to the bargaining table. As Dickson explained in a letter to a former law clerk: 'The result is to give a green light to the federal authorities insofar as legalities are concerned but to give an amber or red light in respect of constitutional convention.'[32] He was describing a classic Dicksonian halfway-house solution that also embodied his ideas about balanced federalism. The Court's message could not be ignored by either the determined Pierre Trudeau or by the provincial premiers. As the Vancouver *Sun* headline proclaimed: 'It's back to compromise.'[33]

Following a month-long flurry of public and private meetings and discussions of provincial officials, a first ministers' conference was convened for 2 November 1981. The prospects for an agreement were not strong and Ottawa refused to renounce the possibility of unilateral action should the conference fail. Trudeau toyed with the option of a constitutional referendum that would go over the heads of the provincial leaders and allow the Canadian people to break the constitutional impasse. Ontario and New Brunswick essentially stood behind the federal proposal, while the remaining eight provinces resisted it, with varying degrees of indignation. Not surprisingly, Quebec's separatist leader, René Lévesque, took the toughest stand, insisting on a veto over any constitutional changes. Quebec strongly opposed the language-rights provisions as a direct assault on its authority to promote the French language in Quebec. Other provinces, Manitoba in particular, took exception to the entrenched Charter of Rights. Alberta insisted upon the principle of provincial equality, a position shared by several other provinces. Quebec's insistence on a veto, combined with the principle of provincial equality, tied the provincial package with a difficult knot, one that Trudeau was not prepared to untie by accepting a provincial proposal to allow opting out of amendments affecting provincial powers with compensation.

Securing Lévesque's agreement for any form of constitutional renewal seemed impossible. He was not prepared to agree to anything that would undermine his separatist project. Quebec's solid membership in the 'gang of eight' stood very much in the way of an accord. However, Trudeau managed to drive a wedge between Quebec and the other seven dissenting provinces by challenging Lévesque to a constitutional referendum, something the other seven dissenting provinces strongly opposed, in large part because of the popularity of the Charter as part of what Trudeau had dubbed 'the people's package.' Without the need to accommodate Lévesque, there was more room to manoeuvre. A formidable trio of attorneys general, Jean Chrétien from Ottawa, Roy Romanow from Saskatchewan and Roy McMurtry from Ontario, found a way out of the impasse with their 'kitchen accord' – a classic Canadian compromise. The main features of the deal were an amending formula that would allow for opting out but without fiscal compensation and an entrenched Charter with provision for a legislative override for certain rights. Mobility rights and minority-language rights would be guaranteed, but with certain significant qualifications, and there would be a federal resolution dealing with natural resources and equalization.

Lévesque bitterly accused his former allies of betrayal during the 'night of the long knives' and warned that the isolation of Quebec from the accord would have dire consequences. Trudeau was not prepared to accept all aspects of the 'kitchen accord,' but neither was he prepared to throw away the prospect of an agreement. He swallowed hard and accepted the notwithstanding clause and abandoned the referendum option in the amending formula. But he obtained important concessions by insisting that the legislative override be subject to a five-year sunset clause and that it not apply to language or mobility rights. Minority-language rights were to be implemented immediately, but with some accommodation for Quebec.

The agreement of nine of the ten provinces assured rapid passage of the Canada Act, 1982 by Westminster, and on 17 April 1982 Queen Elizabeth II gave royal assent to Canada's new constitution.

'Distinct society'

Quebec continued to insist that it had a veto over constitutional amendments. The question was not definitively answered by the Supreme Court's decision in the *Patriation Reference*, but the majority's adoption of the middle ground of 'substantial' provincial agreement strongly suggested that there was no convention giving the province a veto. The Parti Québécois government referred the question to the Quebec Court of Appeal. That court predictably rejected the veto argument.[34] A further appeal was unanimously dismissed by the Supreme Court of Canada in a 'by the Court' opinion written by Beetz.[35] Quebec's argument was based on a 'duality' theory of confederation which claimed for Quebec the status of a 'distinct society,' the 'stronghold of the French-Canadian people' and the 'living heart of the French-Canadian presence in North America.'[36] The Court's decision said little about duality and dismissed Quebec's veto claim since there was no evidence that it had ever been accepted or recognized by political actors, the key requirement for a convention. Dickson's conference notes indicate that there was no doubt about the result, and that the only issue discussed was whether the Court should answer the question. The 1982 constitution was now in place and its legal validity would not be affected by any failure to follow the disputed constitutional convention. However, the majority view was that the Court should give its answer. 'Judge Beetz pointed out that if we refuse to answer the question of the legitimacy of the Constitution it will always be under some sort of cloud.'[37] Unfortunately, the Court's rather terse and formal answer did little to remove the cloud.

Quebec was legally bound by the Charter but there was a widespread sentiment, encouraged by Quebec nationalists and by the federal Progressive Conservatives, that without the agreement of the government of Quebec, the Charter lacked political and moral legitimacy. Brian Mulroney was elected Prime Minister in September 1984 with substantial support from Quebec nationalists on the promise of constitutional accommodation that would 'bring Quebec into the constitution.' The 1985 election of Robert Bourassa as premier of Quebec set the stage for what became know as the 'Quebec round' of constitutional negotiations. These talks, led by Mulroney, produced the Meech Lake accord of 30 April 1987 that would have recognized Quebec as a 'distinct society.' Quebec's veto claim was to be accommodated by allowing all provinces to opt out of amendments with compensation, and where opting out was not possible, by requiring provincial unanimity. Other key elements were limitations on the federal spending power and the appointment of Supreme Court judges from lists supplied by the provinces.

Pierre Trudeau saw the Meech Lake Accord as a constitutional disaster that would Balkanize Canada, weaken the federal government, impose a straitjacket on the amending formula, and undermine the Charter of Rights by subjecting it to the distinct-society clause. He broke his self-imposed silence in retirement with a dramatic attack on the accord and there can be little doubt that his intervention contributed significantly to its demise.

Trudeau Strikes Back

On 21 March 1991, almost ten years after the Supreme Court's decision in the *Patriation Reference*, Trudeau pronounced upon Canada's constitutional state of health. Speaking before a packed audience at the University of Toronto's

Convocation Hall to commemorate the opening of the Bora Laskin Law Library,[38] he chose as his topic 'Patriation and the Supreme Court' and praised Laskin for his 1981 dissent holding that there was no convention requiring substantial provincial consent. Laskin's view, Trudeau asserted, was 'not only the better law, but the better common sense, and consequently it was also wiser politically. Had it prevailed over the majority view, I believe that Canada's future would have been more assured.'[39] Trudeau bitterly resented the majority decision on the constitutional convention as an illegitimate interference with the political process and he blamed the majority for contributing to Canada's continuing constitutional malaise.

Brian Dickson, by then retired from the Court and privately offering advice to Prime Minister Mulroney on the Charlottetown Accord that would contain many of the features of Meech that Trudeau found objectionable,[40] sat in the front row of the audience, a few yards away from Trudeau at the podium. Like Trudeau, Dickson had come to pay tribute to Bora Laskin's legacy. When Trudeau prepared his remarks, he did not know that Dickson, the man he had appointed Chief Justice of Canada, would be present. However, it came as no surprise to Trudeau that Dickson would not like what he was about to hear. It was painfully apparent to everyone in the audience that Dickson was upset by the tone and content of Trudeau's remarks. As Trudeau rolled on with a scornful attack on the majority judgment under the guise of praise for Laskin, Dickson turned red in the face and shuffled in his chair in obvious disagreement. The audience was transfixed with this clash between Canada's two living constitutional giants gathered in memory of the third. Dickson was visibly shaken by Trudeau's venom. Barbara Dickson, seated beside her husband, tried to console and calm him in the wake of Trudeau's attack.

The decision in the *Patriation Reference* was, Trudeau said, 'arguably the most important decision [the Supreme Court] ever rendered or ever will render.'[41] Trudeau did not mince words when it came to the majority opinion on the constitutional convention. The six majority judges, he asserted, had 'fatally tilted the doctrine of Canadian sovereignty away from the people and ... towards one form or other of the compact theory of confederation.' He accused the majority of turning 'a deaf ear and a blind eye to legal arguments which might have led them in another direction.' Conventions, he asserted, are not justiciable, and, by answering the convention question, the Court had allowed itself '"to be manipulated into a purely political role" going beyond the law-making functions that modern jurisprudence agrees the Court must necessarily exercise.' Reverting to an argument John Robinette had abandoned before the Court, Trudeau argued that the federal package did not disturb the existing balance between the federal and provincial governments. The Court, Trudeau asserted, ignored the 'obviously *sui generis*' nature of the federal package 'since no prior constitutional amendment remotely resembled the *Charter of Rights* or the amending formula included in the patriation package.'

Trudeau accused the majority of manipulating and ignoring evidence on the existence of a convention. The majority focused on only five of the twenty-two amendments, and then, realizing that the rule of unanimity their arbitrary selection produced was 'patently repugnant to common sense ... they blatantly decided to *invent* a convention calling for "a substantial degree of provincial consent."' This conclusion, Trudeau argued, was so vague and lacking in precision that it could not possibly be a constitutional convention. 'How can a clear and firm rule be said to exist when "substantial" turned out to mean some unstated number between two and ten?' Then came a passage that amazed the audience and deeply wounded Dickson: '... There seems to be little doubt that the majority judges had set their minds to delivering a judgment that would force the federal and provincial governments to seek political compromise. No doubt believing in good faith that a political agreement would be better for Canada than unilateral legal patriation, they blatantly manipulated the evidence before them so as to arrive at the desired result. They then wrote a judgment which tried to lend a fig-leaf of legality to their preconceived conclusion.'

Trudeau dismissed the argument that the majority had acted responsibly by forcing a political compromise. 'It seemed to me that Canadians had a right to expect a legal decision from their Supreme Court, rather than some well-meaning admonitions about what was politically proper.' Then, almost as an afterthought, Trudeau praised the minority opinion, couched in what had been described as Bora Laskin's '"clearly identifiable drafting style"' as 'not only the better law but also the wiser counsel.'

Trudeau's seething resentment over the majority opinion was unabated, even after ten years. The majority view on the question of convention had strengthened the hand of the provinces and allowed them to extract what he regarded as major, undesirable concessions from Ottawa – the notwithstanding clause, the opting-out amending formula, and the abandonment of a referendum provision. Even more damaging, said Trudeau, was that by insisting on provincial consent, the majority opinion either forced the abandonment of the patriation project or legitimized inevitable disagreement by the separatists and Quebec's consequent posturing as a humiliated victim.

When the two men met after the ceremony, Dickson politely but firmly informed Trudeau that he rejected everything he had said. Trudeau tried to soften the blow he had delivered by reminding Dickson: 'Well, I did appoint you chief justice.' Dickson resented Trudeau's attack, which he thought ill-conceived and in bad taste. 'Violently' disagreeing with Trudeau's legal analysis and considering his language to be 'extravagant,' he 'found Trudeau's address to be profoundly political, out of date and superficial' and 'thought that Trudeau would have been better advised to have maintained his self-imposed vow of silence.'[42]

Dickson disagreed, too, with Trudeau's influential critiques of both the Meech Lake and Charlottetown accords and believed that Trudeau's vehement opposition to the distinct-society clause and renewed federalism was harming the cause of national unity. Nor did he share Trudeau's assessment of the political context and practical consequences of what had happened in 1981. He thought that the majority opinion had salvaged rather than sabotaged Trudeau's constitutional project. A unilateral request could well have floundered at Westminster in the face of strong provincial opposition. The possibility of the United Kingdom saying no to a federal request for patriation would have been humiliating for Canadian nationalists such as Dickson. 'I hesitate to think what might have happened if our judgment had gone the opposite way.'[43]

Dickson decided against making any immediate public response to Trudeau. However, in an article commemorating the work of Jean Beetz written shortly after the Trudeau speech, but not published until 1994, Dickson defended the majority decision as the only position consistent with the federal principle and the maintenance of the rule of law: 'In a country where one of the few constitutional principles that was clear was the federal principle, consensus with respect to change among the members of the federation was a prerequisite for ensuring that change did not lead to chaos.'[44] Dickson referred to Trudeau's own early writings on federalism which defended Privy Council decisions bolstering provincial powers against the attacks of anglophone scholars such as Laskin. In earlier days, Trudeau had written that, if the Privy Council had not leaned in the direction of the provinces, 'Quebec separatism might not be a threat today; it might be an accomplished fact.'[45] Dickson pointedly argued that 'the very same vision of federalism at play in the Privy Council jurisprudence ... helped shape the majority's position in the *Patriation Reference*.'[46]

Trudeau was certainly entitled to disagree with the decision and with the majority's endorsement of the classic federal model in preference to his own centralized vision. But did he not cross the line by accusing the Court of distorting the evidence and deliberately masking a politically motivated judgment with a phoney legal veneer? Trudeau could quarrel with the majority's conclusion, but was it fair or proper for a former prime minister to accuse the judges of overstepping their authority, 'manipulating evidence,' and clothing themselves in 'a fig leaf of legality'? After all, it was the cautious Jean Beetz, a constitutional scholar for whom Trudeau had the greatest respect, who had taken a leading role in crafting the ruling that the unilateral federal plan would violate constitutional conventions. Trudeau refused to acknowledge that he might well have lost the case entirely. Some leading constitutional scholars have argued that the Court gave Trudeau more than he deserved and that the majority should have found that provincial agreement was required as a matter of law not just convention.[47]

Dickson was disturbed by what he regarded as an inappropriate and vicious attack on the integrity of the Court, but he was unshaken in the belief that the majority had done the right thing. What would have happened without the Supreme Court's decision in the *Patriation Reference*? Would the federal government have been able to pull off its unilateral plan? It is impossible to say. We do know that Pierre Trudeau was convinced that, without the Court's intervention, his project would have succeeded. We also know that Brian Dickson was equally convinced that, without the majority ruling, Canada would have been plunged into a potentially disastrous constitutional crisis and possible humiliation by a British refusal to the federal government's request to amend the Canadian constitution. As he put it in a 1985 interview: 'We were asked to do a particular task – to pass upon the legality of a certain course of action which we discharged to the best of our ability and I am personally very pleased with the way things developed subsequently.'[48] In the *Patriation Reference*, as in so many other cases, Dickson believed that he had found a middle-ground, prudent solution to a seemingly intractable legal conundrum.

PART FIVE

Chief Justice and the Charter, 1984–1990

14

Chief Justice

Chief Justice Laskin died in April 1984. His death was a blow for Dickson, who a month later wrote to a friend: 'We are still in the state of shock on the death of Bora. He and I were not only colleagues for some eleven years, but the closest of friends and his passing has left a great void. However, his influence will continue to be felt on the Court.'[1] Laskin's death followed a period of serious illness during which he had been unable to carry out his duties as chief justice. Roland Ritchie, the senior puisne judge, was also in poor health. Dickson was the next most senior judge, and during Laskin's illness he had assumed responsibility for the day-to-day administration of the Court.

Dickson hoped to be appointed chief justice. Seniority favoured him, but there had also been a pattern of alternating the office of chief justice between anglophone and francophone judges. Jean Beetz, the fluently bilingual Montreal francophone, was the next most senior judge after Dickson. Beetz had a strong reputation as a scholar and as a judge and he was well connected to Prime Minister Trudeau. Beetz had hired Trudeau as his first research assistant in 1961 at the University of Montreal.[2] However, Beetz was shy and retiring and he had suffered a heart attack two years earlier. He valued his privacy and had no desire to take on the onerous administrative and ceremonial duties of chief justice. Antonio Lamer offered to help Beetz, telling him: 'I know you don't want to be a Chief Justice, because you don't want the administration. I am ready ... to do all the administration ... All you have to do is sign letters.' But Beetz balked at 'all the speeches' he would have to make, causing Lamer to conclude that 'it was hopeless. He didn't want the job.'[3]

Lamer and the other Quebec judge, Julien Chouinard, were both relatively junior and neither was considered to be a strong candidate for the office at the time. Linguistic considerations apart, Dickson was an obvious choice. He was the most senior judge after Ritchie, and, in the later years of Laskin's tenure as chief justice, he had emerged as the most influential member of the Court jurisprudentially.[4] Dickson also had the administrative experience of running a law office and his organizational abilities and efficiency were legendary.

Though Prime Minister Trudeau had reservations about Dickson because of the *Patriation Reference*,[5] the choices were limited. He could have appointed a Quebec judge, but, in addition to the factors already mentioned, all three Quebec judges had agreed with Dickson in the *Patriation Reference*. Estey, who had supported the federal position on the *Patriation Reference*, was a possibility. He had proven himself an able administrator as chief justice of Ontario and he was very popular with the bar. Trudeau could also have appointed a chief justice from outside the Court, but this had been done only once in the court's history, in 1906, when Charles Fitzpatrick moved from attorney general of Canada to the office of chief justice.

Before making his decision, Trudeau invited Dickson to lunch at 24 Sussex Drive on two occasions. According to Dickson: 'I had lunch with him a couple of times and discussed not only my appointment, but ... who was going to succeed to complete the nine judges.' In the midst of one of these conversations, one of Trudeau's sons ran in, did a cartwheel, and jumped into his father's arms. Dickson described the scene as 'a very spontaneous show of affection ... I was very touched by it.'[6] The conversations with Trudeau went very well. Dickson was appointed as the Supreme Court of Canada's fifteenth chief justice on 19 April 1984, a month before his sixty-eighth birthday. Barbara Dickson was as thrilled as her husband by the honour. She remained fully involved in his judicial work and realized that she would be sharing the burdens of the office.

Dickson's appointment was applauded in the press[7] and in the Canadian legal community. Dickson privately worried that his appointment might offend some in Quebec and was heartened when his appointment was praised by *Le Devoir* and a friend told him that in Quebec his 'competences were perceived as overriding even such powerful concerns as regionalism and alternation.' Dickson was particularly pleased 'with the very warm reception' the announcement of his appointment 'received from the judges and practicing bar in the Province of Quebec.'[8] Samuel Freedman, Dickson's former judicial colleague and one-time rival for a Supreme Court seat, told a reporter: 'There aren't many Brian Dicksons around. I think the Prime Minister made the best choice.'[9]

Dickson's colleagues also welcomed his appointment. Although he had been willing to help Beetz assume the burdens of office, Lamer thought that

Dickson 'was a natural. Everybody rejoiced when he was appointed.'[10] At Dickson's swearing-in as chief justice of Canada on 26 April 1984, both Ritchie and Beetz spoke warmly. Dickson used the occasion to praise Laskin for leading the Court to a threshold of 'new public prominence and stature' that would be crossed as it decided its first Charter cases. Expressing concern about the backlog of cases and the Court's accessibility to all Canadians, as well as his hopes for 'the continuing assistance of the practicing bar and of the Faculties of Law at our universities,' Dickson cautioned that 'the Chief Justice is one judge among nine ... He cannot move mountains. He cannot single-handedly decide a case let alone change the law.'[11]

Administering the Court

Dickson took great care to acquaint himself with all aspects of his new job and to build a team that would enable him to fulfil his many duties efficiently and effectively. As James MacPherson, Dickson's first executive legal officer, observed, 'it would be wrong to say that Dickson was immediately comfortable with all of the aspects of his new position'[12] but he gradually grew into the job and put his own mark on the office.

On the administrative front, Chief Justice Laskin had laid important foundations in 1977 when he secured a change to the Supreme Court Act giving the court's registrar the status of a deputy head of department with budgetary independence and access to the Treasury Board.[13] This made the Court administratively independent from the Department of Justice and meant that the Court, not Justice department officials preoccupied with their own budget, could press the Treasury Board for more resources. After Dickson's appointment as chief justice and the appointment of Guy Goulard as the registrar, the Court fully exploited the possibilities opened by the registrar's change in status. Goulard had served for many years as a family court judge. He took on the role of registrar with gusto and a determination to modernize and professionalize the Court's administration. At the same time, he became adept at Treasury Board politics and was able to get the Court the resources it needed.

As chief justice, Dickson took an active interest in the Court's administration and introduced a number of significant changes.[14] He encouraged Goulard to embark upon an ambitious program to computerize the Court's administration and production of judgments. The Court also embraced modern technology by authorizing oral argument by way of video-conferencing. This innovation was introduced primarily to reduce the cost of leave-to-appeal applications argued by lawyers from outside Ottawa. It was used infrequently, in part because of resistance from the bar, and became redundant shortly after its introduction when oral argument for leave-to-appeal applications was eliminated. However, Dickson was proud of this innovative use of technology since it showed the Court to be a thoroughly modern institution open to change.[15] In the words of a leading scholar on judicial administration, it gave an important signal 'of the willingness of a purportedly conservative institution to embrace new technology and to spend its limited budget to make itself more accessible ...'[16]

Dickson adopted an administrative style that combined consultation with 'substantive decisiveness,' avoiding the extremes of micro-management or administrative indifference that often afflict judges.[17] He was skilful at delegating tasks to others, yet he also maintained a firm grip on the crucial issues and was relentless in his effort to improve the way the Court did its business. While he left many of the details to others, Dickson's attention to detail was well known. He liked to go on unannounced 'walkabouts' to survey the building, greet Court staff members, and spot matters that needed attention. Peter Cory, one of Dickson's colleagues and a fellow Second World War veteran, remembers Dickson as very much the 'commanding officer of the unit' and an 'orderly officer going around seeing that everything is in order ... I remember him coming into the conference room' and finding dirty windows. 'Well! He got the court attendant to bring up maintenance people right away ...'[18]

In the office, his approach was no-nonsense and formal. There was remarkably little small talk and the atmosphere was one of serious business. At the same time, Dickson was unfailingly courteous. When he wanted to see a clerk or a member of the Court staff, he would politely enquire, 'Could you drop by,' or, 'Have you got a moment to see me,' as if the individual might well have more pressing business. There was always a sense of occasion entering his chambers, however frequent the experience, partly because of the aura of the office and partly because of Dickson's own formal style. But despite his formality, he discussed problems in an open manner, and, just as he encouraged his law clerks to find the best legal solutions, he encouraged the members of his staff to seek out and find the best possible administrative solutions. He was unusually well organized and he developed an exceptional ability to get the best out of people. Dickson's administrative style was consultative, influenced by his experience as a corporate director and senior law firm partner where consensus on broad objectives was crucial. It was also strongly influenced by his military experience. With military precision, a problem would be identified, an objective defined, the options discussed, a course of action selected. The administrative officer would be charged with implementation. Dickson would make a notation on one of his many 'to-do' lists and monitor the administrative officer's progress after a decent interval.

Goulard teased out of Treasury Board the resources required to make the staff additions needed to professionalize the Court's operations and handle the increased workload. Lawyers were hired to provide the registrar's office with advice, to prepare objective summaries, and to assist with processing leave-to-appeal applications. Each judge was given a third law clerk to assist in the preparation of judgments. DeLloyd Guth, a professional historian, was hired for a year as the Court's curator to develop a plan for the proper organization and preservation of the Court's records.

Dickson created the position of executive legal officer to assist him generally with his day-to-day work, to assist the Court as a whole, to monitor judgments, to coordinate the law-clerk program, and to serve as the Court's media-relations officer. Here, again, one sees the influence of Dickson's military background and his years as a senior commercial solicitor. He realized that he could not do everything by himself and he built a team of people to help meet the demands of his office. He looked to Goulard to carry the administrative burden and he looked to the executive legal officer for more general support in the many functions of his office. Mark Newman, a former Ritchie clerk, served as Dickson's assistant for several months and in August 1985 James MacPherson became the Court's first executive legal officer. MacPherson had moved from law teaching to the constitutional branch of the Ministry of the Attorney General in Saskatchewan. He had impressed Dickson and the other judges as an outstanding counsel when he argued several early Charter cases. When MacPherson left the Court in January 1988 to assume the position of dean of Osgoode Hall Law School at York University in Toronto, Robert Sharpe, one of the authors of this book, replaced him as the Court's executive legal officer and served until Dickson's retirement in 1990. Dickson's chambers staff also included his highly efficient secretary, Deborah Melanson, upon whom he relied to organize and coordinate a massive workload of correspondence, judgments, agendas, minutes, and travel arrangements. The chambers staff also included Audrey Davis, secretary to the executive legal officer, Dickson's court attendant, Lou Lefebrve, and his driver, Gilles Boisvert.

Improving Media Relations

Dickson was very interested in the media. As a lawyer he had acted for the Winnipeg *Free Press* and before his appointment as chief justice he had decided important cases involving the press. A 1979 case asked whether a newspaper was answerable for defamatory statements in letters to the editor. A local politician sued the Saskatoon *Star-Phoenix*, complaining of a letter to the editor headed 'Racist Attitude' and written by two law students (both of whom later became senior judges)[19] that criticized him and some of his constituents. The *Star-Phoenix* argued that, so long as a newspaper published a letter to the editor in good faith, it should not be required to stand behind the letter as if it were the newspaper's own statement. As Dickson wrote in his conference notes, holding the newspaper to account would curtail the letters-to-the-editor column as a forum for the discussion of various points of view. 'It seems to me that it is no part of the function of a newspaper to publish in the "letters to the Editor" column only material with which he agrees. This puts the editor in a censoring position and does not reflect the role of a newspaper as a disseminator of various and conflicting points of view.'[20] A majority of the Court, including Laskin, disagreed. In his strongly worded dissent, Dickson spoke of the 'right' and the 'duty' of the press 'to act as a sounding board for the free flow of new and different ideas.' He observed that letters to the editor provide a valuable means for 'getting the heterodox and controversial points of view'[21] before the public and that newspapers could not provide that forum if they could publish only letters with which they agree. Richard Malone, publisher of the Globe and Mail, sent Dickson a copy of a letter to the editor that praised the dissent. Dickson warmly replied: 'I read the letter with lively interest because not only did [the letter writer] agree with the views I expressed, but demonstrated her awareness of the issues ... I hope you will give me a call the next time you are in Ottawa.'[22]

Three years later, the Court decided an important media case involving access to court records. In a five-to-four majority judgment that included Laskin, Dickson found that Linden MacIntyre, a well-known investigative journalist, was entitled to inspect a search warrant and the material used to obtain the warrant after it had been executed. Citing Bentham's observation that 'in the darkness of secrecy, sinister interest and evil in every shape have full swing,' Dickson held that 'the curtailment of public accessibility can only be justified where there is present the need to protect social values of superordinate importance.'[23]

One of Dickson's priorities as chief justice was to improve the Court's relations with the media. Dickson agreed with Laskin's concern about the inadequacy of media reports on the Court's work, observing in a 1976 speech: 'This country has consistently failed to develop a tradition of outstanding or even adequately informed reporting on legal issues.'[24] Laskin was relatively open to the media, but, apart from Dickson, his colleagues were not. In November 1975 Laskin and Dickson discussed the possibility of a documentary on the Court with Peter Herndorf, the CBC's director of public affairs.[25] Laskin, who had done an extensive CBC radio interview a few months earlier,[26] thought that a serious program on the Court would enhance public understanding of its work and he hoped his colleagues would agree. Dickson served as the liaison and he invited Herndorf to lunch with the judges at the Rideau Club to discuss the project.[27] Dickson thought the Court should cooperate, but he was in a distinct minority. Pigeon, in particular, was strongly opposed. In Herndorf's presence, Pigeon rebuked Laskin and Dickson for inviting Herndorf to lunch and refused to discuss the idea. The project did not proceed.[28]

At times, even Laskin and Dickson were guarded towards the media. In the spring of 1978 Barbara Amiel suggested an extended *Maclean's* feature on the Supreme Court of Canada as a way to initiate regular coverage of the Court's work. By today's standards, her request was modest. She wanted to interview each judge and describe their education, significant judgments, and areas of expertise 'in professional terms', and to add some brief personal biographical information. 'It is our feeling, and I believe yours, that most Canadians are more familiar with the cases and members of the U.S. Supreme Court than our own.'[29] A similar request by journalist Claire Bernstein was granted ten years later, resulting in the publication of an extended and positive series of interviews.[30] However, in 1978 Dickson toed the party line and refused Amiel's request. He responded in formal terms: 'It is the view, I think, of the members of the Court, that a personal interview with each of the judges would not be possible, but rather that the Chief Justice would be available to discuss with you those matters affecting the Court upon which you might be seeking information.'[31] Amiel wrote a lukewarm feature article on the Court that reflected the judicial reticence towards the press.[32]

Laskin wanted better coverage of the Court's work, but he thought that the problem was that of the press, not the Court: he believed that the solution was for the media to hire legally trained reporters.[33] He also opposed the idea of a Court press officer to assist the media. In a 1977 speech to the annual dinner of the Canadian Press in Toronto, he said that such an officer 'could not be given more than formal information duties' and that 'to go beyond this and to have an official spokesman, someone who would sum up the views of the Court or its members on decisions to the public is, in my view, out of the question. It would not comport with our conceptions of proper judicial behaviour.'[34] In 1979 Laskin learned that reporters sometimes called law clerks for information about cases. He suggested that the Court instruct the clerks 'that if information is sought about any cases on our list or cases in which judgment is pending, they should refer the reporter to [the registrar's office].'[35] Dickson had a more flexible attitude and counselled against 'any hard and fast rule.' He recalled a *Globe and Mail* article that 'dealt competently and accurately with the issues' in a judgment, a result attributable, 'at least in part, to a conversation between the author of the article and [law clerk] Brian Morgan in whose discretion I had, and have, great confidence.' Dickson concluded: 'In my view, in an appropriate case and depending upon the legal secretary [law clerk], it may be desirable to permit some discussion as to the issues involved. On the other hand, I do not think that any such discussion is proper prior to the delivery of judgment.'[36]

Gradually, the Court's icy attitude towards the media began to thaw. In 1980 television cameras were allowed to record the retirement ceremony for Pigeon and the swearing-in ceremony for Antonio Lamer. Dickson favoured this development and described it as 'a new landmark' that would serve to 'invite greater familiarity with, or to spark interest in, the Supreme Court, as one of our fundamental institutions.'[37] As already recounted, the introduction of television cameras to cover the release of the Court's judgment in the *Patriation Reference* was a technological fiasco,[38] but it did show the Court's increasing willingness to modify its traditions to meet the needs of the modern age.

When he became chief justice, Dickson decided that the Court's attitude towards the press had to change. The Court was deciding significant questions of social justice that were of immediate concern to the average Canadian, who could not be expected to read the law reports to find out what the Court was doing. Besides, it was inevitable that the media would shape public opinion about the Court and its work. In these circumstances, Dickson concluded that the Court should be as open and as helpful as possible with the media. In 1984 he made a speech to the Canadian Bar Association urging judges, lawyers, and academics to assist reporters by giving 'comprehensive answers in response to genuine requests for information' and by explaining 'the background that will make sense of a legal issue of current interest.'[39] Dickson later advised Allan McEachern, the sceptical chief justice of the British Columbia Supreme Court, that 'it is important to have legal developments correctly reported' and that he 'could see no objection to giving responsible journalists "background material."' He added that he himself had done this on occasion and 'had never been let down.'[40] Within a few months of becoming chief justice, Dickson decided that 'a public relations officer or a person with some such title should be available at each level of court simply to give a background of the issues in the important cases but without making any attempt to interpret judgments of the court.'[41]

Dickson initiated several changes to make the Court more accessible to the media. Until the mid-1980s, the Court made no provision for reporters. The only place the *Globe and Mail* legal reporter could find to write her stories in the late 1970s was a vanity table outside the stalls in the women's washroom.[42] Dickson established a press room with telephones and a video feed of the oral argument. Reporters could record the oral argument to ensure the accuracy of their stories, and, if they wanted to sit in the courtroom, they had a reserved seating area. In addition, 'objective summaries' providing a description of the basic facts and legal issues of each appeal were provided, as were copies of the factums, and a media-relations committee of judges was established to meet regularly with media representatives. The procedure for releasing judgments was altered to assist the media; several days' advance notice was provided and the Court avoided handing down more than a few judgments at a time. Finally, the executive legal officer's duties included media relations and providing background, off-the-record explanations of judgments.[43] This clashed with the traditional view of Chief Justice Laskin and many of Dickson's colleagues that the Court could speak only through its judgments, and that beyond making the judgments available, no help should be given to the press.[44] Dickson disagreed. 'If we were expecting the press to become better conversant with the work of the Court, then we had to offer them some better facilities.'[45]

In September 1985 the Court agreed to allow CTV's 'W5' program to do a special documentary on the Court and the Charter that included filming some of the judges in the conference room, in chambers, and at leisure.[46] Dalhousie law professor Wayne Mackay wrote an enthusiastic review of the program, praising the informal and human portrayal of six of the nine judges who agreed to be interviewed.[47] He observed that, while viewers might forget the more technical aspects of the show, 'the images of Chief Justice Brian Dickson riding his horse, Justice Antonio Lamer displaying his gun collection and Justice Bud Estey playing tennis, are likely to remain.'[48] A similar request from the Radio-Canada's 'Le Point' was accepted in 1986.[49]

Dickson made a point of getting to know the reporters who covered the Court. He gave a significant number of interviews[50] and provided reporters with advance copies of his speeches. He also had off-the-record discussions with senior editors at the Ottawa *Citizen* and Toronto *Star*.[51] These provoked positive reactions. *Citizen* editor Keith Spicer applauded Dickson's openness: 'I am delighted that you are so open to this kind of informal, and I believe potentially very fruitful, dialogue.'[52] David Vienneau, a senior member of the Parliamentary Press Gallery who regularly covered the Court for the Toronto *Star* during Dickson's time as chief justice, said that Dickson 'realized that we were there trying to do our job the best we could' and that the best way to help us 'was to let us have as much information as possible.'[53] The CBC's legal reporter, Vicki Russell, wrote to Dickson on his retirement: 'You were a friend of the media and we all appreciated your work to help us. It ultimately helped the public, and their understanding of our court system.'[54]

Dickson sometimes had to push his colleagues, not all of whom shared his inclination to respond positively to media requests. In early 1987 David Vienneau asked Dickson to allow the press to attend motions since they often involved significant procedural issues that determined how and when the case would procede. Several judges refused to allow reporters into their offices when they heard motions. Dickson thought the request was justified and he took a firm stand. In a memo to his colleagues, he emphasized 'how troubled I am by this matter.' He feared that, if the Court denied access, 'we will get some quite bad and quite visible publicity' and warned that he had learned that one press organization was contemplating a lawsuit to force the issue. 'I am deeply concerned about the unfavourable publicity that such a lawsuit would entail ... I do not want the Court to be damaged by the accusations of inaccessibility, or worse, by lawsuits against us.'[55]

Bertha Wilson distrusted the media. Perhaps with some justification, she thought that the press treated her unfairly. However, Dickson did not always agree with Wilson's complaints. In October 1984 Wilson gave a conference paper entitled 'State Intervention in the Family' and was dismayed by what she regarded as an unfair press report suggesting that she supported the Liberal government's no-fault divorce proposal. Insisting that her paper was an objective analysis of a developing area of the law and describing the article as a 'completely vicious distortion,' she asked to be removed from the Court's media-relations committee and suggested that the committee's forthcoming dinner meeting with media representatives be cancelled. 'We are bending over to cooperate with them and getting nothing in return.' She asked Dickson to help her with a formal complaint.[56] Dickson was unsympathetic. He thought that a formal complaint would serve no useful purpose, and he also told Wilson that the topic she had chosen 'was somewhat controversial and to an extent invited the sort of press comment which it received ... If there was to be a formal complaint it should go forward from her and not from me.'[57]

A year later, Wilson wrote to the editor of the Ottawa *Citizen* 'to protest most vigorously the complete distortion of my remarks'[58] in an article reporting her Goodman lectures on 'Decision-Making in the Supreme Court'[59] at the University of Toronto in late November 1985. The article described Wilson as a 'rebel' judge and suggested that the Court was suffering under the strains of Charter litigation.[60] Wilson sent her colleagues a copy of her speech 'to set the record straight, at least within the Court,' indicating that she was 'saddened and dismayed by the distortions and out-of-context quotations which coloured the account in the weekend *Citizen*.'[61] These experiences made Wilson extremely guarded with the media, an attitude Dickson did not share.

Modernizing the Court

Dickson wanted the Court to appear to be a modern institution in tune with contemporary Canadian society. He found the label 'puisne,' used for all judges other than the chief justice, unacceptably quaint and obscure. 'It does not refer to physical stature; rather it is an amalgam of two French words, "puis" and "né," meaning born later, and hence junior' – 'a word with which I am not greatly enamoured.'[62] Shortly before he became chief justice, he suggested that the term be eliminated and replaced with 'associate.'[63] While that suggestion went nowhere, he had more success later when the Court dropped the 'Mr.' or 'Madam' before 'Justice.' As he explained to his colleagues: 'We might be accused of aping the United States Supreme Court but if the idea is a worthy one it would not give me any great concern.'[64]

Several procedural changes were introduced during Dickson's tenure as chief justice to streamline and expedite the work of the Court. Dickson eliminated the formal procedure of handing down judgments in open Court to a courtroom full of lawyers, a practice that needlessly added to the cost and delay of litigation. Another important change was the imposition of time limits on oral argument in 1987. Initially, lawyers were asked to give the registrar an estimate of the time they required for oral argument. This proved an ineffective control. Long-winded counsel whose time estimates were excessive exasperated the judges. Estey, formerly a prominent litigator, quipped, 'As in the case of revival meetings, very few souls are saved in the second hour.'[65] In a case argued in October 1986, Estey was dismayed by counsel's estimate that the case would take over five and a half hours. In a memo to his colleagues, he suggested that the case could have been dealt with in an hour and a half and that the case was 'a microcosm' of the 'problem of this Court.' A way had to be found to 'reduce the time of hearings to realistic proportions.'[66] Dickson agreed with Estey and immediately scheduled a Court meeting, at which it was agreed that time limits should be imposed. Estey was able to muster support for time limits from the bar.[67] While many lawyers were dubious about the concept, those who regularly appeared before the Court saw the advantages.[68] If the Court adopted the practice of hearing two appeals a day, its docket would be predictable and lawyers would no longer be faced with a court list that inevitably involved unproductive waiting time. In addition, experienced counsel knew that limited time would serve to focus the argument and that this would be to the advantage of the skilled advocate.

Another important change related to leave-to-appeal applications. From 1975, when the leave-to-appeal requirement was introduced, until 1988, the Court heard oral argument on leave-to-appeal motions in panels of three judges. Brian Morgan, a Dickson clerk, said that sometimes the leave process was 'for both clerks and judges ... like a workout in a mental gymnasium, with legal muscles flexed and tested on a rapid sequence of diverse problems. The cases are digested and judgment calls made – not on the merits, but simply on whether the issues raised are of sufficient importance for consideration by the court.'[69] Oral argument was popular with the bar but time-consuming and costly for the litigants, who had to pay for the lawyer's time and trip to Ottawa. From the Court's perspective, oral submissions on leave applications were not particularly helpful. The Court introduced video-conferencing as a way to reduce cost, but the bar made little use of this technological innovation.

Though the bar also resisted the Court's initiative to decide leave-to-appeal applications on the basis of written argument,[70] the Court got the necessary statutory change. Applications for leave were still decided by panels of three judges, but, before leave was granted, there was an opportunity for all members of the Court to review and comment on the case. Lists of pending applications with summaries of the issues were circulated to the entire Court to afford any judge the opportunity to comment on pending applications. The decision to grant or deny leave was invariably made without reasons. As Dickson explained in 1983 to a Canadian Bar Association meeting, leave-to-appeal decisions were purely discretionary and 'if we were expected to prepare reasons in respect of leave applications I fear we would simply clog the system and delay unduly the decision ...'[71]

Appointments

The early 1980s saw significant changes in the membership of the Court. The retirements of Pigeon, Martland and Ritchie virtually eliminated the Court's conservative wing. Pigeon, described in a history of the Court as 'the conservative philosopher of destruction for the *Bill of Rights*,'[72] was replaced by the reform-minded Antonio Lamer. Martland retired a year later and was replaced by Bertha Wilson.[73] By appointing Lamer and Wilson to replace Pigeon and Martland, Trudeau significantly shifted the balance of the Court.

During Dickson's tenure as chief justice, seven judges were appointed to the Court, one by Trudeau and six by Prime Minister Mulroney. Gerald Le Dain was appointed by Trudeau to fill Laskin's seat a month after Dickson's appointment as chief justice in 1984. Le Dain, then sixty years old, had been a member of the Federal Court of Appeal since 1975. He had grown up in Quebec, was bilingual, and, like Dickson, Lamer, Chouinard, and McIntyre, had served in the artillery. He had a distinguished academic career teaching at McGill in the 1950s and in 1967 he was appointed dean at Toronto's Osgoode Hall Law School. His name became well known to the Canadian public when he chaired the Commission of Inquiry into the Non-Medical Use of Drugs, which recommended the decriminalization of simple possession of marijuana, lighter sentences for other drugs, treatment for heroin addicts, and warnings about the hazards of alcohol and nicotine. Le Dain's name was 'very high on the [Court's] list' and Dickson told Trudeau that 'we would be very happy to have Gerald Le Dain.'[74] Although Le Dain proved to be more cautious than either Lamer or Wilson, his credentials were hardly those of a judicial conservative.

An early and difficult task was urging Roland Ritchie to retire on account of his failing health. Ritchie's daughter understood the problem and helped ease a difficult situation.[75] Ritchie retired in October 1984 and in January 1985 he was replaced by Gérard La Forest, a member of the New Brunswick Court of Appeal since 1981. The press attributed the delay in naming La Forest to a struggle between Justice Minister John Crosbie, pushing for a Newfoundlander, and Prime Minister Mulroney, who wanted La Forest.[76] La Forest, a fluently bilingual New Brunswicker, had studied at Oxford as a Rhodes Scholar, later at Yale, and had a distinguished and varied legal career. He had taught law for several years, served briefly as dean of law at the University of Alberta, and had held senior positions in the federal Department of Justice. La Forest was keenly interested in the process of constitutional change launched by Pierre Trudeau in the late 1960s and early 1970s. He worked as a special advisor to the minister of justice and the prime minister from 1967 to 1970, during the period of the Victoria proposals, and later played a key role in the Canadian Bar Association's effort to provide a model for Canada's constitutional renewal in the late 1970s. As a legal scholar, he wrote widely on the constitution as well as on the rather esoteric subject of extradition. Although a legal scholar at heart, La Forest was no abstract theoretician. He saw law as an instrument of social betterment and was also thoroughly absorbed by the interaction of law and policy making. He had been a member of the Law Reform Commission, together with Antonio Lamer, in its heyday period from 1974 to 1979. La Forest made no secret of his belief that judges had an important lawmaking role. Shortly after his appointment to the Supreme Court of Canada, he gave a lecture on judging in which he described his enjoyment in 'writing judgments, particularly where one can move the law forward for the better ... whenever I come across a case where the law can be refashioned for the public good and private justice, I shall continue to do so – with relish!'[77]

Appointments to the Supreme Court attracted increasing public attention as the Court assumed a higher profile in the 1980s. The legal requirements for appointment are found in the Supreme Court Act, which lays down minimal legal qualifications and requires that three of the Court's nine judges be appointed from Quebec.[78] By convention, three judges come from Ontario, one from the Atlantic provinces, and two from the west. Supreme Court appointments lie within the prerogative of the prime minister. The actual appointment process is shrouded in mystery. The opinion of leading members of the bench and bar is sought, but there is no formal consultation process, nor do provincial governments have any formal say. Parliament has no involvement and American-style public confirmation hearings have no counterpart in Canada. This secretive process was increasingly criticized during Dickson's time as chief justice. The quality of those appointed to the Supreme Court was not questioned, but many critics and editorial writers urged a more open process and provincial governments argued that they should be given a formal role.

An important factor in Dickson's attitude to appointments to the Court was his very positive relationship with Brian Mulroney who was prime minister for all but the first few months of Dickson's time as chief justice. Shortly after Mulroney became prime minister in 1984, Dickson offered to go to Mulroney's office to pay his respects. Mulroney replied: 'No, I will come to your office and pay my respects to you. I am a young lawyer – you are the judge. I have always been taught to respect judges.'[79] Dickson was impressed by Mulroney's gesture. He accepted it as a genuine sign of the prime minister's respect for the courts and the judiciary. The Dicksons were regular guests at functions hosted by the prime minister and Barbara Dickson shared Mila Mulroney's interest in work for the Cystic Fibrosis Foundation. Dickson met regularly with Mulroney and, after his retirement from the Court, worked closely with Mulroney on aboriginal and national-unity issues.[80]

In Dickson's early years on the Court, appointments to the Court were often made without consultation. Dickson and Mulroney, however, established a regular practice of consultation for Supreme Court appointments. As Dickson put it in an interview after his retirement, 'I thought it was a reasonable thing to expect.' Dickson described what happened: 'The minister of justice or the prime minister would usually get in touch, not for nominations, but simply to say, "We are considering so-and-so or so-and-so, and what would be the reaction of the Court?"'[81] Dickson would then share the information with the other judges and report their reaction. Lamer recalls: 'We were always consulted about appointments.'[82]

Dickson put the weight of his office behind the idea of merit-based appointments to all courts. In a 1985 speech to the Canadian Bar Association, he insisted that appointments must be made on the basis of merit, not political affiliation.[83] Minutes of a 1986 meeting with Justice Minister Ray Hnatyshyn indicate that Dickson 'reiterated his view that merit should be the sole factor in appointing judges' and asked to be consulted on judicial appointments generally, 'particularly with regard to the appointment of chief justices because they become members of the Canadian Judicial Council.'[84]

Dickson was sympathetic to a formalized provincial role in Supreme Court appointments and realized that the Court's new role under the Charter was bound to provoke pleas for a more open process. When the Canadian Bar Association was studying how to improve the process for judicial appointments in the mid-1980s, Dickson welcomed measures to ensure proper consultation with the bar but argued strongly against 'American style hearings.' He thought that confirmation hearings 'would lead many, if not most, of the best and most suitable candidates for judicial office to decline a proffered nomination' and would also introduce 'new and very dangerous political forces into the judicial process.'[85] Dickson insisted that he would not have let his name stand under such a process. Before his appointment as a judge, Dickson had refused even to say whether he was interested in being a judge before the minister of justice had confirmed that the appointment was his if he wanted it. Even after he retired, Dickson continued to be adamantly opposed to proposals for giving a strengthened Senate, or indeed any legislative body, a role in the appointment of Supreme Court judges. He believed that nomination hearings would damage the 'mutual respect' between the legislature and the judiciary and that nothing would 'be more likely to bring the administration of justice into disrepute than to subject a nominee for appointment to the Supreme Court of Canada to the degrading, humiliating ordeal to which Professor Bork and Judge Thomas were subjected.'[86] Rob Yalden, who helped Dickson write speeches during his retirement, including a speech in which Dickson denounced confirmation hearings as a 'blood sport' that 'could not but discourage the most eminently suitable candidates from seeking high judicial office,'[87] saw Dickson horrified by the confirmation hearings of Clarence Thomas but also unable to turn off the televised proceedings.[88]

Although Dickson thought that the provinces should be given some role in the appointments process, he was alarmed by the Meech Lake proposal that Supreme Court judges be selected by the federal government from lists of candidates supplied by the provinces. Dickson asked Ontario Attorney General Ian Scott about the proposal and was told that it came from the federal side. In a memo to his executive legal officer, Jim MacPherson, Dickson indicated his concern that the procedure could lead to delay and deadlock: 'I am seriously considering writing to the Prime Minister to express my concerns in this respect, on behalf of the Court, and before the whole thing becomes firmed up in concrete.'[89] There is nothing in Dickson's files to indicate that he did write to the prime minister.

The next appointment after La Forest was that of Claire L'Heureux-Dubé, who replaced Julien Chouinard in April 1987. Chouinard had been a member of the Court since 1979. The Dicksons had developed a close friendship with the Chouinards, and, despite his rather modest jurisprudential contribution, many had seen Chouinard as a possible successor to Dickson as chief justice. However, Chouinard lost his balance while skiing during the 1986 Christmas break and realized that something was drastically wrong. As Dickson recorded in a letter written in mid-January to Douglas Abbott, a retired member of the Court, 'just after Christmas [Chouinard] was advised that he had two tumours in his brain the size of ping-pong balls and that his life expectancy would not exceed two months. I spent some time with him on Sunday and he is obviously deteriorating very rapidly.'[90]

Claire L'Heureux-Dubé was the first woman appointed to the Quebec Superior Court and to the Quebec Court of Appeal and the second woman appointed to the Supreme Court of Canada. She had earned a reputation as an extremely hard-working appellate judge who grilled counsel with tough questions. L'Heureux-Dubé's appointment attracted some controversy. It was widely believed that Mulroney's first choice was Yves Fortier, a highly regarded Montreal lawyer frequently touted as a prospect for the Supreme Court.[91] L'Heureux-Dubé also felt that her appointment was controversial within the Court. She did not know Dickson but she was on friendly terms with McIntyre, who warned her before she accepted the prime minister's offer that 'you will not be welcomed.' In her first encounter with Dickson, she found him to be very cool and peremptory and concluded that 'he was not happy at all about my [appointment].' She felt that she had been thrust on an overburdened and backlogged Court that 'was run like an army ... where the Chief was very angry because it wasn't going at his pace.' However, Bertha Wilson, who had also been met with a cool reception, welcomed and encouraged her. Dickson gradually warmed to L'Heureux-Dubé and he certainly respected her remarkable ability to get her work done. When he told her about a year after her appointment, 'If everybody were like you, it would be a pleasure to be here,' she felt that she had proved herself. L'Heureux-Dubé's admiration for Dickson grew stronger over the years, and, by the time he retired from the Court, she revered him for his intellect, his compassion, and his collegial approach.[92]

In Dickson's last two years on the Court, there were four more appointments, a remarkable turnover in a short space of time. John Sopinka, a leading member of the Ontario bar, replaced Willard Estey in May 1988. Sopinka had made his name as an outstanding advocate, but he was also a man of many talents. He had played professional football, was an accomplished musician, and had written the leading Canadian textbook on the law of evidence. Charles Gonthier, a long-serving trial judge who had been named to the Quebec Court of Appeal only a few months before being named to the Supreme Court, replaced the ailing Jean Beetz in February 1989. On the same day, Peter Cory, an experienced and well-liked Ontario trial and appellate judge, was appointed to replace Gerald Le Dain, who, like Beetz, had retired for reasons of health in late 1988. The addition of these three new judges in fairly rapid succession added significant strength to the Court. Sopinka, Gonthier, and Cory all enjoyed the full confidence of the bar and they came at a time when the Court badly needed an infusion of new blood. Sopinka, who was to die suddenly and prematurely in 1997, applied to judging the same direct, no-nonsense approach he had used as an advocate. Gonthier, a scholarly man who speaks both English and French without a trace of accent, is an acknowledged expert in Quebec civil law. Cory learned French as a trial judge and was fully competent to hear cases in both languages. Revered in the legal community for his gentle and kindly manner, Cory was a dedicated, hard-working, and compassionate judge who, like Dickson, took great pains to make his judgments readable and accessible to ordinary Canadians.

The last judge appointed during Dickson's tenure would later become chief justice. Beverley McLachlin replaced William McIntyre in March 1989. Only forty-five years old at the time of her appointment, McLachlin had a remarkably varied career and had risen rapidly in the judiciary. She had practised law, then taught at the University of British Columbia, and was first appointed to the county court. From there she moved to the Supreme Court of British Columbia, then to the British Columbia Court of Appeal, then back to the Supreme Court of British Columbia as its chief justice, and finally to the Supreme Court of Canada. At her swearing-in ceremony, it was noted that she had been able to move through the judicial hierarchy faster than most litigants. McLachlin quickly proved herself as a decisive, efficient, and hard-working member of the Court. Not long after her arrival in Ottawa, many were predicting that one day she would be appointed chief justice.

First among Equals

Dickson adopted a collegial style of leadership, something of a change from Laskin's more austere and professorial style. As William McIntyre put it, Dickson 'was the first among equals and he did not throw his weight around.' Shortly after his appointment as chief justice, Dickson told a reporter, 'The chief justice may preside at discussions but he doesn't dominate,'[93] and in another interview he described the degree of collegiality on the court as 'reasonable' but 'it could be improved.'[94] Laskin, Wilson recalls, had strong views and was inclined to try to influence the result, while Dickson was 'the opposite.'[95] Beverley McLachlin says that Dickson 'was always very polite,' that 'he really treated everybody with respect,' and that what 'was absolutely foremost ... when he was chairing a meeting [was that] everybody must have their full say.'[96] Dickson impressed his colleagues as being completely open-minded, 'an excellent listener,'[97] and 'truly interested in the views expressed by all members of the Court.'[98] As La Forest put it, Dickson 'sat back and let people say what they had to say.'[99]

Neither Dickson's papers nor interviews with his colleagues reveal any hint of undue lobbying or arm-twisting about how the cases should be decided. Dickson certainly discussed cases and draft judgments with his colleagues, but there was no 'horse-trading' or 'tit for tat' voting, nor did he use the weight or authority of his office as chief justice to coerce a fellow judge. McLachlin, the most junior judge during Dickson's last year on the Court, says that there was no lobbying and that Dickson had no 'buddies.'[100] McIntyre says that lobbying would have been 'absolutely foreign' and that 'I never saw that happen in our court at all, never. I may just have been blind, but I never saw anything of that nature at all.' McIntyre frequently disagreed with Dickson, but Dickson always seemed willing to listen: 'I never had any hesitation to discuss things with Dickson. I remember a case where there was a lot of discussion on a very narrow point ... in criminal law. We were diametrically opposed, we talked about it several times and there was never any difficulty. I never hesitated to disagree or to agree.'[101]

Yet Dickson had a noticeably formal style as chief justice. He never entirely shed his formality, and even outside the courtroom, he maintained a certain distance. This was partly a product of his perception of what the office required, but it was also a product of his private and rather shy nature. Despite his formal veneer and dignified bearing, however, Dickson did convey genuine warmth in his personal relationships. He gave his colleagues, his law clerks, and the Court staff the impression that he was interested in them and that he wanted their views. His family-like relationship with his law clerks has already been described. The same applies to his judicial colleagues. As Antonio Lamer put it, 'he was like a second father to me.'[102] Claire L'Heureux-Dubé says that, Dickson, 'with few words and the type of intonation and the type of gestures (so like a grandfather's),' 'was able to bring the court together.'[103] Dickson made a point of going to his colleagues' chambers when he wanted to discuss something rather than asking them to come to him. They took this as a sign of courtesy and respect. Peter Cory recalls hearing Dickson's limping steps: 'The poor man – the pain he must have been suffering to walk down that long hall.'[104] Dickson also made it his practice to encourage the recently appointed judges, complimenting them on a set of reasons or for making an important point during a Court conference.

Dickson gained the respect of his colleagues with his formal 'chairman of the board' approach to Court business. He had strong personal views about the cases the Court heard, but as chief justice he did his very best to avoid using the weight of his office to impose those views upon his colleagues. Especially with the early Charter cases, Dickson thought it important for the Court to speak as clearly and consistently as possible. One sees the influence of Dickson's experience as a senior corporate lawyer at work here.[105] He was less interested in imposing his own views than in achieving broad consensus; he was looking for clear and practical solutions that would attract the widest possible support from his colleagues and the community at large. He insisted that the Court's decisions be principled, and when he thought the legal principles required him to do so, he was quite prepared to dissent or write his own reasons. However, Dickson's primary instinct was always to search for the middle ground. He was quite prepared to submerge his own ego and to accept limits on what he personally thought would be the ideal solution if to do so would help the Court find a principled, middle-ground position.[106]

In Court, Dickson was polite, patient, and attentive, but he was also very firm and serious, rarely if ever resorting to humour. He strictly enforced time limits and other procedural rules. He set the same tone for Court conferences. Cory says that Dickson 'conducted the conferences just the same way he conducted the Court, with great dignity, great patience and with careful regard to tradition.'[107] He patiently listened to what each member of the Court had to say but, as described by Wilson, his approach was 'very businesslike and very much on the job ... no fun and games.'[108] When it came time to decide who should write, Dickson was 'very careful with regard to assignments'[109] to avoid one member of the Court being unfairly burdened with work. Court conferences on administrative matters tended to be tightly organized with a formal agenda. Some colleagues thought that Dickson took collegial decision making too far in relation to purely administrative matters.[110] As La Forest put it, the discussions were sometimes like 'faculty meetings – need I say more.' But, as La Forest also noted, Dickson's style ensured that everyone was equally involved in the decision-making process.[111]

When the Court was sitting, Dickson took lunch in the judges' dining room where the conversation tended to focus on current affairs rather that the legal points the judges had just heard in court. When not lunching at the Court, Dickson refused to go to public restaurants and stuck to the more private precincts of the Rideau Club or the Cercle Universitaire.[112]

External Duties

As chief justice of Canada, Dickson performed several functions external to the work of the Supreme Court. Not only was he a regular presence at Ottawa ceremonial functions, but as chief justice, he believed that he had a role to play representing Canada to the world. In November 1984 he accepted Prime Minister Mulroney's invitation to join the Canadian delegation led by Foreign Affairs Minister Joe Clark that was to attend the funeral of the assassinated President Indira Gandhi of India.[113] Dickson routinely received foreign diplomats in his chambers. These visits tended to be formal, ritualistic affairs. However, when representatives of the Nicaraguan government came dressed in battle fatigues, Dickson, wearing his usual three-piece suit, took their unconventional behaviour in stride and astonished his visitors by conducting the meeting in Spanish.

Dickson enjoyed the Ottawa social whirl of state dinners and embassy parties and formed close friendships with many foreign ambassadors. As honorary colonel of the 30th Field Regiment (RCA) in Ottawa, he showed great affection for military tradition, he regularly attended regimental functions, and was quite prepared to offer friendly advice to the commanding officer for improvements. His daily agendas for his years as chief justice reveal that, in addition to his busy social life in Ottawa, he frequently travelled to all parts of Canada to receive honorary degrees, attend local bar meetings, visit law schools to lecture or judge moot courts, and participate in judicial conferences. Dickson was also keen on foreign travel and during his time as chief justice he visited judges and courts in the United States, Italy, Austria, the Soviet Union, and Australia. Barbara Dickson was fully involved in these important public duties, invariably at Dickson's side when he travelled, carefully reviewing and commenting on the drafts of his speeches and adding her own grace and charm to the events they attended.

Dickson also had a taste for unconventional and adventurous travel. In May 1987 he eagerly accepted Northwest Territories Justice Minister David Marshall's invitation to join him on the 'Baffin Circuit.' Dickson, Barbara, and James MacPherson arrived in Iqualuit at noon on Dickson's seventy-first birthday. The Dickson party spent the next several days travelling to Pond Inlet, Arctic Bay and Hall Beech with Justice Marshall, his wife, Jill, court staff, and crown and defence lawyers. Unannounced, the chief justice of Canada quietly watched the proceedings in the schools and community halls that served as courtrooms. He was deeply moved by the 'vast and challenging land and a people of distinct culture, language and lifestyle.'[114]

The chief justice of Canada chairs the advisory committee for the selection of recipients of the Order of Canada. Dickson was initially sceptical of this task, seeing the whole exercise as elitist and outdated. Attending an installation ceremony changed his mind. He was touched by the pride and emotion felt by the recipients, particularly the 'members,' many of whom were ordinary people who had 'lived a life of community service and help to others ... the very best of Canadians.'[115] Dickson spent several days each year poring over the files of the many worthy Canadians nominated for the country's highest honour.

Canadian Judicial Council

Dickson's most important duty external to the Court was chairing the Canadian Judicial Council, a statutory body comprised of all provincial superior and appellate court chief justices with a broad mandate 'to promote efficiency and uniformity, and to improve the quality of judicial services' in the courts whose judges are appointed by the federal government.[116] When Dickson assumed office, the Canadian Judicial Council had a relatively low profile. It had been established in 1971 to fill the vacuum that became apparent during the infamous Landreville affair.[117] Leo Landreville, an Ontario High Court judge, faced serious allegations of conflict of interest from his time as mayor of Sudbury. The constitution provides that a superior court judge may be removed only upon a joint address of the Senate and the House of Commons, but it makes no provision for the investigation or processing of complaints against judges. A royal commission, chaired by Supreme Court Justice Ivan Rand, investigated the allegations against Landreville, and it became clear that a more expeditious and less cumbersome procedure had to be found. The Canadian Judicial Council was established and charged with the mandate to investigate complaints against federally appointed judges and, where appropriate, to recommend that the minister of justice initiate the constitutional steps for removal from office.

In addition to dealing with complaints against judges, the council deals with judicial education, makes representations on behalf of judges regarding salaries and benefits, and provides a forum for the discussion of matters pertaining to the delivery of judicial services. In the early years of its existence, relatively little was done in these areas, but under Dickson, the council became more active. Dickson hired Jeannie Thomas, 'a highly intelligent, highly dedicated woman'[118] as the council's executive secretary. Thomas had worked for several years at the Canadian Human Rights Commission, and, like Guy Goulard at the Court, she provided Dickson with the efficient and professional administrative support he needed.

After his first few meetings, Dickson decided that the Council needed to reflect more broadly on its role and mission. He found that 'the agenda ... is often confined to a discussion of a long list of specific items' and believed that the council should 'step back from specific agenda items and ask the broad, and in my opinion, fundamental question of where the Council should be going.'[119] The executive committee was enlarged to make it more representative and structured committees were established to process and coordinate the council's work in education, judicial conduct, salaries and benefits, trial and appellate courts, and the administration of justice.[120] From 1987, the council produced an annual public report detailing its activities and providing details of some complaints. This replaced the chief justice's annual letter reporting on the council's activities sent to all federally appointed judges but unavailable to the public.[121] A Judge's computer advisory committee was established to help bring judges into the age of technology, and the National Judicial Study Leave Fellowship Program offered judges sabbatical leave for study or research at Canadian law schools and brought the experience of the bench to the academy.[122] The council debated many policy issues confronting the courts including the contempt power and sentencing standards, and established a guideline that decisions should be made within six months of hearing. Courts were encouraged to develop media-relations strategies comparable to those of the Supreme Court of Canada, but the council was cool to the idea of cameras in the courtroom. Many other issues were debated by the council during Dickson's time. As one long-time Council member, Chief Justice Constance Glube of Nova Scotia, wrote on Dickson's retirement, he had 'brought [the council] forward in leaps and bounds into the modern age.'[123] Work was begun on a 'Statement of Practical Ethics for Judges' despite Dickson's personal doubts about a code of ethics for judges.[124] A proposal for the interchangeability of judges between provinces to ensure the availability of bilingual judges across the country floundered on constitutional grounds.

Many judges thought that the council paid insufficient attention to judicial salaries and pensions. Chief Justice Laskin did not think that judicial salaries deserved high priority and the concerned judges formed their own association, the Canadian Judges Conference, to lobby the government. Like Laskin, Dickson attracted the criticism of some judges on this issue. In a 1986 judgment, Dickson held financial security to be one of the essential components of judicial independence but refused to rule unconstitutional a law requiring judges to contribute to their generous pension arrangements. 'Canadian judges,' he wrote, 'are Canadian citizens and must bear their fair share of the financial burden of administering the country.'[125] Dickson was probably not surprised to learn that 'a small but vociferous minority of federally appointed judges ... is acutely upset at the perceived unfairness of the contributions we are required to make towards our judicial pensions ... [and that] they are focusing their annoyance and sense of injustice not on Parliament, but instead, on [your] recent decision ...'[126]

Dickson was unwilling to decide cases in a way that would enhance the financial position of judges, but in his capacity as chief justice he was not prepared to surrender the issue to the Canadian Judges Conference and was quite willing to lobby the government. He wanted to respond to the strongly held views of judges across the country and thought it important for judicial morale to show some leadership. Establishing a joint committee comprised of council and conference representatives to present joint submissions to the statutory Triennial Commission, which made recommendations to the government regarding judicial salaries and benefits, Dickson pressed the prime minister and the minister of justice for action on the commission's recommendations. When these pleas did not produce immediate results, Dickson had to quell an incipient revolt by dispirited judges. With a group of trial judges in Quebec threatening a 'work to rule' campaign, Dickson called Chief Justice Larry Poitras and told him to 'tell his people to back off.' Dickson thought that this would be 'the worst possible thing they could have done ... it seemed to me very counter-productive and it was unlikely to improve the chances of getting any benefits.'[127] James Southey, an Ontario judge who worked hard as a member of the Canadian Judges Conference for improvements in judicial salaries and benefits, 'was deeply impressed by [Dickson's] concern for the well-being of the judges of Canada, and the energetic and resolute way in which [he] pressed for improvement of our lot by implementation of the reports of the Triennial Commissions. There is no doubt that the significant results achieved were due in large part to [Dickson's] efforts.'[128]

The number of complaints against judges increased dramatically during Dickson's tenure. Most complaints come from disappointed litigants whose proper recourse is an appeal, but during Dickson's time there were other complaints that had to be taken seriously. He attributed the rising volume of complaints to the higher profile assumed by courts and judges under the Charter and the increasingly litigious nature of Canadians.[129] Complaints frequently concerned judicial remarks during the course of a hearing and, as Dickson observed, 'the public are ready to criticize and to raise complaints even in respect of remarks made from the Bench which have hitherto largely been regarded as free from public criticism.'[130] In the Canadian Judicial Council's 1989–90 annual report, Dickson stated that he did not regard the continuing increase in the number of complaints as 'bad news.' It did not reflect any 'deterioration in the quality of judges' but rather a 'growing awareness of the justice system' and '[l]ike other institutions, the judiciary benefits in the long run from close scrutiny by the public it serves.'

One of Dickson's most significant council initiatives was the establishment of an independent Canadian Judicial Centre, now called the National Judicial Institute, as a permanent national secretariat for judicial- education programs. The creation of such a body was first proposed by Ontario Chief Justice William Howland in 1982.[131] Subsequently in 1986, Alberta Court of Appeal Justice William Stevenson, who later replaced Dickson on the Supreme Court, wrote a detailed report recommending the establishment of a national body to plan and coordinate judicial education. The idea was to bring some order and structure to the hodgepodge of existing programs and institutions. Dickson strongly endorsed the initiative, as did Deputy Attorney General Frank Iacobucci and Justice Minister Ray Hnatyshyn, and in due course a federal-provincial funding agreement was reached. The centre was given a mandate to design and coordinate judicial- education services for both federally and provincially appointed judges, and Justice David Marshall from the Northwest Territories was named the first executive director. The National Judicial Institute now provides a wide range of highly sophisticated programs to both federally and provincially appointed judges.

A Common Touch

During his time as chief justice, Dickson received a large volume of correspondence, some from disappointed litigants and some from those with strong views on agonizingly difficult issues such as abortion and Sunday-closing laws that were coming before the Court under the Charter. There were also letters from young people across the country looking for help or guidance. Dickson took great interest in these letters. Shortly before he retired, he received a letter from a first-year law student. She wrote on behalf of a classmate who was very idealistic but found the law and legal reality harsh and wondered whether she should continue. The student admired Dickson and thought that a letter from him might help her friend. Dickson sent an encouraging reply.

> I firmly believe that the legal profession needs young people of high ideals, sensitivity to the needs and aspirations of others, and a strong social conscience. It is true that at times life in the law appears harsh and that one is often constrained by practical realities. But it is for that very reason that we need in the profession people with high aspirations, committed to improving our legal system and the situation of those who our society has not favoured. I do hope that your friend will not be discouraged and that she will continue in her legal studies. If she remains true to her ideals, one day she will become an important member of the Canadian legal community.[132]

Dickson's advice to the troubled law student described many of the ideals and qualities that brought him to Canada's highest judicial office. At an age when most people are comfortably retired, Dickson assumed his greatest challenge – to lead the Canadian judiciary as it tackled the daunting task of interpreting the Charter of Rights and Freedoms.

15

Building the Foundations

The Charter of Rights and Freedoms became part of Canada's constitution on 17 April 1982, but it took almost two years before the first cases worked their way up to the Supreme Court. Though Dickson welcomed the Charter, he worried that the Canadian judiciary was ill-prepared for the challenges it presented.[1] He recognized that many judges would regard the Charter as a 'heavy' duty and perhaps some would find their responsibilities under it 'uncomfortable.' Believing that it was his role to make sure that all judges were properly prepared for the new legal challenges,[2] he accepted many invitations to speak about the Charter and told judges: 'We face a great challenge; we have been given a weighty responsibility. And the eyes of individual Canadians will be on us as never before.'[3] Dickson urged them to 'exercise reasonable sense, restraint and self-control,' but at the same time he argued that 'constitutionally protected rights and freedoms must not be cut down by any narrow or technical construction' and that the Charter was 'capable of growth and expansion within its constitutional limits.'[4] As he explained in a 1982 address to provincial court judges, 'the Canadian judiciary, and in particular the Supreme Court of Canada, will either breathe life into the Charter or reduce it to a hollow promise of things that may have been.'[5] Dickson was painfully aware that the Court had been almost universally criticized for its restrictive interpretation of the statutory Canadian Bill of Rights. As a signatory to the Court's much criticized 1979 *Bliss* decision that the denial of a benefit on grounds of pregnancy did not amount to sex discrimination, Dickson himself had felt the critics' sting.[6]

Dickson was also concerned about the capacity of the bar and the adversary system to cope with the demands of the Charter. He urged the bar to behave responsibly and mused aloud about whether the courts would have to loosen traditional rules limiting the role of public-interest intervenors and the admissibility of 'statistical, economic and sociological data' to provide the background of 'social context and legislative effect which are necessary for policy making.'[7] Worried that the cost of litigation might make the Charter's lofty promises hollow, he appealed to the legal profession to ensure that disadvantaged Canadians had access to justice. In 1985, the day after the Charter's equality-rights provision came into force, Dickson told a large audience of young lawyers just called to the bar: 'It is profoundly to be hoped that those whose skills have commonly been available only to private and paying clients increasingly will devote some of their skills and talents to extending the blessings of freedom and equality to the legal and social difficulties of the disadvantaged.'[8] He told law professors that the Supreme Court needed their assistance for 'the orderly development of a coherent body of national law' under the Charter.[9]

Despite these reservations about the capacity of Canada's legal establishment to cope with the demands of the Charter, Dickson made no secret of his own determination to breathe life into its vague and general language. He saw the Charter in grand terms. It entrenched 'the foundations of Canadian society: democracy, social justice, freedom and human dignity' and he urged judges, lawyers, and legal academics to meet head-on the challenge of 'advancing the role of law in upholding these principles.'[10] Using language derived from Canadian and American constitutional scholars who pushed for a robust judicial interpretation of fundamental rights and freedoms and that would soon find its way into his own judgments, Dickson told a Calgary audience that 'a constitution is a document designed to grow and develop over time to meet new social, political and historic realities unimagined by its framers.' He warned that the courts would 'have to take a philosophic approach in our interpretive endeavours' and that Charter rights would have to be interpreted in light of 'the purpose of protecting' the right at issue.[11] Dickson told law students at Dalhousie Law School that the meaning of the terms of the Charter 'are not to be found by consulting a dictionary' and Charter interpretation 'requires a philosophic and possibly political theory as context.' The courts, he said, 'will have to go beyond abstract logic and disembodied precedent' and he urged Canada's judges to rise to the challenge: 'When the occasion cries out for new law, let us dare to make it. Let us recognize that the law is a living organism, its purpose is to serve life, its vitality is dependent upon renewal.'[12]

As the first Charter cases were making their way to the Supreme Court, Dickson frequently spoke of the need to develop 'a distinctively Canadian jurisprudence.'[13] This was a familiar theme for Dickson that built upon the efforts of Laskin, Trudeau, and others to break the chains of Canada's colonial past. He had often used the phrase to evoke a spirit of legal growth and renewal, linked to the mandate the Court had been given in 1975 when it gained control over its docket and the right to hear only cases of 'national importance.' As early as 1976, Dickson told law students that 'the increasing bigness in government, business, and labour poses an ever-present threat' to the rights of citizens and that eroding confidence in other institutions created a special responsibility for the Canadian legal community to develop its own distinctive solutions: 'It is your task and mine to ensure that confidence in the administration of justice continues as a unifying force, to which all Canadians can look with confidence for the protection of human rights and individual freedoms, according to law.'[14]

But Dickson's appeal for innovation was carefully blended with his characteristic attention to principle and stability: 'As I see it, the challenge in developing a distinctive Canadian jurisprudence is to combine a respect for recognized rules and established principles with sufficient flexibility to meet the specific needs of an evolving Canadian reality. Change need not, and should not, take place at breakneck speed ... Predictability and certainty are still solid values in the law.'[15] He regarded the Charter as 'a mechanism for peaceful, progressive change' but also as 'an anchor in the storm of social evolution' to ensure that fundamental Canadian values 'are immutable and shielded from encroachment by majority will.'[16]

'The unremitting protection of individual rights and liberties'

The first significant Charter case to reach the Court was *Hunter v. Southam*,[17] argued in late November 1983. The case marked the passage from the era of the pre-Charter, Laskin Court. Laskin, who would have so loved the work of the Charter, was in failing health. He sat the day the case was argued but was too ill to take part in the Court's deliberations and died before the judgment was handed down.

At issue in *Hunter v. Southam* was the constitutionality of a section in the Combines Investigation Act that allowed the director of investigation and research – the government official responsible for investigating corporate wrongdoing – to authorize entry into any premises to search and seize documents.[18] The director suspected that Southam had engaged in anti-competitive activity and he authorized a sweeping search of the Edmonton *Journal*, one of Southam's papers. The officers conducting the search asked for every Southam file except those in the newsroom. Southam resisted the search and sued for an injunction, contending that such an open-ended search, authorized by the prosecuting authority rather than by an independent judicial officer, violated the section 8 Charter guarantee 'to be secure against unreasonable search or seizure.' The case was ideally suited for the Court's early foray into the realm of the Charter. Controlling the powers of law-enforcement officials to conduct searches in private premises was a familiar topic upon which judges had pronounced for centuries. The case did not raise the kind of fundamental, highly contentious social issue that the Court would later face in cases on abortion, mandatory retirement, and hate speech; however, it did require the Court to take an important first step in interpreting a vaguely worded Charter right and to measure the validity of an act of Parliament. The Court was being asked to strike down a law enacted by the elected representatives of the people, and the Court's nerve and mettle was being closely watched. Would the Charter be sheltered in a narrow and legalistic cocoon or would it take flight with generous and expansive judicial interpretation?

After the case was argued, there was an unusually protracted discussion among the judges.[19] Dickson knew that the Court's judgment would be closely parsed by the media as well as by legal scholars. Because of Laskin's illness, Dickson was effectively the acting chief justice, and, before the Court rendered its judgment, he was appointed to the office. Dickson decided that it was especially important to try to achieve a consensus, a view that appears to have been widely shared by the other judges.

At conference after the oral argument, they all agreed on the result: the search violated section 8 of the Charter. There was, however, considerable uncertainty about what the judgment should say. Some judges were inclined to decide the case on a narrow basis and to say as little as possible. Others advocated providing 'some guidelines for the benefit of Parliament as to what might be regarded as minimum standards of a reasonable search and seizure.' It was clear from the discussion that Dickson and Lamer would take a leading role in formulating the Court's response. Lamer was an acknowledged expert in criminal law and procedure and he took a strong interest in how the Charter would affect the criminal law. Dickson was determined to play a leading role in defining the scope and impact of the Charter generally.

It was agreed that the case did not lend itself to the usual treatment of a single conference and that further meetings and discussions would be required. Though the judges often engaged in informal, one-on-one discussions, it was rare to have more than one conference. An ongoing, seminar-type discussion of broad legal issues was virtually unheard of, but, in the early years of the Charter, the Court seems often to have held more than one conference to discuss a case or groups of cases under consideration. The judges were conscious that their early Charter pronouncements would set the tone for the future, and they wanted to sound as clear, confident, and unanimous as possible.

Dickson and Lamer agreed to prepare memoranda that would provide the basis for a detailed discussion of the case in mid-December 1983, when the Court would finish its fall sittings. Lamer was inclined to write narrowly – 'The least said generally about the Charter the better'.[20] – he worried that the Court might unduly limit powers needed by the police in more routine cases. Dickson disagreed. He thought that the Court could not decide the case without setting out some basic principles of Charter interpretation and he did not want the court to lose the opportunity to make its mark. He told his colleagues: 'This is the first clear-cut *Charter* case before this court, and therefore it is desirable, I think, to lay sufficient groundwork for an orderly and logical development of the jurisprudence under section 8 and under the Charter in general.' He identified as the 'major' problem the 'vagueness and openness' of the Charter's text. The American constitution was much more specific and required that searches be authorized by particularized judicial warrants. Canada's section 8 did not arise from 'eighteenth century colonial opposition to certain Crown investigatory practices' and there was no 'particular historical, political or philosophic context capable of providing an obvious gloss on the meaning of the guarantee.' Rather than follow the elaborate American jurisprudence, the Court would have 'to start from first principles.'[21]

Dickson insisted that the Court should look behind the words of the Charter to its underlying principles. He identified the individual's right to privacy as the central concern of section 8. As he saw it, the judgment would turn on the need to balance the privacy interest of the individual against the state's interest in law enforcement. He conceded as problematic the fact that the party seeking Charter protection was a corporation. Anticipating criticism by those who distrusted judicial review and thought that conservative judges would favour the rich and the powerful, Dickson suggested that privacy 'would be less rigorously protected for a corporation than for an individual' but he still insisted that 'a corporation has at least enough of a privacy interest to require some legitimate countervailing governmental interest to justify its being invaded and at least to that extent corporations are entitled to section 8 protection.' As a corporate lawyer who had represented the Winnipeg *Free Press*, Dickson had a keen sense of the enormity of the search involved in the case. In an interview given after his retirement, Dickson remembered that the search powers 'couldn't have been broader ... it was a fishing licence.'[22]

Dickson outlined for his colleagues the crucial points he thought the judgment should make. First, he emphasized the need for prior authorization. He derived this from the common law tradition demonstrating that 'the right to be free from unjustifiable governmental intrusion is predicated on a system of *prior authorization* not one of subsequent validation.' Second was the need for an impartial arbiter. By giving the director the power to authorize the search, the law allowed the government to judge its own case. Third, an objective standard was required to '[eliminate] caprice, uncertainty and variation in the balancing process' between the state and the accused. Taking into account Lamer's concern about routine police investigations, Dickson proposed that the standard could vary with the circumstances. In some situations, requiring prior judicial authorization and the probable-cause standard might be too demanding; he offered the example of border-point customs searches where he thought a more lenient approach would be called for. Dickson wanted to protect privacy but he was no absolutist. He also categorically rejected the suggestion that the Court should rewrite the law by reading into the statute the provisions required by the Charter. Instead, he thought that it should be up to Parliament to draft new legislation.

In the discussions that followed, it was agreed that Dickson should write the Court's judgment, and there was confidence that any differences between Dickson and Lamer could be reconciled. On one point, however, Dickson's views prevailed: the Court's unanimous judgment made some sweeping Charter pronouncements. The opening sentences of Dickson's judgment, although paraphrased from the Charter itself, read like a judicial declaration of what was to come in the years to follow: 'The Constitution of Canada, which includes the *Canadian Charter of Rights and Freedoms*, is the supreme law of Canada. Any law inconsistent with the provisions of the Constitution is, to the extent of the inconsistency, of no force or effect.' Dickson left no doubt that he saw the Charter as conferring an important new mandate on the judiciary. Constitutional interpretation, he wrote, 'is crucially different' than interpreting an ordinary statute that is more specific and 'is easily enacted and as easily repealed.' The constitution is 'drafted with an eye to the future' and aims 'to provide a continuing framework for the legitimate exercise of governmental power.' The purpose of the Charter is 'the unremitting protection of individual rights and liberties,' and, since it 'cannot easily be repealed or amended ... it must ... be capable of growth over time to meet new social, political and historical realities often unimagined by its framers.' Despite his own private doubts on the point, Dickson stated that Canada's judges were ready to assume this awesome task: 'The judiciary is the guardian of the constitution and must, in interpreting its provisions, bear these considerations in mind.'[23]

As he had when reforming family law, Dickson took pains to show that his sweeping pronouncements had a respectable historic pedigree. He noted that 'the need for a broad perspective in approaching constitutional documents is a familiar theme in Canadian constitutional jurisprudence,'[24] and, as an example, he referred to the famous 'living tree' analogy in the 1930 *Person's Case* decision of the Privy Council, which held that women were 'persons' capable of being appointed to the Senate.[25] The constitution is 'a living tree capable of growth and expansion within its natural limits' and judges should not 'cut down' its provisions by a 'narrow and technical construction' but rather should 'give it a large and liberal interpretation.'[26]

Dickson articulated a purposive method of interpreting the Charter that had a fundamental influence on Charter interpretation. The terms of the Charter, Dickson wrote, had to be read and understood in light of the underlying purpose of the right or freedom at issue. 'The Canadian *Charter of Rights and Freedoms* is a purposive document. Its purpose is to guarantee and protect, within the limits of reason, the enjoyment of the rights and freedoms it enshrines. It is intended to constrain governmental action inconsistent with those rights and freedoms ...'[27]

The purposive method was not a new invention. It grew from the writings of legal scholars and from the growing tendency in Canadian law to base decisions more and more upon fundamental legal principles and less and less upon narrow and specific legal rules. In 1982 Dickson urged law students to look behind rules for their purposes, for the interests being protected and balanced, and for the principle that justifies the rules. 'When the legal rules have been milked for their wisdom, usually a fair and just solution will emerge.'[28] In notes he made in preparation for a television interview in 1986, he openly acknowledged that, to decide some Charter cases, the Court had to 'look outside legal materials' and that it was 'important to try to understand the learning of other disciplines such as medicine, economics, history and even philosophy.' He welcomed the challenge: 'I find that to be one of the attractive aspects of being a judge in these early days of the Charter because it increases my own knowledge and understanding of my country and the world around me.'[29]

Dickson identified the protection of privacy as the core purpose of the Charter's guarantee against unreasonable search and seizure. But the right to privacy, he observed, is not absolute. The individual had the right only to a *reasonable* expectation of privacy. As Dickson explained: 'An assessment must be made as to whether in a particular situation the public's interest in being left alone by government must give way to the government's interest in intruding on the individual's privacy in order to advance its goals, notably those of law enforcement.'[30]

These basic principles led Dickson to ask the same three questions posed months earlier in his discussions with his colleagues. First, 'When is the balance of interests to be assessed?'[31] Since the purpose of section 8 is preventive, prior authorization should be required even though it is not mentioned in the constitution's text. This accorded with common law tradition and properly forced the state to justify the intrusion.

The second question was, 'Who must grant the authorization?' Again, the constitutional text was silent, but the answer could be derived from the purpose of the guarantee. The state interest in law enforcement could prevail over the individual's privacy interest 'only where the appropriate standard has been met, and the interests of the state are thus demonstrably superior.' The need for an independent arbiter who could base the decision on the evidence in a neutral and impartial manner was implicit in the right. The person performing the function did not necessarily have to be a judge but 'must at a minimum be capable of acting judicially.'[32]

The third question was, 'On what basis must the balance of interests be assessed?' Here again, the purpose of the right suggested to Dickson the appropriate response. A suspicion in the mind of an investigating officer, however well intended, was not good enough. There had to be an objective standard rising above suspicion. 'The state's interest in detecting and preventing crime begins to prevail over the individual's interest in being left alone at the point where credibly-based probability replaces suspicion.' Dickson found support in both Canadian and American law for a general principle that, to justify a search, there should be reasonable and probable grounds to believe that a crime had taken place and the search would reveal evidence of the crime. At the same time, however, he stated that the standard might be higher or lower depending on the context. An invasion of bodily integrity might require a higher standard while the state's heightened interest in national security might allow for a lower standard.[33]

The Combines Investigation Act search power could not survive scrutiny under these principles. There was no impartial prior authorization and no objective standard. The government's lawyers urged the judges to save the section by either 'reading in' the necessary guarantees or by 'reading down' its broad language to mean only what the Charter would allow. Dickson maintained the view he had earlier expressed to his colleagues and flatly refused the invitation to rewrite the legislation. 'While the courts are guardians of the Constitution and of individuals' rights under it, it is the legislature's responsibility to enact legislation that embodies appropriate safeguards to comply with the Constitution's requirements.'[34]

The judgment in *Hunter v. Southam* was a major achievement. The Court had spoken with a unified and confident voice and had made clear its intention to assume significant power to ensure respect for Charter rights. The purposive approach suggested that Charter rights were going to be interpreted in a generous manner and that there would be no re-run of the Court's disappointing Bill of Rights performance. Advocates of civil liberties and human rights were enthused by the possibilities. However, in some quarters, the judgment was greeted with considerably less enthusiasm. The judgment used the language of individual rights and the sanctity of the home, but the case involved a major corporation trying to avoid state regulation. Charter sceptics, distrustful of judges, put their faith in Parliament and the legislatures to advance social justice, and they feared that this remarkable assertion of judicial power might well do more harm than good.

A Distinctively Canadian Jurisprudence

In *Hunter v. Southam*, in other early Charter judgments, and in his speeches and lectures on the Charter, Dickson emphasized the need for a distinctively Canadian approach and tried to nudge Canadian judges away from their traditional adherence to English jurisprudence. However, he did not want this departure from tradition to lead to the 'Americanization' of Canadian law.

From his days at the Manitoba law school, when he learned from English texts that failed to reflect Canadian values, Dickson's attitude to English authority had been respectful but guarded. As he matured as a judge, and as the Canadian legal community itself matured, Dickson considered English authorities to be of diminishing relevance. At times, his reaction to English pronouncements on Canadian developments was strong. He was outraged by what he regarded as the arrogance of a prominent English judge, Sir John Donaldson, master of the rolls, who had attacked Canada's entrenched bill of rights and the allegedly political role assumed by judges. Dickson told his Supreme Court colleagues: 'I find his address to be ignorant, arrogant and impertinent. He seems to place the blame for the creation of the Charter upon the backs of Canadian judges and then, as I read the latter part of his address, he would suggest that the British judges accomplished the same result through administrative law and judicial review thereby maintaining their apolitical stance and legitimacy.'[35]

Dickson realized that there was a wealth of American experience to draw upon in interpreting the Charter, but he was sensitive to the charge that the Charter would 'Americanize' Canadian law.[36] In a 1983 speech he pointed out that the Charter represented 'a fulfillment of Canada's international obligations respecting human rights,'[37] rather than a copying of the American Bill of Rights, and detailed the significant differences between the Canadian and American constitutions. Among these he listed the absence in Canada of the separation of church and state, the right to bear arms, the protection of property rights, and the right to jury trial in civil matters. Canada's Charter, he pointed out, explicitly contemplated affirmative-action programs and protected freedom of association, mobility, and equal rights for women. Its minority-language and minority-education guarantees had no parallel in the United States, nor did the protection of aboriginal rights and the recognition of Canada's multicultural heritage. These features of the Charter, he said in a 1985 speech, 'manifest a distinctively Canadian social experience, one marked

by a recognition of cultural identity, as well as an awareness of the importance of equality in a multicultural confederation.'[38]

Dickson's proclamations of Canadian legal independence sent the legal
community an important signal as it struggled with the Charter. However, his
message was not narrowly nationalistic. He thought that Canadian judges and
lawyers should become more eclectic and look to the experience of other
human rights regimes. In his own case, despite his guarded approach to
American legal authority, Dickson worked hard to establish a relationship
with the United States Supreme Court. In September 1985 he gave Chief Justice Warren Burger royal treatment on a four-day visit to Canada that included
dinners with the prime minister and the governor general and a visit to Wark-
worth Penitentiary. Burger even sat on the bench with the Court when it delivered judgments. Plans for an honorary degree at Queen's University produced
a strongly negative reaction from members of the Queen's law faculty who
considered Burger to be a reactionary conservative and were outraged at the
prospect of honouring a judge who, during his seventeen-year tenure as chief
justice, had led the United States Supreme Court away from the liberal constitutionalism of the Warren Court of the 1950s and 1960s. Burger did receive an
honorary degree, but it came from the more compliant Law Society of Upper
Canada. For his part, Dickson was charmed by Burger's personal warmth and
unconcerned by the significant differences in their judicial philosophies. In a
letter to Burger thanking him for the visit, Dickson's affection was effusive:
'During the course of a rather lengthy lifetime, I have enjoyed many pleasures
but none exceeded the pleasure of welcoming you and Mrs. Burger to Canada
and the joy of being in your company for several memorable days.'[39]

Burger's visit was a social success but it had little impact upon Canadian
jurisprudence. While the American chief justice was in Ottawa sitting on the
bench with his Canadian counterparts, Lamer was putting the finishing
touches on a decision that rejected a controversial and influential American
doctrine that the courts were bound by the 'original intent' of the drafters of
the constitution.[40] Two months before Burger's arrival, Edwin Meese, Ronald
Reagan's attorney general, had accused some American Supreme Court justices of adopting their own 'policy choices' and ignoring the 'original intention' of the framers of the constitution. Meese argued that the Court should
'resurrect the original meaning of constitutional provisions.'[41] Justice William
Brennan, one of the liberal members of the Court, responded that it was
impossible to know how the framers would deal with 'problems unforeseen
two centuries ago.'[42] In Canada, only two years, not two centuries, had
passed since the adoption of the Charter, but Lamer and his colleagues agreed
with Brennan that a narrow appeal to 'original intention' was a hopeless trap.
In a decision released on 17 December 1985, the Supreme Court refused to be

bound by evidence that government officials who drafted the Charter had intended the section 7 guarantee not to be deprived of 'life, liberty and security of the person ... except in accordance with the principles of fundamental justice' to be exclusively procedural. The adoption of the Charter, Lamer wrote, was a complex process, involving many individuals and institutions, and 'the comments of a few federal civil servants' could not be determinative. The Charter was intended to be an enduring document and 'the rights, freedoms and values' it embodies should not, Lamer stated, 'become frozen in time to the moment of adoption with little or no possibility of growth, development and adjustment to changing societal needs.'[43]

The Burger visit was followed by an even more ambitious Canadian-American legal exchange two years later in the autumn of 1987 that involved leading lawyers and judges from both countries in reciprocating visits to Washington and Ottawa. Three of the Canadian participants, John Sopinka, Charles Gonthier, and Beverley McLachlin, were subsequently appointed to the Supreme Court of Canada. The American contingent included Judge Kenneth Starr, who, as the independent counsel investigating the Whitewater affair, would later lead the effort to impeach President Bill Clinton. Dickson established a warm relationship with William Rehnquist, Burger's even more conservative successor as chief justice, and refused to allow jurisprudential differences to interfere with their friendship. 'There are some issues I thought were better not to discuss ... I think he takes a different point of view ... than I would ... on capital punishment ... Another, the matter of abortion, he holds certain views which are maybe somewhat different from the ones that I might harbour.'[44] Rehnquist, a man with a keen sense of history, recognized the enormous challenge the Dickson Court faced under the Charter. In a letter thanking Dickson for the exchange, he wrote: 'I must say, Brian, that I envy the role of you and your Court at the present time. It seems to me that you occupy much the position of Chief Justice John Marshall [the legendary American judge who established judicial review of legislation under the United States Constitution] and his Court in our early constitutional history, and yet you are sitting at a time so vastly different from his in terms of technological development. I shall follow your decisions with great interest during the next few years.'[45] The friendship between the men would continue in the years that followed, with Rehnquist making several private summer trips to Marchmont.

Dickson strongly believed in the development of international human rights norms from which Canada could benefit and to which Canada could contribute, and to the end, his overtures to the American Supreme Court were matched with visits to other supreme or constitutional courts. In June 1983, almost a year before his appointment as chief justice, Dickson travelled to

Italy to accept an honorary degree from the University of Padua on behalf of Laskin, who was too ill to travel. Dickson went to Rome to meet the Italian Constitutional Court, members of which made a return visit to Canada in October. This set the pattern for similar reciprocal visits with the Soviet Constitutional Court in 1988 and the Austrian Constitutional Court in 1989. All of these visits reflected Dickson's love for travel but also his genuinely eclectic approach to law, particularly his belief that lawyers and judges from different countries and different legal cultures have much to learn from each other. Dickson spoke frequently of the judges of two countries coming together 'with no political ends to serve, no differences to compose, no policies to advance, except the highest of all – the policy of understanding and goodwill.'[46] Barbara Dickson was tirelessly at her husband's side on all of these visits, helping with the travel and social arrangements and offering sage advice on speeches, where to go, and whom to see.

'If I am a Jew or a Sabbatarian or a Muslim'

Dickson's second major Charter judgment involved the contentious issue of Sunday shopping.[47] The Big M Drug Mart opened its doors for business in Calgary on Sunday, 30 May, 1982, in open violation of the pre-First World War Lord's Day Act that made it unlawful to 'sell or offer for sale or purchase any goods, chattels, or other personal property' on the Christian sabbath. The police entered the store and saw customers buying groceries, plastic cups, and a bicycle lock. Charges were laid and Big M raised a Charter defence. The prohibition of Sunday shopping, Big M argued, enforced religious observance and that was contrary to the Charter's guarantee of freedom of religion.

Once again, the discussion at conference[48] left no doubt that the Court would strike down the law despite the Court's 1963 judgment under the Canadian Bill of Rights that the Lord's Day Act did not violate freedom of religion.[49] Roland Ritchie, who had written the 1963 decision, assured his colleagues that 'he would never overrule' the earlier case, but even Ritchie had to concede that 'the Charter has given rules to a different game.' Ritchie's failing health spared him from participating in the judgment, but his comment at conference was prophetic. The Court's enthusiastic embrace of the Charter as the proclamation of a new era of rights protection meant that it would have no hesitation in discarding the 1963 decision as a product of the inadequacy of the Bill of Rights.

Dickson undertook to write the judgment. Appreciating the historic significance of the task, as well as how sensitive and controversial the issue of Sunday closing was, he took great pains drafting his reasons. The judgment would be the Court's first pronouncement on freedom of religion, a more contentious area than powers of search and seizure, and the case was being closely watched by the legal community as a sign of how far the Court would take the Charter's 'fundamental freedoms' of religion, expression, and association.

As in *Hunter v. Southam*, a corporation was claiming a Charter right. Lawyers for the federal government argued that as an impersonal legal abstraction, a corporation could not claim religious freedom. Once again, however, Dickson insisted that the Charter applied. Big M, he pointed out, did not initiate the case but was dragged into court charged with a criminal offence. As Dickson saw it, Big M's right to defend itself engaged the rule of law: a court could not countenance a conviction under a law that itself violated the fundamental rights guaranteed by the Charter. The constitution is the supreme law and, Dickson ruled, 'no one can be convicted of an offence under an unconstitutional law.' To Dickson, the issue of whether a corporation could enjoy freedom of religion was irrelevant: 'Any accused, whether corporate or individual, may defend a criminal charge by arguing that the law under which the charge is brought is constitutionally invalid.' The question for the Court was 'the nature of the law, not the status of the accused.' It was open to any accused, whether 'a Christian, Jew, Muslim, Hindu, Buddhist, atheist, agnostic or whether an individual or a corporation,' to defend the charge on the ground that the law itself was unconstitutional.[50] While this aspect of the case does not seem to have troubled Dickson at the time, the success of corporations as Charter litigants did not go unnoticed. The first two major Charter 'winners' were two corporations, fuelling the concerns of some Charter sceptics that constitutional rights might do more for the rich and powerful that for the disadvantaged members of society.

The real question for Dickson was the validity of the Sunday-closing law. He pored over the extensive briefs that had been filed. Wanting no stone left unturned, he asked the Supreme Court Library to prepare a bibliography on freedom of religion, and, when that arrived, he asked for copies of the books and articles that looked interesting.[51] Dickson loved history and he enjoyed tracing legal doctrines back to their beginnings. He examined the roots of mandatory observance of the sabbath, from the Fourth Commandment to the early English and American statutes that were the models for the Lord's Day Act. His historical review left no doubt that, when enacted, the Sunday-closing law had a religious purpose: it was designed to compel observance of the Christian sabbath. Dickson knew first hand the meaning of compelled religious observance from his own quiet childhood Sundays.

Government lawyers argued that, whatever its origins, the Lord's Day Act now had a valid modern secular purpose, namely, to provide a common day of rest. This submission provoked a debate between Dickson and Wilson on a basic issue of Charter interpretation – should the law be assessed under the

Charter on the basis of its purpose or on the basis of its effects? The debate was more than legal nit-picking. Parliament almost always has a valid purpose in mind when enacting a law. Usually, the question is whether, despite its valid purpose, the law has the effect of impinging unduly upon a fundamental right or freedom.

Sunday-closing laws provide a good example of the difference between purpose and effects analysis. If, as Dickson thought, the purpose of the law was to compel a form of religious observance, that purpose was inimical to freedom of religion. However, if, as the crown argued, the purpose of the law was to provide for a community-wide common day of rest to enhance family values and recreational activities, it would be necessary to consider the more difficult question of its effects. Non-Christian merchants whose faith required observing another sabbath could argue that a Sunday-closing law put them at a disadvantage and had the effect of burdening their religious freedom.

Dickson wanted to keep the case as simple as possible. If the law's purpose was at odds with a Charter right, he saw no need to go any further. The law could not survive, whatever its effects. Wilson worried that this would send the wrong message. She knew that, if Charter analysis focused on the purpose of laws rather than their effects, the Charter would have little bite. In a memorandum to Dickson commenting on his draft judgment, she argued that it would be 'very unlikely that the purpose of legislation would be to violate the *Charter*' and that the more usual situation would be that 'otherwise validly enacted legislation' would have the 'effect' of interfering with a Charter right.[52]

Dickson was hoping for a unanimous judgment, but he was determined to adhere to what he saw as a logical preference for deciding the case on the basis of an obviously unacceptable purpose rather than engaging in a more contentious debate about effects. In his response to Wilson, Dickson referred to the historical record that made it clear that the Lord's Day Act was enacted for a religious purpose and that 'purpose remains the best indication of what it is the legislation was intended to accomplish.' He saw purpose as 'the "primary" test in the sense that it is the first subject of inquiry. When the legislation's purpose offends the Charter, there is simply no need to go further and examine its effect.'[53] Dickson elaborated his point in his final judgment. If the law's purpose is contrary to the Charter, the violation of the protected right was clear, and, as he saw it, deciding the case on the ground of an improper purpose 'will provide more ready and more vigorous protection of constitutional rights by obviating the individual litigant's need to prove effects violative of *Charter* rights.'[54] In the end, Dickson was unable to persuade Wilson of the correctness of his approach and she wrote a separate judgment, concurring in the result.

Dickson was also confronted with a memorandum from Gérard La Forest, who had been appointed to the Court after *Big M* was argued but before it was decided. Although he could have no formal say in the decision, La Forest was a scholar of constitutional law with an extensive background in government. From the start, La Forest had a clear approach to the Charter. He believed strongly in the importance of maintaining respect for basic legal rights, especially privacy rights. At the same time, he felt that rigid Charter doctrines could unduly impair the difficult art of governing the nation, particularly when it involved the distribution of scarce resources. La Forest disagreed with Dickson's outright rejection of the idea that the purpose of a law might shift over time. He pointed out that, while 'shifting purpose' might save some laws, it could also be fatal to others. 'I can foresee the possibility,' he said, in his memorandum to Dickson, 'that a better factual understanding of a situation over time may possibly justify a holding that a statute once thought to be constitutional is no longer so.'[55]

Despite La Forest's arguments, Dickson insisted that the Court should never find that the purpose of legislation has been transformed by changed social conditions.[56] He feared that accepting the 'shifting purpose' doctrine could have major implications for federalism, where constitutional validity essentially turns on the purpose of the law. Allowing the purpose of a law to shift over time would, he thought, introduce an unacceptable element of uncertainty. A law judged constitutional today could be invalid tomorrow since 'no legislation would be safe from a revised judicial assessment of purpose. Laws assumed valid on the basis of persuasive and powerful authority could, at any time, be struck down as invalid.'[57] Dickson's insistence on this point is significant. Although he was writing a decision that demonstrated that the Court would wield the power of judicial review under the Charter, he remained mindful of the concern he expressed years earlier in *Harrison v. Carswell* about the need to maintain the stability of law.

The *Big M* judgment went through many drafts, with Dickson writing and rewriting the crucial passages and reviewing, revising, and polishing the final product with the help of his law clerks. Determined to express himself in clear language, making the judgment accessible to all, he searched for elegant phrasing and language that would convey the profound message of the Charter in a moving and enduring fashion. There can be little doubt that he succeeded.

Dickson picked up on the theme he had introduced in *Hunter v. Southam*. The Charter was to be interpreted in a purposive fashion. The purpose of a Charter right 'is to be sought by reference to the character and the larger objects of the Charter itself, to the language chosen to articulate the specific right or freedom, to the historical origins of the concepts enshrined, and where applicable, to the meaning and purpose of the other specific rights and freedoms with which it is associated within the text of the Charter.' The interpretation should be 'a generous rather than a legalistic one, aimed at fulfilling the purpose of the guarantee and securing for individuals the full benefit of the Charter's protection.' However, Dickson warned, 'it is important not to over-shoot the actual purpose of the right or freedom in question, but to recall that the Charter was not enacted in a vacuum, and must therefore ... be placed in its proper linguistic, philosophic and historical contexts.'[58]

Dickson described freedom as being 'primarily ... the absence of coercion or restraint' and the protection from compulsion and restraint as being 'one of the major purposes of the *Charter*.' The Charter, he ruled, protects against both direct and indirect forms of compulsion or control. He saw freedom in grand liberal terms: 'Freedom in a broad sense embraces both the absence of coercion and constraint, and the right to manifest beliefs and practices. Freedom means that, subject to such limitations as are necessary to protect public safety, order, health, or morals or the fundamental rights and freedoms of others, no one is forced to act in a way contrary to his beliefs or his conscience.'[59]

Then, in a striking passage, Dickson, a Christian who had held high positions in the Anglican Church, placed himself in the position of an adherent to a minority religion. 'If I am a Jew or a Sabbatarian or a Muslim, the practice of my religion at least implies my right to work on a Sunday if I wish. It seems to me that any law purely religious in purpose, which denies me that right, must surely infringe my religious freedom.'[60] This sent a powerful message. It told judges that, to assess Charter claims fairly, they had to put themselves in the shoes of the person claiming the Charter's protection. It offered minority groups and other Charter claimants hope that their pleas would be understood.

At the same time, Dickson anticipated criticism from some sectors of the Christian community. He tried to assure that constituency that he understood their perspective as well and insisted that neither he nor the Charter were opposed to the idea of Sunday being spent as a religious day: 'It is recognized that for a great number of Canadians, Sunday is the day when their souls rest in God, when the spiritual takes priority over the material, a day which, to them, gives security and meaning because it is linked to Creation and the Creator. It is a day which brings a balanced perspective to life, an opportunity for a man to be in communion with man and with God.'[61] But, in the end, Dickson left no doubt that while he understood the depth of feelings engendered by religious debates, there could be no state-sanctioned religion in Canada: '... the diversity of belief and non-belief, the diverse socio-cultural backgrounds of Canadians make it constitutionally incompetent for the federal Parliament to provide legislative preference for any one religion at the expense of those of another religious persuasion.'[62]

Dickson knew that, though Charter enthusiasts would be pleased to see the

Court take such a decisive stand, striking down the law would raise hackles in some quarters. With an eye to those who would say that striking down the law was anti-democratic, he attempted to explain the importance of individual rights and Charter review to the democratic tradition. By striking down the law, Dickson asserted, the Court was actually striking a blow in favour of democracy. The rights of 'individual conscience and individual judgment,' he argued, lie 'at the heart of our democratic political tradition. The ability of each citizen to make free and informed decisions is the absolute prerequisite for the legitimacy, acceptability, and efficacy of our system of government.' As Dickson saw it, 'the rights associated with freedom of individual conscience both to basic beliefs about human worth and dignity and to a free and democratic political system ... are the *sine qua non* of the political tradition underlying the *Charter*.'[63]

Dickson was plainly conscious of the historic significance of his *Big M* judgment. The day before *Big M* was to be released, he travelled to Princeton University, where his son Brian had studied, to give a lecture on the Charter. There, he spoke of a 'dramatic new chapter in Canada's constitutional and jurisprudential evolution' and of an emerging 'distinctively Canadian constitutional jurisprudence, basically British in orientation but drawing freely upon the experience and teachings of other jurisdictions, including the United States.' Dickson explained the evolution of the Canadian constitution and the Charter, the Patriation Reference, and the new role of the Supreme Court of Canada. He said that he was 'inspired by the task' of Charter decision making 'even as I stand awed by its magnitude.'[64] At dinner, he mentioned *Big M* to one of the professors: 'Just think, now I am the John Marshall of Canada.'[65]

Reaction to the Court's decision in *Big M* was generally positive. A Vancouver *Sun* editorial proclaimed: 'Good riddance to the *Lord's Day Act*. The only pity about the demise of that archaic piece of bluenose law is that it took so long. But then that had to await the arrival of the *Charter of Rights* and the constitutional guarantee of religious freedom ...'[66] Toronto's *Globe and Mail* welcomed the decision because the Lord's Day Act 'sounded a sour note in a pluralistic society.'[67] The Toronto *Star* also applauded the decision and joined the *Globe and Mail* in pointing out that provincial Sunday-closing laws remained on the books and that Ontario's complex package of prohibitions and exceptions was 'unacceptably arbitrary and unfair.' The *Star* called for the repeal of provincial Sunday-closing laws, noting that those laws had survived Charter challenge in the Ontario courts but that 'a 1983 Gallup Poll reported that 51 percent of Ontario residents were unreservedly in favour of Sunday openings.'[68]

However, support for the Court's ruling was by no means unanimous. Some commentators were concerned by the strong assertion of judicial power to set aside the laws enacted by democratically elected legislatures. Bob Bettson, a Calgary *Herald* columnist, warned: 'If the *Charter of Rights* is used to trample on the rights of the majority [Christian Sunday observers] to an excessive degree as it has been used in this case, it needs changing.'[69] Fred Cleverly, writing in Dickson's hometown Winnipeg *Free Press*, agreed: 'We are entering a period in which those we elect to govern us will do their best to reflect public opinion, only to be second guessed by the courts.'[70] Dickson also received many critical letters from Christian groups concerned that he had devalued their sabbath.

In practical terms, *Big M* did not end the Sunday-closing debate. Complex and controversial issues remained to be resolved. Federal Justice Minister John Crosbie thought that most Canadians favoured Sunday closing, but he urged respect for the Court's ruling: '... We have to observe the rights of minorities and those who might have objections on religious grounds. We have a *Charter of Rights* now and we have to play by the new rules.'[71] Roy Romanow, the former attorney general of Saskatchewan who had been a key player in the constitutional debates of the early 1980s that led to the adoption of the Charter, believed that the decision was 'probably the most dramatic example of the kind of involvement and decision making capacity that the court now has as a result of the *Charter of Rights.*'[72] In Alberta, a Conservative backbencher urged the adoption of the notwithstanding clause to protect the sanctity of Sunday, while the provincial attorney general, Neil Crawford, indicated that the government would leave it to municipalities to administer Sunday-closing laws at the local level. As with so many Charter issues, opinions cut across traditional party lines. Ontario's Conservative premier, Frank Miller, observed that 'most of us are in favour of a common day of pause,' a view shared by Bob Rae, leader of the provincial NDP, who spoke from the perspective of the workers: 'The principle of Sunday closings – to protect ... people having a day off – is pretty sound.'[73] Shirley Carr, secretary-treasurer of the Canadian Labour Congress (CLC), echoed this view: 'What I am concerned about is the protection of the people that have to work any of these new hours. I just hope they're not going to abuse the work force out there.'[74]

Cruise Missiles over Canada

On 15 July 1983 the federal cabinet decided to permit the United States to test cruise missiles on Canadian territory. The decision provoked an outcry from peace and disarmament groups. 'Operation Dismantle,' a coalition of trade unions, disarmament, and peace groups claiming to represent over one and a half million Canadians, banded together to fight cruise testing on Canadian soil. It launched a Charter challenge asserting that the cruise missile increased the risk of nuclear war by frustrating surveillance and verification systems, heightening international tension, and raising the possibility of precipitous attack. The anti-cruise forces also claimed that permitting American testing on Canadian soil made Canada a more likely target for nuclear attack. They contended that the cabinet's decision to allow cruise-missile testing threatened the life and the security of all Canadians and so was contrary to the Charter's section 7 promise of the right to 'life, liberty and security of the person.'

The case became a focal point for the tensions created by increased media interest in the work of the Court. Some lawyers arguing high-profile Charter cases used the press as a way of attracting public attention to their clients' causes and to themselves. Most judges thought that it was improper for a lawyer to argue his or her case in the media and this strict standard was breached even if the lawyer simply tried to explain what the case was about. Interviews by gowned lawyers in the precincts of the courthouse were particularly galling to the traditionalists.

The leave-to-appeal motion was heard in 1983 while Laskin was still chief justice. Lawrence Greenspon, lawyer for the coalition of public-interest groups mounting the challenge, gave reporters an interview outlining the basis of his client's case. However innocuous this might now seem, it seriously perturbed Laskin, who was usually supportive of the media. He sternly reprimanded Greenspon: 'Are you arguing this case in the press or before the courts? You are pretty close to contempt, you know. This is not very professional conduct.'[75] Laskin's former student, civil libertarian Alan Borovoy, came to Greenspon's defence, pointing out that the case was complicated and, by giving an interview, Greenspon might have helped foster public understanding of the case and the role of the Court. 'It's hard to fathom why it was wrong for Greenspon to grant media interviews about the case.'[76]

When the appeal was heard in late December 1983, the traditionalist judges, especially Ritchie and Estey,[77] were disturbed when Greenspon and the highly respected Gordon Henderson conducted a television interview on the front steps of the Court. This was regarded as a serious transgression, so serious as to require a Court conference where it was decided that videotapes of the interviews should be reviewed. Some judges wanted to take a hard line and treat the lawyers' behaviour as contempt. Fortunately, cooler heads prevailed. Estey, Ritchie, McIntyre, and Wilson met with Ontario's Law Society to urge it to tighten the rules of professional conduct. The Law Society then adopted a new rule which said that public appearances were acceptable if they were approved by the client, in the client's best interest, and not used by the lawyer for self-promotion.[78] Estey was disappointed. He thought that the rule should cover 'conduct of members of the profession related to interviews with journalists and broadcasters before, during and after a court hearing period.'[79]

Dickson, for his part, believed that a lawyer should 'be scrupulously careful not to give the impression that he is touting or attempting to try the client's case in the press,' but he recognized that freedom of expression had to be respected and he thought that lawyers could assist the media by answering genuine requests for information.[80]

The appeal,[81] argued in February 1984, raised fundamental questions. Could the Court make the difficult decision about how best to protect Canada from the threat of nuclear war? Does the Charter restrict the hand of the government in shaping Canada's foreign policy? Does the Charter even apply to cabinet decisions?

Dickson was a keen observer of national and international affairs and he held strong personal views on Canada's defence and foreign policy. Certainly not a pacifist or an advocate of disarmament, he was proud of Canada's military past and he believed that Canada should assume responsibility for its own defence; he thought that it would be wrong to take the benefit of American nuclear protection without shouldering a fair share of responsibility. Five of the other judges who sat on the case – Ritchie, Estey, McIntyre, Chouinard, and Lamer – had also served in the armed forces. Wilson, the seventh judge, had not served but she was no stranger to military conflict. She had lived through the Second World War in Scotland, and her husband, John, had been a pacifist during the war but later served as a chaplain with the Canadian forces in Korea in the early 1950s. There can be little doubt that, of all the judges who sat on the case, Wilson was the most sympathetic to the anti-nuclear, pro-disarmament cause, on account of her own social-democratic views.

At conference after the case was argued, it was clear that none of the judges thought that the Court should accept the invitation to become embroiled in debates about foreign policy and the perils of nuclear war.[82] At the same time, there was a general consensus that the Court should, as Dickson put it, 'maintain our right to supervision of Cabinet decisions which may offend the *Charter.*' The difficult question was how to decide the case without limiting the reach of the Charter. Wilson, the junior judge and the first to speak, thought that the issue was 'inherently non-justiciable' – in other words, not capable of being considered legally and determined by the application of legal reasoning.[83] As the discussion moved around the table, the other judges tended to agree with Wilson's suggested approach. Dickson was non-committal. He thought that the Court could 'dispose of the case either on the matter of non-justiciability or on the basis that the claims made in the statement of claim and the facts pleaded do not engage s. 7.' At the same time, however, he wanted to avoid 'a lengthy exegesis on the important question of s. 7 and its relationship with other sections of the *Charter.*' Dickson was firm on one point: 'We should try and issue one judgment which would be signed by all members of the

Court.' Since Wilson's view seemed to attract general support, she was assigned the task of writing first reasons.

Wilson's draft judgment took a very different line than the one she had expressed at conference. She began by insisting that the Court could deal with the factual issues and she flatly rejected the argument that there were certain decisions beyond the reach of the Charter and the courts. If a decision of the cabinet, even one in relation to Canada's foreign or defence policies, violates a Charter right, Wilson wrote, it is the duty of the courts to intervene. She had reversed her position at conference and now rejected the ill-defined and shaky concept of 'non-justiciability,' favouring a strong assertion of the Court's power to vindicate Charter rights even where highly contentious political issues were in play. The crux of Wilson's carefully constructed opinion, supported by references to leading political and legal philosophers, rested on her conception of the fundamental nature of rights in a civil society. Wilson found that, even if the anti-cruise advocates could show an increased risk of nuclear war, the resulting general and undifferentiated threat to all Canadians did not amount to a violation of a Charter right. No Charter right is absolute, and, Wilson wrote, all Charter rights must 'take account of the political reality of the modern state.'[84] Many government decisions – setting speed limits on highways and declaring war – affect the lives and safety of all citizens. Wilson argued that, although decisions of this nature may well affect the lives or the security of all Canadians, they do not violate the individual rights guaranteed by the Charter. They are, rather, the inevitable result of living with others in a civil state. Wilson concluded that, since the cabinet decision arguably exposed us all to a risk, none of us could complain that our Charter rights had been violated.

When Wilson circulated her draft reasons, Dickson was initially positive: 'I have read with interest your reasons in the *Operation Dismantle* appeal and I think they are excellent.'[85] But, after further reflection and perhaps some discussion with his clerks and other colleagues, Dickson had reservations. He agreed with the way Wilson had put to one side the issue of 'non-justiciability'; however, he was uncomfortable with her rather philosophical approach to the right to life, liberty, and security of the person. Dickson worried about the long-term impact of Wilson's sweeping statements limiting section 7 rights by reference to the general interests of society. Thinking that *Operation Dismantle* was not the best case to deal with the difficult issues posed by section 7, he suggested to Wilson that her reasoning might 'unduly narrow the protection afforded by s. 7.' These rights, he argued, should be limited only by the 'fundamental justice' clause of section 7 or by section 1. 'Competing rights and "benefit to the community" arguments are only properly made with respect to these provisions.' In a later memorandum, he wrote: 'One of the main purposes of the *Charter* is to ensure that the "tyranny of the majority" is not allowed to override fundamental individual rights.' Rights under section 7 'cannot yield to an interpretation ... that allows for their abrogation where it would advance the interests of the community of the whole to do so.'[86]

Dickson recognized that, without using either the 'non-justiciability' argument or Wilson's 'no Charter breach' analysis, it might not be possible to prevent the case from going to trial.[87] The government was trying to shut the case down without a trial on the basis of the pleadings alone. Without a trial they were not entitled to say that the plaintiff's case was so thin on the facts that they were bound to lose. As Wilson had observed in her reasons, 'it is trite law that on a motion to strike out a statement of claim the plaintiff's allegations of fact are to be taken as having been proved.'[88] Dickson was convinced, however, that the plaintiffs had no hope of proving their case. He expressed 'the gravest doubts about the truth of [the plaintiff's] allegations,' but, even assuming their truth, he thought that it would not be possible for the plaintiffs to show a causal link between the government's decision to permit cruise testing and an increased risk of nuclear war. 'It is clear that there must be a sufficient causal connection between an action by the government and an alleged violation of a constitutional right ... I believe the Court should discuss the causal requirements for any finding that the government has violated s. 7 of the *Charter* and should state that these requirements do not appear to be satisfied in the present case.' This, he conceded, would leave the anti-cruise advocates free to proceed to trial if they wished, but with little prospect of success 'since they would have to satisfy the causal requirements laid down by this Court.'

Wilson was not persuaded and she quickly saw that their differences were irreconcilable. In her responding memorandum[89] she indicated that, while she was making some revisions to her draft, she would 'not ... be changing the basic approach since it would appear that there will be more than one set of reasons in this case.' She told Dickson that she thought it was a mistake to import into the Charter the notoriously vague concept of causation but added that she could see the 'political appeal' of causation analysis since 'it would permit us to come out for a large and liberal interpretation of the individual rights themselves.' She pointed out, however, that if Dickson intended to allow the case to proceed to trial, it would be difficult to justify saying anything at all about whether or not the test of causation could be met.

This provoked a further response from Dickson.[90] He did not respond to Wilson's criticism of his causation proposal but reiterated his concern with what he saw as Wilson's use of 'utilitarian considerations' of general community benefit to limit Charter rights. Dickson repeated that he saw it as dangerous to deploy such arguments except under section 7's explicit 'fundamental justice' language or under section 1.

After this flurry of memoranda,[91] it was apparent that unanimity would not be possible. Dickson decided to write what he hoped would be a majority judgment. He based his reasons on the ground he had outlined in his memoranda but, perhaps unsettled by a point made by Wilson, added an important twist. He now thought that the case could be dismissed on the pleadings without a trial since the link between the government's action and the alleged violation of rights was 'simply too uncertain, speculative and hypothetical to sustain a cause of action.' To make out a violation of section 7, he wrote, the plaintiffs would have to prove that the federal cabinet's decision to permit cruise testing increases the risk of nuclear war. 'It is precisely this link between the cabinet decision to permit the testing of the cruise missile and the increased risk of nuclear war which, in my opinion, they cannot establish.' Insisting that he was not basing his opinion on 'non-justiciability,' he hammered away at what he saw as the impossibility of the plaintiff's case. Dickson carefully dissected the anti-cruise arguments and found that they all led to a hopeless dead-end of hypothesis, conjecture, and speculation. All of the plaintiffs contentions, he concluded, were 'premised on assumptions and hypotheses about how independent and sovereign nations, operating in an international arena of radical uncertainty, and continually changing circumstances, will react to the Canadian government's decision to permit the testing of the cruise missile.' These were matters that 'lie in the realm of conjecture, rather than fact. In brief, it is simply not possible for a court, even with the best available evidence, to do more than speculate upon the likelihood of the federal cabinet's decision to test the cruise missile resulting in an increased threat of nuclear war.'[92]

At the same time, Dickson was careful to agree with Wilson's insistence that cabinet decisions, even in the realm of foreign policy, remain subject to the Charter. Dickson made no attempt to refute Wilson's analysis of the nature of section 7 rights; he wanted to avoid the subject and scrupulously omitted any reference to this aspect of Wilson's judgment. The other members of the Court signed Dickson's reasons and Wilson was left alone.

Dickson's reasons for dismissing the case seem less than convincing. The issue was not whether the plaintiffs could prove the necessary causal connection at trial, but whether or not the case should be allowed to go to trial. As Wilson had pointed out, on a motion of this kind, the Court was required to take the allegations of fact as true. Dickson reasoned that the procedural rule 'does not require that allegations based on assumptions and speculations be taken as true.'[93] But how could one know that the case was based 'on assumptions and speculations' without hearing the evidence at a trial? On the other hand, if Dickson meant that the allegations are not capable of proof in a court of law, did that not amount to saying the issue was not justiciable, a doctrine he was at pains to dismiss?

However, from a pragmatic perspective, one can understand why Dickson's approach proved attractive to his colleagues. It allowed the Court to dispose of a case that was politically charged and almost certain to fail, while fully preserving the Court's power to review cabinet decisions. It also avoided what Dickson saw as an ill-timed and ill-advised philosophical debate that might, in the long term, unduly limit the right to 'life, liberty and security of the person.' Dickson failed to achieve unanimity, but, with only one concurring decision, the Court had spoken clearly and decisively on a highly contentious case.

The significance of the Court's decision was not lost on the government. Justice Minister John Crosbie, increasingly sceptical of the Charter and the mandate it conferred on the courts, proclaimed that Canadians 'are now living in a different world' and that because executive decisions could now be reviewed by the courts, 'we've got to govern ourselves accordingly.'[94] Political scientist Peter Russell described the ruling as 'a mighty blow [that] killed totally the dangerous doctrine that the cabinet is above the law.'[95] Counsel Lawrence Greenspon, who could now speak without fear of judicial rebuke, had lost his own battle but had won a larger war. He described the decision as 'one giant step for Canadians forward generally – and one giant step backward for the anti nuclear movement.'[96]

'A stringent standard of justification'

Oakes,[97] Dickson's cornerstone judgment dealing with the limitation of Charter rights, arose from a routine drug prosecution. David Edwin Oakes was picked up by the police outside a tavern in London, Ontario. Oakes was carrying eight one-gram vials of hashish oil and over $600 in cash. The police were unconvinced by Oakes's story that he had bought the hashish for his own use and that he got the cash from a worker's compensation cheque; they charged him with possession of narcotics for the purpose of trafficking, an offence carrying a maximum penalty of up to life imprisonment. The trial followed the two-step procedure set out in the Narcotics Control Act.[98] At the first stage, it was up to the crown to prove beyond a reasonable doubt that Oakes was in possession of narcotics. In the circumstances, this was not a difficult task. At that point, the onus of proof shifted from the crown to the accused. If Oakes failed to prove that he had no intention to traffic in drugs, he would be convicted of the more serious offence.

Section 11(d) of the Charter guarantees the right 'to be presumed innocent until proven guilty according to law.'[99] Oakes's counsel, Geoffrey Beasley, decided that his client's best hope was a Charter attack on the reverse-onus clause, a tactic that would make his client's name go down in history as the label for a fundamental doctrine of Charter interpretation. The trial judge accepted the Charter argument and refused to apply the reverse-onus clause. The crown had no evidence of Oakes's intentions and, without the reverse onus to bolster its case, it could not prove that Oakes intended to traffic. Oakes was acquitted of the more serious charge and convicted of simple possession. The crown appealed but met with no success before the Ontario Court of Appeal.[100] Justice G. Arthur Martin, the acknowledged dean of Canadian criminal law, delivered the court's judgment, holding that a reverse-onus clause could be valid only if there is a rational connection between the proved fact and the presumed fact. Martin reasoned that, where there was only a small quantity of drugs, there was no rational connection between the proved fact of possession and the presumed fact of intention to traffic. It was not for the courts, added Martin, to rewrite the law so that it would only apply to larger quantities.

The crown appealed to the Supreme Court of Canada. The conference discussion was relatively brief. All the judges were impressed with Martin's reasons and they agreed that the reverse-onus provision could not survive. But Martin had written his reasons before the Court had settled some of the basic principles of Charter interpretation. The general view around the conference table was that, while Martin reached the correct result, there was a problem with the way he had approached the case. As Dickson put it in his summary of the conference discussion, '... he tended to collapse s. 1 into s. 11(d) instead of making a determination under the latter section and then going to s. 1.' This was inconsistent with what had emerged as the preferred method of Charter interpretation: give the rights a generous 'purposive' interpretation, and then decide upon the acceptable limits to the rights under section 1. Dickson noted that the failure to keep these two stages distinct would disadvantage those making a Charter challenge. The individual has to prove a violation of the Charter. It is then up to the crown to prove the justification for limiting the right under section 1. If the entire case is decided by interpreting the right without reference to section 1, the crown is relieved of demonstrating that the law is justifiable. However, at the *Oakes* conference, little or no thought was given to the precise test the Court should adopt under section 1.[101] The Ontario courts had not dealt with section 1 and the lawyers arguing the case did not focus on the point. Even as Dickson sat down to write his reasons, his preoccupation was with the reverse-onus provision itself rather than defining the contours of section 1.

Dickson decided that reversing the onus of proof on the accused infringed the presumption of innocence guaranteed by section 11(d), 'a hallowed principle lying at the very heart of criminal law.'[102] As in *Big M*, Dickson took care to describe the right the Charter protected. He assessed the right in human terms from the perspective of the individual who was adversely affected by the law:

> The presumption of innocence protects the fundamental liberty and human dignity of any and every person accused by the State of criminal conduct. An individual charged with a criminal offence faces grave social and personal consequences, including potential loss of physical liberty, subjection to social stigma and ostracism from the community, as well as other social, psychological and economic harms. In light of the gravity of these consequences, the presumption of innocence is crucial. It ensures that until the State proves an accused's guilt beyond all reasonable doubt, he or she is innocent. This is essential in a society committed to fairness and social justice. The presumption of innocence confirms our faith in humankind; it reflects our belief that individuals are decent and law-abiding members of the community until proven otherwise.[103]

Dickson fortified his analysis of the presumption of innocence with reference to a wide range of international sources, including the *International Covenant on Civil and Political Rights*, the *European Convention on Human Rights*, and American case law. As in *Hunter*, he defined the presumption of innocence in the Charter in a manner that drew on the recognition of legal rights before the Charter.

But, as Dickson completed this portion of the draft judgment, he realized that he could only go so far with the interpretation of the right under section 11(b). In the final analysis, as the Court had decided at conference, the fate of the reverse-onus clause would be determined under section 1. The existing case law offered relatively little guidance on the meaning of section 1. Some of the basic groundwork had been laid in *Big M* and the purposive approach suggested that the test should be relatively stringent; however, Dickson decided that a more precise section 1 test was needed. He turned for help to his law clerks, Colleen Sheppard and Joel Bakan, and his executive legal officer, James MacPherson. Sheppard had just completed graduate work at Harvard while Bakan came to Dickson fresh from graduate studies at Oxford. Bakan immersed himself in the European human rights jurisprudence and the limitation of rights under the principle of proportionality; Sheppard provided an American perspective. Dickson worked closely with Sheppard, Bakan, and MacPherson.[104] The final product of their effort was five of the most important pages ever written in Canadian constitutional law.

Section 1, Dickson wrote, guarantees Charter rights and freedoms and 'states explicitly the exclusive justificatory criteria ... against which limitations on those rights and freedoms must be measured.' Charter rights are not absolute, and section 1 recognizes that it may be 'necessary to limit rights and freedoms in circumstances where their exercise would be inimical to the realization of collective goals of fundamental importance.' However, section 1 states that Charter rights are 'subject only to such reasonable limits prescribed by law as can be justified in a free and democratic society.' To Dickson, the words 'free and democratic society' were crucial, and once again, he insisted that 'the very purpose for which the *Charter* was originally entrenched in the Constitution [is that] Canadian society is to be free and democratic.' Dickson wrote that, when assessing limits on a protected right, 'the Court must be guided by the values and principles essential to a free and democratic society which I believe embody, to name but a few, respect for the inherent dignity of the human person, commitment to social justice and equality, accommodation of a wide variety of beliefs, respect for cultural and group identity, and faith in social and political institutions which enhance the participation of individuals and groups in society.' Dickson saw 'the underlying values and principles of a free and democratic society' as both the 'genesis' of Charter rights and 'the ultimate standard against which a limit on a right or freedom must be shown, despite its effect, to be reasonable and democratic.'[105]

Dickson proceeded to describe the 'stringent standard of justification' that must be satisfied to limit a Charter right or freedom. While the party challenging a law bears the initial onus of showing a breach of Charter rights, once a Charter violation is established, the onus shifts to the state to justify limiting the right. First of all, the state must show an objective that relates 'to concerns which are pressing and substantial in a free and democratic society before it can be characterized as sufficiently important.' If an objective of sufficient importance is shown, the state must then satisfy a three-step proportionality test:

> First, the measures adopted must be carefully designed to achieve the objective in question. They must not be arbitrary, unfair or based on irrational considerations. In short, they must be rationally connected to the objective. Second, the means, even if rationally connected to the objective in this first sense, should impair 'as little as possible' the right or freedom in question ... Third, there must be a proportionality between the *effects* of the measures which are responsible for limiting the *Charter* right or freedom, and the objective which has been identified as of 'sufficient importance.'[106]

Dickson concluded that those defending the federal law had failed to satisfy this test. He accepted that the protection of society from 'grave ills associated with drug trafficking' was an objective of sufficient importance, but found that the reverse-onus clause was not rationally connected to this goal. Like Martin, Dickson stressed that the law made the irrational presumption that anyone found with any illegal drugs would sell the drugs.

The *Oakes* decision was front-page news. Police officers complained that the Court had made their job tougher, while defence lawyers suggested that many other reverse-onus clauses would be struck down.[107] Those who hoped for a judicially robust treatment of the Charter were encouraged by these early signals. Others, who feared that judicial power would usurp majority rule were unsettled.

Bold First Steps

In 1984 and 1985 the Court, led by Dickson, took some bold constitutional steps, making it clear that the Charter had ushered in a new era in Canadian law. The Court would not hesitate to strike down laws the judges thought infringed fundamental rights and freedoms. Rights were going to be generously interpreted by means of the 'purposive approach' announced in *Hunter v. Southam* and *Big M.* The Court accepted that Charter rights were not absolute, but the *Oakes* test for the justification of any limitations on rights was tough to satisfy. *Operation Dismantle* established that the Charter applied to all aspects of the government, even the executive decisions of cabinet.

But the Court and the Canadian public had yet to measure fully the Charter's impact. The Court had flexed its Charter muscles but these early cases did not test the limits of the Court's strength or endurance. How far would or should the Court go? What were the limits to the Charter's reach? Would the Court have the nerve to disagree with Parliament or to make law in more contentious areas? Despite the bold start, many questions remained unanswered.

16

Continuity and Change

The Charter of Rights and Freedoms contains a long list of legal rights designed to ensure the fair administration of criminal justice. Most of these rights are derived from the Anglo-Canadian common law tradition and were a feature of our law before the Charter. But the Charter changed certain fundamental rules of the game. Before the Charter, judges – even Supreme Court of Canada judges – applied the law as laid down by Parliament. After the Charter, judges – especially Supreme Court of Canada judges – had the constitutional duty to ensure that Parliament's laws complied with the overriding demands of the constitution. Before the Charter, judges were extremely reluctant to exclude evidence on account of police misconduct or illegal behaviour. After the Charter, judges were required to exclude evidence obtained in violation of these rights if the admission of the evidence in the criminal trial would bring the administration of justice into disrepute. As in other areas of the law, Dickson's views on criminal justice evolved over the years. His approach to the Charter and criminal justice was characterized by both continuity and change. In some areas, Dickson's pre-Charter jurisprudence anticipated the changes that were to come, while in other areas, the Charter forced Dickson to change.

No Fiats for Police Illegality

Dickson's decisions about police powers before the Charter generally reflected his liberal concern about the abuse of state power and his commitment to the rule of law and democracy. Even when this position left him in lonely dissent, Dickson believed that police powers should be based in clear legislation enacted after democratic debate. His approach in these cases may have been influenced by his boyhood memories of a police officer shooting his pet rats without any legal authority, but it was also firmly rooted in fundamental legal principles. In 1979 the Court considered whether a cyclist who ran a red light could be convicted of obstruction of justice for refusing to identify himself to a police officer. The case captured an unusual amount of media attention because the accused, forty-nine-year-old Tim Moore, cycled twenty-nine days from Victoria to Ottawa to attend the Court's hearing. Moore was disappointed after making the long trip because the hearing did not go well for his side. At one point, Louis-Philippe Pigeon 'exploded' at the suggestion that the legislature should be required to pass a law to require people to identify themselves. Pigeon, an expert on statutory interpretation, asked, 'Why is it necessary to spell everything out such that we get unworkable statutes such as the income tax act which runs to whole volumes.' The press reported that Moore consoled himself after the hearing by smoking marijuana in the Supreme Court's parking lot, where he told reporters: 'If the weather is good and I can score some bread then I might stay the summer.'[1]

It is not known whether Moore stayed the summer, but he must have been unhappy when the Court delivered its judgment in October. The majority concluded that he had disrupted the police officer's duties to enforce laws by refusing to identify himself. It stressed how easy it would have been for Moore to have cooperated compared to the 'major inconvenience and obstruction to the police in carrying out their proper duties' caused by his rude refusal to tell the police officer his name.[2] Dickson's conference notes indicate that, from the start, he disagreed with the majority's approach. 'The right to remain silent when questioned on any subject by a police officer is not unlawful unless made so by statute ... A person who fails to cooperate with the police when asked questions cannot be said to be obstructing justice unless there is a legal requirement to answer questions.'[3]

In his judgment, Dickson began from the fundamental premise that individuals maintained their freedom unless a clear legal duty was imposed on them. A failure to act, in the absence of a legal duty, should not be a crime. Dickson followed a traditional and liberal understanding of the rule of law that required all state incursions on freedom to be authorized by law. Although there might be a moral or social duty for Moore to tell the police his name, there was no legal duty because 'the right to remain silent ... does not admit of such erosion.' Dickson emphatically rejected the majority's idea that the general duty of police officers to enforce the law implied a reciprocal duty on individuals to cooperate. Such an approach was not only 'unsound in principle,' but 'unworkable in practice ... The criminal law is no place within which to introduce implied duties, unknown to statute and common law, breach of which subjects a person to arrest and imprisonment.'[4] Dickson's dissenting judgment was praised by most academics as 'well reasoned' and 'clearly superior to the majority decision.'[5] A government lawyer, however, praised the majority for taking a 'law enforcement approach.'[6]

Dickson again found himself dissenting against the expansion of police powers in a 1984 case. The issue was whether a judicial wiretap warrant authorized the police to trespass in order to install the listening device. Relying on an early Dickson judgment that allowed police to enter homes without a warrant to make an arrest,[7] a majority of the Court reasoned that the power to trespass was implicit in the judicial warrant.[8] Dickson saw the issue differently. Unless authorized by law, police officers had no more right to break and enter or trespass than ordinary citizens. 'The right to be free from unwanted intrusion is important and fundamental. It leaves no room for casual inference of Parliamentary sanction of illegality.'[9] It was not the task of courts to infer into legislation a police power to break and enter that had not been clearly articulated by Parliament.[10] Foreshadowing the Court's eventual willingness to go beyond American authorities in interpreting the Charter, Dickson sided with the dissent of Justice William Brennan in a recent United States Supreme Court case that covert entries were not implicitly authorized under similar American wiretap legislation.[11] Although Dickson developed friendships with chief justices Warren Burger and William Rehnquist of the United States Supreme Court, his sympathies on many issues were with the more liberal judges on that Court, such as Brennan, who increasingly wrote in dissent.

Dickson's dissent came after both Quebec and federal royal commissions had revealed that the RCMP had engaged in illegal activities, including break and enters, after the 1970 October Crisis. Although he did not cite these reports, they may have been in Dickson's mind when he raised his concern over giving the police 'a fiat for illegality' that they could use 'whenever the benefit of police action appeared to outweigh the infringements of an individual's rights.' Allowing the police to break and enter in order to install a listening device would also run against 'the traditional legal protection accorded private property and the long-standing refusal of the judiciary to impair that protection when Parliament has not itself done so expressly ... It is for Parliament, not the judiciary, still less the police themselves, to fill any gap in the Criminal Code.'[12] Of course it might have been difficult for the government to authorize police break and enters when memories of RCMP illegalities were still fresh in the minds of many. After Dickson's retirement, the Supreme Court eventually insisted that police lawbreaking be authorized by law, and Parliament responded by giving the police some powers to break the law in the course of their law-enforcement duties.[13] Dickson might have been uncomfortable with such powers, but he would have respected the fact that they had been debated in Parliament and not created by courts.

In 1985 Dickson dissented in a high-profile case involving a challenge by a man named Dedman who had been stopped at a police spot check designed to detect drunk drivers. The majority of the Court, including both Lamer and Wilson, concluded that the police officer's common law duties to prevent crime and protect life and property authorized the random stopping of motorists. It was clear from the conference, however, that Dickson would again dissent on the basis of the principles that he had articulated in his earlier dissents. Once Dickson made up his mind on an important issue of principle, he was often unwilling to abandon his position, even though it may not have been accepted by the majority of the Court. Some believed that Dickson's persistence was in tension with the obligation to follow precedent. For example, McIntyre stated: 'There was one thing about Brian that surprised me ... he would repeat dissents which, in my opinion, an appellate judge should not do ... I don't say that Brian habitually repeated dissents, but there were times when he did.'[14].

Dickson argued in his *Dedman* dissent that 'to find that arbitrary police action is justified simply because it is directed at the fulfillment of police duties would be to sanction a dangerous exception to the supremacy of law. It is the function of the legislature, not the courts, to authorize arbitrary police actions that would otherwise be unlawful as violations of rights traditionally protected at common law.' The case did not involve the Charter, but Dickson believed that Charter rights such as the right against arbitrary detention were already part of 'the long-standing protection accorded individual liberty by the common law,' and that 'individual freedom from interference by the state, no matter how laudable the motive of the police, must be guarded zealously against intrusion. Ultimately, this freedom is the measure of everyone's liberty and one of the corner-stones of the quality of life in our democratic society.'[15] Dickson saw important continuities between the common law and the Charter. In a 1981 address to law students, he argued that the rules of criminal procedure constituted 'a "bill of rights" for persons accused of crime.'[16] Whether before or after the Charter, Dickson required clear legislation to authorize the infringement of rights.

The majority's decision upholding the well-publicized and popular anti-drunk driving program was front-page news and received even more publicity than some of the Court's early Charter cases. The decision was 'welcomed by police and victim support groups,'[17] but there was also support for Dickson's dissent. The *Globe and Mail* criticized the majority's decision for coming to 'the alarming conclusion' that the police could interfere with a citizen's liberty without legislative authorization.[18] The Ottawa *Citizen* also took Dickson's side and argued that 'the Chief Justice zeroes in on the fundamental issue raised by the case – the balance between the interest of the community in law enforcement and the interest of individuals in being free from arbitrary interference with their liberty.'[19] Dickson, a keen reader of newspapers, especially when they mentioned the Court, distributed the favourable editorials to the judges who had joined him in dissent but tactfully did not send them to those who joined the majority judgment.[20]

In 1988, drunk-driving spot checks were again challenged, this time under the Charter. Dickson joined a unanimous judgment upholding the law as a reasonable limit on the accused's Charter right against arbitrary detention.[21] The crucial difference for Dickson was that Ontario had passed a law specifically authorizing the random stops. The legislature, as opposed to the courts, had expanded police powers after democratic debate. The 1988 decision also reflected the Court's increasing willingness to uphold violations of Charter rights as reasonable limits under section 1 of the Charter. Governments were adjusting to their new responsibilities under the Charter and had introduced extensive evidence to demonstrate that drinking and driving was a pressing social problem and that police spot checks were an effective means to deter drunk driving.

Dickson still believed, however, that the police should not have unlimited powers to engage in random stops of cars. In 1990 he dissented from a decision to uphold random-vehicle stops that were not part of an organized campaign to detect drunk drivers. The case reflected a Court closely and almost bitterly split over police powers. A five-judge majority concluded that random stops were justified whenever they were conducted for any traffic-safety reason. Dickson joined Sopinka's strongly worded dissent, which saw 'the roving random stop' as 'the last straw' that would allow the police to stop any vehicle on a whim, perhaps even for discriminatory reasons.[22] At conference, Dickson told his colleagues that the police should 'not have an unrestrictive right to stop each individual without any particular cause.'[23] Both before and after the Charter, Dickson's firm commitment to liberal values of the rule of law made him question unlimited or ill-defined police powers and insist that such powers be clearly articulated and justified in democratically enacted legislation.

Canadians Would Be 'shocked and appalled'

Although Dickson was prepared to take a strong stand against the extension of police powers before the Charter, he was much more reluctant to respond to police illegality by excluding improperly obtained evidence. Excluding relevant evidence went against Dickson's grain. In 1975 he joined a majority judgment that allowed the crown to introduce a breathalyser sample even though the police had failed to inform the accused about his right to a lawyer as required under the Canadian Bill of Rights.[24] Dickson resisted the urgings of both his law clerk[25] and Laskin and Spence in their dissent that the Court should not prefer the state's interest in crime control over the accused's rights. Instead, he signed on to Ritchie's majority judgment that criticized Laskin for trying to import the absolute American exclusionary rule into Canada.

Dickson also joined Martland's 1981 decision in *Rothman* admitting statements that an undercover police officer had tricked from a prisoner.[26] Dickson believed that Estey's bold dissent that the police trick had violated the prisoner's right against self-incrimination was inconsistent with Dickson's 1974 decision which limited the right against self-incrimination to the courtroom.[27] Dickson also warned Estey that his approach might put 'an end to any trickery by the police after they have arrested an accused person. It also seems to sound the death knell for the use of undercover policemen who infiltrate the drug smuggling milieu.'[28]

In the *Rothman* case, Dickson spent much time helping the newly appointed Antonio Lamer draft his judgment in English. Dickson had seen two Quebec judges come and go in rapid succession and he did not want the pattern repeated. He went out of his way to welcome Lamer as a colleague and to assist him in the daunting task of writing his first opinion as a member of the Court. Yet Dickson was not prepared to help Lamer with his vote and he refused to sign the very judgment he had helped Lamer craft. Dickson's refusal to side with Lamer underlines the strength of Dickson's reluctance to exclude relevant evidence. Lamer advanced the moderate proposal that judges should have a common law discretion to exclude statements if their admission would bring the administration of justice into disrepute. In a long memorandum to Dickson, Lamer appealed for support, arguing that Dickson should not be concerned about the absence of precedent for excluding improperly obtained evidence because 'most judges are waiting for this Court to nod one way or the other.' Demonstrating his ability to illustrate his points with vivid and memorable images, Lamer asked Dickson to consider what the courts should do if a police officer tricked a confession from a suspect by dressing up as a priest. Lamer argued that 'the judicial system' required 'a means of self defence' from such misconduct.[29] Despite these strong arguments, Dickson left Lamer, the rookie judge, all alone. Lamer took Dickson's decision in stride. He was more shaken when, with Dickson's permission, he went to Marchmont and shot 'a couple of ducks,' only to discover that Barbara Dickson was quite attached to the ducks and not at all pleased at their demise. Years later, she and Lamer were able to laugh about this memorable incident.[30]

Initial drafts of the Charter would have retained Dickson's position that improperly obtained evidence should not be excluded, but, after the provinces initially refused to agree to the constitutional package, public hearings were held on the draft Charter. Groups representing defence lawyers and civil libertarians complained that this position left people whose rights were violated by the police with no effective remedy, and, in response, section 24 (2) was added. It built on Lamer's *Rothman* dissent and mandated judges to exclude unconstitutionally obtained evidence 'if it is established that, having regard to all the circumstances, the admission of it in the proceedings would bring the administration of justice into disrepute.' Perhaps reflecting on the criticism that it had received from academics and civil-liberties groups for refusing to exclude improperly obtained evidence before the Charter, the Court took this new constitutional mandate seriously.

In one of the first Charter cases challenging police powers, Dickson signed on to a majority judgment, written by Estey, excluding a breath sample obtained when a police officer forgot to inform a drunk driver about his right to counsel a week after the Charter took effect.[31] This decision was the opposite of the result reached by the Court a decade earlier under the Canadian Bill of Rights. Le Dain would not have excluded the breath sample and dissented on the basis that the police officer had acted in good faith. In a memorandum to Le Dain, Dickson explained that he was 'concerned that making good faith a relevant criteria may effectively swallow up the only protection afforded an accused whose right to counsel has been deprived i.e. the exclusion of evidence obtained in violation of his *Charter* right – and therefore render the guarantee rather hollow.'[32] Dickson was determined to renounce the restrictive approach that the Court had taken under the Canadian Bill of Rights.

In 1987 Dickson concurred with an important but controversial Lamer judgment that required courts to exclude in almost all cases evidence obtained from the accused when the right to counsel was violated. Lamer argued that the admission of such evidence 'would render the trial unfair, for it did not exist prior to the violation and it strikes at one of the fundamental tenets of a fair trial, the right against self-incrimination.'[33] By agreeing, Dickson abandoned his 1974 decision that the right against self-incrimination protected the accused only against testimonial compulsion in the courtroom.[34] Dickson accepted that the Charter had fundamentally changed the rules of the game for obtaining evidence from the accused. The strong language used by Estey and Lamer in these early Charter cases caught even some legal academics by surprise. They pointed out that the Court was going as far as, and sometimes beyond, the United States Supreme Court, which enforced its famous *Miranda* right-to-counsel rules with an automatic exclusionary rule.[35]

Gradually, however, Dickson moved away from his initial enthusiasm for excluding evidence to vindicate Charter rights. He worried that the Court's decisions were leaning towards automatic exclusion, and, in the two years before his retirement, he often refused to exclude evidence, especially in drug cases. In a decision dealing with drugs seized by custom officials following a violation of the right to counsel, Dickson argued that section 24 (2) of the Charter was a compromise between the automatic American exclusionary rule and the previous common law rule that all evidence was admissible no matter how it was obtained. He refused to exclude the drugs, stressing that 'the customs officers acted in good faith based on accepted customs procedures.'[36] This seemed to accept the good-faith argument that Dickson had earlier rejected.

Dickson viewed all illegal drugs as a scourge on society and he was reluctant to exclude conclusive evidence of the accused's guilt. Soon, pre-Charter differences with Lamer over the exclusion of improperly obtained evidence started to resurface. Dickson vehemently disagreed with Lamer in one case that involved a rectal search to retrieve a condom containing heroin. Lamer, writing for the majority, held that 'the integrity of our criminal justice system and the respect owed our Charter are more important than the conviction of this offender.'[37] Dickson wrote a vehement dissent which stressed that the police were not motivated by malice and that 'the reasonable person would be shocked and appalled to learn that an accused, unquestionably guilty of importing a sizeable amount of heroin, was acquitted of all charges.'[38] The chief justice's strong words that Canadians would be 'shocked and appalled' by allowing an obviously guilty drug dealer to go free were the lead in press reports of the case.[39] Lamer saw Dickson's position as a sign that he was becoming more conservative in his old age. There may be some truth to that, but it cannot be doubted that Dickson's reluctance to exclude relevant evidence was also a reversion to his earlier, pre-Charter view.

'I have long regarded constructive murder as cruel'

In a 1982 lecture, Dickson told first-year law students: 'You may be surprised to discover that an accused can be convicted of murder even though he did not intend to kill or even wound anyone.'[40] Dickson was referring to the 'constructive' or 'felony' murder provisions in the Criminal Code that made an accused guilty of murder whenever a death resulted during the commission of a serious crime that involved a firearm or violence. Constructive murder was almost universally criticized by academics as the antithesis of the principles of subjective fault that Dickson had championed in the criminal law. Dickson found it especially galling that such an unprincipled and harsh rule should be used to support a conviction for the most serious crime.

The problem before the enactment of the Charter was that Parliament had clearly displaced subjective-fault principles and labelled negligent and accidental killings during the commission of serious crimes as murder. All that Dickson and the Court were prepared to do before the Charter was to chip away at the edges of the constructive-murder offence.[41] In 1983, Dickson even warned trial judges that, despite the 'protracted criticism' of this offence, they could not refuse to instruct juries about it. 'The rule may seem harsh but it is not the function of this Court to consider the policy of legislation validly enacted. So long as the section continues in our Criminal Code it must be given effect in accordance with its terms.'[42] Parliamentary supremacy for Dickson meant that, as a judge, he was required to apply the law, even if he firmly believed it to be unjust.

The enactment of the Charter gave Dickson and his colleagues new tools. Dickson happily signed on to Lamer judgments in 1987 and 1990 that struck the broad constructive-murder offences from the Criminal Code. Dickson's notes record his tongue-in-cheek statement at conference: 'I declared myself biased as I had long regarded constructive murder as cruel.' He was 'influenced by the fact that most other countries have either legislated against felony murder or abandoned it through legal decision.'[43] By his last year on the Court, the Court had made it clear that because of the stigma and penalty attached, a person could be convicted of murder only if the prosecution proved that the accused subjectively knew that the victim would die. The principles of subjective fault that Dickson had long championed were now constitutionalized, at least for the most serious crime of murder.[44] Despite their importance, however, these decisions received surprisingly little publicity, probably because the accused was still guilty of other serious crimes.

In the 1987 case, the federal government did not bother to intervene to defend the Criminal Code provision that treated even accidental killings as murder if they occurred during a serious crime committed with a firearm. At conference, two possible explanations for the federal government's failure to exercise its right to intervene were suggested: '1) that the government does not like constructive murder provisions but, on the other hand, would find it unwise politically to legislate them away preferring, perhaps, that it be done through the legal system; 2) that the Department of Justice does not know what was happening and did not realize the implications of the case.'[45] In any event, the Court cautiously limited its holding to one provision to give the government an opportunity to defend other parts of the constructive- murder law. However, in 1990 the Court struck down the remaining constructive-murder provisions. Lamer stressed that there were less drastic means to deter the use of violence during serious crimes. He and Dickson were not deterred by arguments from McIntyre and L'Heureux-Dubé that they were interfering in parliamentary prerogatives by judging the substantive fairness of crimes and that they were going beyond where the United States Supreme Court had drawn the line when it upheld felony murder laws under the American Bill of Rights.

'The reasonable doubt doctrine is always engaged'

Dickson fully embraced the idea that an accused should be presumed innocent and have the benefit of any reasonable doubt long before those rights were guaranteed under the Charter. In 1978 he ordered a new trial where the trial judge had failed to instruct the jury that the crown must prove beyond a reasonable doubt that the accused did not have a provocation defence. Dickson explained that the jury 'must realize that the reasonable doubt doctrine is always engaged; that it is not displaced with respect to defences. They must be clear in their minds that, if they have a reasonable doubt on any issue, they have the duty to allow the accused to succeed on that issue.'[46] This broad, functional approach to the presumption of innocence also drove Dickson's generous approach to the Charter right to be presumed innocent. As in the police-powers cases, he believed there were important continuities between the common law and the Charter.

Dickson did not regard the idea that the individual should have the benefit of any reasonable doubt as a technical or procedural device; on the contrary, he thought that it reflected the need for the state to treat citizens fairly and respect their dignity. Moreover, these principles did not evaporate even after a person had been found guilty of an offence. In 1982 Dickson extended the reasonable-doubt standard to sentencing. The case involved a man named Gardiner who pled guilty to assaulting his wife and was sentenced to four and a half years. The trial judge had accepted the wife's account of the assault as more probable than the husband's. Dickson believed that the result was unfair. Because 'crime and punishment are inextricably linked,' he insisted that aggravating facts at sentencing should be proved beyond a reasonable doubt. In a statement that built on his generous approach to the rights of prisoners, Dickson concluded that 'upon conviction, the accused is not abruptly deprived of all procedural rights existing at trial.' Concerns about the efficiency of sentencing hearings were 'not sufficient to overcome such a basic tenet suffusing our entire criminal justice system as the standard of proof beyond a reasonable doubt.'[47] Laskin dissented on the basis that the Supreme Court should never hear sentencing appeals, whereas Dickson believed that to decline jurisdiction on important matters of legal principle would be 'to renounce the paramount responsibility of an ultimate appellate court with national authority.' Louise Arbour, then a law professor, praised Dickson's expansive approach to the Supreme Court's jurisdiction as 'wonderful news' that showed a 'willingness to accept responsibility and to exercise power ... on the eve of the Court having to accept the major challenge of enforcing the new *Charter of Rights and Freedoms,*' while she characterized Laskin's dissent as 'impatient ... and abrupt.'[48]

Given Dickson's commitment to a broad approach to the presumption of innocence and the reasonable-doubt standard before the Charter, it was not surprising that he defined the presumption of innocence enshrined in the Charter in eloquent and generous terms in *R. v. Oakes.*[49] After *Oakes*, however, the Court's consensus about how to approach this right broke down in the midst of the larger debate about how to approach Charter interpretation. Some judges, such as McIntyre, wanted to place definitional limits on the right, while others, such as Dickson, wanted to define the right in a broad and generous fashion. A broad approach to the right, however, had implications for how rigorous the test would be under section 1 of the Charter for justifying reasonable limits on the rights. From 1988 to 1990, the Court struggled with many of these difficult questions. Throughout, Dickson maintained a consistent position that the presumption of innocence be interpreted generously so that the reasonable-doubt standard would always apply. At the same time, however, he became increasingly tolerant of laws limiting the broadly defined right.

In the first presumption of innocence case to reach the Court after *Oakes*, Dickson dissented. McIntyre, writing for a three-judge majority, upheld a Criminal Code provision requiring an accused to prove a lawful excuse for possessing housebreaking tools. McIntyre found no violation of the presumption of innocence since the reverse onus applied to a defence and not to an essential element of the offence. 'An accused raising such a defence or excuse is not seeking relief because of an absence of guilt. He seeks relief despite his commission of the offence.'[50] Dickson refused to get bogged down in what he regarded as pointless and technical classifications; instead, he stressed the general and simple principle that the accused should have the benefit of any reasonable doubt on any issue essential for a conviction, including defences.[51] The effect of the presumption forced the accused to testify and this, said Dickson, violated a fundamental value in our society. As he explained in a later decision but again in dissent: 'All substantive issues raised in a criminal prosecution are related to the fundamental issue of guilt and innocence. They should all be decided by the same standard, proof of guilt beyond a reasonable doubt.'[52] Dickson's position was not radical; he had applied similar reasoning long before the enactment of the Charter.

Less than two months later, Dickson's broad approach was accepted by a unanimous Court. The case involved a Criminal Code provision that, in drinking and driving cases, someone found in the driver's seat is presumed to have care and control of the vehicle unless he or she could establish lack of intent to drive the vehicle. Writing for a unanimous Court, Dickson concluded that the presumption of innocence was offended whenever the accused could be convicted despite a reasonable doubt as to guilt, and that the classification of the issue as an element of the offence or as a defence or something else 'should not affect the analysis of the presumption of innocence. It is the final effect of a provision on the verdict that is decisive.'[53] However, Dickson was able to win a majority (which included McIntyre) only by also holding that the government had justified the infringement of the presumption of innocence under section 1 of the Charter. He concluded that the provision was 'a restrained parliamentary response to a pressing social problem' and a reasonable 'compromise' that gave intoxicated people a way out 'when there was a reason for entering the vehicle other than to set it in motion.'[54] The presumption of innocence had never been an absolute right for Dickson. Before the Charter, he had accepted laws in which Parliament had clearly reversed the burden of proof, and in *Sault Ste Marie* he had imposed a burden on the accused to establish a defence of due diligence.

Later that year, however, the tables turned once again. McIntyre, writing for a plurality of the Court, held that the presumption of innocence was not engaged by requiring an accused to produce evidence that he had a valid certificate for the possession of a firearm. Dickson and Lamer both dissented on the basis that a requirement on the accused to produce a firearms certificate violated the presumption of innocence and had not been justified under section 1 of the Charter, albeit for different reasons.[55] Both Dickson and Lamer hunted, and in retirement, Dickson would express misgivings about the federal gun registry.[56] The commentators generally favoured Dickson's more generous approach to defining the presumption of innocence, but they understandably bemoaned the Court's inconsistency on this seemingly basic issue.[57]

In his last year on the Court, Dickson gained acceptance for his constant position that the reasonable doubt is always engaged and that the presumption of innocence is violated when an accused is required to establish a defence. At the same time, however, Dickson and the Court also upheld the reverse onus to establish a variety of defences under section 1 of the Charter. In *Keegstra*, Dickson upheld requiring those charged with the wilful promotion of hate to establish the defence of truth.[58] The law clearly violated the presumption of innocence, but that did not end the Charter analysis. In his section 1 analysis, Dickson stressed that the 'relatively small possibility of truthfulness' did not outweigh 'the harm caused through the wilful promotion of hatred.'[59] McLachlin dissented on the basis that the accused should not have to bear the difficult burden of proving the truth of controversial statements. Dickson also agreed with Lamer's judgment upholding the traditional onus on the accused to establish the insanity defence.[60] In that case, only Wilson was prepared to apply a rigorous version of the *Oakes* proportionality test which would give the accused the benefit of a reasonable doubt that he or she was insane. Dickson's approach to the presumption of innocence was caught up in the dynamics of Charter interpretation. As the Court accepted a broader reading of the right, it also became more willing to find under section 1 that limits on such broad rights were reasonable and justified.

Criminal Justice before and after the Charter

There were elements of both continuity and change in Dickson's application of the Charter to the administration of criminal justice. On some issues – limiting police powers and maintaining the presumption of innocence – the Charter helped Dickson advance ideas that he had already articulated. On other issues, the Charter allowed Dickson to change the law. While Dickson had long thought that the punishment of accidental or negligent killings as murder was cruel, he believed that there was little he could do until the Charter was enacted. The Charter also forced Dickson to change. Before the Charter, he refused to exclude relevant evidence because it was improperly obtained, but the clear mandate in section 24 (2) of the Charter forced him to reach a different conclusion. Near the end of his career, however, Dickson began to revert to his pre-Charter reluctance to exclude relevant evidence.

17

Cracks in the Foundations

Less than a year after *Big M*, the issue of Sunday shopping returned to the Supreme Court in a case known as *Edwards Books*.[1] This time, the fight was led by Paul Magder, a Toronto furrier, who for several years had carried on a relentless struggle to remain open for business in the face of Ontario's Sunday-closing law – a patchwork of prohibitions, exceptions, and exemptions. The Ontario law tried to balance the religious freedom of retailers with the need to ensure retail workers a day of rest with their families, requiring large retailers to close on Sunday while allowing small retail operations to open on Sunday if they closed on Saturday. Magder did not qualify for the exemption. He opened the doors of his Spadina Avenue fur store in Toronto's fashion district every Sunday, defiantly displaying the sign 'Toronto's best known Sunday seller.' Magder, undeterred by hundreds of charges and mounting fines, claimed the benefit of an exemption for tourist areas, but the authorities contended that his business did not qualify.

Three other retailers joined Magder to argue that the law was an affront to freedom of religion. Edward Borins, the son of a well-known Toronto lawyer and the brother of a well-respected Ontario judge, ran three Toronto bookstores with his wife, Eva. Borins decided to defy the law because he thought 'the maze' of regulations and exceptions made the law and its application ludicrous and unfair.[2] His stores specialized in art books and competed with art gallery and museum shops that were free to open on Sundays. Even adult-entertainment parlours selling erotic books and magazines could open on Sunday. Borins complained: 'You can buy a copy of Penthouse or Playboy on Sunday but you can't buy a copy of the Bible unless you shop in a specifically designated book store.'[3] Longo Brothers joined the fight, too. Their Malton fruit market could stay open on Sunday because it fell within an exemption for tourist areas, but their stores in Oakville and Burlington were required to close. Only the fourth challenger, Nortown Foods, a Toronto Jewish meat market and delicatessen, could claim a religious motivation for remaining open on Sundays. Nortown closed it doors on Saturday for religious reasons and was required by law to close on Sunday as well. Small retailers who closed on Saturdays had an exemption for Sunday, but Nortown was too large to qualify for the exemption.

Walter Tarnopolsky, a distinguished civil-liberties scholar before his appointment to the bench, wrote the unanimous judgment of a five-judge panel of the Ontario Court of Appeal.[4] Tarnopolsky accepted Nortown's argument that, under the Charter, retailers who could demonstrate a sincerely held religious belief requiring them to observe another sabbath were exempt from the Sunday-closing law. However, Magder, Borins, and the Longo Brothers were properly convicted, said the Ontario Court of Appeal, since they could not satisfy the religion-based exemption. The decision rejected the plea for wide-open Sunday shopping and added a rather complicated wrinkle to the already complex pattern of exceptions. The unsuccessful defendants appealed to the Supreme Court of Canada. The crown appealed the acquittal of Nortown.

The attack on the Ontario Sunday-closing law presented more difficult issues than those faced by the Court in *Big M*. The holidays chosen by the legislature – Sunday, Christmas and Easter – had an obvious connection with Christianity. But that connection did not defeat the law without further debate. The Ontario law had a secular purpose, namely, to provide retail workers with a common day of rest and recreation.[5] The religious connotation was part of the background of social facts influencing the legislature's choice of a common pause day, but it was not the rationale for the law. As Dickson later explained in his judgment: 'Our society is collectively powerless to repudiate its history, including the Christian heritage of the majority.' Despite the religious connection, the law did not represent 'a surreptitious attempt to encourage religious worship.'[6] As the Ontario Law Reform Commission stated when recommending the law, Sunday had become a worldwide pause day, even in many non-Christian countries.[7]

The difficult Charter issue was not the purpose of the law, but rather its effects, the very issue Dickson had avoided in the *Big M* case despite Wilson's urging. It now had to be faced. A Sunday observer could satisfy both the law and his or her religion by closing on Sunday. A Saturday observer could not. The legislature's benign purpose – to provide a common day of rest – distinguished the decision in *Big M*, but those attacking the law contended that by

choosing Sunday as the day of rest, the law had the constitutionally imper-
missible effect of facilitating the religious practices of the majority and burdening those of non-Sunday observers.

At conference, all of the judges were persuaded that, because the law had a
secular purpose, it should be upheld.[8] It was accepted by all that the legislature's choice of Sunday as the common pause day did not give the law an
unacceptably religious hue. La Forest, who as the Court's junior judge spoke
first, rejected the argument that the effect of the law infringed religious freedom: 'What impels people of the Jewish faith, for example, to keep closed
both Saturday and Sunday is not the law but the religion.' Beetz took a similar
view and suggested: 'We may have to qualify a bit the reference in *Big M* to
"indirect effects."' Surprisingly, Dickson now seemed willing to limit what he
had written in *Big M*. He indicated to his colleagues that he 'shared the views
of Justice Beetz.' No member of the Court supported the exemptions based
on religious beliefs that had found favour with the Ontario Court of Appeal.
Wilson said that she did 'not like the subjective element of "sincerely held
religious beliefs" and that she preferred an objective test.' There was no
discussion of the stringent reasonable-limits test the Court had announced a
week earlier in *Oakes*. Everyone thought that the law should be upheld in its
entirety with the exception of Wilson, who felt that the exemption for those
who close on Saturday was too narrowly drawn. Since she rejected an exemption based on religious belief, she was inclined to strike down the limits on
the exemption and allow any business that closed on Saturday to open on
Sunday.

When the Court released its judgment nine months later – just before Christmas 1986 – the six-to-one split held, but there was significant movement away
from the views expressed at conference. Once again, Dickson wrote the lead
judgment in a landmark case with significant implications for the future
development of Charter principles. But, despite the nearly unanimous result,
the Court was badly split in its Charter analysis. This divergence in approach
signalled disagreements that would pervade the Court's Charter jurisprudence for years to come.

Dickson flatly rejected the argument that the law did not infringe religious
freedom, a significant change from the view he expressed at conference. He
now thought that his original interpretation would unduly limit the Charter's
protection. It implied that rights and freedoms should be narrowly defined to
avoid conflict with legislation. Dickson realized that most Charter cases would
involve the indirect and unintended effect of laws. He became convinced that
it would be a mistake to define Charter rights narrowly, and he insisted that
'indirect coercion by the state is comprehended within the evils from which
s. 2(a) may afford protection.' Demonstrating the same sensitivity to the prac-

tices of non-Christians that he showed in *Big M*, Dickson found that the law did place a burden on the religious beliefs of Saturday observers who had to close one day for religious reasons and another day because of the law. The law also burdened the Saturday-observing customer. 'All coercive burdens on the exercise of religious beliefs are potentially within the ambit of s. 2(a).'[9]

The question was whether the burden the law placed on religious freedom could be justified as a reasonable limit under section 1. Dickson had no difficulty accepting the validity and importance of the law's objective to provide for a common day of rest. Drawing upon his own experience as a boy growing up in Saskatchewan, he described, in near-poetic terms, the joys of a quiet family Sunday: 'A family visit to an uncle or grandmother, the attendance of a parent at a child's sports tournament, a picnic, a swim, or a hike in the park on a summer day, or a family expedition to a zoo, circus or exhibition – these, and hundreds of other leisure activities with family and friends are among the simplest but most profound joys that any of us can know.'[10] The sentiment was sincere, but the irony of working on the judgment with Dickson at Marchmont on a Sunday afternoon did not escape his law clerks.[11]

The next and more difficult issue was whether the Ontario law's limited exemption that applied only to small retailers went far enough to respect the rights of non-Sunday observers. Did the legislature have to do better and provide a more comprehensive exemption that would apply to most, if not all, Saturday observers? Those attacking the law argued that the *Oakes* reasonable-limits test was not satisfied since the legislature had failed to use the 'least restrictive means' to accommodate the religious freedom of all retailers. Those supporting the law argued that a wider exemption would undercut the very idea of a common day of rest and that the court should allow the legislature some latitude and not impose unduly rigid standards.

The case posed the first serious challenge for the *Oakes* test. How perfectly did the legislature have to accommodate and respect the Charter right and how deeply would the Court become involved in the search for the ideal legislative solution? The responses of Dickson, La Forest, and Wilson revealed significant differences on this basic question and demonstrated as well their different approaches to judicial review. Dickson took a characteristically middle-of-the road approach, La Forest urged his colleagues to relax the *Oakes* test, and Wilson advocated a strict application.

The minimal-impairment language of *Oakes* suggested that the Court would be satisfied only with the best possible law, one that impinged upon religious freedom as little as possible. But the *Oakes* test had been criticized by those who feared that it imposed too tight a rein on legislative choice and that it would paralyse the government's day-to-day work of regulating business to protect other important public interests.[12] Dickson was influenced by these criticisms. He realized that, in the regulation and the reconciliation of competing interests, perfection is rarely attainable; he did not want the *Oakes* test to become a legislative straitjacket in which the legislature had no room to manoeuvre, especially when attempting to improve the lot of the less advantaged members of society. In *Edwards Books*, Dickson went out of his way to dispel these fears. As he now saw it, the *Oakes* test had to be applied in a pragmatic way with a view to affording a reasonable measure of legislative choice. 'Legislative choices regarding alternative forms of business regulation do not generally impinge upon the values and provisions of the *Charter*, and the resultant legislation need not be tuned with great precision in order to withstand judicial scrutiny.' Dickson placed great emphasis on the fact that the Ontario Sunday-closing law was designed to protect the interests of retail workers, a particularly vulnerable group. He decided that, if the legislature were not given some leeway, the pursuit of a theoretically pure solution for the protection of religious freedom would defeat the law's objective of giving retail-sales workers a common day of rest with their families: 'In interpreting and applying the *Charter* I believe that the courts must be cautious to ensure that it does not simply become an instrument of better situated individuals to roll back legislation which has as its object the improvement of the condition of less advantaged persons.' Dickson was not prepared to fault the legislature for determining that the protection of 'vulnerable employees in securing a Sunday holiday' ought to be preferred to 'the interests of their employer in transacting business on a Sunday.'[13]

There was no perfect solution to the conundrum of providing retail workers a day of rest and, at the same time, respecting the religious freedom of non-Sunday observers. The exemption based on religious belief favoured by the Ontario Court of Appeal would theoretically protect all those whose religion required the observance of a day of rest other than Sunday. However, a public inquiry into an individual's religious beliefs could itself be invasive of religious freedom and, Dickson wrote, 'state sponsored inquiries into any person's religion should be avoided wherever reasonably possible.' Although it was sadly dated, the evidence led by the Ontario government showed that most Saturday-observing retailers were accommodated by the existing exemption, and Dickson was not prepared to invalidate the scheme. He accepted that there was 'a trade-off between a scheme which provides complete relief from burdens on religious freedom to most Saturday-observing retailers by avoiding a distasteful inquiry, and, on the other hand, an alternative scheme which provides substantial relief from burdens on religious freedom to *all* Saturday-observing retailers.' Both are 'genuine and serious attempts' to minimize effects: 'It is far from clear that one scheme is intrinsically better than the other.' The law's exemption provision, while far from perfect, represented 'a satisfactory effort on the part of the Legislature of Ontario' to alleviate the effects of the law on Saturday observers.[14]

Chouinard and Le Dain agreed with Dickson's judgment. La Forest agreed with the result, but he saw the case as an opportunity to stake out his ground for a much softer *Oakes* test. At a conference held several months after *Edwards Books* was argued, La Forest urged Dickson and the rest of the Court to back away from insisting upon an exemption. He argued that there was no exemption that would please everyone[15] and since there was no obviously preferable solution, the Court should simply leave it to the legislature to balance the competing rights and interests. La Forest made detailed comments on Dickson's draft judgment, but Dickson was unmoved. He told La Forest that he did not think that 'Sunday closing legislation could pass muster without at least some reasonable effort to accommodate Saturday-observing retailers.' Dickson offered the example of the Jewish retailer with no employees other than a spouse. It would, he argued, be difficult to justify requiring such a retailer to close on Sunday: there would be no 'sufficiently important social interest to justify the infringement of that retailer's religious freedom, since there would be no employees adversely affected by their remaining open.'[16]

La Forest insisted that the Court must be 'careful to avoid rigid and inflexible standards' and that 'the legislature must be allowed adequate scope to achieve [its] objective.' As he saw it, achieving the legislative goal of a common day of rest would inevitably affect the rights of some members of society adversely, and there was 'no perfect scenario in which the rights of all can be equally protected.' If the Court were to insist on an exemption, how could the legislature satisfy all the claims from diverse religious groups who observed various sabbaths and religious holidays? He believed that 'a legislature must be given reasonable room to manoeuvre to meet these conflicting pressures.' While Dickson's judgment contained similar language, it is clear that the 'reasonable room' left by La Forest was considerably larger than Dickson was willing to countenance.[17]

In *Edwards Books*, Bertha Wilson emerged as the sole defender of a strict reasonable-limits test. She agreed that the prohibition against Sunday shopping should be upheld but that any business that closed for religious reasons on another day should be exempt. This was the point she made at conference, that the exemption provision in the Ontario law failed to protect religious freedom in a principled fashion. In her view, the exemption crafted by the legislature did not go far enough, and the Charter demanded that the Court insist upon a principled accommodation for religious freedom. In her dissent, described by her biographer as 'outright and indignant,'[18] Wilson advocated striking down the qualifications based on size and number of employees so that any business that closed on Saturday would be free to open on Sunday. 'I do not think that a limit on freedom of religion which recognizes the freedom of some members of the group but not of other members of the same group can be reasonable and justified in a free and democratic society.'[19] As she so often did, Wilson adopted a philosophical approach. Quoting a prominent legal philosopher, Ronald Dworkin,[20] Wilson argued that it was not open to the legislature to create 'a compromised scheme of justice.' She added that the stale and sketchy evidence led to justify the law 'failed totally to discharge [the crown's] burden under s. 1 of the Charter.'[21]

Only a few days before the release of the Court's judgment, Beetz was still wavering. He advised Dickson: 'I have not yet made up my mind as to whether I will agree with you or with La Forest J.'[22] In the end, Beetz agreed with neither and reverted to the view he had expressed at conference. In a short and clear judgment with which McIntyre agreed, Beetz wrote that he saw no problem in the comparative disadvantage faced by non-Sunday observers. He took what might be described as a formal view and reasoned that the law treated all equally: if the non-Sunday observers suffered a disadvantage because they had to close for another day, they did so because of their religion and not because of anything done by the law.

Although the Court had upheld Sunday-closing laws, the judgment was legally controversial. From the perspective of Charter analysis, the serious four-way split in reasoning was more significant that the six-to-one majority in the result. Beetz's judgment was the first sign that the approach set out in *Big M* and *Oakes* would not always prevail. Rather than afford the Charter right generous scope and deal with any limitations under section 1, Beetz opted for a narrow definitional approach that avoided forcing the government to justify the law as a reasonable limit under section 1. While the other judges adhered to a *Big M* 'purposive' interpretation of the right, they were seriously split on the application of the *Oakes* test. La Forest more or less wanted to overrule *Oakes*. Dickson was prepared to soften its impact, and only Wilson was prepared to defend a strict test for laws that impinged upon protected rights.

From a practical perspective, it was clear that the Court's decision would not end the Sunday-closing debate. Sunday-shopping advocates turned from the courts to the political arena. Exhausted and financially drained by his legal battle, Edward Borins held a press conference the day the Court's decision was handed down to announce the start of a 'political battle' to change the law.[23] Borins's stores remained open under the guise of creating a private book club for which over 10,000 members paid 10 cents admission. Within six months, Borins had persuaded the legislature to exempt bookstores from the law, and within a year, the government introduced legislation following the pattern adopted in British Columbia and Alberta, allowing each municipality to decide whether to allow Sunday shopping.

Dickson's decision in *Edwards Books* showed that he was prepared to qualify the rigour of the *Oakes* test. He was sensitive to the critics who accused the Court of a 'power-grab,' and, though he rejected the allegation as being inconsistent with the very notion of a Charter of Rights, he also recognized the need for prudence. He was well aware of the limits of adjudication as a way of making law and he knew that, ultimately, the Court's authority rested on the moral authority of its pronouncements. The Court could take a stand in cases like *Big M* where the law was simply out of step with Canada's religious diversity, but prudence was called for where the legislature was attempting to protect the interests of the vulnerable.[24] In *Edwards Books* he responded as well to the criticism that the Court had favoured corporate interests and undermined regulatory authority. As in his administrative-law decisions, he recognized that the state had an important role to play in regulating society and protecting the disadvantaged. Dickson characteristically refused to be boxed in to a rigid or doctrinaire position and did his best to accommodate legislative authority with the Court's power of judicial review.

Dickson in Dissent: The Labour Trilogy

In June 1985 the Court heard argument in the first of three highly contentious labour cases involving the right to strike.[25] The case involved a challenge to Alberta legislation prohibiting strikes in the public sector and imposing compulsory arbitration to resolve collective-bargaining issues. Two similar cases were argued in October 1985. *PSAC v. Canada* involved an attack on federal legislation that, to combat inflationary wage increases,[26] extended the life of collective agreements of public-sector employees and fixed wages for a two-year period. The third appeal concerned Saskatchewan legislation prohibiting strikes and lockouts in the dairy industry and imposing compulsory arbitration.[27] In all three cases, labour unions argued that the right to strike was constitutionally protected by the Charter's guarantee of freedom of association, and they attacked the legislation curtailing the right to strike as a denial of this fundamental freedom.

It quickly became apparent that, as in *Edwards Books*, these issues would exceed the Court's capacity to achieve consensus. Judgment on the 'Labour Trilogy' – as these cases came to be called – was reserved for almost two years. When the decisions were handed down in April 1987, a few days before the Charter's fifth anniversary, any lingering doubts in the minds of Court-watchers about the highly contentious nature of Charter interpretation were quickly swept away. A majority of the Court refused to recognize the right to strike as a protected freedom under the Charter. The labour movement was bitterly disappointed and, for the first time, Brian Dickson found himself dissenting on an important Charter issue.

At the Court conference after the Alberta case was argued, all judges except

Dickson and Wilson spoke strongly against protecting the right to strike under the Charter. The unions had argued that freedom of association would be a hollow and meaningless guarantee if the constitutional protection extended only to the right to associate and failed to protect the actual activities of the association. McIntyre rejected this argument and warned his colleagues that freedom of association 'does not mean that all objects [of the association] become constitutionally protected. If an association is formed for landholdings does this constitutionally protect property rights?'[28]

Joel Bakan, Dickson's law clerk, had provided a detailed and forceful memorandum urging him to find that the right to strike was protected by the Charter. As a law professor, he would later express his disappointment with the Charter's failure to deal with many issues of social justice.[29] Bakan started his memorandum to Dickson with a candid observation: 'Once again this court is faced with a difficult policy issue on which there is little law and much controversy.'[30] Dickson found the memorandum and the union's arguments persuasive, but, given the force of the views expressed by everyone except Wilson that the legislation should be upheld, he refrained from expressing any definitive view at the conference. By remaining quiet, Dickson preserved his prerogative as chief justice and leading exponent of the Charter to write first reasons, a task he could not have assumed had he taken a strong position at odds with the majority of the Court.

The Court conference after the *PSAC* and Saskatchewan cases produced a similar result. This time it was Le Dain who held sway with the majority. He was strongly of the view that freedom of association did not include the right to strike or the right of collective bargaining. Chouinard, MacIntyre, and Beetz agreed. La Forest thought that freedom of association might be engaged, but that limiting the right to strike could be justified under section 1 as a reasonable limit. Wilson said that she was 'struggling' with the issue and worried that excluding association activities, such as the right to strike, might make freedom of association meaningless. Again, Dickson was not prepared to express a clear view one way or the other on the basic issue of whether the Charter protected the right to strike: 'I wanted to do a great deal more study before expressing my opinion.'[31]

As he worked on the cases, Dickson became convinced that the Court should follow the path of *Hunter v. Southam*, *Big M*, and *Oakes* and give the Charter right a broad and generous interpretation, leaving the limitations on the right and the fine-tuning to section 1. Dickson knew that the labour movement had been highly sceptical of the Charter and of the power it conferred on judges. The Court had generously interpreted freedom of religion in *Big M* and the right to be free from unreasonable search and seizure in *Hunter v. Southam* on behalf of corporate interests. How could the Court now narrowly define the only right that seemed to be intended to protect the interests of trade unions? Dickson decided that the activities of collective bargaining and the right to strike should be protected under freedom of association. For him, the real question was whether the government could justify limiting union rights under section 1. On that issue, he had considerable doubt about how to decide the cases. His drafts and memoranda to and from his law clerks suggest that the matter was one of lively debate in his chambers and the issue remained unresolved in his mind for some time.[32]

Dickson knew from the discussion at conference that he was bound to encounter difficulty trying to persuade his colleagues to go along with his generous interpretation of freedom of association. If he were to circulate a finished draft that went contrary to the drift of the discussion at conference, he would catch his colleagues off-guard, with little hope of persuading them to change their opinion. At the end of November 1985, he took the unusual step of circulating a memorandum providing what he called 'outline summaries of judgments' in the three cases. Dickson made clear the direction he was going.[33] 'Freedom of association,' he argued, would have 'no independent meaning if it does not include, at least to some extent, the freedom of an individual to do in association with others what he or she can lawfully do as an individual. Freedom to join and form an association is meaningless if the association can be prohibited from engaging in the very activities for which it is formed.' He conceded that freedom of association should protect not all the group's activities but 'only those activities which manifest the overall purposes of the *Charter*.' Dickson had no doubt that freedom to engage in collective bargaining and the 'freedom to withdraw services collectively' should be protected since these freedoms 'are recognized as necessary for the protection of employees from unsafe, unhealthy and unfair working conditions.' On the question of whether the laws at issue would survive section 1, Dickson was less clear, but at this point he leaned towards striking down all three laws. While he thought that the legislature could ban strikes by those working in essential services, he said that 'I have not yet made up my mind' whether the Alberta arbitration procedures were 'fair and impartial.' Dickson believed that the Saskatchewan government had failed to prove that the dairy industry was an essential service or that banning strikes was the only way to prevent interruption of dairy production. As for the federal wage-restraint legislation, Dickson felt that it 'is not likely saved by s. 1' since 'it was discriminatory on the part of the federal government to single out federal public sector employees in order to set an example.' This, he wrote, was contrary to the equality provision of the Canadian Bill of Rights and, accordingly, could not be justified as a reasonable limit in a free and democratic society.

Dickson received several helpful suggestions from Julien Chouinard.[34]

Chouinard had been firmly in the 'no right to strike' camp when the cases were argued, but his comments suggest that he was prepared to consider carefully what Dickson was writing. He died before the judgments were released, however, so we do not know whether Dickson would have been able to persuade him in the end. Dickson also adopted helpful suggestions made by Wilson, who was the only member of the Court to agree with him that freedom of association should be broadly defined to include important union activities.[35]

Dickson next circulated a long and ambitious judgment in the Alberta case which made a forceful plea for a generous definition of freedom of association. He referred to a long list of Canadian, American, and English authorities, legal scholars, and international human rights documents, as well as to political philosophers Alexis de Tocqueville and John Stuart Mill. Adopting the purposive approach, Dickson offered generous scope to freedom of association. 'The purpose of the constitutional guarantee of freedom of association is, I believe, to recognize the profoundly social nature of human endeavours and to protect the individual from state-enforced isolation in pursuit of his or her ends.' He emphasized that 'freedom to act with others is a primary condition of community life, human progress and civilized society.' Dickson stressed that group action and activities were extremely important to vulnerable groups in a complex modern world. Freedom of association, he wrote, protected individuals 'from the vulnerability of isolation' and ensured 'the potential of effective participation in society.' It is through association with others that 'individuals are able to ensure that they have a voice in shaping the circumstances integral to their needs, rights and freedoms.'[36]

The constitution, he pointed out, protects many collective or community values – denominational schools, language rights, aboriginal rights, and the nation's multicultural heritage. These rights, he contended, 'embody an awareness of the importance of various collectivities in the pursuit of educational, linguistic, cultural and social as well as political ends.' The individual, he argued, cannot resist political or economic domination without the support of other like-minded persons with similar values or goals. Freedom of association 'has enabled those who would otherwise be vulnerable and ineffective to meet on more equal terms the power and strength of those with whom their interests interact and, perhaps, conflict.'[37]

Against this backdrop, Dickson stressed the particular importance of freedom of association for the labour movement. 'Freedom of association is the cornerstone of modern labour relations. Historically, workers have combined to overcome the inherent inequalities of bargaining power in the employment relationship and to protect themselves from unfair, unsafe, or exploitative working conditions.' Organized labour does not only promote economic interests. 'A person's employment is an essential component of his or her sense of identity, self-worth and emotional well-being.' Association, he wrote, is 'vital as a means of protecting the essential needs and interests of working people.'[38]

Dickson noted that the right to strike was recognized as a fundamental human right in the United Nations *Covenant on Human Rights* and in an International Labour Organization Convention. Canada is a signatory to these instruments and, Dickson wrote, they are 'relevant and persuasive,' albeit not binding, sources. 'I believe that the Charter should generally be presumed to provide protection at least as great as that afforded by similar provisions in international rights documents which Canada has ratified.'[39]

Dickson used unusually strong language to reject what he called the 'constitutive' definition of freedom of association which limits the guarantee to freedom to form or belong to an association and protects only the formal status of the association. 'If freedom of association only protects the joining together of persons for common purposes, but not the pursuit of the very activities for which the association was formed, then the freedom is indeed legalistic, ungenerous, indeed vapid.' The purposive approach, he urged, required the courts to 'give effective protection to the interests to which the constitutional guarantee is directed.'[40]

Dickson concluded that 'effective constitutional protection of the associational interests of employees in the collective bargaining process requires concomitant protection of their freedom to withdraw collectively their services, subject to s. 1 of the Charter.'[41] To Dickson, the right to strike was the essence of the associational activity of a labour union, and, if the courts failed to protect it, freedom of association became an empty shell. Though recognizing that not all group activities gained constitutional protection, he concluded that the group must be at liberty to do collectively what one is permitted to do as an individual. Moreover, as with the right to strike, there are activities that are inherently associational in nature that could not be defined in terms of what an individual could do.

Although he had initially been inclined to dismiss the contention that any of the anti-strike laws could be justified under section 1, in the end Dickson concluded that both the federal anti-inflation law and the Saskatchewan dairy-industry legislation should be upheld as reasonable limits on freedom of association. With regard to the former, it was permissible to limit the right to strike of those providing essential services, 'the interruption of which would threaten serious harm to the general public or to a part of the population.'[42] In the Saskatchewan case, Dickson found that the right to strike could be limited to avoid serious economic harm to farmers who could not cease production and would have to dump their milk and bear the entire brunt of the strike even though they were third parties. To avoid this harm, a fair arbitration procedure could be substituted. However, the Alberta law failed the section 1 reasonable-limits test because the legislature had cast the net too widely, prohibited many non-essential workers from striking, and neglected to provide a fair arbitration procedure as an alternative.

Ever conscious of the federal government's role in regulating the national economy, Dickson was more deferential when it came to the federal anti-inflation wage restraint law. Control of inflation was a pressing and substantial objective and Dickson was not prepared to second-guess Parliament on how to deal with a difficult issue of economic policy. The union argued that it was completely unfair and ineffective to target public-sector employees, but Dickson thought this was a matter for Parliament and not the courts. 'It is not our judicial role to assess the effectiveness or wisdom of various government strategies for solving pressing economic problems.'[43] Given government's leadership role in setting the tone for economic policy, he was prepared to accept Parliament's judgment that selective wage controls would work. Only those parts of the law prohibiting collective bargaining on non-remunerative issues could not be justified.

Dickson's eloquent and forceful plea for the constitutional protection of union activities, balanced with a generous application of the reasonable-limits test, attracted little support. Only Bertha Wilson was prepared to agree with according protection to the right to strike, but, since she was much less willing to allow limits on the right to strike, she was not prepared to sign Dickson's judgments.

McIntyre wrote a fully developed judgment rejecting the proposition that the right to strike was constitutionally protected. It was vintage McIntyre – thorough, well reasoned, fully researched, and sceptical of the Charter as an instrument of legal change. It also reflected his profound doubts about the direction the Court was taking under the Charter. Looking back, several years after his retirement from the Court, McIntyre felt that his colleagues had unwisely abandoned their early agreement to proceed cautiously, that 'they threw caution to the winds and ... that the Court behaved irresponsibly.' In retrospect, he regretted concurring with some of the early far-reaching decisions: 'I agreed with one or two judgments that I would not agree with today ... I think the country was ill-served by the Court in the first ten years of the Charter.'[44]

McIntyre agreed that freedom of association was 'one of the most fundamental rights in a free society ... [it] gives meaning and value to the lives of individuals and makes organized society possible.' But, for McIntyre, the importance of the right did not translate into constitutional protection for all aspects of association. He insisted that rights and freedoms be seen in their historic context, that the Charter 'should not be regarded as an empty vessel to be filled with whatever meaning we may wish from time to time.' Interpretation of the Charter, he wrote, should be 'constrained by the language, structure, and history of the constitutional text, by constitutional tradition, and by the history, traditions, and underlying philosophies of our society.' He refused to expand the concept of 'group rights' beyond the letter of the constitution. Groups were not endowed with rights but rather served as devices 'adopted by individuals to achieve a fuller realization of individual rights and aspirations.' McIntyre regarded the right to strike not as an aspect of the individual's freedom of association but as the product of modern labour-relations legislation.[45]

McIntyre argued that refusing Charter protection was also sound social policy because the delicate balance of conflicting political and economic forces between management and organized labour should not be frozen by the constitution: 'There is clearly no correct balance which may be struck giving permanent satisfaction to the two groups, as well as securing the public interest. The whole process is inherently dynamic and unstable.' Experience had shown that the courts were not the best arbiters of labour disputes. McIntyre urged his colleagues to reject a Charter interpretation that would weight the scales in favour of one side, 'impair the process of future development in legislative hands,' and potentially implicate the courts in the resolution of all strikes.[46]

No other member of the Court who rejected constitutional protection of the right to strike agreed with McIntyre. Beetz and La Forest decided to sign to with Le Dain's brief two-page judgment, obviously written well after Dickson and McIntyre had circulated their opinions. Le Dain rejected the proposition that freedom of association protected the activities of the association. The right to strike, Le Dain found, was not a fundamental right but rather a creature of statute 'involving a balance of competing interests in a field which has been recognized by the courts as requiring a specialized expertise.'[47] It was for the legislature and the legislature alone to define the right depending upon the context. The courts should not curtail legislative choice in this delicate balance by constitutionalizing the right in general and abstract terms. It seems surprising that Beetz and La Forest concurred with Le Dain's terse opinion rather than McIntyre's more developed reasons. Perhaps they thought that Le Dain's judgment had the advantage of cleanly deciding the right-to-strike issue, leaving the broader question of the meaning of freedom of association for another day.

Wilson was the only member of the Court prepared to defend the right to strike to the hilt. She agreed with Dickson's decision in the Alberta case to strike down the law but disagreed that any aspect of the federal legislation could survive: 'Public sector employees should not be deprived of [freedom of association] as a means of government getting across its message, no matter how worthwhile that message may be.'[48] Singling out public-sector workers, she wrote, was arbitrary, unfair, and contrary to the equality guarantee of the Canadian Bill of Rights. She also dismissed the Saskatchewan government's contention that it had made a compelling case for limiting the right to strike in the dairy industry. Here, her attack on Dickson's section 1 analysis was particularly strong. Economic harm to a particular sector did not, Wilson wrote, provide a valid reason to abrogate constitutional rights, and she rejected the proposition that the dairy farmers were third parties since they controlled the cooperative that employed the workers.

The Labour Trilogy was the first significant Charter battle that Dickson lost. The judgments were a bitter disappointment to the unions and fulfilled the worst fears of left-leaning Charter critics. It seemed that the courts were prepared to strike down laws that interfered with corporate interests but held back when legislation affected vital trade-union concerns. The Labour Trilogy proved, if proof were still required, that Charter judging was complex, controversial, and value-laden. The terms of the debate were defined by the constitution, but the results were very much in the hands of the judges. Dickson's powerful dissents represent a remarkable change from his judgment in *Harrison v. Carswell* where he refused the plea of Laskin and striking workers to change the law. More than a decade on, the Court and the enactment of the Charter of Rights had transformed Dickson's attitude.

Dickson never recanted from the pro-union views he expressed in the Labour Trilogy, but he accepted the fact that the opposing view had won the day. In one of his last decisions, handed down shortly after he retired in 1990, Dickson bowed to the rule of precedent by siding with a majority opinion that the Charter's guarantee of freedom of expression does not protect the right to engage in collective bargaining. In a short and reluctant concurring opinion, Dickson made no secret of his unease with the result. After explaining why he thought the case indistinguishable from the Labour Trilogy, he concluded: 'For these reasons, and not without considerable hesitation having regard to the views which I expressed in the labour law trilogy of cases on the scope of s. 2(d) of the *Canadian Charter of Rights and Freedoms*, I have concluded that, short of overruling the reasons of the majority of this Court in the trilogy, this appeal must be dismissed with costs to the respondents.'[49]

Speaking Out

As chief justice, Dickson assumed a much more public role, particularly because the Court's Charter decisions attracted considerable media attention. While he carefully guarded his time and insisted that his primary duty was to be in Ottawa attending to the work of the Court, he loved to travel and he did accept many invitations to speak.

Dickson's speeches and lectures tended to focus on legal topics, and many of them dealt with the Charter and the important new mandate it conferred on the courts. He did his best to avoid controversy and, for the most part, succeeded. However, during the same period the Court was struggling with the contentious issues raised by *Edwards Books* and the Labour Trilogy, Dickson decided to speak out on a non-legal topic and in so doing became embroiled in a controversy. In May 1986 Dickson and Pierre Trudeau received honorary degrees at the University of British Columbia. Dickson decided to speak about the importance of adequate public funding for universities:

> Second-class funding of universities will inevitably lead to second-class teachers, second-class students and, ultimately, a second-class nation. It has been said by many people that education is too important to be left to educators. That may be true. But it is also true that education is too important to be left to Ministers of Finance. Universities desperately require funds to perform their great mission in democratic societies. Governments spend billions of dollars every year on all manner of projects, many worthwhile, others not so worthwhile. In my opinion, money spent on minds will never be money misspent.[50]

Dickson thought that it was a 'motherhood speech' and, before he gave it, had circulated it to some university presidents he knew. 'They all seemed to think it was a good idea.'[51] The speech was well received at the University of British Columbia, but, to Dickson's dismay, the next day it was described on the front page of the Toronto *Star* as 'an uncharacteristically blunt attack.'[52] A business columnist, though agreeing with the views Dickson had expressed, observed that the chief justice had 'put himself smack in the middle of a big, hot issue' and would 'have to take his chances now with everybody else,'[53] a prediction fulfilled when opposition MPs used Dickson's speech to attack Finance Minister Michael Wilson for the government's failure to provide adequate university funding.[54] A critical lead editorial in the Toronto *Globe and Mail* accused Dickson of walking 'too close to the political fire for comfort.'[55] The editorial alleged that Dickson had ignored Bora Laskin's 1982 admonition that judges had to keep their silence on political issues. This message had been directed at Thomas Berger, a highly regarded British Columbia judge, who spoke out in favour of entrenching aboriginal rights in the constitution and according Quebec a veto over constitutional amendments. The Canadian Judicial Council found Berger's comments to be 'unwise and inappropriate' but refused to recommend his removal from judicial office. However, Laskin refused to leave it at that and Berger felt obliged to resign because of Laskin's criticism of his conduct.[56] Dickson, who had told Laskin at the time that he disagreed with the way he handled the Berger issue, thought Laskin's views on judicial speech to be 'extremely narrow' and 'antediluvian.'[57] Still, he was very upset when he read the *Globe and Mail* editorial commenting on his own case.

To make matters even worse, Dickson's speech provoked a complaint to the Canadian Judicial Council. The complaint was promptly dismissed but Dickson was sensitive to any criticism. Even though he thought he had done nothing wrong, the controversy unsettled him. Ten days after the delivery of his speech, Dickson was scheduled to give an address to the Fourth International Conference on Constitutional Law in Quebec City. Jim MacPherson had worked closely with Dickson to prepare a wide-ranging and thoughtful analysis of current human rights issues and travelled to Quebec City with Dickson for the conference. Dickson called MacPherson to his hotel room early in the morning. The speech they had prepared had been cut to shreds. In place of the careful discussion of human rights, Dickson had substituted photocopies of headnotes of the Court's leading Charter decisions. Dickson asked MacPherson what he thought. MacPherson said that, if Dickson did no more than read the audience headnotes, it would be 'one sleepy speech.' Dickson shot back: 'That's exactly what I want, Jim, one sleepy speech.' To MacPherson's surprise, Dickson read the headnotes with great authority and dignity and the international audience warmly applauded his performance. Dickson continued regularly to speak publicly on matters affecting the justice system in Canada, but with a careful eye to avoid anything that might provoke controversy.

Struggling with Charter Application

Another case involving striking workers that presented a contentious issue of Charter interpretation was argued in 1984, but not decided for over two years. Dolphin Delivery, a Vancouver courier company, got an injunction prohibiting locked-out Purolator workers from picketing Dolphin's business. Dolphin made local deliveries for Purolator and the locked-out workers wanted to prevent their employer from shifting work to Dolphin. There was nothing on the statute books to prevent the picketing, but the judge found that Dolphin was entitled to an injunction on the ground that picketing would amount to a common law tort. The union appealed, arguing that the injunction violated the Charter right of freedom of expression.[58]

Before the Court even considered whether the injunction against the secondary picket was or was not a reasonable limit on the striking workers' freedom of expression, it had to decide whether the Charter even applied to a dispute that involved private citizens, not the government. At the time, legal scholars were engaged in a lively debate as to whether the Charter protected rights and freedoms against the actions of private actors. The issue of Charter application had been avoided by agreement of the parties in the lower courts. It was only after the union's lawyer was on his feet to argue the case that Dickson told him that the Court was going to insist on considering the application issue. The case was adjourned for one day, and, when it resumed, the lawyers did the best they could on such short notice to deal with one of the most difficult points of Charter interpretation.[59]

It became clear during the argument that the Court was faced with a very tough issue. If the Court found that the Charter applied, would it follow that all private relationships were subject to the Charter and to judicial scrutiny? On the other hand, if the Charter did not apply, vast areas of the common law, the basic source of private law in all provinces except Quebec, would be exempt from the Charter. Did it make any sense to draw such an important distinction between unwritten common law and statute law? Both, after all, are laws that bind citizens to behave accordingly. But could the Supreme Court say that court orders were exempt from the Charter? This might sound like judicial hypocrisy. All elements of government, including the cabinet, are subject to the Charter, but the judges, who made the rules of the Charter game, would be effectively excusing themselves from Charter compliance.

At the post-hearing conference, the judges agreed that the injunction should stand but there was no consensus on how or why.[60] Le Dain thought that picketing involved freedom of expression but did not think the Charter applied to private acts. Wilson was satisfied that this was a case of freedom of expression and said that she 'would like to have the *Charter* apply to private acts.' However, she also thought that constitutionalizing the common law would be 'horrendous.' She did not think that judges should be seen as part of the structure of government. Chouinard, coming from the civilian tradition of Quebec where the basic source of law was the statutory Civil Code, thought that the Charter should apply to the common law. McIntyre was cautious. He was looking for a way to decide the case on its own facts without making a sweeping pronouncement, but added: 'The Charter has some application to the private sector ... this is particularly the case when s. 15 [the right to equality] comes into play.' Estey thought the whole issue of Charter application could be avoided on the ground that picketing did not amount to expression. Beetz agreed with McIntyre and Estey that the case should be decided on a narrow basis; however, he said that he did not think the Charter applied to civil law or to the Civil Code, only to acts of government. The view Dickson expressed at conference was that 'the *Charter* did apply to the private sector and that peaceful picketing could be an exercise of the right of freedom of expression ...' He added that he would decide the case on the ground that the Charter applied, but that the injunction against secondary picketing was a reasonable limit under section 1.

McIntyre undertook the task of writing the judgment. Respected by his colleagues as a clear-minded and decisive judge, McIntyre found the task of deciding *Dolphin Delivery* to be unusually daunting. He circulated several drafts, changing his mind on key points from draft to draft, and took two years to produce the final product.

On one issue, McIntyre was clear and consistent. Freedom of expression, 'one of the fundamental concepts that has formed the basis for the historical development of the political, social and educational institutions of western society,' should be given a generous interpretation. Quoting the writings of John Milton and John Stuart Mill and the judgments of Oliver Wendell Holmes and Ivan Rand, McIntyre reasoned that picketing should be recognized as Charter-protected expression even if it was a form of action designed to bring economic pressure to bear on the employer. He was equally convinced, however, that if the Charter did apply, the injunction could be justified under section 1 as a reasonable limit. 'It is,' he wrote in his final draft, 'necessary in the general social interest that picketing be regulated and sometimes limited. It is reasonable to restrain picketing so that the conflict will not escalate beyond the actual parties.'[61]

McIntyre could have decided the case on that basis and left the application issue for another day. Since the parties had been taken by surprise when the Court asked them to address the issue, this might have been the more prudent course to follow. However, McIntyre felt compelled to deal with the issue and this is where he and his colleagues encountered difficulty. In the two years that passed from argument to final judgment, his thinking as well as that of Dickson and other members of the Court went through many twists and turns.[62]

In his first draft judgment, circulated to the other members of the Court in mid-April 1986, McIntyre wrote that the Charter did apply to the common law, and that court orders, such as injunctions, were a form of 'government action.' In a memorandum accompanying his draft, McIntyre confessed that he was troubled by the case and that he would welcome comments and discussion. He was 'happy' with the conclusion that the Charter applies to the common law; however, he was 'seriously concerned' about what should be included as government action and worried as well that he was going too far by saying that court orders were included, especially since all judicial orders would be covered. There was 'something offensive to the judicial mind' in classifying court orders as a form of government action and he asked his colleagues to consider whether his approach 'opens the way too widely to private invocation of Charter rights.'[63]

Despite McIntyre's own doubts, Dickson agreed with this version and in early June he sent McIntyre a memorandum stating, 'I am concurring in your reasons in *Dolphin Delivery*,' and offering a few suggestions for improvement.[64] Wilson, however, was not persuaded. She pointed out that it would be difficult to justify holding court-ordered injunctions as being subject to the Charter, but not other court decrees such as damage awards. And, if damage awards were covered, that would mean that the Charter would apply to all private litigation, a result that McIntyre wanted to avoid. Wilson agreed that 'the courts are also subject to the constitution ... and cannot lend themselves to its violation. My only problem is how far this takes you.'[65] Wilson also feared that applying the Charter to the common law would 'do violence to s. 32,' which mentioned only Parliament, the legislatures, and governments. Finally, she was concerned that, if the Charter applied to all common law rules, the Court would be usurping the role of the human rights commissions in dealing with private-sector discrimination.

La Forest provided McIntyre with a five-page memorandum arguing that the Charter should apply only to the legislative and executive branches of government.[66] Drawing upon his pre-judicial work as a senior government lawyer actively engaged in constitutional reform, La Forest explained that in the late 1960s a draft bill of rights that applied to the private sector floundered because it would have covered 'every abuse anyone committed over time' and would have involved the courts in an endless review of the entire body of common and civil law. At the same time, however, La Forest insisted that the courts should have the power 'to mould the common law to fit the values under the Constitution, without direct recourse to it.' This, he argued, reflected the approach of the English common law tradition in which the common law was imbued with basic constitutional values, like freedom of expression, without the formality and rigidity of requiring the courts to act in accordance with the dictates of a written constitution. It also would maintain consistency between the common law provinces and Quebec, where the law is codified. La Forest's 'Charter values' approach would allow the courts to develop the common law and keep it abreast of changes wrought by the Charter but, at the same time, avoid turning every private dispute into a constitutional case.

McIntyre resisted these proposals and circulated two more drafts that went in radically different directions. In his second draft, he changed the analysis but not the result. Though he now rejected the idea that the courts were an arm of government, he argued that the Charter applied to the judge-made common law since it 'is enforceable with all the formal sanctions of government power and authority.'[67] In his third draft, McIntyre abandoned the attempt to make the Charter apply to the common law, except where the government itself was involved in the dispute.[68]

Dickson was uneasy with this change in direction. He asked his law clerk, Stephen Toope, and his executive legal officer, Jim MacPherson, to prepare the outline for a concurring judgment saying that since any violation of freedom of expression could be justified under section 1, it was not necessary to say anything about Charter application.[69] However, Dickson was concerned about the Court's delay in deciding the case. He abandoned the draft, but he did accept Toope's suggestion that he urge McIntyre to consider a compromise that would soften the refusal to apply the Charter to the common law.[70] The idea had been suggested months earlier by La Forest. The Charter would not apply directly to the common law, but the courts would be expected to develop the common law in accordance with Charter values. McIntyre was anxious to get his judgment released and the proposed addition was entirely consistent with his draft. He accepted the suggestion and amended the judgment to say that, although the Charter does not apply to private parties, this was 'a distinct issue from the question of whether the judiciary ought to apply and develop the principles of the common law in a manner consistent with the fundamental values enshrined in the Constitution. The answer to this question must be in the affirmative.'[71]

In *Dolphin Delivery*, the Court had struggled with one of the most difficult issues of Charter interpretation. After two difficult years of drafts, redrafts, and soul-searching, McIntyre, with help from Dickson, La Forest, and Wilson, came up with a resolution that achieved consensus. While one might well criticize the Court for taking two years to decide the case, McIntyre's painstaking search for the best resolution of this difficult issue and his colleagues' willingness to assist him was entirely admirable. The Court did not immediately jump on one side or the other of a serious constitutional debate. Instead, the judges adopted an entirely collegial approach and canvassed every possible solution, and, in the end, McIntyre did his best to craft a principled decision.

Dolphin Delivery has been sharply criticized by some constitutional scholars as conceptually incoherent.[72] Others have argued that the Court was too timid and should have insisted that the Charter does limit private power as well as state authority,[73] though some of these same critics attack the Court in other contexts for excessive Charter zeal. In any event, despite what many may still regard as conceptual weaknesses in the judgment, the 'Charter values' compromise suggested by La Forest and Dickson and accepted by McIntyre had certain advantages. It was another halfway house that, for better or worse, effectively bridged the gap between the extremes of constitutionalizing all human relationships, on the one hand, and ignoring the Charter when developing the private law, on the other.

Struggling with the Backlog

From the moment he was appointed chief justice, Dickson was preoccupied with the Court's backlog. It is generally accepted, especially at the appellate level, that it is not always possible to decide cases on the spot and that a certain amount of delay is inevitable. Time is required for sober reflection, detailed research, and careful reading of a large volume of material. Judgments cannot be released until all members of the Court who sat on the case have signed. Often, the judge circulating a draft judgment will find that the other judges have comments or suggestions for changes or improvements.

But, even with these allowances, in the early 1980s the delay in delivering judgments became chronic. The Court (two of whose judges, Laskin and Ritchie, were seriously ill) consistently failed to meet the six-month guideline suggested by the Canadian Judicial Council, a standard resented by some judges who thought the Supreme Court should be exempted.[74] In 1983 the Court released only seventy-seven judgments and in 1984 only fifty-four, a precipitous decline from the normal pattern of one hundred or so that matched the number of judgments to the number of cases the Court was hearing. Delays of over a year from argument to release of the final judgment were common. With an alarming backlog of reserve judgments just when the Court was meeting the onslaught of difficult Charter cases; it became increasingly apparent that steps had to be taken to expedite the Court's work.

Dickson was deeply concerned about the problem and extraordinarily sensitive to public criticism of the Court's short comings in this area. Shortly after he became chief justice, he made a point of speaking to the bar about his determination to improve the Court's efficiency,[75] and in an effort to deal with the backlog, the Court increased its sitting time by 25 per cent. While this helped to clear the list, more time in court put added pressure on the Court's ability to produce judgments in a timely fashion.

To help remedy matters, Dickson carefully monitored the progress of each case. The registrar's office prepared regular reports, tracking who was writing, how long the case had been under reserve, and whether any reasons had been circulated. Tables were prepared listing each judge's reserve judgments and highlighting problematic cases. Dickson pored over these reports, discussed them with his executive legal officer, and worried about what he could or should do. He looked to the experience of other courts for help.[76] Discouraging lists of reserved judgments were regularly discussed at Court meetings. At the end of June 1986, after Dickson's first full year as chief justice, there were sixty-nine reserves. Dickson urged his colleagues to devote the summer to clearing up the mess 'in order that we may enter the fall term with a reasonably clean slate.'[77] Wilson and Lamer became exasperated by what they regarded as their colleagues' failure to come to grips with the problem. They, like Dickson, delivered draft judgments with great efficiency; attacking their work with enthusiasm and a determination to turn out the best product as soon as possible. Often, however, they would work hard only to find their colleagues unwilling or unable to respond. Weeks and even months would go by without a whisper of either agreement or dissent from some members of the Court.

In February 1985 Wilson had a number of draft judgments in limbo. She sent Dickson a stinging memorandum pointing out that she had written no fewer than six judgments that still awaited the attention of her colleagues. In four cases, she had prepared draft judgments, only to have rehearings or further written submissions ordered because of the failure of the Court to come to agreement: 'I cannot recall a rehearing being ordered on any other cases' for similar reasons. Wilson complained that, through no fault of her own, it took the Court two years to release an important civil judgment she had written[78] and that this unusual delay 'has not gone unnoted in the law journals.' There was no doubting the depths of Wilson's frustration. She wondered whether 'some form of discrimination is at work here' and added: 'Since I am a reasonably conscientious individual I am finding the frustration quite intolerable.' Wilson delivered a thinly veiled threat that she would resign if the situation were not remedied:

Is there any solution to this problem or is it just something the first woman on the Supreme Court is expected to endure? I find that at age 60 one is less disposed to bat one's head up against a stone wall! There are more useful things one could be doing with one's remaining time.

I would appreciate some early action to deal with this situation.[79]

Dickson, who had experienced similar frustrations, responded with an immediate message to the other judges:

I have received a memorandum from Mme Justice Wilson in which she expresses deep concern in her inability to get a number of judgments which she has written released. Mme Justice Wilson mentions that she currently has six in circulation to members of the Court, more than any other member of the Court ...

I would appreciate it very much if all members of the Court would exert a special effort with a view to release in these six cases at the earliest possible date.[80]

The problem was discussed, but it remained unresolved. The situation became even worse in September 1985 when Estey accepted Prime Minister Mulroney's invitation to chair a commission of inquiry into the collapse of Canadian Commercial Bank and the Northland Bank. Only a month earlier, Dickson had told the Canadian Bar Association of his growing concern over the appointment of judges to commissions of inquiry, which, said Dickson, 'presents a serious threat to the reality and image of judicial impartiality and independence.'[81] Estey was anxious to accept the assignment, but Dickson and the other members of the Court were initially strongly opposed. In the past, judicial commissions of inquiry had hurt the Court's reputation. The 1946 Gouzenko espionage inquiry conducted by justices Robert Taschereau and R.L. Kellock attracted widespread criticism for violating civil rights and judicial norms. More recent was the 1966 inquiry by Wishart Spence into the sordid allegations that Conservative cabinet ministers might have revealed state secrets to Gerda Munsinger, a prostitute with Russian connections. It was suggested in the press that Spence, known to have been a strong Liberal, had taken on a partisan political assignment at the government's bidding.[82] There was a consensus that the assignment was 'highly political', and would be bad for the Court's image, and that Estey's absence would impair the Court's ability to get on top of its workload.[83] However, neither Mulroney nor Estey could be moved by these concerns. Mulroney pulled out all the stops. He made a personal visit to Dickson's chambers and pointed out that, in his CBA speech, Dickson had acknowledged that judges might be used in exceptional circumstances. He exerted more pressure at a subsequent meeting with Dickson at 24 Sussex Drive. Both Mulroney and Estey assured Dickson that the inquiry would be completed within three months, a highly unrealistic prediction. In the end, Dickson and the other members of the Court relented and accepted the appointment as more or less inevitable. Estey was lost to the Court for an entire year as it confronted its mountain of work.[84] Within a year, a CBA study on the Court, prompted in large part by the backlog problem, recommended a statutory amendment prohibiting Supreme Court judges from sitting on commissions of inquiry because of the serious disruption to the important work of the Court, a recommendation accepted by the judges 'with one member ... holding a contrary opinion.'[85]

In May 1986 Wilson sent out another plea for an organized and cooperative approach 'to attain a steady flow of judgments going out in rough chronological relationship to the dates of hearing.' To achieve that, she said, it would be necessary for the members of the Court 'to agree to focus on the same judgments within the same time frame. None are going to go out if each judge is doing his or her own thing and not giving priority to the ones which have potential for release on the next judgment day or the succeeding one.' Wilson suggested developing a schedule with projected dates for release based on what seemed to be a reasonable time for the preparation of the judgment. The maximum time, she suggested, should be six months and she thought that most judgments should be delivered in three months. Wilson identified the underlying problem: 'Members of the Court are letting other members' drafts sit while they concentrate on their own. If we all proceed in this fashion inordinate delay in getting judgments out inevitably results.'[86]

Lamer become so exasperated with the failure of his colleagues to deal with draft judgments that in two cases he threatened to send confidential memoranda to the registrar to be placed in the Court file. Particularly galling was the fact that one of the cases dealt with unreasonable delay in the trial court.[87] In the other case,[88] where the judgment was not released until 25 June 1987, Lamer recorded: 'I wish to confirm the following: this case was heard on December 10, 1985 and my reasons were circulated on May 13, 1986.'[89] Lamer told Wilson: 'Something has to be done.'[90] He explained to Dickson his concern over the 'mounting criticism throughout the profession and the public' regarding 'untenable delays' and said that he could not let himself be associated with such delays, especially where he had written his own reasons in a timely fashion. Lamer added: 'In any event, is it not a matter of courtesy to react to a colleague's reasons, at least within six months?'[91]

Upon his return to the Court after completing his work on the banking inquiry, Estey expressed similar concerns, noting that the Court's delays had been the subject of 'journalistic and academic sniping.'[92] He suggested establishing clear target dates for the completion of judgments and reducing the number of hearings in June so that the judges would have time to get their judgments out before the summer. Perhaps more controversial was Estey's suggestion that the Court 'adopt shorter judgments; confine the disposition to the issues which must be decided and no others; and discourage counsel who come here hoping to settle broad areas of the law in one or two appeals. Those expectations should be discouraged.' These suggestions, like many others, were discussed but not adopted.

The delay problem was both structural and personal; there were differences in attitude and work habits that had to be bridged. Two members of the Court, Jean Beetz and Gerald Le Dain, were perfectionists. Their judgments were well-crafted gems, but their style was not well suited to the formidable task of disposing of the one hundred or so cases on the Court's docket each year. They agonized over every case and, at times, were plagued by indecision. Even when they agreed with the result and had only to concur with an opinion written by a colleague, it could take them months to come to grips with having to sign their name. Gérard La Forest was an exceptionally hardworking member of the Court, but he could not resist taking on cases that particularly interested him, even when he already had a lot on his plate. He viewed the urge to expedite matters with suspicion and worried that it threatened to take priority over the quality of the Court's work. Dickson pushed La Forest but he was sympathetic when La Forest told him, 'I just can't get this one out.' Dickson's quick reply was, 'Understood.' La Forest's solution, never accepted by his colleagues at the time, was that the Court should hear fewer cases.[93]

Another factor was illness. Perhaps this was to be expected, given the age of most of the judges and the pressure they worked under, but, for several years running, the Court was plagued by an unusual amount of illness. In the early 1980s it was Laskin and Ritchie. Then Chouinard was struck down with cancer in 1987. Estey was absent for a year on the banking inquiry and then, in the spring of 1987, was again out of commission with a blood clot that damaged his opthomalic nerve. The more serious and debilitating illnesses of Beetz and Le Dain followed in late 1988. As a result, Dickson, Wilson, and Lamer bore a disproportionate burden of the Court's work.[94]

Dickson was plagued by the backlog, and, while he pushed his colleagues to deal with the problem, he did his best to maintain good humour. In 1985 he forwarded to the Court an article sent to him by a Canadian lawyer about the delay problems of India's Supreme Court, which had 136,313 pending cases. Dickson observed: 'I have been somewhat concerned with our Court's backlog of 107 cases waiting to be heard ... By comparison, we are not doing too badly.'[95] Even as chief justice, Dickson could do little more about the delays than exert moral suasion. While the delays were an enormous frustration, he also respected the right and duty of each member of the court to bring his or her own individual judgment to bear on every case. It was simply a fact of life that there were nine strong-willed and strong-minded individuals who worked in different ways and at different speeds. Dickson urged them on, politely and patiently, using his considerable moral authority as a hard-working judge and as the Court's chief justice. Even then, his efforts were resented by some of his colleagues, particularly Beetz and Le Dain.

In the end, however, Dickson's efforts bore fruit. The Court was invigorated in the late 1980s with the appointment of several highly productive judges – John Sopinka, Beverley McLachlin, Charles Gonthier, and Peter Cory, who, together with Lamer, Wilson and L'Heureux-Dubé, shared Dickson's concern for promptness. In 1989 the Court released an astonishing 149 judgments, and another 148 judgments followed in 1990, the year of Dickson's retirement. When he left the chief justice's office, Dickson could proudly claim that the Court was essentially current with its work.

Searching for the Charter Halfway House

The second wave of Charter cases made plain to Brian Dickson and his colleagues the contentious and complex nature of Charter litigation. The initial consensus forged in *Hunter v. Southam*, *Big M*, and *Oakes* began to fracture and the divisions on the Court became apparent. Dickson maintained his insistence on a generous purposive interpretation of Charter rights, but he failed to persuade his colleagues to adopt it with respect to freedom of association and the rights of organized labour. However, by softening the *Oakes* test, Dickson was also starting to build one of his halfway houses. Charter rights would be generously interpreted, but limitations on those rights would be upheld where legislation sought to improve the lot of disadvantaged groups.

More and more, Dickson occupied the middle ground in a complex dynamic of conflicting judicial opinion. Beetz and McIntyre read the Charter narrowly while Wilson and Lamer insisted upon a broad and liberal interpretation. La Forest steadily whittled away at *Oakes*, while Wilson passionately defended it. Dickson's increasingly cautious approach under the Charter was a reversion to his instinctive quest for the middle ground and his constant attempt to accommodate conflicting positions rather than choosing between them.

18

Feeling the Strain

The reaction to the Court's bold steps in the early Charter cases was generally positive and public confidence in the Supreme Court as the final arbiter of fundamental rights and freedoms was high. However, as Charter litigation put the Court at the centre of public debate, its decisions attracted both attention and criticism. Some editorial writers and legal critics thought that the Court was far too eager to strike down laws and feared that its liberal approach to the Charter could undermine laws designed to limit corporate power and protect vulnerable interests.[1] Left-wing critics[2] pointed out that many of the big Charter 'winners' were corporations, while trade unions fared poorly. Conservative critics[3] worried about the erosion of parliamentary sovereignty and feared that the Charter would 'Americanize' Canada's legal and political culture and that special-interest groups would use Charter litigation to achieve a judicially imposed culture of liberal rights.

The Court also faced internal strains. Charter cases were unusually difficult to decide, especially in the early going when so much was riding on the Court's pronouncements. This added burden weighed heavily upon some judges. Even the ebullient Antonio Lamer observed: 'My job description changed overnight.'[4] It took a long time to write some Charter judgments and, as we have explained, the lengthy delays did not go unnoticed.

Judicial Review and Democracy

The most contentious issue Dickson and his colleagues faced under the *Charter* was the claim that the Supreme Court was usurping the role of Parliament.

Dickson himself was conscious of the dangers of excessive enthusiasm for the Charter. As early as 1983, he noted the tendency of governments 'to pass recalcitrant problems to the courts'[5] and of social activists to resort to litigation rather than political action. 'It is presumably easier and cheaper to look to the courts for social changes than to go through the laborious and time-consuming process of persuading legislators.' He worried that 'litigation is being substituted for politics; the judicial process for the political process.'[6] He sometimes wondered whether we 'are expecting too much of the judicial system'[7] and hoped that 'we are not pushing too many problems that are too complex into the courts.' He cautioned lawyers to 'resist the temptation for overkill' since the 'Charter was not intended to provide a full employment program for lawyers or to protect every minor right which people might think themselves ideally to possess.'[8] Speaking at Osgoode Hall Law School, where several vocal Charter sceptics taught, Dickson told the 1985 graduating class to 'consider the merit of legislative as opposed to judicial solutions so that an appropriate balance between the two forums is maintained.' He reminded the fledgling lawyers of the limitations inherent in the judicial process and the advantages of legislation as a way to achieve social justice. 'The courts,' he said, 'are basically reactive; they respond, usually after the event, to remedy situations between two parties.' The legislator had the advantage of 'access to information and material often denied the judge,' and could 'assess the desirability and wisdom of policies in a way the judge may not.' The legislative process allowed for 'consultation, negotiation, mediation, amendment and improvement in a way judicial decisions do not.'[9] In another 1985 speech, Dickson insisted that 'the judicial function is restricted to interpretation and application of the law; it does not include legislating by judges.'[10] Despite his enthusiasm for the Charter, as the years went by, he remained conscious of the dangers of placing too much emphasis on rights. Towards the end of his career on the bench, he worried that Canadians were 'prone to lay greater emphasis upon claims to rights and to pay less heed to the responsibilities which must be shared by all for those rights to become meaningful.'[11]

Dickson recognized that the Charter brought before the Court 'some of the most difficult social, economic, religious and ultimately moral issues of our time'[12] and that the Court was 'compelled to shoulder and resolve questions that evoke strong and potentially divisive sentiment, which present no right answer and no easy solution.'[13] But at the same time he assured Canadians 'that any fears about the emergence of a judicial oligarchy – government by a few judges – are entirely without foundation.'[14] Canada's judges, he often observed, have no 'license to rely on personal, political or philosophical preferences as the basis for interpretation' of the Charter and 'intuitive feelings for justice are a poor substitute for a known rule of law, particularly when we do not all have the same intuition.'[15] To that extent, even under the Charter, Dickson remained faithful to the cautious legalism he had expressed in *Harrison v. Carswell* and in the first *Morgentaler* case.

Yet, notwithstanding his words of caution and restraint, Dickson had no doubt that permitting judges to strike down laws passed by the elected representatives of the people was consistent with Canada's democratic values. Seeing the rule of law and an independent judiciary as essential elements of an ordered democracy, he believed that a liberal structure defining the 'framework for relations among individuals as well as between the individual and the state' and protecting 'individuals from arbitrary and capricious treatment at the hands of government' was essential for social order in a democratic society.[16] The courts' role as guardians of the constitutional order and of the fundamental values necessary to maintain democratic government was, Dickson thought, an essential element of the rule of law. In a 1986 decision, he described the Court as the 'protector of the constitution and the fundamental values embodied in it – rule of law, fundamental justice, equality, preservation of the democratic process, to name perhaps the most important.'[17] Dickson knew that the Court's decisions would not always be popular, but, as he stated in an interview shortly before his retirement, 'we're not here to try to develop popular results. We're here to interpret the Constitution and apply our talents to come up with a jurisprudence the country can be proud of.'[18]

As Dickson saw it, there was nothing new about an independent judiciary with the power of judicial review. Judicial review was implicit in the rule of law and necessary for the realization of the values of federalism, the protection of individual rights and freedoms, the protection of minorities, and the realization of democracy itself. The Charter certainly added to the power of the courts, but, in doing so, it accorded with the swing of history in the rights-conscious world of the second half of the twentieth century. In written notes he prepared for an interview with Radio-Canada's 'Le Point' 1986, Dickson recorded his 'great pride in the *Charter*' since it put 'Canada in the mainstream of the post World War II movement towards conscious recognition of, and protection for, fundamental human rights.' He saw the Charter as 'the logical culmination of Canadian developments in the field of human rights,' building upon the anti-discrimination human rights codes and the Canadian Bill of Rights to protect 'those basic values which most Canadians share and cherish.' Dickson added: 'I am pleased that, in my professional capacity as a judge, I can play a role in protecting and promoting those values.'[19] When speaking about judicial review under the Charter, Dickson would invariably remind his audience that parliamentary sovereignty had never been absolute in Canada because of the division of powers between Parliament and the provinces.[20]

Dickson categorically rejected the contention that Charter adjudication was anti-democratic. As he and some of his colleagues frequently observed,[21] the Charter was a product of democratic choice. The judges of Canada, he pointed out, 'did not ask for the enactment of the Charter. It was thrust upon us.'[22] In Dickson's mind, the language of the Constitution Act, 1982 left no room for doubt that the political actors consciously imposed upon the judiciary the duty to strike down laws that did not meet constitutional muster and to grant appropriate and just remedies to vindicate Charter rights. He told a meeting of Toronto lawyers in May 1985: 'The question of the desirability of constitutional review of government and legislative action has been answered by this country's elected representatives and the judiciary must fulfill the great responsibility they have been given.'[23]

But Dickson was keenly aware of the disappointing record of the Supreme Court under the Canadian Bill of Rights. He had bowed to the Court's narrow interpretation of the Bill of Rights by signing in 1979 the notorious *Bliss* decision, which held that refusing pregnant women unemployment-insurance benefits available to other workers did not amount to sex discrimination.[24] Dickson knew that '*Bliss* came under a tremendous amount of criticism'[25] and he saw the entrenchment of the Charter, with its explicit remedies clauses, as a conscious and deliberate choice by the political actors of the day to reject the approach taken in cases like *Bliss*. The elected representatives of the people were telling the courts something: stop interpreting fundamental rights and freedoms like a contract or an ordinary statute. The generous and liberal interpretation he accorded the Charter was, in Dickson's view, not an unwarranted assertion of judicial power but a direct response to the invitation of the political actors and a fulfillment of the widely held and deeply felt expectations of the Canadian public. As he explained in a 1984 speech: 'Our nation accepted on April 17, 1982, the political proposition that there are some phases of life in Canada that should be beyond the reach of any majority, save by constitutional amendment or by the exercise of the [notwithstanding clause].'[26]

Dickson attributed the apparent public wish for the courts to take an active role under the Charter to the erosion or breakdown of other more traditional institutions. In a 1985 speech he observed that, in an era of drastic social change and eroding established customs, where there seem to be few institutions the ordinary citizen could count on, 'people in increasing numbers are coming to the courts for the assertion of rights to political, economic and social equality.'[27] He saw the 'energetic national debate about social and moral values' engendered by the Charter as a sign of 'the vigour of our democratic institutions and our confidence in their strength and durability.'[28] When Geoffrey Palmer, New Zealand's minister of justice and deputy prime minister, visited Canada while considering a bill of rights for his country, Dickson told him: 'My personal opinion is that our experience under the *Charter* has been a good one ... We respect the values of liberty, equality and diversity ... the *Charter* is an important bulwark of these values.'[29] New Zealand decided to proceed with its own bill of rights modelled partly after the Charter, as did a number of other countries.

Dickson thought that the Charter enhanced rather than detracted from the values of democracy. His vision integrated and harmonized the constitutional protection of minorities and individual rights with the democratic process. It gave democracy a richer meaning than raw majority rule in which the power of numbers prevails over all other values. In his judgments, he often included passages to emphasize the democratic nature of judicial review. For example, in a decision dealing with the presumption of innocence, he described the 'overarching principle of judicial review under the *Charter*' as the need to ensure that legislatures do not infringe upon certain fundamental rights in the name of the broader common good.[30] He recognized that this could be viewed as a challenge to 'the nature of democratic institutions in Canada' since such institutions represented the collective voice of the community. However, he rejected that analysis in favour of one supportive of democracy, insisting that the 'infusion of the spirit of individual and collective democratic aspirations into the process of defining the contours of constitutional guarantees' made the courts 'allies of Canadian democracy' 'by providing a voice and a remedy for those excluded from equal and effective democratic participation in our society.'[31] In short, the courts helped to remedy the institutional weaknesses of democracy.

To those who claimed that judicial supremacy had replaced parliamentary sovereignty, Dickson pointed to section 33: 'Since Parliament can circumvent the *Charter* by no greater effort than an ordinary statutory declaration, it seems necessary to observe that the Canadian judiciary is simply not superior to the legislature, at least not in the tradition of the American constitution.'[32] He pointed out that, just as before the Charter, Parliament had the power to abrogate fundamental rights and that the ultimate safeguard against such action was political, not judicial. Dickson recognized that the courts were not alone in the struggle to protect fundamental rights and freedoms. While he saw the courts as the last resort and ultimate protector of constitutional values, he also regarded Parliament and the legislatures as vital partners. Furthermore, he recognized that the legislators had to be accorded reasonable scope when mediating between competing claims, especially to protect vulnerable groups. As early as 1984, Dickson was describing the dynamic of legislation and judicial review in terms of a dialogue between the courts and the legislatures. He spoke of judicial review by the Courts as 'a kind of policy dialogue with the legislature' and of Charter adjudication as submitting 'the legislative product to a moral critique.' He argued that this 'open give and take between the two branches of government' was 'important for the preservation and advancement of societal values' and that it created 'greater public awareness and understanding of social problems' and promoted 'what might be termed "moral growth."'[33]

Expanding the Procedural Limits

Procedural rules reflect underlying assumptions about the role of the courts. For the most part, the Supreme Court entered the Charter era with traditional procedural rules written for a court that resolved disputes rather than made law. In this classic private-law model of litigation, access to the courts is essentially restricted to the immediate parties with a direct stake in a concrete dispute. Concerned citizens not directly involved in a case are not permitted to intervene to influence the results; the parties and the parties alone control the case and determine what the judge hears. Judges, for their part, resolve these disputes for the benefit of the parties. Judicial decisions become precedents for the future, but, in the classic model, the lawmaking role of the courts is entirely incidental to the central task of dispute resolution.

Standing rules require a litigant to show some specific legal right or interest at stake. Concerned citizens who wish to challenge the constitutional validity of a law are not permitted to do so unless they present a concrete dispute involving their own immediate personal or property rights. Limiting standing before the courts to those with a direct interest is motivated by a fear of 'opening the floodgates' of unnecessary litigation that would politicize the judicial process.

Another rule flowing from the dispute-resolution model of judging is that the courts will not decide cases that are 'moot.' A case is said to be moot if the immediate concrete dispute between the parties no longer exists, even though the underlying legal or constitutional issue remains unresolved.

As the Supreme Court stepped into the bright spotlight of the Charter, there was increasing tension between the Court's new role and the traditional rules of intervention, standing, and mootness. Advocacy groups representing a diversity of conflicting interests and policies turned to litigation rather than politics to advance their interests and, even when not directly involved in cases, insisted on being heard as intervenors. Most members of the Court, including Dickson, were wary of the implications of altering the Court's procedures and practices to accommodate this new style of public-law litigation, but the traditional rules simply failed to reflect the dimensions and implications of a new kind of judicial decision making.

Even before the *Charter*, Bora Laskin had recognized the need for significant procedural change. From the mid-1970s, he pushed the Court to a more open acceptance of its important role as a maker of Canadian constitutional and public law and to rethink its approach to intervention and standing. These innovations, along with the introduction of the requirement for leave to appeal that allowed the Court to decide only cases having 'national importance,' went a long way towards making the Court more orientated to policy making and public law. However, as we shall see, those with a more conservative judicial instinct resisted Laskin's efforts.

Public-Interest Intervenors

Before the Charter era, the Supreme Court of Canada lacked a clear intervention policy. It was assumed that the federal and all provincial governments had a stake in constitutional cases and attorneys general were almost invariably allowed to intervene, but the rules of the Supreme Court were vague about the participation of public-interest groups. The matter was governed by a rule, virtually unchanged from the time it was first enacted in 1878, giving the Court a general discretion to allow interventions.[34] Laskin was favourably disposed to interventions and, influenced by the practice of the United States Supreme Court where 'amicus' briefs were almost automatically accepted, he interpreted the rule generously.[35] He allowed interventions in a number of Bill of Rights cases, most notably in *Lavell*,[36] a 1973 case dealing with equality rights, and the first *Morgentaler* case[37] where pro-choice, pro-life, and other interested groups were allowed to present argument. This practice was followed in several other cases including a case dealing with film censorship in 1976[38] and a case challenging the death penalty as cruel and unusual punishment in 1977.[39] Under Laskin's liberal regime, the Canadian Civil Liberties Association became a familiar presence before the Court. The CCLA had a positive profile in the legal community and the general counsel, Alan Borovoy, had no difficulty in finding lawyers who were prepared to argue an interesting CCLA brief without a fee. However, even Laskin's liberal-minded colleagues remained dubious about intervenors. In the 1977 death-penalty case, Laskin's usual ally, Wishart Spence, reluctantly granted the CCLA, represented by Eddie Greenspan, status to intervene only because all parties consented: 'I am strongly of the opinion that the hearing of an appeal in this Court should never be distorted into a public forum for the advancement of political views. This appeal is an appeal between the parties and the rights of those parties are the paramount and well nigh exclusive concern of the court.'[40]

Dickson's attitude towards intervenors during this period was also guarded. He recognized the advantages but worried about creating a situation where the private litigant would be driven to 'air his case in a public forum in the atmosphere of a semi-political dispute.'[41] 'In principle,' he stated in a 1979 speech, 'our procedure does not allow for participation by representatives of the public. The *amicus curiae* brief is not part of our daily life.' However, he recognized that interventions were possible 'on occasion,' that they could be 'of great help to the Court,' and that they could 'vastly change the nature of the representations, and the materials available to the Court in its law-making role.'[42]

When the Supreme Court revised its rules in January 1983, it retained the old intervention rule with an important addition that seemed to signal a more open attitude.[43] Anyone who had intervened in the lower court was automatically entitled to intervene before the Supreme Court of Canada,[44] and attorneys general could intervene by simply filing a notice with the Court.[45] However, this apparently liberal trend was sharply reversed when the Court flatly refused to apply the new rule in criminal cases. The Court refused to give the CCLA leave to intervene in an appeal involving the use of force to discipline an institutionalized, mentally disabled person. The CCLA had intervened in the lower court and therefore appeared to fall squarely within the new rule. Ritchie's terse ruling on the point simply stated that the new rule 'has no application to purely criminal appeals.'[46] A sentence in Dickson's judgment on the appeal itself perhaps explained the Court's reluctance to allow the intervention. He observed that the case involved the 'sensitive topics' of 'the status and rights of mentally retarded persons, and the limits on the disciplinary prerogatives of persons in authority over those in their charge.' But, he then added: 'Despite this overlay of social concerns it is important to remember that the case before this Court is a criminal one and its resolution must be based on legal principles.'[47] The CCLA was again refused permission to intervene in *R. v. Oakes*, despite the fact that the case raised an important Charter issue and despite the CCLA's successful intervention before the Ontario Court of Appeal.[48] By the end of December 1983, the Court had revoked the rule giving those who had intervened in the courts below automatic status at the Supreme Court.

A lively, behind-the-scenes debate on how to handle interventions ensued at the Court, with some judges expressing unease about the Court's changing role under the Charter. They insisted that cases had to be decided on strictly legal principles. Allowing non-parties to participate, particularly self-styled public-interest groups, could threaten this formal model of judging. In one case refusing a CCLA intervention application, Beetz told counsel Ed Ratushny 'that given the purposes and objectives of the Canadian Civil Liberties Association, there would hardly be any serious *Charter* case in which the Applicant would not be interested.' Beetz 'expressed serious concern' that the CCLA and similar organizations might 'become more or less permanent fixtures of the Court' and that a restrictive intervention policy was required to save the Court's time and to protect its image from being 'perceived by the public as some sort of royal commission.'[49] Willard Estey also thought intervenors added unnecessarily to the length and complexity of appeals. In early 1985, he told his colleagues: 'This Court no longer has the time to fritter away sitting and listening to repetition, irrelevancies, axe-grinding, cause advancement, and all the rest of the output of the typical intervenant.'[50]

Dickson's lack of enthusiasm for intervenors was revealed by his refusal to allow the Seventh Day Adventist Church to intervene in the *Big M Drug Mart* case dealing with Sunday closing.[51] In the next Sunday-closing case, *Edwards Books*, Bertha Wilson allowed a similar application by the Seventh Day Adventists. Knowing that she was bucking a trend and that some of her colleagues would not be pleased, she sent them a memo confessing her sin: 'Yesterday morning I broke all the rules and granted a motion for intervenor status' in the Sunday-closing case.[52] A few days later at the University of Toronto, she made her views publicly known: 'Liberalized intervention, in my view, would ... assist in legitimizing the Court's new role through a more open and accessible court process, and it would go part way to solving the counter-majoritarian problem which some see as inherent in judicial power.'[53]

The divisions on the Court sometimes resulted in inconsistent rulings even in the same case. In 1984 the Court was preparing to hear the appeal in *Ontario Human Rights Commission v. O'Malley*, an important case that would determine the meaning of discrimination. Wilson allowed intervention applications from the Canadian Association for the Mentally Retarded, the Coalition of Provincial Organizations of the Handicapped, and from several provincial human rights commissions.[54] McIntyre, who tended not to favour interventions, was asked to deal with an intervention application from the Retail Council of Canada. He wanted to refuse the application but, in a memo to his colleagues, asked if he should do so after so many other parties had been allowed in.[55] Wilson responded with a defence of the orders she had made. The case raised an important issue for human rights commissions and groups representing the interests of the disabled, as Wilson explained to her colleagues: 'whether an *intention* to discriminate is required for discrimination under Human Rights legislation or whether the fact that the conduct of the defendant has the *effect* of discriminating against a particular group is enough.' She made a strong case for a liberal intervention policy. '... on an important issue like this, applicants directly affected by the result should be heard from so that the Court gets a feeling for the dimension of the problem.' Wilson suggested that it would be only fair to hear the Retail Council: 'I have no doubt their concern will be for shopkeepers if no intention is required. They may, for example, have to install ramps, etc. where they are serving the public including the handicapped.'[56]

Dickson suggested a meeting of the Court to settle the policy on interventions although his own views remained uncertain. 'My own view would be to grant interventions only in rare cases.' He added, however, that if the issue was likely to have adverse financial consequences on the business community, perhaps it was only fair that the Retail Council should be heard. 'I do not see how we can properly grant standing to one side of an issue (which I take it was not an issue which would otherwise be canvassed by the Ontario Human Rights Commission) and deny the other side a right to be heard.'[57] McIntyre refused the application[58] and the matter was further complicated when Estey decided to grant intervenor status in the same case to the Canadian Jewish Congress.[59]

Public-interest litigants were alarmed by the Court's reluctance to allow interventions. The CCLA took the lead in urging the Court to liberalize its practice. Alan Borovoy was determined to get the civil-liberties perspective before the Court, especially in the early cases that would establish the framework for the Charter. In July 1984, after being shut out in *Oakes*, Borovoy sent the Supreme Court a brief urging it to rethink its direction. Borovoy urged the Court to 'develop a rule on interventions which broadens the effective right of constituencies other than the immediate parties to participate in important public interest litigation.' He argued that the issue was one 'of fundamental fairness' and that 'as the entire community will be increasingly affected ... by decisions of the Court, larger sections of the community should be able to participate in the process which produces those decisions.' It was simply not fair, he said, to limit such participation on the basis of the coincidence of which parties litigate first. 'A more inclusive process' was required to ensure 'public respect for both the *Charter* and the Court.' The CCLA made its case in practical terms that would appeal to the conservative judicial mind. Its brief pointed out that an intervenor could provide the court with sensible, middle-ground solutions often ignored or obscured in the traditional two-party model of litigation. A party attacking legislation might argue that legislation should be struck down, while the government would attempt to uphold the law under section 1. An intervenor might present a more nuanced alternative – 'that the government's goal is legitimate but not its means' and that 'a less restrictive means could adequately achieve the same goal.' Conscious of the Court's concern about increasing its workload, Borovoy suggested that intervenors be invited to submit written argument and that the Court selectively determine which intervenors should be heard in oral argument.[60]

The Court did not respond to the CCLA brief. Almost a year after it had been submitted, Dickson's former clerk, Katherine Swinton, by then a law professor and member of the CCLA's Board of Directors, wrote to her former mentor politely but firmly pressing the CCLA's case and asking for 'an opportunity to discuss this matter further with the Court.'[61] Dickson circulated the Swinton letter, provoking a hostile response from Estey. He told his colleagues that the ability of the Court to function was at stake. If the Court's function was to resolve disputes, there was little need for 'this volunteered and self-assessed talent.' If the Court was to become a 'non-elected mini-legislature ... the doors should be open to all.' Estey was contemptuous of groups like the CCLA whom he described as 'self-appointed, self-perpetuating oligarchies of varying degrees of skill, talent and industry.' He saw intervenors as being nothing more than publicity-seeking pressure groups and thought that the CCLA's proposal ignored fundamental aspects of the common law tradition. Estey could envisage no role for them in the judicial process. 'If these volunteers are so vital to the protection of society and the growth of our law, how did the common law ever evolve without their help.'[62]

The British Columbia Civil Liberties Association submitted its own brief, a detailed and scholarly argument prepared by Philip Bryden, a professor at the University of British Columbia and a former Bertha Wilson law clerk.[63] Another well-reasoned submission was made by the Women's Legal Education and Action Fund (LEAF), an organization created specifically to undertake test-case litigation to advance the interests of women.[64] LEAF argued that 'the traditional two party model of litigation is ... structurally inadequate to respond to the diversity of interests arising in ... "public interest" litigation.' A restrictive intervention rule 'will effectively deny the poor and disadvantaged sectors of society, who are least able to initiate the litigation themselves, access to a process which will have a significant impact on their rights.'

The deficiency of the Court's restrictive practice was shown in the Labour Trilogy where the federal government and nine provinces persuaded the Court that the Charter did not protect the right to strike[65] and yet the Canadian Labour Congress had been denied intervention status. As CLC President Shirley Carr would later complain: 'On the most significant *Charter* issue affecting Canadian workers ever to come before the Supreme Court, the central voice of labour was not heard.'[66]

The issue was discussed at various Court conferences, but the Court's policy remained unsettled. Dickson's views on the question were softening and he gradually became receptive to a more liberal policy. He asked James MacPherson for his views, explaining that 'there is a difficult balance to be struck here between, on the one hand, seeking and receiving the best and most creative legal arguments available and, on the other, not further overburdening the already taxed hearing process.' MacPherson advised Dickson that 'at least in the early [Charter] cases, the Court should have a liberal policy with respect to interventions' to ensure that it got the benefit 'of some of the really creative research and thinking that major civil liberties organizations are conducting ... that lawyers in private practice may not have the time or skill to prepare.'[67] Allowing interventions would also balance the scales since governments are freely allowed to intervene and almost invariably argue for a restrictive interpretation of the Charter. MacPherson suggested that the way to avoid overloading the Court's process was to adopt a liberal policy on written briefs but to restrict participation at oral hearings.

The CCLA continued to press for change and, when all else failed, made its concerns known to the public. Kirk Makin wrote a *Globe and Mail* article in early March 1986 based on CCLA associate chair Ken Swan's toughly worded paper alleging that the Court had decided to withdraw intervenor privileges in a manner that is 'almost wholly inarticulate, taken behind closed doors, for no expressed reasons.' Swan speculated that the Court's policy was based on expediency. 'The best guess is that a combination of illness among the judges and a constantly increasing case load had put the court far behind in dealing with its docket.' He complained that the only response the CCLA had received to its earlier submissions was that the matter had been referred to the Supreme Court advisory committee, a body that met privately. 'To date, no response has been received from either the committee or the court. It ... seems wrong that the only forum for approaching the Supreme Court on important questions of policy is a committee whose existence is not widely known.'[68]

The *Globe and Mail* article caught Dickson's attention. He was always sensitive to public criticism of the Court and he seized upon the article as a way of getting the intervention issue resolved. He immediately sent a memorandum to his colleagues: 'I attach a copy of an article which appeared recently in the *Globe and Mail* which you may not have seen, relating to intervenor privileges. I am placing this item on the agenda for the next Conference.'[69] Within a few weeks, he read a well-researched and critical article by Jillian Welch, a University of Toronto law student, urging the Court to adopt a more liberal policy, and again he circulated it to his colleagues.[70]

The Court decided to refer the issue to its liaison committee with the Canadian Bar Association where the Court was represented by Estey, McIntyre, and Chouinard. By October 1986, the committee had come up with a recommendation for a moderately liberalized rule that would allow written argument from intervenors who could demonstrate that the parties to the case would not 'adequately or fully present' the legal arguments the intervenor sought to advance. Oral argument would be allowed only if there were special circumstances.[71] This was too little for both Borovoy and Wilson. Borovoy complained to the minister of justice that the proposal was too narrow and that the Court's process for considering the matter was flawed.[72] He pointed out that, in a challenge to Canada's hate-propaganda law, it would be dangerous for the Court to limit itself to the hatemonger's version of freedom of expression and exclude from consideration other more moderate views. Wilson thought it wrong to limit intervenors to new points of law and responded to Estey's 'reservations about wide open interventions'[73] by reiterating their importance in human rights and Charter cases. She pointed out that the parties tended to focus on the specific facts of the case while intevenors helped the Court understand the broader implications; and she reminded her colleagues how helpful the disabled groups had been in the *O'Malley* case on the issue of indirect or 'effects discrimination.'[74]

By December 1986, the Court had settled on a new rule that at least partially met Wilson's concerns. Intervenors would not have to demonstrate a distinctive legal argument, but only 'reasons for believing that the submissions would be useful to the Court and different from those of the other parties.' Intervenors were not allowed to make oral argument 'unless otherwise ordered by a Judge.'[75]

Perhaps more significant than the text of the rule was the manner in which it was interpreted. The Court began to adopt a much more liberal approach, rejecting a subsequent CBA recommendation to saddle intervenors with costs since these groups typically had limited resources. They should not be penalized 'for doing precisely what the Court wants ... bring[ing] a different perspective and a different legal argument to an appeal.'[76] It was clear that Wilson's views had prevailed, that Alan Borovoy's efforts had borne fruit, and that Dickson's views had changed. In the years to follow, interventions would become commonplace in Charter cases and often the arguments presented by intervenors would influence the result.

Standing and Mootness: Trying to Dodge Foetal Rights

The traditional rules relating to standing and intervention came under severe strain as the Supreme Court of Canada assumed a more overt lawmaking role. Here again Bora Laskin laid some important groundwork. In the mid-1970s, under Laskin's leadership, the Supreme Court developed an important exception to the standing rule for constitutional cases. The Court recognized that there were some situations where laws would be effectively immune from constitutional challenge if concerned citizens with no immediate stake were not permitted to sue. The first case, *Thorson*, involved a challenge to the federal Official Languages Act. The law imposed duties upon governments but conferred no individual rights and imposed no penalties. Given the very nature of the law, it would never give rise to a concrete dispute involving a specific legal right that would satisfy the rules for standing. Laskin's majority judgment refused to countenance a situation in which 'a question of constitutionality should be immunized from judicial review by denying standing to anyone to challenge the impugned statute.'[77] This principle was expanded a year later in *McNeil* when Laskin, writing for the Court, allowed a concerned citizen to challenge the constitutionality of Nova Scotia's scheme of film censorship, used to ban *Last Tango in Paris*.[78]

Anti-abortion crusader Joe Borowski decided to take advantage of the expanded standing rules in a case that he started in the late 1970s and that took him before the Supreme Court on two occasions. Borowski resigned as an NDP provincial cabinet minister in Manitoba in 1971 to protest the government's support for hospital abortion committees, and, shortly before his case reached the Supreme Court, he had gone on an eighty-day anti-abortion hunger strike. He alleged that the Criminal Code provisions dealing with abortion failed to accord adequate protection to foetal rights. The Criminal Code applied only to illegal abortions and Borowski's complaint was that the law did not go far enough. Borowski started his case before the enactment of the Charter, relying on the Canadian Bill of Rights guarantee of the right to life. Because he obviously lacked any immediate personal stake, he sued as a concerned citizen. The attorney general argued that Borowski lacked sufficient interest to sue and attempted to short circuit the case with a preliminary challenge to Borowski's standing. That issue came before the Supreme Court in 1981.

Borowski argued that, if he were not allowed to sue, the issue of protection of foetal rights could never be litigated. Though he cited Laskin's earlier decisions in *Thorson* and *McNeil*, he got an inkling of Laskin's reaction when he rose to object in the middle of the oral hearing and Laskin ordered him removed from the court.[79] Dickson summarized the issue in his conference notes: 'The first and basic question is the extent to which we wish to permit the ordinary citizen without any particular 'special' interest to have standing. If the answer is to encourage this sort of thing then the matter of Borowski's standing presents no problem. We would simply recognize his right to proceed as he has done.'[80]

There was a consensus, not shared by Laskin, that to refuse Borowski, the Court would have to pull back from the *McNeil* decision by excluding Bill of Rights cases or by 'emphasiz[ing] that standing only comes when no other means of challenge is available.' As Dickson noted, even if the second distinction held, 'it is not clear how the validity of the abortion provisions of the Criminal Code could be challenged otherwise than in the manner selected by Borowski.' A second conference was held. Laskin remained adamant that the Court should close the door on Borowski. Although the other members of the Court lacked enthusiasm for allowing Borowski to proceed, they had difficulty seeing how he could be stopped in light of Laskin's earlier rulings: 'The

Chief Justice will try to distinguish the judgments of this Court in *Thorson* and *McNeil*. Most of us think that this will be a rather difficult task.'[81] Laskin did his best to distinguish the earlier cases, but only Lamer agreed with him. Martland wrote a strong opinion stating that Borowski's case fell squarely within the precedents. Dickson was undecided. Less than two weeks before the judgment was released, he told Laskin: 'I am still struggling with this one.'[82] In the end, Dickson agreed with Martland's majority judgment that Borowski had standing and refused to join Laskin's passionate dissent that Borowski's 'emotional response' to the legislation was not enough.[83]

The *Borowski* case went back to the Saskatchewan courts where his plea for foetal rights failed.[84] By the time the matter reached the Supreme Court again in the summer of 1988, there had been two important developments. The Charter had been enacted and in the second Morgentaler case the Supreme Court had struck down Canada's abortion law.[85] Borowski tried to turn both developments to his advantage. The Charter's constitutional protection of the right to life was a more powerful tool than the statutory Bill of Rights and the demise of the Criminal Code abortion provisions in *Morgentaler II* meant that there was a complete vacuum of legal protection for the unborn. Once again, the attorney general tried to derail Borowski's constitutional challenge. Initially, government lawyers asked Dickson, as chief justice, to postpone Borowski's appeal indefinitely since the abortion law had been struck down in *Morgentaler II* and Parliament was debating other options presented by the Mulroney Conservative government. Although such motions were usually heard in chambers, Dickson made a point of hearing the government's request in an open court and he allowed all the intervenors to make submissions. Dickson questioned why the government had not brought a formal motion to declare the case moot. In the end, he refused the federal government's request for an adjournment.

This brought the politically contentious abortion issue back to the Court's docket in the fall of 1988. It soon became apparent that the judges wanted to avoid the issue of foetal rights at all costs. Dickson went into the hearing armed with a forceful bench memorandum from his law clerk, Martha Shaffer, arguing that the Court should refuse to hear Borowski's appeal. The case Borowski was now presenting was very different from the one he had presented at trial. Borowski was attempting to transform what had been framed as an attack on the specific legislation the Court had already struck down into 'a highly abstract case for a positive declaration of foetal rights.' Shaffer arged that 'this metamorphosis would represent a fundamental change between the case he argued in the courts below and the case he is presenting at the Court.'[86] Dickson's conference notes indicate that Wilson and L'Heureux-Dubé were inclined to decide the case on the merits and hold that the foetus was not protected under the Charter, but that the other judges were determined to avoid the thorny and loaded abortion issue. Led by John Sopinka, the prevailing view at conference was that the case should be dismissed on the ground that, since the Criminal Code abortion provisions Borowski attacked had been struck down in *Morgentaler II*, the issue was now moot and Borowski had 'lost his standing.' 'If we sought to give a "yes" answer to the s. 7 question,' argued Sopinka, 'the ramifications would be incalculable ... What is required is legislation by Parliament and cooperation with the provinces. There can be no balancing within s. 1 because there is no legislation.' McIntyre took an even stronger stand: 'It would be the height of irresponsibility to get into the merits.'[87]

Sopinka agreed to write the judgment and he was able to convince all members of the Court, including Wilson and L'Heureux-Dubé, that Borowski's case should be dismissed without any decision on foetal rights. Sopinka wrote that answering the abstract legal question of foetal rights under the Charter would 'pre-empt a possible decision of Parliament by dictating the form of legislation it should enact. To do so would be a marked departure from the traditional role of the court.'[88]

However, the issue of foetal rights simply would not go away. Within a few months of the release of *Borowski*, the Court was again asked to decide the issue, this time on an emergency basis. In July 1989 Jean-Guy Tremblay was awarded an injunction to prevent his former girlfriend, Chantal Daigle, from obtaining an abortion. Tremblay, a former nightclub bouncer, had proposed marriage to Daigle. She had turned him down and reported him for physical abuse. A divided Quebec Court of Appeal upheld Tremblay's injunction. The case was argued under Quebec's Civil Code and Charter of Human Rights and Freedoms, but it clearly had implications for the Charter issue the Court had ducked in *Borowski*.

The case arose in the summer when the Court was not scheduled to sit and when most of the judges were far from Ottawa on vacation. Dickson was determined to have the Court move with uncommon speed to hear the appeal. He immediately recalled five judges for an expedited hearing to decide whether the Supreme Court should hear the case. On 1 August 1989 Dickson, Wilson, Sopinka, Gonthier, and Cory granted leave to appeal. Since Daigle was already in the twenty-first week of her pregnancy, they ordered that the appeal be heard one week later. Dickson assembled the remaining judges for the hearing. He reached Lamer on his yacht at the foot of the Statute of Liberty. McLachlin rushed back from a European vacation. During the week leading up to the hearing, the Court granted intervenor status to LEAF, the Canadian Abortion Rights Action League, and the Canadian Civil Liberties Association, all supporting Chantal Daigle's position, and Campaign Life, REAL Women, and Physicians for Life, all supporting Jean-Guy Tremblay's position. Even in an emergency, the Court now welcomed the assistance of intervenors.

The Court heard argument from Daigle's lawyers on the morning of 8 August. As Dickson's bench notes indicates, Daigle's lawyers argued that, as a result of the injunction, she was the only woman in Canada who could not have an abortion. Daigle swore an affidavit stating that she did not wish to have any contact with Tremblay nor did she want to bear his child. She argued that a decision to prevent her from having an abortion would cause her 'irreparable psychological and moral harm in the future' and that she feared that any child would not be brought up 'in a serene stable family environment in which there is no violence.'[89]

After the lunch break, Daigle's lawyer, Daniel Bedard, returned to Court completely shaken. He informed the court's registrar, Guy Goulard, that he had some unexpected news for the Court. When Court resumed, Bedard told the judges that he had just learned that his twenty-one-year-old client had decided to take the law into her own hands: she had had an abortion in the United States. Bedard apologized to the court, saying: 'I am not asking for understanding. I am not saying this is acceptable behaviour.'[90]

Daigle's action gave the Court the chance once again to dodge the issue of foetal rights. She had procured the abortion she wanted and, so far as she and Tremblay were concerned, there was nothing more to litigate. The Court could follow the course it had taken in *Borowski* and leave the controversial issue for another day. Tremblay's lawyers, eager to preserve their win before the Quebec Court of Appeal, argued that the case was now moot and should not be decided. Daigle's lawyers, however, reminded the Court that other courts had granted injunctions and that other women would be affected in the future.

The Court retired to consider the matter. Dickson was furious and he wanted to end the case on the spot. He had taken the unusual step of convening the Court in the summer months only to have Daigle thumb her nose at the whole process. Dickson had always reacted strongly to deliberate and calculated decisions to break the law. It was entirely possible that the Court could have ended the hearing as moot at that point. Had that occurred, Daigle might also have been found in contempt of court.

A comment by Beverley McLachlin, however, seems to have changed Dickson's mind. She suggested that the Court put themselves 'in Daigle's shoes.' Daigle's pregnancy was already well past three months. She was a desperate young woman who did not want to have the child of the man who had abused her. Daigle had no idea when she would have an answer from the Court and likely knew that the judges could take months to decide such a difficult issue. Could she really be blamed for going to the United States to have her abortion? McLachlin's plea carried the day: 'I thought I could almost see [Dickson's] face change, I don't want to attribute this to my eloquence, there was nothing eloquent to what I said, but he was seeing it from her point of view.' The experience convinced McLachlin 'that you need a different variety of perspectives on the Court ... you never know when the critical thing could be someone ... saying. "Well, maybe you need to look at it from that point of view, maybe in this case, a woman's point of view." Not that a man couldn't have seen it that way – ultimately they did, but it wasn't the way it immediately hit them.' The exchange also revealed that there were 'many elements of [Dickson's] personality; he was angry because this was not the respectful way to treat a Court ... but he was also capable of coming right around and seeing the situation' from another perspective.[91] The man who had grown up with parents who differed on the emotional issue of Ireland's relation to the United Kingdom, and who had spent much of his career on the Supreme Court seeking halfway houses of compromises, could see both side of this difficult issue. The Court decided to resume the hearing. At the end of the long and surprising day, Dickson announced: 'We are all of the view that the appeal should be allowed. The Court will give reasons at a later date for this conclusion.'[92] Despite taking the law into her own hands, Daigle had won the day since the Court was convinced that there was no legal authority supporting her ex-boyfriend's injunction preventing her from obtaining an abortion.

Reactions to the Court's decisions that day were mixed. Speaking to reporters, Tremblay threatened contempt proceedings. Daigle, he said, had 'killed my child ... I do what a father has to do. The fight's not over.' Tremblay's own lawyer, however, suggested that a contempt-of-court charge would only make Daigle 'a hero.' Henry Morgentaler applauded the ruling: 'It's a happy day for women in Canada and especially for the women of Quebec, who up to now could have had doubts in their minds about if they could have an abortion.'[93] The *Globe and Mail* praised the Court for ending the case 'with merciful dispatch' and argued that 'now the abortion debate should return to the proper forum for contentious matters – the Parliament of Canada.'[94]

Dickson undertook the task of writing. He felt obliged to deliver the Court's written judgment quickly and, if possible, unanimously. In a memo to the Court in October 1989 that accompanied his draft judgment, Dickson stated: 'I am sure that we all would like the judgment delivered before the introduction of legislation in Parliament.'[95] He had earlier told his colleagues that 'the focus' of his judgment would be 'the question of whether or not a foetus is a "person" under either the Quebec Civil Code or the Quebec Charter' and that his answer would be no. Dickson also proposed to say that a foetus had no legal status under section 7 of the Charter, but that, as discussed in *Morgentaler II*, the protection of the foetus could be a valid governmental objective under section 1.[96] When Dickson circulated his draft judgment along these lines,[97] La Forest immediately indicated that did not think it appropriate for the Court to deal with the issue of foetal rights under the Charter and that he would be writing on narrower grounds.[98]

This prompted Dickson to pull back. He did not want a divided opinion. Although it seems possible that he might have attracted a majority of the Court on his more broadly based draft, he preferred an immediate and unanimous decision on narrower grounds. After a series of meetings with his colleagues and by making substantial concessions to La Forest and to Gonthier, who shared La Forest's concerns, Dickson was able to achieve a unanimous consensus. In the final version, styled 'by the Court' but written by Dickson, he removed the discussion of foetal rights under section 7 of the Charter.[99] The Charter was mentioned but avoided on the ground that, since the suit was one between private parties, it did not apply. *Borowski* was also cited as justification for not deciding the issue of whether the foetus had rights under the Charter. The Court had decided the legal issue of whether the Quebec legislature had intended to give the foetus the rights of a person, but it refused to 'enter the philosophic and theological' or 'scientific' debates 'about whether or not the foetus is a person' on the ground that 'decisions based upon broad social, political, moral and economic choices are more appropriately left to the legislature.' Dickson declined to adopt La Forest's suggestion that the case be decided on the even narrower basis that an injunction was not an appropriate remedy since it amounted to an invasion of Parliament's criminal-law power. He convinced his colleagues that it was appropriate to decide that there was no substantive basis under Quebec law for the injunction 'in order to try to ensure that another woman is not put through an ordeal such as that experienced by Ms. Daigle.'[100]

Although the judgment was considerably less expansive than Dickson had first proposed, perhaps even less expansive than the majority judgments in *Morgentaler II*, it did establish that the foetus was not included in the reference to a human being under Quebec's Civil Code or in the term 'human being' used in the Quebec Charter. The Court also stressed that not one single case supported the idea that the father had a right in the foetus. The Charter had been avoided, but the judgment certainly hinted that the issue of foetal rights would likely be decided the same way under the Charter.

Prudent Judicial Lawmaking

Daigle showed how far the Court had moved away from some of its earlier concerns about judicial lawmaking. Realizing the importance of the case, the Court made itself available on short notice, listened to a wide range of intervenors, and resisted the temptation to avoid deciding the case when it became moot. At the same time, however, at La Forest's urging, the Court had acted prudently, avoiding sweeping pronouncements that would later tie its hands or the hands of Parliament. As in *Morgentaler II*, the Supreme Court had respected Parliament's lawmaking role and left it considerable room to enact a new abortion law. The Mulroney Conservative government introduced a bill that would allow abortions if a doctor concluded that the continuation of the pregnancy would threaten the life or physical, mental, or psychological health of the woman. In 1991, the year after Dickson retired from the Court, this proposal floundered on a tied vote in the Senate, with pro-life and pro-choice senators opposing the new law as either too liberal or too restrictive. To this day, Canada does not have a criminal law governing abortion, not because the Supreme Court said that constitution does not allow it, but because the legislative process failed to reach consensus.

19

Equality Rights

Equality is universally recognized as a fundamental human right and essential democratic value. But equality means different things to different people and Canada's conception of equality has evolved over time. Defining equality and mapping out the best path to its achievement is a difficult and contentious topic of philosophical, political, and legal debate.

As a law student, Dickson was imbued with the model of formal equality – the idea that the same standards should be applied to all citizens in an even-handed manner. Immediately after the Second World War, the focus shifted to equal opportunity with an emphasis on legislation to eradicate the evils of racism and other forms of direct discrimination. In the Charter era, equality advocates focused their attention on systemic discrimination and the adverse effects of apparently neutral criteria. The courts and the judiciary replaced the legislatures as the primary initiators of equality.

Before his appointment to the bench, Dickson lived a life of affluence and privilege, associated with powerful business interests and the social elite, hardly the background one would expect of a man who would be attentive to the arguments of disadvantaged minorities. However, from his early years as a judge, Dickson was at the liberal edge of judicial thinking on equality and his general jurisprudential outlook was informed by his views on equality. His Manitoba Court of Appeal judgment in *Canard*, striking down a section of the *Indian Act* that deprived an aboriginal widow of the right to administer her husband's estate as contrary to the Canadian Bill of Rights, indicated his early opposition to formal discrimination, while his trial decision upholding the collective rights of the Hutterites, as well as his decision in *Big M*, demonstrated his respect for religious minorities. Other early decisions revealed Dickson's concerns for the rights of disadvantaged groups such as prisoners and farm women. But, as in so many other areas, Dickson's thinking on equality was far from static. Bertha Wilson, the Court's leading exponent of equality during Dickson's time on the Court, thought that among her colleagues, Dickson 'changed the most.'[1]

Women's Rights: Pregnancy and Sex Discrimination

The evolution in Canadian law and social attitudes, as well as in Dickson's own thinking, is evident in his treatment of women's rights. From the perspective of women's rights, he certainly did not steer an entirely steady course. Strongly influenced by the examples of his own mother and of Barbara, he instinctively wanted to treat women as equals. His sense of fairness and decency was offended when Helen Rathwell, Rosa Becker, and Mary Sorochan were denied their equitable share of the farms they had helped build upon family breakdown.[2] Yet many women found him to be excessively preoccupied with the rights of the accused in sexual-assault cases[3] and unsympathetic to abortion rights in the first *Morgentaler* case.[4] Furthermore, in 1979, Dickson signed the Supreme Court's unanimous but controversial *Bliss* judgment,[5] which held that denying pregnant women unemployment-insurance benefits available to other workers did not amount to sex discrimination.

Roland Ritchie, author of the famous *Drybones* decision[6] that had breathed life into the Canadian Bill of Rights, also wrote the Court's unanimous judgment in *Bliss*. Adopting a very formal definition of equality, Ritchie ruled that the law distinguished between unemployed workers not on grounds of their sex but on grounds of pregnancy and that there was nothing wrong with that. The Court solemnly proclaimed: 'Any inequality between the sexes in this area is not created by legislation but by nature.' Ritchie also held that government-conferred benefit schemes could not be challenged and limited the protection of equality to 'denial of equality of treatment in the administration and enforcement of the law before the ordinary courts of the land as was the case in *Drybones*.'[7] The judgment in *Bliss* was a low point for the Supreme Court. To find a judgment more disappointing to those who fought for women's equality rights, one would have to go back to the Court's 1928 decision that the constitution's provision for the appointment of 'qualified Persons' to the Senate did not include women.[8]

Ten years after *Bliss*, the Court heard two appeals from Dickson's former judicial home, the Manitoba Court of Appeal, involving similar issues of gender discrimination. The first case, *Brooks v. Canada Safeway Ltd.*,[9] revisited the issue of pregnancy and sex discrimination. The second, *Jansen v. Platy Enter-*

prises Ltd.,[10] asked whether sexual harassment amounted to sex discrimination under human rights legislation.

Pregnant women employed by Canada Safeway, one of Dickson's former clients, were denied certain accident and sickness benefits available to other workers under the company's benefit plan. Three part-time cashiers challenged the exclusion as sex discrimination under Manitoba's Human Rights Act.[11] They were aided by LEAF, a highly successful feminist litigation and lobby group that had played an influential role when the Charter was drafted. Faced with *Bliss*, the complaint of discrimination failed before the Human Rights Board of Adjudication[12] and in the Manitoba courts.[13] Patricia Allen, one of the complainants, explained that she had applied for benefits when her doctor advised her to avoid standing on her feet at the checkout counter because it affected her blood and weight. She thought it 'incredibly unfair' when she was denied sickness benefits simply because she was pregnant; after all, she said, 'women having babies is a fact of life.'[14] That was precisely the conclusion reached by the Supreme Court. After the case had been argued, the conference discussion was brief and decisive: *Bliss* had to be overruled.[15] Dickson explained in his conference memo: 'As Beetz and I are the sole survivors of the *Bliss* case, it was felt that either one of us should write and I volunteered.'

Although *Bliss* had been decided only ten years earlier, Dickson overruled it as reflecting the thinking of another age: 'I am prepared to say that *Bliss* was wrongly decided or, in any event, that *Bliss* would not be decided now as it was decided then.' Given the participation of women in the labour force, Dickson held that society had to accommodate the combination of 'paid work with motherhood' and 'the childbearing needs of working women.' Echoing the language of *Morgentaler II*, Dickson wrote: 'It is only women who bear children; no man can become pregnant.' A distinction based on pregnancy could affect only women and therefore amounted to sex discrimination. It would, Dickson believed, be profoundly 'unfair to impose all of the costs of pregnancy upon one half of the population.' While pregnancy is voluntary and not an illness, to exclude it as a valid health-related reason for being absent from work would, said Dickson, defy social reality: 'Viewed in its social context pregnancy provides a perfectly legitimate health-related reason for not working and as such it should be compensated.'[16]

In the companion case, Dianna Platy, a waitress in a Winnipeg restaurant, had quit her job when her employer failed to deal with the conduct of the cook who repeatedly grabbed her legs and touched her knee, rear, and crotch area. When she resisted his sexual advances, he told her she would be fired and yelled at her in front of other staff, criticizing her work. Another female employee, Tracy Govereau, made a similar complaint against the same employer. Platy and Govereau alleged that the acts of sexual harassment amounted to sex discrimination. The Manitoba Human Rights Act did not explicitly deal with sexual harassment, but the human rights adjudicator found that the employer's conduct amounted to sex discrimination.[17] The Manitoba Court of Appeal disagreed and ruled that sexual harassment was a wrong done to an individual rather than to women as a group and that it did not amount to discrimination on grounds of sex.[18]

Dickson rejected that argument and applied the reasoning in *Brooks*. Only women can become pregnant and, as a matter of social reality, only women run the risk of sexual harassment. 'To argue that the sole factor underlying the discriminatory action was the sexual attractiveness of the appellants and to say that their gender was irrelevant strains credulity. Sexual attractiveness cannot be separated from gender.' Dickson adopted the argument made by LEAF in support of Jensen and Govereau that 'sexual harassment is a form of sex discrimination because it denies women equality of opportunity in employment because of their sex.'[19]

Brooks and *Jansen* represented major victories for the women's movement. Economic disadvantage flowing from pregnancy and the care of children was and still is a fundamental problem for women. Although the decision in *Bliss* had long been discredited, it remained the law of the land and stood in the way of full recognition of equality rights for women until it was reversed by the supreme court. Similarly, sexual harassment in the workplace is an all too prevalent practice that harms female workers. The refusal of the Manitoba Court of Appeal to recognize sexual harassment as a form of sex discrimination was out of line with academic opinion and the prevalent line of lower court authority, but, until the Supreme Court spoke, the matter was not finally resolved. By overruling *Bliss* and so strongly endorsing the concept that discrimination law would not tolerate burdening women unfairly as a result of pregnancy, or with the indignity and humiliation of sexual harassment, Dickson had sent a clear message. His judgments echoed the arguments advanced by feminist advocates who applauded the rulings as 'a tremendous leap forward for sexual equality' since they 'will increase women's ability to participate more fully in the workplace.'[20] Litigant Patricia Allen, who had fought for seven years to reach the nation's highest court, said: 'I'm glad we did it because, for pregnant women, this is a great thing.'[21] Dickson's former law clerk, Katherine Swinton, who years earlier had convinced him to adopt gender-neutral language in his judgments, observed: 'There's been a real education in rights and equality concepts, both in society and in the courts.'[22] The nation's chief justice and the other members of its highest court understood and were sympathetic to the legitimate concerns of the modern Canadian women who sought equality in the workplace.

'To break a continuing cycle of systemic discrimination'

Dickson's thinking on equality was undoubtedly influenced by his war injury. He knew from his own personal experience about suffering and the limitations a disability could impose. Bertha Wilson thought that Dickson's war injury was a powerful force that made him sympathetic to the claims of the vulnerable or disadvantaged.[23] Yet the way Dickson dealt with his injury might suggest that he would not be particularly sympathetic to affirmative measures designed to accommodate difference. Dickson adamantly refused to be identified as 'disabled' and resented any efforts at accommodation that would draw attention to his amputation. He was determined to live his life unaided as if he were completely able-bodied. This remained true even as he neared retirement and had greater difficulty walking. Antonio Lamer could see that the shiny granite floor outside the judges' chambers on the second floor of the Supreme Court Building was like a sheet of ice for Dickson. But he knew that any suggestion that carpet be installed for Dickson's benefit would be firmly rebuffed. So he resorted to a ruse. When Lamer complained about the noise from the clicking heels of women's shoes. Dickson responded: 'You can't ask them to wear running shoes.' Lamer replied: 'No [but] we could have a nice carpet that would go all around.' Dickson agreed and a regal red carpet was installed.[24]

Dickson, however, did not transfer his attitude towards his own physical disability when it came to disadvantages faced by others. He confronted the contentious issues of systemic discrimination and affirmative action in *C.N.R. v. Canada (Human Rights Commission)*, better known as *Action Travail des Femmes*,[25] decided in June 1987. Women then comprised only 6 per cent of Canadian National's workforce, well below the 13 per cent national average for women in blue-collar jobs. A Human Rights Tribunal found that discriminatory attitudes prevailed. Women were regarded as 'disruptive,' not 'tough enough to handle supervisory jobs,' and having 'no drive, no ambition, no initiative.'[26] One male worker was quoted as saying that a 'big problem to adding women to train crews would be policing the morals in the cabooses.' Another summed it up this way: 'Railroading is a man's sport.' The tribunal concluded that CN's recruitment and hiring policies discouraged women from applying and that no real effort was being made by CN to deal with the problem. Believing that a special employment program was needed, it ordered CN to hire at least one woman in four to fill positions not traditionally held by women until the national average was reached. The Federal Court of Appeal allowed CN's appeal on the ground that the tribunal had no power to impose an equity program designed to prevent future discrimination as a cure for past wrongs.[27]

At conference,[28] all nine judges agreed that the Human Rights Tribunal's order had to be restored, and that Dickson would write the judgment, but the Court was divided on how to approach the case. As Dickson put it: 'Should we write on the narrow basis or broadly or somewhere in between?' Lamer and McIntyre were inclined to decide the case on purely administrative-law grounds – that the Human Rights Tribunal's decision was not 'patently unreasonable' and therefore the Federal Court of Appeal should not have interfered. This would allow the Court to avoid discussing the thorny issue of affirmative action. Wilson, however, disagreed and urged her colleagues to say something positive about affirmative action.

Dickson was non-committal at conference, but he was attracted by Wilson's argument. As he recorded in his conference memo: 'At lunch, I asked Justice Wilson to give me a memorandum of her views so that I could give them full consideration when drafting the reasons.' In her memorandum, Wilson argued that the parties had come all the way to the Supreme Court, at great cost, and they were entitled to a full explanation of the powers of the Human Rights Commission. In the face of the rather firm pronouncement by the majority of the Federal Court of Appeal against affirmative-action measures, a decision reversing on the ground that the Tribunal's decision was not 'patently unreasonable' would be a feeble response. Wilson urged Dickson to take a stand and to disagree expressly with what the Federal Court had said. She conceded that, strictly speaking, it was not necessary to say anything definitive about affirmative action, but she added that while the Court's comments might be *obiter*, 'it will be pretty persuasive *obiter* if it is contained in a unanimous judgment of this Court!' She also said that, if the other judges could not be persuaded, 'I will, of course, go along (if somewhat sheepishly) with the narrow basis for the decision.'[29]

Stephen Toope, Dickson's law clerk, recommended strongly that he follow Wilson's advice and approach the case from a broad perspective, addressing the 'jurisdictional and substantive question whether a Tribunal appointed under the Canadian Human Rights Act may issue an "affirmative action" order to deal with the problem of systemic discrimination.'[30] Dickson decided to write a strong endorsement of the authority of the Human Rights Commission to impose employment equity. Human rights legislation, Dickson insisted, has to be given a generous interpretation. Its purpose is to prevent discrimination, not punish wrongdoing. A 'fault based' approach would make anti-discrimination laws ineffective. It is difficult to prove intent, and to focus on deliberate wrongdoing would fail 'to respond adequately to the many instances where the effect of policies and practices is discriminatory even if that effect is unintended and unforeseen.'[31]

Dickson accepted the concept of systemic discrimination, adopting the analysis suggested by Rosalie Abella in *The Report of the Commission on Equality in Employment* (1984). He also shared the view that 'systemic discrimination' results from 'the simple operation of established procedures of recruitment, hiring and promotion, none of which is necessarily designed to promote discrimination.' The resulting exclusion of the disadvantaged group reinforced the discrimination 'because the exclusion fosters the belief, both within and outside the group, that the exclusion is the result of "natural" forces, for example, that women "just can't do the job."' In addition, Dickson found that, 'to combat systemic discrimination, it is essential to create a climate in which both negative practices and negative attitudes can be challenged and discouraged.'[32]

The Human Rights Act authorized remedies 'to prevent' discrimination and Dickson agreed with the dissenting judgment of former justice minister Mark MacGuigan in the Federal Court of Appeal that the employment-equity program ordered by the Human Rights Tribunal could be justified as a forward-looking, preventive measure 'to break a continuing cycle of systemic discrimination.' Dickson emphasized that the goal of employment equity was not to compensate victims of discrimination or to deal with the plight of specific individuals but 'to ensure that future applicants and workers from the affected group will not face the same insidious barriers that blocked their forebears.' Employment equity, he wrote, defeats intentional discrimination, provides women and other victims of stereotypical attitudes an opportunity to show their worth and disprove the stereotype, and helps create a 'critical mass' of the target group to pave the way for others.[33]

Dickson's efforts proved attractive to his colleagues and the judgment was unanimous. *Action Travail des Femmes* marked an important step in the evolution of Canadian human rights law. The Court had endorsed the concept of systemic discrimination and the need to focus on actual outcomes rather than abstract generalizations. Dickson's judgment recognized affirmative-action measures as a legitimate remedial and preventive tool.

Dickson consistently supported the liberal rulings from human rights commissions, even when doing so led him to dissent. In *Bhinder*,[34] the Canadian Human Rights Commission had ruled that Canadian National's hard-hat rule discriminated against a Sikh who wore traditional headdress. In separate majority judgments, Wilson and McIntyre held that, because the hard-hat rule met the statutory exemption for a bona fide occupational requirement, CN was under no duty to accommodate Bhinder's religious practice; and that, by insisting that he comply with the hard-hat rule, CN was not guilty of religious discrimination. Dickson disagreed with his colleagues that the statutory defence of bona fide occupational requirement was intended 'to obliterate the duty to accommodate.' He thought that the majority's reasoning significantly undermined 'the effectiveness of the Act in curbing adverse effect discrimination ... contrary to the express and implied purposes of the Act.'[35] Since CN could not show that it would suffer undue hardship if required to accommodate the religious practice, Dickson thought that Bhinder's right to be free of discrimination should prevail. His dissent was driven by his profound respect for religious difference and his concern with the discriminatory effects that seemingly neutral rules have on minorities. His position was vindicated five years later in one of his last cases when Wilson reversed her position and the Court reversed *Bhinder*.[36]

Equality and the Criminal Law

Dickson did not write in the Supreme Court's early cases dealing with equality rights under section 15 of the Charter. He made his only direct contribution to section 15 jurisprudence in a series of related decisions involving young offenders[37] that he wrote almost by accident. Federal legislation provided for an alternative-measures program offering various non-custodial sanctions for young offenders. It was left to the provinces to implement these programs. Most provinces implemented the scheme but Ontario decided not to do so. Several young offenders challenged Ontario's decision on various grounds, including the contention that the province's failure to provide an alternative-measures program violated section 15. When the cases were argued in March 1989, there was no doubt expressed at conference that the constitutional challenge failed. La Forest agreed to write.[38] However, seven months later in October, La Forest was bogged down with other judgments and Dickson took on the task.[39]

Dickson's judgments provide an interesting window on his views of the relationship between federalism and the Charter. The argument that the alternate-measures scheme violated equality rubbed against the grain of Dickson's concept of federalism. He construed the federal legislation as being permissive, offering the provinces a choice, and found that to require uniformity across the country under the equality guarantee would be to deny both the permissive nature of the federal legislation and the inherent diversity of federalism. As his *Hauser* judgment showed, he believed strongly in the local application of the criminal law to accommodate local conditions.[40] Citing an academic paper by his former law clerk, Katherine Swinton,[41] Dickson wrote: 'The federal system of government itself demands that the values underlying section 15(1) cannot be given unlimited scope.' Drawing upon the division of powers in relation to the criminal law, he pointed out that 'differential application of federal law can be a legitimate means of forwarding the values of a federal system.'[42]

Dickson was more willing to accept equality arguments in criminal cases that affected the interests of disadvantaged groups. A 1984 Dickson decision involved a caregiver named Ogg-Moss who was charged with assault after he struck a twenty-one-year-old resident on the head five times. The victim had an IQ of 20, could not speak, and had spilt his milk in order to get Ogg-Moss' attention. Ogg-Moss relied on section 43 of the Criminal Code, which authorized schoolteachers, parents, and those standing in their place to use reasonable force 'by way of correction toward a pupil or child' in their care. Even though he was in a minority at conference,[43] Dickson wrote first reasons that became the Court's unanimous judgment upholding the conviction and giving the defence of use of force a narrow interpretation. It was one thing to excuse parents and teachers for 'what would otherwise be criminal force by one group of persons against another,' but quite another to deprive children and the disabled of 'the equal protection we normally assume is offered by the criminal law.'[44] Dickson saw the equality implications of the case at a time when equality was rarely considered in criminal law cases: 'I cannot believe that it is the intention of the *Criminal Code* to create such a category of permanent second-class citizens on the basis of a mental or physical handicap.'[45]

Dickson changed his mind on another important criminal-law case with equality implications. At conference he voted to overturn the acquittal of Lyn Lavallee, a battered woman, who had shot her abusive husband in the back of the head after he had threatened her with yet another beating. This initial position was consistent with other cases in which Dickson held that intentional killings should be treated as murder if the accused had engaged in excessive self-defence.[46] Bertha Wilson believed that case raised some important equality issues and accepted the assignment to write the first judgment. She remembered Dickson's initial scepticism about her more lenient view. As they rode the elevator together back to their offices, Dickson 'asked with astonishment, "Why on earth would you volunteer to write on that one?" ... He thought it was an open and shut case. That she [Lavallee] had had it.'[47]

Wilson then drafted a landmark judgment in which she held that evidence heard at trial about battered woman's syndrome was relevant to Lavallee's self-defence claim. She also stressed that the requirement of reasonable conduct for self-defence should be judged on a standard that reflected the gender and experiences of the accused, arguing that 'the definition of what is reasonable must be adapted to circumstances which are, by and large, foreign to the world inhabited by the hypothetical "reasonable man."'[48] Although Dickson had decided, over a Wilson dissent, that it was not necessary to tell the jury to consider a reasonable person of the same gender and age as the accused in a provocation case four years earlier,[49] he changed his mind and concurred with Wilson. Wilson recalls the case as an example of Dickson's open mind and willingness to be persuaded that his initial impression was wrong: 'He came back later ... when he saw the draft' to tell her 'he had been thinking' and that he now agreed with her. 'It was funny because he was of such a strongly opposite view originally.'[50] *Lavallee* demonstrates Dickson's growing attachment to Wilson's equality views and his receptivity to her feminist perspective, which re-examined traditional legal doctrines in light of their effect on women.

Keeping an Open Mind

Dickson did indeed have a remarkable ability to keep an open mind. He was persuaded that *Bliss* was wrong and he said so. He listened to Beverley McLachlin in the *Daigle* case,[51] and to Bertha Wilson in *Action Travail des Femmes* and *Lavallee*. His law clerks were amazed at his intellectual openness.

Perhaps no case illustrates this better than *Gay Alliance*, a case decided in 1979 well before the Charter and the explosion of equality litigation.[52] The British Columbia Human Rights Commission ruled that the Vancouver *Sun* was guilty of discrimination when it refused to carry an advertisement for a gay-rights publication. Dickson's first impression was that the commission's ruling amounted to a serious interference with freedom of the press. He prepared a strongly worded draft judgment, insisting that the Human Rights Code did not permit 'a government agency, by express command, to compel editors and publishers of newspapers to publish what they otherwise would not publish.'[53] In this early draft, he insisted that the 'government agency' should not be allowed to sit 'in the editorial room with a hand on the editor's shoulder.' The draft contained a detailed discussion of American law and a ringing endorsement of freedom of the press. Dickson showed the draft to Laskin, who urged him to reconsider: 'I think, if I may say so, that your judgment is much too strong for the homely set of facts. I still do not see how a mere classified advertisement which expressed no editorial opinion can be said to jeopardize freedom of the press.'[54] Law clerk Rollie Thompson wrote memoranda arguing that the Human Rights Code applied and that the commission's decision should be respected.[55] Although his initial draft reflected the view of the majority of the Court at conference, Dickson reflected on what Laskin and Thompson were saying and did a complete about-face. He became convinced that his initial enthusiasm for freedom of the press was misplaced in this case and that his first draft was inconsistent with the deference he usually accorded administrative tribunals in general and human rights commissions in particular. He rewrote his judgment as a dissent, foregoing the majority he could have secured with his first draft.[56] He now insisted that the decision of the Human Rights Commission was entitled to deference, and he drew a distinction between the newspaper's editorial content, which was protected by freedom of the press, and advertising, which was not.

Hate Speech, Human Dignity, and the Values of Democracy

Dickson's last judgments were released in December 1990, several months after his retirement and only days before the end of the six-month grace period allowed for retired judges to complete their work. They dealt with the constitutionality of hate-propaganda laws, and Dickson gained a four-to-three majority to uphold the laws as reasonable limits on freedom of expression under section 1.[57] The leading judgment, *R v. Keegstra*,[58] is remarkable in many ways. It is one of Dickson's longest: his reasons take up almost one hundred pages in the Supreme Court Reports and they are followed by McLachlin's seventy-page dissent. The background research was unusually broad and eclectic, with Canadian, American, and European authorities canvassed. The judgment surveyed the history of hate-propaganda laws and cited a rich body of legal, philosophical, and historical literature ranging from the liberal perspectives of poet John Milton, philosopher Isaiah Berlin, and civil-liberties activist Alan Borovoy to the critical-race theory of Mari Matsuda and Richard Delgado. But perhaps most remarkable of all is the quality of the debate between Dickson, the retiring chief justice, and McLachlin, a future chief justice. Dickson emphasized the values of equality that motivated the legislation. He urged his colleagues to uphold the anti-hate laws in the name of protecting vulnerable minorities from vilification and defending the values of equality. Dickson thought that, by protecting respect and tolerance for minority groups, the anti-hate law fostered essential democratic values and should be upheld. McLachlin also focused on essential democratic values, but she saw the case essentially in terms of freedom of expression. She argued with equal force that the laws should be struck down as an unjustifiable interference with free and open debate.

James Keegstra taught social studies at a high school in Alberta, and his teaching was strongly influenced by his anti-Semitic views. He taught his students that Jews were deceptive, secretive, and evil and that they sought to destroy Christianity. He blamed Jews for creating economic depressions, wars, and revolutions and asserted that they had created the myth of the Holocaust to gain sympathy. The local school board warned Keegstra that these teachings were unacceptable. He refused to change and was dismissed. Keegstra was then charged with wilful promotion of hatred under the Criminal Code.[59] Keegstra argued that the hate-speech offence should be struck down because it infringed the Charter guarantee of freedom of expression. Dickson and

McLachlin agreed that, despite its vile message, hate speech was a form of expression and that it was protected by section 2(b) of the Charter. The issue that would decide the case was whether the hate speech law could be justified under section 1 as a reasonable limit on freedom of expression. McLachlin agreed with Dickson that, in view of Canada's multicultural and multiracial social fabric, the promotion of tolerance, equality, and non-discrimination and the protection of minority groups from vilification, humiliation, and degradation were sufficiently important to override a protected right or freedom. But there the agreement ended. Dickson insisted that the hate-propaganda law could be upheld as a properly proportional response to a pressing social problem, while McLachlin concluded that it could not.

McLachlin found that the anti-hate laws were not rationally connected with Parliament's laudable goals. She wrote that the anti-hate law prosecutions had the perverse effect of spreading hate rather than curtailing it. Criminal prosecutions against hatemongers served only to give them a platform and level of publicity they could never achieve if left to their own devices, and, furthermore, attempts at suppression did nothing but create martyrs. The vigorous prosecution of anti-hate laws in pre-Nazi Germany was offered as evidence that such laws were at best ineffective and at worst counter-productive. McLachlin also found that the anti-hate laws were not sufficiently precise to survive the minimal impairment test. Again, she called on the lessons of history. Anti-hate laws, she contended, were all too susceptible to misuse. She cited many instances where prosecutions had been brought or threatened against forms of expression plainly tolerable in a free society. Even if such prosecutions might well fail, the very threat of prosecution could have a chilling effect and stifle debate on controversial matters.[60] Race, religion, and cultural difference are issues of significant public concern and often give rise to heated debate; sensitivities run high and some individuals will take offence at what others regard as fair debate. McLachlin wrote that the anti-hate law failed to identify with sufficient precision that which is reprehensible, with the result that it posed an undue risk to vigorous but genuine debate.

In an early draft of *Keegstra*, Dickson had written that hate speech was far from the 'core' of freedom of expression but at the 'periphery' and that a softer section 1 test should apply. Bertha Wilson wanted to uphold the anti-hate law, but she had consistently supported a relatively strict application of the section 1 test and had always shied away from agreeing that there could be varying degrees of scrutiny under section 1. Wilson took issue with Dickson's draft. In a memorandum to Dickson, she stated that she had serious reservations about a 'core' and 'periphery' of freedom of expression. It looked too much like the discredited American 'levels of scrutiny' theory she had been at pains to avoid. She suggested concentrating on the harmful effects of hate propaganda and avoiding reference to the core and peripheral values of section 2(b). 'I can see this core/peripheral distinction taking off if we endorse it in this case and foresee its being applied to *Charter Rights and Freedoms* generally.' Wilson also took issue with a line in Dickson's draft that seemed to be saying that a reason for upholding the law was that it had been passed by a democratically elected legislature. 'I tend to see the *Charter* as an anti-majoritiarian document and the role of the Court to ensure that minorities are not sacrificed to the majority will.' For Wilson, the fact that the legislation had been passed by Parliament was 'a completely neutral factor in the s.1 weigh scales.'[61]

Dickson was prepared to meet Wilson's concerns, since he needed her support to gain a majority and, in any event, thought her comments valid. He rebuilt his section 1 analysis around a contextual approach more likely to find favour with Wilson and expressly rejected 'an inflexible "levels of scrutiny" categorization of expressive activity.' Hate speech qualified as expression and, Dickson conceded, 'I cannot conclude that hate propaganda deserves only marginal protection under the section 1 analysis.' However, Dickson stuck to the central point that he presented in his first draft and that he needed to make to sustain his section 1 analysis. He saw hate speech as inimical to values underlying freedom of expression, and as a consequence, he thought that restictions on hate speech were more easily justified. Dickson refused to accept the civil-libertarian argument that the anti-hate law unduly inhibited democratic debate. In his view, respect for the autonomy and dignity of every participant was a precondition for genuine democratic debate. Hate speech attacked the autonomy and the dignity of members of religious and racial minorities and, Dickson wrote, Parliament was entitled to limit the hatemonger's expression in order to enhance the right of all Canadians to participate in democratic debate. Hate speech also attacked the autonomy rights of those who are its targets. Dickson rejected the contention that the anti-hate law failed the rational-connection test; the very fact of the criminal prohibition had a significant signalling effect. As Dickson put it, 'hate propaganda legislation and trials are a means by which the values beneficial to a free and democratic society can be publicized.' The law's condemnation of the hatemonger's message comforted members of identifiable minorities, reminded the community as a whole of the importance of respecting Canada's diversity, and emphasized the value of equality and the worth and dignity of each individual. Dickson also drew on international law, in particular the *International Convention on the Elimination of All Forms of Racial Discrimination*, to show the importance attached to legal sanctions against racist speech.[62]

Dickson found that anti-hate laws were drawn with sufficient precision to survive the minimal-impairment test. The Criminal Code offence did not apply to private communications, and the prosecution had to prove that the speaker intended the wilful promotion of hatred. The accused is afforded a number of defences, including truth; the good-faith expression of opinion on a religious subject; the reasonable belief in the truth of statements relevant to the public interest, the discussion of which is for the public benefit; and the conviction that the statement was intended in good faith to remove feelings of hatred. Dickson was unmoved by the argument that past experience had shown that the anti-hate law was susceptible to overzealous and inappropriate use by the authorities and that fear of prosecution would chill legitimate expression on sensitive and controversial matters. On his interpretation, 'only the most intentionally extreme forms of expression' were prohibited and 'the possibility of *illegal* police harassment clearly has minimal bearing on the proportionality of hate propaganda legislation to legitimate Parliamentary objectives ...'[63]

Perhaps the most significant feature of Dickson's hate-law judgment was his assessment of the democratic values at issue. Dickson saw the anti-hate law as a legislative initiative to enhance the universal right to equal dignity and respect, the right of minority groups to be free from discrimination, and the right of all citizens to full participation in the social and political life of the community without vilification. He refused to accept that the values of democracy were exclusively embraced by freedom of expression and insisted that respect for the equality of all citizens was also an essential condition for a true democracy and for truly democratic debate. Dickson found that the harm caused by the hatemonger's message ran 'directly counter to the values central to a free and democratic society, and in restricting the promotion of hatred Parliament is therefore seeking to bolster the notion of mutual respect necessary in a nation which venerates the equality of all persons.' Dickson refused to place expression above other Charter values in the pursuit of democracy: 'Expression can work to undermine our commitment to democracy where employed to propagate ideas anathemic to democratic values.' Since hate propaganda subverts the democratic process, he found it to be a 'brand of expressive activity ... wholly inimical to the democratic aspirations of the free expression guarantee.'[64]

'The capacity to put himself in others' shoes'

Dickson's significant contribution to equality jurisprudence could hardly have been predicted in 1963 when he was first appointed to the bench, and perhaps not even in 1973 when he was appointed to the Supreme Court of Canada. Lynn Smith, a leading equality scholar and advocate, now a judge, who argued many equality cases before the Supreme Court, including both *Bliss* and *Brooks*, observes that Dickson's decisions on equality rights for women 'seem to disprove the hypothesis that direct experience is the only way to gain a meaningful understanding of inequality ...' She credits Dickson with 'the capacity to put himself in others' shoes ...'[65] a quality that Beverley McLachlin also observed from the other side of the bench.[66]

Dickson did not come to the bench with an 'agenda' of equality, nor did he subscribe to any identifiable theory or vision of equality. He saw equality cases in the human terms of the litigants. What motivated his significant contribution to Canada's equality jurisprudence was his profound belief in the importance of allowing diverse and distinctive communities to flourish on the basis of the inherent right of every individual to be fully accepted. When law clerk Stephen Toope used the word 'tolerance' in a draft convocation address, Dickson scratched it out and wrote 'not enough.' He explained to Toope that he did not like the idea of tolerance because it was only the first step. In a diverse society, differences had to be accepted, not merely tolerated.[67]

Even after his retirement from the bench, Dickson's thinking on equality continued to evolve. As a wounded veteran after the war, he refused to be identified as physically disabled and he resented any effort to accommodate his war injury. Yet later, as an older man, he was prepared to identify with the disabled community and to speak out on its behalf. In 1992 he urged university administrators to 'adopt a leadership role in opening up your universities' to previously excluded groups, especially the disabled, 'to ensure that they too are full members in our educational communities. Let us deal with these challenges before we are shamed into doing so.'[68] In 1998 he put the full weight of his name and reputation behind the formation of the 'Dickson Circle,' a group of lawyers prepared to argue disability-rights cases pro bono. Citing the Supreme Court's decision requiring hospitals to provide sign-language interpreters for the hearing impaired, he observed: 'The courts may have an important role to play in addressing the longstanding exclusion experienced by many persons with disabilities.'[69] That same year, Dickson wrote a strongly worded Toronto *Star* column urging the Ontario government to enact the legislation it had promised requiring the removal of discriminatory barriers faced by persons with disabilities to avoid costly litigation that might 'put a strain on the moral authority of the courts.'[70] For Dickson, this was unusual conduct and unusual language, a mark of his profound personal commitment to the ideal of equality for all members of Canadian society.

20

Language Rights and National Unity

Language has been a persistent source of division and tension in Canada. The accommodation of linguistic differences lies at the root of our nation, yet we continue to struggle with the problems that emerge from Canada's complex web of majority- and minority-language groups. The language debate is a familiar and distinctive theme in Canadian law and politics with profound significance for Canadian national unity. It has proved most difficult to resolve and was one of the Supreme Court of Canada's constitutional preoccupations during the Dickson era.

Bilingualism

Brian Dickson was firmly committed to the principles of bilingualism. Before his appointment as a judge, as noted earlier, he made a concerted effort to learn French, and by 1963, when he was appointed to the Manitoba Court of Queen's Bench, he described his proficiency in French as 'moderate.'[1] Despite the cool reception to bilingualism in Manitoba, Dickson made a point of encouraging young lawyers to learn French. In 1967 he told a group of lawyers about to be called to the bar that 'those who wish to practice law with full vigour in this province should take steps to become familiar with the French tongue' and added that proficiency in both languages was essential 'if one seeks to cut a wide swath at the national level, whether in business or in one's profession or in politics.' As he later showed in his Supreme Court judgments, Dickson believed bilingualism to be essential for Canadian national unity: 'The purpose of language is to permit conversation – not to constitute a barrier. The purpose of language is to create greater amity and understanding – not to be a source of irritation or hostility.'[2]

After his appointment to the Supreme Court of Canada, Dickson took regular lessons from a French-language tutor and participated in summer immersion programs for judges, including a session at Laval University when he stayed with a French family. His modest proficiency in French perhaps never quite matched his genuine enthusiasm for bilingualism, but, in his early years on the Court, the other anglophone judges had such limited capacity in French that he regularly sat on leave applications and appeals from Quebec. He asked Chief Justice Gérard Fauteux, who served as chief justice for less than a year after Dickson's appointment to the Court, whether he should spend his time learning civil law or French and 'he very strongly advised learning some more French.'[3] He prepared himself for hearing Quebec appeals with meticulous care, even to the extent of figuring out the questions he would pose to counsel and having his questions translated in advance of the oral hearing.[4] He even wrote a short judgment in French, with much help from Pigeon.[5] Dickson saw the confluence of the common law and civilian traditions at the Supreme Court as a great strength in Canada's legal culture, and he hoped that 'the relations between the two great language groups of Canada' could be helped 'through the activities of the Bar and the work of our jurists.'[6]

A Bilingual Judiciary?

Dickson's jurisprudential commitment to bilingualism was unwavering. He had a strong belief in the importance of respecting and building upon the historic rights of Canada's French-speaking population, and he saw language as 'more than a mere means of communication, it is part and parcel of the identity and culture of the people speaking it.'[7]

In an early Charter decision, *Société des Acadiens v. Association of Parents*,[8] decided in May 1986, Dickson wrote a dissenting judgment that, if adopted by the majority, would have required a bilingual judiciary The case involved the right of New Brunswickers to use either official language in the courts of the province.[9] The majority judgment, written by the fluently bilingual Jean Beetz, rejected the proposition that this right meant that the litigant was entitled to have the case heard by a judge who could understand the litigant's language of choice without the aid of an interpreter.[10] In his strongly worded dissenting judgment, Dickson disagreed with the majority view that language rights were to be narrowly interpreted since they were the product of political compromise, as distinguished from other Charter rights, 'which tend to be seminal in nature because they are rooted in principle.' Dickson wrote of 'linguistic duality' as 'a long-standing concern in our nation' which has 'both French and

English solidly embedded in its history.' Dickson viewed the constitution's language protections as reflecting 'continued and renewed efforts in the direction of bilingualism' and he urged 'special care to be faithful to the spirit and purpose of the guarantee of language rights enshrined in the *Charter*.'[11]

Three years earlier, Dickson had told a CBA meeting that it was 'reasonable to envisage that because of the bilingual nature of this country, all [Supreme Court] judges will be fluent in both official languages.'[12] Now he was prepared to make that a constitutional requirement. In his draft dissent, he wrote that it is 'fundamental ... to any effective and coherent guarantee of language rights in the courtroom that the judge or judges understand ... the language chosen by the individual coming before the court.'[13]

Dickson softened the impact by affording each judge considerable latitude in deciding his or her own level of comprehension. Dickson asked La Forest, who did not sit on the case,[14] to comment on a draft judgment. La Forest pointed out that the sentence quoted had 'serious implications for this Court' and that, if adopted, it could cost the Court 'good judges' who might fail to meet the test. La Forest may well have been thinking of Dickson himself when he observed that bilingualism 'may be understood quite differently by people who are not really fluent in both languages and those who are.' La Forest agreed with Dickson that the Court should do what it could to promote bilingualism, but that there was 'danger in achieving that goal if the Court attempts to move faster than is possible under the present political and social reality.'[15]

Dickson and Wilson, who also dissented, seemed to be advocating a constitutional interpretation that potentially threatened their own ability to continue as members of the Supreme Court. Dickson decided to qualify the point by adding that the constitutional requirement would be met if a judge could 'understand either directly or through other' means, but this sat uneasily in the context of an opinion that proclaimed the importance of bilingualism. Wilson had a passage in an early draft approving of simultaneous translation, but she took it out.[16] In the final version of her reasons, she tried to finesse the problem by relying on a 'growth principle' to limit the current ambit of language rights to existing social expectations but also to allow for their expansion over time as society moved towards the goal of a truly bilingual judiciary. This probably would have saved Dickson, but, in a memorandum to Wilson, he refused to accept it: 'I am concerned about the implications of telling a litigant that his or her rights are being violated in an absolute sense, but that social expectations have not progressed far enough to allow for a remedy.'[17] Wilson responded by explaining that, under her concept of the 'growth principle,' it would be acceptable today if a judge could read and understand the other language but not engage in dialogue with counsel. She thought that the Charter 'recognizes these present deficiencies but points us in the direction we should be moving. As long as we are moving in that direction at a pace which reflects social expectations from time to time there is no violation of the *Charter*.'[18] Dickson probably had a sufficient level of French to survive under Wilson's 'growth principle,' but it would likely have stretched her own limited capacity in French for Wilson herself to qualify.[19]

'The rule of law will not tolerate such chaos and anarchy'

Manitoba struggled with the language issue from its earliest days. Francophone rights were enshrined in the constitution yet were steadily eroded by the growing anglophone majority. The controversies surrounding the plight of Manitoba's French-speaking population have aroused passions throughout Canadian history; indeed, at times, Confederation itself has been shaken and threatened by the Manitoba language issue. French-speaking Metis, fur traders and settlers, once a majority, still formed a significant portion of the provincial population when the province joined Confederation in 1870. The terms of union closely followed the provisions of the Constitution Act, 1867 relating to language rights in Quebec and the Parliament of Canada.[20] Both English and French could be used in the debates before the legislature or in the courts of Manitoba and the laws of the province were to be published in both languages. Twenty years later, after the second Riel uprising, many of the French-speaking Metis had moved away from Manitoba and the predominantly English-speaking settlers vastly outnumbered the province's francophone population. The provincial government purported to alter the 1870 constitutional guarantees by passing the Official Language Act, 1890, an ordinary act of the legislature, providing that only English could be used in the legislature and before the courts and that the laws of the province would be published only in English.[21] The province also repealed the education rights of the province's Catholic and francophone minority, provoking the infamous Manitoba schools crisis.

Manitoba's Official Language Act, 1890 was successfully challenged in two cases in the lower courts,[22] but these decisions apparently went unnoticed. They were not reported in the usual manner, nor were they appealed. The Manitoba government blithely ignored them and life went on as if the 1890 act were perfectly valid until the Franco-Manitoban community began to assert itself more forcefully in the 1970s and 1980s. The 1890 act was again declared unconstitutional by a county court judge in 1976.[23] This time the decision was reported, but again, the Manitoba government ignored it and nothing changed. By 1979, that case had reached the Supreme Court of Canada and in a unanimous judgment, the Court declared that the Official Language Act, 1890 was unconstitutional and invalid.[24] The province could not ignore this pronouncement, but it still refused to accept the bilingual require-ments of the 1870 terms of union. It passed another statute stating that 'any statute or law to the contrary notwithstanding,' only English was to be used in the legislature and in the courts and that the laws of the province would be published only in English.[25]

As another case was making its way to the Supreme Court,[26] Premier Howard Pawley and the NDP government of Manitoba attempted a rap-prochement with the province's francophone minority. The cost of translating all the laws from 1890 forward would be enormous and Pawley concluded that the money could be better spent on services that would meet the day-to-day needs of Franco-Manitobans. In cooperation with the federal Liberal govern-ment, Pawley proposed a constitutional amendment that would limit the laws to be translated but that would provide more French-language government services. This move towards official bilingualism provoked a storm of anti-French protest and was abandoned when the Conservative opposition refused to vote and allowed the division bells to ring for over two hundred hours, forc-ing the legislature to prorogue.

In 1979, the Supreme Court had ruled that the Parti Québécois govern-ment's attempt to avoid Quebec's obligation to publish its laws in both lan-guages conflicted with section 133 of the Constitution Act, 1867 and was unconstitutional.[27] Quebec had immediately complied with the Court's ruling and re-enacted its French-only statutes in both official languages. The federal government could hardly let Manitoba off a similar constitutional hook but there was little political support for bilingualism in Manitoba. In almost thirty municipal elections conducted in 1983, plebiscites were included asking vot-ers if they agreed with the Pawley government's bilingualism policy. Seventy-six per cent of voters said no to bilingualism. The popular rejection of the Pawley government's constitutional proposal represented to some extent a rejection of the federal Liberal bilingualism policy. The federal government could not force Manitoba to act, but it decided that the question had to be resolved. The federal cabinet directed a reference, asking the Supreme Court to decide whether Manitoba was constitutionally required to pass its laws in bilingual form. If yes, what were the consequences of failing to do so? Were the province's unilingual laws completely invalid or did they retain some legal force?

The *Manitoba Language Reference* was clearly a politically loaded case. For those, like Dickson, who supported the ideal of a bilingual Canada, the refusal of Manitoba to respect its constitutional obligations was an affront, while the collapse of Premier Pawley's effort to render the 1870 guarantee into terms more meaningful for the twentieth century was a profound disappointment. For those who opposed bilingualism as an inappropriate imposition from

Ottawa, the idea of declaring all the province's laws unconstitutional or requiring the province to translate all its laws for the benefit of a dwindling francophone population more or less fully fluent in English seemed absurd.

The case was argued in mid-June 1984. It was clear from the discussion at conference[28] that the Court was firmly of the view that Manitoba's unilingual laws failed to satisfy the demands of the constitution. Dickson had no difficulty in concluding that the purpose of section 23 of the Manitoba Act, 1870, like section 133 of the Constitution Act, 1867, 'was to ensure full and equal access to the legislatures, the laws and the courts for francophones and anglophones alike' and that 'the fundamental guarantees contained in the sections in question are constitutionally entrenched and are beyond the power of the provinces of Quebec or Manitoba to amend unilaterally.'[29]

The much more difficult question was what to do about Manitoba's steadfast refusal to comply with its constitutional obligations. The case raised agonizingly difficult constitutional issues with profound implications for the Court. Were all the province's laws unconstitutional? It seemed difficult to avoid that conclusion, yet the result would be truly alarming. Manitoba would be in a state of virtual anarchy, its statute book wiped clean with a single stroke of the Court's constitutional pen. If all of Manitoba's laws enacted since 1890 were invalid, would not the validity of all transactions and rights of property based on those laws be undermined? The present legislature had been elected on the basis of the province's unilingual election legislation – would there even be a legislature in place that could take the legal steps required to remedy the constitutional problem? How could it be legally possible to give unconstitutional laws lawful force? Could the Court in effect suspend the constitution? Was there some way the Court could apply the letter of the constitution and declare the laws invalid but at the same time avoid a situation of legal chaos for the province?

Another difficult question was how far the Court could or should go in ordering the province to rewrite its statutes. Did the Court have the power to force Manitoba to comply with its constitutional obligations? It was unheard of for the Court to require the legislature to enact laws of a certain kind, yet that would be the result of finding that, cover to cover, Manitoba's statute book was invalid. Ordinarily, when a court finds a law unconstitutional, that specific law is struck down. The matter is then in the hands of the legislature. It can simply get on with other business or it can try to enact another law that achieves the same objective but avoids the constitutional difficulty. But here, the situation was drastically different. If the Court were to strike down all the laws of the province, would it not have to involve itself in the difficult process of legal reconstruction?

At conference, some of the judges were dubious that, in the face of such a clear constitutional violation, 'necessity' would allow the Court to save Manitoba's laws in some form. Lamer said that he had 'a hard time finding necessity. If Manitoba wants chaos, let them have chaos.' If the laws were constitutionally invalid, how could the Court do anything to save them? Others, including Beetz and Dickson, worried about making an order that would, in effect, create an impossible situation for the province. Dickson mused that perhaps 'necessity' was not the word, but, as he put it, 'the integrity of the legal system is a logical postulate. It can even be read ahead of the Constitution. If there is no legal system there is nothing upon which the Constitution can operate.'[30] It was agreed that Dickson would prepare the Court's judgment, and, although the final product was styled 'by the Court,' he was the author, albeit with considerable input from his colleagues.

Dickson worked long and hard on the necessity issue. Was there, he asked his law clerks, a law above the law, in other words some 'higher law' that could justify suspension of the constitution and validate invalid laws for a period of time?[31] Some thought the idea indefensible, but others supported it. Various memoranda were produced by Dickson's clerks and by the clerks of other judges.[32] An influential memo from Peter Benson, Le Dain's clerk, containing references to Kelson, Hegel, Locke, Rousseau, and Kant, identified the 'principle of legal continuity' as 'the supreme juridical principle because it articulates the presupposition of every constitutional regime,' and argued that the final purpose of law is 'the creation and maintenance of an actual order of positive laws which preserves and embodies the rule of law.'[33]

Dickson produced a first draft in March 1985. It was a strongly worded judgment that detailed the sorry history of French-English relations in the province and concluded that 'as a result of the persistent violation by the Manitoba legislature of s. 23 of the *Manitoba Act, 1870*, the Franco-Manitoban community has been discriminated against in that they have been denied access to the law on an equal footing with the majority.' Dickson found that rights and obligations that arose under the invalid laws from 1890 to the present were saved by the de facto doctrine that protects acts done under apparent legal authority. This, he wrote, did not 'involve giving effect to unconstitutional laws' but rather it 'recognizes and gives effect only to the justified expectations of those who have relied upon the statute's apparent validity.'[34] At this stage, Dickson was prepared to use the de facto doctrine to save everything that had been done under the regime of unconstitutional law. This included the election of the current members of the legislature. However, the de facto doctrine would cease to operate once the Court's judgment was pronounced, since then the apparent authority of the earlier regime would cease.

Dickson did not hold back on the remedy. A year or so earlier, he had told an audience of Manitoba lawyers that remedial questions under the Charter would 'offer a test of the creativity of the legal mind' and that the problems were particularly vexing 'where positive action is needed to correct the denial of constitutional rights.'[35] His draft judgment certainly showed a brave and creative judicial mind at work. In the face of Manitoba's refusal to abide by the constitution, Dickson wanted to impose a direct command that the province act. The rule of law required that 'this Court order that the legislature of Manitoba act *affirmatively* to remedy its past non-compliance, by taking steps to translate and re-enact all of its unilingual legislation in both languages.' Plainly impatient with Manitoba's failure to respect the rights of its French-language minority, he added: 'Ninety-five years of persistent constitutional violations have gone unchecked: matters must be set right.'[36] He recognized that this was a highly unusual remedy, but he insisted that nothing else would do: 'It must, however, be recognized that the imposition of affirmative duties on the Manitoba legislature is, in this case, the *only* means by which constitutionality can be assured. The power of this court to use such extreme measures flows from the recognition of this Court as the protector and preserver of the Constitution. The duty of this Court to uphold the constitution of Canada necessarily implies that it have the means to do so ... If there ever was a case for the imposition of positive remedies in constitutional law, this is it.'[37] Dickson then applied the doctrine of state necessity to give temporary life to the invalid laws. 'The solution must be to declare the unilingual laws of Manitoba dead and then retroactively to breathe life into them, for a temporary period, in order to avoid transgressing the Rule of Law.'[38]

Despite the concerns he had expressed at conference, Lamer sent a memo to Dickson enthusiastically supporting the draft judgment, especially the part that dealt with 'necessité constitutionelle.'[39] But other members of the Court thought that Dickson's first draft went too far. Beetz and Estey both took the unusual step of discussing the case with Joel Bakan, Dickson's law clerk. According to Bakan, Estey was 'just apoplectic' about the remedy.[40] Estey had previously delivered a speech in which he had been highly critical of the American experience with court-ordered remedies and had argued that 'no amount of prodding by our law schools, professors and commentators will bring this kind of litigation through the doors of our courtrooms.'[41] La Forest also suggested that Dickson tone down the language of the judgment to make it less emotive and more legalistic.[42] Wilson, too, was concerned with the tone of Dickson's draft. Uneasy with the idea of the Court ordering the province to translate its laws, she also thought that it was a bit early in the game for the Court to be flexing its constitutional muscles. 'Although we are "the guardians of the Constitution" in one sense, the Court is a child of the Constitution and dependent upon it for its authority. It is the Constitution which is supreme and not the Court.' Wilson argued for an approach that would respect the traditional roles of the courts and the legislatures. The Court should declare the laws invalid and let the legislature read the judgment and decide what to do about it. 'I would prefer to assume that any government will act in a responsible fashion and, it is only if they don't, that the Court needs to take steps to compel it to do so.'[43]

Beetz agreed with La Forest's suggestion that the language be toned down, and he also shared Wilson's concerns. He noted that the case came to the Court on a reference and asked whether there was any legal authority to impose a mandatory order: 'Our power is confined to answering the constitutional questions.' Beetz noted as well that there had been no request for an injunction and no argument on the point: 'Such an injunction in my opinion, given without jurisdiction, would considerably weaken the legitimacy and even constitutionality of our judgment.' Beetz argued that Dickson's order assumed bad faith on the part of the Manitoba government and that it 'might create the very chaos we wish to avoid if the order is not complied with.' He urged Dickson to amend the draft to declare that the province had a duty to act, that the Court presumed good faith, and 'that, as with a state of emergency, the responsible Legislature and Government should be the first judges of the question when the state of necessity has ceased, subject to ultimate judicial control ... And I would leave it at that.' Beetz also suggested a refinement to Dickson's necessity analysis. Rather than declare the laws invalid and then temporarily resurrect them, Beetz suggested declaring them invalid but having full legal force and effect 'for so long as the state of necessity requires it, because of the state of necessity and the Rule of Law. The practical effect would be the same, but the solution would be more elegant and more sound in legal terms.' He also urged Dickson to take out the detailed historical section which Beetz thought unnecessary and contentious.[44] Le Dain, writing years later, said that several members of the Court were 'strongly opposed ... for jurisdictional and constitutional reasons,' to an order requiring the province to translate its laws and thought that this 'would considerably weaken the legitimacy and even constitutionality of our judgment.'[45] Dickson took these comments to heart and sat down to revise the judgment. He deleted both the lengthy historical discussion and the uncompromising mandatory order; he adopted the suggestion made by Beetz, Wilson, and La Forest that the de facto doctrine be trimmed to apply only to acts of officials and not to the province's laws; and he refined the analysis justifying the temporary validity of the unconstitutional laws.

The challenge was to find a way that would uphold the constitution yet avoid creating 'a legal vacuum' and 'consequent legal chaos in the Province of Manitoba.' With the help of his colleagues' comments, Dickson concluded that the way out of the impasse could be found in the rule of law: a fundamental, yet unwritten, constitutional principle. 'The rule of law,' Dickson wrote, 'must mean at least two things.' The first is that 'arbitrary power' is precluded and that 'the law is supreme over officials of the government as well as private individuals.' The second meaning had a direct bearing on the Manitoba situation: 'The rule of law requires the creation and maintenance of an actual order of positive laws which preserves and embodies the more general principle of normative order. Law and order are indispensable elements of civilized life.'[46]

The rule of law has long been regarded as a fundamental concept in the Anglo-Canadian constitutional tradition. In the *Manitoba Language Reference*, Dickson transformed the rule of law from a vague abstraction to an operative constitutional principle. He cited legal and political philosophers on the nature of law and civil society and the decisions of the Privy Council and the courts of the United States and other Commonwealth countries dealing with situations of 'necessity,' but he knew that to base the Court's decision on such an abstract principle would require justification in the constitution's text and in the jurisprudence of the Court. A textual basis was found in the preamble to the Constitution Act, 1982: 'Whereas Canada is founded upon principles that recognize the supremacy of God and the *rule of law.*' The preamble itself does not have operative force, but Dickson reasoned that the rule of law 'is clearly implicit in the very nature of a Constitution.' The underlying premise of the constitution is 'that Canada be a society of legal order and normative structure: one governed by rule of law. While this is not set out in a specific provision, the principle of the rule of law is clearly a principle of our Constitution.' Dickson refused to 'take a narrow and literal approach to constitutional interpretation' and insisted that 'the jurisprudence of the Court evidences a willingness to supplement textual analysis with historical, contextual and purposive interpretation in order to ascertain the intent of the makers of our Constitution.'[47]

The constitution required the Court to declare Manitoba's unilingual laws of no force and effect, but the principle of the rule of law precluded the legal vacuum that such a declaration would entail. 'A declaration that the laws of Manitoba are invalid and of no legal force or effect would deprive Manitoba of its legal order and cause a transgression of the rule of law. For the Court to allow such a situation to arise and fail to resolve it would be an abdication of its responsibility as protector and preserver of the Constitution.' Dickson concluded that the Court had a constitutional duty to declare Manitoba's unilingual laws to be invalid and of no force, but also 'to take such steps as will ensure the rule of law in the Province of Manitoba.' Failure to safeguard the rule of law would be an abdication of judicial responsibility: 'The constitutional guarantee of rule of law will not tolerate such chaos and anarchy.'[48]

Dickson elaborated a new constitutional remedy that would avoid directly ordering the legislature to enact laws and also resolve the impasse between enforcing the letter of the constitution and maintaining legal order. By issuing a temporary declaration of validity, the Court was able to preserve legal order in Manitoba but, at the same time, create a virtually irresistible pressure on the legislature to bring the province's statutes up to constitutional muster. Although Manitoba's unilingual laws were invalid, it will be necessary, wrote Dickson, to deem them temporarily valid and effective 'for the period of time during which it would be impossible for the Manitoba Legislature to fulfil its constitutional duty.'[49]

The reaction to the Court's judgment was generally positive. Winnipeg *Free Press* editorials praised the judgment for resolving 'the doubt which formerly afflicted some Manitobans about the reality of bilingualism in the province's constitution' and urged the government to expand bilingual services.[50] Dickson's old friend George Tritschler, by then retired as chief justice of the Manitoba Court of Queen's Bench, wrote Dickson to praise the Court for solving 'what seemed to be an insoluble puzzle in a practical way and above all, in language which an intelligent layman should understand.'[51] In a sentence, Tritschler had summed up Dickson's approach to judgment writing, no doubt a style that the old mentor had imparted. Dickson enjoyed the intellectual challenge of a difficult legal issue, but he did not approach his task from a purely intellectual perspective. He insisted upon a practically workable result that could be explained in language understandable to the ordinary Canadian. Tritschler's letter meant a great deal to Dickson and he circulated it to his colleagues, fondly describing Tritschler as 'one of the finest jurists Canada has produced.'[52]

But the reaction to the Court's decision was not entirely favourable. As Dickson knew full well, bilingalism was not universally popular in his native Manitoba. He received a number of critical letters complaining that the Court was forcing people to learn French and basing its decisions on century-old facts rather than present-day realities. The most surprising criticism came from Joseph O'Sullivan, an eccentric and often erratic judge of the Manitoba Court of Appeal. In a completely unrelated case, O'Sullivan attacked the Supreme Court's judgment, describing it as 'truly revolutionary' and asserting that the Supreme Court did not have the power to require the translation of the laws because such a power would infringe on parliamentary prerogatives. Chief Justice Alfred Monnin was dismayed by his colleague's outburst and, in a concurring opinion, rebuked O'Sullivan for making comments that had 'nothing to do with the case at hand' and were 'gratuitous, unnecessary, injudicious and perhaps impertinent. I disassociate myself entirely from them.'[53]

Un Visage linguistique

The political and social reawakening of Quebec in the early 1960s was the first act in a constitutional drama that would preoccupy Canada for the next thirty years. Language was – and is – of primordial importance to the province's francophone majority, who are intent upon resisting the pull of assimilation into the sea of English speakers in the rest of North America. The 'Quiet Revolution' of the Jean Lesage Liberals and their cry of *maîtres chez nous* in the 1960s was followed by the more strident nationalism of René Lévesque and the separatist Parti Québécois in the 1970s and 1980s.

Pierre Trudeau and the federal Liberals confronted the rise of Quebec nationalism with the promise of a bilingual, pan-Canadian citizenship. Trudeau refused to see the nation divided into distinctive linguistic communities and insisted upon a bilingual Canada in which all Canadians would be at home in all corners of the land. Francophone minorities outside Quebec embraced bilingualism as their salvation. However, Quebec nationalists saw bilingualism as a hollow promise, little more than a recipe for the eventual assimilation of Canada's French-speaking minority. They believed that the French language and culture could survive only under a policy of vigorously enforced unilingualism within Quebec, and eventually a sovereign and independent Quebec.

As we saw in chapter 13, Trudeau's agenda for constitutional reform and the election of René Lévesque and the Parti Québécois in 1976 set the stage for the major constitutional battles that would follow. The separatist tide was turned back in the 1980 referendum and Trudeau secured his significant constitutional achievement in 1982. Over howls of protest from Lévesque and the separatists, Trudeau's package of constitutional reform patriated the Canadian constitution and entrenched the Charter of Rights and Freedoms. Quebec was legally bound by the 1982 constitution but there remained a lingering perception in many quarters that it lacked political and moral legitimacy without Quebec's agreement. The election of Brian Mulroney in 1984 with the strong support of Quebec nationalists, combined with the defeat of the separatists and the election of Robert Bourassa in Quebec in 1985, set the stage for the 'Quebec Round' of constitutional negotiations and the Meech Lake Accord in late April 1987. The federal government and the ten provinces agreed at Meech Lake to accommodate Quebec's key demands for constitutional renewal, including recognition of Quebec as a 'distinct society.'

Bourassa attempted to bridge the divide between Quebec nationalism and federalism. He first came to power as leader of the Quebec Liberal Party in 1970 at the age of thirty-six, suffered a humiliating defeat at the hands of Lévesque and the Parti Québécois in 1976, but then made a remarkable comeback by winning the 1985 election with a promise of constitutional accommodation for Quebec. During his first term in office in 1974, Bourassa introduced Bill 22, Quebec's *Loi sur la langue officielle*,[54] making French the official language of Quebec, restricting access to English-language schools, and requiring the use of French on public signs, posters and advertising. Later, in 1977, the Parti Québécois replaced this measure with the more ambitious Charte de la langue francaise.[55] Colloquially known as Bill 101, Quebec's language charter flatly rejected official bilingualism and called for the aggressive enforcement of a French unilingual-language policy for the province.

Quebec's unilingual-language policy proved to be a popular measure with the francophone majority, supported by separatists and federalists alike. The anglophone minority resented the policy, however, and, from the start, the law was attacked in the courts. A provision in Bourassa's Bill 22 restricting access to English-language schools was struck down in 1984 by the Supreme Court of Canada as contrary to the Charter's section 23 guarantee of minority-language education rights.[56] Subsequently, a provision in Lévesque's Bill 101 providing that the laws of Quebec be enacted only in French was also struck down by the Supreme Court as contrary to the requirement of section 133 of the Constitution Act, 1867 that the laws of Canada and Quebec be published in both French and English.[57]

At times, the debate over Bill 101 seemed to ignore linguistic facts. By the late 1970s, Quebec's anglophone minority had fully accepted French as the province's primary and day-to-day language, just as the francophone majority respected the rights of the anglophone minority. Quebec anglophones enjoyed far better access to schools, hospitals, and other public services in their own language than did the francophone minorities in other parts of Canada.

However, a continuing source of irritation and resentment for Quebec's English-speaking minority was Bill 101's requirement of French-only signs. The sign law was contentious because of its symbolism for both sides of the linguistic divide. From the francophone perspective, it was essential to present Quebeckers with a French 'visage linguistique.' Requiring that all public and commercial signs be in French conveyed the important message that life in Quebec was to be lived in French. The problem was particularly acute in bilingual Montreal where the province's anglophone minority was concentrated and where the streets bore the lingusitic marks of North America's predominantly English-speaking commercial and cultural domination. Bill 101's French-only sign law was designed to resist that enormous force and to convey the essential message that, within Quebec, language and culture are different from the rest of North America. From the perspective of the English-speaking minority, the denial of the right to use one's own language was perceived as an insult.

In the aftermath of the constitutional debates that led to the enactment of the Charter in 1982, Lévesque's Parti Québécois government invoked section 33 of the Charter – the 'notwithstanding clause'. Although Quebec was constitutionally bound by the Charter, Quebec nationalists had never accepted its legitimacy and were intent on resisting what they saw as the Charter's centralizing influence and denial of Quebec's distinctive linguistic and political culture. Lévesque decided to make the most of section 33 and the Quebec National Assembly enacted a sweeping 'omnibus' declaration that all the province's laws would be operative notwithstanding relevant Charter rights. This declaration applied retrospectively to 17 April 1982, the date the Charter came into force, but under the 'sunset' clause in section 33, it would expire five years after its enactment, on 23 June 1987. The Parti Québécois government later enacted an override declaration in similar terms, but with specific reference to the Charter of the French Language, that would not expire until 1 February 1989.

The Parti Québécois was defeated in the 1985 election and Robert Bourassa made his comeback as premier of the province. During the election, Bourassa had promised to soften Bill 101 and to allow bilingual signs. However, he backed away from his election promise when he met a wave of opposition to bilingual signs.

Several English-speaking merchants who carried on small retail businesses and catered primarily to English-speaking customers decided to take the issue to court. They asserted that the Quebec law forbidding commercial signs in English violated their freedom of expression, and that Quebec's omnibus override overstepped the constitutional line and did not shield the language law from Charter review. However, under Quebec law, they had another argument too. Quebec's Charter of Human Rights and Freedoms, enacted by the Bourassa Liberals in 1975, also guaranteed freedom of expression, and the Quebec Charter was not subject to any override.

The English-speaking merchants were successful in the Quebec courts.[58] The Quebec government appealed and the cases came to the Supreme Court in mid-November 1987. The Court sat for an entire week to hear argument in three appeals from Quebec. *Ford v. Quebec (Attorney General)*[59] and its companion case, *Devine v. Quebec (Attorney General)*,[60] involved Bill 101. The Court joined these appeals with *Irwin Toy v. Quebec (Attorney General)*,[61] a toy manufacturer's challenge to another Quebec law that restricted advertising aimed at children. Despite the importance of the cases, only seven judges sat. Gérard La Forest was unable to sit, and, to avoid an even number, the most junior judge, Claire L'Heureux-Dubé, did not sit.

The questions posed by these cases were both legally difficult and politically sensitive. From a legal perspective, the Court had to provide an analytic framework for the Charter guarantee of freedom of expression, which lies at the heart of our democratic tradition and is vital to a free and open society. The cases also presented the Supreme Court with a chance to stake out the reach and the limits of freedom of expression under the Charter. Quebec asserted the right to enact laws to enhance its distinctive French language and culture and to protect vulnerable children from manipulative advertising. All of the cases dealt with commercial speech. Does advertising deserve the protection of the Charter? Even if it does, may the state not limit commercial expression to protect other interests and values?

The legal challenge was compounded by the unusually charged political context. The debate surrounding Bill 101 aroused all the passions of Canada's acrimonious language debate, and the political context was further complicated by the uncertainties surrounding the Meech Lake Accord. Prime Minister Brian Mulroney and Premier Robert Bourassa saw the accord as the way to heal the wounds of 1982 by incorporating in the constitution a recognition of Quebec's status as a 'distinct society,' a change that would allow Quebec to accept the Charter politically. In these circumstances, a Charter ruling by the Supreme Court impairing Quebec's capacity to nurture and protect the French language or limiting Quebec's right to invoke the notwithstanding clause could stir nationalist fervour at the very moment that the Bourassa and Mulroney governments were working towards constitutional accommodation. On the other hand, a narrow ruling on freedom of expression would cripple a vital element of the Charter and inflame those who were opposed to any special accommodation for Quebec and who saw Quebec's language laws as an unjustifiable assault on the rights of the province's English-speaking minority.

The attack on the sign law was based on both the Canadian and the Quebec Charters. The lawyers for the English-speaking merchants argued that the law violated freedom of expression, while the attorney general of Quebec contended that, since the sign law related only to commercial advertising, it did not involve a kind of expression that deserved constitutional protection. The attorney general argued as well that freedom of expression protected only the right to convey a message and did not protect the speaker's choice of language. Bill 101 did not prevent anyone from saying anything, it merely required them to say it in French. To bolster this argument, the attorney general noted that language rights were explicitly and expressly dealt with elsewhere in the constitution and that it was not for the courts to expand language rights under the guise of some other right or freedom. Quebec's insistence upon a narrow protection for language rights was consistent with the nationalist vision that the survival of French language and culture is threatened by bilingualism and depends upon a unilingual Quebec. Quebec also attempted to justify its law under section 1 of the Canadian Charter, as well as under section 9.1 of the Quebec Charter, which provides that rights must be exercised in a manner that maintains 'a proper regard for democratic values, public order and the general well-being of the citizens of Quebec.' Finally, the attorney general for Quebec turned to the notwithstanding clause, urging the Supreme Court to reverse an earlier decision of the Quebec Court of Appeal that Quebec's omnibus override of the Canadian Charter was invalid because of its generality and lack of specificity.[62]

When the Court conference to discuss these appeals was held on 15 December 1987,[63] Le Dain came fully prepared with a detailed analysis. Dickson, realizing that Le Dain was anxious to write the judgments, gave him the green light, undoubtedly with mixed feelings. Le Dain was a distinguished constitutional lawyer and no one would question his intellectual capacity to take on the daunting task of writing these landmark judgments. However, Le Dain could be very slow to complete his work and at times was plagued by indecision.

While there remained many details to be resolved, Le Dain's broad outline of how he proposed to decide the case attracted general support. Freedom of expression under both the Canadian and the Quebec Charters would be defined to include commercial speech and the speaker's choice of language, but the province would be given considerable latitude under section 1 to protect other interests. The Court would recognize that Quebec's right to protect the French language could justify limiting the use of English, but it would strike down the sign law on the ground that Quebec failed to demonstrate that a total ban of English was justifiable under the minimal-impairment test. Le Dain thought that the Court should avoid dealing with the issue of the notwithstanding clause on the ground that it was 'moot.' The five-year sunset clause period had expired for the general omnibus measure exempting all Quebec statutes, and, while the override applicable to Bill 101 was still alive, the Court could decide the case under the Quebec Charter. However, if he had to deal with section 33, Le Dain said that he would affirm the right of the province to use the notwithstanding clause in an omnibus way and give it retroactive effect. There seemed to be a general consensus that, because the section 33 issue was moot, the Court should avoid dealing with it. However, neither Beetz nor Dickson was prepared to accept that the section 33 override could be applied retroactively.

Estey Resigns

In mid-April 1988, before Le Dain had produced a draft judgment in the Quebec sign case, Willard Estey announced his retirement from the Court. Estey had always said that he would serve for only ten years. At age sixty-eight and after eleven years in Ottawa, he decided that it was time to move on. He was clearly anxious to leave the Court while he still had the energy to pursue another career. In a handwritten note to Dickson announcing his intention to retire, Estey mentioned his long-standing plan to serve on the Court for ten years. He told Dickson that he had not taken on any new responsibilities since that would be contrary to his position as a sitting judge, but that he expected 'to do so shortly after the effective date of retirement, 22 April 1988.' Explaining that he was not going to a law firm but might take on some part-time work in the world of commerce, he also assured Dickson that he would complete his work on the Court's reserve judgments in accordance with the provision in the Supreme Court Act that gives retired judges six months to complete their work on reserved judgments.[64] 'Please be assured that I shall take on nothing which will impede the discharge of my remaining responsibilities in the work of the Court within the time limit prescribed by the Act.'[65]

Dickson called Estey and tried to persuade him to stay. Estey had sat on no fewer than twenty-five appeals for which judgment had been reserved. Dickson thought that the loss of an experienced, efficient, and productive judge of Estey's standing would be a blow to the Court at this moment. Neither Beetz nor Le Dain enjoyed good health and both were flagging under the unrelenting pressure of work. William McIntyre was also making noises about retiring. The Court still faced its backlog problem and could not afford to lose as many as four of its nine members.

Estey could not be dissuaded. In a memorandum to Dickson, he mentioned Dickson's call and stated: 'I reflected on the matter once again and, not without regret, came to the same conclusion, namely that this is an appropriate time for me to retire.' Estey again assured Dickson that he fully intended to deal with the cases on which he had sat. 'I will devote sufficient time before and after retirement and within the limits prescribed by the Act to discharge my obligations in a quick and orderly way as best I can.'[66]

Estey's assurances proved to be unreliable. It soon became apparent that he was not going to spend the next six months in a corner of the Supreme Court building working away quietly on reserved judgments. Estey was anxious to go into business as chairman of Guaranty Trust Company and as a member of the board of the highly successful and aggressive Central Capital Corporation. He proceeded to give interviews with the Toronto *Globe and Mail*'s legal reporter Kirk Makin[67] and the Toronto *Star*'s David Vienneau,[68] making it quite clear that he was headed for the world of business. 'I have the same feeling as when I left Camp Borden after the war – thank God I came but I ain't coming back. I wouldn't mind divorcing myself completely from the law. It is good for your outlook and your brains to move around.' Estey lambasted Ottawa, the Supreme Court, and his judicial colleagues. Ottawa, he said, was 'so overloaded with civil servants that, as one wag said, it takes 10 to do the work of one.'

He debunked the notion that there was anything special about the Charter. 'It is not a fantastic era. It's the same old era. The Charter is mostly a codification of what we already got.' Asked about Antonio Lamer's recent statement that Charter decisions were gruelling because judges have to anticipate future developments and future cases, Estey retorted: 'Those statements make me ill. The magic of common law is step-by-step development. Anybody who looks down the road to see what cases will be affected is doing what Einstein couldn't do. And I haven't seen too many Einsteins around lately.' Estey proceeded to blast 'gutless' judges who refuse to get tough with criminals.[69] He described the *Morgentaler* abortion decision as probably 'the most futile' because of the problem of determining when the foetus becomes a person. 'The search has gone on since the last ice age and will go on until the next ice age.' Estey was also harshly critical of what he described as his more academically inclined colleagues, blaming them for excessively long and complicated opinions. 'The system breeds delays. What happens is Joe Blow is assigned to write a decision, but he has other things to do. When it finally comes out, it is a 60-page monstrosity and the others have forgotten all about it. Finally, they recycle it and out comes their version ... . There are too many concurring opinions. I think we should have fewer and fewer concurring opinions by returning to the original, primordial philosophy that the law should be simple so people understand it.' He claimed that his role had been to emphasize 'the need for simplicity, practicality and workability.'

As if this were not enough, Estey decided that the time had come to offer his thoughts on some important current issues of public policy. He pronounced himself in favour of free trade, the main issue in the 1988 federal election held six months later. 'I believe in free trade. It will wake us up out of necessity. We're going to go out of business it we don't compete with those guys. For the first six years they'll eat us alive. Then we'll get up off the floor and we'll get going.'[70]

Of greater concern were his comments on the Meech Lake Accord. Estey was strongly opposed to Meech. A year earlier, on 19 May 1987, he had written a scathing memorandum to his colleagues strongly disagreeing with the Meech Lake proposals. He told them that he found it difficult to believe that the accord 'has had the benefit of the attention of a single legal mind' and he offered a detailed list of what he perceived to be drafting flaws in the provisions dealing with the Supreme Court of Canada. Estey was highly critical of the idea of giving the provinces a say in Supreme Court appointments and he thought that the proposed amendment formula was flawed. However, he concluded that it was probably the case 'that the judicial branch has no right or mandate to speak out on constitutional proposals unless and until they are submitted to the Court according to the rules of the Constitution.' He hinted that perhaps a retired judge could speak, adding: 'Unless some member is prepared to volunteer his resignation, the group is left without a spokesman.'[71] Now that he was about to step down from the Court, he decided to let his views be known. He told the *Globe and Mail* reporter: 'My instinct is that it [Meech Lake Accord] is decentralizing, and should therefore be viewed by Canadians with some suspicion. You could ruin Confederation – there is no question about it. That is why it is being nibbled at and attacked. I think we would be better off to stay where we are.'

Estey's comments provoked a storm of protest. Morris Manning, Morgentaler's counsel, wrote a letter to the editor describing Estey's outburst as 'offensive' and 'insulting' and saying that the retired judge had 'trivialized' the Court's judgment.[72] Robert Decary, a prominent Hull lawyer who appeared regularly before the Supreme Court and who later became a judge of the Federal Court of Appeal, suggested that Estey's comments rendered him unfit for further service as a judge. Decary wrote in *Le Devoir* that Estey's comments, particularly his opposition to Meech Lake, made it unacceptable for him to participate in the twenty-five cases on which he sat and for which judgment had been reserved.[73] Estey tried to laugh off Decary's comments – 'How can I disqualify myself? I retired last Friday' – and he added that none of the cases on which he sat involved Meech Lake. Decary responded with a formal complaint to the Canadian Judicial Council asking that Estey's conduct be investigated and that he be relieved of any remaining judicial functions. Estey saved himself and the Court from a potentially embarrassing investigation by withdrawing from any further participation in the Court's work.

Illness Strikes

By the summer of 1988, Le Dain had circulated a draft judgment in the Bill 101 case.[74] It followed the general plan he had outlined at conference with two significant differences. Interpreting freedom of expression to protect both commercial speech and choice of language, Le Dain wrote that language was the instrument by which a people may express its cultural identity and by which individuals may express their personal identities and sense of individuality. Freedom of expression should not be compartmentalized because 'the factors that bear on the individual and societal interests in freedom of expression are much too complex, inter-related and overlapping for that.' However, Le Dain then qualified this generous approach in a way that concerned some of the other judges. He wrote that certain negative effects or limits could take expression outside the protection of section 2(b). He listed three factors. First, 'the particular expression claiming constitutional protection must not prevent the exercise of a protected right or freedom by another.' Second, 'it must not cause clearly established harm or injury to another.' Third, 'it must not undermine the political, social or legal order for which the protection of freedom of expression exists and by means of which it is ensured.'[75]

The second significant difference was that Le Dain had decided to deal with the notwithstanding clause. It had been fully argued and had to be resolved at some point since there were other cases pending in which the issue was not moot. Le Dain's draft held that section 33 laid down requirements of form only and that courts should not review the legislature's use of the notwithstanding clause. He refused to interfere in any way with the highly contested omnibus law exempting all Quebec statutes from the Charter to the maximum degree possible. This aspect of Le Dain's draft seems to have attracted no immediate attention; however, with the aim of preventing the legislature from protecting past Charter violations, it would later be modified to forbid retroactive use of the notwithstanding clause.

Wilson disagreed with Le Dain's approach to freedom of expression.[76] She thought that introducing the three negative factors at the definition stage was inconsistent with the direction the Court had taken in other cases where it had required all limits to be justified under section 1. Beetz paid Le Dain a compliment, 'I have just completed a first reading of your masterly reasons,' but added that he would have to wait to see what Wilson had to offer on Le Dain's limits at the definition stage.[77] Otherwise, both Wilson and Beetz were prepared to concur with Le Dain's draft.

Tragically, Le Dain's Bill 101 draft opinion would be his last. An outstanding constitutional lawyer and a proud anglophone Quebecker, Le Dain was all too painfully aware of the significance of the Bill 101 judgment. For this intense man, who held himself to the highest standards, the burden of writing the Bill 101 judgment proved to be the breaking point. In the late summer of 1988, he suffered a major depressive illness.[78] He never returned to the Court. By the fall, he was hospitalized and completely unable to function. His wife Cynthia, encouraged by Le Dain's psychiatrist, hoped that he would recover and return to work. It was apparent, however, that even on the most optimistic prognosis, Le Dain's recovery would be slow at best. Dickson was not prepared to wait. He decided early on that Le Dain was incapable of ever resuming his judicial duties. Furthermore, despite Le Dain's outstanding legal ability, from Dickson's perspective he had not been the easiest colleague. Le Dain's painstaking work habits made him very slow with his judgments and at times he suffered mood swings that seemed to affect his ability to function. All the while, the Court was under considerable pressure to come to grips with its long list of reserve judgments.

Dickson advised Le Dain's wife that he would insist upon the strict application of the Judges Act, which, at the time, required an order-in-council where a judge is absent from judicial duties for more than three months.[79] Le Dain, his family, and some of his former colleagues from the Federal Court bitterly resented what they perceived as Dickson's precipitous action, a view shared by at least one of Le Dain's colleagues on the Supreme Court.[80] They thought that Le Dain should have been given time to recover. However, Dickson was persuaded that Le Dain's prognosis was poor and that his recovery and the time it would take were so uncertain that the Court simply could not afford to wait. He consulted his colleagues on what to do and, although it was a difficult and distasteful decision, they fully supported him.[81] As William McIntyre put it: 'I think he did what he had to do' and 'what he did was in Le Dain's interest.'[82]

The Court was further hit by illness when Jean Beetz, sixty-one years old, was diagnosed with cancer and unable to sit for the fall term in 1988. With both Le Dain and Beetz out of commission, steps had to be taken to come to grips with the Bill 101 judgment. Only seven judges had sat on the case. Estey was already gone and Le Dain was not able to perform his judicial functions. In view of Beetz's illness, the situation was precarious. The panel that heard the Bill 101 case could be reduced to four judges, one less than a quorum. The Supreme Court Act allows four judges to render a judgment in such circumstances, but only with the consent of the parties.[83] In view of the volatile and politically sensitive issue, the Court obviously did not want to risk having to ask for consent. Meanwhile, a federal election was called for 21 November 1988. By then, eight provinces had ratified Meech Lake, but support for it seemed to be eroding and its adoption was by no means certain. And, in the midst of this, Bill 101 continued to provoke acrimonious debate in Quebec and the Court's decision was anxiously awaited.

Bill 101 Falls, Notwithstanding Stands, Meech Lake Collapses

Le Dain's draft provided the basic elements of the judgment, but much work remained. Though there was no doubt about the result the Court would reach on Bill 101, the Le Dain draft did not provide an entirely satisfactory general framework for the analysis of freedom of expression. Lamer, with considerable help from Wilson, undertook the task of converting the draft into a finished product. On reviewing Le Dain's working files, Lamer saw Le Dain's painstaking work and the torment the case had caused him: 'He was arguing with himself and sending himself memos and raising issues he didn't really have to raise.'[84] Lamer worked closely with Le Dain's clerks, who were familiar both with the draft and with Le Dain's thinking, and it was decided that

...........t should focus on the language-law appeals in order to dispose of the Bill 101 issues as soon as possible. The Court's detailed framework for analysis of freedom of expression would be left to the lower-profile *Irwin Toy* judgment, which dealt solely and squarely with advertising.

Lamer was convinced that Le Dain had been right to deal with the notwithstanding clause. La Forest, who had not sat on these appeals but took an active interest in the draft judgment, disagreed. He doubted the wisdom of sanctioning Quebec's omnibus invocation of the override and thought that the Court was giving too much away needlessly. In early November 1988 he circulated a memorandum to his colleagues urging them reconsider. He contended that section 33 was intended to be an exception while Quebec had made it the rule: 'I fail to see this as an exception. I think an exception to the *Charter* was meant to stand out by a specific decision on the legislature that is obvious to the public.' La Forest suggested that, because the point was moot, the best course was to avoid it: 'Why should those who would wish to ignore the *Charter* be instructed that they can do so? ... I would be much happier, since it can be avoided, not to underline how few clothes the emperor has.'[85]

Le Dain's clerks responded with a memorandum explaining that Le Dain decided to deal with the point because it had been fully argued and had continuing significance for other cases.[86] Lamer agreed with the clerks and disagreed with La Forest. He pointed out that the cases had been under reserve for almost a year and that many prosecutions under the Quebec sign law were being held in abeyance awaiting the Court's ruling. 'We cannot leave these prosecutions in limbo pending another test case slowly making its way up to us. If a majority is for leaving it unanswered, I will write concurring reasons answering it.'[87] McIntyre quickly agreed with Lamer[88] and, it would seem, the point was put to rest. Despite the views that had been expressed at conference, and over La Forest's objection, the Court would decide the section 33 issue in Quebec's favour.

There was another reason for dealing with section 33 which was never referred to in the memoranda but which may have influenced the judges. The blow of striking down an important part of Bill 101 would be considerably softened by a section 33 ruling allowing Quebec to exempt its language laws from the reach of the Charter. From a legal perspective, the Court could justify answering the section 33 question by saying that it was giving valuable guidance on a point that had been fully argued. From a political perspective, the Court could tell Quebec that, whatever the scope of the individual rights guaranteed by the Charter, the province had all the tools it needed to promote and protect the French language within its borders.

By mid-November, while Lamer and Wilson were putting the finishing touches to the judgment, Dickson had some misgivings since the draft seemed to extend full constitutional protection to commercial expression.[89] Wilson, for her part, worried that Dickson's suggested differential treatment for commercial expression might introduce the discredited American 'levels of scrutiny' approach.[90] She was to express similar concerns the next year about Dickson's *Keegstra* judgment.[91] In both cases, Dickson agreed to downplay any suggestion that different types of expression received different levels of protection from the Court.[92]

Before the draft was completed, Jean Beetz retired from the Court for health reasons at the age of sixty-one after fifteen years on the Court.[93] Two weeks later, Gerald Le Dain also resigned for health reasons at the age of sixty-four. Le Dain's illness precluded him from signing the judgment that had driven him to retirement; however, Beetz was able to participate in reserve judgments for the statutory six-month period and, despite his retirement, the Court's quorum for the Bill 101 judgments was assured.

When the Court gave notice that its long-awaited judgment would soon be released, media reports speculated that the Court would strike down the requirement for French-only signs. Some thought that the Court might adopt an 'inside-outside' solution, allowing bilingual signs inside shops but requiring French exterior signs.[94] The situation in Montreal was tense. In September a bomb had exploded at a Montreal office of Lise Bacon, who, as minister for cultural affairs, was responsible for the administration of Bill 101. Shops displaying bilingual signs in defiance of the law were vandalized, and Quebec nationalists were already lobbying Bourassa to invoke the notwithstanding clause in anticipation of an adverse judgment from the Supreme Court.

The Supreme Court released its carefully crafted decisions on the sign-law cases on 15 December 1988. Neither side could claim total victory. The Court ruled that Bill 101's requirement of French-only signs and French-only firm names violated the guarantee of freedom of expression in both the Canadian Charter and Quebec's own Charter of Human Rights and Freedoms. The attorney general of Quebec's argument that freedom of expression should be interpreted narrowly was deemed to be inconsistent with the large and liberal interpretation of Charter rights the Court had adopted in earlier cases. Commercial speech, said the Court, has 'intrinsic value as expression,' hardly a surprising conclusion in the context of the case being fought primarily to vindicate issues of linguistic respect rather that merely commercial interests. The Court also noted that the constitution protects the rights of listeners as well as speakers and that commercial speech 'plays a significant role in enabling individuals to make informed economic choices, an important aspect of individual self-fulfillment and personal autonomy.'[95]

More important, the Court also ruled that freedom of expression included the right to use the language of one's choice. It distinguished the specific language rights of the Charter, which require affirmative measures from government to ensure the provision of certain services in both official languages, from the sign law, which constrained the individual's freedom of choice. The Court described the reason for protecting choice of language in eloquent terms: 'Language is so intimately related to the form and content of expression that there cannot be true freedom of expression by means of language if one is prohibited from using the language of one's choice. Language is not merely a means or medium of expression; it colours the content and meaning of expression. It is, as the preamble of the *Charter of the French Language* itself indicates, a means by which a people may express its cultural identity. It is also the means by which the individual expresses his or her personal identity and sense of individuality.'[96]

The Court also dismissed the attorney general's argument that the sign law could be justified as a reasonable limit on freedom of expression. It accepted Quebec's right to take steps to protect the French language but ruled that a complete ban on English simply went too far. The Court held that a less intrusive law, allowing some English but 'requiring the predominant display of the French language, even its marked predominance,'[97] would satisfy Quebec's legitimate objective to preserve and enhance the use of French language yet also respect the rights of the English-speaking merchants.

While the decision struck down the existing law, the Court's section 1 analysis gave Quebec considerable latitude to pursue a vigorous language policy favouring the use of French. The Court dismissed the argument that the French-only law was discriminatory and, in the *Devine* appeal, rejected the contention that Quebec lacked competence under the division of powers to enact the Charter of the French Language. The Court had virtually adopted the Meech Lake 'distinct society' principle by recognizing Quebec's special place as the cradle of French language and culture in North America and by holding that the province could limit Charter rights to preserve and enhance the French language within its borders. The Court explicitly gave the green light to measures that would achieve the legitimate goal of presenting to all Quebeckers a 'visage linguistique' and thereby conveying a clear and strong message to all its citizens that it is a society that aspires to be predominantly French speaking. In his retirement, Dickson indicated that he had no reservations about the controversial 'distinct society' clause that many opposed and argued that Quebec was already treated as a distinct society in Canadian constitutional law.[98]

The Court also refused to review Quebec's use of the notwithstanding clause. The Court overruled the Quebec Court of Appeal judgment that had found that the legislature was required to use specific language linking the specific Charter rights being overridden with the specific provisions being immunized from Charter scrutiny.[99] That, said the Supreme Court, would invite substantive judicial review of override declarations, whereas section 33 'lays down requirements of form only,' leaving 'no warrant for importing into it grounds for substantive review of the legislative policy in exercising the override authority in a particular case.'[100] Years later, Dickson described the notwithstanding clause as 'an anomaly because the whole purpose of the Charter is to take away the limitation of the rights out of government, the party in power, and place it with the court.'[101] However, in 1988, he put his personal views to one side and signed the judgment. The omnibus declaration exempting all provincial statutes from the reach of the enumerated sections of the Charter was upheld, leaving Quebec virtually unlimited power to overcome Supreme Court decisions under the Charter. This represented a significant win for the nationalist forces willing to assert the will of the majority to override the rights of the anglophone minority. The only judicial constraint the Court was prepared to impose on the notwithstanding clause was to hold that it could not be invoked retroactively to validate a past violation of constitutional rights.

The Court's decision was welcomed by some as a sensible middle-ground solution. It recognized the rights of the anglophone minority but, at the same time, afforded the francophone majority generous scope to take measures to ensure the vitality of the French language and culture. The Montreal *Gazette* proclaimed that 'there is a quality of true grandeur' in the judgment, which it described as 'a model of clarity, logic, fairness and sensitivity' that 'reflects not only the letter of the law, but the finest spirit of this country's needs and aspirations.'[102]

However, the decision provoked a predictable storm of protest from others. Some nationalists, blind to the subtleties of the judgment and intent on gaining maximum political mileage by portraying the decision as a provocation, painted it as a general attack on Quebec's language laws. The Quebec teachers' union, Centrale des enseignants du Québec, labelled the Supreme Court's decision 'a declaration of war' on French Quebec. The Mouvement National des Québecois claimed that the judgment signalled 'a day of mourning for the Quebec nation, a day on which an attempt is being made to force our people to abandon its advance towards its affirmation and go back to the ghetto of survival.' The group warned that 'the anger of the people will not go unnoticed.' Veteran nationalist labour leader Louis Laberge said that the judgment represented a threat to social peace and 'put Quebec back 20 years.'[103] Prominent Quebec writers and artists expressed dismay[104] and Gilles Rhéaume, leader of the Parti Indépendantiste, said: 'Only one word expresses our needs. It is called independence.'[105]

On the other side, some English-rights advocates were bitterly disappointed that the Court left Quebec with so much room to manoeuvre. One spokesman described the decision as a 'tremendous setback for the cause of two equal and official languages.' Morton Brownstein, the owner of La Chaussure Brown (Brown's Shoes), won his case but sensed that the war was not yet over: 'It's not a victory because it can be overruled by the premier of the province.' Complaining that he had received bomb threats, Brownstein promised not to put up English signs until Bourassa announced the government's intended response to the decision. 'We will not contravene the law or do anything to upset the sensitive balance that exists in the province right now.' Another litigant, seventy-six-year-old Allan Singer, was bitterly disappointed since he had clearly lost his ten-year fight to have an English-only sign. He told a news conference: 'It's incredible that my language is disallowed in any part of Canada.'[106]

Premier Bourassa came under immediate and intense pressure from both pro-nationalist and pro-anglophone forces within his own cabinet. The nationalists urged him to invoke the notwithstanding clause while English-speaking cabinet ministers threatened to resign if that step were taken. Moderate voices pointed to the Court's willingness to accept a law that required a 'marked predominance' of French as offering a middle-ground solution, one that seemed to tempt the cautious and conciliatory Bourassa. La Presse continued to advocate the 'inside-outside' solution of French exterior signs and bilingual interior signs, but debated whether the notwithstanding clause would be needed to sustain it.[107] Le Devoir urged respect for minority rights. The headline to its lead editorial proclaimed: 'Le français partout mais sans brimer les droits des autres communautés.'[108]

Parti Québécois leader Jacques Parizeau urged Bourassa to invoke the notwithstanding clause and, in his characteristically bombastic style, warned English-speaking merchants not to inflame the situation by erecting English signs before the issue was finally resolved: 'For God's sake, hold your horses for a little while. No provocation.'[109] At the same time, Parizeau urged Montrealers to attend a public meeting at the nationalist shrine, Paul Sauvé arena, to protest the threatened demise of Bill 101. At a rally held on 18 December 1988, Parizeau told the crowd that the Court's decision underscored the importance of achieving independence for Quebec and he urged Bourassa to invoke the notwithstanding clause.

National political leaders, sensitive to volatility in Quebec, were cautious. The day after the judgment was released, Prime Minister Mulroney said that he had not yet read the Court's pronouncement, but he chided those who had so quickly condemned it, observing: 'It would be helpful if people read the judgment first before they speak on it.'[110] Opposition leader John Turner refused to comment, as did NDP leader Ed Broadbent.

In less than a week, Bourassa announced that he would use the notwithstanding clause to introduce a new bill requiring French-only exterior signs but allowing bilingual signs inside shops so long as French predominated. The issue was too emotive and the political pressure too great to make compromise possible. Bourassa's solution was too little for some Quebec nationalists and too much for the anglophone community. Parizeau accused Bourassa of betraying Quebec by caving in to bilingual signs while three of Bourassa's four anglophone cabinet colleagues resigned in protest against the banning of English exterior signs and the invocation of the override.

Although Dickson, as a sitting judge, kept his views to himself at the time, he was disappointed by Bourassa's use of the notwithstanding clause. He thought that it undermined support for bilingualism elsewhere in Canada and that it undermined the authority of the Supreme Court:

> I was saddened ... because I think it had, from a political point of view, a very serious impact upon people in Western Canada who had been very supportive of bilingualism, but when this action was taken denying the right of English ... The reaction was very, very negative, and continues to be negative to some extent. The other thing I think was unfortunate was in effect overriding the decision of the Supreme Court of Canada which I could not really feel was the best thing for the Province of Quebec or for Canada, or particularly for the Supreme Court of this country.[111]

Dickson's misgivings about Quebec's use of the override were matched by the deep concern he expressed about Manitoba's defiance of constitutional bilingualism. He believed that Canada would be better off if both bilingualism and the Court's decisions were willingly accepted in all parts of the country.

Bourassa defended the use of the override by referring to the Meech Lake Accord's 'distinct society' clause, causing alarm among those in the rest of Canada who feared that this vague clause would give Quebec too much latitude to trample individual rights in the name of preserving Quebec's cultural heritage. It quickly became apparent that Bourassa would pay an enormous political price for invoking the notwithstanding clause. Two provinces, Manitoba and New Brunswick, had yet to ratify the Meech Lake Accord, the cornerstone of Bourassa's constitutional position. Manitoba Premier Gary Filmon described Bourassa's decision as a 'national tragedy' and stated bluntly that he would not push for the ratification unless Quebec changed its language policy. New Brunswick Premier Frank McKenna called for a first ministers' conference to amend the accord to guarantee the rights of linguistic minorities. Without a doubt, then, Bourassa's use of the override contributed to the demise of the Meech Lake Accord and moved the country towards yet another national unity crisis, one that preoccupied Dickson in his retirement years.

'This nation's commitment to the values of bilingualism and biculturalism'

Dickson's final word on language rights came in 1990 in the *Mahé* case from Alberta.[112] A group of francophone parents in Edmonton complained that Alberta's education legislation failed to accord them adequate management and control of the French-language education to which their children were entitled under the Charter's minority-language education guarantee.[113] The long list of counsel who argued *Mahé* included two future Supreme Court justices, Jack Major and Michel Bastarache. Major argued in favour of limiting minority-language education rights while Bastarache urged their expansion. Nine years later, however, as Supreme Court justices, they would co-author a judgment overruling the narrow approach to the interpretation of language rights in *Société des Acadiens*.[114]

Beetz, who had written the majority opinion in *Société des Acadiens*, had retired by the time *Mahé* was argued. It soon became clear from the conference discussion that there would be a decided shift away from the narrow approach he had taken in *Société des Acadiens*. As Dickson's conference memorandum stated: 'The Court seems to be very much of one view with minor variations.'[115] Peter Cory spoke first. As a trial judge, Cory had worked hard to become bilingual, and, as a member of the Ontario Court of Appeal, he had decided a minority-language case in Ontario.[116] Cory spoke 'in favour of encouraging bilingualism and biculturalism' and giving the francophone population a significant role in the management and control of instruction and available educational facilities.

Gonthier agreed: he said that section 23 'is a remedial section which should have a purposive and broad interpretation.' Like the other judges, Gonthier was sensitive to the political consequences of according generous interpretation to language rights. He observed that 'a greater degree of French language teaching in Western Canada would encourage mobility and the movement of francophones from Quebec to the West.' Sopinka, too, agreed 'that we should take a special approach to s. 23. It should receive a broad interpretation.' La Forest pushed for a generous interpretation of management and control: 'The whole system cannot function without giving the minority interest positive say in the management and the education.'

Dickson referred to the divisive effect of Quebec's refusal to accept the minority-language education guarantee: 'I felt the action of Mr. Bourassa ... had done great damage to the attitude of Western Canadians towards encouragement of bilingualism.' He added that 'the judgment will have to be very carefully drafted' and that he was 'fully in accord with the views expressed by all members of the Court that bilingualism should be encouraged and that a proper educational facility be provided for the minority group where numbers warrant it.'

Dickson agreed to write the judgment. His comments at conference and the judgment he prepared reflect his strongly held view that the rights of minority-language groups must be respected, particularly in light of the Quebec separatist movement. Dickson described minority-language education rights as the 'linchpin in this nation's commitment to the values of bilingualism and biculturalism.' The general purpose of these rights, he wrote, 'is to preserve and promote the two official languages of Canada, and their respective cultures, by ensuring that each language flourishes, as far as possible, in provinces where it is not spoken by the majority of the population.' Dickson found that the Charter entitled minority-language communities to a significant level of management and control of their children's schools on the basis of a 'sliding scale approach' that guarantees a level of rights and services appropriate to the number of students involved. He refused to be tied down by the narrow approach of the majority in *Société des Acadiens*, stressing the remedial component of the section 23 guarantee and the importance of schools as community centres for linguistic and cultural activities. He interpreted language rights as having a significant cultural component: 'Language is more than a mere means of communication, it is part and parcel of the identity and culture of the people speaking it.' While accepting that language rights were different from other rights and that they were to be carefully interpreted, he held that 'this does not mean that courts should not "breathe life" into the expressed purpose of the section, or avoid implementing the possibly novel remedies needed to achieve that purpose.'[117]

Dickson was alive to the political realities of minority-language education rights. Aware that he was treading on very sensitive political ground, he took pains to base the Court's decision on the fundamental political choice of the framers of the Charter 'to remedy the perceived defects of these regimes by uniform corrective measures.' He accepted the francophone parents' contention that 'history reveals that s. 23 was designed to correct, on a national scale, the progressive erosion of minority official language groups and to give effect to the concept of the "equal partnership" of the two official language groups in the context of education.'[118] Perhaps recalling the opposition that his proposed mandatory remedy in the *Manitoba Language Reference* had received from his colleagues, Dickson was cautious about the terms of the Court's order. He stressed that the Court would only declare in general terms what section 23 of the Charter required. This would leave the government with the flexibility necessary to fashion the best response in the circumstances, but the Court also made it clear that it expected the government to act promptly and in good faith. Alberta Premier Don Getty, however, called for 'bilingualism by choice, not law' and minority-language school legislation was not enacted for three and half years after the Court's decision.[119]

Language Rights and National Unity

Dickson's strong commitment to bilingualism was a product of several factors. First and foremost, he saw bilingualism as a key element to Canada's national unity. He believed that the survival of the country depended in large part upon respecting language rights, and he saw Manitoba's refusal to honour the historic rights of its francophone minority, the failure of Quebec to respect the rights of English-speaking merchants, and the unwillingness of Alberta to live up to its constitutional obligations to provide adequate schools for its francophone citizens as denials of the rights enshrined in the constitution that could threaten Canada's continued existence if not remedied judicially. Ill-treatment of linguistic minorities also offended Dickson's sense of fairness, or what Charles Gonthier called Dickson's 'preoccupation for the underdog.'[120] As La Forest puts it: 'It was part of his very strong feeling for human rights generally, but it was more than that – his generosity and sense of unfairness ... A sense of injustice, as you know, is more important than a sense of justice.'[121] Dickson's strong support for language rights was also a product of the complex weave of individualism and communitarianism in his thinking. He considered language to be a central element of individual identity and the means by which one expresses one's own identity and individuality. Dickson also saw language as vital to the needs and interests of distinctive communities. Language is the 'glue' that holds communities together and Dickson thought that communities should be nurtured. He was prepared to assert judicial power to protect vulnerable minorities, and, as with equality rights and aboriginal rights, he was not prepared to defer to legislative authority where the majority trampled on minority rights.

21

The Honour of the Crown

Dickson wrote judgments in almost every aboriginal-rights case of significance during his seventeen years on the Court. As the Court's representative
from the prairies, he often volunteered to write in decisions that came from the
western provinces, but his geographical origins alone cannot explain a genuine interest in aboriginal issues that would continue even after his retirement.
In part, he was influenced by his experience in Manitoba with aboriginal people. As already recounted, the Dicksons employed Joseph Wawence from the
Whitedog reserve and tried to help the Wawence family when their daughter
became seriously ill, and they also established scholarships at a Winnipeg private school for aboriginal children. These encounters may seem minimal and a
product of a certain sense of noblesse oblige, but they contributed to Dickson's
understanding of the disadvantage suffered by aboriginal people in Canadian
society.

Gérard La Forest, who co-authored a landmark case on aboriginal rights
with Dickson, thought that Dickson believed that aboriginal people 'needed to
be taken care of in a way' and that sometimes Dickson 'was too good to them
for their own good.'[1] History was important to Dickson and he very much
believed that the honour of the crown was at stake in determining the scope of
aboriginal rights. His approach reflected the precarious position of aboriginal
interests in law and he imposed duties of fairness on governments in part
because they exercised extraordinary powers over aboriginal people. Near the
end of his judicial career, Dickson was increasingly willing to integrate aboriginal perspectives into the law. Later, after his retirement from the bench, he
consulted widely with aboriginal people and concluded that aboriginal self-

government should be the central focus for the Royal Commission on Aboriginal Peoples which the Mulroney government established in 1991. As in so many other areas, Dickson's thinking evolved over time.

Dickson's approach to aboriginal rights provides further indication that there were communitarian elements in his thought. In this respect, his later judicial decisions and his post-retirement belief in the need for aboriginal self-government may be contrasted with the scepticism of liberal individualism towards treaty and self-government rights. Pierre Trudeau argued in 1969 that 'we must be all equal under the laws and we must not sign treaties amongst ourselves and many of these treaties indeed would have less and less significance in the future anyway.' Trudeau also opposed the aboriginal self-government provisions in the 1992 Charlottetown Accord on the basis they imposed a 'hierarchy ... of citizens' and allowed 'collective rights [to] take precedence over individual rights.'[2] Dickson, on the other hand, accepted group rights tied to aboriginal ancestry and historical treaties and believed that aboriginal rights to fish and hunt should have priority over other uses of the land.

The 'biases and prejudices of another era ... [are] no longer acceptable'

In 1983 Dickson persuaded the entire Court to agree to the principle that statutes and treaties should be interpreted generously, with ambiguities being resolved in favour of the Indians.[3] Just how far Dickson was prepared to take this principle remained to be seen since the 1983 case involved clear statutory language exempting Indians from taxation on reserves. Two years later, Dickson's reading of the 1752 Treaty of Peace and Friendship between the British crown and the Mi'kmaq demonstrated that he was prepared to take the principle a very long way.

The Nova Scotia courts had taken a hard line in rejecting claims based on the 1752 treaty. The trial judge bluntly held that 'the right to hunt no longer exists because the land has been settled and occupied by the white man for purposes of farming.'[4] The Court of Appeal went further. It refused to view the 1752 agreement as a treaty made by competent parties. In any event, any agreement was, in its view, terminated by subsequent hostilities between the Mi'kmaq and the crown. Finally, the accused had failed to establish his descent from the Indians who signed the agreement. Dickson also originally had doubts about the case. The accused Simon, a member of the Shubenacadie band, was found in possession of a rifle on a public road near his reserve without a proper hunting licence and during a closed hunting season. Dickson's initial view was to maintain the tough stance he had taken in such cases in the past.[5] At conference, he told his colleagues: 'A treaty does not extend to unlimited hunting. It is subject to implied conditions that hunting rights must be reasonably compatible with public claims and demands. It is impliedly revoked by the opening of the highway.'[6] Dickson prepared a partial draft convicting Simon, but then he asked himself whether he was paying adequate attention to the principle he had announced two years earlier when he persuaded the Court to adopt the canon of liberal and generous interpretation of treaties. That would require him to resolve every doubt in Simon's favour, and in the end he acquitted Simon.

A 1929 Nova Scotia decision held that the Indians did not have sufficient status or capacity to enter into a treaty. The judge had argued in that case that 'the Indians were never regarded as an independent power. A civilized nation first discovering a country of uncivilized people or savages held such country as its own ... The savages' rights of sovereignty even ownership were never recognized.'[7] Dickson's law clerk, Colleen Sheppard, drew his attention to the offensive assumptions underlying the 1929 case. Sheppard, who had worked with aboriginal organizations before her clerkship and later became a law professor specializing in equality rights, wrote a memo arguing that the 1929 case 'contains some very racist and out-dated language.' She was concerned that in his early draft, Dickson made no comment about these 'blatant anti-Indian biases,' and she urged him 'to condemn explicitly the attitudes.'[8] Dickson always encouraged his law clerks to be candid and this was not the first or the last time that a clerk would help educate Dickson about changing social attitudes and sensibilities. He decided to repudiate both the language and assumptions of the 1929 decision as reflecting 'biases and prejudices of another era in our history. Such language is no longer acceptable in Canadian law and indeed is inconsistent with a growing sensitivity to native rights in Canada.'[9] He concluded that the Mi'kmaq chief had the authority and capacity to enter into a treaty.

Dickson turned to the contention that the governor, who had not secured the agreement of Great Britain, did not have the authority to enter into a treaty. Here he attempted to view the matter from the aboriginal perspective and again relied on the new principle of resolving doubts in favour of the Indians: 'It is fair to assume that the Micmac would have believed that Governor Hopson, acting on behalf of His Majesty the King, had the necessary authority to enter into a valid treaty with them. I would hold that the Treaty of 1752 was validly created by the competent parties.'[10] Dickson also rejected the idea that the Indians must give up land to enter into valid treaties, as was the norm on the prairies. He recognized that long before such treaties were signed, the white man had relied on the goodwill of aboriginal people not only for peace and friendship but for survival.

Dickson interpreted the reference to hunting 'as usual' in the 1752 treaty in a generous manner. He rejected the government's attempt to freeze the type of weapons the Indians could use to hunt as 'an unnecessary and artificial construct out of keeping with the principle that Indian treaties should be liberally construed.' The treaty right should 'be interpreted in a flexible way that is sensitive to the evolution of changes in normal hunting practices.' Judges should make sure that the treaty would 'continue to be an effective source of protection of hunting rights' in the future. This was the same broad and forward-looking approach that Dickson was applying to Charter rights. He described the evidence that the treaty had been terminated by subsequent hostilities between the Mi'kmaq and the British as 'inconclusive and conflicting.' Employing the principle that doubts should be resolved in favour of the Indians, he concluded that the crown had failed to prove that the treaty was terminated. 'Given the serious and far-reaching consequences of a finding that a treaty right has been extinguished, it seems appropriate to demand strict proof of the fact of extinguishment.'[11] This was an extremely important finding. The 1982 constitution protected only existing aboriginal and treaty rights that had not been extinguished and the Court had been evenly divided in the 1973 Nisga'a land-claims cases on the proper test for extinguishment.[12] Dickson's judgment meant that the Court now accepted the stricter test championed by Dickson's predecessor, Emmett Hall. A clear and plain intent was now necessary to establish extinguishment of aboriginal rights. A task force reviewing federal land-claims policy later that year concluded that Dickson's judgment meant that the government would now have the burden of 'strict proof' that any aboriginal rights had been extinguished. In the wake of Dickson's judgment, 'the proposition that aboriginal title can be implicitly superseded by law lacks a solid legal basis.'[13]

Dickson dismissed the technical argument that Simon had not properly proven his line of Mi'kmaq descent. This finding also had broader implications since he was prepared to make allowance for the fact that 'Micmac traditions are largely oral in nature.' Dickson pointed out that 'to impose an impossible burden of proof would, in effect, render nugatory any right to hunt.'[14] Treaty rights, just like Charter rights, should not be interpreted in a restrictive way that would render them meaningless.

Simon shows Dickson at his open-minded best. He paid heed to his law clerk's perceptive comments, reconsidered his initial inclination to convict Simon, and resolved the case by applying the principle that doubts should be resolved in favour of the Indians. *Simon* demonstrated a generous approach to defining and interpreting treaties as solemn commitments that could not easily be extinguished and would provide meaningful and evolving protections in the future. It was praised by most commentators and welcomed by aboriginal people as a sign that courts would take their treaty rights seriously.

'Equity will not countenance unconscionable behaviour'

Long before he became a judge, Dickson believed that aboriginal people had often been taken advantage of and gotten a bad deal.[15] A landmark 1984 case demonstrated what he was prepared to do to ensure that aboriginal people were treated fairly and honourably. In 1957 the Musqueam band surrendered 162 acres of prime land in Vancouver to the crown, which then leased it to the Shaughnessy Heights Golf Club for a seventy-five-year period. This procedure was required by a basic principle of aboriginal title, which requires all dealings in Indian lands to be conducted through the crown. The Crown negotiated a long-term lease on terms extremely favourable to the golf club, with the band not even being given a copy of the lease until 1970.[16] In 1984 the Golf Club paid only $33,000 a year to lease some of the most valuable land in Vancouver. The band believed that a fairer rent would have been $1.9 million a year.[17]

The band, led by its chief Delbert Guerin, took the government to court. The trial judge found the crown liable for breach of trust and awarded the band $10 million in damages. In a judgment written by Gerald Le Dain before his appointment to the Supreme Court, the Federal Court of Appeal reversed on the basis that the crown's statutory discretion to deal with surrendered lands from Indian reserves as it saw fit was incompatible with holding the crown liable for breach of trust. Dickson's conference notes indicate that all members of the Court agreed that the terms of the lease were 'disgraceful' and that the Musqueam's appeal should be allowed. Dickson believed that Le Dain had taken a 'a very technical view of things.'[18]

The Court was badly divided over the proper approach to be applied. Wilson was assigned the task of preparing first reasons and she held that the crown breached an 'express trust' when it had leased the land surrendered by the band at such unfavourable terms. In her view, there was 'no magic to the creation of the trust' and one had been created by the band's surrender of the land to the crown.[19] Dickson agreed with the result, but he thought that Wilson was stretching the law of trusts beyond the breaking point. He accepted law clerk Mark Freiman's assessment that it was 'entirely unnecessary to stretch and, with respect, deform the laws of trusts to this extent to arrive at an equitable solution.'[20] Dickson also disagreed with Estey's solution based on the law of agency. Dickson knew that he would not be able to persuade Wilson to abandon her reasons, and so, gently, and without success, he attempted to persuade Estey to abandon his: 'Ultimately I am concerned that the Court in allowing the claim of the Indian Band would be permitting recovery on three very different legal bases. So far as is humanly possible, I think we should seek to speak as one voice.'[21]

Dickson decided the case on the theory that the crown owed the band a fiduciary duty. This approach was more rooted in the unique nature of aboriginal land interests than Estey's agency approach or Wilson's trusts approach. It also provided more guidance for less egregious cases of abuse of the relationship between the crown and First Nations. Dickson started his judgment from the proposition that the Musqueam had a 'pre-existing legal right'[22] to the land by virtue of their prior occupancy of the land. He reached this conclusion without regard to any statute or treaty and even though six years earlier he had avoided recognizing such a pre-existing aboriginal legal right in another case from British Columbia.[23] Dickson stressed that the right was 'unique' and only roughly analogized to general property law. The key features of aboriginal title was that it could not be sold or given to anyone but the crown. Both the Royal Proclamation of 1763 and the Indian Act prevented Indians from selling their land to private persons and required that the crown interpose itself 'between the Indians and prospective purchasers or lessees of their land, so as to prevent the Indians from being exploited.'[24] Dickson responded to this imbalance of power by holding that the courts had an equitable duty to 'supervise the relationship' by requiring the crown to treat the Indians with the utmost fairness. The precarious nature of aboriginal title for Dickson triggered the Court's equitable jurisdiction to ensure that the crown's considerable powers were not abused.

Dickson sought to avoid some of the paternalistic overtones of the fiduciary-duty approach. He stressed that the crown had breached its fiduciary duty not because it had misjudged what was in the band's best interests but because it had not consulted the band about the terms of the golf-course lease.[25] Viewed in this light, the imposition of a fiduciary duty was not a paternalistic edict to the government to take care of the Indians, but rather a means to ensure that aboriginal people were consulted and could participate before the crown made decisions that affected their interests.

Fiduciary duties had previously only arisen in private law and Dickson knew that he was breaking new ground. He stressed that the fiduciary duty imposed on the federal crown was not a duty of either public or private law but a unique duty that stemmed from the special status of Aboriginal title: 'I repeat, the fiduciary obligation which is owed to the Indians by the Crown is sui generis. Given the unique character both of the Indians' interest in land and of their historical relationship with the Crown, the fact that this is so should occasion no surprise.' He had no doubt that the conduct of the crown fell below the required standard. The crown promised the band a favourable lease but then negotiated unfavourable terms without consulting the band. 'Equity will not countenance unconscionable behaviour in a fiduciary, whose duty is that of utmost loyalty to his principal.'[26]

The decision in *Guerin* was hailed by the chief of the Musqueam as 'a great victory for the Musqueam people' and for 'all bands across the country' because it established the principle of a legally enforceable relationship of trust between the crown and aboriginal people. Commentators noted, too, that the Court's new fiduciary duty would influence close to ninety outstanding claims between bands and the crown.[27] The decision also influenced the way the Dickson and the Court were to interpret the aboriginal-rights provisions which, along with the Charter, were added to the constitution in 1982.

'A solemn commitment that must be given meaningful content'

A last-minute addition to the patriation package provided in section 35(1) of the Constitution Act, 1982 that 'the existing aboriginal and treaty rights of the aboriginal peoples of Canada are hereby recognized and affirmed.' No provision for aboriginal and treaty rights had been included in the package introduced by Prime Minister Trudeau in September 1980; many provinces feared the implications of entrenching such rights and Trudeau was prepared to leave them out to obtain provincial agreement. After a special joint committee heard from many aboriginal groups, however, the federal government agreed in early 1981 to recognize aboriginal and treaty rights in the constitutional package. But, when negotiations resumed after the Supreme Court's decision in the *Patriation Reference*, aboriginal rights were again deleted, largely at British Columbia's insistence.[28] In the end, they were restored but subject to the qualification that only 'existing' rights were to be protected. Many worried that the courts might find that many aboriginal and treaty rights had been extinguished before 1982, or that they would be defined to incorporate the largely unfettered ability that legislatures enjoyed before 1982 to regulate, infringe, and even extinguish them.

The Supreme Court heard its first case interpreting the new provision in November 1988. Because of the illnesses of Jean Beetz and Gerald Le Dain, only seven judges sat. The final judgment was not released under the end of May 1990, after William McIntyre had retired, reducing the panel to six. Dickson's conference notes reflect the many unsettled questions about the ambiguous provision: 'The main question is what is the effect of s.35(1)? Does it change the position of the Indians or does it not? It is obvious that the section has vast applications beyond fishing rights and during argument it was mentioned that half the city of Montreal is being claimed under it and part of Vancouver and three-quarters of Winnipeg. It is, therefore, important that we write narrowly.'[29] Dickson's initial inclination may have been to keep the decision narrow, but in the end he worked hard to ensure that the decision laid the same strong foundations for aboriginal rights as his early decisions had for Charter rights.

Like so many other landmark aboriginal-rights cases, this one came from British Columbia. It involved a member of the Musqueam band, Ronald Sparrow, who was charged with fishing with a drift net that was longer than allowed under the band's food fishing licence. With the exception of Bertha Wilson, who thought that the crown had not justified the net-length restriction on the basis of conservation, the consensus at conference was that although Sparrow might have an aboriginal right to fish for food, the regulation was probably justified and he should be convicted. La Forest, who, Dickson noted, was 'anxious to write,' was assigned the task of preparing the judgment. He had a deep knowledge of regulations affecting the fishery which he would bring to bear on the case.

In September 1989 La Forest circulated a draft judgment which would have convicted Sparrow of fishing in violation of the net-length restrictions. He explained in an accompanying memorandum that he had found an aboriginal right to fish for food and ceremonial purposes even though this would 'give rise to serious allocation and management problems.' However, he drew the line at aboriginal rights to fish for commercial purposes: 'It would effect a drastic reallocation of the fishing industry in British Columbia if one took the view that it was commercial.'[30] He insisted that 'the federal power to regulate continues. That is absolutely essential and nothing in the Constitution suggests otherwise.' This rendered aboriginal rights entirely subject to regulation and reflected La Forest's conviction that the courts were ill-equipped to second-guess the reasons of government for regulating complex issues of fishery management. It also mirrored the deferential approach to limitations on Charter rights under section 1 that he had consistently urged.[31]

La Forest's draft was not well received in all quarters of the Court. Dickson found it too narrow and decided to write his own reasons. In March 1990 Wilson sent La Forest a memorandum copied to the Court, indicating that she was 'very uncomfortable' with his approach. She feared that La Forest had interpreted the aboriginal right to fish in a way that did not account for the 'changed lifestyle for Indians in the 20th Century.' Wilson was also concerned that La Forest had imposed too low a burden for the government to justify limitations of aboriginal rights. She thought that the test for limiting rights should incorporate the federal government's fiduciary relationship with the band and the idea that aboriginal fishing should have priority. Wilson argued, 'surely the Indian right must be the last to abate and it seems to me that it ill becomes the federal government to allege otherwise.' She questioned whether La Forest's approach would not make the constitutional recognition of aboriginal rights meaningless. If the federal government was able to erode aboriginal rights in the same manner as before 1982 'one wonders what the Indians got as a result of s.35(1) for which they fought so hard.'[32]

A month later, Wilson directed another memorandum to Dickson. She stressed a number of important points that are reflected in the Court's final judgment. She rejected the idea that existing aboriginal and treaty rights were frozen or should be defined by reference to the powers that governments had before 1982 'so as to cut down those rights. These past regulations may not have been justified. They may have been in violation of the Federal Government's fiduciary duty.' Wilson saw 'no reason to constitutionalize what has been done on the assumption that it was all legal. If we do that, it means that native people start off in 1982 with diminished rights, not "treaty" rights.'[33] Wilson insisted that aboriginal rights be interpreted in the same generous and purposive manner as *Charter* rights.

Wilson also returned to the theme that any limitation on aboriginal rights must be consistent with the crown's fiduciary duty as recognized in *Guerin*. 'I am strongly of the view that the Government cannot pass regulations at will without regard to their impact on the Indians.' Such an unfettered approach would make aboriginal rights 'completely illusory in the sense that they are subject to total defeasance at the hands of those obliged to protect them.'[34] As she had with *Charter* rights, Wilson insisted on a rigorous test to determine whether limitations on aboriginal rights were justified.

Less than a week later, La Forest interrupted his work on other judgments to respond. Following a line of reasoning that he would also take (over Wilson's dissent) in one of these cases, involving mandatory retirement,[35] La Forest warned about the distributive and regulatory consequences of allowing aboriginal rights to evolve to protect commercial fishing. He stressed the disruptive effects that such rights would have on the important non-aboriginal commercial fishery, foreshadowing the controversies that would erupt in the Maritimes several years later after another Supreme Court decision that recognized some aboriginal commercial fishing rights: 'I am always concerned about disrupting individuals as opposed to governments. I fear anything that may detrimentally affect the public's goodwill towards Indians.'[36] La Forest argued that the Court should defer to government attempts to regulate aboriginal rights as long as they were undertaken in good faith. To impose a strict standard of justification would result in 'a perfect nightmare for the regulator' and could result in 'an extremely unwise use of judicial resources' that would second-guess experts. He warned that regulating the fishery was more complex than hunting, in which 'you shoot one animal at a time.' He also expressed doubt that aboriginal people had special knowledge about managing the fishery.[37]

These memoranda reveal Dickson mediating between the strongest poles of his Court – the restrained deference of La Forest and the principled activism of Wilson. They also demonstrate how the approaches of all three judges to the Charter influenced their approach to aboriginal rights. Dickson leaned towards Wilson's more robust approach to defining rights, but he was not entirely unsympathetic to La Forest's caution. In the end, he bridged the gap and, with the help of both La Forest and Wilson, fashioned a judgment for a unanimous Court. The judgment was a halfway house that was strong enough, both in its definition of aboriginal rights and in the onus it placed on governments to justify limitations, to satisfy Wilson, but sufficiently qualified to win La Forest's support. The judgment was issued under the names of both Dickson and La Forest. Wilson, who had contributed significantly to the final judgment, believed that it should have gone out under only Dickson's name because 'it reflects the position you have taken on the appeal from the outset subject to some suggestions from the rest of us including, I am sure, La Forest J.'[38] For his part, La Forest was entirely sympathetic to Dickson's attempts to forge a consensus, especially since the Court was down to six judges. He told Dickson that he refrained from going it alone 'because it might split the Court down the middle ... I am sympathetic to the general balancing you propose, and that is the essence of the case. This time we can avoid our specific views of the nature of aboriginal rights themselves. We should fight that in another context where we do not have an even Court.'[39]

Sparrow was handed down at the end of May 1990. The judgment is consistent with Dickson's purposive and generous approach to the interpretation of Charter rights and his relatively strict approach to their limitation. The Court rejected the notion that aboriginal rights were frozen in the state that they existed in 1982. Such an approach 'would incorporate into the Constitution a crazy patchwork of regulations' and result in arbitrary differences that would not accord with the status of aboriginal rights as constitutional rights. 'Far from being defined according to the regulatory scheme in place in 1982, the phrase "existing aboriginal rights" must be interpreted flexibly so as to permit their evolution over time.'[40] The rejection of the idea of frozen rights reflected the same flexible and 'living tree' approach that Dickson had taken to the interpretation of Charter rights. The Court also rejected the government's argument that the Musqueam's fishing rights had been extinguished because they had been subject to detailed and restrictive regulation and licensing prior to 1982. This argument 'confuses regulation with extinguishment.'[41] The Musqueam were particularly pleased with this part of the ruling and stated that 'it confirms our belief and stated position over countless years that our aboriginal rights to fish, hunt, possess lands etc. ... have never been surrendered or extinguished.'[42] Georges Erasmus, national chief of the Assembly of First Nations, praised the Court for accepting 'that our rights are real and must be fully respected.'[43]

As Wilson had urged, the Court clearly stated that aboriginal rights should be defined in a 'generous, liberal' manner because section 35 'represents the culmination of a long and difficult struggle in both the political forum and the courts for constitutional recognition of aboriginal rights' and 'a solemn commitment that must be given meaningful content.'[44] The Court cited extensive academic argument to the effect that the entrenchment of aboriginal rights in 1982 '"renounces the old rules of the game."' Perhaps reflecting some of Dickson's own movement on aboriginal rights, the Court noted the distance travelled since 1969 when the federal government argued that aboriginal claims to land 'are so general and undefined' that they lacked any legal force and projects such as the James Bay Development could be commenced 'without regard to the rights of the Indians that lived there.'[45]

But parts of the final decision also reflected La Forest's more cautious approach. The Court stressed that the 'salmon fishery has always constituted an integral part of [the Musqueam's] distinctive culture' and that it did not extend to commercial fishing. The Court noted that it had heard 'from numerous interveners representing commercial fishing interests'; that it was aware of the 'possibility of conflict between aboriginal fishing and the competitive commercial fishery with respect to economically valuable fish such as salmon'; and that this conflict might intensify 'as fish availability drops, demand rises and tensions increase.'[46]

The Court also concluded that aboriginal rights were not absolute or immune from 'government regulation in a society that ... is increasingly more complex, interdependent, and sophisticated and where exhaustible resources need protection and management.' Although the reasonable-limits clause of section 1 of the Charter did not apply to aboriginal rights, the Court concluded that 'rights that are recognized and affirmed are not absolute.'[47] The idea that aboriginal rights could be subject to justified restrictions was a compromise between unregulated and absolute aboriginal rights and weak aboriginal rights that would be subject to whatever regulation was in place in 1982. This halfway-house approach appealed to Dickson and was also consistent with his long-time belief that aboriginal rights could be limited for reasons of conservation. The Court stressed that any justified limitation must, as under *Oakes*, relate to a compelling and substantial governmental objective. Conservation and the prevention of harm were valid objectives, but the 'public interest' was too vague. The Court added that conservation of limited resources was 'consistent with aboriginal beliefs and practices, and, indeed, with the enhancement of aboriginal rights.'[48]

Under section 1 of the Charter, something more than an important governmental objective was required to justify the limitation of a right. In place of the section 1 proportionality analysis, the Court incorporated the crown's trust-like relationship and fiduciary duty towards aboriginal people, as Wilson had urged. In language similar to Dickson's judgment in *Guerin*, the Court warned that 'the honour of the Crown is at stake in dealings with aboriginal peoples. The special trust relationship and the responsibility of the government vis à vis aboriginals must be the first consideration in determining whether the legislation or action in question can be justified.'[49] Consistent with *Guerin*, the Court encouraged the crown to consult with aboriginal people about proposed limitations on their rights. Dickson subsequently explained that the case urged 'those charged with making regulations' to 'sit down with the Native people and discuss what is reasonable having regard to the fish stocks available and the necessity for some degree of conservation in the interests of everybody ... it shouldn't be simply a matter of dictating from above, but ... a matter of co-operation between the various competing claims ...'[50] La Forest recalled that Dickson saw the need to consult aboriginal people as a matter 'of good manners.'[51]

The justification process was not a simple matter of balancing the conflicting claims. Following Dickson's dissent in *Jack*,[52] the Court indicated that aboriginal fishing rights should have priority over non-aboriginal fishing. 'The constitutional nature of the Musqueam food fishing rights means that any allocation of priorities after valid conservation measures have been implemented must give top priority to Indian food fishing.' Reflecting Dickson's and Wilson's understanding of rights, such a priority was necessary to ensure that aboriginal rights 'are taken seriously' and respected by 'the government, courts and indeed all Canadians.'[53] The most difficult issues of giving aboriginal uses of scarce resources priority over non-aboriginal uses of the same resources were, however, avoided by the Court's decision, at La Forest's insistence, that aboriginal fishing rights were limited to food fishing and did not extend to commercial fishing. The limited nature of the ruling avoided the type of split in the Court that Dickson, Wilson, and La Forest all wanted to avoid.

'A Honoured Elder' Sets up the Royal Commission on Aboriginal Peoples

The Court's decision in *Sparrow* was released in the early summer of 1990. By the end of the summer, almost 4,000 troops had been deployed in response to demonstrations and an armed occupation by the Mohawk in Oka, Quebec, during the course of which one police officer was killed. The focus of the Oka dispute was a proposed expansion of a golf course over aboriginal burial grounds. A year later, a parliamentary committee reviewing 'the summer of 1990' found that tensions were still running high. It was 'struck by the fact that several key parties involved in the standoff have indicated that they would not change their actions if they faced the same situation again. In this sense, while everyone deplores the use of violence and deplores the loss of life, neither side to the dispute has taken much responsibility for ensuring history does not repeat itself. The Committee believes this is not a conclusion that Canadians will accept.'[54] The other important event in the summer of 1990 was the death of the Meech Lake Accord. Elijah Harper, an aboriginal member of Manitoba's Legislative Assembly, played a key role in this story by refusing to consent to an expedited vote on the ratification of the accord because the accord did not deal with aboriginal issues. In doing so, Harper became a hero for many aboriginal people.

In the still charged aftermath of Oka and the failure of the Meech Lake Accord, Prime Minister Brian Mulroney announced in April 1991 that the government would appoint a royal commission on aboriginal people. This initiative formed part of Mulroney's overall strategy to secure agreement to a new constitutional accord acceptable to Quebec, aboriginals, and the rest of the country. Mulroney hoped that the proposed royal commission and his stated support for aboriginal self-government would appeal to aboriginal leaders and that they would take up his invitation to work together as partners with government to 'reinforce the unity and integrity of Canada.'[55] Mulroney's proposal for a royal commission was, however, initially not well received. A week after the speech, Mulroney received a letter from Georges Erasmus, the grand chief of the Assembly of First Nations, Viola Robinson, head of the Native Council of Canada, and Rosemarie Kuptna, the head of the Inuit Tapirisat. These leaders of key aboriginal organizations told the prime minister that 'the lack of consultation prior to your announcement of this proposal raises questions about how you intend the Royal Commission to proceed. We are concerned that a Royal Commission could delay further action to adequately settle Aboriginal constitutional, land, social and economic issues.'[56]

The prime minister had a major problem on his hands. A refusal by powerful aboriginal organizations to cooperate with the royal commission would put even more strain on already tense relations and might undermine attempts to win aboriginal support for any new constitutional package. Mulroney's response was to enlist Brian Dickson, the recently retired chief justice, to consult with aboriginal people in drafting the mandate and determining the composition of the royal commission. Dickson had become something of a hero for many aboriginal people because of his strong stand on issues of aboriginal rights, culminating in the decision in *Sparrow*.[57] In less than two weeks, Mulroney answered the aboriginal leaders: 'I can think of few Canadians who could undertake the responsibilities of such consultations better than the former Chief Justice. I know that he will want to speak to you in fulfilling his mandate ...'[58]

Dickson accepted the arduous and somewhat risky task of devising the mandate and composition of the royal commission for a number of reasons. For one thing, he was genuinely interested in the issues. As a judge, he had 'spent long weeks, sometimes months, researching aboriginal history and traditions and their relationship to contemporary social, cultural, economic and political issues. This process of research, reflection, and writing prompted in me a great interest in our aboriginal people, their history, their current frustrations and their aspirations for a better future.' The prime minister's request also appealed to Dickson's devotion to public service. Dickson sounded like a loyal soldier: 'I believe that if a Prime Minister asks one for advice and assistance, one should do his or her best to provide them.' Finally, Dickson believed that Canada was in a state of crisis and he wanted to help. Profoundly concerned by the failure of Meech, the crisis at Oka, and the prospect that Quebec might vote to separate, Dickson felt 'deeply that this wonderful country is at a crucial juncture in its history. One of the major reasons for this fragility is a deep sense of alienation and frustration felt by, I believe, the vast majority of Canadian Indians, Inuit and Métis.'[59] This was no time to say no to the country that he loved.

Dickson's reputation endowed the royal commission with legitimacy and his involvement was a key factor in convincing aboriginal leaders to accept a commission they originally did not want. Michael Mitchell, grand chief of the Mohawk Council of Akewesasne, wrote: 'I initially had little confidence in the idea of a commission which would only tell us that we are economically, socially and politically deprived. Your appointment, however, as advisor to the Prime Minister on the Terms of Reference and the credibility you have among aboriginal peoples, has given me renewed hope that not only will we be heard, but that our ideas will be acted upon.'[60] Joseph Norton of the Mohawk Council of Kahnawake similarly viewed Dickson's 'appointment as a positive signal that the government is sincere in this initiative. Further, your commitment to consultation is a welcome change to the manner in which aboriginal issues are usually addressed.'[61] Viola Robinson of the Native Council of Canada told Dickson that his advice to the prime minister would carry 'unimpeachable weight ... I leave you with the good wishes and respect owed you as a honoured elder and I ask simply that you remember that the suggestions you make will help to determine the life of the people yet unborn.'[62]

Immediately after accepting Mulroney's request, Dickson told reporters that 'there is no point in dilly-dallying ... The sooner the royal commission gets going the better'. He promised 'to consult as broadly as possible with the various native groups, the Indians, the Métis and the Inuit and non-native groups who have an interest in this matter.' With the openness to assistance from all quarters that characterized his work on the bench, Dickson added: 'If any

Canadian wants to contribute something, I'd welcome it.'[63] Dickson made good on these promises. He met with the leaders of six different aboriginal groups and all seven aboriginal parliamentarians. He made a special effort to send letters to 1,682 aboriginal people but received only 153 replies.[64]

Dickson had an open-door policy and met with every aboriginal group and individual who requested a meeting during the month of June. Stephen Toope, his former law clerk who, along with James MacPherson, assisted Dickson during the summer of 1991, describes the many meetings:

> I would sit in on these meetings with people who had every reason to be com-
> pletely cynical and doubtful about this process, but because he was doing it
> they weren't ... I don't think there was a single negative meeting ... People
> would always start in a very respectful fashion by commenting on the impor-
> tant role that he played in the life of Aboriginal people and they would always
> refer to certain cases, if they were fairly sophisticated. But even less sophisti-
> cated people knew of him and saw him as an elder ... He was perceived as an
> elder and treated as such. He was completely comfortable in those meetings, he
> handled them just beautifully, I was so impressed ... It was actually extremely
> moving.[65]

Dickson discussed his new project with Barbara and they had Grand Chief Ovide Mercredi and his daughter for a meal at Marchmont.[66] Dickson was impressed by Mercredi, whom he described as 'very eloquent' and 'very thoughtful' and committed to his cause. Although the memories of the confrontation at Oka were still fresh, Dickson felt that he received cooperation from everyone he consulted: 'Whether you are a Native or non-Native the feeling was, lets see what the problems are and let's avoid a repetition of that sort of violent action.'[67]

Dickson spoke at the Assembly of First Nations' annual meeting in Winnipeg in June 1991. Mercredi felt comfortable enough with Dickson to introduce him as 'Mr. Sparrow,' in reference to the Court's landmark decision delivered a year earlier, and he told Dickson that he was among friends 'because you have been a leader in de-colonizing Canadian law.' Dickson then told the audience of over four hundred chiefs that 'I have lived some 41 years in Manitoba and I'm quite familiar with the local situation.' He added that the aboriginal leaders he had talked with 'all seem upbeat, they all seem positive, optimistic ... feeling that this Royal Commission can really accomplish something and I share that view ... the country has never been more receptive to this sort of hearing ... the goal shared across the country is the full participation of Canada's aboriginal people in Canada's economic prosperity and political life ... a very great deal can be accomplished for the betterment of the aboriginal people and for the betterment of our great country.'[68] The assembled chiefs greeted Dickson warmly but also made their concerns known. One Ontario chief told Dickson, 'We have reached our breaking point.' Mercredi stressed that 'we're going to make sure the mandate is clear, it is comprehensive and it's ours ... We're not interested in a study about Indians, but more a study of Canada and its treatment of Indians.' As would happen countless times that summer, Dickson was warned of the danger that the royal commission's report will 'go on another shelf in Ottawa and collect dust.' Dickson responded that the commission was 'regarded as something of great importance to Canada by those in a position of power.'[69]

By the end of the summer Dickson had proposed a massive mandate for the royal commission. The breadth of this mandate reflected the depth of the problems that aboriginal people had told Dickson they faced. It also reflected Dickson's own approach to aboriginal issues.[70] As in many of his aboriginal-rights judgments, he started with the history of the relationship between aboriginal people and the Canadian government and society. In Dickson's view, 'the essential task is to break the pattern of paternalism which has characterized the relationship between aboriginal peoples and Canadian governments.'[71] Dickson believed that self-government was the answer to breaking the bonds of paternalism, and on this point the commission's mandate reflected his own changing views. As a judge, he had stressed the need for the government to treat aboriginal people fairly, but the consultations during the summer of 1991 convinced him to move beyond fair treatment towards empowerment so that aboriginal people could pursue their own priorities and aspirations.

The commission's mandate covered most of the legal, social, cultural and economic dimensions of aboriginal life in Canada. It demonstrated Dickson's interest as a lawyer in the justice system and the treaties and also many other subjects, including economics, cultures, education, and the north, a part of Canada that fascinated him. In 1987, travelling in an old DC-3, Dickson had gone on circuit in the western Arctic, and, after his retirement, he braved travel in an even smaller plane to go on circuit in the eastern Arctic. Dickson, who loved the outdoors, was fascinated by the extremes faced by those who lived in the Arctic and he believed that the royal commission should devote considerable time studying the north and travelling to remote aboriginal communities.

With his experience in the business world, Dickson did not believe that the commission should focus simply on matters of legal, political, social, and cultural justice. In his view, aboriginal self-government was 'tied intimately to land and economic issues. It is not a purely constitutional question.' He believed that aboriginal governments should benefit from Canada's 'well-established tradition of wealthier regions and populations providing assistance to poorer regions and population groups.'[72] He also recommended that the disadvantages faced by aboriginal women should be one of the commission's areas of study, something he backed up by his recommendation of two aboriginal women to serve on the commission. Reflecting his belief in the importance of language, Dickson also recommended that the preservation of aboriginal languages be another focus of the commission's research.

The commission's broad mandate was a matter of some controversy. At their first meeting, the commissioners proposed a prize for the first person to think of something that Dickson had left out. No one won.[73] Certainly, the mandate increased the cost and time required for the commission to complete its work: Dickson had told prospective commissioners that the inquiry would be completed in around two years but it took five. Some have argued that the mandate placed too much emphasis on self-government while others wonder whether the massive mandate made it easier for governments to neglect the commission's extensive recommendations. Dickson had no regrets. At a speech at the release of the five-volume final report, running close to 4,000 pages, he acknowledged that 'there is no doubt that the terms of reference I established for the Commission imposed substantial and difficult duties on the Commissioners. Those terms dealt with virtually every historical, political, legal, cultural, economic and social aspect of the lives of our aboriginal peoples. However, in setting such comprehensive terms of reference, my sincere hope was that progress could be made on many fronts so that there would never be a need to appoint another Royal Commission on Aboriginal Peoples.'[74]

Dickson assembled files on over 480 people who had been nominated to serve on the commission, and he recommended seven people to be named commissioners. Four of the seven were aboriginal and they represented the diversity of Canada's aboriginal population. He explained to the prime minister that 'Aboriginal people are obviously going to be most directly affected by the recommendations of the Commission. Moreover, if "self-government" means anything, it must mean that aboriginal perspectives are central to any redefinition of the relationship between native communities and the Canadian polity as a whole.'[75]

Dickson's selections were politically shrewd.[76] As co-chairs, he recommended former Assembly of First Nations Grand Chief Georges Erasmus and Quebec judge René Dussault. Erasmus was a well-respected aboriginal leader who had originally complained to Mulroney about the lack of consultation before the commission was announced. Dussault was added as a co-chair near the end of the process to ensure a strong presence from Quebec; the violence at Oka had occurred in Quebec and aboriginal claims would be important in the next Quebec referendum on separation from Canada. Dickson's first choice for the non-aboriginal co-chair of the commission had been Bertha Wilson who graciously agreed to serve on the commission in any event even though some press reports had already named her as the co-chair.[77] Dickson greatly respected and admired his former colleague, and he knew of her genuine interest and respect for aboriginal people. In one of the last aboriginal-rights cases that they sat together on, Wilson had written a memorandum about the need for sensitivity to aboriginal spirituality: 'I would not want to tell the Indians what was or was not an Indian religious practice in 1760 and for that matter today.'[78]

Three of the seven commissioners recommended by Dickson were women. One, as already noted, was Bertha Wilson. Another was Viola Robinson, the Nova Scotia Mi'kmaq who, as head of the Native Council of Canada, had complained to Mulroney about the lack of consultation before the royal commission was announced. Robinson had also written Dickson a long and thoughtful letter about the importance of the commission. The third woman recommended by Dickson, was Mary Sillett, a social worker from Labrador who had been president of the Inuit Women's association and vice-president of the Inuit Tapirisat, another organization that had complained about Mulroney's initial lack of consultation. Dickson's recommendation that there be two aboriginal women among the seven commissioners was wise given the concerns that some aboriginal women had about self-government.[79]

Given his long-standing connections with the University of Manitoba, it was not surprising that Dickson recommended the head of its native-studies program, Paul Chartrand, a Metis, to the commission. This would ensure that the aboriginal commissioners reflected the definition of aboriginal people in the 1982 constitution as including Indians, Inuit, and Metis. Dickson also recommended Allan Blakeney, the respected former NDP premier of Saskatchewan. Blakeney could draw on his wealth of practical political experience to make sure that the commission's recommendations were practical and would not sit on the shelf. Blakeney, like Chartrand, came from the prairies where aboriginal issues were particularly urgent. As it turned out, however, Blakeney would resign from the commission after about two years and was replaced by Peter Meekison, an academic and senior civil servant from Alberta.

Dickson had lunch with Mulroney near the end of the summer of 1991 to present his recommendations. Mulroney accepted them all. In a successful attempt to win aboriginal support for the commission, the prime minister had effectively delegated to the retired chief justice the power to determine the commission's membership and terms of reference.

Although his official work was done, Dickson continued to take an interest in the work of the royal commission. A month after the commission had released an interim report on the inherent right of aboriginal self-government – a report that some had criticized in the press as a 'blank cheque'[80] – Dickson made a strong speech in favour of self-government. Dickson had recommended that the commission make such interim reports as a means of influencing the policy process, including the ongoing negotiations about a new constitutional package. He reminded the Conference on First Peoples and the Constitution that the commission's terms of reference – terms he had drafted – required the commission to examine 'the recognition and affirmation of aboriginal self-government, its origins, content and strategy for progressive implementation.' He noted that the commission was not alone in its support of the inherent right of aboriginal self-government and had received support from many committees, commissions, and academics. He argued: 'Canadians must begin to question why we found it so easy to justify asserting sovereignty over aboriginal people, and justified taking aboriginal land. The answers are not too easy to digest.'[81]

After the release of the commission's final report in late 1996, and in the midst of much criticism of the cost and time required to fulfil its massive mandate, the eighty-year-old Dickson urged 'all Canada's governments ... to carefully consider the Report of the Commission and to implement its recommendations. This report must not gather dust on government shelves. I truly hope that all governments will approach it in the same spirit of deep commitment and generosity of spirit as the Commissioners. I trust that today will mark a new and historic beginning between Canada and its Aboriginal Peoples ... I hope that other Canadians will lend their active support, as aboriginal rights continue to be the most pressing human rights issues facing Canadians.'[82]

From Paternalism to Empowerment

As in other areas, Dickson's approach to aboriginal issues evolved over time. In the 1970s, he made generous allowance for private property rights and parliamentary supremacy when interpreting aboriginal hunting rights.[83] In the early 1980s, he established a principle that treaties and laws should be interpreted generously to resolve any ambiguity in favour of the Indians.[84] In the mid-1980s, he fashioned important precedents stressing the obligations of the crown to treat aboriginal people honourably and to take aboriginal rights seriously. These decisions won Dickson trust and respect from aboriginal people. The final steps in Dickson's journey on aboriginal issues was his acceptance of aboriginal self-government, as reflected in the mandate of the Royal Commission on Aboriginal Peoples and, as will be seen in the next chapter, his defence of the 1992 Charlottetown Accord, which constitutionally recognized the principle of native self-government. Dickson's constant starting point was sympathy towards aboriginal people, but his views, like those of Canadian society, took shape gradually, moving from paternalism towards respect, understanding, and a desire that aboriginal people be empowered to govern themselves. As in so many other areas, Dickson's journey was part of Canada's journey.

PART SIX

Retirement, 1990–1998

22

Dickson of Canada

On 4 April 1990 Dickson asked his driver to take him from Marchmont to the prime minister's residence at 24 Sussex Drive. Brian Mulroney greeted Dickson warmly. Dickson handed Mulroney a letter to confirm what he had already told the prime minister: he intended to retire from the bench at the end of the Court's term in June 1990. Dickson next went to the Court where he dictated a memo to the staff. He asked his colleagues to convene in the judges' conference room. He told Court staff that he wanted them 'to know of my decision before it is announced publicly and to express my appreciation to you for the support you have given me during my tenure.'[1] The message caused many tears as the news spread through the building. Claire L'Heureux-Dubé, who had been taken aback by Dickson's military manner when she joined the Court, wept when Dickson broke the news of his retirement.

Dickson was not required to retire until 25 May 1991, his seventy-fifth birthday, but, after discussing the matter at length with Barbara, he decided that 'in fairness to whoever succeeded me as Chief Justice I should retire at the end of the preceding term which was in effect the end of June of 1990' and not in 'the middle of the busiest term of the court.' It was a difficult decision, but he supported mandatory retirement for judges and even wondered whether a retirement age of seventy years of age might be more appropriate given the increasing workload at the Court and 'the stress and strain of the work.'[2]

'You will be remembered as the greatest Chief Justice'

Dickson received many tributes once his retirement was announced. One newspaper observed that 'under his leadership, the court has breathed life into the *Charter* – and given the people a real forum for the protection of their rights.'[3] Judges, lawyers, law professors, law students, and friends from across Canada and in many other countries wrote congratulating him on his career and extending best wishes for his retirement. He was particularly touched by a card signed by all the law students at the University of Manitoba and kind notes from his colleagues and former colleagues on the Court. Dickson replied to all the letters, explaining why he was 'hanging up my skates' and often noting that he was leaving the Court with 'some regret' and 'mixed feelings.' He wrote that he would miss the challenging work and close association with so many fine colleagues but that he and Barbara anticipated enjoying an active retirement, full of travel and more time with their four children and five grandchildren. In these letters, Dickson often commented on the privilege it had been to serve on the Court for seventeen years and how time had passed quickly.[4]

Within a few weeks of Dickson's announcement, the Mulroneys hosted the Dicksons and their guests for a dinner at 24 Sussex celebrating his career. Antonio Lamer, Dickson's successor as chief justice, had already given a speech late in 1989 stating that, when Dickson 'retires, he will stand out as our most important judge ever.'[5] Claire L'Heureux-Dubé wrote Dickson a fond note stating, 'You will be remembered as the greatest Chief Justice of all times, progressive yet not radical, firm but humane. Those who, like me, have had the privilege to serve under your leadership will also praise your thoughtfulness and dedication.'[6] Former colleagues Ronald Martland and William McIntyre also wrote letters praising Dickson for his service to the country and the Court. Jean Beetz, the person who had served with Dickson the longest and who would die of cancer the next year, at only sixty-four years of age, wrote expressing gratitude for Dickson's 'devotion to the Court and to your colleagues, and for your extraordinary contribution to the law, to justice and to the good of Canada, this free but fragile and precious country.'[7] Beetz's eloquent, handwritten letter adverted to the national-unity debate that would very much preoccupy Dickson during his retirement.

The Court held a retirement ceremony for Dickson on 21 June 1990. Dickson fell badly just before the judges were about to enter the courtroom for the ceremony. He was already in pain from a fall on the ice a few months earlier when he broke one of his vertebrae, an injury that had prevented him from going on his beloved early morning horse rides.[8] His colleagues tried to convince him to sit down for a moment to collect himself, but he adamantly refused and insisted upon going into Court immediately so the proceedings would not be delayed. Lamer spoke first about Dickson's contributions to many areas of the law and how the Court under Dickson's leadership had gotten rid of an eighteen-month backlog of cases. Minister of Justice Kim Campbell next described

Dickson as 'the father of *Charter* interpretation, and it is for this that history will best remember you ... Under you, the Court has helped reshape Canadian life.' She added that Dickson's judgments were characterized by their clear, direct, and memorable language and their intelligence, humanity, and embrace of human dignity and equality. The president of the Law Society of Manitoba commented on how Dickson 'made time to engage in public service for the welfare of the Manitoba community' and how these 'human concerns ... were reflected from the bench.' In his own remarks, Dickson emphasized the profound changes that the Court had undergone during his seventeen years in Ottawa, beginning with the amendment to the Supreme Court Act that enabled it to gain control of its docket in 1975 and culminating with the enactment of the Charter in 1982. 'As Canada's court of last resort, we sit in final judgment of the rights of all those who make their home in this magnificent land. The trust imposed in us by our fellow citizens is enormous, and the intellectual and moral challenge we face daily is, to say the least, exhilarating. The ideals we seek to uphold, justice and the rule of law, are among the most noble human aspirations. I am thankful to my country that I have been allowed to participate as a judge for these past almost 23 years.'[9]

The Supreme Court Act, as already explained, gives a retired judge six months to dispose reserved judgments. Dickson dreaded the publication of a judgment with a 'star' beside his name to show that he sat on the case but could not participate in the result because of his retirement and he drove his colleagues very hard to avoid the possibility. As Wilson joked with La Forest, 'That wasn't nice of Brian!'[10] Many of these judgments, released in the last half of 1990, were highly important. They included Dickson's judgment in *Keegstra* upholding hate propaganda offences under section 1 of the Charter, the Court's judgment upholding mandatory retirement as a reasonable limit on equality rights, and a judgment on the insanity defence in which the Court accepted one of Dickson's earlier dissents.[11] Bertha Wilson surprised many by joining Dickson in retirement less than a year later, well before her seventy-fifth birthday. The departure of these two judicial giants seemed to many, both within and outside the Court, to mark the end of an era.

'I'd love to be there again'

Dickson sorely missed his life as a judge, and Barbara could see that her husband missed the Court every day of his retirement.[12] At the same time, however, Dickson remained active and committed to public service for Canada until his death in 1998. As discussed in the previous chapter, he played an important role during the summer of 1991 in establishing the mandate and composition of the Royal Commission on Aboriginal Peoples. He sat as an arbitrator and helped the Canadian Bar Association with a civil-justice reform project. He was a member of one of the first panels to hear a dispute under the North American Free Trade Agreement. The dispute involved Canadian wheat and Dickson, the proud Canadian and westerner, was very happy when he managed to persuade the panel to rule unanimously in Canada's favour.[13] As previously discussed, Dickson began to speak out on the need to treat disabled people fairly, and he also gave speeches throughout Canada, in the United States, and in Hong Kong on the Charter. Like his eldest son, Brian, who continued his career as a senior diplomatic officer, the retired judge who had always relished foreign travel took pride in representing Canada abroad. He prepared for these trips with the same systematic and obsessive attention to detail he had devoted to his judicial work.

Still taking a keen interest in details of life at the Court, Dickson regularly called Lamer, his successor, to comment on matters such as the colour of the Christmas lights and typographical errors in the Court's bulletin of proceedings,[14] and he continued to follow closely the Court's judgments. Peter Cory and Frank Iacobucci visited him at Marchmont, and Dickson called former colleague Gérard La Forest to comment on the Court's work.[15] Shortly before he died, Dickson was asked what he missed about the bench. He replied: 'Everything. I'd love to be there again.'[16]

Return to Duty

In his retirement and until his death, Dickson took on a number of important and demanding assignments involving the Canadian Forces. In 1995 he accepted a special commission to examine and make recommendations regarding the role of Canada's military reserve forces. Dickson undertook this assignment together with one of Canada's leading military historians, Professor J.L. Granatstein, and retired Lieutenant-General Charles Belzile. As part of this inquiry, in June 1995 the seventy-nine-year-old Dickson went on a ten-day 'western swing.' For four days in a row, Dickson and his fellow commissioners held hearings in Winnipeg, Regina, Edmonton, and Calgary. In each city, the hearings lasted into the evening. Dickson, accompanied as always by Barbara, then moved on to Vancouver, where the gruelling schedule eased with two days of hearings and two free days. They needed some rest because the next day there was a 5:45 A.M. departure, an hour that Dickson underlined in his itinerary, for a seven-hour passage on a navy ship through the Straits of Juan de Fuca to Victoria, where they would have three hours of public hearings in the afternoon and another two hours in the evening. The next day, the tour of duty was over and the Dicksons flew home to Ottawa and Marchmont.[17]

Dickson followed this rigorous, military-style schedule with great relish.

The commission heard over three hundred witnesses in fourteen cities across Canada, received hundreds of written submissions, held over fifty technical briefings, and, to Dickson's great satisfaction, accomplished its work more than a quarter of a million dollars under budget. The commission's report, delivered on 30 October 1995, recommended treating the reserves as full members of the defence team, with improved pay and benefits, the opportunity to become active in day-to-day operations of the Canadian Forces, and job-protection legislation to allow reservists to train and serve for extended periods without jeopardizing their civilian employment. Defence Minister David Collenette announced the government's intention to implement most of the Committee's recommendations.[18]

In January 1997 Minister of Defence Doug Young appointed Dickson to chair a special advisory group on military justice and the military police. This assignment came in the wake of the killing of a defenceless young Somali by Canadian peacekeepers in 1993, the appointment of a major royal commission to investigate, and the disbandment of the Canadian Airborne Regiment. Dickson and the other members of the special advisory group – retired Lieutenant General Charles Belzile and retired politician Bud Bird – were given only three months to complete the report. They travelled across the country and held public hearings from Halifax to Vancouver. Their report reflected Dickson's continued pride in the military and spoke of 'the generally high calibre of men and women of all ranks and in all services of the Canadian military establishment with whom we have come in contact during the course of our study.'[19] The military, reeling under an onslaught of criticism associated with the killing of a prisoner in Somalia, must surely have been grateful for these words of confidence. The report outlined a number of reforms that would ensure that military justice and investigations by the military police were carried out in accordance with the rule of law and the Charter of Rights and Freedoms. It stressed the need for independent prosecutors, defence lawyers, and judges to remove courts martial from the chain of command and provide oversight and complaint procedures. It also recommended the abolition of the death penalty, still an available court-martial penalty. Although he had once held that the death penalty did not violate the Canadian Bill of Rights,[20] Dickson's views continued to evolve. He ended his life as an adamant opponent of the death penalty and it was on his recommendation that the last vestiges of the death penalty were removed from Canadian law.[21]

The report also recognized that, at times, military justice had to be expeditious. It stressed the importance of summary trials that would allow 'the chain of command to administer discipline and justice in a swift, decisive and final matter, both under combat circumstances in times of war and in training circumstances in time of peace.'[22] Dickson believed that it was vitally important to remove any doubt about the validity of summary trials under the Charter. This led to recommendations for reducing the severity of punishment, providing some legal assistance to the soldier charged, and better training of the presiding officer. At a news conference at the National War Museum when the report was released, Dickson stressed that summary trials 'were an essential instrument to maintain discipline within the units.' Even in peacetime, 'the integrity of the chain of command can only be preserved if discipline is inculcated at each level of the military hierarchy.'[23] Dickson knew from painful personal experience the costs of breakdown in military discipline, but he also believed that soldiers and officers alike should be treated fairly at all levels of military justice.

Once again, Dickson proudly noted that the report was completed on time and under budget. The minister of defence immediately gave him another assignment, this time to review the minister's own quasi-judicial powers. Dickson's report, again on time and under budget, proposed giving independent judges, rather than the minister, the power to make most military-justice decisions. The recommendations were accepted by the government and became law.[24]

These military assignments brought Dickson full circle. He treated military personnel of all ranks with dignity and respect and he believed that it was his duty to assist and support the military in a time of crisis. In 1997 he received the Vimy Award in recognition of his service to Canada and its military during the Second World War and in his retirement. He looked forward to the awards ceremony at the Chateau Laurier for two hundred guests in black tie and full military dress. He even enquired whether it would be appropriate for his youngest grandchild, Brian, then only eight years old, to attend and was delighted that the boy could join the other members of the family for the evening. Dickson was proud to receive the award, but he also used his acceptance speech to defend the military from what he believed was unfair criticism in the wake of the Somalia scandal. He noted how impressed he was 'with the men and women who are engaged in the service of our nation, both as regular and reserve members of the Canadian Forces. They are intelligent, articulate – often in both official languages – well trained and ambitious. They are also fervent advocates of our nation' who are committed 'to the defence of this nation and the preservation of its democratic ideals.' Dickson viewed the harsh public criticisms of the military through the eyes of both a loyal retired soldier concerned with the status of the military in Canada and a retired judge concerned with fairness. After characteristically editing out even stronger criticism, Dickson declared himself 'deeply saddened' by the media coverage that had 'savagely attacked' and 'destroyed' the careers of several individuals. Dickson, who, as a judge, had stressed the importance of democratic values and fairness, argued that 'democracy implies self-restraint in our judgment of others, just as surely as justice entails the presumption of innocence in our criminal law. For it is just as serious a matter to send a man to jail who has not committed a crime, as it is to destroy his reputation because he could not be heard over the din of knee-jerk public condemnation.'[25]

'This free but fragile and precious country'

The judge who had been moved to tears at the playing of 'O Canada' shortly after the victory of the 'No' side in the 1980 referendum on Quebec sovereignty was in his retirement a citizen who could offer his advice to governments and speak publicly on contentious national-unity issues. The collapse of the Meech Lake Accord in 1990 and opposition to the constitutional recognition of Quebec as a distinct society fuelled sovereignist sentiment in Quebec. Lucien Bouchard left the Conservative government to form the separatist Bloc Québécois and the Quebec National Assembly enacted a law that required a referendum on Quebec sovereignty to be held by 26 October 1992.[26] A concerned Dickson became deeply engaged on the unity file as the country he loved so dearly lurched from crisis to crisis.

Shortly after Dickson delivered his report establishing the Royal Commission on Aboriginal Peoples to the prime minister at the end of the summer of 1991, Mulroney sought Dickson's advice on new constitutional proposals that the government was developing, proposals that would culminate in the Charlottetown Accord of 1992. Although he had maintained appropriate judicial silence at the time, Dickson supported Meech and he believed that former prime minister Pierre Trudeau's opposition to the accord 'had been very unhelpful to the country.'[27]

Dickson took Mulroney's request for advice seriously and in reply wrote the prime minister a fourteen-page, single-spaced letter that went through many drafts. He argued that 'a resurgent sentiment of nationalism, separatism and sovereignty in Quebec' was producing a crisis in Canada, one that he traced to three events: Quebec's refusal to agree to the patriation of the constitution and the Charter in the early 1980s, its use of the override to reverse the Supreme Court's decision striking down part of its language legislation, and the defeat of Meech Lake, 'an event, in my view, to be deplored and with potentially tragic consequences for our country.'

Dickson told Mulroney that he was 'greatly saddened' by the fact that many in Quebec were accepting separation 'as a fait accompli.' Concerned that after separation neither Quebec nor the rest of Canada 'would have the economic footing to compete in the global market place,' he believed that 'the acrimony which would undoubtedly accompany divorce, and the settlements of accounts consequent thereon' would have 'the most serious consequences' for all Canadians. As a former chief justice of Canada, Dickson was worried that one of the many 'catastrophic' effects of separation would be that the Supreme Court of Canada, which by law requires three judges to be members of the Quebec bar, would 'as we know it ... no longer exist.'[28]

Dickson's constant concern about the rule of law, as well as his passionate determination that Canada should not be broken apart, led him to propose to Mulroney that the federal government challenge Quebec's claim to be able to separate without the agreement of the rest of Canada. Dickson indicated to Mulroney that 'although I have only seen but one or two brief references to the point, I am at a loss to know how, under the present Constitution, to which Quebec is subject, that the province could legally secede from the rest of the country.' The retired chief justice pointed out to the prime minister that: 'our Constitution makes no mention of the right of a province to withdraw from the federation. The patriation of our Constitution was delayed for some fifty years because the federal authority and the provinces were unable to agree on the language of an amending formula. That is a small change compared with the suggestion that a province can unilaterally, and perhaps against the will of the rest of the country, leave the federation and become an independent state.'[29] Dickson's thinking foreshadowed the tougher and more legalistic 'Plan B' approach which he would later advocate to a different government.

Mulroney's immediate priority was not to mount a legal challenge to Quebec's claims but to fashion a new constitutional package that would win over both Quebec and aboriginal people. Dickson said that he was sympathetic with Mulroney's attempt to build and expand on the defeated Meech Lake Accord. Unlike Trudeau, Dickson had no trouble with the recognition of Quebec as a distinct society because in his view 'Quebec has been a distinct society socio-logically and constitutionally since the *Quebec Act* of 1774.' Dickson also believed that Quebec's Civil Code was an important reason for that province's distinct status within Canada. He accepted, too, constitutional recognition of aboriginal self-government and advised Mulroney that 'the aboriginal people should be assured' that any delay in the implementation of the right 'is not ... to delay, but, on the contrary, to affirm self-government within a finite period.'[30]

Although Dickson had a deep commitment to the rights of the individual, he was also sympathetic to the collective claims of aboriginal people and Quebec's special role in the Canadian federation. He was instinctively sympathetic to Mulroney's attempts to accommodate competing demands. Throughout his career, Dickson had mediated between the competing views of Laskin, who favoured a strong central government, and Beetz, who supported strong provincial governments, as well as between the insistence of Wilson and Lamer that the courts actively enforce Charter rights and the more cautious approach of La Forest and McIntyre who argued that courts should often defer to governments. It was not a huge step for Dickson to sympathize with Mulroney's attempts to broker an inclusive constitutional package that would meet what he believed were grave threats to the continued existence of the country. For Dickson, halfway houses of accommodation and compromise suited the complex Canadian reality.

Dickson was not opposed in principle to a provincial role in appointing judges to the Supreme Court of Canada. After all, he was a westerner who had some sympathy with western feelings of alienation from Canada's federal institutions. Yet he worried about the details – would the northern territories be involved? Would all or only some western provinces submit a short list when a western seat on the Court became vacant? Drawing on his difficult experience as chief justice with a short-handed Court, Dickson warned Mulroney that that the Court was 'crippled when there is a vacancy.' Mulroney took Dickson's concerns seriously. The eventual Charlottetown Accord allowed the chief justice of Canada to appoint an interim judge if a Supreme Court vacancy was not filled in ninety days.

Dickson also supported Mulroney's proposal to entrench property rights, but he suggested that property be defined. People should continue to receive compensation for expropriated land, but property rights should not adversely affect the development of public policy on matters such as environment protection, land claims, and gun and rent controls. Dickson had always been concerned about property rights, but he accepted the regulatory and redistributive roles of the modern state.

All in all, Dickson was highly supportive of Mulroney's proposals and expressed the hope that they 'will help to heal the wounds from Meech Lake and will lead to a new and unified country, and a more prosperous future for all Canadians.'[31] He later made several speeches in defence of key elements of the eventual Charlottetown Accord. These speeches reaffirmed Dickson's passionate commitment to aboriginal people, Canadian federalism, the Charter, halfway houses of accommodation, and, most of all, Canada.

'I am passionately in love with my country'

Dickson's first public intervention in the national-unity debate was made at the Conference on First Peoples and the Constitution in March 1992 in Ottawa. Aboriginal self-government was then under active consideration and the leaders of national aboriginal organizations had a seat at the table with the first ministers. In February, the Royal Commission on Aboriginal Peoples had released an interim report in favour of recognizing the inherent right of aboriginal self-government.[32] There was, however, significant opposition to aboriginal self-government and the commission's report, like the demands of aboriginal leaders, was controversial.

Dickson waded into the controversy and defended aboriginal self-government. He spoke of how the many aboriginal people whom he had consulted in setting up the Royal Commission on Aboriginal People 'felt that their historical position in Canada, their traditions and values, and their aspirations are not well understood by most non-native Canadians, and that they are not respected and supported by Canadian governments. The breadth and depth of this frustration troubled me deeply.' For Dickson, 'any process of change or reform in Canada – whether constitutional, economic or social – should not proceed, and cannot succeed, without aboriginal issues being an important part of the agenda.'[33]

Dickson was touched by the fact that, despite their frustration, hardly any of the aboriginal people he had met were cynical. 'The reason for the absence of cynicism was, I believe, that most Canadian natives are remarkably decent, fair, tolerant and compassionate people. There was a palpable integrity about virtually all the native people I met during my consultations ... I was very impressed with their dedication, eloquence and common sense. I was moved by the place that a sense of history and spirituality played in their professional lives.'[34] Dickson intended these words as a compliment to the aboriginal people he had met, but they also described values that Dickson thought were important in any person and that he himself had lived by. Although he did not speak publicly about his religion, the Anglican Church was very important for Dickson and his wife knew that her husband had a serious spiritual side.[35] His Christian faith, combined with his respect for minorities, would have helped him appreciate aboriginal spirituality. At the same time, fairness, common sense, tolerance, integrity, and compassion had been the animating values of Dickson's entire life, from his youth on the prairies during the Depression through his service in the war and subsequent service to the community and during his twenty-seven-year career as a judge.

Dickson also spoke of his understanding of Canada. He argued that 'the establishment of Aboriginal government is not as alien to Canadian tradition as some would have it.' Here Dickson may have been thinking of some critics who, inspired by Trudeau, were arguing that aboriginal self-government would subordinate individual rights to collective groups. Dickson returned to the idea that had animated his decisions in the *Patriation Reference*: 'Canada is a federal country.'[36] He argued that 'Canada already has a well-established tradition of multiple sovereignties, namely, its tradition of federalism.' In Dickson's view, it was not a radical step to add aboriginal self-government to Canada's 'overlapping collective identities and multiple sites of political sovereignty.'

Dickson, the practical man of commerce, noted that aboriginal self-government would not work without a land base. He appealed to Canadian traditions of sharing resources with the less fortunate. Economic support from the better-off jurisdictions of Canada to the less well-off ones, including aboriginal governments, was consistent with Canada's 'well-established tradition of wealthier regions and populations providing assistance to poorer regions and population groups.'[37] This view, too, accorded with the way he lived his own life. Although he never sought publicity for it, Dickson was known as 'a very generous man'[38] who made large and private donations to a broad range of charities. He was wealthy, but he never forgot the situation of the less fortunate. In the words of one colleague, Dickson's 'wealth did not interfere with his philosophy, as it does with some people. He wasn't insensitive to the fact you didn't have money.'[39] As another colleague described him, Dickson was a man of the 'so-called privileged classes' who believed that he should 'watch out for the disadvantaged' and be 'very mindful of the underdogs.'[40]

Dickson also waded into another controversy, namely, whether the Charter should apply to aboriginal governments. A month earlier, Georges Erasmus, the co-chair of the royal commission, had expressed some scepticism about applying the Charter to aboriginal self-government.[41] If Dickson's support for aboriginal self-government risked the ire of some non-aboriginal Canadians, his defence of the Charter ran the risk of offending some aboriginal people. Describing the Charter as 'one of the great watershed events in the political and legal life of our country,' Dickson had no hesitation in saying that 'the fundamental value' of Canada was 'a deep respect for basic human rights.' He added: 'As a former Chief Justice closely associated with expansive interpretations of rights and freedoms, I must say that I am concerned that any new constitutional arrangements take due cognizance of the important values of the *Charter*.'[42] Speaking at a workshop during the conference, Dickson made the widely quoted remark that 'I think the *Charter* should be applicable to all Canadians because it's a great document that we should be very proud of.'[43] Dickson also suggested that he believed the courts had a special role to play in protecting minorities. 'Perhaps courts, rather than political institutions, are better suited to protect people who are at the margins of power.'[44] Dickson remained strongly committed to the Charter and the role of the independent judiciary in listening to claims about oppression and unfairness.

Dickson's support for aboriginal self-government subject to the Charter was another one of his halfway-house compromises. He appreciated the need for aboriginal people to have a vehicle for the expression of their collective identity and values, but he also believed that it was important for all individuals and minorities to have recourse to the courts because of the possibility that any government and any majority might abuse their powers.

Dickson ended his speech with a passionate plea for Canadian unity. His notes for the speech include an undated, handwritten note marked 'P.M,'[45] which may well have recorded a conversation with Prime Minister Mulroney.[46] Mulroney publicly praised Dickson's speech a few days after it was given, a fact which suggests that he may have taken a special interest in Dickson's speech.[47] In any event, Dickson's single page of notes marked 'P.M.' reflected the gist of the passionate closing remarks Dickson made in his March 1992 speech.

Dickson pointed out that a recent poll in *Le Devoir* had indicated that 58 per cent of Quebeckers supported sovereignty-association. Dickson, who always closely read the financial pages, argued: 'The recent downward pressures on the Canadian dollar reflect the increasingly perilous state of our country.' Finance was important, but the country was even more important. 'What was hitherto unthinkable is now thinkable – the break-up of a proud and glorious nation, the envy of every other country in the world. The referendum on Quebec sovereignty is expected to be held in October of this year. The clock is ticking. The hour is late. We Canadians are slow to voice patriotism but I want to say that I believe deeply in Canada, I am passionately in love with my country.'[48] He warned that the 'aboriginal agenda' will fail if the country was not kept together. He urged all Canadians to 'work together as nation builders ... with vision and courage, with generosity and mutual respect. Let us have faith in Canada and its future, for ourselves, our children and our grandchildren.'[49]

Dickson's love of Canada reflected many of his experiences, most notably his wartime service. In June 1992, in a speech before awarding the Vimy Award to General John de Chastelain, he noted that the award was named after 'the first battle in which Canadians fought as an independent force.' Over 7,000 Canadian soldiers were wounded and 3,598 died. Dickson stated that 'those heroic men, French Canadians, English Canadians, Canadians of every language and culture, fought side by side and died side by side. They fought for Canada, a United Canada, not for a fragmented Canada or for any one part or region of Canada.'[50] Although he was speaking about Vimy and the First World War, Dickson was also thinking of his own experience in the Canadian army in the Second World War. In an interview the day after the speech, Dickson stated: 'I spent roughly five years fighting for freedom and for Canada in the Second World War and I fought with French Canadians, I fought with other Canadians, they were representing a country, we weren't representing any section of the country.'[51] Dickson's former law clerk Stephen Toope related Dickson's pride in being Canadian to Dickson's experience in the military, when 'people from an enormous diversity of backgrounds' participated 'in a common experience.'[52] Dickson's colleague and fellow Second World War veteran Peter Cory recalled that Dickson's experiences in the military 'were very vivid for him' and 'very important to him from the point of view of Canadian contribution and how much was done by so many. I know how proud he was to have been Canadian and to have seen what was done by Canadians ...' Cory added that Dickson was 'happy to be involved in serving his country again' in his retirement.[53] In his 1992 speech, Dickson suggested that 'it is not difficult to link the 1917 battle ... to today's struggle for national unity.' He quoted Mulroney, who had argued in a recent speech that 'Canadians owe a great debt to those whose heroism allowed a colony to become a nation. Now it's our turn to make our infinitely more modest sacrifices to strengthen Canada's unity and to honour the memories of those who paid the ultimate price at Vimy so that today, Canada could be strong and free.'[54] The prime minister's words had a more powerful meaning coming from Dickson, the wounded soldier.

'I don't want to swim that river and find I'm in a foreign country'

The Charlottetown Accord was signed by all first ministers, the leaders of the territories, and the leaders of the four aboriginal organizations on 28 August 1992, just a month before Quebec's referendum on sovereignty was scheduled to be held. The accord recognized Quebec as a distinct society and the inherent aboriginal right of self-government and increased the role of the provinces in national institutions. Dickson agreed to be part of a 'yes' committee for the Ottawa/Carlton region and 'tried to give whatever support I could.' The distinguished chief justice and companion of the Order of Canada, who always respected the common sense of the people, even gave a speech at a local fair in favour of the accord.[55] In a candid interview during the summer of 1992, Dickson had described the possible break-up of Canada in emotional terms. 'I don't see how one can take one quarter, a third out of a body and still have any viable things.' The prospect of Quebec separating was personal for Dickson. 'I live on the Ottawa River and across the river is the province of Quebec. One of the most beautiful parts of our country, with the hills, and it's beautiful in every season of the year. I have swam over, but when I arrive I like to feel I'm still in Canada and I don't want to swim that river and find I'm in a foreign country.'[56] Dickson mentioned the break-ups that were happening at the time in Yugoslavia and Czechoslovakia. He also spoke of how 'the position of the natives will suffer tremendously' should Quebec separate and of the 'tremendous' contribution of the French language and culture to 'the quality of life in Canada.' Dickson told the interviewer: 'I think we want to recognize the position of Quebec as a distinct society within Canada. I think we want to entrench aboriginal rights.'[57]

Less than a month before the national referendum on the Charlottetown

Accord, Dickson made another speech at a formal awards ceremony where he was presented with the prestigious Royal Bank Award for Canadian Achievement. The timing of Dickson's speech was nothing less than dramatic. Less than a week earlier, Pierre Trudeau had delivered his famous La Maison Egg Roll speech in which he denounced the Charlottetown Accord as 'a mess' that created a 'hierarchy of citizens.' The recognition of Quebec as a distinct society, for Trudeau, meant that 'collective rights, as voted into law by the majority of the National Assembly of Quebec, must guide judges in their interpretation of the *Charter of Rights and Freedoms* and, in fact, of the Constitution in its entirety.' Trudeau had also expressed concerns about the accord's provisions for aboriginal self-government: 'They want to give governments and legislatures to aboriginal people, and they say there are eleven principal native languages in Canada, in addition to forty tribes and six hundred bands.' Trudeau argued that 'there is only room for the provinces and the aboriginals' in the accord and that it weakened the federal government and institutions. He even predicted that the powers of the provinces to participate in the appointment of Supreme Court judges would mean that 'the judges will always hand down judgments in favour of the provinces.'[58] These final comments would have angered Dickson almost as much as Trudeau's speech a year earlier criticizing Dickson's decision in the *Patriation Reference*.

Dickson would use his own speech to present a very different view of Canada and the Charlottetown Accord. The retired chief justice, always mindful of proprieties and always holding his emotions strictly in check, would carefully avoid mentioning the retired prime minister by name. He also edited out statements in earlier drafts of his speech that the accord would not harm women's rights and that, if Meech had been approved, 'Canada would have been spared the traumatic constitutional debate of the past two years and a very uncertain future.' He toned down some of his rhetoric, but he wanted his defence of the Charlottetown Accord to be publicized and he made sure that at least one reporter knew the exact time when he would make his speech.

Rising to give his speech at the black-tie dinner, and with his family in attendance along with a number of his former colleagues on the Court, Dickson spoke of his pride in Canada, of how 'our people of different cultures and languages worked and fought to see Canada emerge as a great nation' and how Canada had recently been ranked first in the world in its quality of life. He spoke of Canada's 'rich heritage of two great legal systems, the confluence of the common law of England and the civil law of France,' and the fact that the constitution protected democratic, equality, and aboriginal rights. Dickson told the audience: 'Today we face the most serious constitutional crisis in our history. Many look only at imperfections in the Constitutional Accord which was hammered out after days, weeks, and months of negotiations by eleven first ministers, two territorial leaders, and four aboriginal leaders ... I believe the history and success of this great nation is firmly rooted in tolerance, mutual respect, sharing, generosity, accommodation and compromise.' Dickson, who as a judge had engineered many creative and sensitive halfway houses of accommodation and compromise, quoted Sir John A. Macdonald who said of Confederation that 'the whole scheme bears upon its face the marks of compromise' and 'mutual concession.' Dickson opposed Trudeau's doctrinaire insistence on individual rights as well as the equally extreme view that collective rights in Quebec or aboriginal societies should not be subject to the Charter.

Dickson ended his speech with an unabashed appeal to Canadians to pull together and approve the Charlottetown Accord. 'I sometimes think we Canadians are far too shy when it comes to expressing pride of country, manifesting our patriotism ... Let us have pride in what we and our forbears have accomplished, pride in ourselves, pride in others.' The consequences of separation for Dickson would be severe: 'As a trial judge, I sat in divorce court for five years and I cannot recall one so-called "friendly" divorce ... After 125 years of shared history, growth and success, a divorce within the Canadian federation would be a profound tragedy ... If we succeed, it will be a symbol of hope to the world. Failure is unthinkable.' Dickson concluded: 'I think it can be done. I think it will be done. I have faith in our political leaders ... elected in a free and democratic society, who worked so hard to reach the Charlottetown Accord. Time is drawing short. But with our active support and commitment the dream of a strong United Canada will surely come true.'[59] Dickson's warnings about the dangers of rejecting the Charlottetown Accord were reported the next day, albeit not as prominently as Trudeau's speech criticizing the accord.[60] His role in building the foundations of Charter jurisprudence made Dickson arguably the most important judge in Canada's history, but he did not attract the same attention as the still dashing former prime minister who had insisted that the Charter be enacted.

Plan B

Later that month, 55 per cent of Canadians voted against the Charlottetown Accord. The 'no' vote was strongest in the west, with over 60 per cent voting 'no' in Dickson's native Manitoba. The 'yes' forces won a narrow victory in Ontario, but less than 46 per cent of Quebeckers approved the accord. Three years later, with the federal liberals under Jean Chrétien now in power, Dickson watched in horror as Quebeckers came within a few thousand votes of authorizing their government to negotiate sovereignty-association with the rest of Canada. The close call of 1995 led to a new federal strategy based on legal and political opposition to Quebec's claims to be able to make a unilateral declaration of independence. Dickson had already discussed such a strategy in 1991 with Mulroney but now the time was ripe to act on it.

In June 1996 Dickson prepared a confidential thirteen-page opinion for Minister of Justice Allan Rock which advocated the tougher 'Plan B' approach to Quebec separatism that he had discussed with Mulroney five years earlier. Dickson argued that a unilateral declaration of independence would be an illegitimate and 'revolutionary breach of Canadian constitutional law, international law and legal convention.' In reference to a possible close Quebec vote in favour of separation, he added that 'it seems inconceivable that less than 12% of a population could literally break up the country which the United Nations has regarded as first in the world.' Newly elected Quebec Premier Lucien Bouchard's assertion of the right to declare sovereignty regardless of a court ruling was, in Dickson's view, 'very dangerous talk inviting confrontation, civil unrest and probable violence.' To Dickson, a unilateral declaration of independence reflected a 'complete denigration of the Canadian Constitution and a spurious attempt to legislate far beyond the limits of provincial powers.'[61] In informal discussions, Dickson spoke of using the Canadian Forces to prevent the break-up of the country in the event of a unilateral declaration of independence.[62]

The idea of a unilateral declaration of Quebec sovereignty offended Dickson's commitment to the rule of law, his commitment to the crown upholding its honour in its dealing with aboriginal people, and his strong sense of nationalism. Dickson collaborated with Peter Hogg, Canada's leading constitutional-law scholar, on an article that argued that allowing Quebec to separate without aboriginal consent would violate the federal government's fiduciary duties to the James Bay Cree and the Inuit of Nunavik, as well as the James Bay land-claims agreement.[63]

At the same time, Dickson also believed that it was important to pursue a softer strategy that would 'persuade Quebecers ... that there are benefits and advantages associated with remaining in Canada, rather than simply focus on the alleged disaster that awaits anyone who questions the merits of the status quo.' Dickson argued that 'the act of friendship of recognizing Quebecers as a distinct society would cost the rest of Canada absolutely nothing.'[64] In 1996 he gave a public speech in Winnipeg in which he argued that it was necessary to show 'Quebecers that change is possible within the federation.' He applauded the federal government's commitment not to create new shared-cost programs in areas of provincial jurisdiction without provincial consent. Noting that the constitutional recognition of Quebec as a distinct society 'remains a matter of some controversy in Western Canada,' Dickson clearly stated he himself had 'no difficulty' with the idea.

In this, his last speech on national unity, Dickson also returned to the tougher 'Plan B' approach. In the event of a 'yes' vote in Quebec, the rule of law must still be respected. Quoting from his judgment in the *Manitoba Language Reference*, he emphasized that 'the rule of law expresses a preference for law and order within a community rather than anarchy, warfare and constant strife.'[65] Dickson was an influential proponent of the federal government's 'Plan B' strategy, which included a reference to the Supreme Court on the legality of a unilateral declaration of independence. As in the *Patriation Reference*, the Court was again asked in 1998 to decide vital issues relating to the very meaning and survival of Canada. The Court's decision followed the Dickson legacy by stressing in clear and understandable language that Canada stood for the basic values of democracy, federalism, the rule of law, and minority and aboriginal rights.[66] In a Dicksonian move towards a halfway house of compromise and accommodation, the Court indicated that Quebec did not have a power under constitutional law or international law to separate from Canada unilaterally, but that Canada could not ignore a clear vote on a clear question in favour of independence.[67]

'Being a fair man was very, very important to him'

Dickson's interventions in the national-unity debate reveal a good deal about the man and the journey that he had taken during his lifetime. They demonstrate Dickson's genuine respect for and concern about aboriginal people and his appreciation of the special place of Quebec and the French language and culture within Confederation, aspects of his thinking that rested on his belief that Canada is a federal country with traditions of respect and accommodation. Dickson's interventions also reveal his commitment to the rule of law and his sense that the Charter and judicial enforcement of the human rights had become a defining feature in Canada during his years as chief justice of Canada. And they point as well to his deep commitment to the Supreme Court, which, since his appointment in 1973, had emerged as one of Canada's most important national institutions. Dickson believed that it was the special role of the judge to listen to the concerns of the less powerful and to intervene and provide remedies for abuse of power and oppression.

Dickson's national-unity speeches also indicate the importance he placed on integrity, fairness, and compassion as personal values. He hoped that Canadians would have the generosity of spirit to accept halfway houses that were respectful of all legitimate positions. He believed that all Canadians, like judges, should try to appreciate the different sides of a dispute, and that it was unwise to insist on undiluted individual or collective rights. Most of all, these national-unity speeches demonstrate Dickson's intense pride in his country and the lasting but often unmentioned impact of his wartime experience. Dickson almost died for his country and he emerged from the experience with a passionate love for Canada and a determination to continue to serve it as best he could.

Dickson died in his sleep on 17 October 1998, at eighty-two years of age. He had not shown signs of illness and was scheduled to leave the next morning on a gruelling journey that would take him to Victoria, Edmonton, and Winnipeg to conduct an audit of the military police as a follow-up to one of the three military inquiries he had chaired during his retirement. The Dicksons' bags were packed and in the hall so that they could leave bright and early in the morning. Dickson had worked on the military assignment the day before. Charles Belzile, who served with Dickson on the inquiry, told reporters that Dickson 'was fine yesterday. It was a long day, but he was in a great mood. We were supposed to leave together as a team this morning at nine o'clock but Mrs Dickson called me at about six to tell me he had passed away.' He added that Dickson 'was an outstanding Canadian, just thoroughly committed to the nation. I think the country lost a great man.'

The man who had so narrowly avoided death in fighting for his county in war served that country to the end. General Lewis MacKenzie remembered Dickson as 'a great war hero ... He was a tough guy and it wasn't easy for him in terms of his health in the last years but that didn't slow him down. He was easy to get to know and easy to like and a very honourable individual.' The head of the War Amps remarked that 'when Canadians read his obituary, I hope they will realize that his many postwar achievements were accomplished while bearing a war-incurred disability ... yet he could outthink, outwork and outperform many of Canada's brightest.'[68] Brian Mulroney stated that he 'had the high privilege of knowing and working with him, and can say that Canada has lost one of her most distinguished sons.' Peter Russell, one of Canada's leading political scientists, called Dickson 'one of our great statesmen ... You have to rank him up there with our greatest prime ministers in terms of what he gives to the country for the longer term.'[69]

Jurists and scholars commented on Dickson's many contributions to the law and his empathy and compassion for the less fortunate. Chief Justice Lamer observed that Dickson's judgments 'now form part of our legal bedrock,' and he described Dickson's judicial career as a continuation of a tradition of service 'to protect others by going to war, serve where there is a flood, serve in hospitals, in schools, in churches, serve the poor and needy ...'[70] Dickson's approach to the law and life, however, was best captured by his son Barry. He said that his father 'loved law and he loved life. Being a fair man was very, very important to him.'[71]

Notes

A Note on Sources

Unless otherwise noted, all references to original sources are to the Brian Dickson Papers, National Archives of Canada, MG 31, E 85.

Brian Dickson was interviewed over the course of several days from 25 February 1991 to 1 March 1993 at Marchmont for the Osgoode Society Oral History Project (referred to in the notes as 'Dickson Interview'). Transcripts of those interviews have been deposited with the Dickson Papers in the National Archives of Canada. An additional interview with Dickson for this book was conducted on 23 August 1993 at Marchmont. We thank Gordon Bale and Philip Girard for providing us with transcripts of interviews of Dickson in April 1984 and October 1985. Although he was not formally interviewed, many conversations with James MacPherson during the project have also been an invaluable source. The following additional interviews were conducted by the authors:

Bakan, Joel. 16 November 2000, Vancouver
Cory, Peter. 6 September 2000, Toronto
Dickson, Barbara. 13–14 December 2002, Louisville, Kentucky
Dickson, Brian Jr. By telephone, 22 August 2002, from Ottawa
Freiman, Mark. 6 November 2000, Toronto
Gonthier, Charles. 18 October 2000, Ottawa
Goudge, Stephen. 14 June 2000, Toronto
Herndorf, Peter. 11 October 2002, Stratford, Ontario
Iacobucci, Frank. 17 October 2000, Ottawa

La Forest, Gérard. 22 February 2003, Fredericton
L'Heureux-Dubé, Claire. 23 October 2000, Toronto
Lamer, Antonio. 17 October 2000, Ottawa
MacAulay, Blair. 30 November 2001, Toronto
McIntyre, William. 16 November 2000, Vancouver
McLachlin, Beverley. 16 October 2000, Ottawa
Monahan, Patrick. 13 December 2000, Toronto
Morgan, Brian. 18 December 2000, Toronto
Morse, Peter. 27 December 2002, Winnipeg
Pratte, Guy. 4 April 2003, Toronto
Sheppard, Colleen. 14 February 2003, Montreal
Swinton, Katherine. 11 December 2000, Toronto
Thompson, Rollie. 30 January 2003, Toronto
Toope, Stephen. 24 January 2002, Toronto
Yalden, Rob. 14 February 2003, Montreal
Wilson, Bertha. 21 September 2000, Ottawa

Chapter 1: A Judge's Journey

1 As quoted in R. Yalden, 'Before the Bench: Brian Dickson as Corporate Lawyer,' in D. Guth, ed., *Brian Dickson at the Supreme Court of Canada. 1973–1990* (Winnipeg: Faculty of Law, University of Manitoba 1998), at 18.

2 Part I of the Constitution Act, 1982 being Schedule B of the Canada Act, 1982 (U.K.) 1982, c.11.

3 Criminal Code, R.S.C. 1970, c.34 s.251.

4 F.L. Morton, *Morgentaler v. Borowski* (Toronto: McClelland and Stewart, 1992) c.5.

5 Ibid. at 61–2.

6 R.I. Cheffins, 'The Supreme Court of Canada: The Quiet Court in an Unquiet Country' (1966), 4 *Osgoode Hall Law Journal*, at 259.

7 S.C. 1960, c.44.

8 410 U.S. 113 (1973).

9 *R. v. Drybones*, [1970] S.C.R. 282.

10 *Canard v. Canada*, [1972] 5 W.W.R. 678 (Man. C.A.).

11 'Morgentaler defence move fails; full 9-man court will hear appeal,' *Globe and Mail*, 3 October 1974.

12 Unreported judgment, 2 October 1974, vol. 11, file 21.

13 'Abortion law unconstitutional, Morgentaler lawyer tells court,' *Globe and Mail*, 4 October 1974; 'Abortion law applied unequally, violates Bill of Rights, Morgentaler appeal is told,' *Globe and Mail*, 5 October 1974.

14 E. Pelrine, *Morgentaler: The Doctor Who Couldn't Turn Away* (Toronto: Gage Publishing 1975), at 144, 146.

15 *Morgentaler v. The Queen*, [1976] 1 S.C.R. 616 at 629, 633, 636 [hereafter *Morgentaler I*].

16 Orchard to Dickson, 1 October 1974, vol. 11, file 23.

17 La Forest interview.

18 'Quebec court's action in Morgentaler case questioned by judges,' *Globe and Mail*, 8 October 1974.

19 Dickson conference memo, 7 October 1974, vol. 11, file 21.

20 Dickson cited the work of Cambridge law professor Glanville Williams in recognizing the defence of necessity, but he noted that other academics in Britain and the United States did not agree with Williams's position and that Williams did not believe that a threat of suicide was sufficient. G. Williams, 'The Law of Abortion' (1952), 5 *Current Legal Problems*, 128 at 133.

21 Dickson draft judgment, undated, vol. 11, file 21.

22 Herman to Laskin, 22 January 1975, vol. 11, file 21.

23 *Morgentaler I*, at 676–7.

24 On 14 March, 1975, shortly before the release of the judgment, Dickson added a preface to his discussion of the necessity defence noting that he was 'assuming the theoretical possibility of such a defence.' He indicated that this change was made at the request of de Grandpré, who had drafted the addition. See Dickson to Court, 14 March 1975, vol. 11, file 21; *Morgentaler I* at 680.

25 Ibid. at 678.

26 Ibid. at 676.

27 Ibid. at 669–70.

28 Ibid. at 654, 650.

29 [1976] 2 S.C.R 200. This famous disagreement between Laskin and Dickson is discussed in chapter 7.

30 'Morgentaler's conviction upheld,' *Globe and Mail*, 27 March 1975.

31 Pelrine, *Morgentaler*, at 154–5.

32 Dickson conference memo, 16 December 1981, vol. 55, file 6. The case was *Abbey v. The Queen*, [1982] 2 S.C.R. 24, where Dickson, on behalf of the Court, ordered a new trial even though the accused was clearly guilty.

33 Dickson interview at 280.

34 C. Dunphy, *Morgentaler: A Difficult Hero* (Toronto: Random House 1996), at 149.

35 B. Dickens, 'The Morgentaler Cases: Criminal Process and Abortion Law' (1976), 14 *Osgoode Hall Law Journal*, 229.

36 Dickson interview at 278.

37 *R. v. Morgentaler* (1984), 14 C.C.C. (3d) at 282, 302, 313 (Ont. H.C).

38 Morton, *Morgentaler v. Borowski*, at 190–1.

39 *R. v. Morgentaler* (1985), 22 C.C.C. (3d) 353 at 378 (Ont. C.A).

40 Ibid. at 395 citing *Bliss v. A.G. Canada*, [1979] 1 S.C.R. 183 at 190.

41 *R. v. Perka*, [1984] 2 S.C.R. 232, discussed in chapter 11.

42 K. Makin, '*Charter*'s meaning at issue in Morgentaler case,' *Globe and Mail*, 7 October 1986.

43 'Ottawa aiming to get more girls involved in sport,' *Globe and Mail*, 7 October 1986; 'Women now closer to full combat role,' *Globe and Mail*, 11 October 1986.

44 'Sex education for prepubescent boys, girls urged at conference,' *Globe and Mail*, 3 October 1974; 'Beauty queen loses Crown, mother says contest unfair,' *Globe and Mail*, 2 October 1974.

45 Scarborough to Dickson, 6 November 1985, MacPherson to Scarborough, 13 November 1985, vol. 132, file 8.

46 Bartel to Dickson, 20 February 1986, MacPherson to Bartel , 10 April 1986, vol. 132, file 8.

47 Dunphy, *Morgentaler*, at 297.

48 K. Makin, 'State use of abortion possible, court told,' *Globe and Mail*, 8 October 1986.

49 Morton, *Morgentaler v. Borowski*, at 224.

50 K. Makin, 'Court is skeptical on "right" to ignore law on abortion,' *Globe and Mail*, 9 October 1986.

51 K. Makin, 'Supreme Court grills Crown lawyer in Morgentaler abortion appeal,' *Globe and Mail*, 10 October 1986.

52 K. Makin, 'Crown rejects abortion law compromise as hearing ends,' *Globe and Mail*, 11 October 1986.

53 Dickson conference memo, 16 October 1986, vol. 99, file 11.

54 Ibid. at 7.

55 Ibid. at 9.

56 K. Makin, 'Crown rejects abortion law compromise as hearing ends,' *Globe and Mail*, 11 October 1986.

57 K. Makin, 'And the verdict is,' *Globe and Mail*, 23 January 1988.

58 Dickson memo to Court, 30 July 1987, vol. 99, file 14.

59 Supreme Court of Canada Act, s.10.

60 *R. v. Morgentaler*, [1988] 1 S.C.R. 30 at 46 [hereafter *Morgentaler II*].

61 Ibid. at 53, 56.

62 Ibid. at 61.

63 Ibid. at 68–9.

64 Ibid. at 77.

65 Ibid. at 183, 171–2.

66 McIntyre to Dickson, 14 August 1987, vol. 99, file 11.

67 *Morgentaler II* at 137–8.

68 *Globe and Mail*, 29 January 1988.

69 As quoted in E. Anderson, *Judging Bertha Wilson: Law as Large as Life* (Toronto: University of Toronto Press 2001), at 233.

70 Makin, 'And the verdict is.'
71 'Winnipeg clinic likely to be first to open,' *Globe and Mail*, 29 January 1988.
72 'Rocks smash windows at Morgentaler abortion clinic,' Montreal *Gazette*, 30 January 1988.
73 Dickson to Court, 30 July 1987, vol. 99, file 14.
74 Morton, *Morgentaler v. Borowski*, at 248.

Chapter 2: Prairie Upbringing

1 Speech in Ottawa, 18 January 1901, quoted in *The Oxford Dictionary of Quotations*, 5th ed. (Oxford: Oxford University Press 1999), at 454.
2 The social and cultural pattern of immigration and integration is discussed in Edward N. Herberg, *Ethnic Groups in Canada: Adaptations and Transitions* (Scarborough: Ont.: Nelson 1989), at 61–4; and Howard Palmer, 'Strangers and Stereotypes: The Rise of Nativism, 1880–1920,' in R. Douglas Francis and Howard Palmer, ed, *The Prairie West: Historical Readings* (Edmonton: Pica Pica Press 1985), 309 at 312.
3 Nancy M. Sheehan, 'Education, the Society and the Curriculum in Alberta, 1905–1980: An Overview,' in Nancy M. Sheehan et al. ed., *Schools in the West: Essays in Canadian Educational History* (Calgary: Detselig Enterprises 1986), at 41–2.
4 *The Wynyard Story*, 1955 (no author or publisher given).
5 John S. Moir, *Enduring Witness: A History of the Presbyterian Church in Canada*, 2nd ed. (Toronto: Presbyterian Publications 1987), at 237.
6 'Manitoba's newest judge learned trade as Boy Scout,' Winnipeg *Tribune*, 5 November 1963.
7 Dickson interview at 36.
8 Ibid. at 22.
9 W.T. Easterbrook and Hugh G.J. Aitken, *Canadian Economic History* (Toronto: University of Toronto Press, 1988), at 490.
10 Letter from A.C. Stewart to R.B. Bennett, 26 May 1931, reprinted in M. Horn, ed., *The Dirty Thirties: Canadians in the Great Depression* (Toronto: Copp Clark 1972), at 96.
11 Desmond Morton, *A Short History of Canada*, 5th ed. (Toronto: McClelland and Stewart 2001), at 216–17.
12 Reprinted in Horn, ed., *The Dirty Thirties*, at 189–90.
13 Millar to Dickson, 12 June 1990, vol. 158, file 6.
14 Dickson interview at 25–6.
15 J.M. Barrie, *The Plays of J.M. Barrie* (New York: Charles Scribner's Sons 1930), at 781.
16 The following description is based on W.A. Riddell, *Regina: from Pile O'Bones to Queen City of the Plains* (Burlington, Ont.: Windsor Publications 1981), at 97–8; and E.G. Drake, *Regina: The Queen City* (Toronto: McClelland and Stewart 1955), at 187–8.

17 M.A. MacPherson, 'About Brian, Bill and Me: Regina Collegiate,' in D. Guth, ed., *Brian Dickson at the Supreme Court of Canada, 1973–1990* (Winnipeg, Faculty of Law, University of Manitoba 1998), at 4.

18 Jack Batten, *Judges* (Toronto: Macmillan 1986), at 331.

19 MacPherson, 'About Brian, Bill and Me,' at 5.

20 W.H. McConnell, *Prairie Justice* (Calgary: Burroughs 1980), at 194–7, provides a biographical sketch of Murdoch MacPherson.

21 Batten, *Judges*, at 331.

22 MacPherson, 'About Brian, Bill and Me,' at 4.

23 See Dickson, 'Remembering Bill Lederman' (1994), 19 *Queens Law Journal*, 1.

24 W.L. Morton, *One University: A History of the University of Manitoba, 1877–1952* (Toronto: McClelland and Stewart, 1957), at 143–7.

25 Clarence Shepard, 'Treasured Memories: Law, Love and War,' in Guth, ed., *Brian Dickson*, at 9–14.

26 Ernest Sirluck, *First Generation* (Toronto: University of Toronto Press 1996), at 42, quoting Philip Marchand, *Marshall McLuhan: The Medium Is the Messenger* (Toronto: Random House 1989), at 15.

27 Dickson 23 August 1993 interview.

28 P. Axelrod, 'The Student Movement of the 1930s,' in P. Axelrod and J.G. Reid, ed., *Youth, University and Canadian Society: Essays in the Social History of Higher Education* (Montreal: McGill-Queen's University Press 1989), 216–46.

29 University of Manitoba Archives.

30 Dale and Lee Gibson, *Substantial Justice: Law and Lawyers in Manitoba, 1670–1970* (Winnipeg: Peguis Publishers 1972), at 256.

31 Ibid. at 258–65.

32 Ibid. at 288.

33 W. Wesley Pue, '"The Disquisitions of Learned Judges": Making Manitoba Lawyers, 1885–1931' in G. Blaine Baker and Jim Phillips, ed., *Essays in the History of Canadian Law* Vol. VIII – *In Honour of R.C.B. Risk* (Toronto: University of Toronto Press Osgoode Society for Canadian Legal History 1999), 512 at 533–7.

34 Remarks at Osgoode Hall Graduation Dinner, Toronto, 15 June 1990, vol. 140, file 19.

35 C.A.W. Manning, ed., *Salmond on Jurisprudence*, 8th ed. (London: Sweet and Maxwell 1930).

36 F. Pollock, *A First Book of Jurisprudence*, 3rd ed. (London: Macmillan 1911).

37 R.C.B. Risk, 'Volume One of the Journal' (1987), 37 *University of Toronto Law Journal*, 193 at 207–8.

38 Roscoe Pound, 'Liberty of Contract' (1909), 18 *Yale Law Journal*, 454 at 462.

39 Risk, 'Volume One of the Journal'; R.C.B. Risk, 'The Many Minds of W.P.M. Kennedy' (1998), 38 *University of Toronto Law Journal*, 353.

40 Cecil Wright, 'The American Law Institute's Restatement of Contracts and Agency' (1935), 1 *University of Toronto Law Journal*, 17 at 43, 47.

41 See John Willis, 'Three Approaches to Administrative Law: The Judicial, the Conceptual, and the Functional' (1935), 1 *University of Toronto Law Journal*, 53.

42 Dickson interview at 77.

43 I. Abella, 'The Making of a Chief Justice: Bora Laskin, the Early Years' (1990), 24 *Law Society of Upper Canada Gazette*, 187 at 190.

44 'Remarks to the Call to the Bar Ceremony' (1985), 19 *Law Society of Upper Canada Gazette*, 118.

45 Dickson interview at 79.

46 Dickson interview, 23 August 1993.

Chapter 3: Off to War

1 C.P. Stacey, *Official History of the Canadian Army in the Second World War – Volume 1: Six Years of War: The Army in Canada, Britain and the Pacific* (Ottawa: Queen's Printer 1966), at 79–80.

2 Ibid. at 132–3.

3 *The History of the Third Canadian Light Anti-Aircraft Regiment from 17 August 1940 to 7 May 1945, World War II* (Calgary: Kellaway Publishing 1955)), at 4–5.

4 Ibid. at 5.

5 C.P. Stacey, *Official History*, Volume 1, at 193.

6 Remarks at luncheon held at Government House and Naval Mess Dinner, HMCS *Provider*, Victoria, British Columbia, 31 August 1985, vol. 139, file 29.

7 Dickson interview, 23 August 1993.

8 C.P. Stacey, *Official History*, Volume 1, at 231.

9 Dickson interview at 67.

10 Ibid. at 69–70.

11 Remarks to Canadian Armed Forces, Brandon, Manitoba, vol. 140, file 23.

12 Dickson interview at 73.

13 John A. Macdonald, 'In Search of Veritable: Training the Canadian Army Staff Officer, 1899 to 1945,' Royal Military College of Canada, MA thesis, 1992, at 2–3.

14 Ibid. at 48.

15 Remarks on the Occasion of 50th Wedding Anniversary, 12 June 1993, vol. 140, file 42.

16 Ibid.

17 C.P. Stacey, *Official History – Volume 1*, at 128.

18 Macdonald, 'In search of Veritable, at 142–3.

19 Ibid. at 126.

20 Ibid. at 127.

21 Dickson interview at 74–75.

22 Clarence Shepard, 'Treasured Memories: Law, Love and War' in D. Guth, ed., *Brian Dickson at the Supreme Court of Canada, 1973–1990* (Winnipeg: Faculty of Law, University of Manitoba 1998), at 12.

23 Dickson interview 23, August 1993.
24 Remarks delivered at the Mess Dinner, Royal Military College, Kingston, Ontario, 31 October 1986, vol. 139, file 64.
25 Dickson interview at 80.
26 Dickson interview, 23 August 1993.
27 Meyer was prosecuted for executing Canadian prisoners of war: B.J.S. Macdonald, *The Trial of Kurt Meyer* (Toronto: Clark, Irwin 1954). He was convicted and sentenced to death, but the sentence was commuted and he was later transferred to a prison in Germany and eventually released.
28 The following is based on C.P. Stacey, *Official History of the Canadian Army in the Second World War – Volume 3: The Victory Campaign: The Operations in North-West Europe, 1944–1945* (Ottawa: Queen's Printer 1960), at 236–45; Denis and Shelagh Whittaker, *Victory at Falaise: The Soldiers' Story* (Toronto: Harper Collins 2000); Reginald H. Roy, *1944: The Canadians in Normandy,* Canadian War Museum Historical Publication no. 19 (Toronto: Macmillan 1984); George G. Blackburn, *The Guns of Normandy: A Soldier's Eye View, France 1944* (Toronto: McClelland and Stewart 1995), at 407–19.
29 Brian Dickson, Jr., interview.
30 Dickson interview at 87–8.
31 The 14 August 1944 'friendly fire' incident is fully documented in Stacey, *Official History – Volume 3*, at 243–5; and Whittaker, *Victory at Falaise*, at 169–81.
32 Stacey, *Official History – Volume 3*, at 243.
33 Ibid. at 243–4. See also Blackburn, *The Guns of Normandy*, at 411–12, reporting a post-war lecture given by General Simonds explaining the causes of the error.
34 Ibid. at 243–5; Whittaker and Whittaker, *Victory at Falaise*, at 169–81.
35 Quoted in Whittaker and Whittaker, *Victory at Falaise*, at 181.
36 Stacey, *Official History – Volume 3*, at 244.
37 M.A. MacPherson, 'About Brian, Bill and Me: Regina Collegiate' in Guth, ed., *Brian Dickson*.
38 Clarence Shepard, supra at 12–14.
39 W.R. Feasby, ed., *Official History of the Canadian Medical Services 1939–1945, Volume 2: Clinical Subjects* (Ottawa: Queen's Printer 1953), at 24–6.
40 Dickson interview at 85–6.
41 Feasby, *Canadian Medical Services*, at 240.
42 Dr D.G. Revell to Dickson, 18 October 1985, private collection. Revell administered the anesthetic.
43 Quoted in John Martinson, ed., *We Stand on Guard* (Montreal: Ovale Publications 1992), at 303.
44 Barbara Dickson interview.
45 Lamer Interview.
46 McLachlin interview.

47 L'Heureux-Dubé interview.
48 La Forest Interview.
49 Joel Bakan Interview.
50 Stephen Toope interview.
51 *Globe and Mail*, 9 November 1985, quoted in Lee Gibson, *A Proud Heritage: The First Hundred Years of Aikins, MacAulay and Thorvaldson* (Winnipeg: n.p., 1993), at 131.
52 Peter Morse interview.
53 Brian Dickson, Jr, interview.
54 Dickson to Lt.-Col. B.E. Stephenson, 13 January 1984, vol. 156, file 7.
55 Müller wrote to Dickson to congratulate him on his retirement: 7 May 1990, vol. 158, file 6.
56 Wilson interview.

Chapter 4: Law and Business

 1 See Lee and Dale Gibson, 'Sir James Aikens' Seamless Web: Finding Fortune and Fame as a Lawyer in the Adolescent Canadian West' (1992) 21 *Manitoba Law Journal*, 161; Lee Gibson, *A Proud Heritage: The First Hundred Years of Aikins, MacAulay and Thorvaldson* (Winnipeg: n.p., 1993).
 2 W. Wesley Pue, '"The Disquisitions of Learned Judges": Making Manitoba Lawyers, 1885–1931,' in B. Baker and J. Phillips, ed, *Essays in the History of Canadian Law, volume VIII – In Honour of R.C.B. Risk* (Toronto: University of Toronto Press Osgoode Society for Canadian Legal History 1999), 512.
 3 James Aikens, 'Address on Opening of Manitoba Law School, 1914,' quoted in Pue, '"The Disquisitions of Learned Judges,"' at 512.
 4 Remarks to the Executive of the Canadian Bar Association on the Court's Tasks, 1984, vol. 139, file 3.
 5 Dickson interview, 23 August 1993.
 6 Ibid.
 7 Gibson, *A Proud Heritage*, at 131.
 8 Ibid.
 9 Peter Morse interview.
10 Dickson interview at 113.
11 Ibid. at 115.
12 Winnipeg *Free Press*, 6 May 1950.
13 Dickson interview at 117.
14 Gerald Friesen, *The Canadian Prairies: A History* (Toronto: University of Toronto Press, 1984), at 420.
15 Dickson interview at 111.
16 Gibson, *A Proud Heritage*, at 130, 149.
17 Ibid. at 131.

18 Gibson, *A Proud Heritage*, at 174.
19 R. Yalden, 'Before the Bench: Brian Dickson as Corporate Lawyer,' in D. Guth, ed., *Brian Dickson at the Supreme Court of Canada. 1973–1990* (Winnipeg: Faculty of Law, University of Manitoba 1998), 15 at 20.
20 *Globe and Mail*, 3 April 1961.
21 Blair MacAulay interview.
22 Quoted in Yalden, 'Before the Bench,' at 28.
23 1955, c.80.
24 *Financial Post*, 3 December 1955.
25 1956, c.70.
26 *Financial Post*, 6 December 1958.
27 Dickson interview, 23 August 1993.
28 Ibid.
29 Yalden, 'Before the Bench,' at 26–7.
30 *The Link*, vol. 36, no. 1, January 1960.
31 However, when Dickson left the firm in 1963, there were fourteen lawyers, none of whom was a woman: Lorne Campbell to Dickson, 1 October 1990, vol. 159, file 17.
32 Yalden, 'Before the Bench,' at 29.
33 David Matas, quoted in 'The New Face of the Law,' *Maclean's*, 30 April 1984.
34 Blair MacAulay interview.
35 Dickson interview, 23 August 1993.
36 Ibid.
37 Brian Dickson, Jr, interview.
38 Barbara Dickson interview.
39 Dickson interview at 326; Barbara Dickson interview.
40 Dickson interview at 327.
41 Call to the Bar Ceremony, Winnipeg, 2 June 1967, vol. 138, file 5.
42 Dickson interview at 263–4.
43 Dickson interview at 97.
44 Brian Dickson, Jr, interview.
45 Ibid.
46 Ibid.
47 Brian Dickson interview at 559.
48 Barbara Dickson interview.
49 Dale Gibson, 'Manifest Justice: A Biographical Sketch' (1991), 20 *Manitoba Law Journal*, 268 at 273–5.
50 See C. Ian Kyer and Jerome E. Bickenbach, *The Fiercest Debate: Cecil A. Wright, the Benchers, and Legal Education in Ontario, 1923–1957* (University of Toronto Press/Osgoode Society for Canadian Legal History 1987).
51 Minutes of the Special Meeting of the Benchers of the Law Society of Manitoba, 16 November 1962, Public Archives of Manitoba, Legal-Judicial History.

52 'Legal Education' (1986) 64 *Canadian Bar Review* 374 at 376.

53 Gibson, *A Proud Heritage* at 274.

54 R.D. Gibson, 'Preface' (1962), 1 *Manitoba Law Journal* 1.

55 Kyer and Bickenbach, *The Fiercest Debate*.

56 J.D. Arnup to Dickson, 17 May 1963, Public Archives of Manitoba, Legal-Judicial History.

57 Gibson, *A Proud Heritage*, at 275.

58 Dickson interview at 97–8.

59 Dickson to Manfred Gollub, 22 June 1995, vol. 158, file 11.

60 Dickson interview at 100–1.

61 Minutes of Benchers Meetings, 31 May 1962, Public Archives of Manitoba, Legal-Judicial History.

62 Ibid., 25 October 1962, 7 August 1962.

63 Blair MacAulay interview.

64 Ibid., and Yalden, 'Before the Bench,' at 30.

65 Blair MacAulay interview.

66 Peter Morse interview, 27 December, 2002.

67 Barbara Dickson interview.

68 'The Public Responsibilities of Lawyers' (1983) 13 *Manitoba Law Journal* 174.

69 'Counsel's Duty to the Court and to His Client,' Continuing Legal Education Society, Halifax, 17 November 1984, vol. 139, file 6.

70 Ibid.

71 Call to the Bar Ceremony, Winnipeg, December 1963, vol. 138, file 4.

72 'Call to the Bar Ceremony,' 1968, vol. 138, file 9.

73 Anthony Kronman, *The Lost Lawyer* (Cambridge:, Mass.: Harvard University Press 1995), at 12; William Rehnquist, 'The Lawyer-Statesman in American History' (1986), 3 *Harvard Journal of Law and Public Policy*, 537; Robert Gordon, 'Corporate Law Practice As a Public Calling' (1990), 49 *Maryland Law Review*, 255.

74 McLachlin interview.

75 John Lamont, quoted in 'The New Face of the Law,' *Maclean's*, 30 April 1984.

76 Gibson, *A Proud Heritage*, at 131.

77 Remarks to the Osgoode Hall Graduation Dinner, 15 June 1990, vol. 140, file 19.

Chapter 5: Queen's Bench

1 Samuel Freedman, 'A Mirror for Modern Magistrates,' in D. Guth, ed., *Brian Dickson at the Supreme Court of Canada, 1973–1990* (Winnipeg: Canadian Legal History Society 1998), at 43–4.

2 Dickson interview at 121.

3 George E. Tritschler, 'Trial Judge: The Manitoba Court of Queen's Bench, 1963–1967' in Guth, ed., *Brian Dickson*, at 35.

4 Dickson interview at 122.
5 Ibid. at 122, 128.
6 Winnipeg *Free Press*, 2 December 1963.
7 Lee Gibson, *A Proud Heritage: The First Hundred Years of Aikens, MacAulay and Thorvaldson* (Winnipeg: n.p., 1993), at 172.
8 Winnipeg *Free Press*, 5 November 1963.
9 Winnipeg *Tribune*, 5 November 1963.
10 Tritschler, 'Trial Judges,' at 36.
11 Dickson interview at 126, 123, 130.
12 'The Role and Function of Judges' (1980), 14 *Law Society of Upper Canada Gazette*, 138 at 141.
13 Dickson interview at 136.
14 Dickson to file, 24 June 1986, vol. 132, file 15.
15 'The Role and Function of Judges,' at 142.
16 Barbara Dickson interview.
17 Dickson interview at 135.
18 Ibid. at 123–4.
19 Ibid. at 124.
20 'The Role and Function of Judges,' at 144.
21 Dickson interview at 124–5.
22 Ibid.
23 'The Role and Function of Judges,' at 146–7.
24 Ibid. at 144–5.
25 Guth, 'Introduction,' in Guth, ed., *Brian Dickson*, at xxxi.
26 'The Role and Function of Judges,' at 150.
27 *R. v. Acoby*, unreported, 8 March 1965, Bench Book Circuit no. 2, vol. 1, file 2.
28 'The Role and Function of Judges,' at 150.
29 Dickson interview at 151–2.
30 Ibid.
31 Ibid. at 153.
32 Stephen Toope interview.
33 Dickson interview at 154–5.
34 See chapter 22.
35 Dickson interview at 155–6.
36 Ibid. at 157.
37 'The Role and Function of Judges,' at 144.
38 Dickson interview at 151–2.
39 Ibid. at 163–4.
40 Ibid. at 163–6.
41 'The Role and Function of Judges,' at 147.
42 *Wilson v. Wilson*, unreported, 17 January 1965, Bench Book Civil no. 8, vol. 2, file 7.

43 *Taraszcuk v. Taraschuk*, unreported, 14 December 1966, Bench Book Civil no. 11, vol. 3, file 1.

44 *Stoberman v. Buttner*, unreported, 29 September 1965, Bench Book Civil no. 7, vol. 2, file 6.

45 *Lathlin v. Manitoba (Registrar of Motor Vehicles)* (1964), 49 W.W.R. 351; Bench Book Circuit no. 2, vol. 1, file 2.

46 *Bates v. Bihum and Lloyds*, unreported, 17 April 1967, Bench Book Civil no. 12, vol. 3, file 2.

47 Dickson interview at 139.

48 Ibid.

49 'The Role and Function of Judges', at 148.

50 R. Rees Brock, 'An Autobiographical Memoir upon Arrival in Ottawa,' in Guth, ed., *Brian Dickson*, at 69.

51 *Saari v. Sunshine Riding Academy Ltd.* (1967), 65 D.L.R. (2d) 92; Bench Book Civil no. 14, vol. 3, file 4.

52 65 D.L.R. (2d) at 98.

53 'The Role and Function of Judges,' at 149–50.

54 Dickson interview at 144–5.

55 Ibid. at 146.

56 *Gilroy v. Portage Animal Hospital*, unreported, 23 November 1964, Bench Book Circuit no. 2, vol. 1, file 2.

57 *Peters v. North Star* (1965), 53 W.W.R. 321, Bench Book Civil no. 4, vol. 2, file 3.

58 *Saari v. Sunshine Riding Academy.*

59 Tritschler, 'Trial Judge,' at 39.

60 See, for example, *Rudy v. Petersen* (1965), 54 W.W.R. 641 at 643: 'I have studied the cases to which counsel have referred me, and others.'

61 *Rudy v. Petersen.*

62 See, for example, *R. v. Gibbon, Bell and Faryon* (1965), 51 W.W.R. 243, holding that certiorari may be used to challenge a committal for trial, rejecting the crown's contention that the only remedy was habeas corpus with certiorari in aid, and requiring the accused to be in custody. See also *R. v. Patzer, Clark and Warren* (1964), 50 W.W.R. 58, dealing with multiple counts of rape.

63 *Continental Insurance Company et al v. Prudential Insurance Co. Ltd.* (1965), 52 W.W.R. 526 at 534.

64 *Hudson Bay Mining and Smelting Co. Ltd. v. Flin Flon Base Metal Worker's Federal Union No. 172* (1966), 58 W.W.R. 165 at 171.

65 Ibid. at 170.

66 (1967), 61 D.L.R. (2d) 429.

67 [1968] S.C.R. 113.

68 'The Role and Function of Judges,' at 138–9.

69 (1966), 59 D.L.R. (2d) 723.

70 In 1965 the Supreme Court upheld an Alberta law that restricted Hutterite prac-
    tices of collective ownership: *Walter v. Alberta (Attorney General)*, [1969] S.C.R. 383.
71 59 D.L.R. (2d) 723 at 732. Dickson relied upon a turn-of-the-century House of Lords
    decision arising from a schism in the Church of Scotland: *General Assembly of Free
    Church of Scotland v. Lord Overtoun*, [1904] A.C. 515.
72 (1967), 65 D.L.R. (2d) 607 (Man. C.A.); [1970] S.C.R. 958.
73 Dickson interview at 210.

Chapter 6: Court of Appeal

1 Dickson interview at 171–2.
2 See Bench Book Ad Hoc, vol. 4, file 4.
3 (1966) 55 W.W.R. 257.
4 Ibid. at 282.
5 Ibid. at 284, 281.
6 (1966) 57 W.W.R. 736, [1966] S.C.R. v.
7 A.F. Sheppard, 'Dickson on Evidence,' in D. Guth, ed., *Brian Dickson at the Supreme
   Court of Canada, 1973–1990* (Winnipeg: Faculty of Law, University of Manitoba,
   1998), 213 at 218, referring to the Canada Evidence Act, R.S.C. 1985. c. C-5, s.16(2).
   Dickson reached a similar conclusion in *R. v. Taylor* (1970), 75 W.W.R. 45.
8 *R. v. Horsburgh* (1965), 55 D.L.R. (2d) 289 at 305.
9 McLachlin interview.
10 Farewell to Manitoba Court of Queen's Bench, 1967, vol. 138, file 7.
11 Barbara Dickson interview.
12 Dickson interview at 184.
13 Ibid. at 176.
14 See Vivian Rachlis, 'A Biographical Note,' in C. Harvey, ed., *Chief Justice Samuel
    Freedman: A Great Canadian Judge* (Winnipeg: Law Society of Manitoba, 1983), 1.
15 'The Public Responsibilities of Lawyers' (1983), 13 *Manitoba Law Journal*, 175.
16 'The Role and Function of Judges' (1980), 14 *Law Society of Upper Canada Gazette*,
    138 at 160.
17 Ibid. at 156, 158.
18 *R. v. McAmmond* (1969), 69 W.W.R. 277 at 278.
19 *Dahlberg v. Naydiuk* (1969), 72 W.W.R. 210.
20 Address to the Canadian Institute for the Administration of Justice Seminar on
    Judgment Writing, 2 July 1981, vol. 138, file 28.
21 *Genovese v. York Lambton* (1969), 67 W.W.R. 355, aff'd [1969] S.C.R. vi; *Chuckry v. The
    Queen*, [1972] 3 W.W.R. 561.
22 *Chuckry*.
23 Ernest Sirluck, *First Generation: An Autobiography* (Toronto: University of Toronto
    Press 1996), at 324–5.

24 [1976] 2 S.C.R. 200 discussed in detail in chapter 7.

25 (1974) 48 D.L.R. (3d) 137.

26 *Genovese v. York Lambton Corporation Ltd.* (1969), 67 W.W.R. 355.

27 *Winding-up Act*, R.S.C. 1952, c.296, s.127.

28 *Genovese* at 373–4.

29 *R. v. Vogelle and Reid* (1969), 70 W.W.R. 641. *Stone v. Stone and Bedford* (1969), 71 W.W.R. 589; *Welbridge Holdings Ltd. v. Metropolitan Corporation of Greater Winnipeg* (1970), 72 W.W.R. 705, aff'd [1971] S.C.R. 957.

30 *R. v. Great West News Ltd* (1970), 72 W.W.R. 354; *R. v. Prairie Schooner News* (1970), 75 W.W.R. 585.

31 *Canadian Acceptance Corporation Ltd. v. Regent Park Butcher Shop Ltd. and Gauthier* (1969), 67 W.W.R. 297.

32 *Clark's-Gamble of Canada Ltd. v. Grant Park Plaza Ltd.* (1966), 57 W.W.R. 27.

33 Ibid. at 45, 39.

34 Compare, however, *Re Pfrimmer Estate* (1968), 66 W.W.R. 574, where, in a short opinion, Dickson reversed the trial judge and made a dependant's relief order.

35 *Barr v. Barr* [1972] 2 W.W.R. 346.

36 Ibid. at 351.

37 *Dahlberg*.

38 *School Division of Assiniboine South, No. 3 and Hoffer v. Greater Winnipeg Gas Company Limited*, [1971] 4 W.W.R. 746.

39 *Welbridge Holdings Ltd.*

40 *Wiswell et al. v. Metropolitan Corporation of Greater Winnipeg* (1964), 45 D.L.R. (2d) 348 (Man. C.A.) affd. [1965] S.C.R. 512.

41 *Hedley Byrne & Co. Ltd. v. Heller & Partners Ltd.*, [1964] A.C. 465.

42 *Koshurba v. N. Kildonan (R.M.) and Popiel* (1965), 51 W.W.R. 608, aff'd (1965) 53 W.W.R. 380.

43 *Welbridge Holdings Ltd.* at 714.

44 Dickson interview at 181.

45 *R. v. Hennessey, Williams and Kumka* (1968), 66 W.W.R. 383 at 384.

46 *R. v. Arenson* (1970), 75 W.W.R. 328; *R. v. Evanson*, [1973] 4 W.W.R. 137; *R. v. Taylor*.

47 See, for example, *Attorney-General of Canada v. Advance T.V. and Car Centre Ltd.* (1968), 66 W.W.R. 595; *R. v. Born*, [1972] 2 W.W.R. 467; *Wright v. Robinson*, [1973] 2 W.W.R. 190; *R. v. Willms*, [1973] 4 W.W.R. 143.

48 But not always: see *R. v. Vogelle and Reid*; *R. v. Pawlowski*, [1972] 1 W.W.R. 481; *R. v. Lepare* (1969), 69 W.W.R. 408 at 411; 'I am not prepared to hold that this court lacks power to remedy such an obvious injustice.'

49 Call to the Bar Ceremony, 1970, vol. 138, file 11.

50 J.R. Colombo, ed., *New Canadian Quotations* (Edmonton: Hurtig 1987), at 311.

51 H.L.A. Hart, *Law, Liberty and Morality* (London: Oxford University Press 1963); Patrick Devlin, *The Enforcement of Morals* (London: Oxford University Press 1968).

52 Criminal Law Amendment Act, S.C. 1968–9, c.38, s.7.

53 *R. v. P.* (1968), 63 W.W.R. 222 at 236, 240.

54 G.E.P[arker], 'Regina v. P,' (1967–8) 10 *Criminal Law Quarterly,* 376 at 378.

55 *R. v. Heffer* (1969), 71 W.W.R. 615.

56 S. 164 (1).

57 'Court's blow for civil rights,' Winnipeg *Tribune,* 29 November 1969.

58 *R. v. Heffer* at 619.

59 Ibid. at 621.

60 Dickson interview at 189.

61 'Address at the University of Winnipeg,' 30 January 1970, vol. 138, file 12.

62 *R. v. Fuller* (1968), 67 W.W.R. 78.

63 Ibid. at 78–9, 81.

64 (1970), 72 W.W.R. 354.

65 Ibid. at 356, 365.

66 *Towne Cinema Theatres Ltd. v. R.,* [1985] 1 S.C.R. 494.

67 *Great West News* at 362, 355.

68 Devlin, *The Enforcement of Morals,* at 15.

69 *R. v. Prairie Schooner News Ltd. and Powers* (1970), 75 W.W.R. 585.

70 *Great West News,* at 354.

71 *Prairie Schooner News* at 604.

72 Ibid. at 604.

73 *Stone v. Stone and Bedford* (1969), 71 W.W.R. 589 at 597.

74 [1972] 5 W.W.R. 678.

75 *R. v. Drybones,* [1970] S.C.R. 282.

76 *Canard* at 688–9.

77 Ibid. at 689.

78 See, for example, *Canada (A.G.) v. Lavell,* [1974] S.C.R. 1349.

79 [1976] 1 S.C.R. 170.

80 Sally M. Weaver, *Making Canadian Indian Policy: The Hidden Agenda, 1968–70* (Toronto: University of Toronto Press 1980).

81 *Vandenburg v. Guimond* (1968), 66 W.W.R. 408 at 409–10.

82 *Reference re Provincial Control of Agricultural Products,* [1971] 3 W.W.R. 204; See also Paul Weiler, *In the Last Resort* (Toronto: Carswell 1974), at 156–7.

83 *Reference re Provincial Control of Agricultural Products* at 211.

84 *Manitoba (Attorney General) v. Manitoba Egg and Poultry Assn.,* [1971] S.C.R. 689.

85 Within a year of the Supreme Court's decision, the provinces and the federal government came together with a joint egg-marketing scheme that imposed provincial quotas, a scheme the Supreme Court found constitutional several years later: *Reference re Agricultural Products Marketing Act, 1970,* [1978] 2 S.C.R. 1198.

86 *Gersham Produce Co. Ltd. v. Manitoba (Marketing Board),* [1971] 4 W.W.R. 50.

87 *Manitoba (Attorney General) v. Burns Foods Ltd.,* [1973] 5 W.W.R. 60 at 71.

88 P. Russell, R. Knopff, and F.C. Morton, eds., *Federalism and the Charter: Leading Constitutional Decisions* (Ottawa: Carleton University Press 1989), at 204.

89 *Manitoba (Attroney General) v. Burns Foods Ltd.*, [1975] 1 S.C.R. 494.

90 Chapter 12.

91 'Address at the University of Winnipeg,' 30 January 1970, vol. 138, file 12.

Chapter 7: Starting Slowly

1 P. Weiler, *In the Last Resort: A Critical Study of the Supreme Court of Canada* (Toronto: Carswell/Metheun 1974), at 4. See also the strong criticisms of Peter Hogg that the Court's reasons for its decisions 'are often woefully inadequate ... brief and in some cases even perfunctory.' P. Hogg, 'The Supreme Court and Administrative Law: 1949–1971' (1973), 11 *Osgoode Hall Law Journal*, 187 at 222. Hogg also noted that the Court never referred to secondary literature. In contrast, between 1985 and 1990, Hogg was cited forty-six times by the Supreme Court. V. Black and N. Richter, 'Did She Mention My Name' (1993), 16 *Dalhousie Law Journal*, 377 at 390.

2 Ontario bencher and future judge Bert MacKinnon as quoted in I. Bushnell, *The Captive Court* (Montreal: McGill-Queen's University Press, 1992), at 370.

3 *Supreme Court Act* R.S.C. 1970 c.s-19, s.36(a).

4 W. Tarnopolsky, 'The Supreme Court and the Canadian Bill of Rights' (1975), 53 *Canadian Bar Review*, 648.

5 *Reference re Truscott*, [1967] S.C.R. 309; *A.G. Canada v. Lavell; Issac v. Bedard*, [1974] S.C.R. 1349; *Calder v. British Columbia* [1973] S.C.R. 313. On Hall, see D. Gruending, *Emmett Hall: Establishment Radical* (Toronto: Macmillan 1986); F. Vaughan, 'Emmett Mathew Hall: The Activist As Justice' (1972), 10 *Osgoode Hall Law Journal*, 411.

6 B. Dickson, 'Remarks at a Dinner in Honour of Retired Justice Emmett Hall,' 25 October 1986, vol. 139, file 63.

7 R. Corelli, 'There's a new order coming to our highest court,' Toronto Star, 12 January 1974.

8 See D. Gibson, 'Unobtrusive Justice' (1974), 12 *Osgoode Hall Law Journal*, 339 at 339, 355.

9 O. Lang, 'Speech at Dickson Swearing in,' 28 March 1973, vol. 194, file 4.

10 Report of the Mackenzie Valley Pipeline Inquiry, *Northern Frontier, Northern Homeland* (Ottawa: Supply and Services 1977) at appendix I.

11 B. Dickson, 'Call to the Bar Address,' 2 June 1967, vol. 138, file 5.

12 Lamer interview.

13 Dickson interview at 559.

14 Ibid.

15 Ibid. at 562.

16 B. Dickson, 'Speech to Federal Lawyers Club' 1974, vol. 138, file 16.

17 We are indebted to Professor Philip Girard for this information.

18 Dickson interview at 220–1.
19 B. Dickson, 'Tribute to the late Chief Justice Laskin' February 1984, vol. 138, file 49.
20 R. Balcome, E. McBride, and D. Russell, *Supreme Court of Canada Decision-Making* (Toronto: Carswell 1990), at 254, 256
21 P. McCormick, *Supreme at Last: The Evolution of the Supreme Court of Canada* (Toronto: James Lorimer 2000), at 66.
22 D. Gibson, 'And One Step Backward: The Supreme Court and Constitutional Law in the Sixties' (1975), 53 *Canadian Bar Review*, 622 at 633; A. McCabe, 'Former justice slams Charter,' Calgary *Herald*, 12 February 1982; W. Monopoli, 'The view from inside the Supreme Court of Canada: Interview with Mr. Justice Martland,' *Financial Post*, 27 March 1982.
23 *Murdoch v. Murdoch*, [1975] 1 S.C.R. 423 at 436 per Martland J.; at 451 per Laskin J. Note that this and other cases not reported in the official Supreme Court law reports until 1975 was actually decided and released in 1973.
24 W.G. Charlton, 'The dangerous precedent that Trudeau set,' *Globe and Mail*, 2 February 1974.
25 Dickson interview at 229.
26 D. Guth, 'Introduction' in D. Guth ed., *Brian Dickson at the Supreme Court of Canada, 1973–1990* (Winnipeg: Faculty of Law, University of Manitoba 1998), at xxi–xxii.
27 Dickson interview at 230.
28 R. Corelli, 'Social issues split Canada's Supreme Court,' Toronto Star, 7 June 1975.
29 Dickson interview at 217
30 *R. v. Drybones*, [1970] S.C.R. 282; *A.G. of Canada v. Lavell and Bedard*, [1974] S.C.R. 1349; *Bliss v. Canada (A.G.)*, [1979] 1 S.C.R. 183. Ritchie's closest colleague was Martland, who recalled that Ritchie was 'a thorough-going lawyer who applied the law as he saw it ... a lot of academics seem to think we should be changing the law. But we saw the rigorous application of the law to every case as our job.' J. Meek, 'The Novascotian,' Halifax *Chronicle Herald*, 5 January 1985.
31 T. Stinson, 'Mr. Justice Roland Ritchie: A Biography' (1994), 17 *Dalhousie Law Journal*, 509.
32 Elizabeth Ritchie to Dickson, 14 June 1988, vol. 134, file 3.
33 'Remarks by Chief Justice Brian Dickson,' in E. Caparros et al., *Melanges Louis-Philippe Pigeon* (Montreal: Wilson and Lafleur 1989), at 50.
34 McCormick, *Supreme at Last*, at 94.
35 B. Dickson, 'Federalism, Civil Law and the Canadian Judiciary: An Integrated Vision' (1994), 28 *Revue Juridique Thémis*, 457 at 459.
36 *A.G. Canada v. Canard*, [1976] 1 S.C.R. 170
37 Dickson interview at 249–51.
38 B. Dickson, 'The Supreme Court of Canada as a Functioning Institution,' Dalhousie Law School, 28 October 1976, vol. 138, file 19.
39 B. Dickson with R. Brock, 'An Autobiographical Memoir upon Arrival in Ottawa,' in Guth, ed., *Brian Dickson* at 71.

40 Report of the Special Committee of the Canadian Bar Association on the Caseload of the Supreme Court of Canada, included as annex A, Legal and Constitutional Affairs Committee, 12 November 1974, at 1.38–1.39.

41 Ibid.

42 R.L. Kellock, 'Supreme Court: "Keep it freely available"' *Globe and Mail*, 2 Febuary 1974; R. Corelli 'Social issues.'

43 An Act to Amend the Supreme Court Act S.C. 1974–75–76, c.18, s.5; *Hansard*, 12 December 1974, at 2193.

44 Bushnell, *The Captive Court*, at 370.

45 Weiler, *In the Last Resort*, at 231.

46 Only Gordon Fairweather mentioned Weiler's proposal for abolition of appeals as of right during the debates, and he quickly added: 'I must say I do not agree with everything that Professor Weiler says.' *Hansard*, 12 December 1974, at 2195.

47 B. Laskin, 'The Role and Function of Final Appellate Courts: The Supreme Court of Canada' (1975), 53 *Canadian Bar Reivew*, 469 at 475.

48 B. Dickson, 'The Supreme Court As a Functioning Institution;' 'Convocation Address,' University of Saskatchewan, 19 May 1978, vol. 138, file 21.

49 B. Dickson, 'Speech to the Newfoundland Branch of the Canadian Bar Association,' 25 June 1980, vol. 138, file 16.

50 Dickson with Brock, 'An Autobiographical Memoir upon Arrival in Ottawa,' at 68.

51 J. Snell and F. Vaughan, *The Supreme Court of Canada* (Toronto: University of Toronto Press/Osgoode Society for Canadian Legal History 1985), at 24–5, 148.

52 *Edmonton Country Club Ltd. v. Case*, [1975] 1 S.C.R. 534 at 546.

53 Ibid. at 550–1.

54 *Barnett v. Harrison*, [1976] 2 S.C.R. 531 at 558.

55 *Turney v. Zhilka*, [1959] S.C.R. 578 at 583.

56 Dickson conference memo, 20 June 1974, vol. 12, file 14.

57 *Barnett v. Harrison* at 559.

58 Ibid. at 550.

59 A. Weinrib, 'Laskin and Property Law' (1985), 35 *University of Toronto Law Journal*, 542 at 553.

60 S. Waddams, *The Law of Contracts*, 4th ed. (Aurora, Ont: Canada Law Book 1999), at 610; G. Fridman, *The Law of Contract in Canada*, 4th ed. (Toronto: Thompson 1999), at 460.

61 Katherine Swinton interview.

62 [1976] 2 S.C.R. 200.

63 *Harrison v. Carswell* (1974), 48 D.L.R. (3d) 137 (Man. C.A.).

64 Dickson conference memo, undated, vol. 12, file 22.

65 *Peters v. The Queen*, (1971), 17 D.L.R. (3d) 128 (S.C.C.) affirming (1970), 16 D.L.R. (3d) 143 (Ont. C.A.).

66 Dickson conference memo.

67 *Harrison v. Carswell* at 205.

68 Ritchie to Dickson, 5 March 1975, vol. 12, file 22.
69 B. Laskin, 'Picketing: A Comparison of Certain Canadian and American Doctrines' (1937), 15 *Canadian Bar Review*, 10. On Laskin's approach to labour law and the influence of his post-graduate education at Harvard see W. Hunter, 'Bora Laskin and Labour Law: The Formative Years' (1984), 6 *Supreme Court Law Review*, 431.
70 *Harrison v. Carswell* at 202.
71 Ibid. at 206.
72 Ibid. at 205.
73 Ibid. at 209.
74 Dickson interview with Wayne MacKay, October 1985.
75 Wilson interview.
76 *Harrison v. Carswell* at 218.
77 Labour Code of British Columbia, S.B.C. 1973, c.122, s.87
78 *Harrison v. Carswell* at 219.
79 Dickson draft judgment, undated, vol. 12, file 22. His notes also contain a quotation from Justice Holmes to the effect that judges should not implement their 'economic or social beliefs' into law.
80 Ritchie to Dickson, 5 March 1975, vol. 12, file 22.
81 *Harrison v. Carswell* at 217.
82 Dickson interview at 272; Dickson interview with Gordon Bale, 9 April 1984.
83 See Dickson memo to Court, 6 June 1975, vol. 12, file 22.
84 The quotes were taken Lord Reid's decisions in *Myers v. D.P.P.*, [1964] 2 All E.R. 881 at 885, and *Pettitt v. Pettitt*, [1969] 2 All E.R. 385 at 390. Dickson went on in the deleted passage to argue that a creative decision reforming the law of evidence (*Ares v. Venner*, [1970] S.C.R. 608) 'did not impair the validity' of Lord Reid's distinction or his conclusion that Carswell's case involved public policy as opposed to lawyer's law.
85 *B.C. Motor Vehicle Reference*, [1985] 2 S.C.R. 486 at 503.
86 J. Ulmer, 'Picketing in Shopping Centres: The Case of Harrison v. Carswell' (1976), 13 *Osgoode Hall Law Journal*, 879; J. Colangelo, 'Labour Law: Harrison v. Carswell' (1976), 34 *University of Toronto Faculty of Law Review*, 236
87 P. Weiler, 'Of Judges and Scholars: Reflections in a Centennial Year' (1975), 53 *Canadian Bar Review*, 563 at 566n.5.
88 B. Dickson, 'Comment,' in Allen Linden, ed., *The Canadian Judiciary* (Toronto: Osgoode Hall Law School 1976), at 81–2.
89 B. Dickson, 'The Supreme Court as a Functioning Institution.'
90 Dickson, 'Comment,' at 82–4.
91 B. Dickson, 'Convocation Address' (1978), 43 *Saskatchawan Law Review*, 1 at 5–6.
92 *Myran v. The Queen*, [1976] 2 S.C.R. 137 at 145.
93 *The Queen v. Mousseau*, [1980] 2 S.C.R. 89 at 92.
94 Dickson conference memo, undated, vol. 40, file 4.
95 Dickson conference memo, 10 May 1977, vol. 19, file 25.

96 *Frank v. The Queen*, [1978] 1 S.C.R. 95 at 101.

97 *R. v. Horseman*, [1990] 1 S.C.R. 901.

98 *Kruger and Manuel v. The Queen*, [1978] 1 S.C.R. 104 at 114.

99 A. Jordan, 'Government, Two–Indians, One' (1978), 16 *Osgoode Hall Law Journal*, 709 at 722.

100 *Kruger and Manuel v. The Queen* at 109.

101 A. Stalker, 'Chief Justice Dickson's Principles of Criminal Law' (1991), 20 *Manitoba Law Journal*, 308 at 322.

102 D. Stuart, 'Chief Dickson and Criminal Law: Cheers, Brickbats and Regrets' (1991), 20 *Manitoba Law Journal*, 288 at 307.

103 [1975] 2 S.C.R. 402.

104 Dickson conference memo, 24 October 1973, vol. 6, file 32.

105 *Hill v. The Queen* at 408–8, 412.

106 *Queen v. Pierce Fisheries Ltd*, [1971] S.C.R. 5; *O'Grady v. Sparling*, [1960] S.C.R. 804. See D. Stuart, *Canadian Criminal Law*, 2nd ed (Toronto: Carswell 1987), at 160–5.

107 *R. v. Sault Ste Marie*, [1978] 2 S.C.R. 1299, as discussed in chapter 11.

108 *Leblanc v. The Queen*, [1977] 1 S.C.R. 339 at 346, 356.

109 In 1989 Dickson joined a judgment of Bertha Wilson that interpreted criminal negligence as requiring a minimal subjective awareness of the prohibited risk. See *R. v. Tutton*, [1989] 1 S.C.R. 1392.

110 *Adgey v. The Queen*, [1975] 2 S.C.R. 426 at 432.

111 *Brosseau v. The Queen*, [1969] S.C.R. 181.

112 D. Gibson, 'Unobtrusive Justice' (1974), 12 *Osgoode Hall Law Journal*, 338 at 355.

113 *Marcoux and Solomon v. The Queen*, [1976] 1 S.C.R. 763 at 765–6.

114 Dickson conference memo, 31 October 1974, vol. 11, file 11.

115 See, for example, *R. v. Leclair and Ross*, [1989] 1 S.C.R. 3.

116 P. Weiler, *In the Last Resort*, at 117.

Chapter 8: Gaining Ground

1 B. Dickson, 'Convocation Address,' University of Saskatchewan, 19 May 1978, vol. 138, file 21.

2 Dickson interview at 318.

3 G. Horwitz, *Canadian Labour in Politics* (Toronto: University of Toronto Press 1968).

4 Joel Bakan interview.

5 See chapter 11 for a discussion of a number of cases in which Dickson refused to compromise his insistence on proof of subjective fault in criminal law.

6 C. Dunphy, *Morgentaler: A Difficult Hero* (Toronto: Random House 1996), at 297.

7 L. Gibson, *A Proud Heritage: The First Hundred Years of Aikens, MacAulay and Thorvaldson* (Winnipeg: n.p., 1993), at 131. See the discussion of Dickson as a 'lawyer statesman' in chapter 4.

8 Barbara Dickson interview.

9 *Evans v. Public Service Commission Appeal Board*, [1983] 1 S.C.R. 582 at 602.

10 See, for example, R. Price, 'Bringing the Rule of Law to Corrections' (1974), 16 *Canadian Journal of Criminology* 209; R. Price, 'Doing Justice to Corrections? Prisoners, Parolees and the Canadian Courts' (1977), 3 *Queen's Law Journal* 214; D. Cole and A. Manson, *Release from Imprisonment: The Law of Sentencing, Parole and Judicial Review* (Toronto: Carswell 1990), at 182–6.

11 Dickson interview at 318.

12 J. Zambrowsky, 'Anger towards Criminals Does Not Provide a Solution,' *John Howard Society of Quebec Quarterly Journal*, vol 1, No. 3, vol. 37, file 5.

13 *Hatchwell v. The Queen*, [1976] 1 S.C.R. 39 at 43.

14 Ibid. at 44.

15 Ibid. at 48.

16 *Solosky v. Canada*, [1980] 1 S.C.R. 821 at 839–40.

17 B. McLachlin and J.C. Thomas, 'Solosky and Prisoner Mail-Opening: A New View of Solicitor-Client Privilege' (1981), 2 *Supreme Court Law Review*, 386 at 399.

18 In his conference memo, Dickson noted that the issue would be determined by 'a balancing process': conference memo, 13 June 1979, vol. 38, file 2. McLachlin noted in her comment that Dickson's approach was 'relative and utilitarian' and was 'not absolute as is the evidentiary rule of privilege; nor is it a right of property': B. McLachlin and J.C. Thomas, 'Solosky and Prisoner Mail-Opening,' at 394.

19 *Solosky v. Canada*, at 836, 841.

20 *Howarth v. National Parole Board*, [1976] 1 S.C.R. 453 at 457.

21 Ibid. at 472.

22 'Parole and the rule of law,' *Globe and Mail*, 29 July 1974. The clipping and a covering memo that Dickson circulated to the Court is contained in Dickson's case file, vol. 10, file 2.

23 *Howarth v. National Parole Board*, at 470, 459, 468, 461, 467.

24 Ibid. at 467.

25 P. Garant, 'L'arret Howarth: une decision regrettable qui confirm l'influence du juge Pigeon,' vol. 10, file 2.

26 S. Silverstone, 'Case Comment' (1975), 63 *Canadian Bar Review*, 92 at 101. Another academic observed that 'all but too few judges (happily, Dickson J. among them) seem aware of the problems which many academics ... have found in this area of present administrative law.' See D. Jones, 'Case Comment' (1975), 21 *McGill Law Journal*, 434 at 440.

27 M. Bloodworth, 'Case Comment' (1976), 8 *Ottawa Law Review*, 70 at 81; Mullan, 'Case Comment' (1978), 24 *McGill Law Journal*, 92 at 105, commenting on *Mitchell v. The Queen* [1976] 2 S.C.R. 570.

28 M. Jackson, 'Justice behind the Walls' (1974), 12 *Osgoode Hall Law Journal*, 1 at 36.

29 *Martineau and Butters v. The Matsqui Institution Inmate Disciplinary Board*, [1978] 1 S.C.R. 118 at 133 (henceforth *Martineau I*).

30 Dickson conference memo, undated, vol. 19, file 2.

31 *Martineau I* at 123, 125.

32 Dickson conference memo, undated, vol. 26, file 11.

33 *Nicholson v. Haldimand-Norfolk Regional Board of Commissioners of Police*, [1979] 1 S.C.R. 311 at 328, 322.

34 House of Commons Subcommittee on the Penitentiary System in Canada, *Report to Parliament* (Ottawa: Supply and Services 1977), at 85–6.

35 [1978] 2 F.C. 637 at 641 (C.A.).

36 Dickson conference memo, undated. vol. 37, file 7.

37 *Martineau v. Matsqui Institution Disciplinary Board*, [1980] 1 S.C.R. 602 at 622 (henceforth *Martineau II*).

38 Ibid. at 622.

39 K. Norman, 'Case Comment' (1981), 45 *Saskatchewan Law Review*, 157 at 163.

40 D. Mullan, 'Developments in Administrative Law: The 1979–80 Term' (1981), 2 *Supreme Court Law Review*, 1 at 27; D. Cole and A. Manson, *Release from Imprisonment* (Toronto: Carswell 1990), at 63. See also M. Jackson, *Justice behind the Walls* (Vancouver: Douglas and McIntrye 2002), at 54–8.

41 *Martineau II* at 629–30.

42 J. Grey, 'The Duty to Act Fairly after Nicholson' (1980), 25 *McGill Law Journal*, 598 at 600.

43 *Martineau II* at 619, 629–30.

44 *Evans v. Public Service Commission Appeal Board*, [1983] 1 S.C.R. 582 at 601–2. Dickson's judgment provided all of these details. Estey's majority judgment referred only to the guards '"insulting remarks"' to the inmates.

45 Ibid. at 619, 611–12.

46 See chapter 17.

47 *King v. University of Saskatchewan*, [1969] S.C.R 678.

48 D. Jones, 'Case Comment' (1981) 19 *Alberta Law Review*, 483.

49 *Harelkin v. University of Regina*, [1979] 2 S.C.R. 561 at 607.

50 Dickson conference memo, 14 June 1978, vol. 30, file 6.

51 *Harelkin v. University of Regina*, at 605.

52 *Kane v. Board of Governors of the University of British Columbia*, [1980] 1 S.C.R. 1105 at 1112–13.

53 Ibid at 1116.

54 Dickson conference memo, 7 May 1974, vol. 10, file 1.

55 *The Law Society of Upper Canada v. French*, [1975] 2 S.C.R. 767 at 783–4.

56 Ibid. at 773.

57 *Ringrose v. College of Physicians and Surgeons of Alberta*, [1977] 1 S.C.R. 814 at 817–18.

58 *MNR v. Coopers and Lybrand*, [1979] 1 S.C.R. 495 at 503.

59 *Martineau II* at 627.

60 *Service Employees International Union Local No. 333 v. Nipawin District Staff Nurses Association*, [1975] 1 S.C.R. 382 at 389.

61 Dickson, undated handwritten note on Court stationary, vol. 6, file 18.

62 *Jacmain v. A.G. of Canada and Public Service Staff Relations Board*, [1978] 2 S.C.R. 15 at 40, applying *Bell v. Ontario Human Rights Commission*, [1971] S.C.R. 756.

63 Dickson conference memo, 29 April 1977, vol. 21, file 6.

64 *Jacmain v. A.G. Canada*, at 29.

65 Dickson draft judgment, 28 July 1977, vol. 21, file 9.

66 N. Fera, 'Case Comment' (1980), 5 *Dalhousie Law Journal*, 364 at 387.

67 Dickson conference memo, undated, vol. 30, file 10.

68 Dickson handwritten note, undated, vol. 30, file 10.

69 *Canadian Union of Public Employees Local 963 v. New Brunswick Liquor Corporation*, [1979] 2 S.C.R. 227 at 233.

70 Ibid at 237.

71 Dickson interview at 320.

72 D. Mullan, 'Developments in Administrative Law' (1980), 1 *Supreme Court Law Review*, 1 at 22.

73 *CUPE v. The Labour Relations Board (Nova Scotia)*, [1983] 2 S.C.R. 311 at 335.

74 *Syndicate des employés de production du Québec et de l'Acadie v. Canadian Labour Relations Board*, [1984] 2 S.C.R. 412 at 441.

75 *Telecommunications Workers Union v. British Columbia Telephone Company*, [1988] 2 S.C.R. 564.

76 *Slaight Communications v. Davidson*, [1989] 1 S.C.R. 1038 at 1061 per Beetz, at 1075 per Lamer.

77 Ibid. at 1051.

78 *Jack v. The Queen*, [1980] 1 S.C.R. 294 at 299.

79 Ibid. at 314, 299, 302, 311.

80 Ibid. at 311, 313.

81 See chapter 7.

82 *The Queen v. Sutherland*, [1980] 2 S.C.R. 451 at 455.

83 See the discussion of the *Manitoba Language Reference* case in chapter 20.

84 *The Queen v. Sutherland*, at 460–1.

85 Ibid at 460.

86 See chapter 6.

87 See chapter 17.

88 *Nowegijick v. The Queen*, [1983] 1 S.C.R. 29 at 36.

89 See chapter 21.

Chapter 9: Compassion and Equity

1 B. Dickson, 'An Address to the Canadian Institute for the Administration of Justice Judicial Conference on Family Law,' Vancouver, 29 August 1981, vol. 138 file 29.

2 *Murdoch v. Murdoch*, [1975] 1 S.C.R. 423 at 451.

3 Ibid. at 436.
4 'The Law As Male Chauvinist Pig,' *Time Canada*, 24 March 1974, as quoted in J. Snell and F. Vaughan, *The Supreme Court of Canada* (Toronto: University of Toronto Press/Osgoode Society for Canadian Legal History 1985), at 310; Law Reform Commission of Canada, *Report on Family Law* (Ottawa: Information Canada 1976), at 2–3, as quoted in R. Balcome, E. McBride, and D. Russell, *Supreme Court of Canada Decision-Making* (Toronto: Carswell, 1990), at 326.
5 I. Bushnell, *The Captive Court* (Montreal: McGill-Queen's University Press 1992), at 391.
6 Dickson interview at 298.
7 Ibid at 297.
8 B. Dickson, 'Speech at University of Western Ontario Law School and University of Manitoba,' fall 1976, vol. 138, file 20.
9 Dickson conference memo, 17 May 1977, vol. 23, file 4.
10 *Rathwell v. Rathwell* (1974), 14 R.F.L. 297 at 304 (Sask. Q.B.).
11 Dickson conference memo, 17 May 1977, vol. 23, file 4.
12 As quoted in *Rathwell v. Rathwell*, [1976] 5 W.W.R. 148 at 159 (Sask. C.A.).
13 *Rathwell v. Rathwell*, [1978] 2 S.C.R. 436 at 443, 445–6, 447.
14 As Paul Weiler observed in 'Of Judges and Scholars: Reflections in a Centennial Year' (1975), 53 *Canadian Bar Review*, 563 at 568. Throughout his judgment, Laskin 'beats the theme of the "extraordinary" contribution of Mrs Murdoch, the fact that "her labour is not simply housekeeping, which might be said to be merely a reflection of the marriage bond."' Fifteen years later, in *Peter v. Beblow*, [1993] 1 S.C.R. 980 at 993, Beverley McLachlin would recognize for the Court that the idea that domestic services were not deserving of recognition was a 'pernicious' one that 'systematically devalues the contributions which women tend to make to the family economy.'
15 *Rathwell v. Rathwell* at 448, 455.
16 Denning would have relied on 'the simple test: What is reasonable and fair in the circumstances as they have developed, seeing that they are circumstances which no one contemplated before.' *Appleton v. Appleton*, [1965] 1 All E.R. 44 at 46 (C.A.).
17 *Rathwell v. Rathwell* at 448.
18 Dickson's law clerk Joe Magnet, wrote him a memorandum arguing that Dickson's attempt to distinguish *Murdoch* 'could attract the comment in the law journals that the Court is trying to save face in the presence of an embarrassing precedent' and urged Dickson to overrule *Murdoch*: Magnet to Dickson, undated, vol. 23, file 3. Another Dickson clerk, Brian Morgan, similarly argued that *Murdoch* should be overruled 'for the sake of judicial and intellectual honesty. However it may be necessary to distinguish it rather than overrule it in order to gain support.' Morgan to Dickson, 9 September 1977, vol. 23, file 7.
19 D. Waters, 'Comment' (1975), 53 *Canadian Bar Review*, 366 at 368.

20 J. McCamus and L. Taman, '*Rathwell v. Rathwell*: Matrimonial Property, Resulting and Constructive Trusts' (1978), 16 *Osgoode Hall Law Journal*, 741 at 754. See also R. Walker, 'Case Comment' (1978), 1 *Canadian Journal of Family Law*, 303.

21 G. Maurice, 'Case Comment' (1978–9), 43 *Saskatchewan Law Review*, 161 at 162.

22 A.B. McGillivray to Dickson, 20 January 1978, Dickson to McGillivray, 1 February 1978, vol. 132, file 16.

23 D. Waters, 'Chief Justice Dickson, the Court, and Restitution' (1991), 20 *Manitoba Law Journal*, 368 at 372.

24 *Rathwell v. Rathwell*, at 456.

25 *Pettkus v. Becker*, [1980] 2 S.C.R. 834 at 853.

26 Ibid. at 845.

27 *Becker v. Pettkus* (1978), 87 D.L.R. (3d) 101 (Ont C.A.); E. Anderson, *Judging Bertha Wilson* (Toronto: University of Toronto Press/Osgoode Society for Canadian Legal History 2001), at 103.

28 *Seneca College v. Bhadauria*, [1981] 2 S.C.R. 181.

29 B. Dickson, 'Madam Justice Bertha Wilson: Trailblazer for Justice' (1992), 15 *Dalhousie Law Journal*, 1.

30 Laskin to the Court, 20 June 1980, vol. 44, file 8.

31 'A "Laskin Court" at last?' *Macleans*, 17 October 1977.

32 Dickson interview at 357.

33 *R. v. Miller*, [1977] 2 S.C.R. 680, affirming (1975) 24 C.C.C. (2d) 401 at 459ff. (B.C.C.A.).

34 Dickson interview at 365.

35 On McIntyre, see W.H. McConnell, *William McIntyre: Paladin of the Common Law* (Montreal: McGill-Queen's University Press 2000).

36 Lamer interview.

37 *Pettkus v. Becker*, at 850–1.

38 Dickson to Jamie Cameron, 23 June 1980, vol. 44, file 8.

39 Dickson, undated draft judgment, vol. 44, file 9, and Dickson to Donovan Waters, 11 March 1983, vol. 134, file 12.

40 *Pettkus v. Becker*, at 848.

41 *Pettkus v. Becker*, at 856, 859.

42 B. Dickson, 'An Address to Judicial Conference on Family Law,' 29 August 1981, vol. 138, file 29. See also B. Dickson, 'The Judiciary – Law Interpreters or Law-Makers' (1982) 12 *Manitoba Law Journal*, 1 at 6.

43 *Pettkus v. Becker*, at 847–8.

44 *Cie Immobilière Viger Ltee v. Lauréat Giguere*, [1977] 2 S.C.R. 67 at 76; B. Dickson 'Federalism, Civil Law and the Canadian Judiciary: An Integrated Vision' (1994), 28 *Revue Juridique Thémis*, 457 at 475. See also G. Klippert, *Unjust Enrichment*, (Toronto: Butterworths 1983), at 370–2; and L. Smith, 'The Mystery of "Juristic Reason"' (2000), 12 *Supreme Court of Law Review* (2d), 211 at 215–19. We are indebted to Pro-

fessor Nicholas Kasirer, of McGill's Faculty of Law and a former Beetz clerk, for bringing this point to our attention.

45 P. Trudeau, *Against the Current* (Toronto: McClelland and Stewart 1996) at 267.

46 B. Dickson, 'Opening Address,' in General Reports of the 13th International Congress of the International Academy of Comparative Law.

47 Dickson did not follow the prevailing English law at the time. Nor did he adhere to the prevailing American law, although he was influenced by the influential American restatement. See P. Maddaugh and J. McCamus, *The Law of Restitution* (Aurora, Ont.: Canada Law Book 1990), at 21.

48 J. McLeod, 'Annotation' (1980), 19 R.F.L. (2d) 166 at 168.

49 'Fair shares,' *Globe and Mail*, 27 December 1980.

50 'Common law wife awarded half of farmer's worth,' *Globe and Mail*, 19 December 1980.

51 D. Anderson, 'The Supreme Court and Women's Rights' (1980), 1 *Supreme Court Law Review*, 457 at 459.

52 N. Bala, '*Pettkus v. Becker*: Equity Aiding the Common Law Spouse' (1981), 6 *Queen's Law Journal*, 514 at 514, 526–7.

53 'Common law wife awarded half of farmer's worth.'

54 Rosa Becker to Dickson, 28 May 1984, Suzanne D'Aoust to Rosa Becker, 4 June 1984, vol. 132, file 6.

55 Anderson, *Judging Bertha Wilson*, at 104.

56 *Sorochan v. Sorochan* [1986] 2 S.C.R. 38; J. MacPherson, 'Working within the Dickson Court' (1991), 20 *Manitoba Law Journal*, 519 at 526.

57 Colleen Sheppard interview.

58 D. Vienneau, 'Rights of common-law wives backed,' Toronto Star, 1 August 1986.

59 B. Dickson, 'The Law and Compassion,' Convocation Address, University of Toronto, vol. 139, file 51.

60 50th Wedding Anniversary Speech, vol. 194, file 23.

61 *Veinot v. Kerr-Addison Mines Ltd.*, [1975] 2 S.C.R. 311 at 313, 322, 320.

62 J. Maclaren, 'The Dickson Approach to Liability in Tort,' in D. Guth, ed., *Brian Dickson at the Supreme Court of Canada, 1973–1990* (Winnipeg: Faculty of Law, University of Manitoba, 1998), at 277.

63 Dickson conference memo, 30 May 1974, vol. 12, file 7.

64 *Paskivski et al v. Canadian Pacific Ltd et al.*, [1976] 1 S.C.R. 687 at 688–9, 708.

65 Dickson notes, undated, vol. 12, file 7.

66 *Paskivski et al v. Canadian Pacific Ltd.* at 701.

67 Dickson interview at 291.

68 *Haig v. Bamford*, [1977] 1 S.C.R. 466 at 475–6, 484.

69 Dickson conference memo, 17 June 1977, vol. 22, file 18.

70 *Andrews v. Grand and Toy Ltd.*, [1978] 2 S.C.R. 229 at 242–3.

71 B. Dickson, 'Law and Medicine: Conflict or Collaboration,' Address to the American Association of Neurological Surgeons, 25 April 1988, vol. 139, file 43.

72 Ibid; Dickson interview at 295.

73 *Andrews v. Grand and Toy Ltd.* at 261.

74 Ibid at 236.

75 Ibid at 236–7.

76 *Lindal v. Lindal,* [1981] 2 S.C.R. 629 at 635.

77 Ibid. at 635.

78 *The Queen v. Sault Ste Marie,* [1978] 2 S.C.R. 1299, discussed in chapter 11.

79 *The Queen v. Saskatchewan Wheat Pool,* [1983] 1 S.C.R. 205 at 209–11.

80 Ibid.

81 B. Dickson, 'Breach of Statutory Duty as Foundation for Cause of Action for Damages,' 1938, University of Manitoba Archives, UA 43 072, Research Papers – LLB LLM theses, at 1.

82 *The Queen v. Saskatchewan Wheat Pool* at 211.

83 Dickson, 'Breach of Statutory Duty,' at 28–9.

84 Lamer to Dickson, 31 January 1983, vol. 58, file 12.

85 Linden to Dickson, 18 February 1983, Dickson to Linden, 15 March 1983, vol. 132, file 6.

86 M. Mathews, 'Negligence and Breach of Statutory Duty' (1984), 4 *Oxford Journal of Legal Studies,* 429 at 431; W. Rogers, 'Rusty Beetles in the Elevator' [1984] *Cambridge Law Journal* 23 at 25; John Fleming, *The Law of Torts,* 7th ed. (Sydney: Law Book 1987), at 115. Even critics who believed that it was unwise to 'submerge breach of statute into the common law of negligence' admitted that 'the clarification of the law ... is certainly welcome.' A. Brudner, 'Case Comment' (1984), 62 *Canadian Bar Review,* 668 at 679.

87 *Nepean v. Ontario Hydro,* [1982] 1 S.C.R. 347 at 412.

88 Ibid. at 349, 371, 363, 364.

89 Swan to Dickson, 19 March 1982, vol. 132, file 6.

90 Dickson to Swan, 29 March 1982, vol. 132, file 6.

91 *Air Canada v. British Columbia,* [1989] 1 S.C.R. 1161 at 1199.

92 Dickson to Swan, 5 August 1982, vol. 134, file 13.

93 B. Dickson, 'Remarks to the Executive of the Canadian Bar Association on the Court's Tasks 1984,' vol. 139, file 3.

94 B. Dickson, 'Supreme Court of Canada as a General Court of Appeal,' County of York Law Association, 30 May 1985, vol. 139, file 19.

95 P. Russell, *The Judiciary in Canada* (Toronto: McGraw-Hill 1987), at 347.

96 Quoted in Dickson's letter to Williams, 25 September 1986, vol. 142, file 4.

97 Ibid.

98 Williams to Dickson, 24 October 1986, vol. 142, file 4.

99 David Nuttall to Dickson, 11 May 1987, vol. 132, file 4.

100 Dickson to Nuttall, 10 June 1987, vol. 132, file 4.
101 Nuttall to Dickson 16 June 1987, vol. 132, file 4.
102 Dickson to Eric Gertner, 20 March 1985, vol. 132, file 7. The case involved a litigant who was denied the benefit of the Court's more generous approach to statute of limitations. Dickson defended the Court's decision to deny leave, but he also saw the case as evidence that 'we should go ahead with obtaining some form of computer control of pending cases' so as to avoid similar problems in the future. Dickson to Guy Goulard, 20 June 1985, vol. 132, file 1.

Chapter 10: Write and Rewrite

1 One counting reveals only thirty-six academic citations for all of 1967, 1968, and 1969, with only two of these citations being legal periodicals. P. McCormack, 'Do Judges Read Books Too? Academic Citations by the Lamer Court 1991–1996' (1998), 9 *Supreme Court Law Review*, 2nd Series, 463 at 467.
2 Dickson interview at 258–9.
3 B. Dickson, 'Address to the Canadian Institute for the Administration of Justice Seminar on Judgment Writing,' 2 July 1981, vol. 138, file 28.
4 *Black and Decker v. The Queen*, [1975] 1 S.C.R. 411 at 422.
5 Lamer to Dickson, 31 January 1983, vol. 58, file 12.
6 McIntyre interview.
7 La Forest interview.
8 B. Dickson, 'Address to the Canadian Institute for the Administration of Justice Seminar on Judgment Writing.'
9 Ibid.
10 *Rathwell v. Rathwell*, [1978] 2 S.C.R. 436 at 442–3.
11 *Pettkus v. Becker,* [1980] 2 S.C.R, 834 at 838.
12 McIntyre interview; McIntyre as quoted in W.H. McConnell, *William R. McIntyre: Paladin of the Common Law* (Montreal: McGill Queens' University Press 2000), at 219.
13 Lamer interview.
14 B. Dickson, 'Address to the University of Manitoba Law School,' fall 1977, vol. 138, file 20.
15 Ibid.
16 Bernard Hofley to Dickson, 17 November 1982, vol. 150, file 14.
17 Dickson to Goulard, 20 June 1985, vol. 150, file 10.
18 The correlation is not perfect, depending on how the volumes are counted. See M. McInnes, J. Bolton and N. Derzko, 'Clerking at the Supreme Court of Canada' (1994), 33 *Alberta Law Review*, 58.
19 Katherine Swinton interview; Patrick Monahan interview.
20 See vol. 150, files 8, 9, 10, 13, especially memo from Mark Newman to Dickson, 27 March 1985, vol. 150, file 13.

21 B. Dickson, Remarks to the Law Society of Newfoundland, 11 May 1988, vol. 139, file 96.

22 Dickson interview at 542.

23 B. Morgan, 'A View of Clerking at the Supreme Court of Canada' (1978), 3 (2) *Hearsay* [Dalhousie Law School Alumni Magizine], 6. See also M. Herman, 'Law Clerking at the Supreme Court of Canada' (1975), 13 *Osgoode Hall Law Journal*, 279.

24 La Forest interview.

25 Dickson 'Remarks to the Law Society of Newfoundland.'

26 Dickson to Peter Rogers and Stephen Toope, 16 September 1986, vol. 132, file 15.

27 Morgan ' A View of Clerking at the Supreme Court of Canada.'

28 L. Sossin, 'The Sounds of Silence: Law Clerks, Policy Making and the Supreme Court of Canada' (1996), 30 *University of British Columbia Law Review*, 278 at 299–300.

29 McInnes, 'Clerking at the Supreme Court of Canada,' at 62.

30 Lamer interview.

31 Memo, Dickson to Peter Rogers and Stephen Toope, 16 September 1986, vol. 132, file 15.

32 Joel Bakan interview.

33 Morgan, 'A View of Clerking at the Supreme Court of Canada.'

34 Law clerks to Dickson, 21 June 1984, vol. 150, file 15.

35 Morgan, 'A View of Clerking at the Supreme Court of Canada.'

36 Katherine Swinton interview; Rollie Thompson interview.

37 Dickson interview at 540–1.

38 Dickson's law clerks were: 1972–3: Bill Estey; 1973–4: Gilles Desrosiers; 1974–5: Vince Orchard; 1975–6: Katherine Swinton; 1976–7: Joseph Magnet; 1977–8: Brian Morgan; 1978–9: Rollie Thompson; 1979–80: Jamie Cameron; 1980–1: Patrick Monahan; 1981–2: Cally Jordan; 1982–3: Ian McGilp, Dianne Pothier; 1983–4: Mark Freiman, Tom Mundell; 1984–5: Catherine Kennedy, Joel Bakan; 1985–6: Colleen Sheppard, Peter Rogers; 1986–7: Stephen Toope, Patrick Macklem; 1987–8: Tom Irvine, Martha Shaffer; 1988–9: Craig Scott, Stephen Smith; 1989–90: Carl Stychin, Shauna Van Praagh, David Layton. In later years, some of Dickson clerks were employed for the calendar year while others were employed on the more traditional basis of starting in the summer after the end of the academic school year.

39 Dickson interview at 542.

40 B. Dickson, Remarks to the Canadian Law Deans, 5 November 1987, vol. 139, file 83.

41 Katherine Swinton interview.

42 B. Dickson, 'Remarks to the Annual Meeting of the Canadian Bar Association,' 23 August 1989, vol. 140, file 8.

43 Dickson to Jamie Cameron, 18 July 1986, vol. 149, file 9.

44 Monahan to Dickson, 2 May 1986, vol. 149, file 17; Dickson to Monahan, 15 May 1986, vol. 149, file 17.

45 B. Dickson, 'The Importance of Universities,' 30 May 1986, vol. 139, file 48.

46 G.V. Nicholls, 'Legal Periodicals and the Supreme Court of Canada' (1950), 28 *Canadian Bar Review*, 422.

47 B. Dickson, 'Address to Canadian Judicial Council Seminar for Newly Appointed Federal Judges,' 12 March 1982, vol. 138, file 34.

48 B. Dickson, 'The Role and Function of Judges' (1980), 14 *Law Society of Upper Canada Gazette*, 138.

49 Dickson to Frank Iacobucci, 12 November 1980, vol. 134, file 11.

50 J. MacPherson, 'Economic Regulation and the British North America Act' (1980–1), 5 *Canadian Business Law Journal*, 172 at 174.

51 D. Waters, 'Trusts Law and Tax Law: A Growing Conflict' (1981), 19 *University of Western Ontario Law Review*, 111.

52 Dickson to Donovan Waters, 28 July 1982, vol. 132, file 6.

53 Jacob Ziegel to Dickson, 29 October 1980, vol. 146, file 3.

54 Barry Reiter to Dickson, 19 July 1982, vol. 132, file 16.

55 Dickson to Reiter, 26 July 1982, vol. 132, file 16.

56 *R. v. Edwards Books*, [1986] 2 S.C.R 713. See A. Petter 'The Politics of the Charter' (1986), 8 *Supreme Court Law Review*, 473; P. Monahan and A. Petter, 'Developments in Constitutional Law: the 1985–1986 Term' (1987) 9 *Supreme Court Law Review*, 69.

57 *R. v. Keegstra*, [1990] 3 S.C.R., 697 at 741.

58 Dickson, 'Address to Canadian Judicial Council Seminar for Newly Appointed Federal Judges.'

59 B. Dickson, 'The Relationship of Judges and Law Schools – Allies in a Common Cause,' Dalhousie University, 19 November 1981, vol. 138, file 31.

60 B. Dickson, 'Remarks to the Advocates Society,' 21 June 1984, vol. 139, file 2.

61 McIntyre interview.

62 Gordon Bale interview of Brian Dickson, 9 April 1984, at 10.

63 Michael Jackson to Dickson, 24 June 1991, vol 170, file 8.

64 'Special Issue: The Dickson Legacy' (1991), 20 *Manitoba Law Journal*, 263–561; D. Guth, ed., *Brian Dickson at the Supreme Court of Canada*, 1973–1990 (Winnipeg: Faculty of Law, University of Manitoba 1998).

Chapter 11: Fault and Free Will

1 B. Dickson, 'Criminal Law Lectures,' 8–10 September 1982, University of Western Ontario, vol. 138, file 35.

2 B. Dickson, 'Swearing-in Speech,' 1973, vol. 138, file 14.

3 *Hill v. The Queen*, [1975] 2 S.C.R. 402, discussed in chapter 7.

4 L. Arbour, '"The Oracle of the Criminal Code"' (1975), 13 *Osgoode Hall Law Journal*, 315 at 317.

5 *R. v. Sault Ste Marie*, [1978] 2 S.C.R. 1299 at 1305.

6 Dickson handwritten notes, vol. 24, file 19.

7 Law Reform Commission of Canada, *Strict Liability* (Ottawa: Supply and Services 1974).

8 Dickson handwritten notes, vol. 24, file 19.

9 *R v. Sault Ste Marie* at 1309–10.

10 *Strasser v. Roberge*, [1979] 2 S.C.R. 953 at 992–3. Dickson dissented in this case because he thought that the Court was diluting the principle of subjective fault as it applied to true crimes.

11 *R. v. Sault Ste Marie* at 1327.

12 Ibid. at 1310.

13 Ibid. at 1311–12.

14 *R. v. Sault Ste Marie* at 1325, 1331.

15 Draft Estey dissenting judgment, undated, at 12, vol. 24, file 19.

16 Dickson to Court, 20 April 1978, vol. 24, file 19.

17 *R. v. Sault Ste Marie* at 1324.

18 A. Hutchinson, 'Sault Ste Marie, Mens Rea and the Halfway House' (1979), 17 *Osgoode Hall Law Journal*, 415 at 421.

19 *R. v. Sault Ste Marie* at 1325.

20 Law Reform Commission of Canada, *Strict Liability*, at 10.

21 *The Queen v. Chapin*, [1979] 2 S.C.R. 121 at 127, 133, 132.

22 *Reference re S. 94(2) of the Motor Vehicle Act*, [1985] 2 S.C.R. 486 at 521.

23 *R. v. Wholesale Travel Group Ltd.*, [1991] 3 S.C.R. 154.

24 *Dunlop and Sylvester v. The Queen*, [1979] 2 S.C.R. 881 at 896.

25 Dickson conference memo, 22 October 1979, vol. 40, file 6.

26 *Morgan v. The Queen*, [1976] A.C. 182; *The Report of the Advisory Group on the Law of Rape* (The Heilbron Report), cmnd. 6352 (1976).

27 Dickson conference memo, 22 October 1979; Estey to Dickson, undated, vol. 40, file 6.

28 *Pappajohn v. The Queen*, [1980] 2 S.C.R. 120 at 138, 148, 150–1.

29 Ibid at 155–6.

30 Ibid at 163, 155.

31 Larry Still, 'Rapists' Charter?' Vancouver *Sun*, 14 June 1980; Elizabeth Grey, 'Courting Regression on Rape,' *MacLeans*, 26 July 1980. An original copy of the womens' groups' letter to the editor is found in Dickson's case files at vol. 40, file 6.

32 Dickson to Jamie Cameron, 21 October 1980, vol. 134, file 11.

33 D. Stuart, 'Pappajohn: Safeguarding Fundamental Principles' (1981), 26 *McGill Law Journal*, 348.

34 T. Pickard, 'Culpable Mistakes and Rape: Relating Mens Rea to the Crime' (1980), 30 *University of Toronto Law Journal*, 75; T. Pickard, ' Culpable Mistakes and Rapes: Harsh Words on *Pappajohn*' (1980), 30 *University of Toronto Law Journal*, 415.

35 Criminal Code, s.265(4) This was upheld from Charter challenge in *R. v. Osolin*, [1993] 4 S.C.R. 595.

36 Dickson to McIntyre, 7 May 1985, vol. 75, file 13.
37 *Sansregret v. The Queen*, [1985] 1 S.C.R. 570 at 587.
38 D. Stuart, *Canadian Criminal Law*, 2nd ed. (Toronto: Carswell 1987) at 144.
39 Criminal Code, s.273.2.
40 *R. v. Darrach*, (1998) 13 C.R. (4th) 283 (Ont. C.A.) aff'd [2000] 2 S.C.R. 443.
41 *Leary v. The Queen*, [1978] 1 S.C.R. 29 at 52.
42 Ibid. at 42.
43 *Leary v. The Queen* at 34.
44 Ibid. at 43.
45 Ibid. at 44–7.
46 Dickson conference memo, 9 December 1987, vol. 105, file 3.
47 La Forest interview.
48 Dickson interview at 305.
49 *R. v. Bernard*, [1988] 2 S.C.R. 833 at 880.
50 Ibid. at 884.
51 Ibid. at 843.
52 *R. v. Daviault*, [1994] 3 S.C.R. 63 at 71.
53 Criminal Code, s.33.1.
54 B. Dickson, 'Criminal Law Lectures.'
55 *Mulligan v. The Queen*, [1977] 1 S.C.R. 612 at 627 (emphasis in original).
56 *Schwartz v. The Queen*, [1977] 1 S.C.R. 673 at 701.
57 Ibid. at 688.
58 G. Williams, *Criminal Law*, 2nd ed. (London: Steven and Sons 1961) at 493–4.
59 P. Weiler, 'The Supreme Court of Canada and the Doctrines of Mens Rea' (1971), 49 *Canadian Bar Review*, 280 at 352.
60 Dickson conference memo, 8 June 1990, vol. 130, file 5.
61 *R. v. Chaulk*, [1990] 3 S.C.R. 1303.
62 *Cooper v. The Queen*, [1980] 1 S.C.R. 1149 at 1170, 1163.
63 *The Queen v. Abbey*, [1982] 2 S.C.R. 24 at 26.
64 La Forest interview.
65 *Rabey v. The Queen*, [1980] 2 S.C.R. 513 at 520.
66 Ibid. at 547–8, 527, 533.
67 *R. v. Stone*, [1999] 2 S.C.R. 290. The decision was a close five-to-four decision and the dissent, which followed Dickson's dissent in *Rabey*, has been much more widely praised in the scholarly literature.
68 Chapter 1.
69 *Perka v. The Queen*, [1984] 2 S.C.R. 232 at 249, 261.
70 Ibid. at 276.
71 Dickson to Wilson, 17 July 1984, vol. 70, file 2.
72 In 1985 the Ontario Court of Appeal applied Dickson's more restrictive approach to hold that Morgentaler could not claim the necessity defence for his deliberate

decision to violate the abortion law: *R. v. Morgentaler* (1985), 22 C.C.C. (3d) 353 (Ont. C.A.). Dickson would have undoubtedly affirmed this decision on appeal if he had not struck down the abortion law.

73 Toope to Dickson, 26 January 1987, vol. 132, file 14.
74 Macklem to Dickson, 26 March 1987, vol. 132, file 14.
75 *The Queen v. Faid*, [1983] 1 S.C.R. 265 at 271.
76 John Holland to Dickson, 31 March 1983, Dickson to Holland, 12 April 1983, vol. 132, file 6.
77 Dickson conference memo, 20 May 1981, vol. 53, file 16.
78 *Vetrovec v. The Queen*, [1982] 1 S.C.R. 811 at 823, 831.
79 B. Dickson, 'Criminal Law Lectures.'
80 *The Queen v. Hill*, [1986] 1 S.C.R. 313 at 320.
81 Ibid. at 324–5, 332, 334.
82 Dickson conference memo, 25 February 1985, vol. 84, file 4.
83 *R. v. Lavallee*, [1990] 1 S.C.R. 852 at 883.
84 *Thibert v. The Queen*, [1996] 1 S.C.R. 37 at 49.
85 *R. v. Corbett*, [1988] 1 S.C.R. 670 at 691–2
86 La Forest interview.
87 Manitoba Aboriginal Justice Inquiry, *The Justice System and Aboriginal People, Vol. 1* (Winnipeg: Queen's Printer 1991), at 378.

Chapter 12: Balanced Federalism

1 For a recent comprehensive history, see John T. Saywell, *The Lawmakers: Judicial Power and the Shaping of Canadian Federalism* (Toronto: Univeristy of Toronto Press Osgoode Society for Canadian Legal History 2002).
2 Bora Laskin, '"Peace, Order and Good Government" Re-examined' (1947), 25 *Canadian Bar Review* 1054.
3 Jean Beetz, 'Les attitudes changeantes du Québec à l'endroit de la Constitution de 1867.' In P.-A. Crépeau and C.R. Macpherson, ed., *The Future of Canadian Federalism* (Toronto: University of Toronto Press 1965); L.-P. Pigeon, 'The Meaning of Provincial Autonomy' (1951), 29 *Canadian Bar Review*, 1126.
4 B. Dickson, 'The Development of a Distinctively Canadian Jurisprudence,' Faculty of Law, Dalhousie University, Halifax, 29 October 1983, vol. 138, file 48.
5 B. Dickson, 'The Rule of Law: Judicial Independence and the Separation of Powers,' Canadian Bar Association, 21 August 1985, vol. 139, file 27.
6 B. Dickson, 'The Role and Function of Judges' (1980), 14 *Law Society of Upper Canada Gazette*, 138 at 173.
7 *Amax Potash Ltd. v. Saskatchewan*, [1976] 2 S.C.R. 576.
8 Dickson conference memo, 10 June 1976, vol. 17, file 9.
9 *Amax Potash* at 590.

10 In writing this chapter we have drawn heavily on K.E. Swinton, *The Supreme Court and Canadian Federalism: The Laskin–Dickson Years* (Toronto: Carswell 1990); K.E. Swinton, 'Dickson and Federalism: In Search of the Right Balance' (1991), 20 *Manitoba Law Journal*, 483.

11 *Di Iorio v. Warden of the Montreal Jail*, [1978] 1 S.C.R. 152 at 200.

12 *General Motors of Canada Ltd. v. City National Leasing Ltd.*, [1989] 1 S.C.R. 641

13 Ibid. at 670, citing P. Hogg, *Constitutional Law of Canada*, 2nd ed. (Toronto: Carswell 1985), at 334.

14 *Multiple Access Ltd. v. McCutcheon*, [1982] 2 S.C.R. 161 at 182, adopting W. Lederman, 'Classification of Laws and the British North America Act,' in *The Courts and the Canadian Constitution* (Toronto: McClelland and Stewart 1964), 177 at 193.

15 Ibid. See also *Rio Hotel Ltd. v. New Brunswick (Liquor Licencing Board)*, [1987] 2 S.C.R. 59

16 See, for example, *General Motors* at 669.

17 *Multiple Access* at 180–1, quoting W. Lederman, 'The Concurrent Operation of Federal and Provincial Laws in Canada' (1963), 9 *McGill Law Journal*, 185.

18 Dickson interview at 347.

19 *Multiple Access* at 197.

20 Swinton, *The Supreme Court and Canadian Federalism*, at 222, 259.

21 See Dickson's tribute to Beetz: 'Federalism, Civil Law and the Canadian Judiciary: An Integrated Vision' (1994), 28 *Revue Juridique Thémis*, 447.

22 [1976] 2 S.C.R. 373. For the political context of this decision, see P. Russell, 'The Anti-Inflation Case: The Anatomy of a Constitutional Decision' (1977), 20 *Canadian Public Administration*, 632.

23 Saywell, *The Lawmakers*.

24 Laskin, '"Peace, Order and Good Government" Re-examined.' See also Swinton, *The Supreme Court and Canadian Federalism*, chapter 8.

25 Beetz, 'Les attitudes changeantes du Québec à l'endroit de la Constitution de 1867.' See also Swinton, *The Supreme Court and Canadian Federalism*, 9.

26 'The Meaning of Provincial Autonomy.'

27 *Ontario (A.G.) v. Canada Temperance Federation*, [1946] A.C. 193 at 205 (J.C.P.C.).

28 4 June 1976, vol. 17, file 2.

29 'The Role and Function of Judges,' at 188.

30 See P.W. Hogg, 'Proof of Facts in Constitutional Cases' (1976), 26 *University of Toronto Law Journal*, 386 at 406.

31 See P. Patenaude, 'The Anti-Inflation Case: The Shutters Are Closed but the Back Door Is Wide Open' (1977), 15 *Osgoode Hall Law Journal*, 397.

32 13 September 1976.

33 Bora Laskin, 'Public Perceptions of the Supreme Court of Canada,' Address at the Annual Dinner of the Canadian Press, 20 April 1977, vol. 201, file 7.

34 Gerald Le Dain, 'Sir Lyman Duff and the Constitution' (1974), 12 *Osgoode Hall Law Journal*, 261.

35 William Lederman, 'Unity and Diversity in Canadian Federalism: Ideals and Methods of Moderation' (1975), 53 *Canadian Bar Review*, 597.

36 *Anti-Inflation Reference* at 458.

37 Judson, Spence, and Dickson agreed with Laskin; De Grandpré agreed with Beetz. Ritchie wrote short separate reasons agreeing with Laskin on the emergency power point and with Beetz on the national dimension point. Martland and Pigeon agreed with Ritchie.

38 Swinton to Dickson, 2 June 1976, vol. 17, file 3.

39 Dickson interview at 281. Twelve years later, Dickson concurred in Le Dain's majority judgment in *R. v. Crown Zellerbach*, [1988] 1 S.C.R. 401, upholding federal jurisdiction over ocean pollution under the national concern doctrine. Beetz concurred with La Forest's dissent.

40 Dickson conference memo, 10 November 1976, vol. 22, file 4.

41 *Canadian Industrial Gas & Oil Ltd. v. Saskatchewan*, [1978] 2 S.C.R. 545 at 573–4.

42 See especially *Central Canada Potash Co. v. Saskatchewan*, [1979] 1 S.C.R. 42, where Dickson concurred in a unanimous judgment by Laskin.

43 In *Re Exported Natural Gas Tax*, [1982] 1 S.C.R. 1004, Dickson joined the majority in striking down a federal tax on provincially owned natural gas.

44 Barbara Dickson interview.

45 s.92a.

46 *Capital Cities Communications Inc. v. Canadian Radio-Television Commission*, [1978] 2 S.C.R. 141; *Public Service Board v. Dionne*, [1978] 2 S.C.R. 191. Compare, however, *A.G. Quebec v. Kellogg's Co.*, [1978] 2 S.C.R. 211, upholding provincial regulation of television advertising directed at children. See also *Irwin Toy v. Quebec (A.G.)*, [1989] 1 S.C.R. 927.

47 Dickson conference memo, *Public Service Board v. Dionne*, 8 June 1977, vol. 22, file 9.

48 *Radio Reference*, [1932] A.C. 304.

49 Quoted in Saywell, *The Lawmakers*, at 269: See also K. Lysyk, 'Reshaping Canadian Federalism' (1979), 13 *University of British Columbia Law Review*, 1 at 16–21.

50 Bora Laskin, 'Judicial Integrity and the Supreme Court of Canada' (1978), 12 *Law Society of Upper Canada Gazette*, 116 at 121. The charge was also answered in a scholarly article: P.W. Hogg, 'Is the Supreme Court of Canada Biased in Constitutional Cases?' (1979), 57 *Canadian Bar Review*, 721.

51 [1978] 2 S.C.R. 662.

52 [1978] 2 S.C.R. 770.

53 R. J. Sharpe, 'Bora Laskin and Civil Liberties' (1985), 35 *University of Toronto Law Journal*, 632.

54 Dickson conference memo, 25 May, 1977, vol. 23, file 1.

55 Dickson conference memo, 29 April, 1977, vol. 23, file 2.

56 P.W. Hogg, 'Is the Supreme Court of Canada Biased in Constitutional Cases?' 721 at 737.

57 Dale Gibson, 'And One Step Backward: The Supreme Court and Constitutional Law in the Sixties' (1975), 53 *Canadian Bar Review*, 622.

58 P. Russell, R. Knopff, and F.L. Morton, ed. *Federalism and the Charter* (Ottawa: Carleton University Press 1989), 204 at 333.

59 *R. v. Wetmore*, [1983] 2 S.C.R. 284 at 305.

60 [1978] 1 S.C.R. 152.

61 Dickson conference memo, 21 November 1975, vol. 15, file 12.

62 R. J. Sharpe, 'Bora Laskin and Civil Liberties.'

63 *Di Iorio* at 207.

64 Although there were three separate opinions by Dickson, Pigeon, and Beetz in addition to Laskin's dissent.

65 [1979] 1 S.C.R. 984.

66 Dickson conference memo, 1 June 1978, vol. 30, file 17.

67 Martland, Ritichie, and Beetz agreed with Pigeon. Pratte agreed with Dickson. Laskin did not sit on the case. Spence upheld the federal prosecution policy under s.91 (27).

68 *Hauser* at 1055.

69 *Russell v. The Queen* (1882), 7 A.C. 829 (J.C.P.C.). However, Laskin, who did not sit in *Hauser*, stated his disagreement with Pigeon's approach in *Schneider v. British Columbia*, [1982] 2 S.C.R. 112.

70 *Hauser* at 1028.

71 See Swinton, The Supreme Court and Canadian Federalism, at 305–10; *Reference re Residential Tenancies Act, 1979*, [1981] 1 S.C.R. 714; *Reference re Ownership of the Bed of the Strait of Georgia and Related Areas*, [1984] 1 S.C.R. 388.

72 *Hauser* at 1032, 1049.

73 *AG Alberta v. Putnam*, [1981] 2 S.C.R. 267.

74 Ibid. at 281.

75 [1983] 2 S.C.R. 206.

76 Dickson to file, 27 September 1982, vol. 62, file 7.

77 *Wetmore* at 305, 299, 306.

78 P.W. Hogg, *Constitutional Law* (Toronto: Carswell, looseleaf edition), at 19.6(b); A. Petter, 'Constitutional Law: Rearranging the Administration of Justice' (1985), 63 *Canadian Bar Review*, 162; J.D. Whyte, 'The Administration of Criminal Justice and the Provinces' (1984), 38 *Criminal Reports* (3d) 184.

79 *Citizens Insurance Company of Canada v. Parsons* (1881), 7 App. Cas. 96.

80 *R. v. Loblaws Groceterias Co. Ltd.* (1969), 69 W.W.R. 511; *Reference re Provincial Control of Agricultural Products*, [1971] 3 W.W.R. 204; *Gershman Produce Co. Ltd. v. Manitoba Marketing Board*, [1971] 4 W.W.R. 50; *Manitoba (Attorney General) v. Burns Foods Ltd.*, [1973] 5 W.W.R. 60, discussed in chapter 6.

81 *Canadian National* at 267.

82 *Canadian National* at 277.

83 *General Motors* at 660.

84 Dickson had concurred in *Labatt Breweries of Canada Ltd. v. A.G. Canada*, [1980] 1 S.C.R. 914, a controversial Estey decision that seemed to mark a significant set-back for federal trade and commerce power. However, in 1980, he refused to go along with *Dominion Stores v. The Queen*, [1980] 1 S.C.R. 844, another highly contentious Estey decision curtailing federal regulatory authority, siding instead with Laskin in dissent.

85 *Canadian National* at 259.

86 *MacDonald v. Vapor Canada Ltd.*, [1977] 2 S.C.R. 134.

87 *General Motors* at 662.

88 *R. v. Crown Zellerbach Canada Ltd.*, [1988] 1 S.C.R. 401.

89 [1989] 1 S.C.R. 641.

90 Dickson conference memo, 18 May 1988, vol. 108, file 3.

91 *General Motors* at 660, 669.

92 Ibid. at 674, 677, 680.

93 *OPSEU v. Ont. (A.G.)*, [1987] 2 S.C.R. 2.

94 In all constitutional cases, the rules of the Supreme Court require the statement of the precise constitutional questions the Court will be asked to answer. This is done so that all attorneys general can be notified of the issues and given the opportunity to appear and present arguments in the case. Constitutional questions are determined on a motion before the chief justice well in advance of the hearing of the appeal proper.

95 Stephen Goudge interview.

96 Dickson conference memo, 19 March 1986, vol. 95, file 6.

97 Ibid.

98 *MacKay v. The Queen*, [1965] S.C.R. 798.

99 *OPSEU* at 25.

100 *Commission du Salaire Minimum v. Bell Telephone Co.*, [1966] S.C.R. 767.

101 *OPSEU* at 18.

102 Ibid. at 22.

103 *Commission du Salaire Minimum v. Bell Telephone Co.* and *MacKay v. The Queen*.

104 Beetz to Dickson, 2 March 1987, vol. 96, file 6.

105 Dickson to Beetz, 2 March 1987, vol. 96, file 6. Dickson perhaps proved his point when he concurred with Beetz in the *Labour Trilogy*: *Bell Canada v. Quebec*, [1982] 1 S.C.R. 749; *Canadian National Railway v. Courtois*, [1988] 1 S.C.R. 868; *Alltrans Express Ltd. v. B.C.*, [1988] 1 S.C.R. 897. See also Dickson's decision in *Alberta Government Telephones v. Canada (RTTC)*, [1989] 2 S.C.R. 225, holding a provincial telecommunications undertaking subject to exclusive federal jurisidiction.

106 *OPSEU* at 57.
107 B. Dickson, 'Dalhousie Law School's Centenary Anniversary,' November 1984, vol. 139, file 7.
108 *General Motors* at 663.
109 Dickson, 'The Role and Function of Judges,' at 188.
110 Swinton, *The Supreme Court and Canadian Federalism*, especially at 315–17.
111 B. Dickson, 'Operations and Practice: A Comparison of the Role of the Supreme Court in Canada and the United States' (1980), 3 *Canada United States Law Journal*, 86.
112 Chapters 13, 20, and 22.
113 Barbara Dickson interview.

Chapter 13: Patriation of the Constitution

1 Transcript of interview of Brian Dickson for Royal Bank Award, 16 June 1992, vol. 193, file 14.
2 The Installation of Mrs. Agnes Benedickson as Chancellor of Queen's University, 24 October 1980, vol. 138, file 30.
3 *Reference re Legislative Authority of Parliament to Alter or Replace the Senate*, [1980] 1 S.C.R. 54 at 78.
4 *The Amendment of the Constitution of Canada* (Ottawa: Queen's Printer 1965), at 15.
5 (1981) 117 D.L.R. (3d) 1.
6 (1981) 118 D.L.R. (3d) 1.
7 (1981) 120 D.L.R. (3d) 385.
8 Patrick Monahan interview.
9 Dickson interview at 353.
10 'He'll feel like bowing out if package is rejected: PM,' *Globe and Mail*, 26 September 1981.
11 Transcript of interview with Greg Frenette, 15 February 1985, vol. 148, file 4.
12 Ian Bushnell, *The Captive Court: A Study of the Supreme Court of Canada* (Montreal: McGill-Queen's University Press 1992), at 430
13 Dickson, 'Federalism, Civil Law and the Canadian Judiciary: an Integrated Vision' (1994), 28 *Revue Juridique Thémis*, 447 at 467.
14 Dickson interview at 282.
15 *Reference re the Amendment of the Constitution of Canada*, [1981] 1 S.C.R. 753 at 784, 801, 807 [hereafter *Patriation Reference*].
16 W.R. Lederman, 'The Process of Constitutional Amendment in Canada' (1966–7), 12 *McGill Law Journal*, 371; and 'Constitutional Amendment and Canadian Unity' [1978] Law Society of Upper Canada, Special Lectures 17.
17 W.R. Lederman, 'The Supreme Court of Canada and Basic Constitutional Amend-

ment,' at 180, in K. Banting and R. Simeon, eds., *And No One Cheered: Federalism, Democracy and the Constitution Act* (Toronto: Methuen 1983).

18 'W.R. Lederman: Scholar and Friend' (1993), 19 *Queen's Law Journal*, 1.

19 *Patriation Reference* at 883, 880.

20 Ibid. at 905–6.

21 Ray Romanow, John Whyte, and Haward Lesson, *Canada ... Notwithstanding: The Making of the Constitution*, 1976–82 (Toronto: Carswell/Methuen 1984), at 179.

22 *Patriation Reference* at 905.

23 Lederman, 'The Supreme Court and Basic Constitutional Amendment,' at 182.

24 *Patriation Reference* at 871.

25 Ibid. at 858.

26 Ibid. at 869, 871, 872.

27 'Trudeau responds from Seoul,' *Globe and Mail*, 29 September 1981.

28 'Confusing BNA judgment spells national crisis ahead,' Montreal *Gazette*, 29 September 1981.

29 'We'll use "all legitimate means" to block BNA package: Lévesque' Montreal *Gazette*, 29 September 1981.

30 'Lyon calls ruling vindication,' Winnipeg *Free Press*, 29 September 1981.

31 'Lougheed feels provinces won,' Calgary *Herald*, 6 October 1981.

32 Dickson to Jamie Cameron, 6 October 1981, vol. 149, file 9.

33 Vancouver *Sun*, 29 September 1981.

34 *Re Attorney General of Quebec and Attorney General of Canada* (1982), 134 D.L.R. (3d) 719.

35 *Reference re Objection to a Resolution to Amend the Constitution*, [1982] 2 S.C.R. 793.

36 Ibid. at 813, quoting from Quebec's factum.

37 Dickson conference memo, 17 June 1982, vol. 57, file 19.

38 The speech is published in (1991), 41 *University of Toronto Law Journal*, 295, and also in Pierre Elliot Trudeau, *Against the Current: Selected Writings 1939–1996* (Toronto: McClelland and Stewart 1996).

39 (1991), 41 *University of Toronto Law Journal*, at 295.

40 See chapter 22.

41 (1991), 41 *University of Toronto Law Journal*, at 296.

42 Dickson to John Aird, 15 April 1985, vol. 158, file 1.

43 Dickson interview at 355–6.

44 Dickson, 'Federalism, Civil Law and the Canadian Judiciary,' 447 at 468.

45 Pierre Elliot Trudeau, *Federalism and the French Canadians* (Toronto: Macmillan 1968), at 198.

46 Dickson 'Federalism, Civil Law and the Canadian Judiciary,' at 469, n.27.

47 Lederman, 'The Supreme Court and Basic Constitutional Amendment'; Peter Russell, 'Bold Statecraft, Questionable Jurisprudence,' and Gil Rémillard, 'Legality, Legitimacy and the Supreme Court,' in Banting and Simeon ed., *And No One Cheered*.

48 Transcript of interview with Greg Frenette.

Chapter 14: Chief Justice

1 Dickson to Beryl Plumptre, 10 May 1984, vol. 134, file 1.
2 Dickson, 'Federalism, Civil Law and the Canadian Judiciary: an Integrated Vision' (1994), 28 *Revue Juridique Thémis*, 447.
3 Lamer interview.
4 This is borne out both by the quality of Dickson's judgments, reviewed in the preceding chapters and by the quantitative method of counting citations: Peter McCormick, *Supreme at Last: The Evolution of the Supreme Court of Canada* (Toronto: James Lorimer 2000), at 98– 101.
5 Ed Ratushny to Dickson, 17 May 1990, vol. 158, file 6: 'I recall speaking with Mr. Trudeau a few years ago and telling him that he had chosen well in selecting you as Chief Justice because of the way in which the Court was handling the Charter cases. He reminded me that he had not been terribly pleased by the position you took on the Constitutional Reference and had some reservations.'
6 Brian Dickson interview at 372–3.
7 See, for example, 'The New Face of the Law,' *Maclean's*, 30 April 1984.
8 Peers to Dickson, 2 May 1984, Dickson to Peers, 15 May 1984, vol. 134, file 1.
9 'The New Face of the Law.'
10 Lamer interview.
11 Remarks on the Occasion of the Installation of The Right Honourable Brian Dickson as Chief Justice of Canada, 26 April 1984, vol. 138, file 54.
12 James C. MacPherson, 'Working within the Dickson Court' (1991), 20 *Manitoba Law Journal*, 519 at 520–1.
13 Carl Baar, 'The Chief Justice as Court Administrator 1984 – 1990,' in D. Guth, ed., *Brian Dickson at the Supreme Court of Canada 1973–1990* (Winnipeg: Faculty of Law, University of Manitoba, 1998), at 304.
14 Ibid.
15 'Recent Developments in the Supreme Court of Canada and Some of the Problems Facing the Court,' Address to the Council of the Canadian Bar Association, Quebec City, 30 August 1983, vol. 138, file 41.
16 Barr, 'The Chief Justice as Court Administrator,' at 312.
17 Ibid. at 304.
18 Cory interview.
19 Constance Hunt of the Alberta Court of Appeal and Jacqueline Dorgan of the British Columbia Supreme Court.
20 Dickson conference memo, n.d., vol. 27, file 9.
21 *Cherneskey v. Armadale Publishers Ltd.*, [1979] 1 S.C.R. 1067 at 1096–7.
22 Dickson to Richard Malone, 19 January 1979, vol. 132, file 16.
23 *A.G. (Nova Scotia) v. MacIntyre,* [1982] 1 S.C.R. 175 at 183, 186–7.
24 'The Supreme Court of Canada as a Functioning Institution,' Annual Dinner of the Dalhousie Law School, 28 October 1976, vol. 138, file 19.

25 Laskin to the Court, 12 November 1975, vol. 156, file 15.

26 Elizabeth Gray to Laskin, 6 February 1975, and CBC press release regarding 'Tuesday Night,' n.d., vol. 156, file 16.

27 Dickson to the Court, 16 April 1975, vol. 156, file 16.

28 Peter Herndorf interview; Laskin to Herndorf, 7 July 1975, vol. 156, file 15; copy of letter from Herndorf to Fred Vaughan, 26 May 1975, vol. 156, file 15.

29 Amiel to Laskin, 6 April 1978, vol. 132, file 16.

30 'How top judges came to grips with Charter,' Toronto Star, 20 May 1990; 'The weighty process of deciding how justice should be done,' Toronto Star, 21 May 1990; 'Behind the scenes with judges who rule Canada's highest court,' Toronto Star, 22 May 1990.

31 Dickson to Amiel, 16 April 1978, vol. 132, file 16.

32 'Nine men in search of even-handed justice,' Maclean's, 12 February 1979.

33 Bora Laskin, 'Public Perceptions of the Supreme Court of Canada,' Address at the Annual Dinner of the Canadian Press, 20 April 1977, vol. 201, file 7.

34 Ibid.

35 Laskin to the Court, 2 February 1979, vol. 159, file 5.

36 Dickson to Laskin, 9 February 1979, vol. 159, file 5.

37 'Address to the Summer Convention of the Newfoundland Branch of the Canadian Bar Association,' St John's, 25 June 1980, vol. 138, file 26.

38 See chapter 13.

39 B. Dickson, 'The Path to Improving the Accessibility of the Law in Canada' (1985), 8 Provincial Judges' Journal, 2.

40 Memo to file, 18 September 1984, vol. 150, file 19.

41 Dickson to Nemetz, 13 September 1984, vol. 150, file 19.

42 Peter Calamai, 'The Media and the Court's Public Accountability,' in Guth, ed., Brian Dickson, at 289.

43 Robert Sharpe, 'The Tasks and Role of a Media Spokesperson for the Courts' (1991), 1 Media and Communications Law Review, 271.

44 Calamai, 'The Media and the Court's Public Accountability,' at 292; Dickson interview at 378, 533.

45 Dickson interview at 378.

46 D.G. McQueen to Dickson, 20 September 1985, vol. 156, file 13.

47 Wayne Mackay 'The human portrayal of Supreme Court Judges,' Halifax Chronicle-Herald, 9 July 1986.

48 The program won the Gordon Sinclair Prize for Excellence in Broadcasting: Dickson to Jim Reed, 9 December 1986, vol. 156 file 13.

49 Dickson to Lamer and MacPherson, 3 December 1986, vol. 156, file 13.

50 See vol. 148, files 4 to 8.

51 Dickson to Ian Urquhart, 23 March 1987, vol. 142, file 5.

52 Spicer to Dickson, 29 February 1988, vol. 136, file 6.

53 Calamai, 'The Media and the Court's Public Accountability,' at 292.
54 Russell to Dickson, 24 April 1990, vol. 158, file 7.
55 Dickson to the Court, 19 February 1987, vol. 132, file 4.
56 Wilson to Dickson, 29 October 1984, vol. 134, file 7.
57 Dickson to file, 6 November 1984, vol. 134, file 7.
58 Ottawa *Citizen*, 5 December 1985.
59 (1986), 36 *University of Toronto Law Journal*, 227.
60 'Justice Bertha Wilson: odd judge out in the Supreme Court,' Ottawa *Citizen*, 30 November 1985.
61 Wilson to the Court, 2 December 1985, vol. 134, file 7.
62 B. Dickson, Operations and Practice: A Comparison of the Role of the Supreme Court in Canada and the United States' (1980), 3 *Canada United States Law Journal*, 86.
63 Dickson to Registrar Hoffley, 16 February 1983, vol. 143, file 12.
64 Dickson to the Court, 3 March 1986, vol. 159, file 5.
65 Quoted in 'Remarks at the luncheon with the Judges of the British Columbia Court of Appeal, 8 May 1986, vol. 139, file 46.
66 Estey to the Court, 6 October 1986, vol. 132, file 2.
67 Estey to Dickson, 6 January 1985, vol. 142, file 13; Minutes of the C.B.A.–S.C.C. Liason Committee Meeting, 27 February 1986, vol. 142, file 13.
68 Estey to Dickson, 5 February 1986, vol. 142, file 13. See also Canadian Bar Association Special Committee Report, *The Supreme Court of Canada* (Ottawa: Canadian Bar Association 1987), at 53–5, accepting the need for some 'guidelines.'
69 B. Morgan, 'A View of Clerking at the Supreme Court of Canada' (1978) 3(2) *Hearsay*.
70 Estey to the Court, 9 October 1986, vol. 143, file 9, reporting on a meeting with the Advocates Society in Toronto; Howard Bebbington, Dept. of Justice, to Guy Goulard, 2 July 1986, ibid., referring to strong opposition in British Columbia.
71 B. Dickson, 'Recent Developments in the Supreme Court of Canada and Some of the Problems Facing the Court,' Address to the Council of the Canadian Bar Association, Quebec City, 30 August 1983, vol. 138, file 41.
72 Ian Bushnell, *The Captive Court: A Study of the Supreme Court of Canada* (Montreal: McGill-Queen's University Press 1992), at 441.
73 For a full account, see E. Anderson, *Judging Bertha Wilson: Law as Large as Life* (Toronto: University of Toronto Press/Osgoode Society for Canadian Legal History 2001), chapter 5.
74 Dickson interview at 428.
75 Lamer interview.
76 'PM, Crosbie disagree on Supreme Court appointee,' Ottawa *Citizen*, 10 January 1985.
77 Gérard La Forest, 'Some Impressions on Judging' (1986), 35 *University of New Brunswick Law Journal*, 145 at 156.

78 Supreme Court Act, R.S.C. 1985, c.S-26, ss.5, 6.

79 Quoted by Dickson, speech at dinner at 24 Sussex, 24 April 1990, vol. 158, file 7.

80 Chapters 20 and 22.

81 Dickson interview at 233–4.

82 Lamer interview.

83 B. Dickson, 'The Rule of Law: Judicial Independence and the Separation of Powers' (1985), 9 *Provincial Judges' Journal*, 4.

84 Minutes of meeting with minister of justice, 23 September 1986, vol. 142, file 18.

85 B. Dickson, 'Remarks to the Executive of the Canadian Bar Association on the Court's Tasks,' 1984, vol. 139, file 3. Dickson discussed confirmation hearings with Chief Justice Warren Burger, who was 'very vocal' in expressing his negative views: Dickson to MacPherson, 14 August 1986, vol. 147, file 2.

86 Dickson interview at 237.

87 B. Dickson, 'Ten Years of the Charter – Its Impact on the Law,' Department of Justice, Ottawa, 16 November 1992, vol. 140, file 39.

88 Yalden interview.

89 Dickson to MacPherson, 8 May 1987, vol. 142, file 16.

90 Dickson to Abbott, 15 January 1987, vol. 133, file 4.

91 *Maclean's*, 27 April 1987.

92 L'Heureux-Dubé interview.

93 'The New Face of the Law.'

94 Memorandum re Interview with Ontario Lawyer's Weekly,' 7 July 1984, vol. 148, file 6.

95 Wilson interview.

96 McLachlin interview.

97 Gonthier interview.

98 Antonio Lamer, 'Remarks at Retirement Ceremony of the Right Honourable Brian Dickson, P.C.,' 21 June 1990, vol. 140, file 21.

99 La Forest interview.

100 McLachlin interview.

101 McIntyre interview.

102 Lamer interview.

103 L'Heureux-Dubé interview.

104 Cory interview.

105 Robert Yalden interview.

106 Prime examples of this are *Daigle v. Tremblay*, discussed in chapter 18, and *Sparrow*, discussed in chapter 21.

107 Cory interview.

108 Wilson interview.

109 Cory interview.

110 Lamer interview; La Forest interview.

111 La Forest interview.
112 Lamer interview.
113 See vol. 147, file 18.
114 Dickson to Marshall, 3 June 1987, vol. 146, file 5.
115 Dickson interview at 511.
116 Judges Act, s.39(2).
117 William Kaplan, *Bad Judgment: The Case of Leo A. Landreville* (Toronto: University of Toronto Press 1996).
118 Dickson interview at 579.
119 Dickson to Chief Justice Constance Glube and Chief Justice Allan McEachern, 24 March 1988, vol. 153, file 1.
120 Nathan T. Nemetz, 'Defining the Canadian Judicial Council,' in Guth, ed., *Brian Dickson*, at 306.
121 McPherson to Ian Greene, 25 June 1986, vol. 151, file 2.
122 This proposal appears to have been initiated by Bora Laskin: Mark MacGuigan (minister of justice) to Laskin, 25 March 1983, vol. 156, file 2.
123 Glube to Dickson, 15 June 1990, vol. 158, file 6.
124 Dickson interview at 604–5.
125 *Beauregard v. Canada*, [1986] 2 S.C.R. 56 at 76.
126 Mark de Wert to Dickson, 7 November 1986. vol. 151, file 2.
127 Dickson interview at 623.
128 Southey to Dickson, 24 May 1990, vol. 158, file 6.
129 Dickson interview at 620.
130 Memo to file, 15 November 1984, vol. 150, file 21.
131 Vol. 56, file 2.
132 Dickson to Gerry Thomas, 20 March 1989, vol. 136, file 10.

Chapter 15: Building the Foundations

1 Brian Morgan interview.
2 B. Dickson, 'The Opening of the Cambridge Lectures,' Cambridge, England, 15 July 1985, vol. 139, file 25.
3 B. Dickson, 'Judging in the 1980s' (1982), 6 *Provincial Judges' Journal*, 18.
4 B. Dickson, 'On the Supreme Court of Canada,' Regina Bar Association, Regina, 15 October 1982, vol. 138, file 37; B. Dickson, 'The Public Responsibilities of Lawyers' (1983), 13 *Manitoba Law Journal*, 175 at 186.
5 B. Dickson, 'Judging in the 1980s.'
6 See chapter 19.
7 B. Dickson, 'The Public Responsibilities of Lawyers,' at 187.
8 B. Dickson, 'Remarks at the Call to the Bar Ceremony, Osgoode Hall Law School, Toronto, 18 April 1985, vol. 139, file 15.

9   B. Dickson, 'The Opening of the Cambridge Lectures.'

10 Ibid.

11 B. Dickson, 'The Supreme Court of Canada and the Canadian Charter of Rights and Freedoms,' Calgary, September 1983, vol. 138, file 46.

12 B. Dickson, 'The Development of a Distinctively Canadian Jurisprudence,' Faculty of Law, Dalhousie University, Halifax, 29 October 1983, vol. 138, file 48.

13 Ibid.; B. Dickson, 'Opening of the Cambridge Lectures,' 'Notes for a CBC Sunday Morning Interview,' October 1984, vol. 148, file 16.

14 'Address at the University of Western Ontario Law School,' 28 October 1976, vol. 138, file 18.

15 B. Dickson, 'Dalhousie Law School's Centenary Anniversary,' November 1984, vol. 139, file 7.

16 B. Dickson, 'Lawyers as Law-Makers – The Challenge of Change,' Convocation, Osgoode Hall Law School, Toronto, 21 June 1985, vol. 139, file 23.

17 [1984] 2 S.C.R. 145.

18 Combines Investigation Act, R.S.C. 1970, c.C-23, s.10.

19 Dickson conference memo, 23 November 1983, vol. 69, file 10.

20 Dickson conference memo, 19 December 1983, vol. 69, file 10.

21 Dickson to the Court, 14 December 1983, vol. 69, file 10.

22 Dickson interview at 389.

23 *Hunter*, at 148, 155.

24 Ibid. at 155

25 *Edwards v. Attorney-General for Canada*, [1930] A.C. 124 at 136.

26 *Hunter*, at 156.

27 Ibid.

28 B. Dickson, 'The Relationship between Judges and Law Schools,' University of Western Onatrio, 8 September 1982, vol. 138, file 35.

29 'Questions and answers Le Point,' n.d., vol. 156, file 13. Other correspondence makes it clear that these notes were prepared in late 1986 or early 1987.

30 *Hunter*, at 159-160.

31 Ibid. at 160.

32 Ibid. at 161, 162

33 Ibid. at 165, 167.

34 Ibid. at 169.

35 Dickson to the Court, 21 August 1987, vol. 142, file 4, referring to a speech by Donaldson at Cambridge lectures, 13 July 1987, 'The Judiciary, The Legislature, The Executive and Politics.'

36 B. Dickson, 'Has the Charter "Americanized" Canada's Judiciary?' (1992), 26 *University of British Columbia Law Review*, 195.

37 Dickson, 'The Supreme Court of Canada and the Canadian Charter of Rights and Freedoms.'

38 Dickson, 'The Opening of the Cambridge Lectures.'
39 Dickson to Burger, 26 September 1985, vol. 147, file 2.
40 *Reference re s. 94(2) of the Motor Vehicle Act (B.C.)*, [1985] 2 S.C.R. 486.
41 'Meese, in Bar group speech, criticizes High Court,' New York *Times*, 10 July 1985.
42 'The 20th century justice,' New York *Times*, 15 October 1985.
43 *Reference re s. 94(2)* at 508, 509.
44 Dickson interview at 660.
45 Rehnquist to Dickson, 10 September 1987, vol. 147, file 13. On John Marshall, see Jean Smith, *John Marshall: Definer of a Nation* (New York: H. Holt 1998).
46 B. Dickson, 'Canadian American Legal Exchange: The Supreme Court of Canada' (1988), 22 *Law Society of Upper Canada Gazette*, 53.
47 *R. v. Big M Drug Mart Ltd.*, [1985] 1 S.C.R. 295
48 Dickson conference memo, 7 March 1984, vol. 74, file 3.
49 *Robertson and Rosetanni v. The Queen*, [1963] S.C.R. 651.
50 *Big M* at 313, 314.
51 Mary Jane Sinclair to Dickson, 8 November 1984, vol. 74, file 8: Dickson to Sinclair, 19 November 1984, vol. 74, file 8.
52 Wilson to Dickson, 26 February 1985, vol. 74, file 3.
53 Dickson to Wilson, 1 March 1985, vol. 74, file 3.
54 *Big M* at 332.
55 La Forest to Dickson, 5 March 1985, vol. 74, file 3.
56 Dickson to La Forest, 10 April 1985, vol. 74, file 3.
57 *Big M* at 334.
58 Ibid. at 344.
59 Ibid. at 336–7.
60 Ibid. at 338.
61 Ibid. at 350–1.
62 Ibid. at 351.
63 Ibid. at 346–7.
64 B. Dickson, 'The Canadian Charter of Rights and Freedoms and Its Interpretation by the Courts,' Princeton Alumni Association, Princeton, N.J., 25 April 1985, vol. 139, file 16.
65 Stan Katz, e-mail message, 23 October 2002.
66 24 April 1985.
67 26 April 1985.
68 25 April 1985.
69 4 May 1985.
70 3 May 1985.
71 Toronto *Star*, 25 April 1985.
72 Winnipeg *Free Press*, 25 April 1985.
73 Toronto *Star*, 25 April 1985.

74 Winnipeg *Free Press*, 25 April 1985.

75 'Cruise missile opponents win another day in court,' Ottawa *Citizen*, 21 December 1983.

76 'Changes sought by MacGuigan,' Vancouver *Sun*, 23 January 1984.

77 'Aide memoire' from Estey, 6 March 1984, vol. 132, file 16.

78 *Rules of Professional Conduct*, Rule 21.

79 Estey to the Court, 12 October 1984, vol. 133, file 6.

80 B. Dickson, 'Counsel's Duty to the Court and to His Client,' Continuing Legal Education Society, Halifax, 17 November 1984, vol. 139, file 6.

81 *Operation Dismantle v. The Queen*, [1985] 1 S.C.R. 441.

82 Dickson conference memo, n.d., vol. 75, file 4.

83 David M. Walker, *The Oxford Companion to Law* (Oxford: Oxford University Press 1980).

84 [1985] 1 S.C.R. at 488.

85 Dickson to Wilson, 21 February 1985, vol. 75, file 5.

86 Dickson to Wilson, 1 April 1985, vol. 74, file 4.

87 Dickson to Wilson, 12 March 1985, vol. 75, file 5.

88 *Operation Dismantle* at 464.

89 Wilson to Dickson, 22 March 1985, vol. 75, file 4.

90 Dickson to Wilson, 1 April 1985, vol. 74, file 4.

91 Wilson also sparred with La Forest, who did not sit on the case but who referred Wilson to an article he had written on the Charter ('The Canadian Charter of Rights and Freedoms: An Overview' [1983], 61 *Canadian Bar Review*, 19 at 27–8) and urged her to offer a wide definition of 'law' that would include the common law, thereby anticipating the debate that would emerge in *Dolphin Delivery*, discussed in chapter 17: La Forest to Wilson, 15 March 1985, Wilson to La Forest, 22 March 1985, La Forest to Wilson, 26 March 1985, vol. 75, file 6.

92 *Operation Dismantle* at 447, 451, 454.

93 Ibid. at 455.

94 'Supreme Court says cabinet must abide by rights *Charter*,' Toronto *Star*, 10 May 1985.

95 'Court allows challenges to cabinet,' Montreal *Gazette*, 10 May 1985.

96 'A check on cabinet powers,' *Maclean's*, 20 May 1985.

97 *R. v. Oakes*, [1986] 1 S.C.R. 103.

98 R.S.C. 1970, c.N-1, s.8.

99 S.11(d).

100 (1983) 2 C.C.C. (3d) 339.

101 Dickson conference memo, 12 March 1985, vol. 83, file 5.

102 *Oakes* at 119.

103 Ibid. at 119–20.

104 Joel Bakan and Colleen Sheppard interviews.

105 *Oakes* at 135, 136.

106 Ibid. at 138, 139.

107 Mark Hume, 'Defence lawyers hail court killing of top drug law,' Vancouver *Sun*, 1 March 1986; Marina Strauss, 'Court strikes down law making accused prove innocence,' *Globe and Mail*, 1 March 1986.

Chapter 16: Continuity and Change

1 B. Hill, 'Court rule on bicyclist reserved,' Ottawa *Citizen*, 8 June 1978. This clipping is contained in Dickson's case files, vol. 26, file 30.

2 *Moore v. The Queen*, [1979] 1 S.C.R. 195 at 204.

3 Dickson conference memo, n.d., vol. 26, file 21.

4 *Moore v. The Queen* at 206, 213.

5 A. Grant, 'Moore v. The Queen: A Substantive, Procedural and Administrative Nightmare' (1979), 17 *Osgoode Hall Law Journal*, 459 at 463. See also E. Ratushny, 'Police powers: A case that asks who's in charge,' *Globe and Mail*, 3 October 1978.

6 E. Ewaschuk, 'Annotation' (1979), 5 C.R. (3d) 307 at 312.

7 *Eccles v. Bourque*, [1975] 2 S.C.R. 739. One commentator criticized Dickson's decision on the basis that it could lead to an 'abuse of power.': J. Manley, 'Case Comment' (1975), 7 *Ottawa Law Review*, 649 at 656. In *R. v. Landry*, [1986] 1 S.C.R. 145, Dickson upheld the common law power to conduct warrantless home entries to make arrests, despite a dissent that the decision violated the warrant requirement in *Hunter v. Southam*, [1984] 2 S.C.R. 145. After Dickson's retirement, the Supreme Court held in *R. v. Feeney*, [1997] 2 S.C.R. 13 that the common law rule did not give enough weight to the Charter. The decision was controversial and Parliament responded by authorizing warrantless entries into homes in exigent circumstances. Criminal Code, R.S.C. 1985, c.C-46, s.529.3, as am. S.C. c.39, s.2.

8 *Lyons v. The Queen* [1984] 2 S.C.R. 633 at 657.

9 *Wiretap Reference*, [1984] 2 S.C.R. 697 at 727.

10 Ibid. at 706–7.

11 Dickson noted voluminous criticisms of the decision in *Dalia v. United States* 441 U.S. 238 (1979) in the American law reviews. Ibid. at 712–14.

12 Ibid at 719, 722, 727.

13 *R. v. Campbell*, [1999] 1 S.C.R. 565. See now Criminal Code, s.25.1, as amended S.C. 2001, c.32, s.2.

14 McIntyre interview.

15 *Dedman v. The Queen*, [1985] 2 S.C.R. 2 at 10, 15, 17 19.

16 B. Dickson, 'Criminal Law Lectures,' University of Western Ontario, 1981, vol. 138, file 35.

17 'Split Supreme Court upholds police powers to spot check,' *Globe and Mail*, 1 August 1985.

18 'In the absence of law,' *Globe and Mail*, 2 August 1985.
19 'A court divided on police power,' Ottawa *Citizen*, 2 August 1985.
20 Dickson to Beetz and Chouinard, 6 August 1985, vol. 79, file 1.
21 *R. v. Hufsky*, [1988] 1 S.C.R. 621.
22 *R. v. Ladouceur*, [1990] 1 S.C.R. 1257 at 1264.
23 Dickson conference memo, 7 November 1989, vol. 122, file 1.
24 *Hogan v. The Queen*, [1975] 2 S.C.R. 574.
25 Magnet to Dickson, n.d., vol. 8, file 20.
26 *Rothman v. The Queen*, [1981] 1 S.C.R. 640.
27 *R. v. Marcoux and Solomon*, [1976] 1 S.C.R. 763, as discussed in chapter 7.
28 Dickson to Estey, 26 November 1980, vol. 46, file 2.
29 Lamer to Dickson, 26 November 1980, vol. 46, file 2.
30 Lamer interview.
31 *R. v. Therens*, [1985] 1 S.C.R. 613.
32 Dickson to Le Dain, 20 March 1985, vol. 76, file 5.
33 *R. v. Collins*, [1987] 1 S.C.R. 265.
34 *Marcoux and Solomon v. The Queen*, [1976] 1 S.C.R. 763, discussed in chapter 7.
35 M. MacCrimmon, 'Developments in the Law of Evidence: The 1985–86 Term' (1987), 9 *Supreme Court Law Review*, 363; D. Paciocco, 'The Development of *Miranda*-like Doctrines under the Charter' (1987), 19 *Ottawa Law Review*, 49; K. Jull, '*Clarkson v. R.*: Do We Need a Legal Emergency Department?' (1987), 32 *McGill Law Journal*, 359. R. Harvie and H. Foster, 'Ties That Bind? The Supreme Court of Canada, American Jurisprudence and the Revision of Canadian Criminal Law under the Charter' (1990), 28 *Osgoode Hall Law Journal*, 729.
36 *R. v. Simmons*, [1988] 2 S.C.R. 495 at 534–5. See also *R. v. Jacoy*, [1988] 2 S.C.R. 548 at 559–60.
37 *R. v. Greffe*, [1990] 1 S.C.R. 755 at 799.
38 Ibid at 770.
39 D. Vienneau, '"Obviously guilty" drug dealer free, Court ignores plea to forget technicality,' Toronto *Star*, 14 April 1990.
40 Dickson, 'Criminal Law Lectures.'
41 *Swietlinski v. The Queen*, [1980] 2 S.C.R. 956; *The Queen v. Vasil*, [1981] 1 S.C.R. 469.
42 *The Queen v. Farrant*, [1983] 1 S.C.R. 124 at 129–30.
43 Dickson conference memo, 11 December 1986, vol. 98, file 14.
44 *R. v. Vaillancourt*, [1987] 2 S.C.R. 636; *R. v. Martineau*, [1990] 2 S.C.R. 633.
45 Dickson conference memo, 11 December 1986, vol. 98, file 14.
46 *Linney v. The Queen*, [1978] 1 S.C.R. 646 at 650.
47 *The Queen v. Gardiner*, [1982] 2 S.C.R. 368 at 415–16.
48 L. Arbour, 'Developments in Criminal Law and Procedure' (1983), 5 *Supreme Court Law Review*, 166 at 169–70.
49 *R. v. Oakes*, [1986] 1 S.C.R. 103, as discussed in chapter 15.

50 *R. v. Holmes*, [1988] 1 S.C.R. 914 at 948.

51 Ibid. at 934.

52 *R v. Schwartz*, [1988] 2 S.C.R. 443 at 478, 463 (dissenting).

53 *R. v. Whyte*, [1988] 2 S.C.R. 3 at 18.

54 Ibid. at 26.

55 *R v. Schwartz*, at 443. In that case, Dickson held that there was no section 1 defence; however, he did not take as demanding an approach as Lamer, who decided that there was not even a sufficient objective to justify the violation. Lamer interview.

56 Guy Pratte interview.

57 D. Stuart, *Charter Justice in Canadian Criminal Law* (Toronto: Carswell 1991), at 252–9.

58 *R. v. Keegstra*, [1990] 3 S.C.R. 697 at 793.

59 Ibid. at 793.

60 *R. v. Chaulk*, [1990] 3 S.C.R. 1303.

Chapter 17: Cracks in the Foundations

1 *R. v. Edwards Books and Art Ltd.*, [1986] 2 S.C.R. 713.

2 Toronto *Star*, 18 December 1986.

3 Ibid.

4 *R. v. Videoflicks et al.* (1984), 48 O.R. (2d) 395.

5 Retail Business Holidays Act, R.S.O. 1980, c.453.

6 *Edwards Books* at 743, 744.

7 *Report on Sunday Observance Legislation* (Toronto: Department of Justice 1970).

8 Dickson conference memo, 7 March 1986, vol. 88, file 11.

9 *Edwards Books* at 758, 759.

10 Ibid. at 770.

11 Colleen Sheppard interview.

12 See for example, A. Petter 'The Politics of the Charter' (1986), 8 *Supreme Court Law Review*, 473; P. Monahan and A. Petter 'Developments in Constitutional Law: The 1985–86 Term' (1987), 9 *Supreme Court Law Review*, 69.

13 *Edwards Books* at 772, 779.

14 Ibid. at 779, 780, 781, 782.

15 Dickson memo to file, 8 September 1986, vol. 88, file 11.

16 Dickson to La Forest, 23 October 1986, vol. 88, file 17.

17 Edwards Books at 794, 795.

18 E. Anderson, *Judging Bertha Wilson: Law as Large as Life* (Toronto: University of Toronto Press 2001), at 178.

19 *Edwards Books* at 808.

20 R. Dworkin, *Law's Empire* (Cambridge, Mass.: Harvard University Press 1986) at 179.

21 *Edwards Books* at 810.

22 Beetz to Dickson, 2 December 1986, vol. 88, file 13.
23 Toronto *Star*, 18 December 1987.
24 See also *Slaight Communications Inc. v. Davidson*, [1989] 1 S.C.R. 1038.
25 *Reference re Public Service Employee Relations Act*, [1987] 1 S.C.R. 313.
26 *PSAC v. Canada*, [1987] 1 S.C.R. 424.
27 *RWDSU v. Saskatchewan*, [1987] 1 S.C.R. 460.
28 Dickson conference memo, vol. 91, file 7.
29 Bakan, *Just Words: Constitutional Rights and Social Wrongs* (Toronto: University of Toronto Press 1997).
30 Bakan to Dickson, 24 June 1985 vol. 91, file 7.
31 Dickson conference memo, 28 June 1985, vol. 91, file 11.
32 vol. 92, file 5.
33 Dickson to the Court, 25 November 1985, vol. 91, file 12.
34 Dickson to Chouinard, 2 July 1986, vol. 91, file 12.
35 Wilson to Dickson, 29 July 1986, vol. 91, file 12.
36 *Public Service Employee Relations Act* at 365, 334, 364, 365, 366.
37 Ibid. at 364, 365, 366.
38 Ibid. at 334, 368.
39 Ibid. at 349.
40 Ibid. at 362–3.
41 Ibid. at 371.
42 Ibid. at 375.
43 *PSAC* at 442.
44 McIntyre interview.
45 *Public Service Employees Relations Act* at 393, 394, 397.
46 Ibid. at 414, 415.
47 Ibid. at 391.
48 *PSAC* at 457.
49 *Professional Institute of the Public Service of Canada v. Northwest Territories (Commissioner)*, [1990] 2 S.C.R. 367 at 374.
50 B. Dickson, 'The Importance of Universities,' Convocation Address, University of British Columbia, 30 May 1986, vol. 139, file 48.
51 Dickson interview at 602.
52 'Universities "desperate" for money judge says,' Toronto *Star*, 31 May 1986.
53 'Chief Justice is right about education,' Toronto *Star*, 3 June 1986.
54 'Wilson rejects plea to aid universities,' Toronto *Star*, 3 June 1986.
55 'A judge speaks out,' *Globe and Mail*, 3 June 1986.
56 'Report and Record of the Committee of Investigation into the Conduct of the Hon. Mr Justice Berger and Resolution of the Canadian Judicial Council' (1983), 28 *McGill Law Journal*, 378 at 391; T. Berger, *One Man's Justice: A Life in the Law* (Seattle: University of Washington Press 2002), at 146–64.

57 Dickson interview at 536–7.
58 *Dolphin Delivery Ltd. v. Retail, Wholesale & Department Store Union, Local 580*, [1984] 3 W.W.R. 481.
59 Peter Gall to the authors, 2 April 2003. Gall was counsel for the employer.
60 Dickson conference memo, 11 December 1984, vol. 89, file 11.
61 *Retail, Wholesale & Department Store Union, Local 580 v. Dolphin Delivery Ltd.*, [1986] 2 S.C.R. 573 at 583, 591.
62 Vol. 89, file 12 contains copies of McIntyre's drafts. There is also a memo from Stephen Toope to Dickson, 31 October 1986, vol. 89, file 11, summarizing the various drafts.
63 McIntyre to the Court, 18 April 1986, vol. 90, file 1.
64 Dickson to McIntyre, 4 June 1986, vol. 89, file 12.
65 Wilson to McIntyre, 29 April 1986, vol. 89, file 12.
66 La Forest to McIntyre, 2 May 1986, vol. 89, file 12.
67 14 July 1986, vol. 89, file 12 at 23–4
68 15 September 1986 vol. 89, file 14.
69 Vol. 89, file 14.
70 Toope to Dickson, 8 December 1986, vol. 89, file 14.
71 *Dolphin Delivery* at 603.
72 D.M. Beatty, 'Constitutional Conceits: The Coercive Authority of Courts' (1987), 37 *University of Toronto Law Journal*, 183.
73 A.C. Hutchinson and A.J. Petter, 'Private Wrongs/Public Wrongs: The Liberal Lie of the Charter' (1988), 38 *University of Toronto Law Journal*, 278.
74 Dickson interview at 600.
75 B. Dickson, 'The Path to Improving the Accessibility of the Law in Canada' (1985), 8 *Provincial Judges' Journal*, 2.
76 See, for example, Goulard to Dickson, 28 May 1986, vol. 132, file 2, summarizing the literature from the United States on ways to expedite appeals.
77 Dickson to the Court, 15 July 1986, vol. 132, file 15.
78 *Kamloops v. Nielsen*, [1984] 2 S.C.R. 2.
79 Wilson to Dickson, 28 February 1985, vol. 134, file 7.
80 Dickson to the Court, 28 February 1985, vol. 134, file 7.
81 B. Dickson, 'The Rule of Law: Judicial Independence and the Separation of Powers' (1985), 9 *Provincial Judges' Journal*, 4.
82 J. Snell and F. Vaughan, *The Supreme Court of Canada: History of the Institution* (Toronto: Univeristy of Toronto Press 1985), at 158, 230–1.
83 Dickson handwritten memo, n.d., vol. 142, file 15.
84 Dickson interview at 437–41.
85 Canadian Bar Association Special Committee Report, *The Supreme Court of Canada* (Ottawa: Canadian Bar Association 1987), at 41 and Appendix 1: 5.
86 Wilson to Dickson, 12 May 1986, vol. 132, file 2.
87 *R. v. Rahey*, [1987] 1 S.C.R. 588.

88 *R. v. Smith*, [1987] 1 S.C.R. 1045.
89 Lamer to Goulard, 27 February 1987, vol. 133, file 8.
90 Lamer, handwritten note, no date, vol. 133, file 8.
91 Lamer to Dickson, 27 February 1987, vol. 133, file 8.
92 Estey to Dickson, 3 October 1986, vol. 132, file 2.
93 La Forest interview.
94 Peter McCormick, *Supreme at Last: The Evolution of the Supreme Court of Canada* (Toronto: James Lorimer 2000) at 114.
95 Dickson to John McAlpine, 21 January 1985, vol. 132, file 16.

Chapter 18: Feeling the Strain

1 Jeffrey Simpson, 'Rule of the Courts,' *Globe and Mail*, 7 May 1986; Robert Fulford, 'Charter of Wrongs' (1986), 101 (12) *Saturday Night*.
2 See, for example, A. Petter, 'The Politics of the Charter' (1986), 8 *Supreme Court Law Review*, 473; P.J. Monahan and A. Petter, 'Developments in Constitutional Law: The 1985–86 Term' (1987), 9 *Supreme Court Law Review*, 69.
3 F.L. Morton and R. Knopff have been especially prominent: see F.L. Morton and L.A. Pal, 'The Impact of the Charter of Rights and Freedoms on Public Adminstration' (1985) 28 *Canadian Public Administration*, 221; F.L. Morton, 'The Political Impact of the Canadian Charter of Rights and Freedoms' (1987), 20 *Canadian Journal of Political Science* 31; Rainer Knopff and F.L. Morton, *Charter Politics* (Scarborough: Nelson Canada 1992).
4 'How top judges came to grips with Charter,' Toronto *Star*, 20 May 1990.
5 B. Dickson, 'Recent Developments in the Supreme Court of Canada and Some of the Problems Facing the Court,' Address to the Council of the Canadian Bar Association, Quebec City, 30 August 1983, vol. 138, file 41.
6 B. Dickson, 'The Public Responsibilities of Lawyers' at 187.
7 B. Dickson, 'Recent Developments' (1983), 13 *Manitoba Law Journal*, 175.
8 B. Dickson, 'The Public Responsibilities of Lawyers,' at 187, 186.
9 B. Dickson, 'Lawyers and Law-Makers – The Challenge of Change,' Convocation, Osgoode Hall Law School, Toronto, 21 June 1985, vol. 139, file 23.
10 B. Dickson, 'The Rule of Law: Judicial Independence and the Separation of Powers' (1985), 9 *Provincial Judges' Journal*, 4.
11 B. Dickson, 'Rights and Responsibilities,' Ashbury College, Ottawa, 10 June 1989, vol. 140, file 6.
12 B. Dickson, 'Questions and Answers Le Point,' n.d., vol. 156, file 13.
13 B. Dickson, 'Remarks at Dinner in Honour of Governor General Jeanne Sauvé,' 19 December 1984, vol. 139, file 9.
14 B. Dickson, 'Address to the Montreal and Quebec Law Associations,' 29 November 1984, vol. 139, file 8.

15 B. Dickson, 'Remarks at Luncheon, Lawyer's Inn, Vancouver, 17 June 1985, vol. 139, file 22.
16 Dickson, 'The Rule of Law.'
17 *Beauregard v. Canada*, [1986] 2 S.C.R. 56 at 70.
18 'The weighty process of deciding how justice should be done.' Toronto *Star*, 21 May 1990.
19 Dickson, 'Questions and Answers Le Point.'
20 Dickson, 'Remarks at Luncheon, Lawyer's Inn.'
21 See, for example, *Reference re s. 94(2) of the Motor Vehicle Act (B.C.)*, [1985] 2 S.C.R. 486 at 497, per Lamer J.
22 B. Dickson, 'Remarks at the Luncheon with the Judges of the British Columbia Court of Appeal,' 8 May 1986, vol. 139, file 46.
23 B. Dickson, 'Supreme Court of Canada as a General Court of Appeal,' County of York Law Association, 30 May 1985, vol. 139, file 19.
24 *Bliss v. The Attorney General of Canada*, [1979] 1 S.C.R. 183, discussed in greater detail in Chapter 18.
25 Dickson interview at 476. For a detailed critique, see Marc Gold, 'Equality before the Law in the Supreme Court of Canada: A Case Study' (1980), 18 *Osgoode Hall Law Journal*, 336.
26 Dickson, 'Remarks at Dinner in Honour of Governor General Jeanne Sauvé.'
27 B. Dickson, 'Canada's Charter and the Supreme Court of Canada,' 1985. vol. 139, file 12.
28 B. Dickson, 'The Canadian Charter of Rights and Freedoms and Its Interpretation by the Courts,' Princeton Alumni Association, Princeton, N.J., 25 April 1985, vol. 139, file 16.
29 B. Dickson, 'Remarks at Dinner in Honour of Mr. Geoffrey Palmer, Deputy Prime Minister and Minister of Justice, Government of New Zealand,' 16 September 1985, vol. 139, file 32.
30 *R. v. Holmes*, [1988] 1 S.C.R. 914 at 931.
31 Ibid. at 932.
32 B. Dickson, 'Judging in the 1980's' (1982), 6 *Provincial Judges' Journal*, 1.
33 B. Dickson, 'Address to Quebec Provincial Court Judges, 3 November 1984, vol. 139, file 5. For a full account of the dialogue metaphor, see Kent Roach, *The Supreme Court on Trial: Judicial Activism or Democratic Dialogue* (Toronto: Irwin Law 2001).
34 Rule 60.
35 Laskin asked Justice Byron White of the United States Supreme Court for information on the American practice: see White to Laskin, 16 March 1976, vol. 132, file 17.
36 [1974] S.C.R. 1349.
37 [1976] 1 S.C.R. 616.
38 *Nova Scotia Board of Censors v. McNeil*, [1976] 2 S.C.R. 265.
39 *Miller and Cockriell v. The Queen*, [1977] 2 S.C.R. 680.

40 Chambers Decision, n.d., vol. 17, file 13.
41 B. Dickson, 'The Supreme Court of Canada as a Functioning Institution,' Annual Dinner of the Dalhousie Law School, 28 October 1976, vol. 138, file 19.
42 B. Dickson, 'Operations and Practice: A Comparison of the Role of the Supreme Court in Canada and the United States' (1980) 3 Can. U.S. L.J. 86.
43 The following discussion draws upon J. Welch, 'No Room at the Top: Interest Group Intervenors and Charter Litigation in the Supreme Court of Canada' (1985) 43 *University of Toronto Faculty of Law Review*, 204. The Court's policy on intervention has attracted considerable criticism from Charter sceptics; see especially Ian Brodie, *Friends of the Court: The Privileging of Interest Group Litigants in Canada* (Albany: State University of New York Press 2002); F.L. Morton and Rainer Knopff, *The Charter Revolution and the Court Party* (Peterborough, Ont.: Broadview Press 2000).
44 Rule 18.
45 Rule 32.
46 *Ogg-Moss v. R.*, [1984] 2 S.C.R. 171.
47 Ibid. at 173.
48 [1983] S.C.B. 1068.
49 Beetz to the Court, 10 May 1983, vol. 144, file 8, regarding his decision to refuse the CCLA leave to intervene in *R. v. Marlene Moore*, [1983] S.C.B. 439.
50 Estey to the Court, 30 January 1985, vol. 144, file 11.
51 [1984] S.C.B. 79.
52 Wilson to the Court, 21 November 1985, vol. 132, file 1.
53 B. Wilson, 'Decision-Making in the Supreme Court' (1986) 36 *University of Toronto Law Journal*, 227 at 243.
54 [1983] S.C.B. 756, 778.
55 McIntyre to the Court, 7 March 1984, vol. 133, file 16.
56 Wilson to McIntyre 8 March 1984, vol. 133, file 16.
57 Dickson to McIntyre, 14 March 1984, vol. 133, file 16.
58 [1984] S.C.R. 254
59 [1985] S.C.R. 8; Estey to the Court, 17 January 1985, vol. 144, file 11.
60 A. Borovoy, 'Submission to Supreme Court of Canada re Interventions in Public Interest Litigation,' 17 July 1984, vol. 144, file 10.
61 Swinton to Dickson, 14 June 1985, vol. 144, file 10.
62 Estey to Dickson, 3 July 1985, vol. 144, file 10.
63 P. Bryden, 'Public Interest Intervention in the Courts,' May 1986, vol. 144, file 10.
64 n.d., vol. 144, file 9.
65 See chapter 17.
66 Carr to Justice Minister Ray Hnatyshyn, 26 May 1987, vol. 144, file 9.
67 MacPherson to Dickson, 7 October 1985, vol. 144, file 10.
68 K. Swan, 'Intervention and Amicus Curiae Status in Charter Litigation,' in R.J. Sharpe, ed., *Charter Litigation* (Toronto: Butterworths 1987) 27.
69 Dickson to the Court, 4 March 1986, vol. 144, file 10.

70 Dickson to the Court, 15 April 1986, vol. 144, file 10, attaching Welch, 'No Room at the Top.'

71 Report of the Canadian Bar Association – Supreme Court of Canada Liaison Committee, 22 October 1986, vol. 142, file 12.

72 Borovoy to Justice Minister Ray Hnatyshyn, 23 December 1986, vol. 142, file 12.

73 Estey to the Court, 6 November 1986, vol. 144, file 9.

74 Wilson to Estey, 6 November 1986, vol. 144, file 9.

75 Rule 18, amended 21 May 1987.

76 Canadian Bar Association Special Committee Report, *The Supreme Court of Canada* (Ottawa: Canadian Bar Association 1987), at 41 and Appendix 1: 8.

77 *Thorson v. Canada (Attorney General)*, [1975] 1 S.C.R. 138 at 145.

78 *Nova Scotia Board of Censors v. McNeil.*

79 'Strode up to judge, Borowski told to leave,' *Globe and Mail*, 29 May 1981.

80 28 May 1981, vol. 50, file 18.

81 1 June 1981, vol. 50, file 18.

82 Dickson to Laskin, 18 November 1981, vol. 50, file 18.

83 *Minister of Justice of Canada v. Borowski*, [1981] 2 S.C.R. 275.

84 *Borowski v. Canada (Attorney General)* (1983), 4 D.L.R. (4th) 112 (Sask. Q.B.); (1987) 39 D.L.R. (4th) 731 (Sask. C.A.).

85 See chapter 1.

86 Shaffer to Dickson, 29 September 1988, vol 106, file 13.

87 Dickson conference memo, 4 October 1988, vol. 106, file 13.

88 *Borowski v. Canada (Attorney General)*, [1989] 1 S.C.R. 342 at 346.

89 *Tremblay v. Daigle*, [1989] 2 S.C.R. 530 at 537.

90 'Court lifts injunction after Daigle abortion,' *Globe and Mail*, 9 August 1989.

91 McLachlin interview.

92 'Judgment of the Court,' 8 August 1989, vol. 110, file 2.

93 'Court lifts injunction after Daigle abortion.'

94 'Quashing the Injunction,' *Globe and Mail*, 10 August 1989.

95 Dickson to the Court, 10 October 1989, vol. 110, file 2.

96 Dickson to the Court, 14 August 1989, vol. 110, file 2.

97 There is no copy of the draft in Dickson's files, but it is clear from the memoranda that he did write along these lines.

98 La Forest to the Court, 13 October 1989, vol. 110, file 2.

99 Dickson to the Court, 8 November 1989, vol. 110, file 2.

100 *Tremblay v. Daigle* at 571, 552, 550, 572.

Chapter 19: Equality Rights

1 Wilson interview.

2 See chapter 8.

3 See chapter 11.

4 See chapter 1.

5 *Bliss v. Attorney General of Canada*, [1979] 1 S.C.R. 183.

6 *R. v. Drybones*, [1970] S.C.R. 282.

7 *Bliss* at 190, 192.

8 *Reference as to the Meaning of the Word 'Persons' in Section 24 of the British North America Act, 1867*, [1928] S.C.R. 276, reversed by *Edwards v. A.G. Canada*, [1930] A.C. 124 (J.C.P.C.).

9 [1989] 1 S.C.R. 1219.

10 [1989] 1 S.C.R. 1252.

11 S.M. 1974, c. 65.

12 (1985), 6 C.H.R.R. D/2560 and D/2840.

13 (1986), 42 Man. R. (2d) 27 (C.A.) affirming (1985), 38 Man. R. (2d) 192 (Q.B.).

14 'Can't discriminate against pregnant staff, court rules,' Toronto *Star*, 5 May 1989.

15 Dickson conference memo, 16 June 1988, vol. 109, file 3.

16 *Brooks* at 1243, 1237.

17 (1985), 6 C.H.R.R. D/2735, affd. (1985), 24 D.L.R. (4th) 31 (Man. Q.B.).

18 (1986), 33 D.L.R. (4th) 32 (Man. C.A.).

19 *Jensen* at 1290, 1291.

20 'Pregnant women win legal equality,' Toronto *Star*, 5 May 1989.

21 'Can't discriminate against pregnant staff, court rules.'

22 'Pregnant employees must have all rights Supreme Court rules,' Montreal *Gazette*, 5 May 1989.

23 Wilson interview.

24 Lamer interview.

25 [1987] 1 S.C.R. 1114.

26 Ibid. at 1120.

27 (1985), 20 D.L.R. (4th) 668.

28 Dickson conference memo, 7 November 1986, vol. 94, file 7.

29 Wilson to Dickson, 10 November 1986, vol. 94, file 7.

30 Toope to Dickson, 3 February 1987, vol. 94, file 15.

31 *Action Travail* at 1135.

32 Ibid. at 1139.

33 Ibid. at 1143, 1144.

34 *Bhinder v. Canadian National Railway Co.*, [1985] 2 S.C.R. 561.

35 At para. 14.

36 *Central Alberta Dairy Pool v. Alberta (Human Rights Commission)*, [1990] 2 S.C.R. 489.

37 *R. v. Sheldon S.*, [1990] 2 S.C.R. 254; *R. v. Jeffery P,* [1990] 2 S.C.R. 300; *R v. Angeline T.*, [1990] 2 S.C.R. 304; *R . v. James B.*, [1990] 2 S.C.R. 307; *R. v. Gregory S.*, [1990] 2 S.C.R. 294.

38 Dickson conference memo, 28 March 1989, vol. 122, file 11.

39 La Forest to Dickson, 13 October 1989, vol. 122, file 11.

40 See chapter 12.

41 K. Swinton, 'Competing Visions of Constitutionalism: Of Federalism and Rights, in K. Swinton and C. Rogerson, eds., *Competing Constitutional Values: The Meech Lake Accord* (Toronto: Carswell 1988).

42 *Sheldon S.* at 288, 289.

43 Dickson conference memo, 17 September 1984, vol. 69, file 14.

44 *R. v. Ogg Moss*, [1984] 2 S.C.R. 173 at 183. Fifteen years later, the same section was unsuccessfully challenged as a denial of equality rights: *Canadian Foundation for Children, Youth and the Law v. Canada (Attorney General)* (2002), 57 O.R. (3d) 511 (C.A.) leave to appeal granted [2002] S.C.C.A. No. 113.

45 *Ogg-Moss* at 187.

46 Dickson conference memo, vol. 119, file 2.

47 E. Anderson, *Judging Bertha Wilson* (Toronto: University of Toronto Press/Osgoode Society for Canadian Legal History 2001), at 219.

48 *R. v. Lavallee*, [1990] 1 S.C.R. 852 at 874.

49 *R. v. Hill*, [1986] 1 S.C.R. 313.

50 Wilson interview.

51 See chapter 18.

52 *Gay Alliance Towards Equality v. The Vancouver Sun*, [1979] 2 S.C.R. 435.

53 Dickson draft judgment, vol. 33, file 3.

54 Laskin to Dickson, 4 May 1979, vol. 33, file 4.

55 Thompson to Dickson, n.d., vol. 33, file 4.

56 Martland wrote the majority opinion holding that the Human Rights Commission had gone too far in interfering with freedom of the press and that it could not compel the newspaper to accept the advertisement. Laskin wrote a separate dissent.

57 Wilson, L'Heureux-Dubé, and Gonthier agreed with Dickson while La Forest and Sopinka agreed with McLachlin.

58 [1990] 3 S.C.R. 697.

59 S.319. See also s.318, the related provisions prohibiting the wilful promotion of genocide.

60 The American courts have tended to strike down restrictions on racist speech: see *Collin* v. *Smith*, 578 F.2d 1197 (1978); *R.A.V.* v. *City of St. Paul*, 112 S.Ct. 2538 (1992).

61 Wilson to Dickson, 28 November 1990, vol. 128, file 1.

62 *Keegstra* at 767, 766, 769.

63 Ibid. at 783.

64 Ibid. at 756, 764.

65 L. Smith, 'The Equality Rights' (1991), 20 *Manitoba Law Journal*, 377 at 391.

66 McLachlin interview.

67 Toope memo to the authors, 27 March 2003.

68 B. Dickson, 'Freedoms and Responsibilities in the Universities' Response to a Multicultural Society,' The National Symposium on Institutional Strategies For Race

and Ethnic Relations at Canadian Universities, Queen's University, Kingston, Ontario, 3 February 1992, vol. 140, file 29.

69 'Jurist backs worthy legal cause,' Toronto *Star*, 20 June 1998.
70 'Disabilities Act must have teeth,' Toronto *Star*, 7 October 1998.

Chapter 20: Language Rights and National Unity

1 'Manitoba's newest judge learned trade as Boy Scout,' Winnipeg *Tribune*, 5 November 1963.
2 Call to the Bar Ceremony, Winnipeg, 2 June 1967, vol. 138, file 5.
3 Dickson interview at 265.
4 Brian Morgan interview.
5 Rollie Thompson interview.
6 B. Dickson, 'Address to the Federal Lawyers Club,' 1974, vol. 138, file 16.
7 *Mahé v. Alberta*, [1990] 1 S.C.R. 342 at 362.
8 [1986] 1 S.C.R. 549.
9 S. 19 (2).
10 In *MacDonald v. City of Montreal*, [1986] 1 S.C.R. 460, a judgment handed down the same day, the Court held that section 133 of the Constitution Act, 1867 does not require the courts of Quebec to issue bilingual documents.
11 *Société des Acadiens* at 578, 564.
12 B. Dickson, 'Recent Developments in the Supreme Court of Canada and Some of the Problems Facing the Court,' Address to the Council of the Canadian Bar Association, Quebec City, 30 August 1983, vol. 138, file 41. He seemed to back away from that claim in a 1985 interview: 'It is difficult to pass a rule saying you must be bilingual because that cuts out a lot of very fine people who are not bilingual.' Transcript of interview with Greg Frenette, 15 February 1985, vol. 148, file 4.
13 *Société des Acadiens* at 566.
14 While on the New Brunswick Court of Appeal, La Forest had sat on a procedural motion in the case.
15 La Forest to Dickson, 26 March 1986, vol. 85, file 2.
16 Wilson to the Court, 22 November 1985, vol. 85–6, file 6.
17 Dickson to Wilson, 28 November 1985, vol. 85, file 2.
18 Wilson to Dickson, 4 December 1985, vol. 85, file 2, referring to s.16 (3).
19 E. Anderson *Judging Bertha Wilson: Law as Large as Life* (Toronto: University of Toronto Press/Osgoode Society for Canadian Legal History 2001), at 186.
20 Manitoba Act, 1870, s.23; Constitution Act, 1867, s.133.
21 An Act to Provide That the English Language Shall Be the Official Language of the Province of Manitoba, 1890 (Man.), c.14.
22 *Pellant v. Hebert* (County Court), first published in *Le Manitoba* (a French-language newspaper), 9 March 1892, reported in (1981), 12 *R.G.D.* 242; *Bertrand v. Dussault*, 30 January 1909, County Court of St Boniface (unreported), reproduced in *Re Forest*

and Registrar of Court of Appeal of Manitoba (1977), 77 D.L.R. (3d) 445 (Man. C.A.), at 458–62.

23 *R. v. Forest* (1976), 74 D.L.R. (3d) 704 (Man. Co. Ct.).

24 *Attorney General of Manitoba v. Forest*, [1979] 2 S.C.R. 1032.

25 An Act Respecting the Operation of Section 23 of *the Manitoba Act in Regard to Statutes*, 1980 (Man.), c.3.

26 *Bilodeau v. Attorney General of Manitoba*, [1981] 5 W.W.R. 393 (Man. C.A.); [1986] 1 S.C.R. 449.

27 *A.G. Quebec v. Blaikie (No. 1)*, [1979] 2 S.C.R. 1016; *A.G. Quebec v. Blaikie* (No. 2), [1981] 1 S.C.R. 312.

28 Dickson conference memo, n. d., vol. 76, file 13.

29 *Reference re Language Rights under s. 23 of Manitoba Act, 1870 and s. 133 of Constitution Act, 1867*, [1985] 1 S.C.R. 721 at 739.

30 Dickson conference memo.

31 Cathy Kennedy to Dickson, 21 September 1984, vol. 77, file 3.

32 In Dickson's chambers, Mark Frieman, Cathy Kennedy, Thomas Mundell, and Joel Bakan all wrote significant memoranda. From other chambers, Peter Benson and Elizabeth Elliott made significant contributions.

33 Benson memo, 'A Contribution to the Analysis of the Manitoba Reference,' August 1984, vol. 78, file 7.

34 '1st Draft Circualted,' 14 March 1985, vol. 77, files 10 and 11 at 95, 67.

35 B. Dickson, 'The Public Responsibilities of Lawyers' (1983), 13 *Manitoba Law Journal*, 175 at 187.

36 '1st Draft,' at 80–1.

37 Ibid. at 81–2.

38 Ibid. at 115.

39 Lamer to Dickson, 22 March 1985, vol 77, file 1.

40 Joel Bakan Interview.

41 W. Estey, 'The Law of Remedies – An Overview,' in Law Society of Upper Canada, *New Developments in the Law of Remedies* (Toronto: Butterworths 1978), at 19.

42 La Forest to Dickson, 29 March 1985, vol. 77, file 5.

43 Wilson to Dickson, 3 April 1985, vol. 77, file 5.

44 Beetz to Dickson, 3 April 1985, vol. 77, file 5.

45 Gerald Le Dain, 'Jean Beetz as Judge and Colleague,' in *Mélanges Jean Beetz* (Montreal: Éditions Thémis 1995), at 675.

46 *Manitoba Language Reference* at 747, 748, 749.

47 Ibid. at 751.

48 Ibid. at 753, 754, 758.

49 Ibid.

50 'There is still a better way,' Winnipeg *Free Press*, 14 June 1985; 'A time for leadership,' Winnipeg *Free Press*, 15 June 1985.

51 Tritschler to Dickson, 23 June 1985, vol. 132, file 10.

52 Dickson to the Court, 5 July 1985, vol. 132, file 10.

53 *Yeryk v. Yeryk*, [1985] 5 W.W.R. 705.

54 S. Q. 1974, c.6.

55 R.S.Q. c.C-11.

56 *Quebec (Attorney General) v. Quebec Association of Protestant School Boards*, [1984] 2 S.C.R. 66.

57 *Blaikie (No. 1); Blaikie (No. 2)*.

58 *Ford et al. v. Attorney General of Quebec* (1984), 18 D.L.R. (4th) 711 (Que. S.C.); *Attorney General of Quebec v. La Chaussure Brown's Inc.* (1986), 36 D.L.R. (4th) 374 (Que. C.A.).

59 *Ford v. Quebec (Attorney General)*, [1988] 2 S.C.R. 712.

60 *Devine v. Quebec (Attorney General)*, [1988] 2 S.C.R. 790.

61 [1989] 1 S.C.R. 927.

62 *Alliance des Professeurs de Montreal et al. v. Attorney General of Quebec* (1985), 21 D.L.R. (4th) 354 (Que. C.A.).

63 Dickson conference memo, vol. 104, file 15.

64 Supreme Court Act, R.S.C. 1985, c.S-26, s. 27 (2).

65 Estey to Dickson, 14 April 1988, vol. 133, file 5.

66 Ibid.

67 Toronto *Globe and Mail*, 27 April 1988. Quotations are from the *Globe* unless otherwise indicated.

68 Toronto *Star*, 27 April 1988.

69 Ibid.

70 Ibid.

71 Estey to the Court, 19 May 1987, vol. 143, file 17.

72 *Globe and Mail*, 4 May 1988.

73 *Le Devoir*, 2 May 1988.

74 There is no copy of the draft in the file. The following is based on law clerk Craig Scott's memorandum to Dickson summarizing Le Dain's draft, vol. 104, file 16.

75 Quoted in Scott memo.

76 Wilson to Le Dain, 30 August 1988, vol. 104, file 16, Wilson to the Court, 19 October 1988, vol. 104, file 16.

77 Beetz to Le Dain, 1 September 1988, vol. 104, file 16.

78 Le Dain's illness is fully documented in vol. 133, file 12.

79 S.35. Two orders-in-council giving Le Dain successive one-month leaves of absence were requested and granted. S.35 has since been repealed and replaced by s.54, which allows a chief justice to grant a leave of absence for up to six months.

80 L'Heureux-Dubé interview.

81 La Forest interview.

82 McIntyre interview.

83 Supreme Court Act, R.S.C. 1985, c.S-26, s.29.

84 Lamer interview.

85 La Forest to the Court, 2 November 1988, vol. 104, file 15.

86 Lisa Brownstone and Richard Janda to Lamer, 10 November 1988, vol. 104, file 15.

87 Lamer to the Court, 15 November 1988, vol. 104, file 15.

88 McIntyre to the Court, 16 November 1988, vol. 104, file 15.

89 Dickson to the Court, 22 November 1988, vol. 104, file 15.

90 Wilson to the Court, 23 November 1988, vol. 104, file 15.

91 See chapter 19.

92 Dickson to McIntyre, Lamer, and Wilson, 24 November 1988, vol. 104, file 15.

93 Beetz retired to a life of quiet seclusion in Montreal where he died three years later in September 1991.

94 *La Presse*, 15 December 1988.

95 *Ford* at 767.

96 Ibid. at 748–9.

97 Ibid. at 780.

98 See chapter 22.

99 *Alliance des Professeurs*.

100 *Ford* at 740.

101 Dickson interview at 420.

102 'With justice to all,' Montreal *Gazette*, 16 December 1988.

103 Toronto *Star*, 16 December 1988.

104 'Les artistes québécois sont en colère,' *Le Devoir*, 16 December 1988.

105 'Students cheer nationalist heroes,' Montreal *Gazette*, 16 December 1988.

106 Montreal *Gazette*, 16 December 1988.

107 'Montréal doit demurer ville française,' 'La 'solution Dion' peut-elle s'appliquer avec ou sans clauses nonobstant?' *La Presse*, 16 December 1988.

108 *Le Devoir*, 17 December 1988.

109 Toronto *Star*, 16 December 1988.

110 Ibid.

111 Dickson interview at 420.

112 *Mahé v. Alberta* at 362.

113 S.23

114 *R. v. Beaulac*, [1999] 1 S.C.R. 768.

115 Dickson conference memo, 25 June 1989, vol. 115, file 16.

116 *Reference re Education Act of Ontario and Minority Language Rights* (1984), 10 D.L.R. (4th) 491 (Ont. C.A.).

117 Mahé at 350, 362, 365.

118 Ibid. at 364.

119 I. Urquhart, 'Infertile Soil? Sowing the Charter in Alberta,' in D. Schneiderman and K. Sutherland, ed., *Charting the Consequences: The Impact of Charter Rights on Canadian Law and Politics* (Toronto: University of Toronto Press 1997), at 40.

120 Gonthier interview.

121 La Forest interview.

Chapter 21: The Honour of the Crown

1 La Forest interview.
2 S. Weaver, *Making Canadian Indian Policy* (Toronto: University of Toronto Press 1981), at 179; P.-E. Trudeau, *A Mess That Deserves a Big No* (Toronto: Robert Davies Publishing 1992), at 12–13.
3 *Nowegijick v. The Queen*, [1983] 1 S.C.R. 29, as discussed in chapter 8.
4 *The Queen v. Simon*, [1985] 2 S.C.R. 387 at 392–3.
5 *The Queen v. Mousseau*, [1980] 2 S.C.R. 89, as discussed in chapter 7.
6 Dickson conference memo, 1 November 1984, vol. 80, file 14. (The quote is taken from Dickson's description of Le Dain's position, with which he agreed.)
7 *R. v. Syliboy*, [1929] 1 D.L.R. 307 at 313–4 (N.S. Co. Ct.).
8 Sheppard to Dickson, 12 September 1985, vol. 80, file 14.
9 *The Queen v. Simon*, [1985] 2 S.C.R. 387 at 399.
10 Ibid. at 401.
11 Ibid. at 405–6.
12 *Calder v. British Columbia*, [1973] S.C.R. 313.
13 Task Force to Review Comprehensive Claims Policy, *Living Treaties: Lasting Agreements* (Ottawa: Department of Indian Affairs and Northern Development, 1985), at 45. See also D. Ginn, 'Indian Hunting Rights' (1986), 31 *McGill Law Journal*, 527 at 550.
14 *Simon v. The Queen* at 408.
15 Barbara Dickson interview.
16 *Guerin v. The Queen*, [1984] 2 S.C.R. 335 at 370.
17 'Musqueams relish getting $10 million,' Vancouver *Sun*, 4 November 1984; '$10 million is awarded B.C. band in lawsuit,' *Globe and Mail*, 2 November 1984.
18 Dickson conference memo, 16 June 1983, vol. 70, file 13.
19 *Guerin v. The Queen* at 355.
20 Freiman to Dickson, 5 March 1984, vol. 71, file 6.
21 Dickson to Estey, 27 September 1984, vol. 70, file 13.
22 *Guerin v. The Queen* at 379.
23 *Kruger and Manuel v. The Queen*, [1978] 1 S.C.R. 104 at 109–10, as discussed in chapter 7.
24 *Guerin v. The Queen* at 383.
25 Ibid. at 384, 388.
26 Ibid. at 387–9.
27 'Musqueam Indian band wins $10 million in golf club land suit,' Vancouver *Sun*, 1 November 1984; 'Indian award clears the way to more claims,' *Globe and Mail*, 2 November 1984.
28 R. Romanow, J. Whyte, and H. Leeson, *Canada ... Notwithstanding: The Making of the Constitution, 1976–1982* (Toronto: Carswell Methuen 1984), at 209.

29 Dickson conference memo, 4 November 1988, vol. 119, file 7.

30 La Forest to Court, 20 September 1989, vol. 119, file 1.

31 *R. v. Edwards Books*, [1986] 2 S.C.R. 713, as discussed in chapter 17. On La Forest, see R. Johnson et al. ed., *Gérard V. La Forest at the Supreme Court of Canada 1985–1997* (Winnipeg: Supreme Court of Canada Historical Society 2000).

32 Wilson to LaForest and the Court, 13 March 1990, vol. 119, file 1.

33 Wilson to Dickson, 5 April 1990, vol. 119, file 1.

34 Ibid.

35 *McKinney v. University of Guelph*, [1990] 3 S.C.R. 229.

36 *R. v. Marshall*, [1999] 3 S.C.R. 456; *R. v. Marshall*, [1999] 3 S.C.R. 533. See generally K. Coates, *The Marshall Decision and Native Rights* (Montreal: McGill-Queen's University Press 2000).

37 La Forest to Dickson, 11 April 1990, vol. 119, file 1.

38 Wilson to Dickson, 16 May 1990, vol. 119, file 1. La Forest wrote a memorandum to Dickson on the same day indicating that he had put 'in a lot of work' on the judgment in 'the clear expectation that we were writing' a joint judgment. La Forest to Dickson, 16 May 1990, vol. 119, file 1.

39 La Forest to Dickson, 20 April 1990, vol. 119, file 1.

40 *Sparrow v. The Queen*, [1990] 1 S.C.R. 1075 at 1091, 1093.

41 Ibid. at 1097, 1099.

42 'Natives hail aboriginal-rights ruling,' Montreal *Gazette*, 1 June 1990.

43 'Governments cannot ignore aboriginal rights, court rules,' Toronto *Star*, 1 July 1990.

44 *Sparrow v. The Queen* at 1105, 1106 1108.

45 Ibid. at 1104.

46 Ibid. at 1101.

47 Ibid. at 1109.

48 Ibid. at 1114. In subsequent years, however, the Court would accept a broader range of factors as capable of justifying limitations on aboriginal rights: *R. v. Vanderpeet*, [1996] 2 S.C.R. 507; *Delgamuukw v. British Columbia*, [1997] 3 S.C.R. 1010.

49 *Sparrow v. The Queen* at 1114.

50 Dickson interview at 334.

51 La Forest interview.

52 [1980] 1 S.C.R. 294, as discussed in chapter 8.

53 *Sparrow v. The Queen* at 1119.

54 Report of the Standing Committee on Aboriginal Affairs, *The Summer of 1990* (May 1991), at 30, 171–3.

55 Speech by Brian Mulroney, 23 April 1991, vol. 172, file 10.

56 Letter to Brian Mulroney, 2 May 1991, vol. 171, file 10. The aboriginal leaders added: 'If we are to move ahead on this proposal then we must open lines of communication to reach agreement on the possible composition, duration, mandate,

budget, appointees, staffing and terms of reference of a Royal Commission and related initiatives.'

57 Dickson had also spoken in support of special programs to encourage more aboriginal law students. B. Dickson, 'Speech at Conference on Legal Education,' 26 October 1985, vol. 139, file 37.

58 Mulroney to Erasmus et al. 14 May 1991, vol. 171, file 10.

59 Dickson to Mulroney, 2 August 1991, vol. 167, file 3.

60 Mitchell to Dickson, 17 June 1991, vol. 171, file 3.

61 Norton to Dickson, 3 June 1991, vol. 171, file 11.

62 Robinson to Dickson, 2 July 1991, vol. 171, file 7.

63 D. Vienneau, 'Native affairs troubleshooter promises "no dilly-dallying,"' *Toronto Star*, 15 May 1991.

64 B. Dickson, 'The Genesis of the Royal Commission on Aboriginal Peoples,' n.d., vol. 167, file 10.

65 Stephen Toope interview.

66 Barbara Dickson interview.

67 Dickson interview at 343.

68 Transcript of Assembly of First Nations meeting, Winnipeg, 12 June 1991, vol. 173, file 11.

69 D. Henton, 'Natives at "breaking point," chief says,' Toronto *Star*, 13 June 1991.

70 Stephen Toope interview.

71 B. Dickson, 'Report of the Special Representative respecting the Royal Commission on Aboriginal Peoples,' 2 August 1991 vol. 167, file 3.

72 B. Dickson, 'First Peoples and the Constitution Conference Report' (13–15 March 1992), at 61, vol. 173, file 15.

73 E. Anderson, *Judging Bertha Wilson: Law as Large as Life* (Toronto: University of Toronto Press, Osgoode Society for Canadian Legal History 2001), at 356.

74 B. Dickson, 'Speech on Release of the Report,' n.d., 1996, vol. 167, file 9.

75 B. Dickson, 'Report of the Special Representative.'

76 Dickson interview at 337.

77 B. Cox, 'Ex-Indian leader, retired judge to head native probe,' *Waterloo Record*, 3 August 1991.

78 Wilson to the Court, 10 May 1990, vol. 119, file 6.

79 An aboriginal woman's group subsequently brought an unsuccessful Charter challenge when they were excluded from the constitutional discussions leading to the Charlottetown Accord: *Native Women's Association of Canada v. Canada*, [1994] 3 S.C.R. 627.

80 W. Johnson, 'A blank cheque,' Montreal *Gazette*, 14 February 1992, vol. 173, file 15. The interim report was *The Right of Aboriginal Self-government and the Constitution*, 13 February 1992.

81 B. Dickson, 'First Peoples and the Constitution Conference Report,' at 59.

82 B. Dickson, 'Speech on Release of the Report.'

83 *Myran v. The Queen*, [1976] 2 S.C.R. 137; *Frank v. The Queen*, [1978] 1 S.C.R. 95; *Kruger and Manuel v. The Queen*, [1978] 1 S.C.R. 104, as discussed in chapter 7.

84 *Jack v. The Queen*, [1980] 1 S.C.R. 294; *Nowegijick v. The Queen*, [1983] 1 S.C.R. 29, as discussed in chapter 8.

Chapter 22: Dickson of Canada

1 Dickson to all Court employees, 4 April 1990, vol. 158, file 6.
2 Dickson interview at 625.
3 'Dickson steps down,' Toronto *Star*, 5 April 1990.
4 The many retirement letters Dickson received, as well as his replies, are contained in vol. 158, files 6, 7 and 8.
5 D. Vienneau, 'Dickson ruled tops by a jury of his peers,' Toronto *Star*, 5 Nov. 1989.
6 L'Heureux-Dubé to Dickson, 4 April 1990, vol. 158, file 8.
7 Beetz to Dickson, 5 April 1990, vol. 158, file 8.
8 Dickson to David Peterson, 10 May 1990, vol. 158, file 7.
9 'Retirement Ceremony of The Right Honourable Brian Dickson, P.C.' 21 June 1990.
10 La Forest interview.
11 *R. v. Keegstra*, [1990] 3 S.C.R. 697; *McKinney v. University of Guelph*, [1990] 3 S.C.R. 229; *R. v. Chaulk*, [1990] 3 S.C.R. 1303.
12 Lamer interview.
13 Guy Pratte interview.
14 Lamer interview.
15 La Forest interview.
16 'Double Take,' *Maclean's*, 10 August 1998.
17 'Itinerary Western Swing Special Commission on Reserves,' 11–21 June 1995, vol. 193, file 5.
18 'National Defence News Release,' 7 May 1996, vol. 187, file 13.
19 'Report of the Special Advisory Committee on Military Justice and Military Police,' vol. 187, file 14.
20 The case was decided a year after Parliament had abolished the death penalty and the Court was unanimous in its decision not to invalidate the death penalty under the statutory Bill of Rights: *R. v. Miller*, [1977] 2 S.C.R. 680. The Supreme Court, like Dickson, subsequently changed its position and indicated that extradition to face the death penalty will generally be inconsistent with the Charter: *United States of America v. Burns and Rafay*, [2001] 1 S.C.R. 283.
21 Guy Pratte interview.
22 'Report of the Special Advisory Committee.'
23 'Chief Justice Brian Dickson's Opening Remarks, Press Conference, National War Museum,' 25 March 1997, vol. 188, file 8.
24 'Report of the Special Advisory Committee on the Minister of Defence's Quasi-Judicial Reforms,' vol. 187, file 14.

25 B. Dickson, 'Remarks at Vimy Award,' 22 November 1997, vol. 194, file 1.
26 K. McRoberts and P. Monahan ed., *The Charlottetown Accord, the Referendum and the Future of Canada* (Toronto: University of Toronto Press 1993).
27 Patrick Monahan interview.
28 Dickson to Mulroney, 25 October 1991, vol. 165, file 13.
29 Ibid.
30 Ibid.
31 Ibid.
32 Royal Commission on Aboriginal Peoples, *The Right of Self-Government and the Constitution: A Commentary* (Ottawa: Royal Commission on Aboriginal Peoples, 13 February 1992).
33 B. Dickson, *First Peoples and the Constitution Conference Report*, 13–15 March 1992, at 56–57, vol. 173, file 15.
34 Ibid at 57.
35 Barbara Dickson interview.
36 See chapter 13.
37 Dickson, *First Peoples and the Constitution Conference Report*, at 60–1.
38 La Forest interview.
39 Lamer interview.
40 Gonthier interview.
41 Erasmus had stated: 'In the best of all worlds the aboriginal people themselves will have to design their own constitution and the kinds of rights they will recognize internally.' D. Henton, 'Don't reject Charter, natives told,' Toronto *Star*, 18 February 1992, vol. 173, file 15.
42 Dickson, *First People and the Constitutional Conference Report*, at 61. A few days before the speech, Dickson's former clerk Stephen Toope had warned him to stay away 'from any precise statement on the relationship between the Charter and aboriginal communities.' Faxed note from Toope to Dickson, 10 March 1992, vol. 175, file 20.
43 J. Brydon, 'Limit native self-government, former chief justice says,' Waterloo *Record*, 16 March 1992.
44 Dickson, *First Peoples and the Constitution Conference Report*, at 55.
45 The note is contained in vol. 175, file 19. It mentions the *Le Devoir* poll and included these comments: 'natives have put their agenda ahead of national agenda,' 'if one leaves, native agenda will fail if votes to separate, all over,' 'can be in leadership role, keeping Canada together,' 'national builders – can win everything or lose everything,' 'pressure on $,' 'we want it all perfection perfection enemy of good, 1867, 1982, 1990 Meech all imperfect,' 'this matter extremely serious will be no one to look after them.'
46 Dickson had access to Mulroney and regularly visited and talked with him. Guy Pratte interview; Barbara Dickson interview.

47 'Define your terms, PM says,' *Hamilton Spectator*, 18 March 1992.

48 Dickson, *First Peoples and the Constitution Conference Report*, at 61.

49 Ibid. at 62.

50 Dickson, 'Remarks at Vimy Award Ceremony,' 15 June 1992, vol. 193, file 17.

51 Transcript of interview of Brian Dickson for Royal Bank Award, 16 June 1992, vol. 193, file 14.

52 Stephen Toope interview.

53 Peter Cory interview.

54 Dickson, 'Remarks at Vimy Award Ceremony.'

55 Dickson interview at 661.

56 This incident was confirmed in an interview with Brian Dickson, Jr, who swam the Ottawa river with his father.

57 Transcript of interview for Royal Bank Award, 16 June 1992.

58 P.-E. Trudeau, *A Mess That Deserves a Big No* (Toronto: Robert Davies Publishing, 1992), at 14–15, 25, and 63. See also 'Without equality, "one has dictatorship" – Trudeau,' Toronto *Star*, 3 October 1992.

59 Dickson, 'Speech on Receiving Royal Bank Award for Canadian Achievement,' 8 October 1992, vol. 193, file 14.

60 D. Vienneau, 'Ex-chief justice warns of "gravest crisis,"' Toronto *Star*, 9 October 1992.

61 Dickson to Sheila Purdy, senior policy adviser, Office of the Minister of Justice, 17 June 1996.

62 Guy Pratte interview.

63 B. Dickson and P. Hogg, 'Rules for a Referendum on Quebec Sovereignty,' 2nd draft, 21 Oct. 1996. See also P. Hogg, 'Principles Governing the Secession of Quebec' (1997), 8 *National Journal of Constitutional Law*, 19.

64 Dickson to Sheila Purdy.

65 B. Dickson, 'Brian Dickson: Two Modest Views,' *Globe and Mail*, 5 July 1996.

66 R.J. Sharpe, 'The Constitutional Legacy of Brian Dickson' (2000) 38 *Osgoode Hall Law Journal*, 189.

67 *Reference re Secession of Quebec*, [1998] 2 S.C.R. 217. The federal government subsequently introduced a law concerning the various procedures to be followed in the event of another referendum on Quebec sovereignty. *Clarity Act*, S.C. 2000, c.26.

68 G. Hughes, 'War hero "gave his life to law,"' Ottawa *Citizen*, 18 October 1998.

69 Ibid.

70 'Remarks of Chief Justice Lamer, Ceremony in Memory of the Right Honourable Brian Dickson, P.C.,' 2 November 1998.

71 T. MacCharles, 'Brian Dickson blazed a trail as chief justice,' Toronto *Star*, 18 October 1998.

Illustration Credits

Michael Bedford, Ottawa: Brian Dickson, 1984; Supreme Court of Canada, 1989

Barbara Dickson: Lillian Gibson; Thomas Dickson; Lillian and Thomas Dickson with Brian; Brian and Thomas Dickson; Brian and Tom riding a pony; Thomas and Brian in Saskatchewan; Brian and Tom, circa 1932; Family picnic; Regina, 1932; Law school graduation; In training camp; Canadian Officer Training Corps; Wedding day; Louis St Laurent and Dickson; Winnipeg Flood HQ; Deborah, Barbara, and Brian; Brian Dickson at Aikens MacAulay; Mianki; Visit by Chief Justice Burger; Brian Dickson, Jr, hooding his father; Riding at Marchmont; At Marchmont with Derry; Pierre Trudeau and Brian Dickson; Pierre Trudeau, Faculty of Law, University of Toronto; Fortieth wedding anniversary; Fifty-fifth wedding anniversary

National Archives: Queen's Bench judge, 1963 (PA 212781); Supreme Court of Canada, 1973 (PA 212784); Supreme Court of Canada, 1975 (PA 212790); Supreme Court of Canada, 1977 (PA 212791); Supreme Court of Canada, 1987 (PA 212787); Supreme Court of Canada, 1989 (PA 212786); Mulroneys and Dicksons

National Film Board: Supreme Court of Canada, 1977

Supreme Court of Canada: Supreme Court building (Philippe Landreville); Chief Justice Laskin, 1975; Main courtroom, Supreme Court of Canada (Philippe Landreville); Judges' Conference Room, Supreme Court of Canada (Philippe Landreville)

Toronto Star: Gowning for court, June 1990 (Erin Combs); Riding with grandchildren at Marchmont (Erin Combs)

Index

1981   David H. Flaherty, ed., *Essays in the History of Canadian Law: Volume I*
1982   Marion MacRae and Anthony Adamson, *Cornerstones of Order: Courthouses and Town Halls of Ontario, 1784–1914*
1983   David H. Flaherty, ed., *Essays in the History of Canadian Law: Volume II*
1984   Patrick Brode, *Sir John Beverley Robinson: Bone and Sinew of the Compact*
       David Williams, *Duff: A Life in the Law*
1985   James Snell and Frederick Vaughan, *The Supreme Court of Canada: History of the Institution*
1986   Paul Romney, *Mr Attorney: The Attorney General for Ontario in Court, Cabinet, and Legislature, 1791–1899*
       Martin Friedland, *The Case of Valentine Shortis: A True Story of Crime and Politics in Canada*
1987   C. Ian Kyer and Jerome Bickenbach, *The Fiercest Debate: Cecil A. Wright, the Benchers, and Legal Education in Ontario, 1923–1957*
1988   Robert Sharpe, *The Last Day, the Last Hour: The Currie Libel Trial*
       John D. Arnup, *Middleton: The Beloved Judge*
1989   Desmond Brown, *The Genesis of the Canadian Criminal Code of 1892*
       Patrick Brode, *The Odyssey of John Anderson*
1990   Philip Girard and Jim Phillips, eds., *Essays in the History of Canadian Law: Volume III – Nova Scotia*
       Carol Wilton, ed., *Essays in the History of Canadian Law: Volume IV – Beyond the Law: Lawyers and Business in Canada, 1830–1930*
1991   Constance Backhouse, *Petticoats and Prejudice: Women and Law in Nineteenth-Century Canada*
1992   Brendan O'Brien, *Speedy Justice: The Tragic Last Voyage of His Majesty's Vessel Speedy*
       Robert Fraser, ed., *Provincial Justice: Upper Canadian Legal Portraits from the Dictionary of Canadian Biography*
1993   Greg Marquis, *Policing Canada's Century: A History of the Canadian Association of Chiefs of Police*
       F. Murray Greenwood, *Legacies of Fear: Law and Politics in Quebec in the Era of the French Revolution*
1994   Patrick Boyer, *A Passion for Justice: The Legacy of James Chalmers McRuer*
       Charles Pullen, *The Life and Times of Arthur Maloney: The Last of the Tribunes*
       Jim Phillips, Tina Loo, and Susan Lewthwaite, eds., *Essays in the History of Canadian Law: Volume V – Crime and Criminal Justice*
       Brian Young, *The Politics of Codification: The Lower Canadian Civil Code of 1866*
1995   David Williams, *Just Lawyers: Seven Portraits*
       Hamar Foster and John McLaren, eds., *Essays in the History of Canadian Law: Volume VI – British Columbia and the Yukon*
       W.H. Morrow, ed., *Northern Justice: The Memoirs of Mr Justice William G. Morrow*
       Beverley Boissery, *A Deep Sense of Wrong: The Treason Trials and Transportation to New South Wales of Lower Canadian Rebels after the 1838 Rebellion*